MOON

COLOMBIA

ANDREW DIER

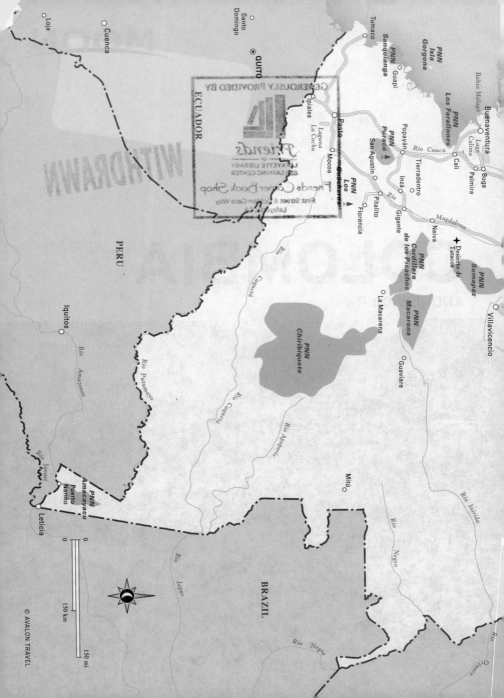

ECUADOR

PERU

BRAZIL

COLOMBIA

Quito

Loja

Cuenca

Santo
Domingo

Tumaco

Guapi

Ipiales

Laguna
La Cocha

Mocoa

Pasto

San Agustín

Popayán

Inzá

Tierradentro

Cali

Buga
Palmira

Buenaventura

Lago
Calima

Bahía Málaga

PNN
Sanquianga

PNN
Isla
Gorgona

PNN
Los Farallones

PNN
Puracé

PNN
Los
Guácharos

Pitalito

Florencia

Gigante

Neiva

Río Cauca

Magdalena

Desierto de
Tatacoa

PNN
Sumapaz

Villavicencio

PNN
Cordillera
de los Picachos

PNN
Macarena

La Macarena

Guaviare

Río Magdalena

Iquitos

Río Amazonas

Río Putumayo

Río Caquetá

Río Caquetá

Río Apaporis

PNN
Chiribiquete

Mitú

Río Inírida

Río Negro

Leticia

PNN
Amacayacu

Puerto
Nariño

Río Javarí

Río Amazonas

Río Japurá

Río Negro

Río Negro

Río Orinoco

0   150 km

0   150 mi

© AVALON TRAVEL

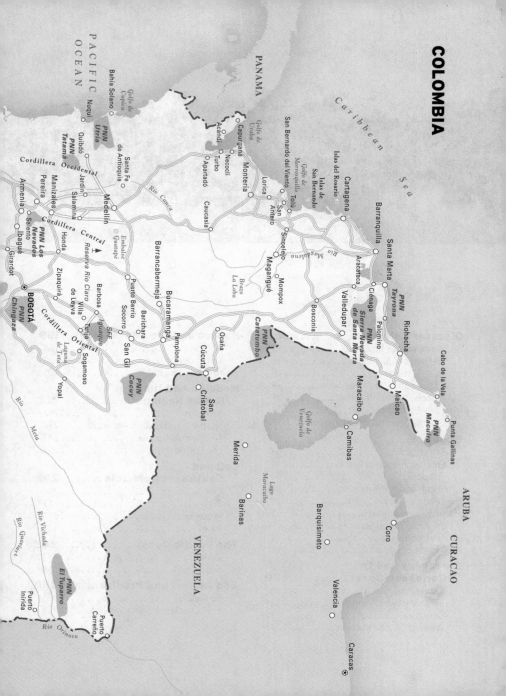

Contents

DISCOVER
Colombia

dyllic colonial towns, fast-paced cities, stunning archaeological sites, jaw-dropping scenery, and secluded beaches should be enough to put Colombia on your must-see list. But what really seals the deal is the contagious *alegría* (happiness) of the people you will meet along the way.

Bogotá offers all the architecture, culture, restaurants, and nightlife that you would expect in any major city, while growing Medellín is known for its can-do spirit, transformative infrastructure projects, and perfect weather. These are destinations in their own right. But they are also excellent bases for visitors who wish to enjoy creature comforts while exploring the rest of the country.

Cartagena, Villa de Leyva, and Barichara will transport you back to the 18th century, when the region's citizens were ruled by a king in Madrid. Cartagena never fails to seduce those who stroll along its narrow cobblestone streets adorned by bougainvillea cascading from balconies above.

The Andes Mountains combined with Colombia's tropical location mean that every possible natural setting is within reach. The Sierra Nevada del Cocuy offers incredible trekking amid glaciers and snowcapped peaks. Coffee farms are nestled in verdant valleys abundant with fruit trees and bamboo forests. Los

Clockwise from top left: traditional Colombian snacks; Bogotá; coffee beans; bougainvillea spilling onto the streets of Cartagena; Puente Navarro, Honda; Sierra Nevada del Cocuy.

Llanos, Colombia's eastern plains, and the dense jungles of the Amazon basin are tropical wonderlands, with innumerable opportunities for nature and wildlife viewing.

Even the beaches here are varied. Colombia is the only country in South America with both Caribbean and Pacific coastlines. The Caribbean coast features gems like Parque Nacional Natural Tayrona, where glacier-fed streams flow from snowcapped mountains into the sea. The Pacific coast offers solitude and a chance to spot humpback whales breaching. And, far from the mainland in the Caribbean, the islands of San Andrés and Providencia are a sultry respite.

Colombia is one of the most biodiverse countries on the planet. Its people are just as diverse. Beyond differences in language, dialects, and accents, you can tell where someone is from by the songs they sing, the instruments they play, and the dances to which they move. In Cali, salsa—with its fancy footwork, color, and hypnotic percussion—is nothing less than an obsession. In Los Llanos, *joropo* is a tribute to Colombian cowboy tradition. *Vallenato* music, heard along the Caribbean coast, relates tales of lost love accompanied by instruments with African, indigenous, and European roots.

Forward looking and hopeful, Colombia has turned the page from its past. Now is a great time to experience this change firsthand. Colombia has laid out its welcome mat and beckons: ¡*Bienvenidos!*

Clockwise from top left: humpback whale; beach in Providencia; golden tanager; young Colombian musician.

Planning Your Trip

Where to Go

Bogotá

Against the backdrop of the Andes Mountains, the country's cool capital is a **cosmopolitan melting pot.** It's a city of stunning colonial and modern **architecture,** art and culture, **glitzy shopping, five-star dining,** and **euphoric nightlife.**

Cartagena and the Caribbean Coast

Cartagena is the seductive, **colonial jewel** of the Caribbean. Beyond, the Caribbean coastline runs the gamut from the eerie **desert landscapes** of **La Guajira** in the far north to the **untamed jungles** near **Capurganá** along the Panamanian border. In between are the tropical jungles and the ruins of the Tayrona indigenous settlement of **Ciudad Perdida** in the **Sierra Nevada de Santa Marta.**

Boyacá and the Santanderes

The cradle of Colombian independence, the departments of Santander and Boyacá are graced with **stunning countryside,** from the awe-inspiring **Cañón del Chicamocha** to the snow-capped peaks of the **Sierra Nevada del Cocuy. San Gil** is the outdoor adventure capital, while nearby **Barichara** is one of the most beautiful **colonial pueblos** in the country. The sacred **Laguna Iguaque** and the nearby town of **Villa de Leyva,** with its serene whitewashed buildings and cobblestone streets, are truly picturesque.

Cañón del Chicamocha

IF YOU HAVE...

- **ONE WEEK:** Visit Medellín, stay at a coffee farm, and fly to Cartagena.

- **TWO WEEKS:** Add the Caribbean coast, then Bogotá and colonial Villa de Leyva.

- **THREE WEEKS:** Add Cali and Popayán or the Pacific coast.

- **FOUR WEEKS:** Add an excursion to the Amazon or Los Llanos.

Medellín and the Coffee Region

Ambitious Medellín is known for its **temperate climate** and **fun nightlife**. For a break from the city, the **Reserva Natural Río Claro** makes a fantastic midweek distraction. Photogenic Paisa pueblos abound, with **Jardín, Jericó, Salamina,** and **Salento** some of the most colorful. Stay at one of countless **coffee haciendas** in the lush rolling hills. The landscape is dotted with towering wax palms and brightly colored birds. The snow-covered volcanic peaks of **Parque Nacional Natural Los Nevados** beckon mountain climbers.

Cali and Southwest Colombia

Colombia's third-largest city is a joyous one, filled with music and dance. When the sun goes down

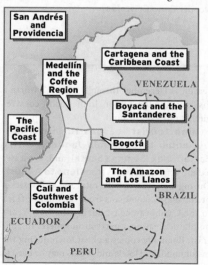

it's hard to resist Cali's hypnotic salsa rhythms. To the west, beyond the **endless sugarcane fields** of the **Valle de Cauca,** stands the White City of **Popayán,** a **historic colonial city** of presidents and poets. It makes a great base from which to explore the archaeological sites of **Tierradentro** and **San Agustín.** Under the looming shadow of **Volcán Galeras, Pasto** is known for its raucous Carnaval de Negros y Blancos in January. In the **bucolic countryside** south toward Ecuador are **mountains** and **emerald-green lakes.**

The Pacific Coast

The Pacific is Colombia's wild coast, where the thick jungles of **Chocó** meet the beaches and endless ocean at wonderfully remote **Bahía Solano** and **Nuquí.** Warm Pacific waters are a playground for **humpback whales** that spend July through October here. Sea turtles are return visitors, too. Serious divers will want to make the journey to **Santuario de Flora y Fauna Malpelo,** where schools of hammerhead sharks slowly circle.

San Andrés and Providencia

The paradises of English-speaking San Andrés and Providencia offer everything you'd expect from a Caribbean island vacation. **Fantastic diving** will keep you occupied for days off of sunny San Andrés. The daily routine of lounging on **remote beaches,** eating fresh seafood, lazing in hammocks, and **stargazing** on the beach in rustic Providencia will have you hooked.

hammocks and hats for sale

orchid

The Amazon and Los Llanos

The Amazon **rainforest** is the lungs of the world. Visit an eco-lodge on the **Río Javari,** where you can take canoe rides above the treetops in the flooded jungle. Observe birds and pink dolphins by day and look for crocodiles as darkness falls.

Spend a couple of days in the Ticuna village of **San Martín** and enjoy the blissfully car-free hamlet of **Puerto Nariño.** In Los Llanos, take in the astonishing wildlife at **Hacienda La Aurora.** Bathe in the **multicolored waters** of natural wonder **Caño Cristales.**

When to Go

Because Colombia straddles the equator, the temperatures and length of days are nearly constant year-round. There are, however, distinct dry and rainy seasons. Throughout most of the country, the months of **December through February** and **July through August** are considered *verano* (dry season). *Invierno* (rainy season) is usually between **April and May** and again between **September and November.**

In San Andrés and Providencia, June through November is rainy and from February through April it's drier. In the Amazon the drier months are between June and September and the rainy season is December through May. It's worth a visit during either season. In the Pacific coast region, it rains year-round.

High tourist seasons run from **mid-December through mid-January,** during **Easter week (Semana Santa),** and, to a lesser extent, school vacations from **June to August.** During high season, hotel rates and airline ticket prices soar. Colombians from the interior flock to the Caribbean coast during the New Year's holidays, creating a party atmosphere. In contrast, Bogotá becomes a ghost town during the major holidays. Hotels and flights may be hard to come by during the 10 or so *puentes* (long weekends) of the year.

Many of the major **festivals and celebrations** take place between December and February: the Feria de Cali, the Carnaval de Negros y Blancos in Pasto, Hay Festival in Cartagena, and the Carnaval de Barranquilla.

Easter week celebrations are popular in colonial cities such as Popayán, Mompox, Pamplona, and Tunja, while during that time every two years Bogotá puts on the Festival Iberoamericano de Teatro. **Humpback whales** make their appearance off the Pacific coast from **July to October.**

Before You Go

Passports and Visas

Travelers to Colombia who intend to visit as tourists for a period of under 90 days will need only to present a **valid passport** upon entry in the country. You may be asked to show **proof of a return ticket.** Tell the immigration officer if you intend to stay up to 90 days, otherwise they will probably give you a stamp permitting a stay of 60 days. Language schools and universities will be able to assist those who may require a yearlong **student visa.**

Vaccinations

There are **no obligatory vaccination requirements** for visiting Colombia. However, proof of the **yellow fever vaccine** may be requested upon arrival at the Parque Nacional Natural Tayrona or at the Leticia airport in the Amazon. This vaccination can be obtained at Red Cross clinics throughout the country. If you are traveling onward to countries such as Brazil, Ecuador, or Peru, you may have to provide proof of the vaccine upon entry to those countries.

Salento

The Centers for Disease Control and Prevention (CDC) recommends that travelers have all the **basic vaccinations** updated. In addition, for most travelers to Colombia, the CDC recommends the **hepatitis A** and **typhoid** vaccinations. **Hepatitis B, rabies,** and **yellow fever** vaccinations are recommended for some travelers. If you plan to visit the Amazon region, **antimalarial drugs** may be recommended. With infections of **mosquito-borne illnesses** such as malaria, dengue, chikungunya, and Zika possible in tropical areas of the country, visitors are encouraged to keep mosquito repellent close at hand.

Transportation

Most travelers arrive by plane to Colombia, with the vast majority arriving at the modern **Aeropuerto Internacional El Dorado** in Bogotá. There are numerous **daily nonstop flights** into Bogotá from the eastern seaboard of the United States, as well as from Houston, Dallas, Los Angeles, and Toronto. The cities of **Medellín, Cali, Cartagena, Barranquilla,** and Armenia are also served by nonstop flights from the East Coast of the United States.

There are **overland border entries** from **Ecuador** (to Ipiales) and **by boat** from **Peru** or **Brazil** to the Amazonian port of Leticia and, by sea, from **Panama** to Capurganá or Cartagena.

Intra-country flights are easy, safe, increasingly more economical, frequent, and, above all, quick. Taking the **bus** to just about anywhere in the country is an inexpensive and popular but slower option. **Renting a car** is a viable option in the **coffee region** where roads are good. In the **major cities,** there are extensive **rapid bus**

networks, and in **Medellín** there is a clean and efficient **Metro**. **Private buses** and **taxis** are ubiquitous in cities, although cabs should be ordered in advance. The best way to see the sights of most cities is usually **on foot.**

What to Pack

For jungle exploration, **waterproof hiking boots** and **collapsible trekking poles** are musts. For exploring the Amazon, Capurganá, or the Pacific coast, a **waterproof camera bag** and **silica gel** may prevent the heartache of a ruined camera. For caving, visiting the tombs of Tierradentro, and finding your way at night, a **small flashlight or headlight** comes in handy. To spot humpbacks, birds, and other wildlife, **binoculars** will be great to have. If you plan on spending much time on the coast, bring your own **snorkeling gear.** A lightweight **sleeping sack** makes rustic sleeping conditions more comfortable.

To protect against the sun, pack a **wide-brimmed hat**; against the rain, a **lightweight rain jacket** and **compact umbrella**; against mosquitoes, lightweight and light-colored long-sleeved shirts and some strong repellent. For long bus rides, earplugs, eye masks, and **luggage locks** will make the trip more relaxing. A **Latin American Spanish dictionary** will help you get your point across.

Casual attire is fine at most restaurants, theaters, and religious venues. Restaurants in Bogotá and Cartagena may expect more of an effort. In large cities, you'll want to **dress to impress** in bars and clubs. Shorts are generally frowned upon in interior cities.

The Best of Colombia

There's not one clear-cut, common way to visit uncommon Colombia. For a first-time visit, a tour of the coffee region and Cartagena on the Caribbean coast will be a beautiful and easy weeklong introduction to this fascinating country. In two weeks, you can squeeze in Medellín, a Paisa pueblo or two, and the sublime colonial town of Villa de Leyva in Boyacá, and then cap it all off with a weekend in fast-paced Bogotá. With a third week, you can explore the parks of southwest Colombia and salsa the night away in Cali.

Medellín and the Coffee Region

DAY 1

Arrive in the evening at the Aeropuerto Internacional José María Córdova in Rionegro, outside of Medellín. Make the one-hour trip via cab or bus into town. Get settled at **Charlee Lifestyle Hotel,** then linger over perfectly paired Argentinian wine and food at one of the city's most renowned restaurants, **Carmen.**

DAY 2

Discover downtown Medellín by taking a ride on the Metro. Here you can check out the finest art museum in the region, the **Museo de Antioquia,** and have your picture taken in front of your favorite rotund **Fernando Botero** sculpture in the adjacent plaza. Visit the moving **Museo Casa de la Memoria**, the country's first museum dedicated to the memory of victims of Colombia's decades-long armed conflict.

Then check out symbols of the new Medellín: the **Metrocable gondola** network and the **Biblioteca España,** a boldly designed public library built on the side of a mountain. From there, transfer once more to another Metrocable line to the **Parque Arví,** a huge recreational area.

Head back to your hotel and freshen up before checking out a tango show at **Salón Málaga.**

DAY 3

Take the three-hour bus ride through the southern Antioquia countryside to the

one of Medellín's Metrocable gondolas

If you don't have the time for a long overland trip, consider flying to these destinations from Bogotá or Medellín.

Getaways close to airports in larger cities such as Santa Marta, Neiva, Montería, and Yopal are served by various major airlines. Check domestic airlines such as **Satena** (www.satena.com) or **Aerolínea de Antioquia** (www.ada-aero.com) for the smaller destinations.

FROM BOGOTÁ

- **Hacienda La Aurora:** See wildlife like never before at this cattle ranch and nature reserve in the Llanos. (Airport: Yopal)

- **Caño Cristales:** Discover the secret of the multicolored waters at this serene national park in the southern Llanos. (Airport: La Macarena)

- **San Agustín:** You'll be blown away by Colombia's best-preserved archaeological site, nestled in the rolling mountains south of Neiva. (Airport: Neiva)

- **Parque Nacional Natural Tayrona:** Enjoy a quick beach break at the spectacular PNN Tayrona. Be sure to save some time for a jungle hike to **El Pueblito,** remnants of a former Tayrona settlement in the Sierra Nevada de Santa Marta. (Airport: Santa Marta)

FROM MEDELLÍN

- **Pacific Coast:** Breathtaking sunsets, remote beaches, and the chance to see visiting

a Satena airplane

humpback whales make for a memorable getaway from Medellín. (Airport: Bahía Solano or Nuquí)

- **Capurganá:** On the Panamanian border, Capurganá is a Darien Gap outpost, home to tropical rainforest and wild beach landscapes. (Airport: Acandí or Capurganá)

- **Río Cedro:** Rejuvenate at this deserted stretch of beach set against a backdrop of tropical dry forest and banana plantations, home to birds and sloths. (Airport: Montería or Tolú)

---

picture-perfect Paisa town of **Jardín.** Hang out with the locals in the sublime **Parque Principal,** a park bursting with flowers, where you can enjoy a beer or sip a locally produced coffee.

Relax at the low-key hostel **Casa Selva y Café,** a pleasant walk away from the town center. Birding and nature enthusiasts will want to stay at **Hacienda La Esperanza.**

DAY 4
Set off for the coffee region by heading to **Manizales** in the morning on a five-hour bus ride. Once in town, have a coffee under the shadow of the remarkable **El Cable** tower, the gondola system that once transported coffee over the mountains to the Río Magdalena.

Check in to a **coffee farm** in the verdant valleys near Chinchiná such as **Hacienda**

Venecia or **Hacienda Guayabal,** only about a half hour away.

DAY 5
Take a tour of a coffee farm today, and admire the orderly rows of deep green coffee plants adorned with bright red beans. In the afternoon, take a bus to one of the region's cutest pueblos, **Salento,** a five-hour trip.

Stay at the bright orange **Tralala** hostel and have dinner at wonderful **La Eliana,** followed by dessert and coffee at **Café Jesús Martín.**

DAY 6
Hitch a ride on a Jeep Willy through pastureland and tropical forest to the **Reserva Acaime,** where you can watch hummingbirds flit about while you warm up with a hot drink. Then head back down through a wonderland of 60-meter-high (200-foot-high) wax palms, Colombia's national tree, in the **Valle de Cocora.**

Spend the night again in Salento. Before retiring for the night, stroll the atmospheric **Calle Real.**

Cartagena and the Caribbean Coast
DAY 1
From nearby Pereira, fly to **Cartagena,** 1.5 hours away. Once you land and change into the airy attire standard for the sultry city, get to know the area by taking a stroll on the massive ramparts that once protected the city against English pirates.

Have dinner at **La Vitrola,** a Cartagena classic. Spend the night at the boutique beauty **Hotel LM** or the **3 Banderas,** a friendly midrange option.

DAY 2
Walk the Old City streets, getting lost and found again as you amble from the divine **Parque de Bolívar** to the **Plaza Santo Domingo** to **Las Murallas,** the city's walls. Be sure to check out the impressive **Castillo de San Felipe** in the late afternoon.

Go for ceviche at **La Cevichería** and a mojito or two across the street at the historic and elegant **El Coro** in the Hotel Sofitel Legend Santa Clara.

The Valle de Cocora is home to wax palms.

balconies in Cartagena's Old City

DAY 3

For a change of pace, take a cab or bus to **Bocagrande,** Cartagena's version of Miami Beach. A walk along the bay in the Castillo Grande district is a fine way to pass the afternoon.

Spend some time in the hip and happening area of **Getsemaní,** a neighborhood of tapas bars and watering holes. For inventive local cuisine, try **La Cocina de Pepina.**

DAYS 4-6

From the Muelle Turístico in town, take a boat to the beaches of **Islas del Rosario,** the area's finest beaches, and spend a couple of nights at an island hotel. It's worth splurging for the **Hotel San Pedro de Majagua.**

Return to Cartagena in the late afternoon and take one last walk on the walls, enjoying a cocktail and the Caribbean breeze at **Café del Mar.**

EXCURSION TO LA GUAJIRA

If you have 4-5 extra days, consider taking a trip to **La Guajira,** a desert peninsula that is home to the Wayúu people.

Start at the beach in **Palomino** or in **Riohacha,** the departmental capital of La Guajira, and join up with an organized tour group. After a dusty ride past countless cacti and lonely goats, you'll arrive at **Cabo de la Vela,** where you can take a dip in the Caribbean Sea or try your luck windsurfing or kitesurfing.

The next stop is **Punta Gallinas,** the northernmost point of South America. Spend a day or two on a photo safari of the unusual landscape of desert dunes that drop dramatically into the sea.

Take a canoe trip to explore the mangroves, then share a huge, freshly prepared lobster with a friend. Upon your return in Riohacha, and if there's time, check out the **Santuario de Fauna y Flora Los Flamencos** for an early-morning or late-afternoon canoe ride in search of flamingos and other waterfowl.

Bogotá and Boyacá

DAY 1

Fly into **Bogotá.** Set in the Andes at an elevation of 2,625 meters (8,612 feet), the Colombian capital city can be especially cool and the sun particularly potent. Dress in layers and take along sunscreen and an umbrella. In the late afternoon, wander the historic **Candelaria** district and marvel at the treasures of the **Museo del Oro.** Stay at the **Casa Platypus** downtown or **Cité** in the north.

DAY 2

Take a bus or hire a car for the 3.5-hour trip to the low-key pueblo of **Villa de Leyva,** one of Colombia's best-preserved colonial towns, in the department of Boyacá.

Enjoy the unique atmosphere in Villa de Leyva by walking its stone streets. Check out the woolen *ruanas* (ponchos) at **Alieth Tejido Artesanal,** and if you have time, visit the **Convento del Santo Ecce Homo** in the surrounding desert.

Stay at **Renacer,** a friendly hostel, or splurge at the **Hotel Plaza Mayor,** where the views of the plaza can't be beat.

DAY 3

Visit the **Santuario Flora y Fauna Iguaque** just outside of town and hike to the mist-shrouded **Laguna Iguaque** for some morning exhilaration. Relax in Villa de Leyva for the evening.

DAYS 4-5

Return to Bogotá and, if it's a weekend day, go to the top of the **Torre Colpatria** for an incredible 360-degree view of the massive city. Walk along the pedestrianized Carrera 7, spending some time at the fantastic museums of the **Manzana Cultural,** including the **Museo Botero.** Catch a concert in the Florentine **Teatro Colón** or hear the **Orquesta Filarmónica de Bogotá** play at the Universidad Nacional campus.

If the next morning is a Sunday, enjoy the city's **Ciclovía** by renting a bike and joining the thousands of Bogotanos hitting the streets in this

Colombia feels like a celebration year-round, but especially during these colorful music and dance festivals.

CALI

Cali residents boast that their city is the world capital of salsa, and there's no denying that it's an integral part of daily life in Cali. The last week of the year is the **Feria de Cali,** a weeklong event of open-air salsa concerts, parties, and pageantry that takes over the city.

Another major festival worth checking out is the **Festival Petronio Álvarez,** a September celebration of Pacific coast music and culture.

VILLAVICENCIO

On the Llanos, the great eastern plains of Colombia, cowhands work on cattle ranches during the day. At night, they get out their harps and jam a Llanero form of waltz called *joropo.* During the **Torneo Internacional del Joropo** in June, musicians and dancers from across the Llanos converge on Villavicencio, participating in open-air concerts and competitions. Cowboys show their stuff in Llanero rodeos during the weeklong festival.

MEDELLÍN

Tango has a long history in Medellín. The **Festival Internacional de Tango** is held each year in June, offering four days of free concerts and dance performances across the city.

BARRANQUILLA

Colombia's favorite party is the **Carnaval de Barranquilla,** held each year in February.

Carnaval de Barranquilla

Cumbia, an intriguing mix of indigenous, African, and Spanish musical styles, takes center stage at this multiday event of parades, concerts, and revelry.

BOGOTÁ

Typical of the way this metropolis rolls, Bogotá doesn't have just one music celebration. From July to November, the action takes place in the city's largest park, the Parque Simón Bolívar, during the **Festivales al Parque** series: Salsa al Parque, Jazz al Parque, and the thumping Rock al Parque.

weekly ritual. If it's not a Sunday, hike or ride to the top of the **Cerro de Monserrate** for great views of the city.

San Agustín, Popayán, and Cali

DAYS 1-2

Fly into Neiva and immediately head south to **San Agustín,** the most important archaeological site in Colombia. It's the country's version of

Easter Island, set amid lush countryside in the Cordillera Central of the Andes. Take your time visiting the park: Two days should do it.

Stay in one of the cute guesthouses, such as **El Maco,** that dot the lovely countryside.

DAYS 3-4

Contract private transportation or take the scenic route (involving a couple of buses) to the village of

San Andrés de Pisimbalá, at the edge of another important archaeological site, **Tierradentro.** This series of underground burial tombs is spread atop hills in the lush countryside. It's a scenic place, and you should take your time and walk the sites at a leisurely pace, splitting your visit across two days.

Stay in San Andrés de Pisimbalá at the **La Portada** guesthouse.

DAY 5

Take the four-hour scenic bus ride to the historic White City of **Popayán.** Wander the streets and linger in the beautiful **Parque Caldas.**

Stay at the friendly **Hostel Caracol** or at the classic **Hotel Dann Monasterio.** Before retiring, listen to some tango music over a cold beer at **El Sotareño.**

DAY 6

Take the easy two-hour bus ride to Cali. In the late afternoon, enjoy the atmosphere of the **Parque San Antonio,** the best place for people-watching or enjoying the sunset.

Have dinner in one of the cozy restaurants in the sloping San Antonio neighborhood, and stay there, too, at the **Ruta Sur** hostel or the **San Antonio Hotel Boutique.** Later, check out a *salsoteca* (dance club) for a truly authentic Cali experience. Get a good night's rest to prepare for your flight home tomorrow.

Excursions and Side Trips
SAN ANDRÉS AND PROVIDENCIA

If you're looking to get away from it all, go to the island of Providencia, part of the San Andrés Archipelago, off the coast of Nicaragua. Allot at least four days for some solid beach relaxation time.

Fly into San Andrés. To get to Providencia from there, it's just a short flight. Once in Providencia, stay at the **Hotel Sirius,** where dive experts can take you to the reefs for a few underwater adventures. Add 1-2 days in San Andrés if you're into snorkeling, diving, and drinking coco locos.

THE AMAZON

This quick but meaningful Amazon adventure

parrots

beach in San Andrés

Social-Impact Tourism

flamingos at Santuario de Fauna y Flora Los Flamencos

The annual number of international visitors to Colombia increased almost threefold from 2000 to 2012. This boom has fostered a growth of community and ecotourism options. Here are several ways to support the local people, plants, or animals, all while having the vacation of your dreams.

- **Stay in a *posada nativa*.** The interior of **San Andrés** (page 373) is home to *posadas nativas* (native guesthouses) that are owned and operated by locals, many of whom have deep roots on the island. Stay at a *posada nativa* and you'll get to know the local culture.

- **Visit a national park.** Colombia's system of natural parks and protected areas cover around 13.4 percent of the country. The Parks Service actively engages local communities, with much of the ecotourism infrastructure being operated by community-based organizations. Some of the region's best parks are **Parque Nacional Natural Tayrona** (page 128) near Santa Marta and **Parque Nacional Natural Old Providence McBean Lagoon** (page 376) on Providencia.

- **Save the animals.** At the **Bahía de Cispatá refuge** (page 151) in San Antero, local fishers are helping to protect crocodiles and turtles, once hunted for their meat and eggs. Visit the **Santuario de Fauna y Flora Los Flamencos** (page 143), most famously known for its population of migratory flamingos. Here, conservationists also work to keep threatened sea turtles safe.

will require at least four days. Leticia is the gateway to the Colombian Amazon. It's a two-hour flight from Bogotá. At the **Reserva Natural Tanimboca,** you can stay in a treehouse in the jungle, just minutes from town.

For the next couple of days, take a boat up the world's most powerful river and visit the Ticuna community of **San Martín.** Continue onward to the decidedly eco-friendly **Puerto Nariño.**

Alternatively, you can head straight to the eco-lodges along the **Río Javari,** in Brazil, where you can take day and nighttime safaris, discovering the abundant life of the Amazonian rainforest and river.

The Wild Coasts

If you have the time and an adventurous spirit, check out some of Colombia's wildest stretches of coastline, from the rocky Pacific and the Darién to the dry tropical forests of Córdoba.

Caribbean Coast

This ambitious weeklong itinerary takes you to lesser-known points along the Caribbean coast. Be prepared to take several modes of transportation in order to get around. If you don't have a full week to spend here, prioritize a visit to Capurganá or Río Cedro. Waters can be rough between December and February.

DAY 1

From Cartagena, board a bus for the three-hour ride to sleepy **Tolú**. Upon arrival, hop on a tour of the **Islas de San Bernardo.** Soak up the sun, splash about in the Caribbean, and settle in for the night at the resort **Punta Faro** or **Casa en el Agua,** a fun floating hotel.

DAY 2

Today is all about island-hopping. Take a tour of the neighboring islands, including **Santa Cruz del Islote,** considered the most densely populated island in the world.

Take a boat back to Tolú and spend the night at **Villa Babilla,** where you can prepare your own dinner and soak up the silence.

DAY 3

In the morning, take a minibus to **Bahía de Cispatá,** a turtle and crocodile refuge run by local fishers near the town of San Antero. Once you've worked up an appetite, have a fresh seafood lunch at **Pesecar,** which is perched on Bahía de Cispatá.

From here, it's a three-hour trip to **Río Cedro.** Take a minibus from San Antero to Lorica, then transfer to a bus headed for Moñitos. From there, you can arrange for a motorbike to take you to **Reserva Natural Viento Solar.** You'll arrive at this private reserve on undeveloped coastline in

bay near Capurganá

baby sea turtle

Reserva Natural Viento Solar

time to take a walk on the secluded beaches and go for a dip in the calm waters. Settle into one of the thatched-roof cabins, lulled to sleep by the sounds of the jungle and sea.

DAYS 4-5

Wake up early and take a walk through the tropical dry forest of the reserve. If you're lucky, you may spot an *oso perezoso* (sloth) clinging to a tree. Enjoy a quiet breakfast before hitting the road to the **Darién Gap,** a region that straddles the Colombia-Panama border.

It's a multi-hour trip to the beach town of **Necoclí.** Take a motorbike to Montería, then hop on a bus headed for Necoclí. Check into the **Hotel Panorama Suite** for the night.

The next morning, take a fast boat across the gulf to **Capurganá,** which takes about 1.5 hours. Once you arrive in Capurganá, stay at the friendly **Cabañas El Tucán, Cabañas Darius,** or at the secluded, honeymoon-worthy **Bahía Lodge.**

DAY 6

Get up nice and early for a day of hiking and exploration. Hike through the jungle surrounding Capurganá to **El Cielo waterfall** and splash around in the water before heading back into town. Next, take the two-hour hike to the neighboring town of **Sapzurro,** letting the howler monkeys guide you. Have lunch at the **Gata Negra.**

Head back to Capurganá and have a gourmet dinner on the beach at **Donde Josefina.**

For those more interested in exploring the water, spend the day on a **snorkel or dive trip.** This region has over 30 diving sites to choose from, so expect a full day on the water.

DAY 7

Today you return to Cartagena. Take a boat to Necoclí, and then a long bus ride back to Cartagena. Alternatively, you could fly to Medellín if you're traveling onward in Colombia.

Pacific Coast

The Pacific coast is different from the Caribbean side. There are few roads, and the main mode of transportation is by boat. The best way to visit the Pacific is to pick a spot and limit your time to that area. If you make your accommodations arrangements beforehand, your hostel or lodge will pick you up from the airport. Your lodge can also arrange **humpback whale-watching** trips from July to October. Seeing these great creatures is a highlight of any visit to the Pacific.

BAHÍA SOLANO

This town at the fringe of the jungle is a great base for any activity. Go diving or sportfishing, or hike in the jungle or along the beach to crystal-clear swimming holes and waterfalls like the **Cascada Chocólatal.** Or hang out in orderly and walkable Bahía Solano and experience city life, Pacific style.

Spend a few nights at one of Bahía Solano's hotels, like **Posada Turística Rocas de Cabo Marzo** or **Posada Turística Hostal del Mar.**

- **Getting There:** The flight to Bahía Solano from Medellín takes one hour. You can even walk from the airport to your hotel.

EL VALLE

El Valle boasts broad beaches and the fantastic **Estación Septiembre Sea Turtle Hatchery,** where newborn sea turtles are released into the turbulent waters of the Pacific Ocean, as well as unforgettable sunsets over **Playa Almejal.**

Stay the night at one of the several fantastic beachside lodges and hostels of El Valle, or get to know the cultural life of the people of the Pacific by staying at one of the *posadas nativas* (guesthouses owned and operated by locals) here, such as **Villa Maga.**

- **Getting There:** Fly into the Bahía Solano airport. El Valle is home to one of the few roads in this area, so you can hop on a *colectivo* to reach your lodge.

NUQUÍ

Five-star eco-lodges, as well as a few economical options, abound on the coastline near Nuquí. If you stay at one of the eco-lodges, like **El Cantíl** or **Morromico,** you'll quickly become accustomed to being pampered. Their all-inclusive packages include great seafood dinners, access to remote beaches, **guided nature hikes** in search of colorful dart frogs, and day trips to Afro-Colombian and Emberá **indigenous villages.**

sunset on Playa Almejal

Parque Nacional Natural Utría

- **Getting There:** The flight into Nuquí from Medellín takes 45 minutes.

PARQUE NACIONAL NATURAL UTRÍA

This beautiful **national park** between Nuquí and Bahía Solano is the perfect option for those who want to be surrounded by nature. Take a hike, discover a remote beach, or go swimming. At night, you can hunt for glow-in-the-dark mushrooms, then fall asleep to the sounds of the rainforest.

- **Getting There:** You can reach PNN Utría from either the Bahía Solano or Nuquí airport. Park staff will pick you up.

Colonial Towns and Countryside

Gorgeous countryside, historic pueblos and cities, and outdoor adventures: Get a taste of what Bogotá, Boyacá, and Santander have to offer.

Days 1-3

Spend a couple of days in **Bogotá** wandering the **Candelaria,** the capital city's *centro histórico*, then visit the **Quinta de Bolívar,** Simón Bolívar's old country home. Don't miss the **Cerro de Monserrate,** a pilgrimage site with unsurpassed views of the metropolis. Hike up, then take a ride on the gondola or tram back down.

Learn about Colombia's past from the time of the Muiscas to its shaky years as an independent nation in the city's excellent museums, like the extensive art galleries of the **Manzana Cultural** and the mesmerizing **Museo del Oro.**

Days 4-5

After setting off from Bogotá, make your way

to **Tunja**, a three-hour bus ride. Tunja is a city of spectacular **colonial churches**. Spend a few hours checking them out, then head on to the nearby colonial town of **Villa de Leyva**, one of the country's most beautiful and well-preserved pueblos, just 45 minutes away.

Villa de Leyva's charm is in its quiet atmosphere and lovely whitewashed colonial architecture. The **Plaza Mayor** is the top place to experience both. In the countryside nearby, check out the **Santuario Fauna y Flora Iguaque** for a half-day hike to Laguna Iguaque, which was sacred to the Muiscas. In the adjacent arid deserts, visit the lovely **Convento del Santo Ecce Homo**.

Day 6

Today is a travel day. Return to Tunja to catch a bus bound for **Barichara**, which is Villa de Leyva's rival for most beautiful pueblo. Judge for yourself as you walk the stone streets of this old tobacco town in the department of Santander.

Days 7-8

Stroll the famous **Camino Real** to the indigenous village of **Guane** and return to Barichara in time for the spectacular sunset. Stay at the **Color de Hormiga Hostel** or **Posada del Campanario** and wake up to the chirping of colorful birds.

Barichara makes a great base for all sorts of outdoor adventures in and around **San Gil**. Spend a day hiking to waterfalls, rafting, splashing in swimming holes, or caving. Have dinner at **Gringo Mike's** in San Gil.

Day 9

Head north toward **Bucaramanga**. On the way there, visit the **Cañón del Chicamocha** and be blown away by the views. It's a 1.5-hour trip to the canyon. Stay the night at **Hotel Hacienda El Roble**, a coffee farm and guesthouse.

Day 10

On your last morning in the area, cap things off by paragliding at **Mesa de Ruitoque** outside of Bucaramanga. If soaring above the green valleys is too much action, visit the colonial town of **Girón** nearby, and treat yourself with a sweet *oblea* (wafer) dripping in caramel.

From the Bucaramanga airport, catch a flight back to Bogotá.

Excursion to El Cocuy

Got more time and need some mountains to conquer? You can get to the **Sierra Nevada del Cocuy** by land directly from Tunja or from Bucaramanga, going through the highland university town of **Pamplona**. Add at least four more days for this option.

Bogotá

Highlights

★ **Plaza de Bolívar:** Colombia's most important and most photographed plaza is named for Simón Bolívar, the man who gave the country independence (page 34).

★ **Iglesia Museo Santa Clara:** This colonial-era church, an example of Mudejar architecture, is often host to edgy art exhibits (page 37).

★ **Manzana Cultural:** Colombia's tumultuous history has given rise to some noteworthy creative expression that is on display in the art museums of the city's cultural block (page 39).

★ **Museo del Oro:** Anthropology, history, and art combine in this extraordinary presentation of pre-Columbian gold artifacts (page 42).

★ **Cerro de Monserrate:** The views from atop this hill are incredible both by day and by night (page 43).

★ **Ciclovía:** When a city can get a quarter of its population to get out and ride a bike on a Sunday, you know it's doing something right (page 56).

★ **Nemocón:** The plaza and streets of this little-visited salt-mining town are full of charm (page 75).

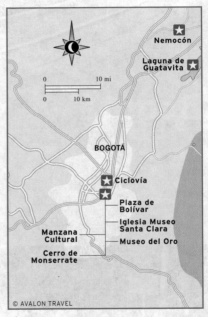

© AVALON TRAVEL

★ **Laguna de Guatavita:** This sacred lake is the source of the El Dorado myth (page 76).

Busy Bogotá is Colombia's cool capital—and not just in terms of its famously chilly nights.

A few years ago, visitors would arrive at the El Dorado airport and spend two days maximum in the Andean metropolis before taking the next flight to Cartagena. Now people are staying awhile, and it's easy to see why.

There is the Museo del Oro, of course, undoubtedly one of the best museums in Latin America. There are precious few reminders of the Muisca settlement of Bacatá in this vast concrete jungle of today, but this museum is a stellar tribute to a people who all but disappeared within decades of the Spanish conquest.

Then there is the living museum that is the historic district, La Candelaria. Every street block has its unique story to tell: the flower vase that changed history, the loyal companion who saved the Liberator's neck, the generosity of a famous painter. Colonial churches surprise with their quiet, steadfast beauty, and grandiose buildings along Avenida Jiménez stand as testament to the aspirations of the "Athens of South America." Red buses, glitzy shopping areas, and stunning libraries set in manicured parks are proof that Bogotá can, with a little investment and good government,

overcome the formidable challenges of its recent past.

A melting pot of nearly eight million, Bogotá is home to Colombians from every corner of the country who come to study, seek opportunity, or crave the freedom and anonymity that this sprawling city offers. It shouldn't come as a surprise that it is the country's culinary and cultural capital as well. This is the place to enjoy nouvelle Colombian cuisine, with flavors from the two coasts served at a host of innovative restaurants. It's the place where there is always something going on—a massive theater festival, a symphony concert, a dance marathon courtesy of a big-name DJ, a gallery opening—it's just a matter of finding out when and where. Bogotanos' reputation for being gloomy and cerebral is unfair. You only need to experience the sheer *alegría* (joyfulness) of Andrés Carne de Res one weekend night for proof.

When the intensity of this over-caffeinated city becomes too much, the *páramos* (highland moors), cloud forests, and mountain lakes of extraordinary natural parks beckon. Parque Nacional Natural Chingaza, Parque

Previous: Biblioteca Virgilio Barco; the Sunday Ciclovía. **Above:** flying kites at the Biblioteca Virgilio Barco.

Bogotá

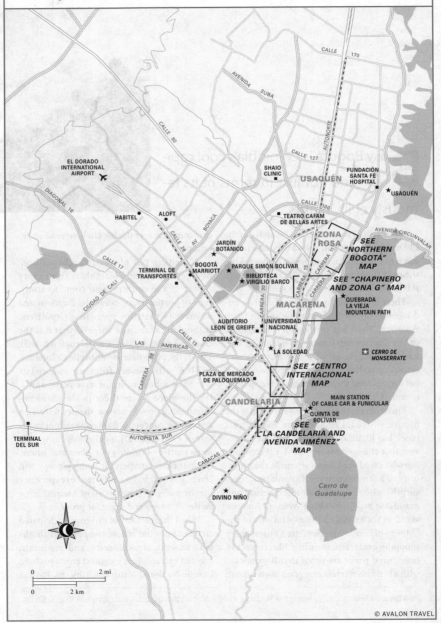

CALLE 170

AVENIDA SUBA

CALLE 80

AUTONORTE

EL DORADO
INTERNATIONAL
AIRPORT

DIAGONAL 16

CALLE 127

SHAIO
CLINIC

FUNDACIÓN
SANTA FÉ
HOSPITAL

USAQUÉN

★ USAQUÉN

CALLE 100

HABITEL

ALOFT

CALLE 26

AV. BOYACÁ

TEATRO CAFAM
DE BELLAS ARTES

ZONA
ROSA

AVENIDA CIRCUNVALAR

*SEE
"NORTHERN
BOGOTÁ"
MAP*

CALLE 17

CIUDAD DE CALI

JARDÍN
BOTÁNICO ★

TERMINAL DE
TRANSPORTES

BOGOTÁ
MARRIOTT

PARQUE SIMÓN BOLÍVAR ★

CARRERA 30

CARRERA 15

CARRERA 11

CARRERA 7

*SEE "CHAPINERO
AND ZONA G" MAP*

BIBLIOTECA
VIRGILIO BARCO ★

MACARENA

★ QUEBRADA
LA VIEJA
MOUNTAIN PATH

CALLE 13

AUDITORIO
LEON DE GREIFF ★

UNIVERSIDAD
NACIONAL

LAS AMERICAS

CARRERA 68

CORFERIAS ★

★ LA SOLEDAD

✚ CERRO DE
MONSERRATE

PLAZA DE MERCADO
DE PALOQUEMAO ■

*SEE "CENTRO
INTERNACIONAL"
MAP*

CANDELARIA

MAIN STATION
OF CABLE CAR & FUNICULAR

★ QUINTA DE
BOLÍVAR

AUTOPISTA SUR

*SEE
"LA CANDELARIA AND
AVENIDA JIMÉNEZ"
MAP*

TERMINAL
DEL SUR

CARACAS

Cerro de
Guadalupe

★ DIVINO NIÑO

☾

0   2 mi

0   2 km

© AVALON TRAVEL

Natural Chicaque, and Laguna de Guatavita are all only about an hour away.

HISTORY

As early as AD 300, the Muisca people settled along the Cordillera Oriental (Eastern Mountain Range) of the Andes Mountains, forming a loose confederation. Bacatá (now Bogotá) was the seat of the Zipa, head of the southern confederation. The Muiscas had an agricultural economy but also extracted salt and emeralds, wove fine textiles, and actively traded for cotton, shells, and gold with other indigenous peoples. The names of many of their settlements—Chía, Suba, Engativá—survive, though no physical traces remain.

Lured by tales of riches, three European armies converged on Muisca territory in 1538. An army headed by Spanish conquistador Gonzalo Jiménez de Quesada arrived from Santa Marta. Another army, headed by Spaniard Sebastián de Belalcázar, approached from the south. A third army, led by German expeditionary Nikolaus Federmann, followed a route from present-day Venezuela.

By the time Federmann and Belalcázar arrived, Jiménez de Quesada had plundered the Muisca lands. In August 1538 Jiménez de Quesada founded a settlement that he named Santa Fe de Bogotá del Nuevo Reino de Granada de las Indias del Mar, and by the late 17th century the town was home to roughly 15,000 people. European diseases had almost completely wiped out the Muisca population by that time, and marriages between Muiscas and the Spanish formed the *mestizo* base of the city.

The city was the seat of the first provisional government established after Colombia's declaration of independence in 1810. In 1819, the name of the city was changed to Bogotá, and it became capital of the newly formed Gran Colombia. The city was not connected by railroad to the outside world until the end of the 19th century—and then only to Girardot, a port on the Río Magdalena.

The early decades of the 20th century were a period of growth and prosperity. The postwar period was a time of rapid, haphazard development that saw the establishment of many new industries. Much of the growth was unplanned, and sprawling slums developed, especially in the south of the city.

By the 1990s, Bogotá had become synonymous with poverty, crime, and urban sprawl. A series of mayors, including Enrique Peñalosa and Antanas Mockus, transformed the city with large projects such as the TransMilenio rapid bus system and by investing heavily in education and basic services. In 2015, the city reelected Peñalosa on his promises of a metro, expanded public services, and greater security.

Despite all its challenges Bogotá continues to be the economic, cultural, and educational powerhouse of Colombia. The city is a magnet for people from all over the country and, in recent years, even from abroad.

PLANNING YOUR TIME

At the minimum, give Bogotá two days. In that short time span, you can cover La Candelaria, head up to Monserrate, discover the Museo del Oro, and enjoy some good meals in the Zona T, Zona G, or the Macarena.

With about five days you can explore neighborhoods like the Macarena, check out the botanical gardens, or make a day trip to the Parque Natural Chicaque or to Laguna de Guatavita. If you're here over a Sunday, you'll absolutely have to head out to the Ciclovía.

If you are staying in Colombia for 10 days, you can try a city-country combo by adding Villa de Leyva. Or make it a city-coast combo, adding a Caribbean coast destination such as Cartagena or Santa Marta.

Many museums are closed on either Monday or Tuesday. The Museo del Oro is closed Mondays and the art museums of the Manzana Cultural are closed Tuesdays. During the end-of-year holidays and Holy Week (Semana Santa), Bogotá becomes a ghost town as locals head for the countryside, the coast, or abroad. There is very little traffic at those times, but many restaurants are closed and nightspots are empty, especially around Christmas. Bogotá is a particularly dull place to be on New Year's Eve. Semana Santa is perhaps less lonely and can be a good time to visit, especially when the biennial theater festival is on. On long weekends, many Bogotanos skip town; those from the provinces come for a visit.

SAFETY

Bogotá is much safer than it once was. The best advice is to, as Colombians would say, *"no dar papaya."* Literally, that translates to "don't give any papayas." Don't hand someone the opportunity to take advantage of you.

While strolling in La Candelaria, keep a watchful eye on cameras and other gadgets. Better yet, leave valuables—including passports—locked away in the hotel safe if possible. Private security guards and police now regularly patrol La Candelaria at night, although it may feel a little spooky after 10pm or 11pm.

Traveling by the city's SITP buses is safe and comfortable. The red TransMilenio buses can get crowded, so be aware of pickpockets. Private buses and *colectivos* are less safe and drivers can be reckless.

Bogotá has had a serious problem with taxi crime, commonly known as *paseo milonario*. But recent technological advances have nearly eliminated these crimes. Tappsi and EasyTaxi are popular and free smartphone apps in which you can request a cab, find out the name of the driver, and have your trip tracked by a friend. Alternatively, you can use ride-sharing apps like Uber. Avoid hailing cabs off the street, particularly when you are alone, when it is late at night, and when you are near nightclubs and up-scale dining areas.

If you are heading out for a night on the town, do not accept drinks from strangers. Leave credit/debit cards, your passport, and expensive cell phones at home.

During an emergency, call 123 from any phone.

ORIENTATION

Sprawling Bogotá covers some 1,776 square kilometers (686 square miles), filling a large part of the *altiplano* (high plateau), or savanna. Much of your time will likely be spent along the corridor that is **Carrera 7** or **Avenida 7** (called the **Séptima**). The Séptima extends, parallel to the eastern mountains, from the Plaza de Bolívar in La Candelaria north through the Centro Internacional and Chapinero, and then to Usaquén and beyond.

Bogotá street addresses are generally easy to figure out. *Calles* (streets) run east-west (perpendicular to the mountains), while *carreras* go north-south (parallel to the mountains). For example, the Museo del Oro address is Calle 16 No. 5-41. This means it is on Calle 16, 41 meters from Carrera 5. The Centro Andino shopping mall is at Carrera 11 No. 82-71, or on Carrera 11, 71 meters from Calle 82. The higher the number of the *calle*, the farther north you are. Similarly, the higher the number of the *carrera*, the farther west you go.

The city planners also created *avenidas* (avenues), *diagonales*, and *transversales*. Both *diagonales* and *transversales* are streets on the diagonal. To add to the fun, some *calles* are also called *avenida calles*, because they are major thoroughfares, and likewise there are some called *avenida carrera*. Avenida Calle 26 is also known as Avenida El Dorado. Carrera 30 is also known as Avenida Quito or NQS. There are some streets that are called *bis*, as in Calle 70A *bis* or Carrera 13 *bis*. It's like an extra half street. Finally, addresses in the south of Bogotá have *sur* (south) in their address. The address for the 20 de Julio shrine is Calle 27 Sur No. 5A-27.

La Candelaria

La Candelaria is the oldest part of town, dating to the 16th century. With the Plaza de Bolívar at its heart, it is a neighborhood full of historic buildings, interesting museums, and hostels. This area, combined with Avenida Jiménez and Centro Internacional, is generally considered Bogotá's downtown or Centro. La Candelaria is bounded by Carrera 10 on the west, Calle 7 to the south, Carrera 1 to the east, and Avenida Jiménez to the north.

Avenida Jiménez

The northern border of La Candelaria, Avenida Jiménez is also known as the Eje Ambiental. This pedestrian street that is shared with a TransMilenio line winds from Carrera 10 eastward to Carrera 3, where it morphs into Carrera 2A. In addition to being the home of the Museo del Oro, colonial churches, the Quinta de Bolívar, and the Cerro de Monserrate, the area is also known for its grand early-20th-century architecture.

Centro Internacional

North of La Candelaria, the Centro Internacional is home to the Museo de Arte Moderno de Bogotá and the Museo Nacional, as well as the bullfighting ring and the iconic Torres del Parque complex. This neighborhood straddles the Séptima (Cra. 7) and spans from Avenida El Dorado (Cl. 26) north to Calle 36.

Just above this is the quirky neighborhood of Macarena, full of art galleries and cozy restaurants.

Chapinero

Most people consider Chapinero to extend from around Calle 45 to about Calle 72, although officially it continues north to Calle 100. Its western boundary is Avenida Carrera 14 (also known as Avenida Caracas), and its eastern boundary pushes up against the mountains.

The neighborhood's eastern half (east of the Séptima) is known as the **Chapinero Alto** and is mostly residential. To the west of the Séptima is a gritty commerce center that is also considered a hub of gay nightlife. There are no major sights in Chapinero.

Northern Bogotá

Northern Bogotá does not have many tourist sights, but it offers myriad options for dining, shopping, and nightlife. This neighborhood has its southern border at Calle 68 and houses pockets of activity in the **Zona G** (between Clls. 69-70 east of the Séptima to Cra. 5), the **Zona Rosa** (between Clls. 81-85 and Cras. 11-15), and the **Parque de la 93 area** (between Clls. 91-94 and Cras. 11-15).

In the Zona Rosa, Calle 82 and Carrera 13 form a T—hence the moniker **Zona T**—and are pedestrian streets lined with restaurants and thumping watering holes.

East of the Séptima between Calles 120 and 125 is **Usaquén,** a once traditional pueblo that has been enveloped by Bogotá. Usaquén is known for its Sunday flea market and restaurants.

Western Bogotá

Western Bogotá (west of Av. Cra. 14) includes the Parque Simón Bolívar, along with the Jardín Botánico and the Biblioteca Virgilio Barco.

Farther west, Avenida Carrera 30 intersects with Avenida El Dorado (Calle 26), which connects the El Dorado airport with downtown. In addition to its TransMilenio line, this nicely designed thoroughfare is lined with hotels, shopping centers, and the fortress-like U.S. Embassy.

Sights

Everything you need to see in Bogotá is downtown, from La Candelaria to the Centro Internacional. Most museums have at least limited English explanations, and some have English-language tours.

LA CANDELARIA

La Candelaria is a living museum. It is a reminder of Spanish power and ambition in the New World; a tribute to the yearning for freedom embodied by Colombia's founding fathers; and a reflection on the tenacity of the independent Colombian republic to persevere in the face of adversity. La Candelaria is a bustling place and has been for centuries. These days, university students, government bureaucrats, tourists, and old-timers who have lived in the area for decades pass each other along the narrow streets and frequent the same cafés.

You could spend a couple of days admiring the colonial churches and exploring the many museums in the area, but if you don't have that much time, three or four hours will give you a good sense of the area and its significance. All of the sights in La Candelaria are easily and best visited on foot. Areas above the Chorro de Quevedo (toward the eastern mountains), as well as some parts to the west, bordering Avenida Caracas, can be a little sketchy and should be avoided.

★ Plaza de Bolívar

Every respectable Colombian city has a Plaza de Bolívar, but none have quite the history of this one. Between Carreras 7-8 and Calles 10-11, the **Plaza de Bolívar** is the natural starting point for any tour of La Candelaria. Originally known as the Plaza Mayor, the plaza has had several reincarnations during its history. In colonial times, it was where the Friday market took place. It was also the setting for executions, including that of independence heroine Policarpa Salavarrieta. Following the death of Simón Bolívar in 1846, Congress renamed the plaza in his honor. A diminutive statue of the Liberator, the first of many Bolívar statues in the world, stands in the middle of the plaza. Today it's the location

Plaza de Bolívar

La Candelaria and Avenida Jiménez

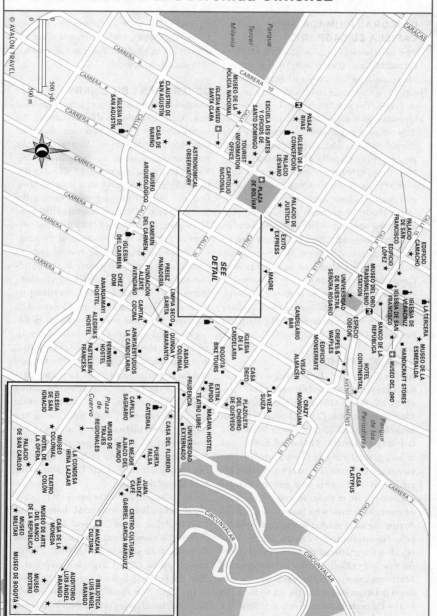

© AVALON TRAVEL

0
0

500 yds
500 m

CARRERA 9
CARRERA 8
CARRERA 7
CARRERA 8
CARRERA 7
CARRERA 6
CARRERA 5
CARRERA 4
CARRERA 3

CARRERA 10
CARRERA 15
CARRERA 13
CARRERA 3

Parque Tercer Milenio
Parque de los Periodistas

CARACAS

CIRCUNVALAR
CIRCUNVALAR

CALLE 9
CALLE 7
CALLE 8
CALLE 10
CALLE 11
CALLE 13
CALLE 15
CALLE 16
CALLE 18

AVENIDA JIMÉNEZ

SEE DETAIL

MUSEO DE LA POLICÍA NACIONAL
IGLESIA MUSEO SANTA CLARA
CLAUSTRO DE SAN AGUSTÍN
IGLESIA DE SAN AGUSTÍN
CASA DE NARIÑO
ASTRONOMICAL OBSERVATORY
PASAJE RIVAS
ESCUELA DES ARTES Y OFICIOS DE SANTO DOMINGO
TOURIST INFORMATION OFFICE
IGLESIA DE LA CONCEPCIÓN
PALACIO LIÉVANO
CAPITOLIO NACIONAL
PLAZA DE BOLÍVAR
PALACIO DE JUSTICIA
ÉXITO EXPRESS
MUSEO ARQUEOLÓGICO
CAMERÍN DEL CARMEN
IGLESIA DEL CARMEN
FUNDACIÓN ALZATE AVENDAÑO
CHEZ DOM
ANANDAMAYI HOSTEL
ALEGRÍA'S HOSTEL
FERNWEH HOSTEL
PASTELERÍA FRANCESA
PRESZ PANADERÍA
LIMPIA SECO SANTA
CAPITAL APARTAESTUDIOS LA CANDELARIA
QUINOA Y AMARANTO
COCINA
ABADÍA COLONIAL
MADRE
IGLESIA DE LA CANDELARIA
BOGOTÁ BIKE TOURS
CANDELARIO BAR
CASA DECO
PRUDENCIA
EXTRA RÁPIDO
TEATRO LIBRE
MASAYA HOSTEL
UNIVERSIDAD EXTERNADO
LA VIEJA SUIZA
PLAZOLETA DEL CHORRO DE QUEVEDO
VIEJO ALMACÉN
CRAZY MONGOLIAN
UNIVERSIDAD DE NUESTRA SEÑORA ROSARIO
MUSEO DEL ORO TRANSMILENIO STATION
ESPACIO ODEÓN
CREPES & WAFFLES
EDIFICIO MONSERRATE
HOTEL CONTINENTAL
BANCO DE LA REPÚBLICA
MUSEO DEL ORO
IGLESIA DE SAN FRANCISCO
MUSEO DE VERACRUZ
LA TERCERA
MUSEO DE LA ESMERALDA
HANDICRAFT STORES
EDIFICIO PALACIO DE SAN FRANCISCO
EDIFICIO LÓPEZ
EDIFICIO CAMACHO
CASA PLATYPUS

Detail:

Plaza de Cuervo

IGLESIA DE SAN IGNACIO
MUSEO COLONIAL
HOTEL DE LA ÓPERA
PALACIO DE SAN CARLOS
CAPILLA DEL SAGRARIO
MUSEO DE TRAJES REGIONALES
CATEDRAL
EL MEJOR AJIACO DEL MUNDO
LA CONDESA IRINA LAZAAR
TEATRO COLÓN
PUERTA FALSA
CASA DEL FLORERO
JUAN VALDEZ CAFÉ
CENTRO CULTURAL GABRIEL GARCÍA MÁRQUEZ
MANZANA CULTURAL
CASA DE LA MONEDA
MUSEO DE ARTE DEL BANCO DE LA REPÚBLICA
MUSEO MILITAR
MUSEO BOTERO
MUSEO DE BOGOTÁ
AUDITORIO LUIS ÁNGEL ARANGO
BIBLIOTECA LUIS ÁNGEL ARANGO

of demonstrations, inauguration ceremonies for the Bogotá mayor, and concerts.

CATEDRAL PRIMADA AND CAPILLA EL SAGRARIO

The neoclassical facade of the **Catedral Primada** (9am-4:30pm daily) dominates the plaza. Built in 1807, the cathedral was designed by Capuchin architect Fray Domingo de Petrés. The tombs of Gonzalo Jiménez de Quesada, founder of Bogotá, and independence figure Antonio Nariño are in a side chapel on the right. Next door to the cathedral is the **Capilla El Sagrario** (Cra. 7 No. 10-40, 8:30am-11:50am and 1pm-4pm Mon.-Fri., 8:30am-5pm Sun.). This chapel was built much earlier than the cathedral, in the 1600s. The interior is decorated with a Mudejar or Moorish-style vaulted wooden ceiling. Along the sides of the cross-shaped chapel are several large works depicting biblical scenes by Colombian baroque painter Gregorio Vásquez de Arce y Ceballos. A ceremony was held here to honor the army and Simón Bolívar following their decisive victory over the Spaniards at the Battle of Boyacá in 1819.

CASA DEL FLORERO

Across Calle 10 on the northeast corner of the plaza is the **Casa del Florero** (Cra. 7 No. 11-28, tel. 1/334-4150, 9am-5pm Tues.-Fri., 10am-4pm Sat.-Sun, COP$3,000), also known as the **Museo del 20 de Julio** or **Museo de la Independencia**. This small house used to be a general store run by a Spaniard, José González-Llorente. The story goes that his refusal to lend a vase to a pair of Creoles sparked the ire of either incredibly sensitive or cunning locals, who launched a protest during the busy market day against Spanish rule. Historians today dispute much of the tale, but the shattered remains of that colorful vase are exhibited today in the museum. Maybe the most interesting exhibit in the museum is a room that shows the transformation of the Plaza de Bolívar over time, with raw footage of two of the most traumatic events in recent Colombian history: the Bogotazo riots following the assassination of Jorge Eliécer Gaitán in 1948 and the siege of the Palacio de Justicia following a takeover by the M-19 guerrilla group in 1985. There are some explanations in English. Tours are also available, usually in Spanish.

GOVERNMENT BUILDINGS

The newest building on the plaza, completed in 1991, is the **Palacio de Justicia** on the north side. Housing the Supreme Court and other high courts, this building replaced the previous structure, which was destroyed following the tragic events of 1985. (That building had replaced a previous justice building that was burned to the ground during the Bogotazo riots.) On November 6 of that year, M-19 guerrillas stormed the building, perhaps in cahoots with infamous drug kingpin Pablo Escobar, killing several justices and holding some 350 people in the building hostage. After an hours-long standoff, the military counterattacked, coordinating its assault from the Casa del Florero. The fight concluded the next day with the building engulfed in flames, the result of a military rocket. More than 100 people were killed, and controversy remains about the tragedy and the government's actions. Five years after the attack the M-19 demobilized, becoming a political movement. Today, it is telling that there is not even a plaque mentioning the tragedy. Nevertheless, clearly some wounds have healed: Former M-19 guerrilla Gustavo Petro was elected mayor in 2011, with his office (*alcaldía*) in the **Palacio Liéviano** on the west side of the plaza.

On the south side of the square is the neoclassical **Capitolio Nacional,** home of the bicameral Colombian Congress. Designed by architect Thomas Reed, the Capitolio took more than 70 years to build, finally being completed in 1926. Gargoyles keep watch atop the building behind the Ionic columns of the front. For about two months in 2009 the entire facade was covered with 1,300 massive ants, a project of Colombian artist Rafael

Golden floral motifs adorn the nave at the Iglesia Museo Santa Clara.

IGLESIA DE LA CONCEPCIÓN

The **Iglesia de la Concepción** (Cl.10 No. 9-50, 7am-5pm daily) was completed in 1595, making it the second-oldest church in the city. Along with a convent, it used to take up an entire block of old Santa Fe. The convent (which no longer exists) was built for the daughters and granddaughters of the conquistadors. The spectacular geometric designs on the ceiling and the polychromatic presbytery are among the most striking aspects of the church. If you pop in, you will see many faithful—most of humble means—in the pews, praying. This city block is called Calle del Divorcio. This refers to a nearby residence for separated or single women who were banished from their homes and not allowed into convents.

Farther down the street beyond the Iglesia de la Concepción is the historic labyrinthine artisans market known as the **Pasaje Rivas.**

MUSEO DE LA POLICÍA NACIONAL

The grandiose Palacio de la Policía, built in the early 20th century, was once the headquarters for the national police and today is home to the **Museo de la Policía Nacional** (Cl. 9 No. 9-27, tel. 1/233-5911, www.policia. gov.co, 9am-5pm Tues.-Fri., free). Tours are given by knowledgeable and friendly cadets who are fulfilling their one-year public service obligation. The museum does have its fair share of guns, but there are also exhibits on different technologies employed by police in pursuit of the bad guys, along with tributes to police dogs. If you go up to the rooftop, you can catch a unique perspective of the city. In the streets nearby are dozens of shops selling police and military uniforms.

★ IGLESIA MUSEO SANTA CLARA

It is easy to overlook the stone exterior of the **Iglesia Museo Santa Clara** (Cra. 8 No. 8-91, tel. 1/337-6262, www.museoiglesiasantaclara. gov.co, 9am-5pm Tues.-Fri., 10am-4pm Sat.-Sun., adults COP$3,000), but that would be a shame: This is one of the most beautiful sights in Bogotá. Once part of a convent for barefoot Franciscan nuns, known as Clarisas, the

Gómezbarros. The work was a commentary on forced displacement resulting from Colombia's armed conflict.

West of the Plaza
ESCUELA DE ARTES Y OFICIOS DE SANTO DOMINGO

One of the best trade schools in Latin America for woodworking, embroidery, silversmithing, and leatherworking is the **Escuela de Artes y Oficios de Santo Domingo** (Cl. 10 No. 8-73, tel. 1/282-0534, www.eaosd.org, 9am-5pm Mon.-Fri., free). Attracting artisans from around the world, this school receives support from the Fundación Mario Santo Domingo. Tours (9am, 10am, 11am, and 3pm Mon.-Fri.) are offered at four different times on weekdays; sign up by phone or email. Classes are open to anyone. The school is housed in two lovely colonial buildings from the 1600s that are connected by a courtyard. A store—which could be mistaken for a design museum—sells items made by students.

little church is an extraordinary example of Mudejar style in Santa Fe. The convent was completed in 1647; it originally housed 12 nuns who were descendants of conquistadors, along with 12 Creole maidens. Perhaps the most stunning design aspect can be admired by craning your neck and looking up: The single nave is beautifully illuminated by hundreds of golden floral motifs. The church is now strictly a museum, and it often hosts edgy contemporary art exhibitions. Admission is free on Sundays.

South of the Plaza
CASA DE NARIÑO

You can have your picture taken with members of the Presidential Guard (they don't mind) at the gates of the neoclassical **Casa de Nariño** (Cra. 8 No. 6-26, www.presidencia.gov.co), home to Colombia's presidents. As its name suggests, the presidential palace stands on the site of the birth house of Antonio Nariño, one of the early voices for independence in New Granada (the name given to the territory by the Spanish). In 1906 Nariño's house was razed to make way for the first presidential palace, which was designed by the same French architect who designed the Palacio Liévano on the Plaza de Bolívar. The palace has served as home for Colombian presidents off and on since 1886. Minutes after the 2002 inauguration of President Álvaro Uribe, the exterior of the palace was slightly damaged by missiles fired by FARC guerrillas. Several missiles landed on humble homes in slums nearby, killing 13.

Tours are given of the Casa de Nariño, but you must make a reservation several days in advance by filling out the form on their website. Even if you don't visit the interior of the palace, you can watch the changing of the Presidential Guard on Wednesdays and Fridays at 2:30pm and on Sundays at 3pm.

Also on the grounds of the Casa de Nariño is the oldest **astronomical observatory** in the New World. This was the initiative of famed botanist and scientist José Celestino Mutis. It was completed in 1803.

IGLESIA AND CLAUSTRO DE SAN AGUSTÍN

Facing the palace on the south side, the **Iglesia de San Agustín** (Cra. 7 No. 7-13, 9am-5pm Mon.-Sun.) was part of the first Augustinian monastery in the Spanish New World, completed in 1668. It is a three-nave temple, which distinguished it from other churches at the time. A 1785 earthquake destroyed the two towers (they rebuilt just one). In 1861, during liberal reforms, the government took control of the church from the Augustinians. The next year the church was the scene of a presidential coup attempt during the Battle of San Agustín, as Conservatives attacked Liberals who were holed up in the church and adjacent monastery (which no longer stands). The church suffered damage yet again during the Bogotazo riots in 1948.

The **Claustro de San Agustín** (Cra. 8 No. 7-21, tel. 1/342-2340, 9am-5pm Mon.-Sat., 9am-4pm Sun., free) didn't serve long as a seminary, and in fact was used as a garrison in which Antonio Nariño was imprisoned. During the Bogotazo rampage, international delegates in town for the 9th Pan-American Conference sought shelter there from the mayhem on the streets. Today this beautiful cloister is run by the Universidad Nacional, which puts on temporary art exhibits and hosts educational activities.

MUSEO ARQUEOLÓGICO

The **Museo Arqueológico** (Cra. 6 No. 7-43, tel. 1/243-0465, www.musarq.org.co, 8:30am-5pm Mon.-Fri., 9am-4pm Sat., 10am-4pm Sun., COP$4,000) holds an extensive and nicely presented collection of ceramic work of pre-Columbian indigenous peoples. There is also a room containing colonial-era decorative arts, in acknowledgement of the history of this 17th-century home of a Spanish marquis. A small café adjoins the museum.

East of the Plaza
MUSEO COLONIAL

Well worth a visit, the **Museo Colonial** (Cra. 6 No. 9-77, tel. 1/341-6017, www.

museocolonial.gov.co, 9am-5pm Tues.-Fri., 10am-4pm Sat.-Sun., COP$3,000) showcases a fine collection of art and religious artifacts from the colonial era, including the largest collection of works by Gregorio Vásquez de Arce y Ceballos. On the bottom floor is an exhibit that explores life in colonial times. The museum courtyard is quiet and green. Admission is free on Sundays.

This museum was historically part of the **Manzana Jesuítica**, a complex that included the adjacent **Colegio Mayor de San Bartolomé** (Colombia's oldest school, built in 1604) and the **Iglesia de San Ignacio**, from 1643.

TEATRO COLÓN

Modeled on the Teatro Santi Giovanni e Paolo in Venice, the **Teatro Colón** (Cl. 10 No. 5-32, tel. 1/284-7420, www.teatrocolon.gov.co) was designed by Pietro Cantini to commemorate the 400th anniversary of Christopher Columbus's 1492 landing in the New World. The theater was closed for several years during a massive overhaul. Today it sparkles. Tours (3pm Wed.-Thurs., noon and 3pm Sat., COP$5,000) are given, but the best way to experience the theater is by enjoying a performance.

PALACIO DE SAN CARLOS

Today housing the Ministry of Foreign Relations, the colonial-era **Palacio de San Carlos** (Cl. 10 No. 5-51, closed to the public) was the home of Colombian presidents from 1825 until 1908. During the Bolívar dictatorship and the turbulent Gran Colombia period, Bolívar's companion Manuela Sáenz earned the nickname "Liberator of the Liberator" for helping him escape through a palace window—saving him from an 1828 assassination attempt. A plaque marking the exact spot draws the curiosity of passersby today.

MUSEUMS

The **Museo de Trajes Regionales** (Cl. 10 No. 6-18, tel. 1/341-0403, www.museodetrajesregionales.com, 9am-4pm Mon.-Fri., 9am-2pm Sat., COP$3,000) showcases traditional costumes from the different regions of Colombia but is best known for being the home of Manuela Sáenz, Simón Bolívar's companion. The museum is next door to the **Plaza de Cuervo**, a tropical patio in the middle of historic Bogotá. Behind the elegant palm trees is the house where Antonio Nariño is said to have translated the Declaration of the Rights of Man from French into Spanish in 1793. After making about 100 copies of it for distribution to rouse the masses, he panicked and began to frantically destroy them. (He would later be imprisoned by the Spanish authorities.)

The **Museo Militar** (Cl. 10 No. 4-92, tel. 1/281-3086, www.museo-militar.webnode.com.co, 9am-4pm Tues.-Fri., 10am-4pm Sat.-Sun., free, must present identification) is in a 17th-century house that was home to independence hero Capt. Antonio Ricaurte. Dozens of mannequins dressed in Colombian military uniforms keep visitors company as they amble the corridors of the museum. One room is dedicated to Colombia's participation in the Korean War, in which 4,300 Colombians fought, with 163 losing their lives. Colombia was the only country in Latin America to send troops in support of the United Nations/United States coalition. Two patios are filled with cannons, tanks, and fighter jets.

The **Museo de Bogotá** (Cra. 4 No. 10-18, tel. 1/352-1864, www.museodebogota.gov.co, 9am-6pm Tues.-Fri., 10am-5pm Sat.-Sun., free) has a permanent exhibition that examines the development of Bogotá through the years, and temporary shows have highlighted photography, historical figures in the city, and neighborhood profiles.

★ Manzana Cultural

The **Manzana Cultural** (Cl. 11 No. 4-41) of the Banco de la República is the most important "Cultural Block" in Colombia. It comprises the Biblioteca Luis Ángel Arango, the library's concert hall, the Museo Botero, the Museo de Arte, the Colección de Arte del Banco de la República, and the Casa de la Moneda.

BIBLIOTECA LUIS ÁNGEL ARANGO

The plain **Biblioteca Luis Ángel Arango** (Cl. 11 No. 4-14, tel. 1/343-1224, www.banrepcultural.org, 8am-8pm Mon.-Sat., 8am-4pm Sun.) is reportedly one of the busiest libraries in the world, with over 5,000 visitors each day. Part of the same complex and located behind the library, the **Casa Republicana** (8am-8pm Mon.-Sat., 8am-4pm Sun., free) often hosts temporary art exhibits. There is also a stunning chamber music concert hall in the large complex.

COLECCIÓN DE ARTE DEL BANCO DE LA REPÚBLICA

With 14 galleries highlighting Colombian art from the 17th century to present day, the **Colección de Arte del Banco de la República** (Cl. 11 No. 4-21, tel. 1/343-1316, www.banrepcultural.org, 9am-7pm Mon. and Wed.-Sat., 10am-5pm Sun., free) is an excellent opportunity to discover Colombian art. Look for the series of "dead nuns." It was customary to paint nuns twice in their lifetimes: once when they entered the convent and once more moments after passing away. The nuns from this series lived at the nearby convent of the Iglesia de la Concepción.

Another highlight is the spectacular—if a tad gaudy—*La Lechuga* monstrance (a monstrance is a receptacle to hold the Host). It's called *La Lechuga,* meaning lettuce, because of its 1,486 sparkling emeralds, but it is also adorned by hundreds of diamonds, rubies, amethysts, and pearls. The Spaniard who created this extraordinary piece charged the Jesuits the equivalent of a cool US$2 million when he finished it in 1707. Hidden away in a vault for over 200 years, it was acquired by the Banco de la República in 1987 for US$3.5 million.

Nineteenth-century landscapes, portraits by impressionist and Bogotá native Andrés Santa María, and works from an array of well-known Colombian artists from the 20th century (including Alejandro Obregón, Eduardo Ramírez, Guillermo Wiedemann, and Luis Caballero) are other museum highlights.

Free guided tours in Spanish are offered several times a day.

MUSEO DE ARTE DEL BANCO DE LA REPÚBLICA

Behind the Colección de Arte, and housed in a brilliantly white boxlike construction, is the **Museo de Arte del Banco de la República** (Cl. 11 No. 4-21, tel. 1/343-1316, www.banrepcultural.org, 9am-7pm Mon. and Wed.-Sat., 10am-5pm Sun., free), which hosts temporary exhibits and has one floor dedicated to 20th-century Latin American and European art from the Banco de la República collection.

MUSEO BOTERO

In the **Museo Botero** (Cl. 11 No. 4-41, tel. 1/343-1316, www.banrepcultural.org, 9am-7pm Mon. and Wed.-Sat., 10am-5pm Sun., free) there are still lifes, portrayals of everyday life in Colombian pueblos, and social commentaries by one of the most well-known contemporary Colombian artists, Medellín-born Fernando Botero. In addition to paintings of corpulent Colombians, there are bronze and marble sculptures of chubby cats and bulgy birds. One side of the lovely colonial house, which surrounds a sublime courtyard, displays the artist's collection of European and American art, including works by Picasso and Dalí—all donated by the *maestro* so that Colombians of all backgrounds could enjoy them without paying a peso. Once the home of archbishops during the colonial era, the building was torched during the 1948 riots of the Bogotazo. It's been painstakingly restored. Guided tours are offered daily.

CASA DE LA MONEDA

Connected to the Museo Botero and the Colección de Arte by patios and a Botero gift shop, the **Casa de la Moneda** (Cl. 11 No. 4-93, tel. 1/343-1316, www.banrepcultural.org, 9am-7pm Mon. and Wed.-Sat., 10am-5pm Sun., free) was where the New World's first gold coins were produced starting in the early 17th century. The museum's **Colección**

Numismática shows the history of the Nueva Granada mint.

CENTRO CULTURAL GABRIEL GARCÍA MÁRQUEZ

Designed by Rogelio Salmona, the **Centro Cultural Gabriel García Márquez** (Cl. 11 No. 5-60, tel. 1/283-2200, www.fce.com.co, 9am-7pm Mon.-Sat., 10:30am-5pm Sun., free) was a gift from the Mexican government in honor of the 1982 Nobel Prize winner for literature, Colombian Gabriel García Márquez. (The author lived in Mexico from the 1960s until his death in 2014.) On the main level, where you can enjoy a sunset view of the cathedral, is a bookstore with an ample selection of books on Colombia. Next to the Juan Valdez Café below is an exhibition space.

AVENIDA JIMÉNEZ

Avenida Jiménez used to be the Río San Francisco and the extreme northern boundary of Santa Fe. Most of the historic buildings on this street can only be enjoyed from the exterior. In 2000, in an effort to reinvent the historic Avenida Jiménez, architect Rogelio Salmona created the **Eje Ambiental** (Environmental Corridor), which extends from the Universidad de los Andes campus to Avenida Caracas. Vehicular traffic is banned here except for the red buses of the TransMilenio. Ample pedestrian space has made this a pleasant place for a stroll.

A fantastic pedestrian zone extends along Carrera 7 from the Plaza de Bolívar to Calle 26. This busy commercial area is a fun way to check out the city's core and do a little shopping, sightseeing, and people-watching.

Historic Architecture

Impressive buildings line the entire length of Avenida Jiménez. Most of these gems were built in the early 20th century. To the west side of the Séptima (Cra. 7) are: the neoclassical **Palacio de San Francisco** (Av. Jiménez No. 7-56), prior home to the Cundinamarca departmental government; the **Edificio López** (Av. Jiménez No. 7-65), by the same construction firm that built the Chrysler Building in New York; and the modernist **Edificio Camacho,** farther down and on the right.

It was on the southwest corner of the Séptima and Avenida Jiménez that populist Liberal Party presidential candidate Jorge Eliécer Gaitán was assassinated on April 9, 1948, the event that sparked the tragic Bogotazo riots. Up to 3,000 were killed in the unrest. This precipitated the bloody

courtyard at the Casa de la Moneda

period of La Violencia that quickly engulfed the entire country. At the present-day McDonald's, a plaque and flowers mark the spot where the tragedy took place. A young Gabriel García Márquez, then a law student at the Universidad Nacional, lived near the Palacio de San Francisco at that time, and with his building in flames, it's said that he and his brother rushed back inside—to save his typewriter.

On the eastern (mountain) side of the Séptima, notable buildings include the modernist **Banco de la República** (Cra. 7 No. 14-78); the **Universidad de Nuestra Señora del Rosario** (Cl. 12C No. 6-25), founded in 1653, which is housed in a colonial building that was originally a monastery; the **Edificio Monserrate** (Av. Jiménez No. 4-49), which was home to *El Espectador* newspaper; the fabulous restored **Hotel Continental** (Av. Jiménez No. 4-19), once the most exclusive hotel in town; the neoclassical **Academia Colombiana de Historia** (Cl. 10 No. 9-95); the 17th-century **Iglesia and Convento de las Aguas** (Cra. 2 No. 18A-58), where Artesanías de Colombia has a store; and finally (at the end of the Eje Ambiental), the campus of the **Universidad de Los Andes,** one of the top universities in Latin America, with several stunning new buildings. Los Andes has around 19,000 students.

Churches

Typical of most all colonial-era churches, the **Iglesia de San Francisco** (Cl. 16 No. 7-35, 6:30am-8pm Mon.-Fri., 6:30am-12:40pm and 4:30pm-8pm Sat.-Sun.) looks somber from the outside, but inside it's adorned with a fantastic golden altar, considered a masterwork of American baroque. This is the oldest of all the churches in the city, built by the Franciscans in 1557. The church is often full of working-class faithful. Adjacent to the San Francisco is the **Iglesia de Veracruz** (Cl. 16 No. 7-19), which is where several independence figures, executed by the Spaniards, are laid to rest.

The third church in this row is called **Iglesia La Tercera** (Cl. 16 No. 7-35, 7am-6pm Mon.-Fri., 11am-1pm Sat.-Sun.), and it is one of the jewels of colonial churches in Bogotá. It was built in the late 18th century, about 50 years before Colombian independence. Architecturally, a highlight is its barrel-vaulted ceiling decorated with geometric designs and altarpieces made of cedar and walnut. Unlike other churches, the interior is not covered with gold leaf.

★ Museo del Oro

Some visitors come to Bogotá specifically to see the world-renowned **Museo del Oro** (Gold Museum, Cra. 6 No. 15-88, tel. 1/343-2233, www.banrepcultural.org/museo-del-oro, 9am-6pm Tues.-Sat., 10am-4pm Sun., COP$4,000). The museum tells the story of how—and why—the native peoples of Colombia created such incredibly detailed and surprisingly modern designs of gold jewelry and religious objects. What's on view is but a fraction of the museum's collection, which begin with its first acquisition in 1939.

What is astonishing about the collection is the sophistication of the work. It is almost all smelted, with Muisca and Sinú peoples employing a "lost wax" technique, with various metals being purposefully alloyed. Here, rather than large, hammered pieces as found in countries like Peru, you will see intricately crafted and designed jewelry.

One of the highlights is the golden raft created by local Muisca people. The raft portrays the ritual of El Dorado, "the Golden One." Another piece to look for is the collection's first acquisition, the Quimbaya Póporo. This was used during religious ceremonies. The unforgettable Offering Room is filled with golden treasures. English explanations are excellent throughout the museum (so is the audio tour). Just beyond the gift shop is a restaurant that specializes in Colombian and Mediterranean cuisine. Saturday is a good day to visit the museum, as there may be fewer school groups visiting. On Sunday, admission is free. There are guided tours (11am, 3pm, and 4pm) daily, some of which are in English.

Museo de la Esmeralda

On the 23rd floor of the Avianca building is the **Museo de la Esmeralda** (Cl. 16 No. 6-66, tel. 1/482-7890, www.museodelaesmeralda.com.co, 10am-6pm Mon.-Sat., COP$5,000). The museum has an impressive re-creation of an emerald mine and several examples of different emeralds from Colombia and elsewhere. Guides, fluent in Spanish and English, will make sure you know that the best emeralds do—without a doubt—come from Colombia, primarily from the Muzo mines in the Boyacá department. Although there is little pressure to do so, you can purchase all different classes of emeralds, and the facility's jewelers can transform the emeralds you choose into rings or earrings within a day. Even if you are not interested in purchasing an emerald it is fun to check out the gems under a magnifying glass, as you learn why some emeralds are much more precious than others. The museum also has a small store on the main floor of the building that sometimes has coupons for discounted museum entry. Security at the Avianca building is stringent, and you will need to bring a photocopy of your passport and produce the telephone number of your hotel for entry.

Quinta de Bolívar

The **Quinta de Bolívar** (Cl. 21 No. 4A-30, tel. 1/336-6410/19, www.quintadebolivar.gov.co, 9am-5pm Tues.-Fri., 10am-4pm Sat.-Sun., COP$3,000, free Sun.) is a lovely country estate that was presented by Francisco de Paula Santander, vice president of the República de Gran Colombia, as a gift to Simón Bolívar in 1820. Bolívar stayed there during his brief and sporadic visits to Bogotá, a city he did not like. He spent approximately 432 nights here, give or take. Built in 1800, the estate is a beautiful example of a late colonial-era house. It's furnished with period pieces and set in a beautiful garden under cypress and walnut trees. It is just a five-minute walk uphill from the Quinta to Monserrate.

★ Cerro de Monserrate

It's worth the ride or hike to the top of **Cerro de Monserrate** (Cra. 2 Este No. 21-48, tel. 1/284-5700, www.cerromonserrate.com, 6:30am-midnight Mon.-Sat., 6:30am-6:30pm Sun.) for memorable views of the city by day or night. There are two different ways to reach the peak, one easier than the other. For the easy way, take either the **funicular tramway** (6:30am-11:45pm Tues.-Fri., 6:30am-4pm Sat., 6:30am-6:30pm Sun., round-trip

Cerro de Monserrate, as seen from the Quinta de Bolívar

COP$19,000) or the **gondola** (6:30am-midnight Mon., noon-midnight Tues.-Sat., 10am-4:30pm Sun., round-trip COP$19,000). It's cheaper on Sundays, so expect long lines.

The second option involves hiking to the top. Due to large crowds on weekends and holidays, this is a good plan for a weekday morning. The path is open 5am-4pm Wednesday-Monday. There is no charge to make the somewhat challenging ascent on foot. Moving at a brisk clip, the walk will take less than 45 minutes.

In the past there have been reports of bandits lingering in the woods along the path, but the security situation has vastly improved. Police cadets are stationed at three or four points along the trail until 4pm, and when there are no police there are plenty of other hikers or vendors selling refreshments.

If you feel as if you have done your exercise for the day once you achieve the peak, you can purchase a one-way ticket at the top to ride either the funicular tramway or the gondola back down.

For some, the white chapel at the top, the **Santuario de Monserrate,** is the goal of this hike. It is not architecturally notable, and it has been destroyed and rebuilt several times since the 1600s, but it is the highest church around, at about 3,152 meters (10,341 feet) above sea level. Inside, a 17th-century sculpture of the Fallen Christ of Monserrate attracts religious pilgrims. Some climb the hill on their knees during Holy Week, believing that the Fallen Christ grants miracles to those who do so.

There are two pricey restaurants on the top of the mountain—a romantic setting for marriage proposals and a favorite spot for locals to bring visitors. These are French-Colombian **Restaurante Casa San Isidro** (tel. 1/281-9270, www.restaurantecasa-sanisidro.com, noon-midnight Mon.-Sat., COP$40,000) and **Restaurante Casa Santa Clara** (tel. 1/745-4628, www.restaurante-casasantaclara.com, noon-5pm Tues.-Fri., noon-4pm Sat.-Sun., COP$25,000), which specializes in Colombian fare.

To the south of Monserrate rises the **Cerro de Guadalupe,** topped by a large statue of the Virgin. It can only be accessed by road and was, until recently, unsafe to visit. If you would like to visit (the views are about the same as from Monserrate), take a microbus on Sunday from the intersection of Calle 6 and Avenida Caracas. As you enter the ticket office at the base of Monserrate, you may see an old photograph of a tightrope walker crossing the 890 meters (2,900 feet) from Monserrate to Guadalupe blindfolded. This stunt was performed by Canadian daredevil Harry Warner in 1895.

CENTRO INTERNACIONAL
Museo de Arte Moderno de Bogotá

Across from the Parque de la Independencia on Avenida 26 is the **Museo de Arte Moderno de Bogotá** (Museum of Modern Art of Bogotá, Cl. 24 No. 6-00, tel. 1/286-0466, www.mambogota.com, 10am-6pm Tues.-Sat., noon-4:30pm Sun., COP$5,000). It often puts on interesting exhibitions highlighting Colombian and Latin American artists. Nicknamed MAMBO, it is a creation of architect Rogelio Salmona.

Torre Colpatria Observation Deck

The **Torre Colpatria Observation Deck** (Cra. 7 No. 24-89, tel. 1/283-6665, 6pm-9pm Fri., 8am-8pm Sat., 8am-5pm Sun., COP$5,000) offers unparalleled 360-degree views of Bogotá. The vista of the city from this 50-story tower is arguably superior to that of the Cerro de Monserrate. At night the tower goes into disco mode, displaying colorful lights.

Parque de la Independencia

The **Parque de la Independencia,** long a favorite for young lovers and those seeking a pleasant stroll under the towering eucalyptus and wax palm trees, was created in 1910 in celebration of Colombia's 100-year anniversary

Centro Internacional

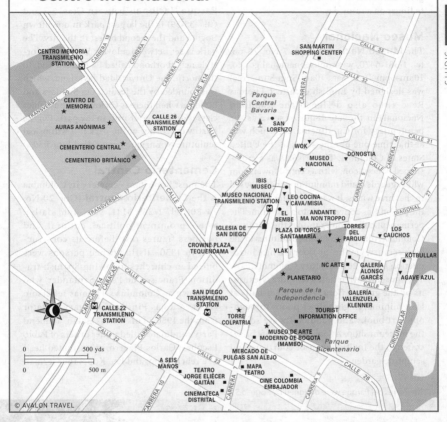

© AVALON TRAVEL

of independence from Spain. The **Quiosco de la Luz** houses a tourist information center (Punto de Información Turística, or PIT). Adjacent to the Parque de la Independencia is the green corridor of the **Parque del Bicentenario**, a long-delayed urban revitalization project that opened in 2016.

Within the park is a planetarium, the **Planetario de Bogotá** (Cl. 26B No. 5-93, tel. 1/281-4150, www.planetariodebogota.gov.co, 10am-5pm Tues.-Sun., COP$5,000). Next to that is the **Plaza de Toros de Santamaría.** The neo-Mudejar brick arena was built in the 1930s by a Spanish architect and was modeled after bullfighting rings in Madrid.

Bullfighting is a controversial topic in Bogotá, and its future is uncertain. But the bullring is photogenic, especially from atop the Torre Colpatria.

About 100 steps up from the bullfighting ring and planetarium are the iconic **Torres del Parque.** These three brick apartment buildings, rising parallel to the eastern mountains, were designed in the 1960s by Rogelio Salmona, the most accomplished architect from Bogotá during the late 20th century. French-born Salmona studied with Le Corbusier and was awarded the Alvar Aalto Prize in 2003 for his lifetime achievements. Public space takes up almost three-fourths of the area in the tower complex, and its art galleries, cafés, and bodegas are nice places to linger on a rainy day.

Museo Nacional

The **Museo Nacional** (Cra. 7 No. 28-66, tel. 1/381-6470, www.museonacional.gov.co, 10am-6pm Tues.-Sat., 10am-5pm Sun., free) was designed by English architect Thomas Reed (who also designed the Capitolio Nacional) in the late 1800s to serve as the penitentiary for Cundinamarca, which was at that time one of nine states of the United States of Colombia. The prison was a cross-shaped panopticon, with a central tower from which guards could monitor prisoners housed in the three wings. It was in the late 1940s that the prison was converted into a museum. The permanent collection examines the history of Colombia from pre-Columbian cultures to the 20th century. On the top floor is a nice introduction to late 20th-century Colombian art. The museum often holds temporary exhibits on the ground floor. There are usually at least minimal English descriptions throughout. Art books and handicrafts are sold at the museum shop. A Juan Valdez Café brews coffee in the inviting interior courtyard and sculpture garden.

Parque Nacional

A center of activity on the weekends, the **Parque Nacional** (between Cras. 5-7 and Clls. 35-39) is the largest park in downtown Bogotá and the second oldest in the city. The park is set between a lovely English Tudor-style neighborhood called La Merced and, to the north, the Universidad Javeriana, which was founded by the Jesuits. On Sundays and holidays when there is Ciclovía, free aerobics classes draw huge crowds in the park. On the northwest corner of the park is a whimsical sculpture by Enrique Grau called *Rita 5:30*.

Cementerio Central

The most important cemetery in Colombia is the **Cementerio Central** (Cra. 20 No. 24-80, tel. 1/269-3141, 9am-4pm daily), where prominent political, cultural, and business figures rest. Before its construction in 1830, distinguished persons were buried in churches following Spanish tradition. Francisco de Paula Santander, who is known as Colombia's Thomas Jefferson; Gustavo Rojas Pinilla, a military dictator from the 1950s; Luis Carlos Galán, a Liberal Party candidate killed under orders of Pablo Escobar; Carlos Pizarro, assassinated head of a rebel group; and Leo Kopp, the German

The Torres del Parque were designed by Rogelio Salmona.

founder of the Bavaria brewery, are all buried here.

There is a part of the cemetery where thousands of victims from the Bogotazo riots from April 1948 are buried, many of them chillingly listed as "N. N." ("no name"). Women sell cut flowers outside of the cemetery gates and graffiti provides bursts of color. Keep your wits about you when walking through the farther expanses of the cemetery, as security guards may not be nearby to ward off pickpockets. This is a popular spot on weekends, but is emptier on week days.

Immediately west of the cemetery is a remarkable art installation called *Auras Anonimas* by Colombian artist Beatriz González. This abandoned columbarium (a structure used to house ashes) is covered with around 9,000 primitive black-and-white paintings of people carrying away the dead. It is a powerful reflection on the human toll of the armed conflict in Colombia.

A memorial to victims of violence of the armed conflict is adjacent to the Cementerio Central. The **Centro de Memoria, Paz y Reconciliación** (Cra. 19B No. 24-86, tel. 1/381-3030, www.centromemoria.gov.co, 11am-1pm and 2pm-4pm Mon., 8am-10am, 11am-1pm, and 2pm-4pm Tues.-Fri., free) is one of the first memorials of its kind in Colombia. It is an educational space, where schoolchildren come to hear firsthand accounts from victims of the conflict.

NORTHERN BOGOTÁ
Parque de la 93
The **Parque de la 93** (between Cras. 11A-13 and Clls. 93A-B) is a manicured park with a playground surrounded by restaurants. Workers from the area stroll the park on their lunch hour. On soccer game days, big screens are set up for fans to watch the match.

Usaquén
Once upon a time, charming **Usaquén** was its own distinct pueblo. Now at the fringes of sprawling Bogotá, Usaquén has somehow retained some colonial charm. It has become a dining and drinking hot spot with many restaurants and bars around the main square. On Sundays the neighborhood comes alive during its popular **flea market** (Cra. 5 at Cl. 119B).

WESTERN BOGOTÁ
The sights of Western Bogotá can be reached by SITP buses Z7 and 59B.

Parque Simón Bolívar
When it was built in the late 1960s, **Parque Simón Bolívar** (between Clls. 53-63 and Cras. 48-68, 6am-6pm daily) was in the countryside. Now, it's the middle of the city. The park is an excellent place for watching Bogotanos at play, especially on the weekends. Numerous festivals and concerts take place here. There are more than 16 kilometers (10 miles) of trails in the park In August, traditionally the windiest month, thousands of families try their luck at catching a breeze with their colorful kites.

Biblioteca Virgilio Barco
With the downtown skyline and mountains providing a picturesque background, the **Biblioteca Virgilio Barco** (Av. Cra. 60 No. 57-60, tel. 1/379-3520, www.biblored.gov.co, 2pm-8pm Mon., 8am-8pm Tues.-Sat., 9:30am-5:30pm Sun.), designed by architect Rogelio Salmona, is one of four fantastic library-parks in the city created by Mayor Enrique Peñalosa. The purpose of these mega libraries is to provide citizens access to books, Internet, and cultural/educational opportunities in a peaceful environment. Green spaces like this are few and far between in lower-income neighborhoods. A bike path encircles the park and is popular with young inline skaters and joggers. The well-maintained grounds are a playground for both the young and the old—and their dogs.

Jardín Botánico
Colombia is one of the most biodiverse countries on the planet, and the **Jardín Botánico** (Botanical Garden, Av. Cl. 63 No. 68-95, tel. 1/437-7060, www.jbb.gov.co, 8am-5pm Mon.-Fri., 9am-5pm Sat.-Sun., COP$2,700) does an

Northern Bogotá

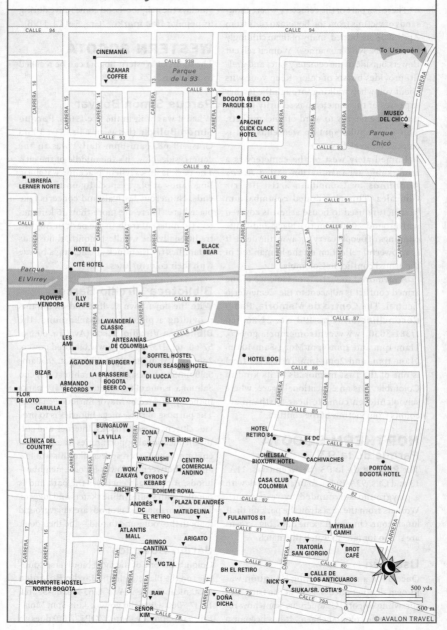

CALLE 94

CINEMANÍA

AZAHAR
COFFEE

CALLE 93B

Parque
de la 93

CALLE 93A

CALLE 94

To Usaquén

BOGOTA BEER CO
PARQUE 93

APACHE/
CLICK CLACK
HOTEL

MUSEO
DEL CHICÓ

Parque
Chicó

CALLE 93

CALLE 93

CALLE 92

CALLE 92

LIBRERÍA
LERNER NORTE

CALLE 91

CALLE 90

CALLE 90

HOTEL B3

CITÉ HOTEL

BLACK
BEAR

Parque
El Virrey

FLOWER
VENDORS

ILLY
CAFE

CALLE 87

LAVANDERÍA
CLASSIC

CALLE 87

ARTESANÍAS
DE COLOMBIA

CALLE 86A

LES
AMI

AGADÓN BAR BURGER

SOFITEL HOSTEL

FOUR SEASONS HOTEL

HOTEL BOG

CALLE 86

BIZAR

LA BRASSERIE
BOGOTA
BEER CO

DI LUCCA

ARMANDO
RECORDS

FLOR
DE LOTO

CARULLA

EL MOZO

JULIA

CALLE 85

BUNGALOW

CLÍNICA DEL
COUNTRY

LA VILLA

ZONA
T

THE IRISH PUB

WATAKUSHI

WOK/
IZAKAYA

GYROS Y
KEBABS

CENTRO
COMERCIAL
ANDINO

ARCHIE'S

BOHEME ROYAL

ANDRÉS
DC

PLAZA DE ANDRÉS

EL RETIRO

MATILDELINA

HOTEL
RETIRO 84

84 DC

CHELSEA/
BIOXURY HOTEL

CACHIVACHES

CASA CLUB
COLOMBIA

CALLE 82

PORTÓN
BOGOTÁ HOTEL

CALLE 82

FULANITOS 81

MASA

CALLE 81

ATLANTIS
MALL

GRINGO
CANTINA

ARIGATO

MYRIAM
CAMHI

TRATORÍA
SAN GIORGIO

BROT
CAFÉ

VG TAL

CALLE 80

CALLE 80

BH EL RETIRO

NICK'S

CALLE DE
LOS ANTICUAROS

CHAPINORTE HOSTEL
NORTH BOGOTA

RAW

CALLE 79

SIUKA/SR. OSTIA'S

0

500 yds

SEÑOR
KIM

CALLE 78

DOÑA
DICHA

CALLE 79A

0

500 m

© AVALON TRAVEL

CARRERA 16
CARRERA 15
CARRERA 14
CARRERA 13
CARRERA 11A
CARRERA 10
CARRERA 9A
CARRERA 9
CARRERA 7
CARRERA 16
CARRERA 14
CARRERA 13A
CARRERA 13
CARRERA 12
CARRERA 11
CARRERA 10
CARRERA 9A
CARRERA 8
CARRERA 7A
CARRERA 14
CARRERA 13
CARRERA 10
CARRERA 9
CARRERA 8
CARRERA 17
CARRERA 16
CARRERA 15
CARRERA 14A
CARRERA 14
CARRERA 13A
CARRERA 13
CARRERA 12A
CARRERA 11
CARRERA 9
CARRERA 7

excellent job of highlighting that diversity. It won't be hard to find the Colombian national tree, the iconic wax palm. And inside the greenhouse, be on the lookout for the official Bogotá orchid. The gardens take visitors on a tour of the many different climate regions in the country—from the *páramos* (highland moors) to cloud forests to tropical jungles. Feel free to stray from the paths and get closer to the plants.

Entertainment and Events

Bogotá is the cultural capital of Colombia. All regions of Colombia are represented in the musical traditions here. Merengue, salsa, *cumbia* (traditional Caribbean music), *vallenato* (love ballads accompanied by accordion): You name it, you can hear it.

NIGHTLIFE

Bogotá has a bar, club, or party for every taste. Popular nightspots are scattered along the Carrera 7 corridor. To get the latest on nightlife, and find out about parties, check out Vive In (www.vive.in) and the magazine *GO* (www.goguiadelocio.com.co), as well as each club's Facebook page.

The largest concentration of nightlife is in Northern Bogotá. There are over 100 gay and lesbian bars and clubs in the city; the Plaza de Lourdes (Cra. 13 and Av. Cl. 63) in Chapinero is a good place to start, as it has a group of gay bars surrounding it.

Expect to pay COP$10,000-30,000 cover at clubs, unless there's a big-name DJ or band, when covers are higher. Covers can include a *consumible* (complimentary drink). Pay for drinks with small bills or exact change, as some wayward bar staff may attempt to keep the change, especially from visitors. Tips are not generally expected at bars.

All electronic music clubs are gay friendly and become even more so as the night wears on. Clubs stay open until 3am generally, with some operating until daylight. After-parties exist, but these can be sketchy affairs.

La Candelaria

Candelario Bar (Cra. 5 No. 12B-14, tel. 1/342-3742, 9pm-3am Fri.-Sat.) gets rowdy, with a student crowd singing and drinking to reggaetón and Latin beats.

Cuban Jazz Café (Cra. 7A No. 12C-36, tel. 1/341-3714, www.cubanjazzcafe.com, 5pm-3am Wed.-Sat.) is a hot spot for mojitos and *son* music. Check out **Viejo Almacén** (Cl. 15 No. 4-30, 6pm-2am Tues.-Sun.), a tango bar named after the famous nightspot of the same name in Buenos Aires.

Avenida Jiménez

Quiebra Canto (Cra. 5 No. 17-76, tel. 1/243-1630, 6:30pm-3am Wed.-Sat., cover COP$10,000) is a classic haunt where jazz, funk, and salsa are often the order of the night. Wednesdays are especially popular at this two-floor joint.

Centro Internacional

In the Macarena, cool **Baum** (Cl. 33 No. 6-24, cell tel. 316/494-3799, 10pm-5am Fri.-Sat., COP$35,000) packs in an enthusiastic crowd of locals and visitors who lose themselves to the beats of top international DJs.

Late-night dancing goes underground at **Vlak** (Cra. 6 No. 26B-61, cell tel. 321/439-7610, COP$25,00), a basement club near the bullfighting ring.

Chapinero

The salsa is hot at **El Titicó** (Cl. 64 No. 13-35, cell tel. 310/696-2240, www.eltitico.com.co, 8pm-3am Fri.-Sat.), a live music and dancing venue in an edgy area of Chapinero.

Video Club (Cl. 64 No. 13-09, www.video-club.com.co, COP$25,000) does electro-house music at its cool location in Chapinero. It's a good idea to wear a long-sleeved shirt, because

Chapinero and Zona G

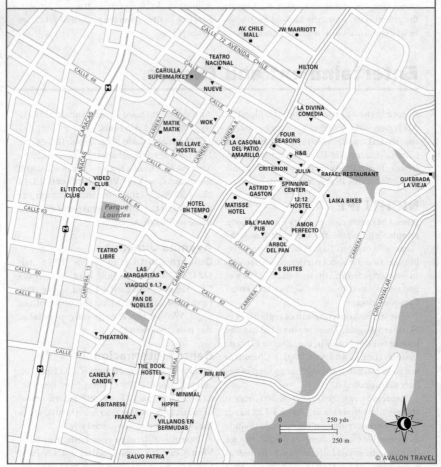

CALLE 72 AVENIDA CHILE
AV. CHILE MALL
JW MARRIOTT
TEATRO NACIONAL
CALLE 71
CARULLA SUPERMARKET
HILTON
NUEVE
CALLE 70
LA DIVINA COMEDIA
CALLE 68
CALLE 69
CARRERA 11
WOK
MATIK MATIK
CARRERA 9
MI LLAVE HOSTEL
LA CASONA DEL PATIO AMARILLO
FOUR SEASONS
CALLE 67
CARRERA 9
H&B
CALLE 66
CRITERION
JULIA
RAFAEL RESTAURANT
QUEBRADA LA VIEJA
CARACAS
VIDEO CLUB
EL TITICÓ CLUB
ASTRID Y GASTON
SPINNING CENTER
12:12 HOSTEL
LAIKA BIKES
CALLE 63
CALLE 64
Parque Lourdes
HOTEL BH TEMPO
MATISSE HOTEL
B&L PIANO PUB
AMOR PERFECTO
CARRERA 1
TEATRO LIBRE
CALLE 65
ARBOL DEL PAN
CALLE 60
CARRERA 13
LAS MARGARITAS
CARRERA 7
CALLE 64
6 SUITES
VIAGGIO 6.1.7
CALLE 59
PAN DE NOBLES
CALLE 62
CARRERA 4
CALLE 61
CIRCUNVALAR
THEATRÓN
CALLE 57
CANELA Y CANDIL
THE BOOK HOSTEL
CARRERA 4A
RIN RÍN
MINIMAL
ABITARE56
HIPPIE
FRANCA
VILLANOS EN BERMUDAS
0   250 yds
0   250 m
SALVO PATRIA

© AVALON TRAVEL

most of the action is on the top-floor terrace. The club hosts special events marketed to gay clientele on Sundays.

Octava (Cra. 8 No. 63-41, www.cluboctava.com, 10pm-6am Fri.-Sat.) has an awesome sound system and sophisticated beats. The crowd is a little older than at most clubs.

A change of pace is on tap at **B&L Piano Pub** (Cra. 4A No. 66-03, cell tel. 322/351-8791, noon-3pm and 6pm-midnight Mon.-Wed., noon-midnight Thurs.-Sat.), where jazz and blues grab the spotlight. This hidden gem in an upper-crust area features live music most nights.

Theatrón (Cl. 58 No. 10-32, tel. 1/235-6879, www.theatrondepelicula.com, 9pm-5am Fri.-Sat., cover COP$30,000) is a giant disco catering to the gay crowd, with about 13 different spaces in its Chapinero location.

Northern Bogotá

Thanks to **Bogotá Beer Company** (www.

bogotabeercompany.com), a successful chain of pubs with several locations throughout the city, sipping on a Candelaria artisan beer has become trendy in Bogotá. They also serve decent burgers. Try one of the northern locations: one on Calle 85 (Cl. 85 No. 13-06, tel. 1/742-9292, ext. 316), and one in the Parque de la 93 area (Cra. 11A No. 93A-94, tel. 1/742-9292, ext. 313).

Sit on the terrace and listen to rock music at always-packed **The Pub Bogotá** (Cra. 12A No. 83-48, tel. 1/691-8711, www.thepub.com.co, noon-close daily, no cover), where you're in a strategic position to watch people cruising the Zona T.

Chelsea Bar (Bioxury Hotel, Cl. 83 No. 9-48, 11th fl., cell tel. 310/325-7674, www.bioxury.com, Thurs.-Sat.) is a happening terrace bar near the Zona Rosa. In the center of the Zona Rosa is **Bungalow** (Cra. 13 No. 83-47, cell tel. 317/369-7889, 7pm-3am Thurs., 5pm-3am Fri.-Sat.), a chic terrace bar with DJs and cocktails. Also in the Zona Rosa, **Armando Records** (Cl. 85 No. 14-46, www.armandorecords.org, hours vary Tues.-Sat., cover COP$15,000) attracts a slightly grungy but cool crowd. The terrace is a fun (but sometimes cold) spot. Live bands and international DJs regularly play here.

La Villa (Cra. 14A No. 83-56, hours vary Tues.-Sat., cover COP$15,000) hosts the popular Gringo Tuesdays parties, but has all kinds of themed parties catering to locals and visitors alike.

Apache (Cra. 11 No. 93-77, tel. 1/635-1916, www.clickclackhotel.com, noon-2am Mon.-Sat.) is the place for music, burgers, and sports on television. It's atop the Click Clack Hotel in the Parque de la 93 area.

The **W Lounge** (Av. Cra. 9 No. 115-30, tel. 1/746-7111, www.wbogota.com, 8pm-1am daily) at the W Bogota Hotel is a swanky space dominated by a graffiti-style mural. On weeknights, the after-work crowd and W guests settle into the sofas here. DJs spin on weekend nights, where an occasional cover is charged.

On Wednesday nights, the place to go is **Cavú Club** (Cra. 15 No. 88-71, tel. 1/249-9987, www.cavuclub.com, 9pm-3am Wed., cover COP$20,000). Here the music played is a mix of pop genres and there is usually a performance by a drag queen.

THE ARTS
Cultural Centers

The **Fundación Gilberto Alzate Avendaño** (Cl. 10 No. 3-16, tel. 1/282-9491, www.fgaa.gov.co, 9am-5pm Mon.-Fri., free) in La Candelaria puts on theater and music performances featuring local talent and hosts art exhibits.

In the gorgeous neighborhood of La Merced, bordering the Parque Nacional, **Cine Tonalá** (Cra. 6 No. 35-37, tel. 1/285-9391, www.cinetonala.com, noon-11pm Sun. and Tues.-Thurs., noon-3am Fri.-Sat.) has a robust program of art films (with beer specials) and hosts cool parties.

Near Centro Internacional, **Casa Kilele Casa Cultural** (Cl. 28a No. 16A-31, tel. 1/487-7921 or cell tel. 320/858-4703) is the funky home of a wide range of parties, concerts, performances, workshops, and yoga classes.

A cool space on pedestrian Avenida Jiménez is **Espacio Odeón** (Cra. 5 No. 12C-73, www.espacioodeon.com, 10am-5pm Mon.-Fri.), where there is often an art installation on view.

Art Galleries

Bogotá is a magnet for artists from across Colombia. There are interesting galleries in neighborhoods across the city that are open to all, not just art buyers. **Artería** (www.periodicoarteria.com) offers fantastic free walking tours of different gallery districts in Bogotá.

In the Macarena, look for **Valenzuela Keller** (Cra. 5 No. 26B-26, tel. 1/661-1961, www.vkgaleria.com, 10am-1pm and 2pm-6pm Mon.-Fri., 11am-4pm Sat.) and **Alonso Garcés** (Cra. 5A No. 26-92, tel. 1/337-5827, www.alonsogarcesgaleria.com, 10am-1pm and 2pm-6pm Mon.-Fri., 10am-2pm Sat.).

In the industrial area of San Felipe in western Bogotá are an astonishing number of galleries. Some of the best include experimental

Galería Beta (Cl. 75A No. 20C-52, tel. 1/255-5902, www.galeriabeta.com, 10am-5pm Mon.-Fri., 2pm-5pm Sat.), **Galería SGR** (Cl. 74 No. 22-28, tel. 1/631-8027, www.sgr-art.com, 10am-6pm Mon.-Fri., noon-4pm Sat.), which highlights renowned contemporary Latin American artists, and nature-focused **Flora Ars + Natura** (Cl. 77 No. 20C-48, tel. 1/675-1425, www.arteflora.org, 2pm-6pm Mon.-Fri., 10am-1pm Sat. by appt.).

Classical Music and Opera

You may not think of classical music when you think Bogotá, or South America for that matter, but the city is home to two excellent orchestras and an opera, and hosts talented performers year-round. As is the case for most concerts and events in Bogotá, purchasing tickets in advance from Tu Boleta (tel. 1/593-6300, www.tuboleta.com) is the most convenient option.

The excellent **Orquesta Filarmónica de Bogotá** (www.filarmonicabogota.gov.co) performs often on the Universidad Nacional campus at the **Auditorio Leon de Greiff** (Cra. 45 No. 26-85, www.divulgacion.unal.edu.co) and occasionally at other venues. The Auditorio León de Greiff is hard to miss: There is a huge stencil of iconic revolutionary Che Guevara on its exterior. There is often an international guest soloist at these concerts. Although tickets are available at the *taquillas* (ticket offices) at these theaters a few hours before performance time, it is recommended to purchase tickets, which are usually inexpensive (COP$20,000), in advance at a Tu Boleta outlet.

The **Sinfónica Nacional de Colombia** (www.sinfonica.com.co, tickets COP$60,000) often performs classical music at the spectacular **Teatro Mayor Julio Mario Santo Domingo** (Av. Cl. 170 No. 67-51, tel. 1/377-9840, www.teatromayor.com) in the western *localidad* of Suba.

At the **Sala de Conciertos Luis Ángel Arango** (Cl. 11 No. 4-14, tel. 1/381-2929, www.banrepcultural.org/musica, ticket office 1pm-8pm Mon.-Fri.) in La Candelaria,

the Teatro Mayor Julio Mario Santo Domingo

chamber music concerts featuring acclaimed international artists are regularly held in the company's spectacular modernist theater in the Biblioteca Luis Ángel Arango.

The **Ópera de Colombia** (tel. 1/608-8752 or 1/608-2860, www.operadecolombia.com), one of the few opera companies in South America, is highly regarded. They perform classic operas during their season, which usually extends from August to October. The **Teatro Jorge Eliécer Gaitán** (Cra. 7 No. 22-47, tel. 1/379-5750, ext. 213, www.teatrojorgeeliecer.gov.co) and the **Teatro Colón** (Cl. 10 No. 5-62, tel. 1/284-7420, www.teatrocolon.gov.co) are two classic venues that host opera performances, as well as other concerts and events.

Theater

The country's most prominent theater company, the **Teatro Nacional** (Cl. 71 No. 10-25, tel. 1/217-4577, www.teatronacional.com.co, tickets COP$70,000) has three different theaters in Bogotá, and regularly puts on comedic and dramatic productions. Their main theater, Teatro Nacional Fanny Mikey, is named in honor of beloved Argentinian actress Fanny Mikey, who moved to Bogotá and started its famed theater festival.

FESTIVALS AND EVENTS

Festival Iberoamericano de Teatro

Every even year during Holy Week, theater and dance take over the city during the **Festival Iberoamericano de Teatro** (www.festivaldeteatro.com.co). Attracting more than 100 prestigious international troupes and companies and over 170 representing Colombia, this festival is a living tribute to Fanny Mikey, an Argentinian actress who adopted Colombia as her home. She started the biennial affair in 1988. Known for her bright red hair and distinctive smile, she passed away in 2008. With over 800 performances in the span of two weeks, this is one of the largest such theater festivals in the world. The festival kicks off with a Saturday parade. There are always theater groups from English-speaking countries, and there are typically many circus and dance performances. To take a break from the show, you can always party at the **Carpa Cabaret** at night, where you can drink and dance alongside actors from across the globe. Besides performances in theaters, there is an impressive series of free performances in parks and plazas in neighborhoods across the city and workshops for acting students.

ArtBo

More than 50 art galleries representing 400 artists from the Americas converge on Bogotá each November during **ArtBo** (www.artboonline.com), known more formally as the **Feria Internacional de Arte de Bogotá**, one of the top contemporary art fairs in Latin America. It is held each year at the Corferias fairground (Cra. 40 No. 22C-67, www.corferias.com).

Feria de Artesanías

In December, and just in time for Christmas, the Corferias fairground (Cra. 40 No. 22C-67, www.corferias.com) is the setting for the fantastic—if overwhelming—**Feria de Artesanías** (www.expoartesanias.com). During two weeks, artisans come from across Colombia to showcase and sell their handicrafts. Many artisans, particularly indigenous peoples and Afro-Colombians from rural areas, have their trip to Bogotá sponsored by Artesanías de Colombia, the event's organizer. Most shoppers plan on multiple visits in order to see everything. The fair is also a great place for tasty Colombian snacks like *patacones* (fried plantains).

Gay Pride

Taking place during either the last weekend of June or first weekend of July and coinciding with a long weekend is Bogotá's **gay pride celebration.** The parade, called La Marcha, kicks off on a Sunday at noon from the Parque Nacional and makes its disorganized but festive way down the Séptima to the Plaza de Bolívar. Anyone can join in the parade. Bars and clubs host pride parties over the long weekend.

Music Festivals

Free music festivals take center stage at the Parque Simón Bolívar (between Clls. 53-63 and Cras. 48-68) during the latter half of the year. The most popular outdoor music festival is **Rock al Parque** (www.rockalparque.gov.co, July), the largest free outdoor rock festival in Latin America. Other festivals include **Gospel al Parque** (Aug.), **Hip Hop al Parque** (Oct.), **Salsa al Parque** (Nov.), and the Colombian music showcase of **Colombia al Parque** (Nov.).

International and Colombian jazz artists perform annually at the long-running **Festival Internacional de Jazz de Bogotá.** Most concerts are held at the **Teatro Libre** (Cl. 62 No. 9-65, tel. 1/217-1988) in Chapinero. The festival usually takes place in early September, with tickets available via Tu Boleta.

Shopping

LA CANDELARIA

The narrow streets of this main tourist neighborhood are lined with small shops specializing in Colombian *artesanías* (handicrafts), the quality of which ranges from trinkets to the refined.

For a fun stop while sightseeing, check out **Pasaje Rivas** (between Cras. 9-10 and Clls. 10-11), a bazaar that dates to the late 19th century. The passages are so narrow that it's impossible to not interact with carpenters selling furniture and women peddling hand-woven baskets and curios. For high-quality hand-carved utilitarian wood items and more, check out the shop of the **Escuela de Artes y Oficios Santo Domingo** (Cl. 10 No. 8-73), a well-regarded school for craftspeople.

AVENIDA JIMÉNEZ

Avenida Jiménez (Calle 13) is a pedestrian thoroughfare that also functions as the northern border of La Candelaria. It winds from Carrera 10 toward the mountains and Carrera 2. The surrounding city blocks are always bustling with shoppers and merchants peddling practically everything.

Surrounding the Plaza de San Victorino (Cras. 11-13 and Clls. 12-13) is the eponymous shopping area of **San Victorino,** known for its vibrant atmosphere and countless shops where locals head for deals on clothing and household goods.

To the north of Avenida Jiménez is a **used book market** (Cra 8A and Clls. 15-16), and on bustling Calle 19 are specialty shopping centers—including the multilevel **Centro Comercial Vía Libre** (Cl. 19 at Cra. 5), almost exclusively devoted to tattoo parlors. There are also some cafés that serve alcohol, providing liquid courage to the soon-to-be tattooed.

Colombia is one of the top emerald-producing countries in the world, and Bogotá is probably the best place in the country to pick up one of those gems. It would be wise to walk into jewelry stores armed with knowledge about gem quality and prices. To get that education, check out the **Museo Internacional de la Esmeralda** (Cl. 16 No.

hand-woven baskets for sale along Pasaje Rivas

6-66, tel. 1/286-4268, 10am-6pm Mon.-Sat.), then visit one of the many stores on the block of Carrera 6 between Calles 10 and 13.

Recommended places to peruse handicrafts include the dozens of small stalls in the **Galería de Artesanías Colombianas** (Cl. 16 between Cras. 5-7), across the street from the Museo del Oro, and the much finer (and more expensive) shop of **Artesanías de Colombia** (www.artesaniasdecolombia.com.co), which is managed by the same entity that hosts the amazing Feria de Artesanías every December. Hammocks, ceramics, woven goods, toys, and jewelry, all meticulously produced by skilled artisans from throughout the country, are sold at their shops. One location is on the grounds of the Iglesia Las Aguas (Cra. 2 No. 18A-58, tel. 1/284-3095, 9am-6pm Mon.-Fri.).

NORTHERN BOGOTÁ

The Zona Rosa, surrounded by upscale wealthy neighborhoods, is mostly known for its glitzy American-style shopping malls. These include the **Centro Comercial Andino** (Cra. 11 No. 82-71, tel. 1/621-3111, www.centroandino.com.co, 10am-8pm Mon.-Sat., noon-6pm Sun.), **El Retiro Centro Comercial** (Cl. 81 No. 11-94, tel. 1/745-5545, www.elretirobogota.com, 10am-8pm Mon.-Sat., noon-6pm Sun.), and **Centro Comercial Atlantis Plaza** (Cl. 81 No. 13-05, tel. 1/606-6200, www.atlantisplaza.com, 8am-1am Mon.-Sat., 11am-1am Sun.). Here you will find dozens of Colombian and international clothing stores for all budgets and a smattering of other specialty shops (books, handicrafts, music, cosmetics, etc.).

Bogotá's high-end jewelers specialize in locally mined gold. In the Centro Comercial Andino are two of the city's best: **Liévano** (Cra. 11 No. 82-71, Local 157, tel. 1/616-8608, 10:45am-7:45pm Mon.-Sat.), which specializes in gold and emerald jewelry and high-end Swiss watches, and **Bauer** (Cra. 11 No.

82-71, tel. 1/478-5454, 11am-7pm Mon.-Sat.), which was founded by a German immigrant in 1893 and is popular for its wedding bands and other pieces of jewelry. **L.A. Cano** (Cra. 11 No. 82-51, shop 2-10, tel. 1/610-1175, 9am-8pm Mon.-Sat.) is known for its gold pre-Columbian motifs.

A short stroll from the Zona Rosa malls is a street dedicated almost exclusively to **antiques**. The **Calle de los Anticuarios** (Cl. 79A between Cras. 7-9) is lined by antique shops as well as some restaurants. **Cinco en Punto** (Cl. 79B No. 8-31, tel. 1/248-9798, 10am-6pm Mon.-Sat.) offers a range of curios, from vases to furniture. **Anticuario Novecento** (Cl. 79B No. 7-60, tel. 1/606-8616, www.anticuarionovecento.com, 10am-6:30pm Mon.-Sat.) has a wide collection that includes religious art from colonial Colombia along with Baccarat crystal from the 1930s. **Bolívar Old Prints** (Cl. 79B No. 7-46, tel. 1/695-5006, www.bolivaroldprints.com, 10:30am-6pm Mon.-Sat.) specializes in old maps from Latin America and is owned by a French expat.

The rich agricultural area of the savanna of Bogotá, on the outskirts of the city, is filled with flower farms. Flower markets in the city provide a glimpse of the country's floral diversity. About a 10-minute walk from the Zona Rosa in the **Parque El Virrey** (Cl. 86 at Cra. 15, daily) is a popular flower market of dozens of stalls. Near the market is a storefront of **Artesanías de Colombia** (Cl. 86A No. 13A-10, tel. 1/691-7149, www.artesaniasdecolombia.com.co, 10am-7pm Mon.-Sat., 11am-5pm Sun.).

Farther north in the colonial neighborhood of Usaquén is the **Mercado de las Pulgas Toldos de San Pelayo** (Cra. 7B No. 124-77, 8am-5pm Sun.), a large flea market held every Sunday. Here, you can expect to find handicrafts, antique furniture, artwork, and artisanal foods, among other items. Bargaining is acceptable and prices are reasonable.

Sports and Recreation

BIKING
★ Ciclovía

At 7am every Sunday and on holidays, about 120 kilometers of Bogotá's roads are closed to vehicular traffic so that cyclists, joggers, dog walkers, skaters, and people-watchers can claim the streets. The **Ciclovía** started in the 1970s as a neighborhood initiative. Today it is an institution, and one of the few spaces in which people of all classes in Bogotá mix. On sunny days, over two million people have participated in the Ciclovía.

The event is most enjoyable on a bike, especially because you can cover a lot more of the city pedaling rather than walking. Two of the most popular routes are Avenida Séptima (Av. Cra. 7) and Carrera 15. It's an excellent way to see parts of the city that you might not have otherwise considered.

The Ciclovía is easy to figure out and do on your own. Helpful staff and volunteers are stationed along the entire route. Bike repair stations are located on all routes; they'll inflate flat tires for about COP$1,000.

The city's weather changes quickly, so pack a lightweight rain jacket and apply sunscreen. Vendors sell freshly squeezed orange juice along the way. Watch the time—at 2pm, the cars come roaring back.

Ciclopaseo de los Miércoles

On Wednesday nights, it's not uncommon to see more than a hundred cyclists of all ages and abilities taking a ride along the *ciclorutas* (bike paths) and streets of Bogotá. The **Ciclopaseo de los Miércoles** has been going strong for about seven years. The group typically meets at bike shops in Northern Bogotá. Find out about the next ride on their Facebook page. There is no charge to join the ride.

Bike Rentals

Some hostels and hotels have bicycles available to their guests for rent.

Bogotá Bike Tours (Cra. 3 No. 12-72, tel. 1/281-9924, www.bogotabiketours.com), run by the attentive American owner, Mike, is a popular agency based in La Candelaria.

An agency that works with many big hotels

The Sunday Ciclovía is a Bogotá institution.

is **Bogotravel Tours** (tel. 1/ 282-6313, www. bogotraveltours.com). They have bikes for rent at the Hilton Hotel (Cra. 7 No. 72-41) and a downtown location (Cl. 16 No. 2-52). They also offer tours.

Laika Bikes (Cra. 4 No. 69-23, cell tel. 310/625-7170, www.laikabikes.com) is another bike store.

HIKING

Bogotá's city limits include a great expanse of rural areas. The mountains surrounding the city are just too inviting to not explore. There are more paths to conquer besides the one to the top of the **Cerro de Monserrate.**

Amigos de la Montaña (www.amigos-delamontana.org) is a group that maintains a couple of mountain trails in the Chapinero area. Most popular is the **Quebrada La Vieja** (Cl. 71 No. 1-45, 5am-9am Mon.-Sat., free), a path along a babbling brook up a mountain that leads to a statue of Mary. The return is by the same path, and it will take about two hours to make the round-trip. It is wildly popular with locals. To get to the beginning of the trail, take a cab. Or, if you're coming from Zona G on foot, walk east along the south side of Calle 72. Follow the sidewalk that parallels a stream until you reach the busy Circunvalar. Continue through the pedestrian tunnel, after which you'll find the entrance gate. No guide is needed for this hike.

Another group, **Camino Bogotano** (cell tel. 300/224-0289, www.caminobogotano. wordpress.com), regularly organizes hikes in the mountains around the city that you can join for COP$30,000. Reserve a spot on their website. Another organization, **Caminar Colombia** (tel. 1/366-3059, www.caminar-colombia.com, COP$45,000 incl. transportation), offers ecological walks, usually on Sunday. On the day of the hike, the group usually meets at 6:30am at the Los Héroes shopping center (Cra. 19A No. 78-85). The TransMilenio station there is called Los Héroes.

The city's environmental office organizes interesting guided **ecological walks** (tel.

1/377-8881, www.ambientebogota.gov.co/ caminatas-ecologicas, free) throughout the city. It may take some time to sign up for the program and for a particular walk.

BIRD-WATCHING

Some serious bird-watching can be done right in the city, in and around the wetlands of the 200-acre **Parque La Florida** (Km. 2 Autopista Medellín, no phone, 7am-5pm daily, free) in western Bogotá. Two endemic species, the Bogotá rail and Apolinar's marsh-wren, are birds to keep an eye out for, but well over 100 species have been documented in the park.

Diana Balcázar, a wetlands bird expert and author of several books, offers interesting morning bird-watching excursions through **Birding Bogotá and Colombia** (cell tel. 310/249-5274, www.birdingbogotaandcolombia.com, hotel pickup included). Tours include a species checklist, breakfast and snacks, and an English-speaking guide.

TOURS
Walking Tours

The **Bogotá Tourism Office** (www.bogotaturismo.gov.co) offers a free two-hour walking tour of La Candelaria in Spanish (10am and 2pm daily) and in English (10am and 2pm Tues. and Thurs.). Tours start at the tourist information office on the southwest corner of the Plaza de Bolívar. To reserve your spot, stop by the office, call (tel. 1/555-7692), or email (informacionturistica@idt.gov.co) a day before you want to go.

One of the city's most popular tours is the **Graffiti Tour** (cell tel. 321/297-4075, www. bogotagraffiti.com, COP$20,000 requested donation). During about 1.5 hours, you'll take a walk through a world you might not have thought much about. Throughout La Candelaria and on the gritty downtown streets, there is some compelling street art to be seen. Tours are given in English by graffiti artists, who will offer their take on Colombian history and politics to boot. The tour's meeting point is usually at Parque de los

Periodistas near Avenida Jiménez—but you'll be notified of the official spot upon making your reservation.

Bus Tours

If your time is limited and you're looking for an easy way to hit the main sights, consider a hop-on, hop-off bus tour. The green double-decker buses of **TurisBog** (El Retiro shopping mall, Entrance 3, tel. 1/467-4602, 9am-5:30pm Wed.-Sat., www.turisbog.com, adults COP$60,000) stop four times a day at each of the route's eight stops, including the Jardín Botánico, Parque de la 93, El Retiro mall, Cerro de Monserrate, the Museo Nacional, and La Candelaria. Included with your ticket is an audio guide and a map.

Bike Tours

If you'd like the camaraderie of a group of other visitors as you get to know the city and get in a little exercise, try one of the many excursions offered by **Bogotá Bike Tours** (Cra. 3 No. 12-72, tel. 1/281-9924, www.bogotabiketours.com). The company offers bike tours around the city and many walking tours, such as an unusual graffiti tour.

Excursion Tours

Many hotels can arrange tours to attractions such as Zipaquirá and Laguna de Guatavita.

There are some extraordinary national natural parks (*parques nacional natural,* or PNN) quite close to Bogotá, making for excellent day hiking. Visits to these parks can be a bit difficult to organize without transportation or familiarity with the area. **Aventureros** (Cra. 15 No. 79-70, tel. 1/467-3837, www.aventureros.co) organizes

the Graffiti Tour

mountain bike trips outside of Bogotá, for instance to the Desierto de Tatacoita near Nemocón. **Ecoglobal Expeditions** (tel. 1/579-3402, www.ecoglobalexpeditions.com) organizes excursions to destinations throughout Colombia, including the famous Caño Cristales and hikes in El Cocuy. They also can organize day trips to parks near Bogotá, such as the Parque Natural Nacional Sumapaz, containing the world's largest *páramo* (highland moor), and the PNN Chingaza. **Colombia Oculta** (tel. 1/630-3172, ext. 112, cell tel. 311/239-7809, www.colombiaoculta.org) is a similar organization, with similar destinations.

Food

The Bogotá dish par excellence is *ajiaco*. This is a hearty potato and chicken soup, seasoned with the herb *guascas*. On a dreary day, there's nothing better. Heated debate can arise about what else to include in the soup. A small piece of corn on the cob usually bobs in the soup, as does a dollop of cream, but capers and avocado slices are controversial additions.

Having just a tiny Asian population, Colombia doesn't have dazzling Asian cuisine, but you'll be pleasantly surprised at the variety in Bogotá.

Reservations are helpful on weekend evenings. Restaurant staff will be more than happy to order a cab for you by phone.

Tap water in Bogotá—*de la llave*—is perfectly safe and good tasting.

LA CANDELARIA
Colombian
The classic place for a huge tamale and a hot chocolate, the **Puerta Falsa** (Cl. 11 No. 6-50, tel. 1/286-5091, 7am-10pm Mon.-Fri., 8am-8pm Sat.-Sun., COP$18,000) claims to be one of the oldest operating restaurants in Bogotá, having opened in 1816. It gets crowded here.

★ **El Mejor Ajiaco del Mundo** (Cl. 11 No. 6-20, tel. 1/566-6948, 11am-7pm Mon.-Fri., noon-6pm Sat., COP$15,000) lives up to its name, which means "the best *ajiaco* in the world." The restaurant's large bowls of *ajiaco* stew are beloved by locals.

International
With exposed beams adding to an unpretentious atmosphere, **Capital Cocina y Café** (Cl. 10 No. 2-99, tel. 1/342-0426, noon-3pm and 6:30pm-9:30pm Mon.-Fri., 4pm-10pm Sat., COP$24,000) serves surprisingly sophisticated dishes at reasonable prices, offering Colombian cuisine as well as dishes like pork ribs and seafood salad. It is vegetarian friendly, and there is often a fish-of-the-day special.

Prudencia (Cra. 2 No. 11-34, tel. 1/394-1678, www.prudencia.net, noon-4pm Mon.-Fri., 12:30pm-5:30pm Sat., COP$28,000) boasts of serving *comida campesina* (country food) from around the world. It's rather elegant for La Candelaria, with an open kitchen and chandeliers. Daily specials depend on what's in season, and there are always vegetarian (and sometimes gluten-free) options. This spot is only open during the week.

Vegetarian
Using Andean ingredients, the tiny **Quinoa y Amaranto** (Cl. 11 No. 2-95, tel. 1/565-9982, 8am-4pm Mon., 8am-9pm Tues.-Fri., 8am-5pm Sat.) is a cozy downtown haven for vegetarians. With three-course lunches for around COP$16,000, it offers bang for your buck.

Pizza
Go find mother if you want pizza in La Candelaria—**Madre** (Cl. 12 No. 5-83, tel. 1/281-2332, www.madre.la, 8pm-2am Mon.-Sat., COP$29,000), that is. The *jamón serrano* pizza gets high marks, along with the gin ice cream. With its great drinks and live music on Friday nights, this spot is bringing cool back to La Candelaria.

Cajun
Cajun food is the thing at **La Condesa Irina Lazaar** (Cra. 6 No. 10-19, tel. 1/283-1573, lunch Mon.-Sat., COP$35,000). This tiny, American-run spot is easy to miss, but if you are in the mood for pork chops or crab cakes, this is the place. There are only six tables, so it's best to make reservations. If you can persuade him, the friendly owner might open the restaurant for you for dinner.

Cafés, Bakeries, and Quick Bites
Preisz Pastelería (Cra. 4 No. 9-66, tel. 1/481-8544, 8am-6pm Mon.-Fri., 10am-4pm Sun.,

COP$14,000) bakes their own bread, and is a cheerful and inexpensive spot for sandwiches and salads. They also serve yerba maté drinks and homemade *alfajores* (sandwich-style cookies with dulce de leche in the middle).

Set in a funky house with an interior patio and nooks for relaxing, ★ **Chez Dom** (Cl. 9 No. 3-11, tel. 1/342-8266, 10am-9:30pm Mon.-Sat., COP$15,000) is a French café that also serves healthy lunches. A small organic market adjoins this cute spot.

AVENIDA JIMÉNEZ AND CENTRO INTERNACIONAL
Colombian

For a hearty meal of *mamona* (grilled meat), run to **Asadero Capachos** (Cl. 18 No. 4-68, tel. 1/243-4607, www.asaderocapachos.com, 11:30am-3:30pm Tues.-Thurs., 11:30am-5pm Fri.-Sun.), an authentic *llanero* (cowboy) restaurant. For under COP$20,000 you get a healthy portion of tender, slow-grilled meat, fried yuca, and a *maduro* (fried plantain), which all goes down well with a beer. On weekends they have live music and dance performances. Vegetarians will have a difficult—but not impossible—time here.

Fish soups, shrimp cocktails, and *arepas de huevo* (corn cakes filled with egg) are some of the dishes on the menu at **Misia by Leo Espinosa** (Transversal 6 No. 27-50, tel. 1/795-4748, 9am-10pm Mon.-Sat., 9am-4pm Sun., COP$25,000). They do fantastic breakfasts and brunches, and you must try the loquat milkshake. Misia is near the Ibis Hotel and Museo Nacional.

Specializing in cuisine from the agricultural region of Boyacá, ★ **Doña Elvira** (Cra. 6 No. 29-08, www.restaurantedonaelvira.com, noon-4pm Mon.-Sat.) serves hearty soups, like *ajiaco*, and lots of potatoes, corn, and beans, as well as dishes like fried catfish. This restaurant has been in the same family since 1934.

Set in what appears to be a crumbling old house is one of the gems of downtown Bogotá. ★ **A Seis Manos** (Cl. 22 No. 8-60,

tel. 1/282-8441, 11:30am-11:30pm Mon.-Sat., COP$24,000) has delicious lunches of Colombian-Mediterranean fusion with a lot of flair. At night it's a major cultural center, with DJs, performances, film screenings, and language exchanges. Visit their Facebook page to find upcoming events.

On a quiet street behind the Museo Nacional, ★ **Donostia** (Cl. 29 Bis No. 5-84, tel. 1/287-3943, noon-4pm Mon., noon-4pm and 7pm-11pm Tues.-Sat., COP$30,000) is a swanky place for tapas and wine. They serve Spanish-Colombian cuisine.

Mexican

In Parque Bavaria, **San Lorenzo** (Cra. 13 No. 28A-21, tel. 1/288-8731, 11am-4pm Mon.-Fri., COP$23,000), on the 4th floor of the old Bavaria brewery, packs in the banking crowd at lunch. This restaurant serves consistently good Mexican food. Sometimes mariachis will serenade diners.

International

In the Macarena neighborhood, it's all about Swedish-style meatballs at innovative **Köttbullar** (Cl. 26C No. 3-05, tel. 1/620-1632, www.kottbullar.co, noon-4:30pm Sun. and Tues., noon-10:30pm Wed.-Sat., COP$19,000), where the dish is served in a multitude of preparations and sauces. The meatballs go well with a locally brewed beer, and Köttbullar even serves some veggie variations on the meatball. This is a cool place.

Breakfast

Pastelería La Florida (Cra. 7 No. 21-46, tel. 1/341-0340, 6am-9pm daily, COP$16,000) is a local institution, a Colombian version of a greasy spoon. Breakfast is big here; options include tamales, eggs, waffles a la mode, and hot chocolate.

Cafés, Bakeries, and Quick Bites

Andante Ma Non Troppo (Cra. 5 No. 26C-57, tel. 1/284-4387, 8am-8pm Mon.-Sat., 8am-3pm Sun., COP$16,000) is a long-running café that serves breakfast, sandwiches, and salads in one of the most iconic buildings in Bogotá, the Torres del Parque. It's more atmospheric than memorable.

Crepes & Waffles (Av. Jiménez No. 4-55, tel. 1/676-7600, www.crepesywaffles.com.co, noon-8:30pm Mon.-Sat., noon-5pm Sun.) is a chain found all over Colombia. Fill up on a *crepe de sal* (savory crepe) for around COP$18,000, or order a mini-waffle with Nutella and vanilla ice cream. This location is in the easy-on-the-eyes Monserrate building on the Eje Ambiental.

CHAPINERO
Colombian

Las Margaritas (Cl. 62 No. 7-77, tel. 1/249-9468, noon-4pm Tues.-Fri., 8am-5pm Sat.-Sun., COP$15,000) has been around for over a century. Try the *puchero,* a meaty stew, on Thursday. The *ajiaco* (chicken and potato soup) is also good.

For the best of original coastal cuisine, try friendly **MiniMal** (Cra. 4A No. 57-52, tel. 1/347-5464, www.mini-mal.org, noon-3pm and 7pm-10pm Mon.-Wed., noon-3pm and 7pm-11pm Thurs., noon-11pm Fri.-Sat., COP$25,000). The stingray *cazuela* (stew) is one of the more exotic items on the menu. There's also a funky gift shop.

Latin American

In a cool setting of exposed brick walls and minimalist design is **Cantina y Punto** (Cl. 66 No. 4A-33, tel. 1/644-7766, noon-10pm Mon.-Sat., noon-6pm Sun., COP$32,000). Top menu items include duck mole, fried tuna, and thirst-quenching margaritas and other tequila drinks.

Classy **Astrid & Gastón** (Cra. 7 No. 67-64, tel. 1/211-1400, www.astridygastonbogota.com, noon-3pm and 7pm-11pm Mon.-Sat., COP$50,000), direct from Lima, and stylish **Rafael** (Cl. 70 No. 4-65, tel. 1/255-4138, 12:30pm-3pm and 7:30pm-11pm Mon.-Sat., COP$45,000) are rivals for the top Peruvian spot in town. At Astrid, try an only-in-Colombia *coca* pisco sour. **La Despensa de**

Rafael (Cl. 70A No. 9-95, tel. 1/235-8878, www.rafaelosterling.pe, 12:30pm-3:30pm and 7:30pm-11pm Mon.-Sat., noon-4pm Sun., COP$38,000) is a Peruvian-fusion bistro in Quinta Camacho run by Rafael.

Arepas La Reina (Cra. 6 No. 57-15, tel. 1/605-1877, 10am-7pm Mon.-Sat.) serves arepas filled with black beans, grilled chicken, or beef with avocado and cheese, just like in Caracas, Venezuela. It's enough for lunch.

International

Salvo Patria (Cra. 54A No. 4-13, tel. 1/702-6367, www.salvopatria.com noon-11pm Mon.-Sat., COP$22,000) is inventive and trendy, serving both Colombian and international cuisine. There's a variety of interesting appetizers, sandwiches, meaty main courses, and vegetarian options. You'll be tempted to try a carafe of gin *lulada* (a drink made with the juice of a *lulo,* a tangy fruit). There's a daily lunch special.

Dishes at **Villanos en Bermudas** (Cl. 56 No. 5-21, tel. 1/211-1259, 7pm-11pm Tues.-Sat., COP$80,000) are works of art. This small-plates place is one of the city's most creative dining spots. Its chefs use fresh, local ingredients in the experimental tasting menu of eight small dishes. You'd never know judging by its ordinary exterior.

★ **Franca** (Cl. 56 No. 6-33, cell tel. 316/880-1627, noon-3pm and 6pm-9pm Mon.-Fri., noon-midnight Sat., noon-6pm Sun., COP$28,000) is a bistro in Chapinero Alto that has great burgers (and veggie burgers) and emanates neighborhood charm. On Sundays they have a barbecue that is also vegetarian friendly.

French

French restaurant **Criterión** (Cl. 69A No. 5-75, tel. 1/310-1377, noon-4pm and 7pm-11pm Mon.-Sat., 9am-1pm and 7pm-11pm Sun., COP$60,000) is the standard-bearer when it comes to haute cuisine in Bogotá. It is the creation of the Rausch brothers, who are among the top chefs in the city.

Tapas

The small, unassuming **Nueve** (Cl. 70A No. 10A-18, noon-4pm and 7pm-midnight Mon.-Sat., COP$42,000) is actually quite sophisticated, serving small plates. Coconut rice cakes with grilled prawns in a lemongrass sauce is a favorite here. Fantastic wines from across the globe are available by the glass.

Italian

Giuseppe Verdi (Cl. 58 No. 5-35, tel. 1/211-5508, noon-11pm Mon.-Sat., noon-9pm Sun., COP$20,000) has been around for over four decades, serving typical Italian dishes featuring house-made pasta. They have added a small terrace café for more informal meals or a glass of wine.

★ **Trattoría de la Plaza** (Cl. 66 No. 22-45, 2nd fl., tel. 1/211-1740, noon-5pm Sat.-Thurs., noon-10pm Fri., COP$48,000) is a sophisticated Italian restaurant that boasts superb presentation and a wide range of wines. Reservations are required at this elegant lunch place.

At **La Divina Comedia** (Cl. 71 No. 5-93, tel. 1/317-6987, noon-3:30pm and 7pm-11pm Mon.-Sat., COP$30,000), go for the divine *tortellata* (a mix of stuffed pastas).

Lebanese

Despite its location on the busy speedway of Carrera 5, intimate **Zátar** (Cra. 5 No. 69-15, tel. 1/317-8974, noon-3:30pm and 6pm-9pm Mon., noon-3:30pm and 6pm-10pm Tues.-Fri., noon-10pm Sat., COP$24,000) is one of the city's best places for Lebanese cuisine.

Asian

The pan-Asian chain **Wok** (Cra. 9 No. 69A-63, tel. 1/212-0167, www.wok.com.co, noon-11pm Mon.-Sat., noon-8pm Sun., COP$23,000) is hard to beat. Don't let the fact that it is a chain dissuade you: The menu is astoundingly extensive, inventive, and fresh. Hearty fish soups and curries based in coconut milk will warm you up, and there are numerous vegetarian dishes, such as a Vietnamese-inspired grilled tofu sandwich. The quality of their sushi is also good. Wok is an environmentally and socially responsible company, working with family farmers and fishers in small communities throughout Colombia. A second location is in the Museo Nacional (Cra. 6 Bis No. 29-07, tel. 1/287-3194) in Centro Internacional.

Vegetarian

Don't be turned off by the name: ★ **Hippie** (Cl. 56 No. 4A-15, tel. 1/675-7154, www.hippie.com.co, 11:30am-11pm Mon.-Fri, 9am-11pm Sat., 9am-5pm Sun., COP$24,000) serves delicious food, and even the most button-downed diners will feel at ease at this cute place in Chapinero Alto. Many menu items have organic ingredients, and there are many vegan and vegetarian dishes. They sell crystals and incense next door.

Burgers

Gordo (Cra. 4A No. 66-84, tel. 1/345-5769, noon-11pm daily, COP$22,000) excels at the basics of hamburgers and french fries. The fried pickles get high marks.

Breakfast and Brunch

Árbol de Pan (Cl. 66 Bis No. 4-63, tel. 1/481-7465, 8am-8pm Mon.-Sat.) is known for almond croissants, mimosas, and brunch.

NORTHERN BOGOTÁ
Colombian

At ★ **Fulanitos 81** (Cl. 81 No. 10-56, tel. 1/622-2175, lunch daily, COP$20,000) there is always a line at lunchtime, and for good reason: This is Cali cuisine at its best. Try the *chuletas de cerdo* (pork chops) or *sancocho* (soup), and have a refreshing *lulada* (a drink made with the juice of a *lulo*, a tart tropical fruit).

For a crash course in Colombian cuisine in an elegant atmosphere, visit **Casa Club Colombia** (Cl. 82 No. 9-11, tel. 1/744-9077, noon-midnight daily, COP$28,000). In a lovely house from the mid-20th century, where the fireplace is always lit, *bandeja paisa* (dish of beans, various meats, yuca, and potatoes) and favorites from all corners of the country are on the menu. This is a great brunch option on weekends.

It's always a celebration at **Andrés Carne de Res,** an obligatory stop for all visitors to Colombia. Music, costumed waiters, samples of Colombian food from across the country, drinks, and dancing is what it's all about here. The original location is **Andrés** (Cl. 3 No. 11A-56, tel. 1/863-7880, noon-3am Thurs.-Sat., noon-11pm Sun., COP$50,000) in the countryside of Chía, about 45 minutes from Bogotá. A more convenient location is **Andrés D.C.** (Cl. 82 No. 12-21, tel. 1/863-7880, noon-midnight Sun.-Wed., noon-3am Thurs.-Sat., COP$35,000), in town. Look for the windmills next to the El Retiro mall. **La Plaza de Andrés** (Cl. 82 No. 11-75, 8am-9pm Mon.-Thurs., 10am-10pm Sat.-Sun., COP$25,000) is also in the mall. It offers the color and diversity of cuisine of the original, but without the raucous atmosphere. This location doesn't have table service, but it's still pretty fun.

Welcome to Bogotá's version of Santa Marta. **Gaira Cumbia Café** (Cra. 13 No. 96-11A, tel. 1/746-2696, www.gairacafe.com, 9am-10pm Mon.-Wed., 9am-2am Thurs., 9am-3am Fri.-Sat., 9am-6pm Sun., COP$25,000) specializes in good Caribbean cuisine that's popular with locals. Musician Guillermo Vives and his mom run the show here, and Guillo often performs. He is the brother of Carlos Vives, the multiple Grammy Award-winning *vallenato* singer. On weekend mornings there are special activities for children, while on weekend nights, reservations are essential, and there may be a cover for live music events. The line between dining and partying gets rather blurry as the night wears on.

Latin American

Delicious margaritas, a fun atmosphere, and tasty tacos are the order of the day or night at ★ **Gringo Cantina** (Cl. 80 No. 12A-29, tel. 1/622-2906, noon-11pm Mon.-Thurs., noon-1am Fri.-Sat., noon-6pm Sun., COP$32,000), a colorful spot that looks like it belongs on a laid-back beach in Mexico. It's popular with gringos and locals alike.

International

Harry Sasson (Cra. 9 No. 75-70, tel. 1/347-7155, noon-midnight Mon.-Sat., noon-5pm Sun., COP$35,000) is named for a celebrity Colombian chef. In a gorgeous house refitted with modern touches, this contemporary classic is a favorite among the city's power players.

Andrés Carne de Res

(You can tell by the serious-looking bodyguards waiting outside in their SUVs.) Try the chestnut prawns. And go for a Hendrick's gin and tonic—a favorite among this crowd.

In a fantastic setting bordering a park, **Black Bear** (Cra. 11A No. 89-06, tel. 1/644-7766, noon-11pm Mon.-Sat., noon-6pm Sun., COP$36,000) packs guests in around its boisterous bar, satisfying appetites with grilled octopus, hearty burgers, and smart cocktails.

European

Not even a sign can be seen at minimalist ★ **Klaas** (Cl. 77A No. 12-26, tel. 1/530-5074, noon-11pm Mon.-Sat., COP$45,000), a restaurant run by a Belgian chef. The weekly menu offers just a few three-course options. It's mostly French-inspired cuisine, and specialties often include *coq au vin* and salmon lasagna. There is always a vegetarian menu, and the wines are thoughtfully paired. In the evenings, look for the candlelit tables on this quiet street 10 minutes from the Centro Comercial Andino.

Italian

At unpretentious **Trattoría San Giorgio** (Cl. 81 No. 8-81, tel. 1/212-3962, noon-10:30pm Mon.-Sat., noon-6pm Sun., COP$22,000), Italian regulars are often found sipping wine and enjoying a multicourse meal.

DiLucca (Cra. 13 No. 85-32, tel. 1/257-4269, noon-midnight daily, COP$25,000) turns out consistently good pastas and pizzas, and also offers delivery. The atmosphere is rather lively inside.

Julia (Cl. 85 No. 12-81, tel. 1/530-2115, noon-10pm daily, COP$30,000) serves delicious thin-crust gourmet pizzas. This spot doesn't disappoint.

Asian

★ **Izakaya** (Cra. 13 No. 82-74, 3rd fl., tel. 1/622-5980, noon-10:30pm Mon.-Sat., noon-8:30 Sun., COP$30,000) is a fantastic Japanese restaurant in the Zona T. Here you feel like you're in Tokyo—except the friendly waitstaff

speak Spanish. Izakaya serves small, beautifully presented dishes and sake.

Excellent service awaits at sleek **Watakushi** (Cra. 12 No. 83-17, tel. 1/744-9097, noon-3pm and 6pm-11pm Mon.-Thurs., noon-11pm Fri.-Sat., noon-5pm Sun., COP$35,000), one of the many restaurants operated by local restaurant wizard Leo Katz. Reservations are needed on weekends.

Don't let the lack of decor and plastic chairs at **Arigato** (Cl. 80 No. 11-28, tel. 1/248-0764, www.restaurantearigato.com, 11am-9pm Mon.-Sat., COP$25,000) turn you off. The food at this family-run Japanese restaurant is authentic. The fresh fish is flown in regularly from the Pacific coast.

★ **Señor Kim** (Cl. 78 No. 12-09, cell tel. 300/218-8175, noon-3pm and 5pm-8pm Mon.-Fri., 1pm-7pm Sat., COP$18,000) is a sweet Korean place run by a friendly Korean-Colombian couple. It's small but popular, and soups like *kimchi jjigae* and noodle dishes like *japchae* are fantastic.

Indian

There are few Indian restaurants in Bogotá, but of those, **Flor de Loto** (Cl. 85 No. 19A-24, tel. 1/383-7543, noon-3pm and 6pm-9pm Mon.-Sat., COP$24,000) is probably the best. The head chef is originally from the Punjab region of India, and this cash-only place feels authentic.

Burgers

Agadón Burger Bar (Cra. 13 No. 85-75, tel. 1/255-4138, noon-10pm Mon.-Sat., noon-6pm Sun., COP$20,000) will leave you satisfied. It's run by a pair of Israelis, and features portobello burgers on the menu. It's across from the Four Seasons.

Vegetarian and Vegan

★ **Raw** (Cra. 12A No. 78-54, cell tel. 304/335-9578, www.hoymesientoraw.com, 8:30am-8:30pm Mon.-Fri., 8:30pm-4pm Sat., COP$22,000) offers fresh and delectable vegan dishes. This delightful café has a daily three-course lunch special, a la carte menu items, and smoothies.

For a delicious vegetarian lunch (usually with a soup of the day, main course, juice, and dessert) or a veggie burger and fries, head to cheerful **VG Tal** (Cra. 12A No. 79-26, tel. 1/316-3538, 9am-7pm Mon.-Fri., 9am-5pm Sat., COP$20,000), on a quiet side street near the Atlantis Plaza shopping mall.

Cafés and Quick Bites

When it comes to *onces* (Colombian tea time), **Myriam Camhi** (Cl. 81 No. 8-08, tel. 1/345-1819, 7am-8pm daily, COP$18,000) takes the cake. The *napoleón de Arequipe* and chocolate flan satisfy a sweet tooth, but healthy breakfasts and lunches, including a decent salad bar, are also featured. Across the street is **Brot Café** (Cl. 81 No. 7-93, tel. 1/347-6916, 7:30am-7pm daily, COP$16,000), a neighborhood spot that does breakfasts, including large fresh fruit bowls and tasty chocolate baguettes. It's open for lunch, but is more popular late in the afternoon.

With benches set up outside, **Siuka** (Cl.

79A No. 8-82, tel. 1/248-3765, 9am-7pm Mon.-Sat., 11am-5pm Sun., COP$14,000) is a welcome midmorning or late-afternoon place to meet for brownies and a barley tea.

If you can find ★ **Les Amis Bizcochería** (Cra. 14 No. 86A-12, tel. 1/236-2124, 8:30am-7:30pm Mon.-Fri., 9am-6pm Sat.), you'll love it. This bakery-café makes delicious French and Colombian pastries and has a couple of tables for clients. It's on the 2nd floor of an ordinary-looking apartment building.

★ **Brown** (Calle 77A No. 12-26, tel. 1/248-0409, www.brownesunareposteria.com, 11am-6pm Mon.-Fri., 11am-4pm Sat.) is intimate and cute as a button and has a light lunch menu (half a sandwich, soup, salad, and drink for COP$16,500) and scrumptious brownies. There are about four tables outside and a couple inside.

Build your own salad, or just stop by for pastry and dessert at **Masa** (Cl. 81 No. 9-12, tel. 1/466-1552, noon-9pm Mon., 7am-9pm Tues.-Fri., 8:30am-9pm Sat., 8:30am-5pm Sun., COP$23,000), a corner restaurant with pleasant open-air seating.

Accommodations

Many visitors choose to stay in the colonial center of La Candelaria, as there is a wealth of hostels along the neighborhood's narrow streets. This area is very quiet, so nighttime incidents of crime are not unheard of. Be cautious when out late at night in this area.

Increasing options are available in other parts of the city for travelers of all budgets and interests. Neighborhoods such as Chapinero Alto (the eastern side of the Séptima in Chapinero) and Zona G are home to cool restaurants and close to easy transportation options on Carrera 7 (the Séptima). For getting around, it's good to be close to that important artery. The same could be said for Avenida Calle 26 (Av. El Dorado), a major thoroughfare that has easy transportation links to the rest of the city.

Some of the best hotels in Bogotá are well-known international luxury brands. There are two superb **Four Seasons** hotels: the **Four Seasons Bogotá** (Cra. 13 No. 85–46) and the **Four Seasons Casa Medina** (Cra. 7 No. 69A-22) near Zona G. Comfort and attention at these cannot be beat. **Hilton** (Cra. 7 No. 72-41) and **JW Marriott** (Cl. 73 No. 8-60) are neighbors along the Séptima not far from Zona G. The **Marriott** (Av. Cl. 26 No. 69B-53), meanwhile, is located on Avenida Calle 26 toward the airport. The **W Bogotá** (Av. Cra. 9 No. 115-30), near Usaquén, is the headquarters of cool when it comes to hotels in Bogotá.

Weekend rates are often less expensive in hotels that cater to business travelers, and may drop even further on *puentes* (long weekends).

LA CANDELARIA

Travelers on a budget will find plentiful friendly options in La Candelaria close to all the important sights. It can feel a little desolate late at night, and there are occasional reports of crime, so be alert.

Under COP$70,000

★ **Fernweh Photography Hostel** (Cra. 2 No. 9-46, tel. 1/281-0218, www.fernwehostel. com, COP$37,000 dorm, COP$110,000 triple w/shared bath) is very cool and laid-back. Stunning photos of Colombia adorn the walls. There are peaceful common areas, including a relaxing backyard patio. A fluffy dog called Wolf protects the guests. Daylong photography workshops are offered for COP$300,000. The two dorm rooms have nine and four beds, and there are two private rooms.

At **Alegria's Hostel** (Cl. 9 No. 2-13, tel. 1/282-3168, cell tel. 313/419-1288, www. alegriashostel.com, COP$35,000 dorm, COP$65,000 d) there are ample common areas with hammocks, and some cozy private rooms with fireplaces. There's a big dorm room with 10 beds and a smaller one with 4 beds.

Set in an old house in La Candelaria overflowing with rustic charm, **Anandamayi Hostel and Hotel** (Cl. 9 No. 2-81, tel. 1/341-7208, cell tel. 315/215-5778, www. anandamayihostel.com, COP$40,000 dorm, COP$140,000 d shared bath) has three interior patios bursting with plants, flowers, and the occasional hummingbird. The atmosphere is warm, despite the chilly nights. There is one large dorm room with 10 beds. The rest of the rooms are private, mostly with shared baths.

Masaya Intercultural (Cra. 2 No. 12-48, tel. 1/747-1848, www.masaya-experience.com, COP$36,000 dorm, COP$110,000 d) near LaSalle University offers different accommodation options depending on your budget or style, from luxurious private rooms to dorms. Guests and students congregate by the bar and restaurant area in front. The common areas, which include outdoor patios, can be social, so bring earplugs. The two dorms rooms have four and six beds and privacy curtains, and there are six private rooms. The staff has tons of information on activities to keep guests occupied.

COP$70,000-200,000

★ **Casa Platypus** (Cra. 3 No. 12F-28, tel. 1/281-1801, www.casaplatypusbogota.com, COP$47,000 dorm, COP$189,000 triple) is a comfortable, clean, and friendly guesthouse with 17 rooms. The rooftop terrace is an excellent place to unwind with a glass of wine after a day hitting the streets. Breakfast gets good marks. Platypus is run by Germán, who was one of the first people to set up a hostel in Bogotá, back when only the intrepid dared to visit. The dorm rooms (only four beds apiece) don't have bunks, which makes late-night arrivals less disruptive.

The **Abadía Colonial** (Cl. 11 No. 2-32, tel. 1/341-1884, www.abadiacolonial.com, COP$150,000 s, COP$200,000 d), an Italian-run midrange option with 12 rooms, is pleasantly quiet around the interior patio. The on-site restaurant specializes in Italian cuisine.

There are 18 rooms at ★ **Apartaestudios La Candelaria** (Cl. 10 No. 2-40, tel. 1/281-6923, www.apartaestudioscandelaria.com, COP$160,000 d), a good and spacious option for those wanting solitude.

COP$200,000-500,000

★ **Hotel de la Ópera** (Cl. 10 No. 5-72, tel. 1/336-2066, www.hotelopera.com.co, COP$350,000 d) still reigns as the luxury place to stay in La Candelaria. The hotel comprises two converted homes, one Republican style and one colonial. There are two restaurants, including a rooftop spot that has one of the best views downtown. The hotel also offers a spa. You can expect very professional service here.

Casa Deco (Cl. 12C No. 2-36 tel. 1/283-7032, www.hotelcasadeco.com, COP$192,000 d) is a nicely refurbished art deco building with 21 well-appointed and spacious, if somewhat chilly, rooms. The terrace is an excellent place for relaxing on a late afternoon.

CENTRO INTERNACIONAL

The TransMilenio line on the Séptima has played a major role in transforming this area into a walkable and well-situated place to stay while discovering the city. There are only a few accommodation options in this neighborhood. The area is perfectly safe during the day, but you'll want to avoid walking around late at night.

COP$70,000-200,000

In the heart of the Centro Internacional, few surprises are in store at ★ **Ibis Museo** (Transversal 6 No. 27-85, tel. 1/381-4666, www.ibishotel.com, COP$120,000), part of a French budget hotel chain. Across from the Museo Nacional, the hotel has 200 small but adequate rooms and a 24-hour restaurant (breakfast not included). Good restaurants like Leo Cocina are nearby, and it's close to all downtown attractions. Just avoid nighttime strolls in this area. This is a nice place to be on Ciclovía Sundays, although they don't provide bikes for guests.

CHAPINERO

Halfway between La Candelaria and the Zona Rosa is Chapinero, straddling either side of the Séptima. On the eastern side of the Séptima is **Chapinero Alto,** a tree-lined residential neighborhood where small, trendy restaurants are cropping up. Stay in this area if you're looking for quiet but still want to be close to the action—either end of town is just a short bus ride away. The western side of the Séptima is a bit grittier and is populated mostly by mom-and-pop shops. There's some activity here at night, as there is a group of gay bars around the Plaza de Lourdes (Cra. 13 and Av. Cl. 63).

Under COP$70,000

A relative newcomer to the area, having opened in 2014, **12:12** (Cl. 67 No. 4-16, tel. 1/467-2656, cell tel. 317/635-4047, www.1212hostels.com.co, COP$38,000 dorm, COP$138,000 d) earns praise from budget travelers who appreciate this hostel's cleanliness, comfort, and attention to details like privacy curtains for beds in the dorm rooms. Some of the dorm rooms are large, with 8-10 beds. It has a nice location near the Zona G restaurant area, and cool, cheery decor in the common areas. There are just two private rooms here.

Mi Llave Hostel (Cra. 10A No. 67-29, cell tel. 316/805-1661, www.millavehostels. com, COP$35,000 dorm, COP$130,000 d) opened in 2015, and has a cute patio in back and good coffee. It's in a great location close to the Zona G.

COP$70,000-200,000

The Viaggio chain has nine reasonably priced furnished apartment buildings in Bogotá. **Viaggio 6.1.7.** (Cl. 61 No. 7-18, tel. 1/744-9999, www.viaggio.com.co, COP$131,000 d) is a high-rise centrally located on the Séptima. Rooms have tiny kitchenettes, but breakfast is included in the price. You can rent rooms on a daily, weekly, or monthly basis.

Classical music fills the air at intimate **6 Suites** (Cra. 3B No. 64A-06, tel. 1/752-9484, cell tel. 315/851-1427, www.6suiteshotel.com, COP$139,000 d), which has exactly that number of rooms in a small house. Some packages include a dinner of Argentine cuisine. There is a Saturday vegetable and fruit market in a small park next to the house, as well as a round-the-clock police station.

On a quiet street but within easy walking distance to restaurants and public transportation, the **Casona del Patio** (Cra. 8 No. 69-24, tel. 1/212-8805, www.casonadelpatio. com, COP$127,000 d) is a comfortable and economical choice, especially for its high-end address. Many of the 24 rooms (several with two twin beds) have natural light and wooden floors.

Two small hotels in appealing English Tudor-style houses make the grade for those on a quest for charm. Near the trendy Chapinero Alto neighborhood, ★ **The Book Hotel** (Cra. 5 No. 57-79, tel. 1/745-9988, www. thebookhotel.co, COP$150,000 d) offers 27 comfortable rooms and a pleasant lobby filled with books.

With just 10 rooms, the **Matisse Hotel** (Cl. 67 No. 6-55, tel. 1/212-0177, cell tel. 300/463-5053, www.matissehotel.com, COP$150,000 d) is a five-minute walk to the Zona G and very close to the busy Séptima. Some rooms may not have windows—or ones that open.

WESTERN BOGOTÁ

There are several international chain hotels close to the airport along Avenida Calle 26 (Av. El Dorado). With a TransMilenio line on this broad, tree-lined thoroughfare, it's easy to hop on one of the red buses and spend the day visiting the major sights in La Candelaria. There are few points of interest in this neighborhood, but there is the **Gran Estación mall** (Av. El Dorado No. 62-47). Plus, along the Avenida and the TransMilenio line is a pleasant bike route and jogging path.

COP$70,000-200,000

In the old, tree-lined neighborhood of La Soledad is the 13-room, family-run **Hotel Parkway Bogotá** (Av. Cra. 24 No. 39B-32, tel. 1/288-5090, www.hotelparkway.com.co, COP$103,000 s, COP$146,000 d). It's ripe for a renovation, but it's friendly. Larger rooms are in the main house, up a retro spiral staircase, with smaller rooms surrounding a huge lawn in back. It's about 15 minutes to La Candelaria from here. Within walking distance are some cafés and cultural centers.

The ★ **Aloft Hotel** (Av. Cl. 26 No. 92-32, tel. 1/742-7070, www.starwoodhotels.com/aloft hotels, COP$169,999 d) is stylish and modern, offering an excellent breakfast buffet with a view, as well as a large lawn set against a backdrop of skyline and mountains. It's in an odd location in a business park, but it is within five minutes of the airports. There are 142 rooms in this property. It's about a five-minute walk to the Portal El Dorado TransMilenio station.

NORTHERN BOGOTÁ

Uptown is a good option if comfort trumps budget and you want to be close to loads of excellent restaurants.

Under COP$70,000

Within walking distance of restaurants and shopping is **Chapinorte Bogotá Guesthouse** (Cl. 79 No. 14-59, Apt. 402, tel. 1/256-2152, cell tel. 317/640-6716, www.chapinortehostelbogota.com, COP$64,000 s with shared bath). There are just a handful of private rooms, most of which have shared baths. There's a kitchen provided for guest use. The hotel is on a popular Sunday Ciclovía route (Carrera 15).

COP$70,000-200,000

On a quiet street in a wealthy neighborhood within easy walking distance to the Zona T, **Retiro 84 Apartasuites** (Cl. 84 No. 9-95, tel. 1/616-1501 www.retiro84.com, COP$173,000 d) has 16 rooms. It's comfortable and is reasonably priced for this high-rent part of town. This spot is popular with business travelers in town for longer stays.

Hotel Le Manoir (Cl. 105 No. 17A-82, tel. 1/213-3980, www.lemanoir-egina.com, COP$120,000 d) is a sound midrange hotel, located in a residential neighborhood between Usaquén and the Parque de la 93 area. There are 52 rooms here.

The ★ **NH Royal Metrotel** (Cl. 74 No. 13-27, tel. 1/657-8787, www.nh-hotels.co, COP$182,000 d) is massive. It has over 300 rooms, and thus is a popular choice for visiting tour groups. It has a similarly large terrace and a gym. It's located in a quiet area about a 10-minute walk to the Zona Rosa.

COP$200,000-500,000

BH (www.bhhoteles.com) is a Colombian chain of business hotels, with several locations throughout the city. **BH Retiro** (Cl. 80 No. 10-11, tel. 1/756-3177, COP$217,000 d) overlooks a busy and delightful park, and is a five-minute walk to the Centro Comercial Andino.

There's not much in the way of services here, but it's clean and comfortable.

Cool ★ **84 DC** (Cl. 84 No. 9-67, tel. 1/487-0909, www.84dc.com.co, COP$248,000 d) blends in well in this upscale neighborhood, just blocks from the Zona T. It has 24 spacious, modern rooms, and the breakfast area downstairs has lots of natural light and a patio.

★ **B3** (Cra. 15 No. 88-36, tel. 1/593-4490, www.hotelesb3.com, COP$260,000 d) is one of the most striking hotels in town, thanks to its wonderful living plant wall. The lobby area is a lively place in the early evening, when guests munch on tapas and sip cocktails at the bar. Upstairs, rooms are minimalist and spacious. The hotel has a few bikes available for guests, and the Ciclovía passes directly in front on Sundays. Joggers can hit the paths of Parque El Virrey next door.

Although it's right next door to the revelry of Zona Rosa, you'd never know it in your quiet, comfortable room at the **NH Royal La Boheme** (Cl. 82 No. 12-35, tel. 1/644-7100, www.nh-hotels.co, COP$250,000 d).

At **B.O.G.** (Cra. 11 No. 86-74, tel. 1/639-9999, www.boghotel.com, COP$420,000 d), every detail has been thought out. The smart restaurant in the lobby, featuring Spanish touches, serves great lemonade. The rooftop pool is luxurious. A giant photograph of an emerald in the gym and spa area downstairs may inspire you to buy one.

Right on Parque El Virrey, the location of ★ **Cité** (Cra. 15 No. 88-10, tel. 1/646-7777, www.citehotel.com, COP$400,000 d) couldn't be better. The terrace of the hotel's restaurant, Le Bistro, is a popular place for Sunday brunch for both guests and non-guests alike. This 56-room hotel has a rooftop pool and bikes for guests to use during the Ciclovía, which passes by every Sunday and holiday.

The discreet **Hotel Portón Bogotá** (Cl. 84 No. 7-55, tel. 1/616-6611, www.hotelportonbogota.com.co, COP$400,000 d) prides itself on its tight security, making it a favorite of visiting diplomats. It has an elegant old-school feel, especially in the restaurant and lounge area, where they light the three fireplaces every evening at 7pm. It's on a quiet street within walking distance to the Zona T.

Information and Services

VISITOR INFORMATION

For information on all things Bogotá, go to a **Punto de Información Turística** (PIT). There is usually someone on staff who can speak English, provide you with a map, and answer questions. In La Candelaria there is a PIT on the southwest corner of the Plaza de Bolívar (tel. 1/283-7115, 8am-6pm Mon.-Sat., 8am-4pm Sun.). Other locations include the **Quiosco de la Luz** (Cra. 7 at Cl. 26, tel. 1/284-2664, 9am-5pm Mon.-Sat.) in the Parque de la Independencia, the international terminal of the airport (T1, no phone, 7am-10pm daily), and at two bus terminals: the Terminal de Transportes (Diag. 23 No. 69-60, Local 127, tel. 1/555-7692, 7am-7pm Mon.-Sat., 8am-4pm Sun.) and the Terminal del Sur (Autopista Sur, Local 67, tel. 1/555-7696, 7am-1pm daily).

TELEPHONES

The telephone code for Bogotá and many surrounding towns is 1. To call a cell phone from a landline, first dial 03 and then the 10-digit number. To do the reverse, call 03-1 (the 1 for Bogotá). When in the city, there is no need to dial 1 before a landline number.

Prepaid cell phones or SIM cards can be purchased at any Claro or Movistar store.

Emergency Numbers

The single emergency hotline is 123. Most

operators don't speak English. You should provide the neighborhood you are in and a precise street number.

U.S. citizens who have health, safety, or legal emergencies can contact the **U.S. Embassy** at 1/275-2000.

NEWSPAPERS AND MAGAZINES

The *City Paper* is a free monthly newspaper in English with information on events, interesting profiles, and essays. It's distributed to hotels, restaurants, and cafés during the first two weeks of the month. Two other free papers, *ADN* and *Metro,* both in Spanish, are distributed on street corners in the mornings. *Cartel Urbano* and *Artería* are free publications covering cultural events. *GO* is a monthly publication on things going on in the city.

El Tiempo and *El Espectador* are the two main newspapers in town, and are good sources for information. *Semana* is considered the best news magazine, and is published weekly.

SPANISH-LANGUAGE COURSES

The Spanish spoken in Bogotá is considered neutral and clear, making the city an excellent place to study Spanish. The best schools are operated by the major universities in town and offer a variety of options, including one-on-one tutoring and larger classroom environments. The city's best schools include the **Universidad Externado** (Centro de Español para Extranjeros/CEPEX, Cra. 1A No. 12-53, tel. 1/282-6066, ext. 1221, www.uexternado. edu.co/cepex, 12-hour course COP$403,000) and the **Universidad Javeriana Centro Latinoamericano** (Transversal 4 No. 42-00 6th fl., tel. 1/320-8320, www.javeriana.edu.co). There are several Spanish-language schools in La Candelaria, like **Spanish World Institute** (Cra. 4A No. 56-56, www.spanishworldin-stitute.com, tel. 1/248-3399, 20-hour course US$245) and **International House Bogotá**

(Cl. 10 No. 4-09, tel. 1/336-4747, www.ihbo-gota.com, US$220/week).

MONEY

ATMs are everywhere throughout the city, and are the best option for getting Colombian pesos. Transaction fees vary. Some ATMs on the streets are closed at night. Be cautious when taking out money.

To change money, try **New York Money** at the Centro Andino mall (Centro Comercial Andino, Av. Cra. 11 No. 82-71, Local 3-48, tel. 1/616-8946, 9:30am-8:30pm daily), Atlantis Plaza (Centro Comercial Atlantis Plaza, Cl. 81 No. 13-05, Local 301-A, tel. 1/530-7432, 10:30am-8pm daily), or at the Granahorrar shopping center (Centro Comercial Avenida Chile, Cl. 72 No. 10-34, Local 320, tel. 1/212-2123, 10am-7pm daily). They are also open on holidays. You'll need to show your passport to change money.

VISAS AND OFFICIALDOM

To stay beyond the 60 or 90 days allowed to visitors from the United States, Canada, Australia, New Zealand, and most European countries, you will need to go to **Migración Colombia** (Cl. 100 No. 11B-27, tel. 1/595-4331, 8am-4pm Mon.-Fri.). It is best to go there a few days before your current visa expires.

HEALTH
Altitude

At 2,580 meters (8,465 feet), Bogotá is the third-highest capital city in the world (behind La Paz, Bolivia, and Quito, Ecuador). It is common to feel short of breath and fatigued during the first two days at the higher altitude. Other symptoms of altitude sickness include headache and nausea. Take it easy for those first few days in Bogotá and avoid caffeine and alcohol. If you are sensitive to high altitude, see a doctor before your trip for a prescription medication to mitigate the effects.

Sunburns are more common at higher elevations, as there's less atmosphere blocking out UV rays. Apply sunblock regularly, even when it's cloudy.

Hospitals, Clinics, and Pharmacies

Bogotá has excellent physicians and hospitals. Two of the best hospitals are the **Fundación Santa Fe** (Cl. 119 No. 7-75, www.fsfb.org.co, emergency tel. 1/629-0477, tel. 1/603-0303) and the **Clínica del Country** (Cra. 16 No. 82-57, tel. 1/530-1350, www.clinicadelcountry.com). For sexual and reproductive health matters, **Profamilia** (Cl. 34 No. 14-52, tel. 1/339-0900, www.profamilia.org.co), a member of the International Planned Parenthood Federation, offers clinical services. It is steps away from the Profamilia TransMilenio station on Calle Caracas.

Mom-and-pop pharmacies are all over the city and can be less stringent about requiring physical prescriptions. **Farmatodo** (tel. 1/743-2100, www.farmatodo.com.co) has around 30 locations in Bogotá; some are open 24 hours a day.

LAUNDRY

Wash-and-dry services that charge by the pound or kilo are plentiful in La Candelaria and Chapinero. This service is often called *lavandería*, as opposed to dry cleaning (*lavado en seco*). In La Candelaria two such services are **Limpia Seco Sarita** (Cra. 3 No. 10-69, tel. 1/233-9980) and **Extra-Rápido** (Cl. 12 No. 2-62, tel. 1/282-1002). In Chapinero there is **Lava Seco** (Cra. 9 No. 61-03, tel. 1/255-2582), another **Lava Seco** (Cl. 66 No. 8-20, tel. 1/249-7072), and **Lavandería San Ángel** (Cl. 69 No. 11A-47, tel. 1/255-8116).

A good dry cleaning service is **Classic** (Cra. 13A No. 86A-13, tel. 1/622-8759).

Transportation

GETTING THERE
Air

Modern and user-friendly **Aeropuerto Internacional El Dorado** (BOG, Cl. 26 No. 103-09. tel. 1/266-2000, www.elnuevodorado.com) is the largest airport in the country. All international and most domestic flights now depart from T1, the main terminal. The following airlines serve domestic locations from T1: Avianca, LATAM, Satena, EasyFly, and Viva Colombia. There is a wealth of services in T1, including a Crepes & Waffles restaurant that's open 24 hours. There are money exchange offices and ATMs just outside of the customs area.

The smaller **Puente Aéreo,** or **T2,** is a secondary terminal used only by Avianca, and it serves smaller domestic destinations. It's less than half a kilometer from T1. All Avianca domestic flights depart from T2, except for flights to Barranquilla, Cartagena, Cali, Medellín, and Pereira. If you have a connection that requires a transfer between T1 and T2, there is a complimentary shuttle bus service provided. Airline staff (usually from Avianca) are available around the clock to assist those needing to transfer terminals.

AIRPORT TRANSPORTATION

Leaving the baggage claim and customs area, you will be approached—insistently—by taxi services, but these are not recommended. Instead, look for the official taxi queue outside the terminal. Metered taxis cost around COP$25,000-35,000 to most points in town.

SITP and TransMilenio bus service is also available, but it can be difficult to purchase a Tullave transit card at the airport. The **16-14 bus** is a free airport shuttle that takes passengers to the Portal El Dorado TransMilenio station, about half a mile from the airport, where Tullave cards can be purchased. From there, catch a red TransMilenio bus (COP$2,000) into the city, about a 30- to 45-minute ride. If you don't have a lot of luggage, this can be an inexpensive way to get into town.

Bus

Bogotá has three bus terminals: the **Terminal del Sur,** the **Portal del Norte,** and the main bus station, the **Terminal de Transportes** in Salitre.

TERMINAL DE TRANSPORTES

The **Terminal de Transportes** (Diagonal 23 No. 69-60, tel. 1/423-3630, www.terminalde-transporte.gov.co) is well organized and clean, and is divided into three "modules," each generally corresponding to a different direction: Module 1 is south, Module 2 is east/west, and Module 3 is north. There are two other modules, 4 and 5, corresponding to long-distance taxi services and arrivals, respectively. All modules are in the same building. Each module has an information booth at the entrance, with an attendant who can point you in the right direction.

In the arrivals module, there is a tourist information office (PIT), where the helpful attendants can give you a map of the city and assist you in getting to your hotel. There is also an organized and safe taxi service and plenty of public transportation options available.

During the Christmas and Easter holidays, the bus terminal is a busy place with crowds and packed buses. This is also true on *puentes* (long weekends).

To take a cab from La Candelaria to the terminal, a trip that takes about 30 minutes, expect to pay COP$15,000.

PORTAL DEL NORTE

The **Portal del Norte** (Autopista Norte with Cl. 174), part of the TransMilenio station of the same name, may be more convenient if you are arriving from nearby destinations such as Tunja or Villa de Leyva.

TERMINAL DEL SUR

The **Terminal del Sur** (Autopista Sur with Cra. 72D) is near the Portal Sur of TransMilenio. This station serves locations in the south of Cundinamarca, such as Tequendama, and then travels farther south to Girardot, Ibagué, Neiva, Popayán, Armenia, and Cali, continuing all the way to Mocoa in Putumayo.

GETTING AROUND
Bus

To ride TransMilenio or SITP buses, you must first purchase a refillable **Tullave card.** One card can be used by multiple passengers. Cards are available for purchase at TransMilenio stations and at *papelerías* (mom-and-pop stationery stores) located near TransMilenio and SITP bus routes. It's easier to purchase the cards at *papelerías* (look for the Tullave decal on storefronts), as lines at TransMilenio stations can be insufferably long. Buying or refilling Tullave cards is cash-only.

TRANSMILENIO

TransMilenio (www.transmilenio.gov.co) is the bus rapid transit (BRT) system that serves Bogotá. Begun in 2000, it has transformed the city, and is the largest BRT system in the world. Over two million Bogotanos use the system each day, and it can be a useful and inexpensive way for visitors to get around. There are more than 100 stations covering much of the city on 12 lines.

There are three TransMilenio lines that are especially useful to visitors. First are the red hybrid TransMilenio buses on Carrera 7 (the Séptima). These are regular-looking buses, not the massive buses commonly associated with TransMilenio. This is the **M line**, and it is the best way to get from downtown to the north. This line has a modern terminal at the Museo Nacional. Going south toward La Candelaria, the M line morphs into the **L line.**

Second is the original **B line** on Avenida Caracas. This extends from downtown to the Portal del Norte bus terminal at Calle 170. An offshoot, the J line, makes a detour toward the Museo del Oro.

The third line of importance is the **K line**

along Avenida El Dorado (Av. Cl. 26), which serves the airport.

The system operates 5am-midnight Monday through Saturday and 6am-11pm on Sunday and holidays. A ride (paid for a with a Tullave card) typically costs about COP$2,000, and transfers (within 75 minutes) on TransMilenio or SITP cost only COP$300.

While riding the buses, keep your wallet in your front pocket and watch your belongings, especially during rush hour. When attempting to board or disembark TransMilenio buses, don't expect other passengers to make room for you. Call out "*permiso, por favor*" and move with purpose.

SITP

Bogotá is gradually modernizing with **Sistema Integrado de Transporte Público** (SITP, www.sitp.gov.co). Most useful for visitors are the blue SITP buses, which cost COP$2,000 per ride. Like the TransMilenio, you'll need a Tullave card to ride. SITP covers pretty much the entire city, so it's helpful to use apps like Moovit to find a bus that can take you where you want to go (but times are usually inaccurate on the app, so don't rely on them). Once you're at a bus stop and you spot

your bus coming, you must flag it down by waving your card at the driver.

Taxis

It's estimated that over a million people take a cab each day in the city. There are around 50,000 taxis (mostly yellow Hyundais) circulating the streets of Bogotá. If you plan on taking a cab, either call one (or have one called) or, better yet, use an app like Easy Taxi, Tappsi, or Uber.

A *taximetro* calculates units, which determine the price. The rates are listed on a *tarjetón* (large card) with the driver's information. That card should always be visible. There are surcharges for cab services ordered by phone, for nighttime rides, and for going to the airport. Taxi drivers do not expect tips, but you can always round up the fare if you'd like. During end-of-year holidays, drivers may ask for a holiday tip.

Walking

You get a real feeling for the city and its frenetic energy by walking its streets. The neighborhoods that make up downtown (La Candelaria, Centro Internacional, and the Macarena) are accessible on foot, and walking is often the best way to get around. The

TransMilenio buses

same holds true for the upscale shopping and residential areas in Northern Bogotá.

The worst thing about walking in the city is crossing its streets. Protected crosswalks are rare, and many drivers have little respect for pedestrians or cyclists. Even if a pedestrian light is green, that doesn't guarantee that traffic will yield. Also, note that when traffic lights turn yellow, drivers may not actually slow down. Finally, keep in mind that, when there is no traffic, like on a peaceful Sunday evening, drivers tend to speed.

Biking

Bogotá has one of the most extensive bike path networks in Latin America, with over 340 kilometers of *ciclorutas* (bike lanes). Bicyclists should take extra care when using the *ciclorutas,* as vehicles may not yield for bikes. A popular, easy, and protected bike path extends along Carrera 11 between Calles 82 and 100.

Ciclovía is a weekly event (occurring on Sundays and holidays) during which usually traffic-filled streets are closed to vehicles, and bicycles take their places. Helmets are not essential in the Ciclovía, but they are advisable on the *ciclorutas.* Never leave a bike unattended.

Car Rental

With more than a million (usually aggressive) drivers on the clogged streets of Bogotá, renting a vehicle is a bad idea for visitors. However, if you are planning to travel to nearby places like Villa de Leyva or would like to take your time touring parks or villages, renting might be a solid option.

National (Cra. 7 No. 145-71, www.nationalcolombia.com), **Avis** (Av. 19 No. 123-52 Local 2, tel. 1/629-1722, www.avis.com), and **Hertz** (Av. Caracas No. 28A-17, tel. 1/327-6700, www.rentacarcolombia.co) have offices in Bogotá. Foreign driver's licenses are accepted in Colombia. It's important to find out your car's vehicle restriction days, which mean you can't drive during business hours for two predetermined days of the week, based on the last digit of your license plate.

Vicinity of Bogotá

ZIPAQUIRÁ

A favorite day trip for visitors to Bogotá is the city of **Zipaquirá** (pop. 112,000). About 40 kilometers (25 miles) from Bogotá, Zipaquirá is known for its Catedral de Sal—a cathedral built in a salt mine. Zipaquirá is named for the the Zipa, the Muisca leader of the Bacatá confederation. The Muisca settlement was very close to the mines, and they traded salt for other commodities with other indigenous groups.

Sights

The **Catedral de Sal** (tel. 1/852-3010, www.catedraldesal.gov.co, 9am-5:30pm daily, COP$20,000) is part of the Parque del Sal. The original cathedral was built by miners in 1951, but due to safety concerns at that site, a new and larger cathedral was built and opened in 1995. The cathedral is indeed an impressive feat of engineering. Tours are obligatory, but you can stray from the group. Masses take place here on Sundays, and they attract many faithful. Other features include a museum, a rock-climbing wall, and a children's 3-D film, which you could skip.

The picturesque main plaza in Zipaquirá, with palm trees rising against a backdrop of green mountains, is always the center of activity in town. Here locals gather to gossip, get their shoes shined, or munch on an *oblea* (wafer) oozing with caramel. Dominating the plaza is a cathedral designed by Friar Domingo de Petrés, who also designed the Bogotá and Santa Fe de Antioquia cathedrals. Construction began in 1805; 111 years later, in 1916, it was completed and dedicated.

Getting There

Zipaquirá is an easy day trip from Bogotá. On weekends, families and tourists alike take the Turistren from the **Usaquén train station** (Cra. 9 No. 110-08, tel. 1/316-1300) at 8:15am or the **Estación de la Sabana** (Cl. 13 No. 18-24, tel. 1/375-0557) near La Candelaria at 9:15am. Bands play Colombian *papayera* music as you slowly chug through the savanna of Bogotá on the three-hour trip. The train returns to Bogotá in the late afternoon, giving you more than enough time to visit the salt mines. Only round-trip train tickets (COP$52,000) are sold.

The company Alianza runs buses (1 hour, COP$4,800) to Zipaquirá's **Terminal de Transportes** (Cras. 6C-7 and Clls. 10-12) from Bogotá's **Portal del Norte TransMilenio station** every 20 minutes or so, all day long. Upon arriving at Portal del Norte, take a left from where you get off the TransMilenio bus and you will see signs pointing the way for "Zipa" buses; the attendants can also direct you. You'll pay the Zipa bus driver directly. The trip takes about an hour and costs COP$6,000.

You can either walk or take a short taxi ride to the Parque del Sal from Zipaquirá's train or bus station.

★ Nemocón

With only 10,000 residents, the sleepy pueblo of **Nemocón** (www.nemocon-cundinamarca.gov.co) is 15 kilometers (9 miles) from Zipaquirá and just 65 kilometers (40 miles) from Bogotá. It is a cute, compact colonial-era town, also home to salt mines, but it does not attract nearly the same number of visitors that Zipaquirá does. That's part of its allure. In pre-Columbian times, this was also a Muisca settlement devoted to salt extraction.

On the plaza, a church is set against a backdrop of eucalyptus-covered hills that are the result of some sort of reforestation effort. There is a small salt museum on the corner, and students will be happy to give you a tour in Spanish. About a 10-minute walk toward the hills are the **salt mines** (www.minadesal.com, 9am-5pm daily, tours COP$22,000). Tours take about 90 minutes. The beautifully renovated section of the mines that you visit is no longer used for salt extraction. In the depths of the mines you will see stalactites and stalagmites. The pools where salt and water were mixed to pump out the salt are a highlight. The reflection of the illuminated vaults on the surface

the sleepy pueblo of Nemocón

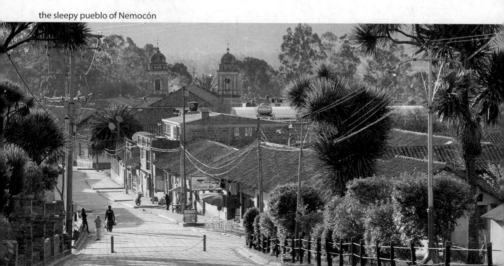

Vicinity of Bogotá

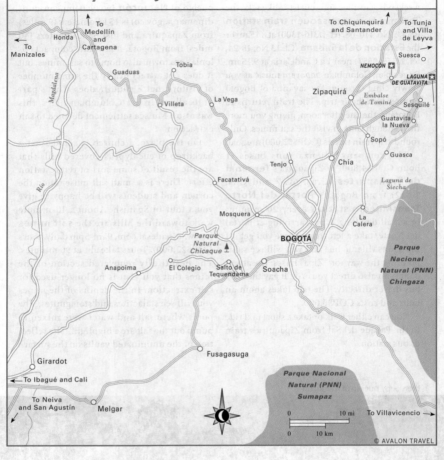

To Chiquinquirá and Santander

To Tunja and Villa de Leyva

Suesca

NEMOCÓN

LAGUNA DE GUATAVITA

Zipaquirá

Embalse de Tominé

Sesquilé

Guatavita la Nueva

Sopó

Guasca

Tenjo

Chía

Laguna de Siecha

Facatativá

Mosquera

La Calera

BOGOTÁ

Parque Nacional Natural (PNN) Chingaza

Parque Natural Chicaque

Anapoima

El Colegio

Salto de Tequendama

Soacha

To Medellín and Cartagena

Honda

To Manizales

Guaduas

Tobia

Villeta

La Vega

Magdalena

Río

Girardot

To Ibagué and Cali

Fusagasuga

To Neiva and San Agustín

Melgar

Parque Nacional Natural (PNN) Sumapaz

0   10 mi
0   10 km

To Villavicencio →

© AVALON TRAVEL

of the pools, combined with the cool lighting, is quite something.

There are simple restaurants with names like the **Venado de Oro** (the Golden Deer) on the plaza or **La Casa de la Gallina** (the Hen House) on Calle 2 (No. 4-24). There's not much in the way of accommodations in Nemocón; most visitors make it a day trip.

The bus company Alianza offers service to Nemocón (1.5 hours, COP$6,700) from the Portal del Norte bus station in Bogotá.

★ LAGUNA DE GUATAVITA

The El Dorado myth, which became an obsession for gold-thirsty Europeans in the New World, is based on a Muisca Indian ritual that took place in this perfectly round mountain lake.

Following the death of the Muisca *cacique* (chief), a nephew would be chosen to succeed him. The day of the ceremony, the nephew would be sequestered in a cave. Then, stripped naked and covered with mud and gold dust, he would be rowed to the center of the sacred lake with incense and music filling the air. Once there, gold, silver, emeralds, and other tributes were tossed into the cold waters, and the *cacique* would dive in.

When Europeans arrived in Guatavita, they drained the lake at least three times, looking for treasure at the bottom of the lake. A giant cut in the lake can be still seen today.

Today **Laguna de Guatavita** (cell tel. 315/831-1086, www.car.gov.co, 9am-4pm Tues.-Sat., non-Colombian adults COP$16,000, free for seniors) is being given the respect it deserves. An environmental agency maintains the park, which is located close to the town of Sesquilé. In order to preserve the lake, the agency has forbidden direct access to it. The lake is much better appreciated from above, on the well-maintained path along the top of the crater. On Saturdays, you must join a tour group (included in admission) to see the lake. Tours leave every 30 minutes and last less than an hour. Guides are knowledgeable and passionate about their work. English tours are possible, especially for larger groups, but those should be reserved in advance. During the week you can amble along the path at your own pace.

While much of the brick path is flat, there is a fairly steep climb, making it difficult for those with physical limitations. At the end of the walk, you can walk or hop on a minibus to the entrance of the park. When Monday is a holiday, the park is open Wednesday-Monday.

Getting There

Getting to Laguna de Guatavita via public transportation is fairly straightforward. The bus company Águila offers service (1.5 hours, COP$8,000) to the town of Nueva Guatavita. At the TransMilenio Portal del Norte station in Bogotá, take a bus bound for Nueva Guatavita. Upon arrival in Nueva Guatavita, contract a taxi driver to take you to the park, wait for you, and bring you back to Nueva Guatavita. Expect to pay COP$60,000 for this service. On weekends, there is a bus service (COP$10,000) from Nueva Guatavita directly to the park that departs at 11am and 1pm.

Another option is to hire a driver out of Bogotá to make the trip to Laguna de Guatavita and back. This trip takes 1.5-2 hours each way. Your hotel or hostel in Bogotá can recommend a private car service, and may even assist with negotiating a price.

PARQUE NACIONAL NATURAL CHINGAZA

Some 75 kilometers northeast of Bogotá, the **Parque Nacional Natural Chingaza** (tel. 1/353-2400, www.parquesnacionales.gov. co, 8am-4pm daily, non-Colombian adults COP$39,500) extends over 76,000 hectares (188,000 acres) and makes for an excellent day trip of hiking among armies of *frailejón* plants through the misty *páramo* (highland moor).

The park limits the number of visitors, so it is best to request an entry permit in advance by calling **Parques Nacionales** (tel. 1/353-2400, www.parquesnacionales.gov.co). They will ask you to send the names of the members of your group in an email and confirm the reservation. They will also provide contact information for the local association of guides. You can save a lot of money, and help the local economy, if you do it this way rather than through an organized private tour. Plan on hiring an experienced guide (COP$50,000/day), as trails are often not obvious. The guides are generally very knowledgeable and friendly. However, they may not speak English.

The hike to the sacred **Lagunas de Siecha**, three mountain lakes called Suramérica, Siecha, and Guascatakes, takes about 3.5 hours. Other excursions within the Parque Nacional Natural Chingaza can be made from different entry points.

Pack rubber boots, as you will be hiking along muddy paths—sneakers just won't do. A light raincoat or windbreaker and sweatshirt are essential, as well as a packed lunch, snacks, and water.

Practicalities

In the town of Guasca you can relax, eat, and stay at the **Posada Café La Huerta** (cell tel. 315/742-0999, www.cafelahuerta.com), where they make great corn bread. If you decide to stay with them for a weekend, they can arrange your transportation and visit to PNN Chingaza.

Getting There

It's challenging, but possible, to get to PNN Chingaza via public transportation. From Bogotá, take a bus to Guasca. Buses to Guasca leave from the Portal del Norte bus terminal as well as from an informal bus pickup area between Calles 72 and 73 at Carrera 14. Once there, ask any taxi or bus driver where to find the right bus.

From Guasca, take a *buseta* (minivan) toward Paso Hondo, about 15 kilometers away. This 20-minute ride (COP$2,000) will leave you at the intersection that leads to the park. From there, you must walk six kilometers (about 90 minutes) to reach the park entrance. *Busetas* leave at 6:30am, 7:30am, and 9:30am.

Leave Bogotá by around 7am to make the 9:30am *buseta*.

If you travel with private transportation, it is possible to drive closer to the park, but only with a four-wheel-drive vehicle. **Hansa Tours** (tel. 1/637-9800, www.hansatours.com) hires out drivers for the day to do this trip.

SUESCA

It's all about rock climbing in Suesca. On the weekends, Bogotanos converge on this little town and head to the rocks. Most climbing takes place along two kilometers' worth of cliffs, called *las rocas,* just behind the town. Some of the cliffs are up to 250 meters (820 feet) high. It's a beautiful setting, and the fresh smell of eucalyptus trees and mountain mist add to the atmosphere.

Several outdoors shops in Suesca rent equipment and organize rock-climbing classes and excursions. **Explora Suesca** (Cra. 6 No. 8-20, cell tel. 311/249-3491 or 317/516-2414) rents rock-climbing gear, teaches classes, and rents out bikes. At **Monodedo** (Cra. 16 No. 82-22, Bogotá, tel. 1/616-3467, cell tel. 316/266-9399, www.mondodedo.com) in Bogotá, expect to pay around COP$60,000 for a three-hour rock-climbing excursion with a guide.

frailejones at the Parque Nacional Natural Chingaza

Food

After all that rock climbing, it's time for some Thai food. Check out **Restaurante Vamonos Pa'l Monte** (Km. 5 Vía La Playa-Suesca, cell tel. 320/856-8992, www.vamonospalmonte.com, 8am-8pm Fri.-Sun., COP$14,000) for Phuket vegetables or pad Thai. It's on the main road and within walking distance of *las rocas*.

Another popular place is **Rica Pizza** (Km. 5 Vía La Playa-Suesca, cell tel. 312/379-3610), on the main road, close to *las rocas*. They serve pizza and more typical Colombian fare.

Accommodations

Many folks make a visit to Suesca a camping weekend. The most popular campground is **Campo Base** (1 km east of Vía La Playa-Suesca, cell tel. 320/290-8291, campsite COP$20,000, tent rental COP$15,000). They've got hot water and a place for cooking, and they rent out tents. They're laid-back here.

The luxurious nine-room bed-and-breakfast **Casa Lila** (cell tel. 320/204-8262 or 300/835-9472, patriciavalenciaturismo@gmail.com, COP$150,000-220,000 d) is so cozy, with fireplaces all around and its own restaurant, that it may be hard to leave. It's right next to an old train station at kilometer 3.

Getting There

Buses from Bogotá regularly serve Suesca (1.5 hours, COP$10,000) from the Portal del Norte station. The bus will drop you at the center of town, near *las rocas*.

You can also contact a Bogotá-based tour company that specializes in rock climbing, such as **Ecoglobal Expeditions** (tel. 1/616-9088, www.ecoglobalexpeditions.com, from COP$130,000), who can also arrange for transportation.

HONDA

The steamy town of Honda, known as the City of Bridges for its 29 spans, rests on the banks of the Río Magdalena, almost exactly halfway between Bogotá and Medellín. Founded in 1539, it was the country's first and most important interior port. From the 16th century until the mid-20th century, the Río Magdalena was the main transportation route connecting Bogotá to the Caribbean coast and the rest of the world. Quinine, coffee, lumber, and slaves were loaded and unloaded along the banks, and steamships would ply the route toward the coast.

In 1919, the Barranquilla-based SCADTA airlines became the first airline of the Americas, bringing seaplane service to Honda. (SCADTA would later become Avianca Airlines.)

Honda and its sleepy streets now make for a nice stopover between Bogotá and Medellín. The steamships and seaplanes no longer make their appearances, but if you head down to the river's edge you can ask a local angler to give you a quick jaunt along the river in his boat. Be sure to walk across the bright yellow **Puente Navarro,** a pedestrian bridge built by the San Francisco Bridge Company in 1898. Check out the **Museo del Río Magdalena** (Cl. 10 No. 9-01, tel. 8/251-0129, 10am-6pm Tues.-Sun., COP$3,000) on the way. It puts the historical and geographical importance of the Río Magdalena into context within the development of Colombia.

A popular weekend destination for Bogotanos in need of *tierra caliente* (hot country) relaxation, the town has some good hotel options. For pampering, try the **Posada Las Trampas** (Cra. 10A No. 11-05, tel. 8/251-7415, www.posadalastrampas.com, COP$230,000 d). For a friendly welcome, stay at the ★ **Casa Belle Epoque** (Cl. 12 No. 12A-21, tel. 8/251-1176, cell tel. 312/478-0173, www.casabelleepoque.com, COP$80,000-110,000 d), a moderately priced hotel popular with international travelers. The staff can arrange boat trips on the Magdalena for guests.

There is plentiful public transportation to Honda. From the Terminal de Transportes in Bogotá it is about a five-hour journey (COP$20,000). The bus station in Honda is outside of town, and it costs COP$4,000 for a taxi from there to town.

Cartagena and the Caribbean Coast

M agical Cartagena wastes no time in seducing its visitors. It's a majestic walled city full of magnificent churches and palaces, picturesque balcony-lined streets, and romantic plazas.

Beyond Cartagena, Colombia's Caribbean coast extends 1,760 kilometers (1,095 miles), from Venezuela to Panama, and is longer than California's coastline. The coastal area varies dramatically, with an astonishing array of landscapes: desolate deserts, snowcapped mountains, lowland swamps, dry savannas, and rainforest.

Colombia's colonial past lives on in Mompox, a once-thriving port on the Río Magdalena where it feels as if time has stopped. The old city of Santa Marta has positioned itself as a great base from which to explore the beaches and mountains of the north-central coast.

Beach options abound here. The most famous are at Parque Nacional Natural Tayrona: glimmering golden sand beaches with the jungle backdrop of the Sierra Nevada. Islands in the Parque Nacional Natural Corales del Rosario y San Bernardo, between Tolú and Cartagena, beckon visitors with their white sandy beaches and five-star hotels.

There are many options for nature lovers. Minca, a small town located on the slopes of the Sierra Nevada not far from Santa Marta, offers unparalleled bird-watching opportunities. In the jungles that envelop Capurganá and Sapzurro, you can go bird-watching, listen to the cries of howler monkeys, and count colorful frogs along jungle paths. Offshore, dive with the occasional sea turtle and observe myriad marine life in nearby waters.

Adventurous types can hike up to Ciudad Perdida in the Sierra Nevada. The views of the Lost City, with its eerie, beautiful terraces set atop the mountain, are simply unforgettable. Travel up the Guajira Peninsula, home of the Wayúu, Colombia's largest indigenous community. Here you'll find Cabo de la Vela, where the desert meets the sea, and stark, magnificent Punta Gallinas, the

---

Previous: Colonial buildings in the historic center of Cartagena; beach on the Bocagrande peninsula.
Above: Iglesia de Santa Bárbara in Mompox.

Look for ★ to find recommended sights, activities, dining, and lodging.

Highlights

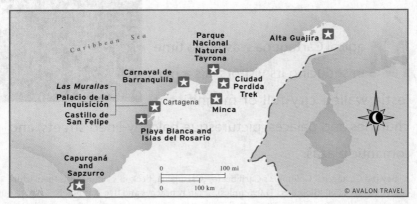

★ **Las Murallas:** Stroll the centuries-old stone ramparts of the Old City and savor the moment with a sundowner cocktail at one of the wall's breezy bars (page 90).

★ **Palacio de la Inquisición:** This spectacular 17th-century building was where Catholic authorities once meted out punishment to accused heretics during the dark days of the Spanish colonial era. Today it's a fine history museum (page 91).

★ **Castillo de San Felipe:** Wander through the tunnels of this 17th-century Spanish fortress built to protect the city and its gold from English pirates (page 92).

★ **Playa Blanca and Islas del Rosario:** Make it a true Caribbean holiday at this group of 25 coral islands, known for their white-sand beaches, turquoise waters, and gentle breezes (page 110).

★ **Carnaval de Barranquilla:** Madcap and euphoric, this is Colombia's most famous celebration. Put on a costume and dance your way down the parade route (page 116).

★ **Minca:** Take a break from the beach and chill in this refreshing town set in the foothills of the spectacular Sierra Nevada de Santa Marta (page 126).

★ **Parque Nacional Natural Tayrona:** Mountains meet jungles meet beaches at this popular national park near Santa Marta (page 128).

★ **Ciudad Perdida Trek:** Climb the thousand-plus stone steps through the cloud forest to the mystical Lost City, the most important settlement of the Tayrona civilization (page 136).

★ **Alta Guajira:** Be mesmerized by the stark beauty of desert landscapes, get to know Wayúu culture, and dine on fresh lobster at the top of South America (page 144).

★ **Capurganá and Sapzurro:** Walk barefoot along deserted beaches, trek through dense rainforest among colorful frogs and howling monkeys, or cool off in a crystalline brook (page 153).

Cartagena and the Caribbean Coast

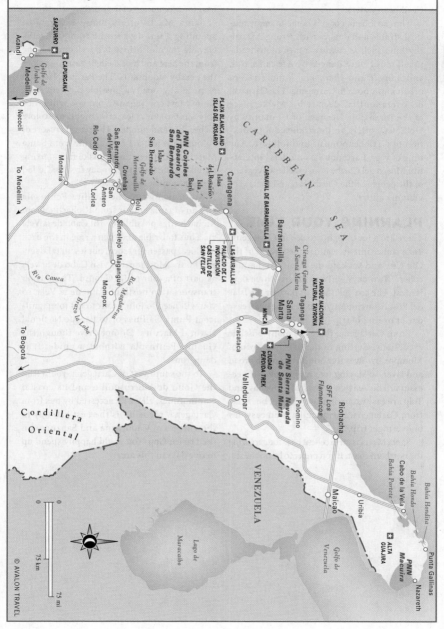

Map labels:

SAPZURRO
Acandí
CAPURGANÁ
Gulfo de Urabá
To Medellín
Necoclí
To Medellín
Montería
Río Cedro
San Bernado del Viento
San Antero
Lorica
Coveñas
Tolú
Sincelejo
Magangué
Río Cauca
Brazo la Loba
Mompox
Río Magdalena
To Bogotá
Cordillera Oriental

Islas San Bernardo
Gulfo de Morrosquillo
PNN Corales del Rosario y San Bernardo
Islas del Rosario
Isla Barú
PLAYA BLANCA AND ISLAS DEL ROSARIO
Cartagena
LAS MURALLAS
PALACIO DE LA INQUISICION
CASTILLO DE SAN FELIPE
CARNAVAL DE BARRANQUILLA

CARIBBEAN SEA

Barranquilla
Ciénaga Grande de Santa Marta
Santa Marta
Taganga
MINCA
Aracataca
CIUDAD PERDIDA TREK
PNN Sierra Nevada de Santa Marta
Valledupar
PARQUE NACIONAL NATURAL TAYRONA
Palomino
SFF Los Flamencos
Riohacha

VENEZUELA
Lago de Maracaibo
Gulfo de Venezuela
Maicao
Uribia

Bahía Hondia
Cabo de la Vela
Bahía Portete
ALTA GUAJIRA
PNN Macuira
Punta Gallinas
Nazareth

0 75 km
0 75 mi
© AVALON TRAVEL

northernmost point in South America, where windswept dunes drop dramatically into Caribbean waters.

The Caribbean coast is home to many musical strains and dances with strong African rhythms, such as *cumbia,* a melodious traditional music once danced by African slaves, and *mapalé* and *champeta,* a more recent urban music born in Cartagena. The Carnaval de Barranquilla, declared a Masterpiece of the Intangible Heritage of Humanity by UNESCO, offers an unparalleled introduction to Caribbean music and folklore. Any time of year, Barranquilla's modern, interactive Museo del Caribe is an excellent overview of the people of the Caribbean and their very vibrant culture.

PLANNING YOUR TIME

There are a lot of sights to see in Cartagena. Take some time to wander the streets of the Old City and soak up the beauty and atmosphere. Two days will suffice, but three days is ideal. The coastal island of Barú or the Islas del Rosario archipelago can be done in an easy day or overnight trip.

From Cartagena, there are many possible excursions. Getting to the riverside town of Mompox involves five hours of travel by road and river, so staying two nights there is necessary. The seaside towns of Coveñas and Tolú are easy excursions with direct bus links from Cartagena. Barranquilla is an easy day or overnight trip.

Santa Marta is an excellent base for exploring the northern coast. If you prefer to be on the sea,

the laid-back seaside village of Taganga, only a short ride from Santa Marta, could also be your base for exploration of the north.

Santa Marta offers many excursions. Spending a few days in the tranquil Sierra Nevada town of Minca is a welcome escape from the heat and an excellent base to explore the nearby mountains. The Parque Nacional Natural Tayrona is a possible day trip from Santa Marta or Taganga, but you will probably want to stay at least two nights to explore its beaches and jungles. The seaside resort of Palomino is just a 1.5-hour ride from Santa Marta. All of these towns make fine starting points for the four- to five-day trek to Ciudad Perdida, a must for any backpacker.

Most visitors to the Guajira Peninsula join an organized tour from Riohacha. From Riohacha it is possible to visit Cabo de la Vela via a bus to Uribia and then a ride in the back of a local passenger truck, but it will take several hours. Most tourists visit Cabo de la Vela as part of a tour of La Guajira. There is no transportation north of Cabo de la Vela, so you will need to join a tour to get to magnificent Punta Gallinas or to Parque Nacional Natural Macuira. Do not drive though the Guajira Peninsula without a guide: It is dangerous.

To the southwest of Cartagena, you'll find the Golfo de Morrosquillo and its coastal communities, all easily accessed by bus from Cartagena. Medellín is the best gateway to the villages of Capurganá and Sapzurro on the Darien Gap. You could happily spend up to five days in this area.

Cartagena

Cartagena de Indias is a sprawling city located on the Caribbean coast of Colombia at the north end of a large bay with the same name.

History

Cartagena de Indias was founded in 1533 by Spanish conquistador Pedro de Heredia on a small Carib indigenous settlement. During the 16th century, the city was sacked by pirates numerous times, most notably by Sir Francis Drake in 1568. Pairs of forts were constructed at various passage points in the harbor to stop intruders. The construction of the fortifications took almost two centuries and was completed by the mid-1700s.

The city prospered as one of the main slave ports in Spanish America. It is estimated that more than one million slaves passed through the city. Slaves often escaped and created free communities known as *palenques,* such as the town of San Basilio, south of Cartagena.

Cartagena formally declared independence from Spain in 1812. In 1815, it was recaptured by the Spanish. Cartagena was retaken by revolutionaries in 1821. During the 19th century, Cartagena lost its status as one of Spain's main ports. The economic decline had one good side effect: preserving the colonial past. The Old City remained largely intact through the 20th century, prompting UNESCO to declare it a World Heritage Site.

Cartagena remained relatively peaceful even during the worst periods of violence in the 1980s and 1990s. In the past decade, Cartagena has become a major international tourist destination, with a proliferation of chic, five-star hotels in the Old City, glitzy condominiums and hotels in Bocagrande, and new resorts along the coast north of the city.

Safety

The crown jewel of Colombian tourism, Cartagena is quite safe to visit. Be mindful while walking on the walls after dark. It's easy to be distracted while strolling the streets, so keep your valuables close to your body.

While reports are rare, police have been known to stop and frisk young non-Colombian men in the evening, purportedly out of suspicion of drug possession—in actuality they are looking for money. This has occurred most commonly late at night in Getsemaní. Some people have found that calling attention to the officer and getting others to record the episode on their phone defuses the situation.

Some of the poor fishing villages on islands near Cartagena, such as Tierrabomba (close to the entrance to Bocachica), are best visited in a group. Keep an eye on drinks at late-night watering holes.

By far the greatest annoyances in Cartagena are persistent street vendors, who have even been known to latch on to walking tours. In the evening, some vendors will pitch less legal items on male passersby. Saying *"No, gracias,"* may or may not help ward off these nuisances. Don't allow them to get under your skin.

Most taxi drivers, bartenders, and vendors are honest, but there are always a few who will try to take advantage of visitors by overcharging or not returning the proper amount of change to a non-Colombian visitor who may not hold a strong grasp of the language. Always try to pay with small notes or coins when possible—keep those COP$20,000 and COP$50,000 notes only for emergencies, or change them. Request to see the drinks menu (*carta de tragos*) at bars before ordering. Before getting into a cab, have an idea of what you'll be paying, and confirm the amount with the driver upfront.

Orientation

The city's tourist focus is a relatively small area: the **Old City,** the original Spanish settlement that was once completely enclosed by massive stone walls. The Old City comprises two main districts: the **Centro,** with

Cartagena

© AVALON TRAVEL

0   0

1 km

1 mi

SEE "CENTRO AND SAN DIEGO" MAP

SEE "GETSEMANÍ" MAP

Caribbean Sea

EL LAGUITO

BOCAGRANDE

To PLAYA BLANCA AND ISLAS DEL ROSARIO

Bocagrande Beaches

AV SAN MARTIN

BOCAGRANDE MALL

HILTON HOTEL

HOSPITAL/ BOATS TO TIERRABOMBA ISLAND

Castillo Grande Jogging Path

Cartagena Bay

NAVAL BASE

MUELLE DE MANGA

CLUB NAVAL/ CASTILLOGRANDE FORT

PRESIDENTIAL GUESTHOUSE/ MANZANILLO FORT

MANGA

CLUB DE PESCA/ PASTELILLO FORT

CARIBE PLAZA MALL

CENTRO

GETSEMANÍ

SAN DIEGO

EL CABRERO

MARBELLA

CASTILLO DE SAN FELIPE

CRUISE SHIP TERMINAL

LA POPA

AVENIDA SANTANDER

DIAGONAL 22

MERCADO DE BAZURTO

AVENIDA PEDRO DE HEREDIA

AIRPORT

To La Boquilla, Las Americas, Playa Manzanillo, and Barranquilla

BULLFIGHTING RING, SOCCER, BASEBALL STADIUM

TRANSVERSAL 54

To Turbaco

To Barranquilla

TERMINAL DE TRANSPORTES (BUS STATION)

Caribbean Sea

PLAYA BLANCA AND ISLAS DEL ROSARIO

Isla de Tierra Bomba

Bocachica

Barú

Bocagrande

Ciénaga de la Virgen

MAP AREA

its magnificent walls, narrow streets, colorful bougainvillea dangling from balconies, activity-packed plazas, and myriad churches and palaces; and **Getsemaní,** an old colonial neighborhood that was also enclosed by its own wall and fortifications. Today it is the hot new address for lodging, restaurant, and nightlife options.

CENTRO

The Centro (from *centro histórico;* also called the Old City or the Walled City) is the historic core of Cartagena; it's surrounded by the most impressive sections of the city walls. This is where most of Cartagena's sights are located, including its most famous churches and museums. Today, the Centro is where many upscale hotels, restaurants, shops, and nightclubs are found.

The northeastern half of the Centro is known as **San Diego.** Here the architecture is more modest. There are a few attractions in San Diego, notably the Iglesia de Santo Toribio de Mogrovejo and Las Bóvedas, a shopping arcade located in a section of the walls. The charm of San Diego lies in its quiet streets and pleasant bars and restaurants, particularly around the Plaza de San Diego.

The Centro is organized in a general grid with numerous plazas. Even many residents don't know or use official street names, as they change from block to block. Orient yourself by identifying the main squares—Torre de los Coches, Plaza de la Aduana, Plaza de Santo Domingo, Parque de Bolívar, and Plaza Fernández de Madrid—and making your way from one to the other. Walking these charming streets (and even getting lost on occasion) is a pleasure.

GETSEMANÍ

The neighborhood of Getsemaní lies to the southeast of the Centro. The architecture here is much more modest than in the Centro. The epicenter of the neighborhood today is the Plaza de la Trinidad, in front of Iglesia de la Santísima Trinidad, where backpackers, street performers, and longtime residents congregate in the evenings.

BOCAGRANDE

South of the Old City is flashy Bocagrande, a skinny peninsula with many high-rise hotels, malls, and residential buildings. The main attractions here are the beaches, which get packed on weekends with Colombian

Plaza de San Pedro Claver, with Bocagrande in the background

Centro and San Diego

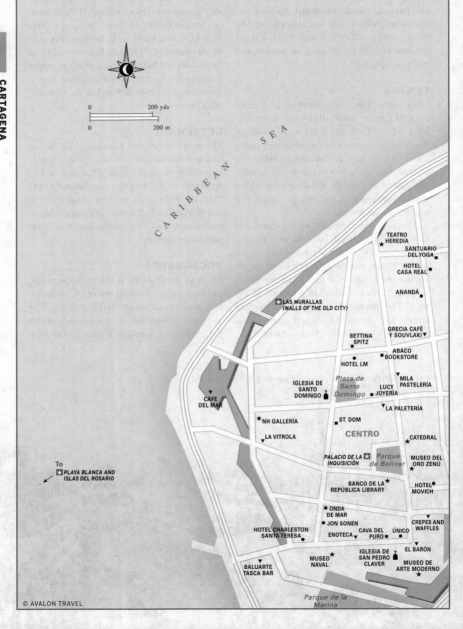

CARIBBEAN SEA

N

0   200 yds

0   200 m

TEATRO HEREDIA ★

SANTUARIO DEL YOGA

HOTEL CASA REAL ●

ANANDÁ ▼

★ LAS MURALLAS (WALLS OF THE OLD CITY)

GRECIA CAFÉ Y SOUVLAKI ▼

BETTINA SPITZ ■

ABACO BOOKSTORE ■

HOTEL LM ●

IGLESIA DE SANTO DOMINGO ♦

Plaza de Santo Domingo

LUCY JOYERÍA ■

MILA PASTELERÍA ▼

CAFÉ DEL MAR ▼

LA PALETERÍA ▼

NH GALLERÍA ★

ST. DOM ■

LA VITROLA ▼

CENTRO

CATEDRAL ★

PALACIO DE LA INQUISICIÓN ✚

Parque de Bolívar

MUSEO DEL ORO ZENÚ ★

BANCO DE LA REPÚBLICA LIBRARY ★

HOTEL MOVICH ●

To
✚ PLAYA BLANCA AND ISLAS DEL ROSARIO

ONDA DE MAR ■

JON SONEN ■

HOTEL CHARLESTON SANTA TERESA ●

ENOTECA ■

CAVA DEL PURO ■

ÚNICO ■

CREPES AND WAFFLES ▼

EL BARÓN ▼

BALUARTE TASCA BAR ▼

MUSEO NAVAL ★

IGLESIA DE SAN PEDRO CLAVER ♦

MUSEO DE ARTE MODERNO ★

Parque de la Marina

© AVALON TRAVEL

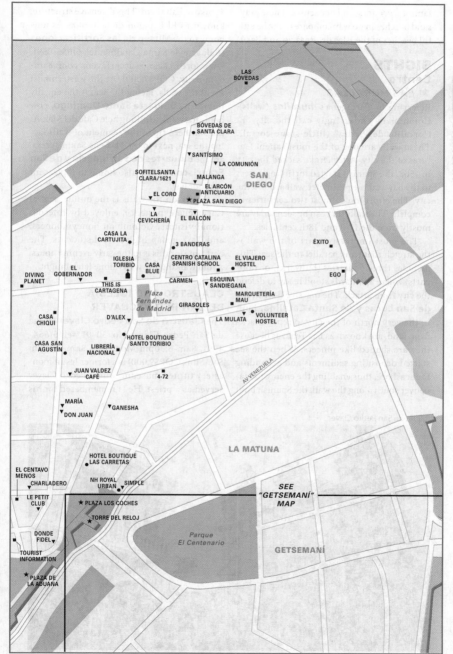

LAS BÓVEDAS

BÓVEDAS DE SANTA CLARA

SANTÍSIMO
LA COMUNIÓN

SOFITELSANTA CLARA/1621
MALANGA
EL ARCÓN ANTICUARIO
EL CORO
PLAZA SAN DIEGO

SAN DIEGO

LA CEVICHERÍA
EL BALCÓN

CASA LA CARTUJITA
3 BANDERAS
ÉXITO

IGLESIA TORIBIO
CENTRO CATALINA SPANISH SCHOOL
EL VIAJERO HOSTEL

DIVING PLANET
EL GOBERNADOR
CASA BLUE
EGO

THIS IS CARTAGENA
CARMEN
ESQUINA SANDIEGANA

Plaza Fernández de Madrid
MARQUETERÍA MAU

GIRASOLES
VOLUNTEER HOSTEL

CASA CHIQUI
D'ALEX
LA MULATA

CASA SAN AGUSTÍN
LIBRERÍA NACIONAL

JUAN VALDEZ CAFÉ
4-72

AV. VENEZUELA

HOTEL BOUTIQUE SANTO TORIBIO

MARÍA
DON JUAN
GANESHA

LA MATUNA

HOTEL BOUTIQUE LAS CARRETAS

EL CENTAVO MENOS
CHARLADERO
NH ROYAL URBAN
SIMPLE

SEE "GETSEMANÍ" MAP

LE PETIT CLUB
PLAZA LOS COCHES

TORRE DEL RELOJ

DONDE FIDEL
Parque El Centenario

GETSEMANÍ

TOURIST INFORMATION
PLAZA DE LA ADUANA

families, vendors, and masseuses. These gray-sand beaches in no way compare to the beautiful beaches of the Islas del Rosario and Barú.

SIGHTS
Centro
★ LAS MURALLAS

Referring to Cartagena's *murallas* (walls), Colombians endearingly call the city "El Corralito de Piedra" (little stone corral). These walls are one of the most salient features of the city. After Drake sacked the city in 1568, the Spanish started fortifying access to the bay and the perimeter wall around the city. The effort took almost two centuries to complete. The walls that can be seen today are mostly from the 17th and 18th centuries.

The most impressive part of the wall is the stretch that runs parallel to the sea. This includes three *baluartes* (bulwarks, or ramparts) where Spaniards stood ready to defend the city from attack. The massive **Baluartes de San Lucas y de Santa Catalina,** built in the very north of the city to repel attacks from land, are known as Las Tenazas because they are shaped like pincers. When the sea started depositing sediments and expanding the seashore, thus enabling the enemy to maneuver south along the wall, the Spanish built

a spike to halt them. This defensive structure, known as El Espigón de la Tenaza, is now home to the **Museo de las Fortificaciones** (Baluarte de Santa Catalina, tel. 5/656-0591, www.fortificacionesdecartagena.com, 8am-6pm daily, COP$7,000). At the westernmost tip of the walls, facing the sea, is the equally impressive **Baluarte Santo Domingo,** now home to swank drinking hole Café del Mar. At the southern tip of the segment of walls facing the sea, next to the Plaza de Santa Teresa, are the **Baluartes de San Ignacio y de San Francisco Javier,** also home to a pleasant outdoor bar.

A walk on the walls is the quintessential Cartagena experience, enjoyed by international visitors, Colombian honeymooners, and Cartagenan high school students. The best time for this is in the early evening hours. Avoid walking the walls alone late at night.

CLAUSTRO AND IGLESIA DE SAN PEDRO CLAVER

The **Claustro de San Pedro Claver** (Plaza de San Pedro Claver No. 30-01, tel. 5/664-4991, 8am-5:30pm Mon.-Fri., 8am-4:30pm Sat.-Sun., COP$9,000) is a former Jesuit monastery turned museum, where Pedro Claver served as a priest. He is remembered for his

Iglesia de San Pedro Claver

Palacio de la Inquisición

Mon.-Sat., 10am-4pm Sun., COP$19,000). This remarkable 18th-century construction, one of the finest extant examples of colonial architecture in the city, was the headquarters of the Spanish Inquisition in Cartagena. In this building was housed the Tribunal del Santo Oficio, whose purpose was to exert control over the Indians, mestizos, and African slaves not only in Nueva Granada but also in New World colonies in Central America, the Caribbean, and Venezuela. The tribunal was active from 1610 until the late 17th century. There were two other tribunals in the New World: one in Lima and another in Mexico City.

The first floor of the building is a museum displaying the weapons of torture employed by authorities as part of the Inquisition. In Cartagena as elsewhere, the most common punishable crime was "witchcraft," and hundreds of supposed heretics (indigenous people were excluded from punishment) were condemned here. On the second floor are exhibition spaces dedicated to the restoration of the building and to the history of Cartagena. Most explanations are written in Spanish; you may decide to hire one of the English-speaking guides (COP$35,000 for a group up to five persons). On your way out, take a right and then another right onto Calle de la Inquisición and look for a small window on the palace wall. This was a secret spot where citizens of colonial Cartagena could anonymously report others for various and sundry heresies.

MUSEO DEL ORO ZENÚ

The **Museo del Oro Zenú** (Cra. 4 No. 33-26, Parque de Bolívar, tel. 5/660-0778, 9am-5pm Tues.-Sat., 10am-3pm Sun., free), on the east side of the Parque de Bolívar, exhibits gold jewelry and funerary objects from the Zenú indigenous people, who were the original dwellers of the Río Magdalena area and Río Sinú valley, to the southwest of Cartagena. It has excellent explanations in both English and Spanish. A smaller version of the Museo del Oro in Bogotá, this museum has a regional focus and is one of the few tributes to indigenous culture in Cartagena.

Getsemaní
IGLESIA DE LA SANTÍSIMA TRINIDAD

The **Iglesia de la Santísima Trinidad** (Plaza de la Trinidad, tel. 5/664-2050, mass 6pm Mon.-Sat., 9am and 6pm Sun.) was completed in the mid-17th century. This bright yellow church of three naves has as its model the city's cathedral. The church is often open during the day, and visitors are welcome to sit on a pew in front of a massive fan and cool off. In the evenings the colorful Plaza de la Trinidad is a hub of activity.

Casa Museo Rafael Núñez

Just beyond the wall in the Cabrero neighborhood is the **Casa Museo Rafael Núñez** (Cl. Real del Cabrero No. 41-89, tel. 5/660-9058, 9am-5pm Tues.-Fri., 10am-4pm Sat.-Sun., free). This is the house of Rafael Núñez, the four-time former president of Colombia, author of the 1886 Colombian constitution, and author of the 11 verses of Colombia's national anthem. Núñez governed Colombia from this, his coastal home. The museum has memorabilia from his political life and is a beautiful example of 19th-century Cartagena architecture. Núñez's grave is in the Ermita de Nuestra Señora de las Mercedes across the street.

★ Castillo de San Felipe

The largest Spanish fort in the New World, the magnificent **Castillo de San Felipe** (Cerro de San Lázaro, east of Old City, tel. 5/656-6803, www.patrimoniodecartagena. com, 8am-6pm daily, COP$25,000) must have given pirates pause as they contemplated an attack on the city. While the walls around the city fended off maritime attacks, this fort was built atop the Cerro de San Lázaro to repel attacks by land at the Media Luna gate. Construction was begun in 1639 and completed more than a century later. Tunnels enabled soldiers to quickly move about without

Getsemaní

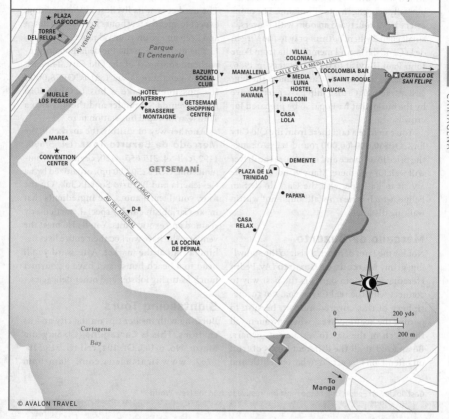

Parque El Centenario

PLAZA LAS COCHES

TORRE DEL RELOJ

AV VENEZUELA

MUELLE LOS PEGASOS

HOTEL MONTERREY

BRASSERIE MONTAIGNE

GETSEMANÍ SHOPPING CENTER

MAREA

CONVENTION CENTER

GETSEMANÍ

CALLE LARGA

AV DEL ARSENAL

D-8

LA COCINA DE PEPINA

BAZURTO SOCIAL CLUB

MAMALLENA

CAFÉ HAVANA

VILLA COLONIAL

CALLE DE LA MEDIA LUNA

MEDIA LUNA HOSTEL

LOCOLOMBIA BAR

SAINT ROQUE

GAUCHA

I BALCONI

CASA LOLA

DEMENTE

PLAZA DE LA TRINIDAD

PAPAYA

CASA RELAX

To CASTILLO DE SAN FELIPE

Cartagena Bay

To Manga

0   200 yds
0   200 m

© AVALON TRAVEL

CARTAGENA
CARTAGENA

being noticed, and cells housed the occasional unlucky prisoner.

Today, visitors ramble through 890 meters (0.5 mile) of tunnels and secret passages (a flashlight will come in quite handy). Views from the highest points of the fort are magnificent. The best time to visit the fort is in the late afternoon, when the intense sun abates. Audio tours (COP$10,000) are available. For many, the view of the fort from a distance suffices, especially at nighttime when it is lit up.

If you want to do things up for a special celebration, you can rent out the entire *castillo* or space on the *murallas*. Contact the **Sociedad de Mejoras Públicas de Cartagena**

(Castillo de San Felipe de Barajas, tel. 5/656-0590, www.fortificacionesdecartagena.com) for more information.

To get to the fort, take a cab (COP$6,000), a bus (COP$1,500) from Avenida Santander, or the TransCaribe (COP$2,000) from Avenida Venezuela.

La Popa

La Popa is a 150-meter-high (500-foot-high) hill east of Castillo de San Felipe, so named because of its resemblance to a ship's stern (*popa* in Spanish). La Popa is home to the **Convento Nuestra Señora de la Candelaria** (Cra. 20A 29D-16, tel.

5/666-0976, 9am-5:30pm daily, COP$5,000), which was built by Augustinian monks, reportedly on a pagan site of worship. The monastery has a courtyard abloom with flowers, a small chapel where faithful pray to the Virgen de la Candelaria, and memorabilia from Pope John Paul II's visit to the monastery in 1986. For many, the view of Cartagena is the biggest attraction. Cruise ship passengers arrive by the busload at La Popa, so be prepared for crowds.

You can take a taxi there from the Old City for COP$50,000-60,000 round-trip. Arrange the price in advance and make sure the driver will wait for you there. Many visitors combine a visit to La Popa with the Castillo de San Felipe, which is nearby (although not within walking distance).

Mercado de Bazurto

Not for the faint of heart, a visit to the sprawling, grimy **Mercado de Bazurto** (Av. Pedro Heredia, 5am-4pm daily) is the best way to connect with the real Cartagena. On the periphery of this covered market, be sure to peruse the seafood area, where women sell the catch of the day to restaurant owners. Be amazed at all the different kinds of fruit on offer. Don't be afraid to barter a little and don't be shy: The hundreds of vendors generally enjoy interacting with foreign visitors. The market is at its liveliest in the morning; expect to spend a few hours here. Dress down and keep an eye on your valuables.

The market is in the Pie de la Popa neighborhood southeast of the Old City. The best way to get there is via taxi (COP$8,000). It's possible to take a bus (COP$1,500) from Avenida Santander and there is also a TransCaribe rapid bus station here.

Another way of visiting the market is the **Mercado de Bazurto Tour** (tel. 5/660-1492, cell tel. 315/655-4120, cevicheria@hotmail.com, COP$250,000 pp), organized by La Cevichería and Bazurto Social Club. On the tour, you'll learn about the ingredients that make Caribbean cuisine special, particularly seafood and exotic fruits. You'll also meet the vendors who have worked their entire lives behind a stall at the market. Afterward you'll head to a beach house and have a gourmet lunch featuring lobster and other delicacies.

Sightseeing Tours

Bursting with insider tips on the city and its environs, **This Is Cartagena** (Cl. Sargento Mayor, No. 6-107, Of. 104, cell tel. 318/516-7767, www.ticartagena.com, 9am-6pm

Castillo de San Felipe, one of the most impressive forts in the New World

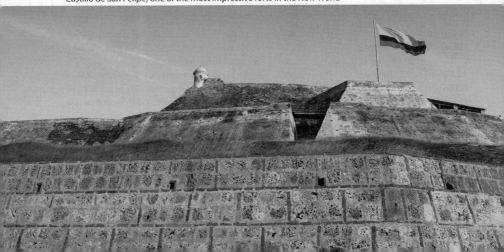

Mon.-Fri.) offers unconventional tours of the city. In addition to a top-notch walking tour of the Old City (US$42), the company also offers a tour devoted to the art scene (US$55), a bizarre-foods tour (US$85), a day of luxurious island-hopping on a yacht (US$750), and a drinking tour (US$75).

A fund-raising project for the nonprofit FEM (www.femcolombia.org), **Cartagena Insider** (Cl. del Quero No. 9-64, tel. 5/643-4185, www.insider.com.co) takes visitors beyond the boutique hotels and fancy restaurants of the Old City to experience the "real" Cartagena and its people. Tour options include a night of salsa, a day trip to La Boquilla fishing community, a walking tour of the Mercado de Bazurto, and a tour focusing on the Champeta music culture unique to Cartagena. Proceeds go directly to the nonprofit's social programs in and around the city. Tours can also be arranged to communities such as Tuchín, Córdoba, Leticia (a town on Barú), Palmerito, and San Bacile de Palenque.

With an extensive array of interesting tours, **Alternative Travel Cartagena** (tel. 5/646-0701, www.alternativetravelcartagena.com) aims to take visitors to lesser-known areas in and around Cartagena for a unique experience. They are based in the fishing village of La Boquilla and offer horseback rides on the beach, cooking classes, and canoe rides through mangroves.

Photographer Joaquin Saramiento offers various tours of the city with **Fototour** (cell tel. 317/635-4021, www.cartagenaconnections.com, US$80), during which amateur photographers can hone their skills, learn about Cartagena's history and culture, and explore the city.

ENTERTAINMENT AND EVENTS
Nightlife

Cartagena's nightspots tend to close at 3am weekdays, with some staying open until 5am on weekends. Expect to pay a cover fee, but groups can ask for a discount. The city's favorite music styles are old-school salsa and *son cubano,* along with the Afro beats of *champeta.*

With the Caribbean breeze kissing your face, enjoying a drink on the *murallas* is an experience that shouldn't be missed. There are three official options for this activity, one of them a cheapie. First, the **Baluarte Tasca-Bar** (Cl. San Juan de Dios, tel. 5/660-0468, 5:30pm-2am daily, no cover) is an open-air restaurant-bar on the wall across from the Plaza de Santa Teresa. It's chilled-out here, not trendy—but the drink prices are on the steep side: COP$24,000 for a margarita. The most happening spot is the **Café del Mar** (Baluarte Santo Domingo, tel. 5/664-6515, 5pm-3am daily, no cover), on the wall near the entrance to the Plaza de Santo Domingo. The music is loungey and electronic, and it stays busy until late. It's a cool place, but it's not great for mingling, as patrons are all seated in bulky furniture, and the drinks are pricey. The third option is also good for your budget: Buy an Águila beer from a roaming vendor (COP$3,000) and wander the walls at your leisure.

SALSA AND *SON CUBANO*

Donde Fidel (Plaza de los Coches, tel. 5/664-3127, noon-2am Sun.-Thurs., noon-3am Fri.-Sat., no cover) is a tiny salsa lovers' spot where the action spills out onto the plaza in front. Good times and cold beer can be found here.

La Esquina Sandiegana (corner of Cl. del Santísimo and Cl. de los Púntales, 5pm-2am Sun.-Thurs., 5pm-3am Fri.-Sat., no cover) is a locals' place, where the music is salsa and the drink is beer. Its walls are decorated with salsa posters, album covers, and photographs of salsa greats. It's a hole-in-the-wall bar in the San Diego neighborhood.

CHAMPETA

Bazurto Social Club (Av. del Centenario No. 30-42, tel. 5/664-3124, www.bazurtosocialclub.com, 7pm-3am Thurs.-Sat., cover varies) is an always-lively restaurant-bar, popular with Colombians and international visitors

Plaza-to-Plaza Walking Tour

Total Distance: 1.6 kilometers (1 mile)
Walking Time: 25-30 minutes
The best way to get to know Cartagena is to go for a morning stroll, finding your way from plaza to plaza, and even getting lost a couple of times. This tour starts in the Centro and ends in San Diego.

Torre del Reloj in the Plaza de los Coches

1. Start at the **Plaza de los Coches** (west of Av. Venezuela, opposite Getsemaní), once the main entry point to the city. It is easily identifiable by the iconic 19th-century **Torre del Reloj** (clock tower) that tops the entrance through the wall. Inside stands a statue of Cartagena's founder, Pedro de Heredia. During the colonial period, this plaza was the site of the city's slave market. Today, the plaza is filled with watering holes catering to visitors. Along the main corridor is the **Portal de las Dulces,** a row of stands where Afro-Colombian women sell homemade sweets, often made from coconut and tamarind.

2. Immediately to the southwest is the large triangular **Plaza de la Aduana,** once the seat of power in colonial Cartagena. It is surrounded by stately colonial mansions. A statue of Christopher Columbus presides in the center. It has its fair share of ATMs and is where the main tourist office is located.

3. Adjacent to Plaza de la Aduana to the southwest is the **Plaza de San Pedro,** a small but charming square, located in front of the imposing **Iglesia de San Pedro Claver** and attached cloister.

4. Walk two blocks north on Calle de San Pedro and you'll arrive at the city's heart, the leafy **Parque de Bolívar,** a shady park with benches, fountains, and a statue of Simón Bolívar in the middle. Surrounding this lovely park are some of the most important buildings of the city, including the **Catedral Basílica Menor** and the **Palacio de la Inquisición.**

5. Continue north on Calle de los Santos de Piedra for one block. Take the first left onto Calle de Ayos. One block west is the **Plaza de Santo Domingo,** in the heart of the former upper-class quarter. You will notice many superb two-story *casas altas* built by rich merchants. The plaza is dominated by the austere **Iglesia de Santo Domingo.** A rotund nude bronze sculpture by famous Colombian sculptor Fernando Botero, live musical performances, and many outdoor cafés liven up the popular plaza.

6. Walk north along Calle de Santo Domingo for a block, then turn right and head east for four blocks on Calle de la Mantilla until you reach Calle Segunda de Badillo. Turn left and half a block north is the large, green **Plaza Fernández de Madrid** in the San Diego district. On the northwest side is the charming **Iglesia de Santo Toribio de Mogrovejo,** with its magnificent wooden ceiling.

7. Head east on Calle del Santísimo for two blocks, then turn left on Calle Cochera del Hobo and go north just over a block to the **Plaza de San Diego,** which is surrounded by inviting restaurants. It's also where artisans sell handicrafts under the shade of a tree.

8. Walk north for one block on Calle de las Bóvedas, which will deposit you at the **Plaza de las Bóvedas** at the extreme northeast of the city. Once the location of a military storehouse, this is where you can browse handicrafts under the golden arched walls of the Galería de las Bóvedas.

alike. Get a taste for Afro-Colombian *champeta* beats, as live acts, including the Bazurto All Stars, often perform here. They also serve food, such as shrimp empanadas and paella. The house drink is the fruity rum *machacos*.

GAY CLUBS

Gay nightlife in Cartagena is not exactly thriving: There are only a couple of spots worth checking out. Crowds are friendly and the scene is mixed.

Brash **D8** (Cl. del Arsenal No. 8B-155, tel. 5/646-0657, 10pm-4am Fri.-Sat.) is the dance club of the moment in Cartagena. To take it down a notch, try **Le Petit Club** (Cl. del Candilejo No. 32-34, 5pm-2am Wed.-Sat.), which has a pub-like atmosphere, especially midweek.

COCKTAIL BARS

In an unassuming corner of the Plaza de San Pedro Claver, **El Barón** (Cra. 4 No. 31-7, tel. 5/664-3105, 5pm-1am Sun.-Mon., noon-1am Tues., noon-2am Wed.-Sat., no cover) is devoted to cocktail culture. The interior is all brass and rustic furnishings, but you can also sip the evening away out on the plaza, where the people-watching is fantastic. Allow the bartender to mix you a gin-basil smash—you can get a beer anytime. Tapas are also on offer.

If you're looking for atmosphere, head to **El Coro** (Cl. del Torno No. 39-29, tel. 5/650-4700, 5pm-2am Sun.-Thurs., 5pm-3am Fri.-Sat., no cover), at the Hotel Sofitel Legend Santa Clara. At this posh bar in a former 17th-century convent, crisply dressed bartenders serve Caribbean cocktails to hotel guests and others while Latin jazz plays in the background. Of the larger convent complex, El Coro is located in the chorus area from where the resident nuns sang while mass was celebrated in the adjacent chapel. Ask to see the crypt, which was an inspiration for Gabriel García Márquez as he wrote *Of Love and Other Demons*.

Festivals and Events

Cartagena feels like a celebration all the time, but it's especially true from November to February, when an array of cultural events are featured. Pick up a copy of **Donde,** a free monthly newspaper with Cartagena event listings. You can find it at the airport and in big hotels.

HAY FESTIVAL

The **Hay Festival** (www.hayfestival.com) is an important international festival that began in Wales nearly 30 years ago. It celebrates literature, music, environmental awareness, and community and is held in various cities across the world, including in Cartagena in late January. Bill Clinton has called it the "Woodstock of the mind." In addition to talks and concerts, the festival holds educational programs for youth in the neighborhoods of Cartagena. It also provides free or discounted tickets to students. Most of the events take place in the **Teatro Heredia** (Cl. de la Chichería No. 38-10, tel. 5/664-6023 or 5/664-9631). While the festival's name is pronounced as the English "hay," in Colombia it's often pronounced as the Spanish *"hay"* ("ai"). Hay Festival is thus a double entendre: *hay festival* in Spanish means yes, there is a festival!

FESTIVAL INTERNACIONAL DE MÚSICA

Over the course of a week in early to mid-January, the churches, plazas, and theaters of the Walled City become the setting for classical music concerts by musicians from all over the world during the **Festival Internacional de Música** (International Music Festival, www.cartagenamusicfestival.com, tickets www.tuboleta.com). Most concerts sell out far in advance, but if you can't get tickets, you might be able to catch a free performance in one of the churches or plazas in the Old City.

FESTIVAL INTERNACIONAL DE CINE DE CARTAGENA DE INDIAS

If you're in town during late February and are looking for an excuse to escape the heat, here it is: the **Festival Internacional de Cine de Cartagena de Indias** (International Film Festival, tel. 5/664-2345, www.ficcifestival.

com). A tradition since the 1960s, this week-long film festival has an interesting program of documentaries, Colombian films, and shorts; a series of roundtable discussions with prominent actors and directors; and educational activities in neighborhoods throughout the city. The venues include historic buildings and plazas.

CONCURSO NACIONAL DE BELLEZA

Beauty contests, and especially the **Concurso Nacional de Belleza** (Miss Colombia Pageant, tel. 5/660-0779, www.srtacolombia. org), are a big deal in Colombia. The coronation of Señorita Colombia takes place every November and is the highlight of Cartagena's Independence Day celebrations. Aspirers for the title represent each of the departments of the country, in addition to some cities. Ladies from the Valle del Cauca and Atlántico have won the most titles (10 each) since the pageant began in the 1930s. In 2001, the first Miss Colombia of Afro-Colombian heritage was chosen: Vanessa Mendoza, who represented the Chocó department. Tickets to the main events—the swimsuit competition at the Cartagena Hilton and the coronation at the Centro de Convenciones—are hard to come by but not impossible to purchase.

ELECTRONIC MUSIC FESTIVALS

In early January every year, especially on the first weekend after New Year's Day, one or two multiday beachside electronic music festivals take place. Drawing a hip and sexy crowd from Bogotá, Medellín, and Cali, as well as international visitors escaping cold winters, the festival of the moment is **Storyland** (www.storyland.com.co). Tickets and information can also be found at Tu Boleta (www.tuboleta.com). Buy your tickets well in advance.

SHOPPING
Centro

The most historic place to pick up some Colombian handicrafts is at **Las Bóvedas** (San Diego, extreme northeastern corner of the wall, 9am-6pm daily). Once a military storehouse, today it's the place to buy multicolored hammocks and all kinds of Colombian *artesanías* (handicrafts) of varying quality.

For men, nothing says Cartagena chic like a crisp guayabera shirt. The typical linen or cotton guayabera has two vertical embroidered stripes and four pockets, and can be worn to a wedding or special event, or even out to dinner at one of the elegant restaurants of the Old City. Tailor Edgar Gómez of **Ego** (Cl. de Portobello No. 10-92, tel. 5/668-6016, 9am-5pm Mon.-Fri.) purportedly once made guayaberas for Bill Gates and the king of Spain.

Along Calle Santo Domingo there are several boutiques of top Colombian designers. Bogotana **Bettina Spitz** (Cl. de la Mantilla No. 3-37, tel. 5/660-2160, www.bettinaspitz.com, 11am-1pm and 2pm-8pm daily) sells casual, beach, and formal clothes for women, as well as an array of accessories, shoes, and some men's items. **Onda de Mar** (Cl. de las Damas, tel. 5/668-5226, 9am-6pm daily) is a Colombian clothing brand that has everything you need for a day at the beach. **St. Dom** (Cl. de Santo Domingo No. 33-70, tel. 5/664-0197, 10am-8pm Mon.-Sat., noon-6pm Sun.) is a boutique that brings together Colombian designers of accessories, clothing, handbags, and jewelry.

Antiques shops provide a glimpse into aristocratic living from the Cartagena of yesteryear. **El Arcón Anticuario** (Cl. del Camposanto No. 9-46, tel. 5/664-1197) showcases Colombian furniture from both the colonial and Republican eras. This is the spot to pick up your very own whimsical Cartagenan doorknocker or chandelier.

Casa Chiqui (Cl. de la Universidad No. 36-127, tel. 5/668-5429, www.casachiqui.com, 10am-6pm Mon.-Sat.) specializes in interesting interior design items, housewares, and furniture from around the world. While Asia, Africa, and the Middle East are represented, there are Colombian handicrafts, such as colorful Barranquillan Carnaval masks, woven handbags, and placemats made from palm leaves, on display as well.

Touches of Cuba are found everywhere here: mojitos, music, and, too, the cigars. At **La Cava del Puro** (Cl. de las Damas No. 3-106, tel. 5/664-9482, www.lacavadelpuro.com, 9am-8pm Mon.-Sat., 10am-8pm Sun.) they don't sell just any old stogie; here the cigars come from Havana and are of the best quality. Smoking is not only permitted here, but in fact promoted. Sometimes a little whiskey is served to perusing clients.

Abaco Libros (Cl. de la Mantilla, tel. 5/664-8290, 9am-9pm Mon.-Sat., 3pm-9pm Sun.) is a cozy bookshop and café with a variety of books on Cartagena, top Colombian novels, and a selection of magazines, classics, and best sellers in English. **Librería Nacional** (Cl. Segunda de Badillo No. 36-27, tel. 5/664-1448, 8:30am-12:30pm and 2pm-6:30pm Mon.-Fri., 8:30am-5pm Sat.) is a chain bookstore with shelves full of Colombian and Spanish-language books, and some books in English.

Getsemaní

For high-quality handicrafts, pay a visit to **Artesanías de Colombia** (Centro de Convenciones, Local 5, tel. 5/660-9615, 10am-7pm Mon.-Sat.). This is a government entity whose mission it is to promote Colombian handicrafts and craftspeople. This store sells handicrafts from across the country but specializes in masks from the Carnaval de Barranquilla, woven *mochilas* (handbags) from indigenous groups in the Sierra Nevada, and the colorful embroidery of *molas* from indigenous groups in the Darién Gap region near Panama.

The most atmospheric book-browsing experience in the city is on the northern edge of the Parque del Centenario in Getsemaní, home to several secondhand **book stalls.** You never know what you might find. Days and hours of operation are irregular, so just stroll by if you're in the area.

SPORTS AND RECREATION
Beaches

Though Cartagena boasts a seaside location, it lacks the spectacular beaches that first-time visitors might be envisioning. Instead, the most popular beaches in Cartagena, located on the Caribbean side of the **Bocagrande peninsula,** feature gray-sand beaches packed with Colombian families and plied by vendors and masseuses. Umbrella rentals are expected,

Mochilas (handbags) are just some of the handicrafts sold in Cartagena.

and usually cost around COP$20,000 for the afternoon. Near the jetties is a gay-friendly section called **Playa Hollywood.** Beyond this point, the beach hangs a sharp left and merges into the beaches of the Laguito neighborhood; there are some waterfront restaurants and windsurfing rentals here.

Bocagrande's beaches are just a 10-minute cab ride from the Old City and offer water that's good for swimming and splashing around—but don't expect the turquoise colors often associated with the Caribbean.

For postcard-perfect white-sand beaches and palm trees, book a day tour or multiday excursion to **Barú** or the **Islas del Rosario.**

Diving

Diving Planet (Cl. Estanco del Aguardiente No. 5-09, tel. 5/660-0450, www.divingplanet. org, 8am-7pm Mon.-Sat.) offers classes and diving excursions to some 25 locations throughout the Parque Nacional Natural Corales del Rosario y San Bernardo. A one-day course costs COP$305,000; a day trip for already-certified divers costs COP$290,000. Discounts are offered for paying in advance online or in cash. Multiday PADI certification courses are also available, some of which include an overnight on the white beaches of the Islas del Rosario. Snorkeling excursions are also available (COP$190,000).

Sailing

It doesn't get much better than renting out a 43-foot catamaran with a captain and crew and sailing around Cartagena and its nearby islands. **Veleros Colombia** (cell tel. 316/528-2413, www.veleroscolombia.com, COP$2,900,000/4 hours) can make that happen. In addition, they offer sailing courses (COP$4,650,000/3-day course) along the Caribbean coast and diving excursions in the Islas del Rosario and the Islas de San Bernardo.

Biking

The best time to explore Cartagena by bike is early on a Sunday morning or on a Sunday or Monday evening when there is little activity and light traffic in the Old City. Many hostels and some hotels have bicycles for rent.

Bicitour Getsemaní (Cl. Don Sancho, Edificio Aqua Marina, cell tel. 300/357-1825, COP$5,000/2-hour rental) rents out bikes and offers guided tours of the Old City, Manga, and Bocagrande. **Velo Tours** (Cl. Gastelbondo, tel. 5/664-9714, www.velotours. com.co, COP$80,000/day) offers several bike tours of the city, including a three-hour nighttime tour (COP$80,000).

FOOD

Seafood reigns supreme in Cartagenan cuisine. Popular fish are *pargo rojo* (red snapper), *corvina* (sea bass), *dorado* (mahimahi), and *sierra* (swordfish). Shellfish include *langosta* (lobster), *langostinos* (prawns), and *chipi chipis* (tiny clams). These main dishes are often accompanied by delicious coconut rice and *patacones* (fried plantains).

On the street, especially in the Old City, there are food and drinks on practically every corner. There's no better refreshment than a cold *agua de coco* (coconut water), either straight from the fruit or out of a plastic bag. Street snacks, popular in the late morning or late afternoon, are called *fritos.* They include items like *arepa de huevo* (fried eggs in a corn arepa), *carimañola* (fried yuca-flour pastry with cheese and meat), and seafood empanadas. Fresh fruit, particularly *mango biche* (green mango served with salt and hot spices), can be a good break from the heavier *fritos.* For a sweet bite, head to the Portal de las Dulces, a traditional sweets market near the Torre del Reloj.

Though many restaurants in the Walled City sport Manhattan prices, an inexpensive meal is not impossible to find. There are still a few mom-and-pop restaurants featuring cheap set lunches for locals who would balk at paying over COP$10,000 for their midday meal.

This Is Cartagena (www.ticartagena. com) offers a reservation service for many of the city's top restaurants.

Centro

CARIBBEAN

Popular ★ **Santísimo** (Cl. del Torno No. 39-62, tel. 5/660-1531, www.elsantisimo.com, noon-11pm daily, COP$40,000) has a religious theme, with candles and an austere interior design. The Plan Milagro ("Miracle Plan," COP$45,000) is a prix fixe meal that's recognized as the restaurant's best deal.

Malanga (Plaza de San Diego No. 8-19, tel. 5/660-1472, noon-midnight daily, COP$22,000) prides itself on serving only the freshest ingredients and regional recipes. Try the mango shrimp ceviche and relax with a glass of sangria. The space is welcoming and intimate, with soft lighting, but most patrons sit outside on the colorful Plaza de San Diego.

Some of the freshest ceviche in town is served at **La Cevichería** (Cl. Stuart No. 7-14, tel. 5/660-1492, 1pm-10:30pm daily, COP$28,000). The restaurant has a creative menu, featuring options with mango and coconut. Its location on a quiet street makes the outdoor seating especially welcoming. Get a little taste of everything by ordering the "Miss-Cellanea" ceviche sampler. You can also pick up a T-shirt at their little shop.

★ **La Mulata** (Cl. Quero No. 9-58, tel. 5/664-6222, noon-4pm Mon.-Sat., COP$18,000) specializes in Cartagenan cuisine. Their seafood dishes feature a perfect mound of coconut rice and a thin, crispy slice of fried plantain on top, to add some height to the presentation. Decorated with names of regional dishes, the restaurant walls provide a vocabulary lesson on Caribbean cuisine. Try the coconut lemonade.

CARIBBEAN FUSION

Fabulous ★ **Carmen** (Cl. de Santísimo, Cl. 38 No. 8-19, tel. 5/664-5116, www.carmencartagena.com, noon-3pm and 6pm-11pm Mon.-Tues., noon-11pm Wed.-Sun., COP$159,000) blends Caribbean with Asian and Middle Eastern cuisine, offering a five-course tasting menu that includes wine. Impeccable service and an unforgettable meal await. Seating is indoors or out on the patio. Reservations are necessary.

For pork ribs in hoisin sauce or a lobster sandwich, visit **María** (Cl. del Colegio No. 34-60, tel. 5/660-5380, www.mariacartagena.com, noon-3pm and 6:30pm-11pm Mon.-Fri., 6:30pm-11:30pm Sat., COP$42,000), a restaurant with nods to Asian cuisine. It's a cheerful, bright space, and the only place in town where you can dine under the glow of a chandelier of ceramic pineapples.

The **1621** (Hotel Sofitel Legend Santa Clara, Cl. del Curato, tel. 5/650-4741, noon-11pm daily, COP$45,000) combines French and Caribbean cuisine in the elegant atmosphere of a classic hotel that was once a 17th-century convent. Desserts are sumptuous, a perfect match for the ambience. Don't miss their extensive wine collection.

★ **El Gobernador by Rausch** (Cl. del Sargento Mayor No. 6-87, tel. 5/642-4100, www.bastionluxuryhotel.com, noon-3pm and 7pm-11pm daily, COP$45,000) is a fancy Mediterranean-Caribbean fusion restaurant with serious chandeliers in the Bastion Luxury Hotel. Favorites on the menu include scallops with pork belly and duck in *corozo* sauce. For dessert, try the piña colada mousse.

Pacific and Caribbean cuisine unite at **La Comunión** (Cl. de las Bóvedas No. 39-116, tel. 5/645-5301, noon-10pm daily, COP$36,000), which is housed in a cheerfully decorated space. The menu features black tamales filled with octopus and squid.

SEAFOOD AND STEAK

Don Juan (Cl. del Colegio No. 34-60, tel. 5/664-3857, www.donjuancartagena.com, noon-3pm and 7pm-11pm daily, COP$40,000) is a sophisticated bistro with high ceilings where you can order seafood, steak, and pasta in an elegant setting. Try the tangy grilled sea bass on lemon risotto.

Transport yourself to the Havana of yesteryear at ★ **La Vitrola** (Cl. Baloco, Cl. 33 No. 2-01, tel. 5/664-8243, noon-3pm and 7pm-midnight daily, COP$35,000), an always-elegant, always-packed restaurant that specializes in Caribbean seafood, such as their popular tuna steak with avocado and mango, as well as pasta dishes. Immaculately dressed bartenders are a blur of constant motion as they mix innumerable mojitos. La Vitrola is pricey, but the atmosphere, with live Cuban music in the evenings, makes it worthwhile. Reservations must be made well in advance.

CASUAL DINING

El Balcón (Cl. Tumbamuertos No. 38-85, cell tel. 300/336-3876, noon-midnight daily, COP$22,000) is a friendly place with a view in Plaza de San Diego. Get here in the early evening and enjoy a sundowner cocktail as you listen to lounge music or have a light meal like a refreshing gazpacho or their shrimp "sexviche."

Casual and cute, **Collage Charladero** (Cl. Roman No. 5-47, tel. 5/660-7672, www.collagecharladero.com, noon-midnight Mon.-Sat., noon-5pm Sun., COP$22,000) serves sandwiches, burgers, falafels, fresh juices (watermelon with lime and mint), and refreshing sangria in a clean and cool environment close to all the historic sites.

Simple (Hotel NH, Plaza de los Coches, tel. 5/645-5051, www.simplecartagena.com, 7am-10:30pm daily, COP$36,000) has Scandinavian interior design and an interesting menu with items like crab tacos and coconut prawns. They also serve fresh pastries at breakfast.

D'Alex (Plaza Fernandez de Madrid, cell tel. 312/883-5925, noon-10pm daily, COP$14,000) is a cheap spot that is popular with the backpacker crowd looking for a bargain on *pescado frito* (fried fish), the restaurant's specialty.

ITALIAN

Twinkling lights and fountains create ambience on the patio of **Enoteca** (Cl. San Juan de Dios No. 3-39, tel. 5/664-3806, www.enoteca.com.co, noon-11:30pm daily, COP$30,000), a Cartagena pizza and pasta institution. The pizzas are better than the pasta. If you want air-conditioning more than atmosphere, grab a table inside.

GREEK

For a change of pace, bright and tiny **Grecia Café y Suvlaki** (Cl. de la Estrella No. 4-47, cell tel. 313/707-7827, noon-10pm Mon.-Sat., COP$15,000) is Greek-run and specializes in gyros and souvlaki.

INDIAN

For a little curry with your shrimp, try **Ganesha** (Cl. del Colegio No. 34-68, tel. 5/660-9165, noon-3pm and 6:30pm-11pm Tues.-Sun., COP$24,000), an authentic Indian restaurant with an extensive menu and many vegetarian options.

VEGETARIAN

The inexpensive set lunches at vegetarian **Girasoles** (Cl. de los Puntales No. 37-01, tel. 5/660-2625, 11am-4pm daily, COP$12,000) are a salvation to many a vegetarian visitor. The usual lunch includes a vegetable soup to start, followed by a main protein dish accompanied by rice and vegetables. You won't leave hungry. This informal lunch counter has many regular customers. Girasoles usually publishes the day's menu on its Facebook page.

BAKERIES AND CAFÉS

One of the best bakery-cafés in town is ★ **Mila Pastelería** (Cl. de la Iglesia No. 35-76, tel. 5/664-4607, www.mila.com.co, 9am-10pm Mon.-Sat., 10am-9pm Sun., COP$17,000), a bright place for sandwiches, tempting desserts, and a late breakfast (served until 11am) for those who slept in too late at the hotel.

SWEETS

A homemade ice cream popsicle from ★ **La Paleterría** (Cl. de Ayos No. 3-86, 11am-11pm daily, COP$10,000) makes a late-afternoon stroll around the steamy city much more enjoyable. At this ice cream stand, order one of the interesting flavors such as *mango biche* (green mango) or Tropical Paradise, a non-dairy option packed with fruit chunks.

Getsemaní

CARIBBEAN

At ★ **La Cocina de Pepina** (Callejón Vargas, Cl. 25 No. 9A-06, Local 2, tel. 5/664-2944, noon-4pm and 6pm-10pm Tues.-Sat., noon-4pm Sun.-Mon., COP$25,000), typical dishes from across the Caribbean coast are thoughtfully reinvented. The *mote de queso*, a thick soup made of salty Costeño cheese and yams, gets rave reviews. It's a cozy place in an alley near Calle del Arsenal.

Unpretentious **Casa de Socorro** (Cl. Larga No. 8B-112, cell tel. 315/718-6666, noon-3pm and 6pm-10pm Tues.-Sat., COP$28,000) may surprise you with its Cartagenan specialties, ceviche, and *limonada de coco* (coconut lemonade). The loyal clientele of locals speaks for itself.

SEAFOOD

Marea by Rausch (Centro de Convenciones, Cl. 24 No. 8A-344, tel. 5/654-4205, www.mareabyrausch.com, noon-3pm and 7pm-10pm Tues.-Sat., 4pm-10pm Sun., COP$52,000) is an ultra-chic seafood restaurant that is the brainchild of the Rausches, two brother chefs from Bogotá. Specialties include tuna tartare and prawns in a coconut and saffron sauce. This restaurant has excellent views of the bay and the Torre del Reloj.

TAPAS

The Plaza de la Trinidad is the beating heart of happening Getsemaní, and it's home to some swanky spots perfect for a small meal and a couple of drinks. Cool **Demente** (Plaza de la Trinidad, cell tel. 311/831-9839, www.demente.com.co, 4pm-2am Mon.-Sat., COP$22,000) specializes in cocktails and tapas. It's an open-air spot with a retractable roof, where the music is funky, the cocktails are chic, and the cigars are Cuban. On the back patio is a beer garden complete with twinkling lights, serving wood-oven pizza

and craft beer. It's a fun place for an evening of small plates and drinks.

ITALIAN

VIPs such as Colombian president Juan Manuel Santos have been known to sample the authentic Italian dishes at **I Balconi** (Cl. del Guerrero No. 29-146, cell tel. 311/392-0936, www.ibalconi.co, 4pm-11:30pm Tues.-Sun., COP$18,000). It gets boisterous here as the evening wears on and the wine flows. Ask for a table on one of the balconies so you can enjoy the street life from on high.

DUTCH-INDONESIAN FUSION

Delightful **Saint Roque** (Cl. Espíritu Santo No. 29-214, cell tel. 317/226-8039, Mon.-Sat. 5pm-10:30pm, COP$24,000) serves Dutch-Indonesian cuisine in an up-and-coming area of Getsemaní. Try the *gado-gado* vegetarian salad with peanut sauce, and choose a candlelit table on the sidewalk.

ARGENTINIAN

Chef Rodrigo at ★ **Gaucha** (Cl. Espiritu Santo No. 29-207, cell tel. 310/648-7942, COP$38,000) knows his *bife de chorizo* (New York strip) from his *vacio* (flank), and it's no wonder this sophisticated restaurant with both sidewalk and indoor seating has become a Cartagena favorite. The waitstaff here is attentive.

FRENCH

Brasserie Montaigne (Cra. 8B No. 25-103, tel. 5/650-3030, noon-3pm and 6pm-11pm daily, COP$28,000) is a classic French restaurant in the Hotel Monterrey. Cordon bleu and crème brûlée are classics on the menu.

Bocagrande

Elegant **Arabe Internacional** (Cra. 3 No. 8-83, tel. 5/665-4365, www.restaurantearabeinternacional.com, noon-3:30pm and 7pm-10pm Mon.-Fri., noon-10pm Sat.-Sun., COP$25,000) has been serving authentic Middle Eastern cuisine since 1965. It's a popular place for the Cartagena business crowd.

Tabetai (Av. San Martín No. 5-145, tel. 5/647-9861, noon-11pm daily, COP$22,000) specializes in Japanese cuisine, specifically sushi. They have fun happy hours most afternoons, often with DJs on the weekend.

Riquisimo BBQ (Cra. 1 No. 1A-148, tel. 5/655-0861, 7:30am-midnight daily, COP$18,000) looks like an American-style coffee shop, but it serves typical Cartagenan fare in addition to sandwiches and fixed-price lunches. Their generously portioned breakfasts are a specialty.

ACCOMMODATIONS

As the top tourist destination in Colombia, Cartagena boasts a large and diverse hotel sector. The Centro and Getsemaní are the top neighborhoods for small, high-end boutique hotels, often occupying well-restored colonial-era homes; many feature rooftop terraces. Being pampered at one of these luxury options—even for just a few nights—will be a highlight of your visit.

Hostels proliferate in the city, especially in Getsemaní. The vast majority offer private rooms with air-conditioning, but these tend to go fast, so plan to reserve at least a few weeks in advance. Some hostel dorm rooms don't have air-conditioning.

Bocagrande, with its high-rise hotels and condos, is more popular with Colombian families than with international visitors. Staying here means proximity to Bocagrande's beaches, cheaper food options, and more space for less money.

For a last-minute deal, visit **COTELCO** (Aeropuerto Rafael Nunez, tel. 5/656-9200, www.cartagena.cotelco.org, 7am-1:30am Mon.-Sat., 8am-5:30pm Sun.) at the Cartagena airport, which is generally open through the last arrival of the day. This association of hotels often has discounted prices for a variety of options in the Centro, Getsemaní, Bocagrande, and Las Américas. Look for them in the baggage arrival area.

For most international visitors, hotels should not charge IVA (sales tax). Inquire about IVA when you make your reservation, and again when you're checking in, to be sure you aren't improperly charged. (For more information on the regulations behind IVA, see the *Essentials* chapter.)

Centro

UNDER COP$70,000

Your stay at the ★ **Volunteer Hostel** (Calle del Quero No. 9-64, tel. 5/643-4185, www.volunteerhostel.org, COP$40,000 dorm, COP$130,000 d) supports an array of social projects in underserved communities in and around Cartagena. Accommodations are basic, but comfortable and clean. One of the other perks is the chance to meet like-minded people from across the globe.

In the Old City, the Uruguayan hostel chain **El Viajero** (Cl. Siete Infantes No. 9-45, tel. 5/660-2598, www.elviajerohostels.com, COP$60,000 dorm, COP$230,000 d) has air-conditioned dorm rooms of various sizes. A handful of private rooms are located across the street in a more subdued environment. A decent breakfast is included in the room rate. Guests enjoy socializing at the bar.

COP$70,000-200,000

Previously a hostel, **Casa Blue** (Plaza Fernández de Madrid, Cl. del Curato No. 38-08, tel. 5/668-6501, COP$200,000 d) is within the Walled City just a few blocks from the Plaza de Santo Domingo. The rooms are private and the hotel markets itself to a budget-conscious business crowd. Its location on a popular plaza means you should expect some noise in the evenings.

A midrange option with a guesthouse feel is ★ **3 Banderas** (Cl. Cochera del Hobo No. 38-66, tel. 5/660-0160, www.hotel3banderas.com, COP$200,000 d). This hotel is housed in a 200-year-old building with two interior patios and a rooftop terrace with a tiny pool. Some of the 24 rooms are small, but it's generally a good value. Request one of the rooms with a small balcony.

Hotel Casa Real (Cl. del Cuartel No. 36-122, tel. 5/664-7089, www.casarealhotel.com.co, COP$180,000 d) has two rooftop terraces, adequate rooms with antiques from old Cartagena, and a central location.

COP$200,000-500,000

With just eight rooms, a pleasant rooftop terrace, and a delicious breakfast, **Hotel Boutique Santo Toribio** (Cl. Segunda del Badillo No. 36-87, cell tel. 317/893-6464, www.hotelsantotoribio.com, COP$350,000) checks off all the boxes for a comfortable stay in the city. Lounge music adds an air of chicness. Bikes are available for rent.

You can't really go wrong at the ★ **NH Urban Royal** (Plaza de los Coches No. 34-10, tel. 5/645-5050, www.nh-hotels.com, COP$443,000 d), one of two locations of the NH Hotels chain in the city. Rooms are equipped with basics, and most offer nice views of the always-busy Plaza de los Coches. The rooftop pool is a welcome sight after a long day—the view is quite something, too—and the included breakfast is ample.

A friendly staff is what sets **Hotel Boutique Las Carretas** (Cl. de las Carretas No. 34-28, tel. 5/660-4853, COP$280,000 d) apart. Rooms are spacious and some have balconies with a street view. On the rooftop you'll find a small pool. The building itself is an architectural mishmash, and the interior design is more folksy than sophisticated.

OVER COP$500,000

The two-story **Bóvedas de Santa Clara** (Cl. del Torno No. 39-114, tel. 5/650-4464, www.bovedasdesantaclara.com, COP$580,000 d) has only 18 rooms, some of which are extremely spacious, and some have views of the water. Guests can use the Hotel Sofitel Legend Santa Clara spa and facilities across the street. The hotel staff can organize day trips to the Hotel San Pedro Majagua in Islas del Rosario. There is no restaurant on-site, although breakfast is served.

The comfort and fabulous location of ★ **Hotel Movich** (Cl. Velez Danies No. 4-39, tel. 5/660-0133, www.movichhotels.com, COP$880,000) make it a good value, even though the rates are steep. Light floods

its spacious rooms, and the rooftop terrace has a refreshing pool and a 360-degree view of the Old City. A 15-minute massage is included with your stay.

The two-story colonial-era **Casa la Cartujita** (Cl. del Curato No. 38-53, tel. 5/660-5248, www.casalacartujita.com, COP$725,000 d) has seven bright-white minimalist rooms and a lovely terrace, a Jacuzzi, a dipping pool, and a pleasant reading room. Rent the entire house and you'll have a personal chef at your service.

The result of a meticulous restoration of three adjacent 17th-century houses, the ★ **Casa San Agustín** (Cl. de la Universidad No. 36-44, tel. 5/681-0000, www.hotelcasasanagustin.com, COP$1,500,000 d) is easily one of the most luxurious addresses in Cartagena, if not all of Colombia. Among the amenities are an inviting pool on the main floor, complimentary afternoon tea in the library, a terrace with a fabulous view, spacious rooms with exposed wood-beamed ceilings, a cozy bar, and the original stone walls. This hotel is a member of Leading Hotels of the World.

Good taste reigns at **Anandá** (Cl. del Cuartel No. 36-77, tel. 5/664-4452, COP$960,000 d), whose name means "maximum state of happiness" in Hindi. It's certainly close to the truth at this gorgeous, meticulously restored 16th-century home. There are 23 rooms of three different styles and a pool, Jacuzzi, and daybeds on the rooftop. Anandá is home to the restaurant Carmen.

The 89-room ★ **Hotel Charleston Santa Teresa** (Plaza de Santa Teresa, tel. 5/664-9494, www.hotelcharlestonsantateresa.com, COP$740,000 d) is steps away from the wall. It was originally built in the 17th century as a convent for Carmelita nuns. In the 1980s it was converted into a hotel. There are two wings to this historic hotel, a colonial one and a Republican-era one dating from the early 20th century. Rooms are nothing short of luxurious, with accommodations in the colonial wing a notch above the more modern ones. The two inner courtyards are lovely, with astounding and ever-changing floral displays. Concierges can arrange any excursion you'd like. The hotel's many amenities—four restaurants (one run by renowned chef Harry Sasson), a rooftop pool, a spa, and a gym—ensure a relaxing stay.

One Old City classic is in San Diego. The 122-room **Hotel Sofitel Legend Santa Clara** (Cl. del Torno No. 39-29, tel. 5/650-4700, www.sofitel.com, COP$780,000 d) is synonymous with class and luxury, though it once served as a convent. The stunning colonial courtyard features tropical plants, a fountain, and modern sculptures. The gorgeous chapel is available for weddings. Be sure to request a tour of the hotel from a staff member to see remnants of the convent. Make time for drinks at the on-site bar El Coro. The pool area is large; during low season, nonguests can obtain day passes.

From the rooftop terrace of ★ **Hotel LM** (Cl. de la Mantilla No. 3-56, tel. 5/664-9100, www.hotel-lm.com, COP$637,000 d), guests enjoy spectacular views of old Cartagena, including the Iglesia de San Pedro Claver. This luxury hotel has seven spacious rooms and an "interactive" kitchen, where guests can participate in food preparation. Rooms are decorated with original artwork. Hotel LM is just around the corner from the Plaza de Santo Domingo.

Getsemaní
UNDER COP$70,000
Australian-run ★ **Mamallena** (Cl. de la Media Luna No. 10-47, tel. 5/670-0499, www.hostelmamallenacartagena.com, COP$35,000 dorm, COP$100,000 d) is a small, attitude-free, friendly place where guests linger over beers at the small bar in front. Air-conditioning is available 24 hours a day, and pancakes are served for breakfast. Tours to area attractions can be arranged. There's a resident dog, a cat, and a couple of tortoises.

Colorful and cheerful **Papaya** (Cl. del Pozo No. 28-36, tel. 5/643-7340, COP$40,000 dorm) only has dorm accommodations and is seconds away from the Plaza Trinidad scene.

Hotel Sofitel Legend Santa Clara

The Shangri-la of backpacker accommodations in Cartagena is the famous ★ **Media Luna Hostel** (Cl. de la Media Luna No. 10-46, tel. 5/664-3423, www.medialunahostel.com, COP$35,000 dorm, COP$120,000 d). Located on the edge of Getsemaní, it's a high-energy kind of place with multicultural socializing (and flirting) centered on the small pool in the courtyard. If you're looking to break out of your shell, this may be the place. It has a capacity of over 100 guests with just a couple of private rooms (book early for those). Note that the vast majority of rooms don't have air-conditioning, which may be a challenge for those unused to the Cartagena heat. The staff organizes lots of activities and bikes are available to rent. There's also an attached burrito stand. Then there's the bar: On Wednesday nights, show up around 9pm for their famous Visa por un Sueño party.

COP$70,000-200,000
★ **Casa Relax** (Calle del Pozo No. 25-105, cell tel. 310/443-1505, www.cartagenarelax.

com, COP$170,000 d) feels like a hostel for adults without the discomfort of dorm accommodations. Here you can make use of the kitchen, have a cocktail by the groovy pool, and socialize a bit. There are 12 rooms.

Low-key **Casa Villa Colonial** (Cl. de la Media Luna No. 10-89, tel. 5/664-5421, www.casavillacolonial.com.co, COP$185,000 d) is a midrange option for those interested in staying close to the Old City. The rooms are basic, with wood furniture and tiled floors. Its rooftop terrace has a pool.

COP$200,000-500,000

Style is the thing at ★ **Casa Lola** (Cl. del Guerrero No. 29-108, tel. 5/664-1538, www.casalola.com.co, COP$374,000 d), designed and managed by a Spanish couple who were some of the first hoteliers in Getsemaní. The hotel, spread over two buildings (one colonial and one Republican-era), has 10 rooms featuring furniture and art from all over the world. Its location near Café Havana means there may be street noise on weekend nights. Casa Lola also offers design-oriented apartments (US$250-450) for rent in the Centro that sleep 4-10 people.

Hotel Monterrey (Cra. 8B No. 25-100, tel. 5/650-3030, www.hotelmonterrey.com.co, COP$290,000) is a classic hotel with a huge rooftop terrace that houses a small pool, perfect for soaking up the views of the Old City. It's on a busy street across from the convention center, but traffic noise isn't an issue. Breakfast is served in a cute interior courtyard.

Bocagrande
UNDER COP$70,000

Relaxed **Hostal Las Velas** (Cl. 1A No. 1-52, cell tel. 300/831-0159, www.hostallasvelas.com, COP$35,000 dorm, COP$100,000 d) opened in 2015. Its location just steps from the beach draws travelers who can't get enough kitesurfing, surfing, and windsurfing. This medium-sized house has one dorm room with eight beds and two private rooms (one with an en suite bathroom). The rooms don't have much flair, but this is a friendly spot in an area not frequented by tourists.

COP$70,000-200,000

Small **Barahona 446** (Cra. 2 No. 4-46, tel. 5/665-6144, www.hotelesbarahona.com, COP$180,000 d) is a bargain spot in the middle of Bocagrande, about a five-minute walk from the beach. The rooms are decent, but don't expect a view. Light sleepers may want to use earplugs, as noise from common areas can be a nuisance.

COP$200,000-500,000

The old classic in town is the **Hotel Caribe** (Cra. 1 No. 2-87, tel. 5/650-1160, www.hotelcaribe.com, COP$480,000 d). These swanky digs, comprising three large buildings, are next to the beach, and they even have a beach club exclusively for guests. The nicest feature here is the garden complete with resident parrots and deer. The 360 medium-sized rooms have views of the sea or the garden. Most visitors enjoy lounging by the pools and drinking a fruity cocktail.

For a no-surprises brand-name hotel experience, the **Hilton Cartagena** (Av. Almirante Brion, tel. 5/665-0660, www.hilton.com, COP$460,000 d) won't fail you. It's at the tip of Bocagrande, isolated from the crowds, and has multiple pools and tennis courts as well as a gym. Rooms feature all-marble bathrooms. President Obama stayed here during the 2012 Summit of the Americas.

INFORMATION AND SERVICES
Tourist Information

In addition to locations at the airport and at the cruise ship terminal, there are city-run **tourist information kiosks** (no phone, 9am-noon and 1pm-6pm Mon.-Sat., 9am-5pm Sun.) near the Torre del Reloj and an air-conditioned main office in the historic **Casa de Marquez Plaza de la Aduana** (tel. 5/660-1583, 9am-noon and 1pm-6pm Mon.-Sat., 9am-5pm Sun.).

Emergency and Medical Services

In case of an emergency, call the **police** at 112. For medical emergencies, call an **ambulance** by dialing 125 or head to **Hospital Universitario** (Cl. 29 No. 50-50, tel. 5/669-7308, 24 hours daily).

Spanish-Language Courses

Cartagena offers many opportunities to take group and individual Spanish classes. Many hostels have local Spanish tutors or can recommend a school or private teacher.

You may want to try out a class before committing to several days' instruction. One recommended school is **Lengua Nativa Spanish School** (cell tel. 304/573-1027, individual class US$15). **Nueva Lengua** (Calle del Pozo No. 25-95, Getsemaní, tel. 5/660-1736) has a solid track record, with locations in various cities. A 15-hour week of classes costs US$200.

Centro Catalina (Cl. Siete Infantes No. 9-21, San Diego, cell tel. 310/761-2157, www. centrocatalina.com) offers small-group classes in a house in the San Diego district.

Volunteering

The **Fundación La Vecina** (La Boquilla, www.fundacionlavecina.com) helps low-income children living in La Boquilla. It was started by a Dutch woman, Nathalie Rietman. The foundation has short-term positions open during school vacations (January, July, and December), in addition to long-term (three months and up) opportunities.

The **Fundación Juan Felipe Gómez** (Cl. 31 No. 91-80, Ternera, tel. 5/661-0937, www. juanfe.org) is the brainchild of Catalina Escobar, a Colombian businesswoman who was nominated as CNN Hero of the Year in 2012 for her tireless efforts to help at-risk teenage mothers. Both short- and long-term volunteers are invited to share their skills with the young women at this impressive center. You can take a public bus or a taxi (20 minutes) from the Centro to the *fundación*.

Founded by Colombian pop singer Shakira in the late 1990s, the **Fundación Pies Descalzos** (Pie de la Popa, www.fundacionpiesdescalzos.com) builds schools, including the stunning Colegio Lomas del Peyé to the northeast of town, which it also operates. See their website for volunteer opportunities as well as fundraising needs.

Cartagena Paws (www.cartagenapaws. com) rescues abandoned dogs, and can always use kind dog walkers.

The **Fundación por la Educación Multidimensional** (FEM, Cl. del Quero No. 9-64, Centro, tel. 5/643-4185, www.femcolombia.org) strives to make an impact on budding entrepreneurs by pairing them with volunteers who have expertise in business, architecture, community development, and other vocations. FEM generally seeks longer commitments of multiple weeks from its volunteers, but some short-term opportunities are occasionally offered.

TRANSPORTATION
Getting There
AIR

Cartagena's **Aeropuerto Internacional Rafael Núñez** (CTG, tel. 5/656-9202, www. sacsa.com.co) is located to the east of the city, about a 12-minute cab ride from Cartagena. Taxis from the airport to the Old City are reliable and regulated. The current fixed rate is COP$15,000.

Delta (www.delta.com) is the latest U.S. carrier to launch nonstop service to Cartagena, offering flights from Atlanta. **JetBlue** (www.jetblue.com) and **Avianca** (www.avianca.com) operate flights between New York-JFK and Cartagena. Nonstop flights from Florida are offered by **Spirit Airlines** (www.spirit.com) via Fort Lauderdale; Avianca has a nonstop out of Miami. **Copa** (www.copaair.com) serves Cartagena from its hub in Panama City, Panama. Charter carrier **Air Transat** (www.airtransat.com) flies nonstop from Montreal to Cartagena from December to March.

The main national carriers, Avianca and **LATAM Airlines** (www.latam.com), operate many flights each day to Cartagena from various Colombian cities. **VivaColombia** (www.vivacolombia.co) often offers inexpensive fares between Cartagena and Medellín, Bogotá, Cali, and Pereira. **ADA** (www.ada-aero.com) serves the city with flights from Medellín, Montería, and Cúcuta. **EasyFly** (www.easyfly.com.co) has a nonstop from Bucaramanga.

BUS

Regular bus service connects Cartagena with all major and coastal cities. The **Terminal de Transportes** (Diag. 56 No. 57-236, tel. 5/663-0454) is a 20- to 30-minute cab ride from the Centro. Expect to pay about COP$20,000 for the trip.

The Terminal de Transportes offers bus service to Bogotá, Medellín, Cali, and other interior cities. However, if you are making your way along the coast, it's quicker and easier to get to Santa Marta or Barranquilla by taking one of the fast *busetas* (large vans) that regularly serve the main Caribbean cities. **Marsol** (Cra. 2A No. 43-11, tel. 5/656-0302, www.transportesmarsol.net) and **Berlinas** (Cl. 46C No. 3-80, tel. 5/693-0006, www.berlinasdelfonce.com) are the top choices and have pickup sites near the Centro in the Marbella neighborhood. Marsol even offers door-to-door service (*puerta-puerta*). The last *buseta* leaves Cartagena around 8pm. It's a decent option to travel after dark—the roads are good and it's safe—as the roadside scenery isn't that impressive, there's less traffic, and you may as well spend the remaining daylight hours enjoying a mojito in the Old City.

CRUISE SHIPS

Cartagena is a major port of call for cruise ships from across the globe, bringing around 350,000 visitors each year. Entry into the Bahía de Cartagena is a dramatic one, as the ships pass through ruins of old Spanish forts.

The city is a living museum, and the best way to get to know it is by walking its narrow streets, getting lost, and finding one's way

again. Be sure to bring some sun protection and water—the sticky midday heat can be sizzling. If you take an organized walking tour, you will likely be hounded by hawkers selling Colombian souvenirs.

Take a cab from the port to the Torre del Reloj, one of the main entrances to historic Cartagena. Pop into a museum and a grandiose colonial-era church, enjoy a delicious meal at one of the many fine restaurants, and cap it all off with a walk and a drink on the *muralla* (wall) facing the Caribbean Sea.

CAR OR MOTORCYCLE

Consider renting a car or motorcycle for overland travel. Hertz and National, as well as local companies, have pickup and drop-off locations at the airport. This could be a good option if you are planning on taking your time getting to know the Caribbean coast or are continuing onward to Colombia's interior. The main road to Barranquilla is mostly four lanes, but shrinks to two lanes farther on to Santa Marta.

Getting Around

Walking is the best way to get around the Old City, Getsemaní, and Bocagrande. Thanks to its narrow streets, scarce parking, and heavy traffic, Cartagena is not a particularly car-friendly city.

TAXIS

For short hops between neighborhoods, cabs are quick and easy. Taxis here do not have meters, so it's possible you won't get the local rate. Before hopping in a cab, ask a local or two the standard rate. From the Old City to Bocagrande, expect to pay around COP$6,000. A ride to the airport will cost COP$15,000, and a trip to the beaches at Las Americas will be COP$12,000. Tipping is not customary. Ride-sharing services such as **Uber** (www.uber.com), **Easy Taxi** (www.easytaxi.com), and **Tappsi** (www.tappsi.co) have arrived in Cartagena, which may help minimize anxiety or confusion about taxi fares.

BUSES

It may seem overwhelming at first, but taking a public bus is a cheap way to get around. To hop on a bus to Bocagrande from the Old City, walk down to Avenida Santander along the sea and flag down just about any bus you see (or look for a sign in the window that reads "Bocagrande"). The ride will set you back COP$1,800. There are a few options for getting off: As you board, tell the bus driver where you would like to be let off; belt out *"¡Parada!"* as you approach your destination; or discreetly exit behind someone else. On the main road (Carrera 11) just to the east of the walls, facing the Monumento India Catalina, is a nonstop parade of buses loading and unloading. From here you can get to the Castillo de San Felipe, the Mercado de Bazurto, or the bus terminal, for the same low price of COP$1,800.

TRANSCARIBE

Launched in December 2015 after more than 10 years in development, the **TransCaribe bus system** (www.transcaribe.gov.co) employs organized stations (rather than standard bus stops). It caters mostly to residents but may be useful for visitors interested in traveling out of the Centro to the city's southern neighborhoods. Some of the major stops are at Muelle de la Bodeguita, La Matuna, Chambacú (Castillo de San Felipe), and Mercado de Bazurto.

The bright-orange bus stations are located along Avenida Venezuela, a thoroughfare between the Centro and La Matuna that extends into the southern neighborhoods. Expect to pay under COP$2,000 for the comfortable ride.

BOCACHICA

Bocachica, which means "Small Mouth," is one of two entrances to the Bahía de Cartagena. It is at the southern end of the bay. The other, much wider entrance is Bocagrande ("Big Mouth"), more familiar as the peninsula southwest of the Old City. In 1640, when three galleons sank at Bocagrande and blocked that passage, the Spaniards decided to fortify the more easily defensible Bocachica.

The **Fuerte de San Fernando** (Isla Tierrabomba, tel. 5/655-0211 or 5/655-0277, www.patrimoniodecartagena.com, 8am-6pm daily, COP$9,000) and **Batería de San José** are two forts at either side of Bocachica, the first line of defense. The Fuerte de San Fernando, at the southern tip of the island of Tierrabomba, is a particularly impressive example of 18th-century military architecture. It is very well preserved and you can still see the barracks, kitchen, storerooms, and chapel enclosed within the massive fortifications. The low-lying Batería de San José is a much more modest affair, and can be visited with a ticket for Fuerte de San Fernando.

The only way to get to Bocachica is by one of the *lanchas* (fast boats, COP$7,000) that depart from the Muelle de los Pegasos, the tourist port in Cartagena near the Torre del Reloj. The 45-minute trip through the bay provides interesting views of Cartagena and the port. The waits between departures can be long, so bring sunscreen and something to do.

In Bocachica, there are a few small, informal restaurants where you can eat fried fish, coconut rice, and *patacones* (fried plantains) and drink a cold beer.

★ PLAYA BLANCA AND ISLAS DEL ROSARIO

South of Cartagena is the elongated island of **Barú,** which is separated from the mainland by the Canal del Dique, an artificial waterway built in 1650 to connect Cartagena with the Río Magdalena. On Barú lies **Playa Blanca,** a Caribbean paradise of idyllic, white-sand beaches bordering warm blue waters. West of Barú and about 25 kilometers (15.5 miles) southwest of Cartagena is the archipelago **Islas del Rosario,** part of the much larger **Parque Nacional Natural Corales del Rosario y San Bernardo.** On Barú and the Islas del Rosario, traditional Afro-Colombian communities with rich cultural heritages share space with the vacation houses of Colombia's rich and famous.

Isla Grande

trip (US$70) features a day at a fab beach resort, lunch, and snorkeling or kayaking, and includes hotel pickup and drop-off. For an unforgettable time, upgrade to the Island Hopping in Style tour, which offers the same activities—from your own personal yacht. This option ranges US$600-6,000, depending on the yacht.

If you are willing to pay more, there are more upscale day tours to the *islas*. One is a day trip to the luxurious beachside **Hotel San Pedro de Majagua** (Cartagena office: Cl. del Torno No. 39-114, tel. 5/650-4464, www.hotelmajagua.com, day trip COP$173,000) on Isla Grande. They take care of transportation from the Muelle de Marina Santa Cruz in Manga (boats leave at 9am, return at 3:30pm daily). The price also includes a seafood lunch and a visit to an aquarium. For an unforgettable sunset experience, try the Neon Sunset Tour on a paddleboard with LED lights, perfect for illuminating bioluminescent plankton. You can also spend the night at this comfortable hotel (COP$350,000 d including transportation).

Food

To enjoy fresh seafood and fabulous cocktails under the sun, **Pescador de Colores** (Km. 3 past Pasacaballos Bridge, Barú, cell tel. 315/394-2374, www.elpescadordecolores.com, 11:30am-5:30pm Wed.-Mon., COP$40,000) is the place to be on Barú. This swanky beach lounge specializes in Euro-Caribbean cuisine, but the biggest attraction is hanging out on a beach bed.

Accommodations

Best known for its location in Cartagena, **Media Luna Hostel** (Playa Bobo, Isla Barú, cell tel. 313/536-3146, www.medialunahostel.com, COP$50,000 dorm) also owns a chill beachside hostel in Barú, which consists of five two-story thatched-roof *cabañas*. Each *cabaña* has four beds and a bathroom and can be either a private room or a dorm, depending on your preference. They will take care

Barú is home to several beautiful beaches. With the exception of Playa Blanca, most of these are inaccessible to the general public. The 25 small coral islands of the Islas del Rosario are a marine wonderland. The once-spectacular coral reefs off of Barú and surrounding the archipelago have been badly damaged by the increased flow of freshwater from the Canal del Dique, which has been dredged in recent years.

Quiet **Isla Grande** in the Islas del Rosario has a handful of hotels and a community group, Nativos Activos, run by Afro-Colombian locals who rent bikes and equipment and can organize tours and other activities. They are always available at Hotel San Pedro de Majagua. Expect to pay COP$20,000 for a bike rental.

This Is Cartagena (Cl. Sargento Mayor No. 6-107, Oficina 104, Centro, tel. 5/660-9128, www.ticartagena.com, 9am-6pm Mon.-Fri.), based out of the Old City, offers fantastic tours to the islands. A standard day of round-trip transportation (COP$60,000) from their Getsemaní location, where pickup is at 9am daily.

Sport Barú (Ensenada del Cholón, Km. 26, Isla Barú, cell tel. 314/506-6520, www. sportbaru.com, COP$800,000 d) is a relaxing beach resort nestled among the mangroves on the quiet side of the Cholón lagoon. There are three cabins with multiple rooms each for rent; the older ones with thatched roofs have more charm. All of them are comfortable, but the Wi-Fi is iffy. A visit here usually includes lounging on the beach in front of the hotel or at Playa Azul, a quick boat ride away. For those staying more than a day, the food can get a little repetitive (lots of fried fish and coconut rice). You can also take a day trip here (COP$145,000), which includes transportation, lunch, and an excursion to Playa Azul.

In a quiet section on the north side of Isla Grande, **Eco Hotel Las Palmeras** (Isla Grande, cell tel. 314/584-7358, COP$75,000 d) is a laid-back and no-frills beachside hostel that has lots of charm, thanks mainly to the nice people who run it. Don't expect luxury here: A shower requires scooping water from a bucket with a coconut shell.

MOMPOX

Mompox was founded in 1540 on the eastern edge of a large island between two branches of the Río Magdalena (the Brazo de Loba and the Brazo Mompox). This lovely town was an opulent center of trade, connecting the interior of the country with Cartagena during the colonial era. But then the mighty river changed its course in the late 18th century and Mompox's importance steadily declined, never to return.

Mompox is what Cartagena looked like before it became a tourist destination, and it's hard to deny the melancholic charm this oppressively hot town retains even today. The attraction here is strolling the wide streets, admiring the whitewashed houses decorated with intricate iron latticework, and watching the river flow by. In 1995, due to its architectural importance, the town was declared a UNESCO World Heritage Site.

The town is spread out along the muddy Magdalena, and the river is its raison d'être. It does not have a central plaza, but rather three squares, each with a church, facing the river. It is believed that each of these squares is on the location of a former indigenous settlement. From south to north, they are **Plaza de Santa Bárbara, Plaza de la Concepción** (also known as Plaza Mayor), and **Plaza de San Francisco.** Three main streets run parallel to the river: Calle de la Albarrada (which corresponds to Carrera 1) facing the river; the Calle Real del Medio, Mompox's main street, one block west of the river; and the Calle de Atrás (literally, the "street behind").

Sights

There are two historic churches worth visiting in Mompox. The riverfront **Iglesia de Santa Bárbara** (Cl. de la Albarrada and Cl. 14, mass 6pm Fri.-Sun.) was built in 1630. The facade is painted a striking yellow, with colorful floral decorations. It has an unusual baroque octagonal tower with a balcony wrapping around it. Inside is a magnificent gilded altar. The church extends from the Plaza de Santa Bárbara to the Plaza de San Francisco. The second noteworthy church is the **Iglesia de San Agustín** (Cl. Real del Medio and Cl. de la Albarrada, mass 4pm daily), which houses the Santo Sepulcro, a gilded reproduction of Christ's tomb. The churches are only open during mass times. Guests of the **Casa Amarilla** (Cl. de la Albarrada No. 13-59, tel. 5/685-6326 or cell tel. 301/362-7065, www. lacasaamaraillamompos.com) can make a request with the hotel to take a quick peek inside the churches.

The only museum in town, which keeps irregular hours, is the **Museo Cultural de Arte Religioso** (Cl. Real del Medio No. 17-07, tel. 5/685-6074, 9am-noon and 3pm-4pm Tues. and Thurs.-Fri., 9am-noon Sat.-Mon., COP$2,000). It's home to displays of gold- and silverwork from the colonial era. Mompox silver- and goldsmiths made a name for themselves with their intricate filigree jewelry.

Another interesting sight is the **Piedra de Bolívar** (Cl. de la Albarrada and Cl. 17), a river-facing monument with a stone slab that lists all the visits Simón Bolívar made to Mompox.

Mompox's atmospheric 19th-century **Cementerio Municipal** (Cl. 18 and Cra. 4, 8am-noon and 2pm-5pm daily, free) is well worth a detour. The cemetery houses the tombs of Afro-Colombian poet Candelario Obeso and General Hermógenes Maza, who fought beside Simón Bolívar. The cemetery is also known for the resident cats that frolic among the graves.

Festivals and Events

Semana Santa (Holy Week), which occurs during late March or April, is the most important celebration in Mompox. Visitors from all over Colombia converge on the town to watch its religious processions and attend concerts. You'll have to book months in advance to get a hotel room during that time.

The **Mompox Jazz Festival** (early Oct.) has become the biggest show in town, with performances by international artists such as Tito Puente selling out far in advance.

Shopping

Mompox is known in Colombia for its intricate gold filigree jewelry. Look for the **Joyería Filimompox** (Cl. 23 No. 3-23, tel. 5/685-6604 or cell tel. 313/548-2322, hours vary), where the staff will explain their craft to you during your visit to their workshop. They accept credit cards.

At the **Escuela Taller de Artes y Oficios de Santa Cruz de Mompox** (Claustro de San Agustín, Cl. 16 No. 1A-57, tel. 5/685-5204, hours vary), young people learn traditional handicrafts. Visitors are welcome to drop by and watch these artisans at work. Inside, there's an interior courtyard, an inviting place to linger for a while.

Food and Accommodations

During low season, restaurant options in Mompox become scarce. With sufficient notice, most hotels will prepare meals. Belgian-run **El Fuerte** (Cra. 1 No. 12-163, tel. 5/685-6762, 6pm-9pm Fri.-Sun., COP$20,000) is the best dining option in town. It's mostly Italian cuisine, and the pizza and pasta are done right. The **Comedor Costeño** (Cl. de la Albarrada No. 18-45, tel. 5/685-5263, 7am-5pm daily, COP$12,000) serves *comida típica* (Colombian fare) overlooking the Magdalena.

On the Plaza de la Concepción, **Khalilieh** (Cra. 1A No. 17A-54, tel. 5/685-5978,

Iglesia de Santa Bárbara

noon-9pm daily, COP$14,000) serves Lebanese food and grilled meats.

During high season, inquire about the **planchon sunset cruise** (three hours, COP$30,000), where passengers enjoy a drink on the river, floating on a wooden barge. For more information, contact Carmen Garrido (cell tel. 310/606-4632) or ask at the Casa Amarilla.

Bioma Hotel Boutique (Cl. Real del Medio No. 18-59, tel. 5/685-6733 or cell tel. 315/308-6365, www.bioma.co, COP$190,000 d) may be one of the most comfortable options in town, as it offers 12 air-conditioned rooms, a dipping pool, and good food.

The ★ **Casa Amarilla** (Cl. de la Albarrada No. 13-59, tel. 5/685-6326 or cell tel. 301/362-7065, www.lacasaamarillamompos.com, COP$25,000 dorm, COP$100,000 d), owned by a British travel writer, is another excellent choice, with accommodations for backpackers as well as private rooms for those seeking more comfort. After a careful restoration, the Casa Amarilla added a luxurious colonial house, the Casa de la Concepción (COP$1,500,000), which has four bedrooms and two interior patio gardens; the second-story balcony provides a lovely view to the plaza below. Best of all, it has a pool.

Casa España (Cl. Real del Medio, tel. 5/685-5373 or cell tel. 313/513-6946, www.hotelcasaespanamompox.com, COP$180,000 d) is a guesthouse with 16 basic rooms, most with two double beds, and an interior courtyard with plenty of rocking chairs in which to relax.

Getting There

Most visitors arrive in Mompox from Cartagena, and there are several ways to make the journey.

There is one direct bus that leaves from Cartagena's **Terminal de Transportes** (Diag. 57 No. 24-236, tel. 5/663-0454) at 6:30am daily. The ride takes eight hours and costs COP$50,000. More comfortable is a door-to-door service with a company like **Toto Express** (cell tel. 310/707-0838, COP$75,000), which takes six hours.

The fastest way involves a van, a boat, and a taxi: Take a van (COP$40,000 pp, 3.5 hours) from outside the Terminal de Transportes in Cartagena to Magangué, a port on the Magdalena; there hop on a *chalupa* boat that will take you to a spot called Bodega de Mompox (COP$7,000, 30 min.); and from there take a shared taxi or *mototaxi* (COP$15,000, 30 min.) to Mompox.

Santa Marta and Vicinity

With a charming historic district, great hotel and restaurant options, and proximity to popular natural attractions, Santa Marta is a major tourist destination. Steamy Barranquilla lies halfway between Cartagena and Santa Marta, and is home to the world-renowned Carnaval de Barranquilla.

BARRANQUILLA

Colombia's fourth-largest city (pop. 1.6 million) is known for its busy port and for the bacchanalian Carnaval de Barranquilla, designated a World Masterpiece of the Oral and Intangible Heritage of Humanity by UNESCO. This, the most famous celebration in Colombia, is a time of music, dancing in the streets, and revelry. Usually occurring in February, it lasts only about four days, but the city pulses with anticipation for days (if not weeks) in advance.

During the rest of the year there's not a whole lot to lure the visitor to Barranquilla. It is not a colonial city, but vestiges of its early-20th-century importance can be seen in its El Prado district.

Barranquilla offers a handful of attractions, including the Museo del Caribe and the quirky Bocas de Ceniza, a jut of land

Barranquilla

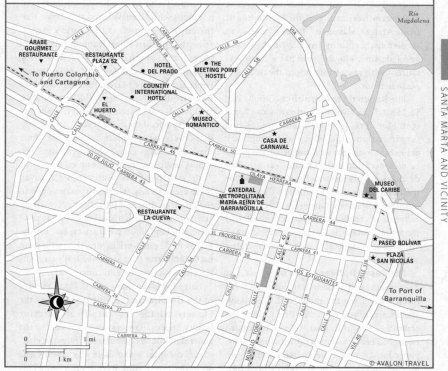

that divides the Río Magdalena from the Caribbean Sea. A wealth of comfortable hotel and restaurant options may be the trick for weary travelers returning from the jungle or beach.

Sights

Two museums lend insight into Barranquilla's people and culture. The first, **Casa del Carnaval** (Cra. 54 No. 49B-39, tel. 5/319-7616, 9am-5pm Mon.-Sat., COP$5,000), is Carnaval headquarters, and its Sala Carnaval Elsa Caridi provides an interactive introduction to the annual event. After a visit here, you'll come to understand the many different components of the celebration, like the different musical styles: *cumbia, mapalé, chandé,* and *son.* While at first blush it may seem that the

Carnaval de Barranquilla is just a big party, there is more to it than meets the eye. Behind every costume, parade, and dance there is a story. Knowledgeable guides will share this story and their genuine enthusiasm for the festival at this well-done museum.

The other top museum is **Museo del Caribe** (Cl. 36 No. 46-66, tel. 5/372-0582, www.culturacaribe.org, 8am-5pm Mon.-Fri., 9am-6pm Sat.-Sun., COP$13,000), one of the finest museums in the country, with a focus on Costeño (Caribbean coast) culture. There is a room dedicated to Gabriel García Márquez, in which characters from the author's books come alive; the exhibit may be hard to follow if your Spanish is less than fluent. There are slide shows on Caribbean ecosystems and exhibits on the people of the

Caribbean, including a fascinating video series on the region's many different indigenous tribes. Of particular interest is a room that examines immigration to the coast, from African slaves to "Turcos," meaning those mostly coming from Syria, Lebanon, and Palestine. The museum has a small restaurant with reasonably priced meals on the plaza in front.

The **Banco de la República** (Cra. 54 No. 52-258, tel. 5/371-6690, 8am-noon and 2pm-6pm Mon.-Fri., free) is the address for culture in Barranquilla. Along with temporary art exhibitions, classical music concerts are held on occasion at the on-site Teatro Amira de la Rosa. This modern theater is noted for the fantastic artwork by modern Colombian painter Alejandro Obregón (1920-1992); called *Se va el caimán*, it's a large and colorful piece that evokes the Caribbean legend of the alligator-man. Check in with a staff member to see it.

The **Paseo Bolívar** (Cl. 34 between Cras. 38-45) is the gritty main drag downtown. It's lined with discount shops and used-book stands, where you can often find Colombian classics—even in English—if you look hard enough. There's always a crowd at the newspaper kiosks, which seems like a scene from a different era. On the restored **Plaza San Nicolás** (between Clls. 32-33 and Cras. 41-42) is the neo-gothic **Iglesia San Nicolás Tolentino** (Cra. 42 No. 33-45, tel. 5/340-2247), which took about 300 years to build. It's usually open, with mass occurring several times a week. Be wary of pickpockets in this part of the city.

Not about roses and chocolates, the **Museo Romántico** (Cra. 54 No. 59-199, tel. 5/344-4591, 9am-11:30am and 2:30pm-5:30pm Mon.-Fri., COP$5,000) is really a history museum of Barranquilla with artwork, old Carnaval costumes, missives signed by Simón Bolívar, and a typewriter used by Gabriel García Márquez. The majestic building, in the posh El Prado neighborhood, was once the home of Jewish immigrants who arrived in Colombia at the turn of the 20th century.

Festivals and Events
★ CARNAVAL DE BARRANQUILLA

For most Colombians, Barranquilla is synonymous with Carnaval, and they boast that the city's celebration is the world's biggest after that held in Rio (although folks from New Orleans may balk at this claim). During the four days prior to Ash Wednesday, in late February or early March, the **Carnaval de Barranquilla** (www.carnavaldebarranquilla. org) is full of Costeño pageantry, with costumes, music, dancing, parades, and drinking. This is the only place in Colombia where the bacchanal is fully celebrated, although some Caribbean cities make an effort.

Prior to the official festivities of Carnaval, there are *verbenas,* which are parties open to the public in different parts of the city. To get an invite to one, ask a local or two. Carnaval officially begins on a Saturday, but on the Friday night one week before, the celebration **La Guacherna** (Cra. 44 and Cl. 70) awakens the city with parades and concerts.

Saturday is the main event. That's the day of the **Batalla de las Flores** (Battle of the Flowers) parade. It's when floats carrying beauty queens, dancers, and members of the general public in *comparsas* (groups) in elaborate costumes make their way down Calle 40 under the sizzling Barranquilla sun. This event dates back to 1903, when it began as a celebration of the end of the Guerra de los Mil Días (Thousand Days' War). Participation in the parades is serious business here, involving planning, practice, money, and, sometimes, connections. However, there is one *comparsa* during the Batalla de las Flores in which just about anyone can participate, and it's one of the most popular: the "Disfrázate como Quieras"—go however you like. Anybody in a costume, from the silly to the sexy, can participate. Check out the Disfrázate como Quieras Facebook page to find out how you can join in the fun.

On Sunday, during the **Gran Parada de Tradición y Folclor,** groups of dancers perform on Calle 40 to the hypnotic music of Carnaval—a mix of African, indigenous, and European sounds. On Monday there is another parade, the **Gran Parada de Comparsas**. Starting in the late afternoon, a massive concert attracts more than 30 musical groups, who compete for the award of Congo del Oro.

On Tuesday, after four days of music and dancing, things wind down with the parade **Joselito Se Va con las Cenizas** (Cra. 54 and Cl. 59). This is when Joselito, a fictitious Barranquillero, "dies" after four days of rumba, and his "body" is carried through the streets as bystanders weep. Joselito is sometimes played by an actor, and other times is a mannequin.

Watch all the action of the parades from the *palcos* (bleachers) that line Calle 40, the only way to spectate. Keep in mind that the parades take place in the middle of the day, meaning lots of sun and heat. Tickets (COP$100,000-300,000) for the *palcos* can be ordered online at **Tu Boleta** (www.tuboleta. com), or your hotel may be able to assist in getting you a ticket.

With regard to Carnaval, it's said that *"Quien lo vive es quien lo goza"* ("Whoever experiences it is who enjoys it"). But to do that, it's crucial to get hotel and flight reservations early—ideally around six months in advance.

Food

Regional standouts include *butifara soledena*, which is a beef and pork sausage normally served with *bollo de yuca*, a boiled ball of yuca. Another meaty dish, popular during Carnaval, is *sancocho de guandú*, a stew of beef, yuca, yams, plantains, and vegetables. For breakfast on the go, Barranquilleros grab an *arepa de huevo* (an egg in a cornmeal arepa that is then fried). Many restaurants are clustered around Carrera 52 between Calles 70-100.

The ★ **Restaurante Bar La Cueva** (Cra. 43 No. 59-03, tel. 5/340-9813, www. fundacionlacueva.org, noon-3pm and 6pm-10pm Mon.-Thurs., noon-3pm and 6pm-1am Fri.-Sat., COP$30,000) has history and lots of character. It was the hangout of Gabriel García Márquez and artists such as Alejandro Obregón in the 1960s. Elephant tracks, memorabilia, and photos make it seem like a museum, but it is still a restaurant, and a popular one at that. The specialty here is seafood. There's live music on Friday and Saturday evenings. Be sure to check out the Obregón work *La Mulata de Obregón,* complete with a bullet hole thanks to a drunken friend of the artist. Reservations are essential on weekend evenings.

Joselito Se Va con las Cenizas, one of the closing celebrations of Carnaval

El Huerto (Cra. 52 No. 70-139, tel. 5/368-7171, 8am-7:30pm Mon.-Sat., 10am-3pm Sun., COP$12,000) offers an inexpensive and healthy all-vegetarian break from the norm with a set lunch menu every day. There is also a small store that sells baked goods and health food products such as quinoa and granola.

Accommodations

Because of its status as a business destination, Barranquilla has a number of hotel options, although hostels are almost nonexistent. Rates at chain hotels can significantly drop on weekends. During Carnaval, prices sky-rocket and hotels sell out months in advance.

Friendly and low-key, the **Meeting Point Hostel** (Cra. 61 No. 68-100, tel. 5/318-2599, www.themeetingpoint.hostel.com, COP$30,000 dorm, COP$100,000 d) is the only hostel catering to international back-packers in Barranquilla. This Italian-run spot has a pizzeria out front. The neighborhood is quiet and green, about a 15-minute walk from El Prado. You may suffer if you don't splurge on a room with air-conditioning.

Country International Hotel (Cra. 52 No. 75-30, tel. 5/369-5900, ext. 120, www.countryinthotel.com, COP$238,000 d) has a nice pool and comfortable rooms. It's located in a good area.

★ **Hotel Estelar Alto Prado** (Cl. 76 No. 56-29, tel. 5/336-0000, COP$292,000 d) is a modern, comfortable, and stylish address in Barranquilla. This is where the Argentinian national soccer club stays when they face off against Colombia.

Transportation
GETTING THERE

Barranquilla's **Aeropuerto Internacional Ernesto Cortissoz** (Soledad, www.baq.aero) offers excellent connections with all major cities in Colombia and a handful of nonstop international flights as well. The airport is south of the city in Soledad. Taxi rides cost about COP$20,000 from the airport to downtown.

Avianca (www.avianca.com) flies nonstop to Barranquilla from Miami, Bogotá, Cali, and Medellín. **LATAM Airlines** (www.latam.com) has flights from Bogotá. On **Copa** (www.copaair.com) there are nonstop flights from San Andrés and Panama City.

VivaColombia (www.vivacolombia.co) flies from Medellín, **EasyFly** (www.easyfly.com.co) has nonstop flights from Bucaramanga and Valledupar, and **ADA** (www.ada-aero.com) flies from Montería.

There is regular bus service to all points in Colombia from the **Terminal Metropolitana de Transportes** (Km. 1.5 Prolongación Cl. Murillo, tel. 5/323-0034, www.ttbag.com.co), which is about 15 minutes from downtown. If you're traveling on to Santa Marta or Cartagena it's more convenient to take a fast van service directly from the city. From their terminals in town, both **Berlinastur** (Cl. 96 No. 46-36, tel. 5/385-0030, www.berlinastur.com) and **MarSol** (Cl. 93 No. 47-13 Local 4, tel. 5/357-6209) make the daily journey to Santa Marta (2 hours, COP$20,000) and Cartagena (1.5 hours, COP$20,000) from early in the morning until around 6pm. They are fast and reliable and usually take credit cards. There's no need to reserve a seat.

GETTING AROUND

Barranquilla is not a pedestrian-friendly city. Unmetered taxi cabs are the most convenient way to get around. Ask a local how much you should expect to pay before stepping into a cab. You should never pay more than COP$13,000 to get to in-town locations. Colombian apps such as Tappsi and Easy Taxi make getting a cab easier, and Uber is also available.

Transmetro (www.transmetro.gov.co, 5am-11pm Mon.-Sat., 6am-10pm Sun., COP$1,600) is the rapid bus system, which runs along two main avenues: Avenida Murillo (also known as Calle 45) and Avenida Olaya Herrera (also known as Carrera 46). There are stations in front of the Museo del Caribe, the cathedral, and the stadium.

Santa Marta

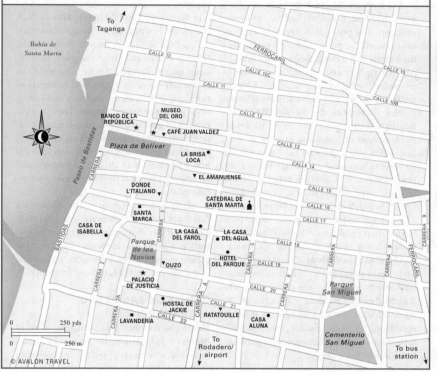

Bahía de
Santa Marta

To
Taganga

CALLE 10
FERROCARRIL
CALLE 10
CALLE 10C
CALLE 11
CALLE 10B
CALLE 12
MUSEO
DEL ORO
BANCO DE LA
REPÚBLICA
★ ● CAFÉ JUAN VALDEZ
CALLE 13
Plaza de Bolívar
LA BRISA ●
LOCA
CALLE 14
▼ EL AMANUENSE
CALLE 15
DONDE
L'ITALIANO ▼
CATEDRAL DE
SANTA MARTA
CALLE 16
SANTA
MARCA
CALLE 17
CASA DE
ISABELLA
LA CASA
DEL FAROL
LA CASA
● DEL AGUA
CALLE 18
Parque
de los
Novios
HOTEL
DEL PARQUE
CALLE 19
★
OUZO
PALACIO
DE JUSTICIA
CALLE 20
Parque
San Miguel
HOSTAL DE
JACKIE
CALLE 21
RATATOUILLE ▼
CASA
ALUNA
LAVANDERÍA
CALLE 22
Cementerio
San Miguel

Paseo de Bastidas
BASTIDAS
CARRERA 1
CARRERA 2
CARRERA 2A
CARRERA 3
CARRERA 4
CARRERA 5
CARRERA 6
CARRERA 7
CARRERA 8
CARRERA 9
FERROCARRIL

0   250 yds
0   250 m

To
Rodadero/
airport

To bus
station

© AVALON TRAVEL

SANTA MARTA

Santa Marta is the logical launching pad for visits to the nearby Sierra Nevada—including Parque Nacional Natural Tayrona and Ciudad Perdida—and is a convenient stop on the way to the Alta Guajira.

The **Centro Histórico** extends from the busy Calle 22 (Avenida Santa Rita) in the west to the Avenida del Ferrocarril in the east, toward the seaside village of Taganga. The southern border ranges from the same Avenida del Ferrocarril in the south to the *malecón* (Carrera 1C/Avenida Rodrigo de Bastidas) in the north. The focal point of the Centro is the Parque de los Novios (Carreras 2A-3 and Calles 19-20). This is a lovely park with pedestrian streets (Calle 19 and Carrera

3) intersecting on its eastern side. Most sights are within a smaller range of streets from Carrera 5 to the water and between Calles 20 and 14.

The **Rodadero district,** with condos and hotels lining the beach, is southwest of downtown Santa Marta, just around the bend on the main highway. Local buses continuously ply the stretch between the Centro Histórico and Rodadero.

SIGHTS
CENTRO HISTÓRICO

The compact Centro Histórico in Santa Marta feels like a living museum, with its mix of colonial and Republican-era architecture. All major sights, save for the Quinta de San Pedro

Alejandrino, are located here and can be visited in one day.

The **Parque de los Novios** (Cras. 2A-3 and Clls. 19-20) is a symbol of the city's rejuvenation. The pedestrian streets (except for one) around the park make a pleasant place for a stroll and a meal. Restaurants line the park's periphery and on the Calle 20 side of the park is the grandiose neoclassical **Palacio de Justicia,** Santa Marta's main courthouse.

The **Catedral de Santa Marta** or **Basílica Menor** (Cr. 5 No. 16-30, tel. 5/421-2434, masses at noon and 6pm Mon.-Sat., 7am, 10am, noon, and 6pm Sun.) took around 30 years to build and was completed in 1794, toward the end of Spanish reign in Nueva Granada, as colonial Colombia was called. It is one of the oldest cathedrals in Latin America. The city's founder, Rodrigo de Bastidas, is buried there, and Simón Bolívar laid in rest there before his body was moved to Caracas.

The **Plaza de Bolívar** (Cras. 1-2 and Clls. 14-15) has a statue of Simón Bolívar on horseback, ready to destroy the oppressors. The **Banco de la República** (Cl. 14 No. 1C-37, tel. 5/421-0251, www.banrep.gov.co, 8:30am-6pm Mon.-Fri., 9am-1pm Sat., free) often has art exhibits and also has a peaceful public library on the third floor.

The **Museo del Oro Tairona** (Cl. 14 No. 1C-37, tel. 5/421-0251, www.banrepcultural. org, 9am-5pm Tues.-Sat., 10am-3pm Sat., free) is in the historic **Casa de la Aduana,** perhaps the oldest customs house in the Americas, dating back to 1531. A smaller version of the famous Museo del Oro in Bogotá, this focuses on the Tayrona people, who were the native settlers of the region and forebears of the Kogis, Arhuacos, Kankuamos, and Wiwas who live in the Sierra Nevada. There are ceramic and gold artifacts on display, and a description of the Ciudad Perdida archaeological site. A visit to this museum may enrich your hike up to the Lost City, as you'll have a better understanding of the people who once inhabited it.

Along the waterfront is the **Paseo de Bastidas** (Cra. 1) boardwalk. A sunset walk along the pier that extends from the boardwalk is a Santa Marta ritual. Check out the great views of the port, the sailboats moored at the Marina Santa Marta, and Isla Morro.

QUINTA DE SAN PEDRO ALEJANDRINO

Simón José Antonio de la Santísima Trinidad Bolívar y Palacios, better known as Simón Bolívar, was instrumental in bringing

Museo del Oro Tairona

independence to several countries in Latin America, including Venezuela, Colombia, Ecuador, Peru, and Bolivia. While awaiting exile to Europe, he passed away at the age of 47 in Santa Marta at the **Quinta de San Pedro Alejandrino** (Mamatoco, tel. 5/433-2995, www.museobolivariano.org.co, 9am-4:30pm daily, COP$21,000). This country estate is now a museum where visitors can see the bedroom in which Bolívar died in 1830. A modern wing houses the Museo Bolivariano de Arte Contemporáneo.

Young guides will offer to take you around the complex for about COP$2,000, but you're probably better off on your own. The *quinta* is set in a manicured botanical garden. There is a small snack bar and gift shop on the grounds.

Shopping

For funky gifts made by local designers, such as T-shirts and art, check out the small shop **Santa Marca** (Cl. 17 No. 2-45, tel. 5/423-5862, 10am-7pm Mon.-Sat.).

El Amanuense (Cl. 16 No. 3-28, tel. 5/420-0993, Mon.-Sat. 9am-5pm) is a tiny bookshop that carries work mostly by Colombian authors. There's also a small café inside.

Go back in time in **Vejeces Casa de Antiguedades** (Cl. 18 No. 7A-64, cell tel. 300/305-3324, 9am-5pm Mon.-Sat.), a quaint Centro shop jam-packed with interesting stuff. While there are some pre-Columbian pieces for sale, note that it is illegal to take these abroad.

El Tiburón (Cra. 2 18-09, tel. 5/421-4301, 10am-6pm daily) makes shocking use of every square inch of its space in the Centro to display Colombian handicrafts and kitsch, and by no small miracle, shop employees seem to know where everything is.

Recreation

There are some terrific diving spots quite close to Santa Marta. **Santa Marta Dive and Adventure** (Cl. 17 No. 2-43, tel. 5/422-6370, www.santamartadiveandadventure.com) is a reputable agency that offers dive tours and courses with some English-speaking instructors. Dive sites are off the coast of Parque Nacional Natural Tayrona, at two shipwrecks near Santa Marta, and offshore from the town of Taganga. A three-day course goes for COP$650,000, a half-day course is COP$200,000, and a diving excursion for certified divers costs COP$160,000.

Food

Most of Santa Marta's finest restaurants can be found in the Centro Histórico, although the Rodadero area is known for its seafood joints. For a delightful ambience, seek out restaurants on pedestrianized streets in the Centro Histórico, such as Carretera 3 between Calles 15 and 16 (Callejón del Correo), Calle 19 between Carreteras 3 and 5, and on the Parque de los Novios.

CENTRO HISTÓRICO

One of the first restaurants to populate Callejón del Correo was ★ **La Casona/ Donde L'Italiano** (Cra. 3 No. 16-26, cell tel. 316/429-1131, 5pm-10pm Mon.-Sat., COP$30,000), a cheerful restaurant where even the standard pasta arrabiata tastes exquisite. The diverse menu offers Caribbean cuisine (with an Italian flair) in addition to traditional pasta dishes.

★ **Ouzo** (Cra. 3 No. 19-29, tel. 5/423-0658, www.ouzosantamarta.com, noon-10:30pm Mon.-Thurs., noon-11pm Fri.-Sat., COP$25,000) consistently ranks as one of the top fine-dining restaurants in Santa Marta. Specializing in Mediterranean fare, Ouzo has brought some class to the Parque de los Novios. Order a plate of sizzling seafood or pasta accompanied by a glass of white wine. **El Balcón de Ouzo** serves tapas and pizza on the rooftop terrace of Ouzo. It's one of the best spots in Santa Marta for a sundowner.

An unassuming bistro, ★ **Ratatouille** (Cl. 21 No. 4-54, tel. 5/421-5356 or cell tel. 300/828-6966, noon-4pm Mon.-Wed., noon-3pm and 6:30pm-10:30pm Thurs.-Sat., COP$22,000) is run by a recent arrival from France, serving traditional French cuisine with some Colombian touches. It's a smart choice for dessert and coffee, too. They hold occasional storytelling events with longtime Santa Marta residents.

For Peruvian food with a Caribbean twist, check out **Rocoto** (Cra. 2 No. 19-15, cell tel. 300/835-8604, noon-3pm and 6pm-10pm Tues.-Sun., COP$35,000), on an edgy street a couple of blocks from Parque de los Novios. The pisco sours (try the passion fruit version) and *causas* (traditional Peruvian potato dish) never disappoint, but there are also other tasty dishes to be tried, such as a steak served with polenta.

RODADERO

For delicious seafood, pasta, and wine in a minimalist setting, try **DiVino** (Cl. 6 No. 1-26, tel. 5/421-3735, noon-11pm daily, COP$30,000), one of the top restaurants in Rodadero.

★ **Donde Chucho** (Cl. 6 No. 2-61, tel. 5/422-1752, 11:30am-10:30pm daily, COP$25,000) is the classic Santa Marta seafood joint. It's so popular it has even opened branches in Bogotá. The original restaurant (there is another location in the Centro) is a casual open-air place filled with photos of Chucho, the owner and chef, posing with Colombian beauty queens, sports stars, and politicians. It's hard to believe that Chucho began this seafood empire with a humble wooden ceviche stand in Rodadero in the 1990s.

The terrace of **Pepe Mar** (Cra. 1 No. 6-05, tel. 5/422-2503, noon-10pm Sun. and Tues.-Thurs., noon-midnight Fri.-Sat., COP$26,000) is the best place for people-watching in all of Rodadero. Try the fried red snapper with coconut rice and a *patacón* (fried plantain) or two. Casual attire, like tank tops and bathing suits, is okay here.

Accommodations

The Centro Histórico offers posh boutique hotels and comfortable hostels. The Rodadero has plenty of high-rise hotels, many of which are all-inclusive. The relaxed beach village of Taganga is very close to the city; some prefer to stay there and visit Santa Marta for its restaurants in the evenings.

UNDER COP$70,000

Many hostels in Santa Marta vie for the title of "party hostel." **La Brisa Loca** (Cl. 14 No. 3-58, Centro Histórico, tel. 5/431-6121, www.labrisaloca.com, COP$45,000 dorm, COP$80,000 d) is a revamped mansion-turned-hostel that has earned its spot as a backpacker favorite. There's a small pool in the main courtyard surrounded by three floors of private rooms and large mixed dormitories (6-10 beds). On the top floor is an excellent bar that, thanks to its daily drink specials, gets jammed with backpackers and locals alike, especially on weekends. Don't expect peaceful sleep here.

Located in a quiet, tree-lined neighborhood about five kilometers (3.1 miles) east of the Centro, **The Dreamer** (Cra. 51 No. 26D-161, tel. 5/433-3264, www.thedreamerhostel.com, COP$40,000 dorm, COP$100,000 d) makes life easy for guests, offering tons of information on day trips and coordination of travel to other destinations (such as their location on the beach in Palomino). All the action here centers on the pool, where there is a bar and restaurant that serves burritos and huge lemonades.

Drop Bear Hostel (Cra. 21 No. 20-36, tel. 5/435-8034, www.dropbearhostel.com, COP$30,000 dorm, COP$60,000 d) is set in a huge house that was built by a drug trafficker in the 1980s. The hotel bar is aptly named the Cartel Bar. Rooms are massive. Perhaps the nicest feature at Drop Bear is the big pool, which is the main gathering area at this sociable place. Ask for a tour of the house, including its secret tunnels and oddities. The hostel is a 10- to 15-minute drive east of the Centro.

★ **Aluna** (Cl. 21 No. 5-27, Centro Histórico, tel. 5/432-4916, www.aluna-hotel.com, COP$30,000 dorm with fan, COP$100,000 d with a/c) is a small, quiet hostel with a mix of dorms and private rooms, all of which are immaculately maintained. Private rooms have their own bathrooms. The hostel's café serves breakfast and snacks.

Hostal Jackie (Cl. 21 No. 3-40, Centro Histórico, tel. 5/420-6944, www.elhostaldejackie.com, COP$36,000 dorm, COP$90,000 d) has dorms of different sizes and private rooms, most with just a fan. The rooftop is a friendly gathering place, and sometimes they have DJs playing at the bar. There is a small pool on the ground floor.

COP$70,000-200,000

The ★ **Hotel del Parque** (Cl. 19 No. 4-45, Centro Histórico, tel. 5/420-7508, COP$90,000 d) on the pleasant pedestrian Calle 19 is a gem. Supremely low-key, this hotel has just a handful of air-conditioned rooms but is very well maintained, and, best of all, it's fairly priced. There's complimentary coffee, but no free breakfast; however, there are many options within walking distance.

COP$200,000-500,000

La Casa del Farol (Cl. 18 No. 3-115, Centro Histórico, tel. 5/423-1572, www.lacasadelfarol.com, COP$317,000 d) was one of the first boutique hotels in the city. It's in an 18th-century house and has six rooms that are named for different cities of the world. From the tiny wading pool on the rooftop you get a nice view of the city. With the same owners and just across the street, **La Casa del Agua** (Cl. 18 No. 4-09, Centro Histórico, tel. 5/423-1572, www.lacasadelagua.com.co, COP$180,000 d) has four rooms of various sizes and styles. Try for one with a balcony. The small pool downstairs is a welcome sight after a day out in the heat.

The 10-room ★ **Casa de Isabella** (Callejón del Río, Cra. 2 No. 19-20, Centro Histórico, tel. 5/431-2082 or cell tel. 301/466-5656, www.casaisabella.com, COP$280,000 d) is a tastefully revamped Republican-era house with nods to both colonial and Republican styles, and it surrounds a tamarind tree that's over 200 years old. The suites on top have fantastic private terraces and hot tubs.

For a beachfront option, check out **Tamacá Beach Resort Hotel** (Cra. 2 No. 11A-98, Rodadero, tel. 5/422-7015, www.tamaca.com.

co, COP$300,000 d). It has 81 rooms with all the usual amenities and a fantastic pool area that overlooks the water. The hotel has two towers, with the beachside tower preferred by most.

Information and Services

In addition to a stand at the airport, there is a **PIT** (Punto de Información Turística, Cra. 1 No. 10A-12, tel. 5/438-2587, 9am-noon and 2pm-6pm Mon.-Fri., 9am-1pm Sat.) tourist information booth along the waterfront.

Lavandería El Paraíso (Cl. 22 No. 2A-46, tel. 5/431-2466, cell tel. 315/681-1651, 9am-6pm Mon.-Fri., 9am-1pm Sat.) will wash your clothes and have them ready for pickup by the next day.

Transportation

Santa Marta is easily accessed by air and land from all major cities in Colombia.

The **Aeropuerto Internacional Simón Bolívar** (Km. 16.5 Troncal del Caribe) is 16 kilometers (10 miles) west of the Centro Histórico. Domestic carriers **Avianca** (www.avianca.com), **LATAM Airlines** (www.latam.com), **VivaColombia** (www.vivacolombia.co), and **EasyFly** (www.easyfly.com.co) connect Santa Marta with the major cities of Colombia. **Copa** (www.copaair.com) has nonstop flights from its hub in Panama City, Panama. Taxis to the Centro Histórico from the airport cost around COP$25,000.

There is hourly bus service to Cartagena, Barranquilla, and Riohacha. Many buses to nearby coastal destinations leave from the market area (Cra. 11 and Cl. 11) in the Centro Histórico. Long-haul buses for destinations such as Bogotá, Medellín, and Bucaramanga depart from the **Terminal de Transportes** (Cl. 41 No. 31-17, tel. 5/430-2040) outside of town.

Taxis to Taganga cost around COP$8,000 and *colectivo* buses are around COP$1,200. These can be found on the waterfront near Parque Simón Bolívar, along Carrera 5, or at the market at Carrera 11 and Calle 11.

The best way to get around the Centro

Histórico is on foot. A recommended **walking tour** (cell tel. 301/485-9222, free) of historic Santa Marta is offered by local Eduardo Riveira. Tips are welcome, and the walks usually take place at 10am on most weekdays.

TAGANGA

This popular beachside community is only about a 20-minute ride northeast through the desert from Santa Marta and is actually considered part of the city. In the 1970s, this sleepy fishing village was discovered by hippie-types looking for an escape from urban life, and it soon evolved into a mecca for backpackers. On any given Saturday along the bayside promenade, you'll brush shoulders with Colombian families, diving fanatics, traveling musicians, and general sunseekers of all ages and nationalities. It's as close as Colombia gets to Venice Beach.

Recreation
DIVING AND SNORKELING

The warm waters (24-28°C/75-82°F) off of Taganga provide some good diving and snorkeling opportunities. Diving excursions take you into the waters off of Parque Nacional Natural Tayrona to the northeast, to Isla

Morro off the coast of Santa Marta, or to a shipwreck near the beaches of Rodadero. The best months for diving here are between July and September.

Tayrona Dive Center (Cra. 1C No. 18A-22, tel. 5/421-5349, cell tel. 318/305-9589, www.tayronadivecenter.com, 8am-noon and 2pm-6pm daily) is a very organized agency that offers PADI certification courses (COP$650,000) over a period of three days with six dives each day, a one-day mini-course (COP$160,000), and diving excursions for those with experience. They also have a hotel (COP$70,000 d) at the same location with six rooms, five with views of the water. Rooms have a safe-deposit box and big refrigerators. The hotel is exclusively for divers during high season (mid-December to mid-January, Holy Week, and mid-June through mid-July).

Oceano Scuba (Cra. 2 No. 17-46, tel. 5/421-9004, cell tel. 316/534-1834, www.oceanoscuba.com.co, 8am-noon and 2pm-6pm daily) offers the whole array of diving activities, from one-day dives for certified divers (COP$110,000) to a one-day beginner's course (COP$180,000) to an open-water PADI certification course (COP$600,000) that lasts three days. Night dives (COP$80,000)—during

The fishing village of Taganga has become a backpacker mecca.

which you might come across eels—and snorkeling (COP$50,000) are also on offer.

Poseidon Dive Center (Cl. 18 No 1-69, tel. 5/421-9224, www.poseidondivecenter.com, 9am-6pm daily) is a third well-established dive center that has English-speaking instructors. They offer dozens of courses, like an open-water diving class (COP$830,000) and tours, such as a 10-dive package (COP$860,000).

BEACHES

The gray, sandy beach in front of the boardwalk attracts hordes of locals, especially on weekends, but the best beaches are outside of town. **Playa Grande,** northwest of town, is the best of the bunch, and it is one of the closest to Taganga. It costs COP$10,000 round-trip to get there by boat. To arrange for boat transportation, just head to the beach in front of the promenade or at La Ballena Azul. There are always boaters waiting for customers. There's a path to Playa Grande from Taganga, which takes 15 minutes to walk. Check with your hotel whether it's open and passable.

Boats can also take you to the beaches of the **Parque Nacional Natural Tayrona** for COP$40,000 round-trip, but you can negotiate that price, especially if you are in a group. Although all visitors to the park are supposed to pay an entrance fee (and it is steep for non-Colombians), some boat captains will take you to beaches without park employee supervision, which park officials rightly do not condone. During the windy months of December-February, boat transportation can be rough, bordering on dangerous.

Food

★ **Babaganoush Restaurante y Bar** (Cra. 1C No. 18-22, 3rd fl. above Taganga Dive Center, cell tel. 318/868-1476, 1pm-11:30pm Wed.-Mon., COP$20,000) is an excellent Dutch-run restaurant and bar with amazing views. It's a true crowd pleaser, with a diverse menu of falafel, seafood, steak, and even a shout-out to Southeast Asia. Go in the evening for the atmosphere, drinks, and sunset.

The daily happy hour (5pm-7pm) is hard to pass up.

Tucked away on a side street a block or two from the beach, **Pachamama** (Cl. 16 No. 1C-18, tel. 5/421-9486 or cell tel. 318/393-9291, COP$24,000) has a sophisticated menu that includes Argentinian steaks, ceviche, pasta, and refreshing cocktails, all skillfully prepared by the French chef.

Direct from Atlanta comes ★ **Taco Beach Bar and Grille** (Cra. 1 No. 18-49, tel. 5/423-3912, noon-8pm daily, COP$15,000). With Tex-Mex delights, happy hours, and sand beneath your feet, this spot is all that you need in a beach bar.

Café Bonsai (Cl. 13 No. 1-07, tel. 5/421-9495, www.cafebonsai.com, 8am-3pm Mon.-Sat., COP$18,000) is a cute place for coffee, freshly baked breads and pastries, and sandwiches and other lunch items.

Accommodations

It's not close to the beach, but **La Casa de Felipe** (Cra. 5A No. 19-13, tel. 5/421-9120, www.lacasadefelipe.com, COP$30,000 dorm, COP$70,000 d) is a spacious and comfortable choice.

If you want backpacker prices without a backpacker scene, check out **Hostal Pelikan** (Cra. 2 No. 17-04, tel. 5/421-9057 or cell tel. 316/756-1312, COP$25,000 dorm, COP$65,000 d), a decent place to stay with a nice terrace for your morning coffee. Breakfast is an additional cost.

La Ballena Azul (Cra. 1 at Cl. 18, tel. 5/421-9009, www.hotelballenaazul.com, COP$173,000 d) is a classic Taganga hotel, started by a Frenchwoman years ago. It's still in the family, and they still serve crepes in their restaurant. Ballena Azul is on the beach, with the best location in town—in the center of activity. Next door, the American-run ★ **Taganga Beach Hotel** (Cra. 1 No. 18-49, tel. 5/421-9058, COP$110,000 d) has seven comfortable rooms, with plans for more, and an awesome little bar in front. It's just steps from the beach.

Probably the most luxurious option in

Taganga is the **Hotel Bahía Taganga** (Cl. 8 No. 1B-35, tel. 5/421-0653 or cell tel. 310/216-9120, www.hotelbahiataganga.com, COP$200,000 d). It's on the northern side of the bay. Head to the pool in the late afternoon and watch the sun slip behind the mountains.

Transportation

Taganga is easily reached from Santa Marta and from points east, such as the Parque Nacional Natural Tayrona and Palomino. Minibuses and buses ply both routes daily.

From Santa Marta's Centro Histórico, you can take a minibuses to Taganga for about COP$1,500. Taxis from Santa Marta cost around COP$12,000, more from the bus terminal or airport. Once in Taganga, you can walk everywhere you need to go.

★ MINCA

If you've had your fill of beaches or the seductive Caribbean cities, maybe it's time for an altitude adjustment. Artists, nature lovers, coffee farmers, and transplanted urbanites in the village of Minca (pop. 500) look down upon their neighbors in nearby Santa Marta—literally. At an elevation of 660 meters (2,165 ft.), midway up the Sierra, you get a bird's-eye view of Santa Marta, just 45 minutes away. You also get a great bird's-eye view of birds, especially higher up at the edge of the Parque Nacional Natural Sierra Nevada de Santa Marta. The blissful routine of mountain hikes, dips in invigorating swimming holes, and sunset ogling may make you want to linger here.

Recreation

In and around Minca there are no safety issues, and you can hike up the mountain on your own without a guide.

The Sierra Nevada de Santa Marta is a renowned coffee-growing region. The **Finca La Victoria** (no phone, 9am-4pm daily, COP$10,000) is a family-run coffee farm that you can visit for a small fee. It is between Pozo Azul and Los Pinos, about a one-hour walk from town. The farm uses an astonishing

peaceful Minca, in the Sierra Nevada de Santa Marta

hydroelectric system and machinery dating back over 100 years. After the tour, save room for lunch at the French-run bistro on the premises. Pick up some of Minca's homegrown beer, made by Happy Toucan, also on the farm's premises.

HIKING

Minca is a paradise for hikers. Nearby are several gentle hikes along tranquil mountain roads and paths to swimming holes of either freezing-cold or wonderfully refreshing pure water, depending on the thickness of your skin. Three popular swimming holes are within easy walking distance from Minca: Balneario Las Piedras (45 min.), Pozo Azul (1 hr.), and the Cascadas Marinka (1 hr.).

BIRD-WATCHING

High in the Sierra Nevada, at an elevation of around 2,400 meters (7,875 feet), the **Reserva El Dorado** (www.proaves.org) is one of the finest bird-watching reserves in the country. For reservations (COP$569,000 3 nights

It Takes an Eco-Village

Visiting an eco-lodge in Colombia is one of the best experiences the country offers. In the jungle outside of Minca, there resides something even better—**Paso del Mango,** an eco-village comprising lodges and nature reserves that all share a commitment to preserving this beautiful land.

The best place to stay in Paso del Mango is the shockingly deluxe **Finca Carpe Diem** (tel. 5/420-9610, www.fincacarpediem.com, COP$17,000 hammocks, COP$35,000 dorm, COP$180,000 luxury cabin), which is perched on the cusp of the jungle. This Belgian-run lodge is also a working farm and a 50-hectare natural reserve, and is home to a tree-planting project. There's a refreshing natural pool, beekeeping classes, and a restaurant onsite, which offers a variety of options in a friendly atmosphere.

To get to Paso del Mango, take a taxi to the village of Bonda (COP$10,000) from Santa Marta. From the soccer field, take a *mototaxi* (COP$8,000) along the scenic road up to the mountains.

all-incl.), contact **EcoTurs** in Bogotá (Cra. 20 No. 36-61, tel. 1/287-6592, info@ecoturs.org) or **Aviatur** (tel. 1/587-5181, www.aviaturecoturismo.com) in Bogotá. The accommodations are excellent, with 10 spacious rooms, great food, and, crucially, hot showers. The area is home to 19 endemic species, including the Santa Marta antpitta, Santa Marta parakeet, Santa Marta bush tyrant, blossom crown, and screech owls. Anybody can stay at El Dorado, even the non-birding crowd.

TOURS

To go on a photo safari in the jungle and improve your skills, check out **Fototrails** (cell tel. 310/650-5200, www.foto-trails. com, COP$45,000-90,000). They offer unique one-day tours for all skill levels. Tours focus on wildlife and nature photography, or feature visits to a Kogi indigenous community or farming families. Tours are led by a native English speaker and professional photographer.

Food

There are a handful of good eateries in Minca, mostly catering to international travelers. Hotels and hostels are always a reliable and reasonably priced option for guests and non-guests alike. They are open every day with lunch hours generally noon-3pm and dinner 6pm-10pm. Main dishes rarely cost more than COP$20,000. Standouts include ★ **Hostal Casa Loma** (50 m above the church, cell tel. 313/808-6134 or 321/224-6632, www.casalomaminca.com) and **El Mirador Hotel** (200 m from town entrance, cell tel. 311/671-3456 or 318/368-1611).

Dining at **Ei Mox Muica** (300 m from town entrance, cell tel. 311/699-6718, 10am-9pm daily, COP$18,000) is like being invited to a friend's house. They only have two tables, which overlook a lush garden. The menu includes a variety of pasta, salads, crepes, and wines. They are into locally produced chocolate here—it might even make an appearance in your pasta.

Tienda Café de Minca (diagonal from police station, cell tel. 312/638-5353, 8:30am-8pm daily) sells snacks (like empanadas), beer, and wine. There is sometimes live music on weekends. It's a good place to find out what's going on in town.

Lazy Cat (across from Tienda Julimar, cell tel. 313/506-5227, noon-9pm daily, COP$15,000) offers a filling meal of pasta or burgers, or just a fruit smoothie. It's in the center of town on the main street.

Acccommodations
UNDER COP$70,000

★ **Hostal Casa Loma** (50 m uphill from a small church, cell tel. 313/808-6134, www. casalomaminca.com, COP$20,000 dorm, COP$80,000 d) is on a hilltop with an impressive vantage point over Santa Marta. It's a friendly place, where delicious food (often vegetarian) is served, and you can mingle with other travelers. Cabins such as the Casa Selva and Casa Luna farther up on the hillside are quieter than the rooms near the main social area, providing the ultimate jungle experience. Camping (COP$15,000) is also available. To get to Hostal Casa Loma, climb a winding path just behind the church. Casa Loma offers yoga classes (COP$20,000) and massages (COP$55,000), and shows two films a week in an outdoor setting.

Oscar's Hostal Finca La Fortuna (400 m from town entrance near casino area, cell tel. 313/534-4500, www.oscarsplace.com.co, COP$20,000 hammock, COP$25,000 dorm, COP$40,000 d) consists of simple and luxurious cabins dramatically set on a bluff with extraordinary views of Santa Marta and the surrounding countryside. Oscar's is completely off the grid, with solar panels providing electricity and rainwater collection and a well accounting for all water. The sunsets here, particularly from mid-June until mid-December, are "living art," as owner Oscar puts it. At times Oscar's can have a party atmosphere.

Hostel Mirador (200 m from town entrance, cell tel. 311/671-3456 or 318/368-1611, http://miradorminca.wordpress.com, COP$25,000 dorm, COP$60,000 d) is an enchanting hostel with a great view, warm hosts, and delicious meals. The hostel has two private rooms and a dorm room with three beds. It's set in a lush garden, and the lovely dining area is open-air. The restaurant is open to the public nightly; meals cost around COP$20,000.

Casa Elemento (cell tel. 313/587-7677, www.casaelemento.com, COP$20,000 hammock, COP$35,000 dorm, COP$100,000 d) has a fantastic location far up the mountain, and is a sociable and fun place to spend a few days. There's lots of hanging out here, both at the bar and in the massive 10-person hammock, and it's so remote that there's nothing much going on. The countryside is inspiring, but a lot of guests are more interested in partying. To get there, hire a *mototaxi* from Minca (COP$20,000).

COP$70,000-200,000
Hotel Minca (near town entrance, cell tel. 321/204-1965, www.hotelminca.com, COP$120,000 d), once a convent, was one of the first hotels in Minca. There are 14 spacious yet basic rooms in this old-fashioned building that boasts broad verandas with hammocks. There's a nature path on the grounds, and numerous hummingbird feeders along the open-air dining area ensure that you'll have a breakfast-time show.

Information and Services
Bring plenty of cash with you to Minca: There are no ATMs here. There is a small **tourist information stand** (near police station, cell tel. 317/308-5270, 10am-6pm daily). It's run by the tour agency **Jungle Joe's** (www.junglejoeminca.com).

Transportation
Minca is easily reached from Santa Marta. *Taxis colectivos* (shared taxis) depart from Santa Marta on a regular basis from the market (Cra. 11 and Cl. 11). These cost COP$7,000; the ride takes about 45 minutes. Private taxis from the airport cost around COP$50,000, and taxis from Santa Marta's Centro Histórico to Minca cost COP$40,000.

★ PARQUE NACIONAL NATURAL TAYRONA
Perhaps the best-known national park in Colombia, the **Parque Nacional Natural Tayrona** (PNN Tayrona, 34 km northeast of Santa Marta on the Troncal del Caribe highway, tel. 5/421-1732, www.aviaturecoturismo.com or www.parquesnacionales.gov.co, 8am-5pm daily, COP$42,000 non-Colombian, COP$16,000 Colombian resident, COP$8,500 children) encompasses gorgeous beaches, tropical rainforests, and archaeological sites.

The park covers 12,000 hectares (30,000 acres) of land from the edge of Taganga in the southwest to the Río Piedras in the east. The southern border of the park is the Troncal del Caribe highway and to the north is the

Caribbean Sea. To the east and south of the PNN Tayrona is the PNN Sierra Nevada de Santa Marta, a much larger national park.

The frequently tempestuous waters of the PNN Tayrona provide dramatic scenery, with palms growing atop massive island boulders and waves crashing against them. More than 30 golden-sand beaches in the park are set dramatically against a seemingly vertical wall of jungle. Although you can't see them from the park, the snow-covered peaks of the Sierra Nevada de Santa Marta are only 42 kilometers (26 miles) from the coast.

The park includes significant tracts of critically endangered dry tropical forests, mostly in its western section; these forests are much less dense than the humid tropical forests. At higher elevations you will see magnificent cloud forests. In addition to beaches, the coast is home to marine estuaries and mangroves. The park is laced with streams fed by chilly waters that flow from high in the sierra. In the western part of the park, many of these run dry during the dry season, while in the eastern sector they have water year-round.

The forest in PNN Tayrona is alive with plant and animal life. Some 1,300 plant, 396 bird, and 99 mammal species have been identified here. Four species of monkeys live in the park, and they can often be spotted. Five species of wild cats have been identified in the park: the margay, jaguar, ocelot, panther, and jaguarundi. Their numbers are few and these great cats are expert at hiding in the jungle—don't count on stumbling across them during your visit. Other mammals include sloths, anteaters, armadillos, deer, and 40 types of bats. Birds include migratory and resident species, such as the rare blue-billed curassow (locally called El Paují), a threatened bird that lives in the cloud forest, as well as toucans, macaws (*guacamayas*), and many hummingbirds.

PLANNING YOUR TIME

The best months to visit the park are February, March, September, and October. There are two rainy seasons: April-June and September-November, with the latter being more intense. During these times, trails can be extremely muddy.

If at all possible, avoid visiting PNN Tayrona during the high seasons of late December through mid-January, during Semana Santa (Holy Week), and, to a lesser extent, during summer school holidays from mid-June until mid-July. During these times, the park is swarmed with visitors. Long

Parque Nacional Natural Tayrona

holiday weekends (*puentes*) are also quite busy here; a weekday visit is by far the best.

While many people visit the park on day trips from Santa Marta, spending one or two nights in the park is recommended, even though accommodations and food can be expensive.

Bring mosquito repellent (especially during rainy season), a flashlight or headlamp, hiking or athletic shoes if you will be hiking to El Pueblito, sunscreen, and cash. Darkness falls around 6pm year-round, and there is not much going on in the park, so bring playing cards and a book to read. Visitors are not permitted to bring alcohol into the park; your bags may be inspected upon entry. Passports are necessary for entry.

ORIENTATION

The majority of visitors see just the extreme northeastern section of the park. This part of the park houses the main entrance, **El Zaino.** From El Zaino, visitors can access the **Cañaveral** area, which includes the Ecohab accommodations; campsites at **Castilletes;** and cabins and campsites at **Arrecifes.** Farther southwest are La Piscina and more campsites at **Cabo San Juan** (also called El Cabo). From Cabo San Juan, there is access to the archaeological site El Pueblito.

Closer to Santa Marta is the **Palangana** entrance, which provides access to Playa Neguanje and other remote beaches. No overnight stays are permitted in this part of the park.

For day-trippers, Bahía Concha and Playa Cristal are accessible by boat from Taganga.

Recreation
BEACHES

The beaches in Parque Nacional Natural Tayrona are spectacular, but though the water may appear inviting, currents are deceptively strong, and, despite the warnings posted on the beach, many people have drowned here. Of the park's 34 beaches, there are only 6 where swimming is permitted. There are no lifeguards on duty in the park, and no specific hours for swimming.

The best swimming beaches are around the Cabo San Juan area, including **Arenilla** and **La Piscina,** inviting coves of turquoise waters that are protected by natural rock barriers. It's a 20-minute walk from Arrecifes to both of those beaches. Cabo San Juan, with a large campground nearby, is a hub of activity in the park. Farther along is a clothing-optional beach, just past Playa Brava.

Some of the other beaches open to swimming are in the less-visited western part of the park. **Playa Neguanje** is accessed by car or taxi (COP$15,000 from Santa Marta) through the Palangana entrance (12 km northeast of Santa Marta). **Playa del Muerto** (Playa Cristal) is another recommended beach in the same area. It's more than 20 kilometers (12.5 miles) from the park entrance to the beach.

It's possible to visit some of the beaches at the western end of the park all the way to Cabo San Juan by boat from Taganga, but park staff prefer that visitors enter the park by land. The waters can also be quite rough, especially between December and February.

HIKING

The best-maintained and most beautiful hike in the park is the underappreciated stretch between **Cañaveral and Arrecifes** (3 kilometers/1.9 miles, one hour). Upon arrival, most visitors take this path to reach campsites or cabins between Arrecifes and Cabo San Juan. Wooden bridges meander through the jungle as you follow the sound of the crashing waves until you reach a beach strewn with massive boulders. To best enjoy this hike, consider sending your luggage onward to Arrecifes by horse (COP$19,000). Be on the lookout for capuchin monkeys, snakes, and birds.

A highlight of any visit to PNN Tayrona is the trek up to **El Pueblito** (also called Chairama, 3 kilometers/1.9 miles, 1.5 hrs. one way from Cabo San Juan), which consists of ruins of what was an important Tayrona settlement. The site contains well-preserved remnants of terraces, and a small Kogi community still lives nearby. The challenging path through the tropical jungle is steep and the stone steps can be slippery, but it's well worth it. Hikers can go up to El Pueblito without a guide, but inquire when you enter the park if you'd like to hire one. El Pueblito is usually accessed from within Tayrona by walking west along the beach from Arrecifes and following the signs from Cabo San Juan. A longer version of this hike can be started from the main highway, the Troncal del Caribe, at the Calabazo entrance to the park, around 24 kilometers (15 miles) northeast of Santa Marta. It's about a 2.5-hour trek from there. There's a good chance of spotting monkeys and birds on this longer hike.

Food and Accommodations

The park has two surprisingly upscale restaurants. One is in Cañaveral, close to the Ecohabs, and the other is in Arrecifes, near the *cabañas*. They are open daily 7am-9pm, and the specialty at each is fresh seafood. Expect to pay around COP$30,000 for a lunch or dinner entrée. Both restaurants accept credit cards. There are some snack bars in the park concentrated around the popular beach and campsites, serving fried fish,

empanadas, and fresh fruit. The snack bars are usually open during daylight hours (9am-6pm daily).

There are numerous lodging options in PNN Tayrona for every budget: high-end Ecohabs, mid-level *cabañas*, and camping. The travel agency **Aviatur** (Bogotá office Av. 19 No. 4-62, tel. 1/587-5181 or 1/587-5182, www.aviaturecoturismo.com) manages most of the lodging facilities in the park. Neither the Ecohabs nor the *cabañas* could be considered a bargain, but the Ecohabs, where you can awake to a beautiful view of the sea, are indeed special, and worth one or two nights. The *cabañas* are set back from the beach but are quite comfortable. Safety boxes are included in all rooms, and can be provided to campers as well. Some visitors prefer to leave a bag or valuables at a trusted hotel in Santa Marta.

The **Ecohabs** (COP$784,000-963,000 pp breakfast incl.), in the Cañaveral sector, consist of 14 private *bohíos* (thatched-roof cabins) that sleep 2-4 people. From a distance they look like giant nests amid the trees, but in reality they are modeled after the thatched-roof houses of the Tayrona people. There are two floors to the Ecohabs: On the first floor is the bathroom and an open-air social area. On

Ecohab at Parque Nacional Natural Tayrona

the second floor is the bedroom. A flashlight is necessary if you need to go to the bathroom in the middle of the night, as you have to go outside and downstairs. This is inconvenient for some.

In nearby Arrecifes, there are six two-story *cabañas* (12 rooms, COP$438,000-602,000 pp breakfast incl.) with a capacity of four persons each. These are like jungle duplexes, with the two units divided by thin walls. There is also a **hammock area** (COP$36,000 pp) in Arrecifes with a capacity of 60 hammocks. Those choosing this option have access to lockers and the safety box at the lobby area.

There are **campgrounds** (COP$20,000 pp) in both Cañaveral and Arrecifes and also at Cabo San Juan, which is a 15-minute walk to the west from the beach at La Piscina. Cabo tends to get very crowded, bordering on unpleasant (thanks to not enough sanitary facilities), during long weekends and holidays. A better camping option is low-key Castilletes, which is just before the entrance to Cañaveral.

Transportation

From Santa Marta you can take any bus eastbound along the Troncal del Caribe to the main entrance (El Zaino). *Colectivo* buses can be caught at the intersection of Carrera 11 and Calle 11 (the market) in Santa Marta, and the trip takes about an hour and costs under COP$5,000. You can also take a cab for about COP$60,000.

Expect a thorough inspection of backpacks and bags upon entering the park. Visitors are not allowed to bring in plastic bags (to protect sea turtles), and no alcohol is permitted (although beer is served at restaurants and snack bars in the park). Be sure to bring bug repellent, a flashlight, and good hiking boots.

Visitors pay the entrance fee at the administrative offices. These fees are not included in the Aviatur package prices.

It's about four kilometers (2.5 miles) from the offices to Cañaveral, and vans travel this route on an ongoing basis (COP$3,000). From there it is 45 sweaty minutes on foot through the jungle to Arrecifes. Mules can be hired to carry your bags, or you can rent a horse for COP$20,000.

PNN Tayrona to Palomino

If you prefer less civilization and more tranquility, the coast between PNN Tayrona and Palomino has some interesting places to hang your *sombrero vueltiao* (Colombian hat) for a few days. Between these two very popular tourist destinations are beaches that are rather overlooked by the masses. Day trips to PNN Tayrona can be easily coordinated from this area.

ACCOMMODATIONS

Impossibly placed atop giant beach boulders, the guesthouse **Finca Barlovento** (Playa Los Naranjos, 40 km east of Santa Marta, Bogotá tel. 1/325-6998, www.fincabarloventosantamarta.com, COP$400,000 d incl. 2 meals) is located between the sea and the Río Piedras. It's an amazing place to stay, and the food's good, too. There are just three rooms and one luxurious cabin here. Jungle excursions can be arranged by the hotel, but be sure to enjoy some beachside afternoons. You'll have the sand mostly to yourself.

The waves are the main draw at ★ **Costeño Beach Surf Camp and Ecolodge** (Playa Los Naranjos, 45 km east of Santa Marta, cell tel. 310/368-1191, www.costenosurf.com, COP$30,000 dorm, COP$80,000 d), but the property also gets exceptionally high marks from its guests for its laid-back atmosphere. Costeño Beach has both dorm and private accommodations on a former coconut farm. It's also solar powered. Rent a board (COP$30,000 per day) or take a class (COP$25,000) to make like the surfers do.

La Brisa Tranquila (45 km east of Santa Marta, Buritaca, cell tel. 321/599-5966, www.labrisatranquila.com, COP$30,000 dorm, COP$140,000 d) is the tamer version of La Brisa Loca in Santa Marta. This beachside hostel is only five kilometers (3.1 miles) from PNN Tayrona. It comprises six private rooms, beach huts, and dorms.

Playa Koralia (50 km east of Santa Marta, cell tel. 310/642-2574 or 317/510-2289, www.koralia.com, COP$209,000 d) is a beach-chic hotel on the water just east of PNN Tayrona. Accommodations are simple but comfortable, meals are healthy, and there's a spa and a bar. It's a popular place for weddings and celebrations for groups from Bogotá. Excursions to Tayrona and other sights can be arranged.

The recipe for pure relaxation, ★ Gitana del Mar (50 km east of Santa Marta, Buritaca, cell tel. 312/293-7053, www.gitanadelmar.com.co, COP$600,000 d with all meals) has six eco-chic bungalows, a stunning beachside location, and a spa and restaurant. There's no air-conditioning and the hotel strives to be as environmentally responsible as possible without sacrificing luxury. The hotel offers a calendar of wellness retreats and regular beachside yoga classes.

The environmentally conscious ★ Quebrada del Plátano (60 km east of Santa Marta, Buritaca, info@quebradadelplatano.com, cell tel. 312/338-4348, COP$80,000 camping, COP$140,000 pp with meals) is a nature reserve and working farm with organic fruit, herbs, coffee, and vegetables. The water here comes from mountain springs, and all electricity is solar powered. Waterfalls and swimming holes are a short walk away. The reserve is located between the Río Buritaca and a smaller creek. There is just one private room, one shared room, and an area for hammocks.

PALOMINO

Swaying coconut palms and uncrowded beaches: That's what the Caribbean is all about, isn't it? And at Palomino that's exactly what you get. This town has become quite a popular destination, particularly with backpackers. Caribbean currents can be frustratingly strong here, but the cool waters of the nearby Río Palomino flowing down from the Sierra Nevada de Santa Marta are always refreshing and much more hospitable. Palomino is a good stop to make between Santa Marta and desert adventures in the Alta Guajira.

Palomino extends out from either side of the main highway, Troncal del Caribe. There are no street names in Palomino; the main points of reference are The Dreamer hostel, the highway, and the gas stations Terpel and Mobil.

Recreation

Recreational activities in and around Palomino include easy walks to the **Río**

beach in Palomino

Palomino, about an hour away, where there is also tubing. Tubing down the river usually takes about 2.5 hours and costs around COP$25,000. Also in the area are the fantastic jungle waterfalls at private nature reserve **Quebrada Valencia** (village of Buritaca, no phone, COP$3,000). All hotels and hostels organize these easy excursions. On the weekends, families from Santa Marta take over the area—it's more peaceful during the week.

Chajaka (office on the south side of the main coastal highway, cell tel. 313/583-3288, calixtoteheran@gmail.com) offers interesting day trips or multiday hiking trips (COP$120,000) into the Sierra Nevada to visit Kogi communities and experience the jungle. Ask for Calixto Teheran, a longtime guide with Chajaka and a friendly expert who knows the Sierra well.

La Sirena Yoga (La Sirena hostel, cell tel. 312/861-4850, COP$18,000) offers 1.5-hour yoga sessions on the beach in front of the hostel of the same name. Class frequency depends on the number of participants, so stop by in advance to inquire about times.

To rent a surfboard, visit **Chill and Surf** (The Dreamer hostel, cell tel. 315/610-9561, www.chillandsurfcolombia.com, 9am-4pm daily). They have a stand on the beach in front of The Dreamer. They also offer classes.

Food and Accommodations

Palomino is well on its way to dethroning Taganga as the deluxe backpacker resort. That's thanks largely to one famous hostel: ★ **The Dreamer** (cell tel. 300/609-7229, www.thedreamerhostel.com, COP$29,000 dorm, COP$110,000 d). This is by far the most social place this side of Santa Marta. Dorm and private accommodations are in *malokas* (cabins) surrounding an always-happening pool area and outdoor snack bar. The Dreamer is not just for partiers: You can always retreat to your cabin for some peace.

There are dozens of hostels that have sprung up in Palomino, all striving to compete with The Dreamer. If The Dreamer is booked, **The Tiki Hut** (cell tel. 314/794-2970,

www.tikihutpalomino.co, COP$35,000 dorm, COP$135,000 d) is a suitable second choice, and it's just next door.

★ **La Sirena Eco Hostel** (cell tel. 310/718-4644, www.ecosirena.com, COP$190,000 d) provides a contrast to the neighboring The Dreamer. Here it's vegetarian food, yoga, reiki, massages, and quiet. The six beachside *cabañas* are simple and gorgeous, and the toilets are dry "eco" models. The restaurant serves delicious healthy breakfasts.

At the **Hotel Hukumeizi** (cell tel. 315/354-7871 or 317/566-7922, www.turismoguajira. com, info@hukumeizi.com, COP$250,000 pp with meals) there are 16 cute, round *bohíos* (bungalows) with a restaurant in the center. If you go during the week, you'll probably have the place to yourself. From here it's about a 15-minute walk along the beach to the Río San Salvador and about an hour to the Río Palomino.

★ **El Matuy (Donde Tuchi)** (Palomino, cell tel. 315/751-8456, www.elmatuy.com, COP$180,000 pp with meals) is a privately owned nature reserve with 12 cabins, each with a hammock out front, set amid palm trees and with no electricity (this means candlelit evenings and no credit card machine). Hotel staff can help organize horseback riding or other activities. Surprisingly, there's Wi-Fi available in the reception area (making it a popular place).

On the southern side of the highway, called La Sierrita, there are a number of options for those who prefer mountains to beaches. **Casa Campestre Ameli** (La Sierrita, cell tel. 311/232-0034, COP$15,000 camping, COP$25,000 private room) is surrounded by beautiful gardens and offers budget-conscious accommodations. **Mamatukua Hostel** (La Sierrita, cell tel. 320/354-8791, www.lasierrita. co, COP$135,000 d) is a sweet, relaxing hostel managed by a pair of Bogotanos. Set amid the trees of the Sierra, the hostel has three rooms (with a shared bath) and a cabin. You'll wake to the sounds of birds chirping. **Jaguar Azul** (La Sierrita, cell tel. 313/800-9925, www.jaguarazulpalomino.com, COP$25,000 dorm,

COP$60,000 d) has a couple of dorms as well as private rooms. This hostel is set among fruit trees, about a 15-minute walk to the beach. It's closer to the beach than Mamatukua. There's parking available.

Transportation

There is regular bus transportation along the Troncal del Caribe between Santa Marta and Riohacha. From Santa Marta, at the market on Carrera 11 and Calle 11, take a bus bound for Palomino. It's about a two-hour trip and costs COP$10,000. On the highway where the bus drops you off, there are young men on motorbikes who will take you to your hotel for about COP$3,000.

PARQUE NACIONAL NATURAL SIERRA NEVADA DE SANTA MARTA

Parque Nacional Natural Sierra Nevada de Santa Marta (www.parquesnacionales. gov.co) has a total area of 383,000 hectares (945,000 acres), making it one of the largest parks in Colombia.

The main attraction is the **Ciudad Perdida (Lost City)**, the most important archaeological site of the Tayrona, the pre-Columbian civilization that inhabited the Sierra Nevada. The Tayrona had a highly urbanized society, with towns that included temples and ceremonial plazas built on stone terraces. There are an estimated 200 Tayrona sites, but Ciudad Perdida is the largest and best known. Many of these towns, including Pueblito (in the Parque Nacional Natural Tayrona), were occupied at the time of the Spanish conquest. Today, an estimated 30,000 indigenous people who are descendants of the Tayronas, including the Kogis, Arhuacos, Kankuamos, and Wiwas, live on the slopes and valleys of the Sierra Nevada de Santa Marta. These people believe that the Sierra Nevada is the center of the universe and that the mountain's health controls the entire Earth's well-being. Many areas of the Sierra are sacred sites to these people and are barred to outsiders.

The Sierra Nevada de Sant[a] described as a giant pyramid[,] dered on the north by the Car[ibbean,] the southeast and southwest [] of northern Colombia. Altho[ugh] lieve that the range is a distan[t] the Cordillera Oriental (Easte[rn] Range) of the Andes, most geologists believe it is a completely independent mountain system.

It is the world's highest coastal mountain range, with the twin peaks of **Pico Cristóbal Colón** and **Pico Bolívar** (the two are called Chinundúa by indigenous groups in the area) reaching 5,776 meters (18,950 feet; Colón is said to be slightly higher than Bolívar) but located only 42 kilometers (26 miles) from the sea. Pico Cristóbal Colón is the world's fifth-most prominent mountain after Mount Everest (Nepal/Tibet, China), Mount Aconcagua (Argentina), Denali (United States), and Mount Kilimanjaro (Tanzania). The range includes seven other snow-covered peaks that surpass 5,000 meters (16,400 feet): Simonds, La Reina, Ojeda, Los Nevaditos, El Guardián, Tulio Ospina, and Codazzi. Treks to these peaks used to be possible from the northern side of the mountains, starting at the Arhuaco indigenous village of Nabusímake (Cesar), but are no longer permitted by the indigenous communities.

The PNN Sierra Nevada de Santa Marta encompasses the entire mountain range above 600 meters (16,400 feet). In addition, a small segment of the park east of the PNN Tayrona, from the Río Don Diego to the Río Palomino, extends to sea level. This means that the park encompasses the entire range of tropical ecosystems in Colombia: low-lying tropical forests (sea level to 1,000 meters), cloud forests (1,000-2,300 meters), high mountain Andean forest (2,300-3,500 meters), *páramo* (highland moor, 3,500-4,500 meters), super *páramo* (4,500-5,000 meters), and glaciers (above 5,000 meters). However, because access to the upper reaches of the park is limited, what visitors will most be able to appreciate is low-lying tropical and cloud forest.

The isolation of the range has made it an

of biodiversity, and it hosts many plant and animal species that are found nowhere else. The Sierra Nevada de Santa Marta is home to 187 mammal species, including giant anteaters, spider monkeys, peccaries, tree rats, jaguars, and pumas. There are 46 species of amphibians and reptiles, including several that live above 3,000 meters (9,840 feet) that are found nowhere else on the planet. There are an astonishing 628 bird species, including the Andean condor, blue-knobbed curassow, sapphire-bellied hummingbird, and black solitary eagle, as well as many endemic species. There are at least 71 species of migratory birds that travel between Colombia and North America.

★ Ciudad Perdida Trek

A highlight for many visitors to Colombia is the four- to six-day, 52-kilometer (32-mile) round-trip trek to the **Ciudad Perdida (Lost City)** in the Sierra Nevada. The Ciudad Perdida is within the confines of the Parque Nacional Natural Sierra Nevada de Santa Marta.

The Ciudad Perdida, called Teyuna by local indigenous tribes and Buritaca 200 by archaeologists, was a settlement of the Tayrona, forebears of the people who inhabit the Sierra Nevada today. It was probably built starting around AD 700, at least 600 years before Machu Picchu. There is some disagreement as to when it was abandoned, although there is evidence of human settlement until the 16th century. The discovery of the site in 1976 marked one of the most important archaeological events of recent years. From 1976 to 1982, archaeologists from the Colombian National Institute of History and Anthropology painstakingly restored the site.

Spread over some 35 hectares (86 acres), the settlement consists of 169 circular terraces atop a mountain in the middle of dense cloud forest. Archaeologists believe that this sophisticated terrace system was created in part to control the flow of water in this area, which receives torrential rainfall for much of the year.

Plazas, temples, and dwellings for tribal

trekking to the Ciudad Perdida

leaders were built on the terraces in addition to an estimated 1,000 *bohíos* (traditional thatched-roof huts), which housed between 1,400 and 3,000 people. Surrounding the Ciudad Perdida were farms of coca, tobacco, pumpkins, and fruit trees. The city was connected to other settlements via an intricate system of mostly stone paths.

PLANNING TIPS

The somewhat challenging hike to the Ciudad Perdida requires no special preparation. Booking your tour a few weeks in advance is necessary if you're planning to travel between mid-December and mid-January, during Semana Santa, or in June and July.

The trek is mostly uphill, starting at an elevation of around 150 meters (490 feet) and ascending to an elevation of 1,100 meters (3,600 feet). The out-and-back trek takes four to six days. Most people opt to make the trek in four days, but talk to your guide if you change your mind mid-trek and want to slow your pace and extend for one more day.

Ciudad Perdida Tour Outfitters

The tour companies who lead Ciudad Perdida treks are all roughly the same. The exception is **Wiwa Tours** (Cra. 3 No. 18-49, Santa Marta, tel. 5/420-3413, www.wiwatour.com), which employs indigenous guides who tend to be more reserved than the guides with other outfits. Other tour companies are listed below.

- **Magic Tour** (Cl. 16 No. 4-41, Santa Marta, tel. 5/421-5820; Cl. 14 No. 1B-50, Taganga, tel. 5/421-9429, www.magic-tourcolombia.com)

- **TurCol** (Centro Comercial San Francisco Plaza, Cl. 13 No. 3-13, Local 115, Santa Marta; Cl. 19 No. 5-40, Taganga, tel. 5/421-2256, www.turcoltravel.com)

- **Baquianos Tour** (Cl. 10C No. 1C-59, Santa Marta, tel. 5/431-9667, www.guiasybaquianos.com)

- **Expotur** (Cra. 3 No. 17-27, Santa Marta, tel. 5/420-7739; Cl. 18 No. 2A-07, Taganga, tel. 5/421-9577, www.expotur-eco.com)

There is one set fee (COP$850,000) for the trek. This does not change, no matter if you're making the trek in four, five, or six days. If you are in very good shape and prefer to go fast, the trek can be done in three nights and four days. This requires six hours of hiking per day and rising early, with daily hiking distances varying from 7.5 kilometers (4.7 miles) to 15 kilometers (9.3 miles).

Thousands of people of all ages traverse the path each year. Each group is usually between 8 and 12 people, the majority being Europeans. Numerous groups populate different parts of the trails at any one time, and campsites can get crowded at night.

Frequent rain showers mean the trail can be muddy, and the weather is extremely humid. There are numerous river crossings to be made, some more thrilling than others, but all manageable. To reach the spectacular terraces of Ciudad Perdida, you will climb about 1,200 often-slippery stone steps. In case of an emergency on the mountain, a burro or helicopter will be sent to retrieve hikers in distress for a fee.

Seasons and Climate

From mid-December through mid-January you'll have plenty of company on the way to the Ciudad Perdida: It's high tourist season. Other high seasons are during Semana Santa and when schools are on summer break, from June through July.

The wettest times tend to be April to May and September to November. Expect a daily downpour and doable, but sometimes treacherous, river crossings. Rainy weather makes the trek more challenging. On the plus side, there are usually fewer crowds on the mountain at that time.

What to Pack

Bring a small to medium backpack, enough to carry a few days of clothes; good hiking boots with strong ankle support; sandals for stream crossings; long pants; mosquito repellent; sunscreen; cash for refreshments to purchase along the way; a small towel; toilet paper; hand sanitizer; a flashlight (preferably a headlamp); sealable bags to keep things dry; a light rain jacket; and a water container.

Assume that everything in your backpack will get wet, but bring along extra plastic bags to minimize damage. If you have them, trekking poles are a nice addition, although it's easy to find a trusty walking stick along the way. There are beds with sheets and blankets provided, but a lightweight sleeping bag or sheet is a good idea, as the cleanliness of the provided bedding is questionable. Consider earplugs and sleeping pills—widely available at Colombian pharmacies. To limit carrying along wet clothes, consider wearing "disposable" T-shirts that can be left behind at the camps (they will be washed and used by locals).

Don't worry about bringing snacks—all meals are provided by your tour operator. Bring a small amount of cash, as some snack breaks at coffee or fruit stands run by local families are not included in the tour price.

To keep you occupied at night, a small paperback and a deck of cards are good to have handy.

Camping

The campsites along the way seem to turn into backpacker villages during high season, with upwards of 60 people there every night, but they are never rowdy. Upon arrival the routine is fairly standard. You'll be able to cool off in the pristine waters of nearby swimming holes, have dinner, and hit the hammocks. Sleeping in hammocks can be uncomfortable for those not used to them, but bunk beds are also available.

The Trek

On the first morning, you will rendezvous with your tour operator either in Santa Marta or in Taganga, meet your fellow trekkers and guides, and take a 1.5-hour minibus ride to the villages of Mamey and Machete, at the edge of the park, where a generous lunch at a small restaurant will be served before you set off.

The first day of hiking, about 3-4 hours, will take you through cleared farmland, not jungle, so be prepared for extensive sun exposure. You'll take a break along the way at a coffee and fruit stall. At your campsite, you will have the opportunity to plunge into a natural swimming hole of cool, crystalline waters.

The second day of the trek is the longest one, and most groups aim for an early start. Under the canopy of the Sierra Nevada, the trail hugs the Río Buritaca for much of the time. There are multiple river crossings, including a swinging bridge. Before arrival at camp, you'll pass by the thatched roofs of the Kogi indigenous settlement Mutanyí. (Your guide will instruct you on photography etiquette.) Kogi children may ask you for *dulces* (candy), but otherwise interaction with the people that live here is unlikely. Your group will arrive at camp after noon. The rest of the day includes lots of downtime.

On the third day, the various groups on the trail jockey to be the first to arrive at the Ciudad Perdida. A 5:30am start is worth it to experience a sense of discovery as you climb the steps to the ancient terraces. Mosquitoes may be out in full force, so apply insect repellent. Leave your pack at camp; just carry your camera, walking stick, and bottle of water. The sun can be quite potent at the ruins, so bring sunscreen as well. After a final water crossing, the famed 1,200 stone steps dramatically appear, a silent invitation to this sacred lost city.

Take your time going up the steps. At the first series of grassy circular terraces, all that remains of the community's commercial center, your guide will give an introduction to the site. From there, climb the Queen's Path to the main site. Colombian soldiers guard the site and are always glad to chat up visitors. Take care when descending the steps on your way back, as they can become slippery.

La Guajira

The vast Guajira Peninsula has some of the most rugged, beautiful landscapes in Colombia. It is home to the Wayúu indigenous people, who have maintained their independent way of life through centuries. Though many Wayúu now live in cities and towns, their traditional *rancherías* (settlements) dot the desert. With the growth of tourism, many have set up lodging using traditional *ranchería* houses made out of *yotojoro,* the dried hearts of cactus plants.

The Colombian side of the peninsula (Venezuela claims the other part) can be divided into three sections. The Baja Guajira (Lower Guajira), near the Sierra Nevada de Santa Marta, is fertile agricultural and cattle-ranching land. The arid middle swath, with the departmental capital of Riohacha and the unlovely towns of Uribia and Maicao, is home to the majority of the peninsula's population. The Alta Guajira (Upper Guajira), from Cabo de la Vela to Punta Gallinas, is sparsely populated and has some other-worldly landscapes. Focus your visit on this last part.

Lack of infrastructure, especially in the north, makes visiting La Guajira a challenge, so most people opt for organized tours. Though it is possible to get to Cabo de la Vela on public transportation, do not travel elsewhere in the Alta Guajira without a dependable local guide. The roads are unmarked tracks in the sand, and getting lost is inevitable.

During the rainy months, September to November, it can be difficult to travel through the desert, which can become muddy to the point of impassability.

History

Spanish navigator Juan de la Cosa, who was a member of Columbus's first three voyages, disembarked in Cabo de la Vela in 1499, making the Guajira Peninsula one of the first places visited by Europeans in South America. It was not until 1535 that explorer Fernando de Enciso founded a settlement near Cabo de la Vela, which became a center of pearl extraction. This early settlement was relocated to Riohacha, which was founded in 1544. The traditional Wayúu inhabitants of the peninsula put up strong resistance to Spanish advances. During the 19th and 20th centuries, the peninsula was used primarily as a smuggling route.

For better or for worse, the fortunes of the Guajira changed in 1975 when the Colombian government entered into an agreement with oil giant Exxon to develop the Cerrejón open-pit coal mine 80 kilometers (50 miles) southeast of Riohacha. This project involved the construction of Puerto Bolívar, a coal port located in Bahía Portete, and of a railway to transport the coal. Production started in 1985. Coal has since become one of Colombia's main exports. The mine has generated more than US$2 billion in royalties for the Colombian government. Little of this wealth has trickled down to the people of La Guajira. The region is the fourth-poorest department in Colombia.

RIOHACHA

Called Süchiimma in the Wayúu language, meaning "city of the river," Riohacha (pop. 231,000), bordered on the east by the Río Ranchería, is La Guajira's slow-paced departmental capital. It is one of the oldest cities in Colombia, but there are few remnants of its colonial past on display.

While it's not a tourist destination in itself, Riohacha is an excellent base from which to launch tours of Alta Guajira or visit the flamingos of the Santuario de Fauna y Flora Los Flamencos. Visitors enjoy strolling the city's boardwalk in the evenings and perusing the colorful *mochilas* (shoulder bags) made and sold by Wayúu women.

La Guajira

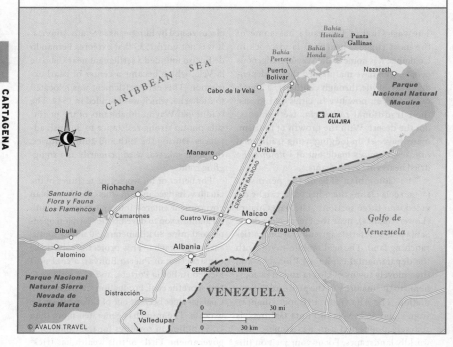

Sights

Parallel to Calle 1, also known as Avenida Marina, is the **Paseo de la Playa boardwalk** (0.8 kilometers/0.5 miles long), where locals and tourists take their evening strolls and enjoy the sea air. Along the way are kiosks where vendors sell ceviche and Wayúu women display brightly colored *mochilas* (traditional woven handbags) on the sidewalk, nonchalantly waiting for customers. The kilometer-long pier known as the **Muelle Turístico** that extends from the midpoint of the boardwalk is another favorite place for a walk, especially in the evening, with the sea breeze providing relief from the heat of the day.

With its striking murals depicting Wayúu culture, it's hard to miss the large **Centro Cultural de la Guajira** (Cra. 15 No. 1-40, tel. 5/727-0990, www.banrepcultural.org/riohacha, 8am-11:30am and 2pm-5:30pm Mon.-Fri., 9am-1pm Sat., free). Inside, the cultural center has a permanent exhibition space that tells the history of the area, from Spaniard pearl harvesters to modern times, when multinationals arrived to extract natural gas and coal. A good portion of the museum discusses Wayúu culture, and includes an exhibit on the area's traditions for Carnaval. The content of the exhibition is quite interesting and is a must-visit for anyone mildly interested in this unusual place. Unfortunately, there are few English-language explanations of the exhibits. The center also houses a small public library.

Parque Padilla (Cl. 2 and Cra. 7), Riohacha's main plaza, is named after favorite son Admiral José Prudencio Padilla, who was the most prominent Afro-Colombian commander in the revolutionary wars. To one side of the plaza is the only remnant of colonial

Riohacha, the reconstructed **Catedral de Nuestra Señora de los Remedios** (Cl. 2 No. 7-13, tel. 5/727-2442, mass 6:30am and 7pm Mon.-Sat., 7am, 11am, and 7pm Sun.). This cathedral was erected in the 16th century, but completely rebuilt in the 1800s. The remains of Padilla repose here. The church is open to the public during mass, and occasionally at other times of the day. In the evening, the plaza buzzes with locals relaxing and catching up with friends and children playing.

Food

There are several seafood restaurants along Avenida Marina/Calle 1. A perennial favorite is **Casa del Marisco** (Cl. 1 4-43, tel. 5/728-3445, 10am-10pm daily, COP$25,000), a restaurant that serves an array of fresh seafood dishes and pastas.

With a modern design, a menu to please most anyone (sandwiches, pizza, crepes, and salads), and outdoor seating, **Lima** (Cl. 13 No. 11-33, tel. 5/728-1313, 10am-10pm Mon.-Sat., COP$15,000) is a crowd pleaser.

The first thing to do at ★ **Yotojoro** (Cl. 7 No. 15-81, cell tel. 315/754-0176, 11am-10pm daily, COP$22,000), a well-known favorite among Riohacha's upper crust, is order a *limonada de coco* (coconut lemonade). Their

specialty is seafood, so go for either the hearty *cazuela de mariscos* (seafood stew) or the signature dish, the *pargo monsenor* (grilled red snapper stuffed with shrimp in a tomato-coconut milk sauce).

★ **Mantequilla** (Cl. 7 No. 11-183, tel. 5/729-1148, cell tel. 301/622-0442, lunch Mon., lunch and dinner Tues.-Sat., COP$15,000) is somewhat fancy by Riohacha standards, and it's a departure from the seafood-centric places that populate the main drag. The options are legion here: Order pasta, goat stew (a Wayúu specialty), or one of the many other menu items. Arrive early to take advantage of the set lunch menu.

The city's best Middle Eastern food can be found at ★ **Al Arz** (Cl. 7 No. 10-115, tel. 5/728-3760, noon-9pm Tues.-Sun., COP$13,000), an authentic, cheerful, and popular place for locals and visitors alike on Calle Ancha. If you've been out and about, get a table close to the air-conditioning unit.

Accommodations

Most visitors stay in Riohacha for only a night or two before heading onward. The options covered in this section are all centrally located, within walking distance of the city's attractions.

CARTAGENA
LA GUAJIRA

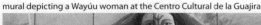

mural depicting a Wayúu woman at the Centro Cultural de la Guajira

Riohacha

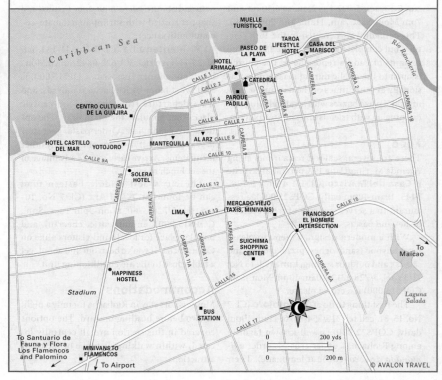

The 46-room ★ **Taroa Lifestyle Hotel** (Cl. 1 No. 4-77, tel. 5/729-1122, www.taroaho-tel.com, COP$260,000) is the swanky option in town, and it's not that expensive. Go for a room with a view of the boardwalk and sea, where you can swing in a hammock to your heart's content. Sip a cocktail on the top-floor terrace and feel the breeze.

Close to downtown, the long-standing **Hotel Arimaca** (Cl. 1 Av. La Marina No. 8-75, tel. 5/727-3515, www.hotelarimaca.com, COP$185,000 d) is a standard Colombian business hotel with 50 rooms. It has a pool.

The helpful and friendly staff at **Happiness Hostel** (Cra. 15 No. 14-51, tel. 5/727-3828, COP$40,000 dorm, COP$140,000 d) makes it the top choice of budget travelers.

The building is spic-and-span and cheerfully decorated with fluorescent colors and whim-sical signs. There are two private rooms; the three dorm rooms can sleep six people apiece. Guests can cook in the outdoor kitchen on the back patio, take a Spanish lesson, or order a drink at the small bar. Staff can assist with travel arrangements to Alta Guajira and the Santuario de Fauna y Flora Los Flamencos.

The **Hotel Castillo del Mar** (Cra. 9A No. 16-150, cell tel. 315/792-4743, castillodelmar-suites@hotmail.com, COP$30,000 dorm, COP$110,000 d, discount for multiple nights) is about a 10-minute walk from the boardwalk in a quiet residential area. There are 11 rooms, some with air-conditioning. Private rooms are spacious and, as the name implies, the build-ing really does resemble a castle.

Information and Services

At discount supermarket **Metro** (tel. 5/728-9670, 8am-10pm Mon.-Sat., 8am-9pm Sun.) in the modern **Centro Comercial Suchiimma** (Cl. 15 No. 8-56, 10am-9pm daily), you can pick up all the provisions you need for a long ride through the desert.

Transportation

Aeropuerto Almirante Padilla (RCH, Cl. 29B No. 15-217, tel. 5/727-3854) is five minutes north of town. There are only one or two flights per day from Bogotá to Riohacha on **Avianca** (www.avianca.com).

The **bus station** (Av. El Progreso and Cl. 11) has frequent service to Albania, Maicao, Santa Marta, and Barranquilla. There is also service to Valledupar, Cartagena, and Bogotá. **Shared taxis** to Uribia (where you can pick up trucks to Cabo de la Vela) leave from the market area (Cl. 15 and Cra. 1) in town. A cab to the bus station from downtown Riohacha will cost only about COP$6,000.

The atmosphere at the bus station is rushed and harried; do your best to not let it stress you out. Standard buses take longer, but are more comfortable. *Busetas* are faster minivans. Then there are shared taxis, which are more uncomfortable but much faster. If you're westbound (to Palomino, Santa Marta, or beyond), the frantic bus station experience can be avoided by turning up at the **Francisco El Hombre traffic circle.** You'll see folks hanging out waiting for transportation here; just ask them which *buseta* is going your way.

Getting around town is easy, and the best way to do so is on foot. Taxis are also considered safe. Popular taxi and ride-sharing apps have yet to arrive in Riohacha.

CROSSING INTO VENEZUELA

For stays less than 90 days, U.S., Canadian, and most European citizens do not require a visa to enter Venezuela. You may be required to show proof of a hotel reservation and proof of an air ticket departing from Venezuela, and your passport must not expire within six months of entry into Venezuela. There is

a Venezuelan consulate in Riohacha for further queries: **Consulado de Venezuela** (Cra. 7 No. 3-08, Edificio El Ejecutivo, Piso 2, tel. 5/727-4076, 8am-noon and 2pm-5pm Mon.-Thurs., 8am-1pm Fri.). There is an entry point to Venezuela at the town of Maicao, but diplomatic tensions sometimes result in border closings.

SANTUARIO DE FAUNA Y FLORA LOS FLAMENCOS

Spotting flamingos is the order of the day at the **Santuario de Fauna y Flora Los Flamencos** (Camarones settlement, www.parquesnacionales.gov.co, 7am-5pm daily, free). This park, 25 kilometers (15.5 miles) southwest of Riohacha, includes the Laguna Navio Quebradado and the larger Laguna Grande, with the fishing settlement of Camarones on the park's eastern side and the Caribbean Sea just beyond the mangroves and tropical dry forests on the north.

The park is home to thousands of American flamingos and up to 180 other species of migratory and resident aquatic birds, such as ibis and storks. Sea turtles also arrive at the lonely beach here, where conservation efforts help keep the threatened animals safe. The 7,000-hectare sanctuary (17,300 acres), which is part of the national park system, encompasses a coastal estuary where the flamingos fish for tiny shrimp in the shallow waters (from whom the birds obtain their gorgeous rose-colored plumage).

The flamingos are migratory, and are most often observed during rainy seasons such as October-November, when their numbers reach into the thousands. During the rest of the year smaller flocks often reside in the park.

To see the flamingos up close, take an hour-long *chalupa* (wooden boat) excursion (COP$15,000 pp), captained by a local, onto one of the lagoons. The price of the excursion is negotiable, and the more people there are in a group, the lower the cost. To protect your skin from the powerful sun and glare off the water, visit the park early in the morning. Ample sun protection and drinking water are essential no matter the time of day.

GETTING THERE

The easiest way to get to the park is to arrange a taxi from Riohacha (COP$15,000 each way). Either request for the driver to wait while you visit the park (additional COP$50,000), or, after finishing your tour of the park, take a *mototaxi* (COP$3,000) to the main road, where buses (COP$2,000) back to Riohacha regularly pass.

To take public transportation both ways, take a bus from Riohacha going toward Camarones for a trip of about 20 kilometers on the main road toward Santa Marta. From Camarones take a *mototaxi* (COP$3,000) to the entrance of the park, or walk the 3.5 kilometers to the park entrance.

To have someone else do the organizing and coordinating, contact **Expedición Guajira** (Cl. 2 No. 5-06, Riohacha, tel. 5/727-2336, cell tel. 311/439-4677 or 301/485-2837, franklin_penalver@yahoo.com), which will take you on an organized tour of the park for COP$80,000 per person. Insist on an early start.

★ ALTA GUAJIRA

The sparsely populated Alta Guajira (Upper Guajira) comprises the peninsula east of Cabo de la Vela and Uribia. The area's three largest settlements, where most of the tourism infrastructure is located, are Cabo de la Vela, Punta Gallinas at the very northern tip, and Nazareth, in the northeast.

The terrain has a striking ochre color, with rocky and sandy patches. The vegetation is mostly shrubs and cacti. The Caribbean coast here is broken by three large bays with stunning turquoise and aquamarine waters: Bahía Portete, Bahía Honda, and Bahía Hondita. The last of these is easily accessible as a day trip from Punta Gallinas. There are a few low mountain ranges, including the Serranía de la Macuira (864 meters/2,835 feet), located in the extreme northeast of the peninsula,

but overall the terrain is low and slightly undulated.

The only destination in the Alta Guajira that is accessible by public transportation is Cabo de la Vela. Though it is possible to contract transportation by land or sea to Punta Gallinas, most visitors choose to visit the region via organized tour, an easy option.

The sands of Alta Guajira are a favorite location for raucous 4x4 races and competitions.

Tours

The typical Alta Guajira tour (COP$380,000 pp, including food and lodging) lasts three days, spending a day each in Cabo de la Vela (with a stop at the now-abandoned salt mines of the Salinas de Manaure) and Punta Gallinas. A longer option (COP$800,000-880,000 pp, including food and lodging) adds two nights in Nazareth to visit the Parque Nacional Natural Macuira. Tours operate out of Riohacha and include SUV transportation.

Inquire before booking how many people will be in your SUV, as tour operators often try to cram seven people into a vehicle, making for an uncomfortable ride. Drivers generally have a limited grasp of English. If you'd like some background information about the region and the Wayúu people before setting off, check out the Centro Cultural de la Guajira in Riohacha first.

The desert countryside seems endless and is beautiful in its own desolate way. You'll be amazed at how these drivers know which way to go, as there are no road signs, only cacti and the occasional goat. Every once in a while, you will have to pay "tolls" to Wayúu children who have set up quasi roadblocks. To gain their permission to cross, drivers hand over crackers, cookies, or candy.

TOUR COMPANIES

Most tour companies are based in Riohacha, but some will take care of transporting you from other origin points, like Palomino, PNN Tayrona, or Santa Marta. Many companies don't regularly accept credit cards for payment; to avoid carrying a lot of cash around, consider making a *consignación* (bank deposit), which can be done anywhere in Colombia. Get the tour company's bank account information and go in person to a branch of their bank, then make a cash deposit of the full trip amount. There are no ATMs in Cabo de la Vela or Punta Gallinas.

Franklin Peñalver and the Wayúu guides of **Expedición Guajira** (Cl. 2 No. 5-06, Riohacha, tel. 5/727-2336, cell tel. 311/439-4677 or 301/485-2837, franklin_penalver@yahoo.com) know the desert like the backs of their hands. A three-day tour that includes stops in Cabo de la Vela and Punta Gallinas costs COP$550,000 per person. A two-day tour of Cabo de la Vela costs COP$230,000. Tours include food and lodging. It's also possible to craft a custom private tour. A two-person personalized tour will tend to be priced at the standard four-person rate.

Kai Eco Travel (Av. 1A No. 4-49, Riohacha, cell tel. 311/436-2830, www.kaiecotravel.com) has a range of tours for those who don't mind a group setting (maximum 6-8 people per group). A quick two-day jaunt to Cabo de la Vela costs around COP$220,000, with an extra night in Punta Gallinas bumping that up to COP$500,000. If you're up for the real Guajira experience of sleeping in a *chinchorro*

(hammock), the rates decrease slightly. Get details from Francisco at the Hotel Castillo del Mar in Riohacha.

Kaishi (Cl. 11B No. 16-125, Riohacha, cell tel. 311/429-6315, www.kaishitravel.com, adelgadorozco@yahoo.com) is another agency with a very good reputation. They only offer private tours. The per-person price decreases as the passenger list expands, so it behooves you to go with a larger group of friends. A five-day private tour for two people that includes Cabo de la Vela and Punta Gallinas costs COP$2,000,000 per person. The shorter three-day tour to Punta Gallinas with a brief stop in Cabo de la Vela costs COP$1,300,000 per person.

Cabo de la Vela

Cabo de la Vela (known as Jepira in the Wayúu language), 180 kilometers (111 miles) north of Riohacha, is a small Wayúu fishing village spread along the Caribbean Sea. It comes as a pleasant shock to finally arrive at the waters of the Caribbean after several hours driving through the Guajira's arid landscape. Here the beaches are nice, the views otherworldly, and the atmosphere peaceful. Cabo de la Vela is a destination for windsurfers and kiteboarders, thanks to its smooth waters

beach near Cabo de la Vela

and ample winds that provide near-perfect conditions.

There are several excursions around Cabo; organized package tours should include all of them in the price. One is to **El Faro,** a lighthouse on a high promontory with nearly 360-degree views of the surrounding ocean. Another is to the **Ojo del Agua,** a small but pleasant beach near a freshwater spring. Farther afield is the **Pilón de Azúcar,** a high hill that affords incredible views to the surrounding region. Nearby is the **Playa de Pilón,** a beautiful ochre-colored beach. To the west is the **Jepirachi Wind Farm,** the first of its kind in Colombia; the turbines make for a somewhat surreal sight in the midst of this barren territory. For travelers not on an organized tour, any Cabo hotel can arrange an SUV tour to these sights for around COP$20,000 per site, per person.

RECREATION

Cabo de la Vela is an excellent place to learn how to kiteboard or windsurf, as there's a good breeze here most of the year (the exception being September through November).

There are two excellent schools offering courses and equipment rental. **Eoletto** (10-min. walk from Ranchería Utta, cell tel. 321/468-0105 or 314/851-6216, www.windsurfingcolombia.com) is a windsurfing and kitesurfing school that also offers accommodations in hammocks (COP$22,000) in a quiet spot facing the water. An eight-hour windsurfing course costs COP$450,000; kitesurfing is COP$800,000. Rentals are available for COP$50,000 per hour.

Kite Addict Colombia (cell tel. 320/528-1665, www.kiteaddictcolombia.com) offers a 10-hour, three- to four-day basic course for COP$800,000, has *chinchorro* accommodations (COP$10,000 pp), and does kitesurfing excursions to Punta Gallinas. Kite Addict is located between the Mana shop and Posada Pujurú. It's the only hut with a second story.

ACCOMMODATIONS

Family-run guesthouses are plentiful in Cabo de la Vela, and are quite rudimentary. Freshwater is scarce here in the desert, so long showers are not an option. Floors are usually sandy, and electricity is limited. The street in Cabo de la Vela along the sea is lined with about 15 guesthouses. There are a few lodgings outside of town toward El Faro, such as Ranchería Utta.

The ★ **Ranchería Utta** (300 m northwest of town, Vía al Faro, cell tel. 312/687-8237 or 313/817-8076, www.rancheriautta.com, COP$15,000 hammock, COP$35,000 bed pp) is a nice place to stay. It is just far enough from Cabo de la Vela that you can experience the magic of being far away from civilization. Cabins are simple, with walls made from the hearts of *yotojoro* (cacti), a traditional form of construction in the desert. There are 11 *cabañas* with a total of 35 beds and plenty of inviting *chinchorros* (hammocks) for lazing about. Being on the beach at night, looking up at the stars, and listening to the sound of gentle waves breaking nearby is unforgettable. A pleasant restaurant at the hotel serves breakfast (COP$7,000), lunch (COP$18,000), and dinner (COP$20,000). The fare is mostly seafood (lobster is a favorite but will cost extra), but they can accommodate vegetarians.

Hospedaje Jarrinapi (cell tel. 312/600-2884, 321/831-7850, or 310/643-2786, www.hospedajejarrinapi.amawebs.com, COP$12,000 hammock, COP$35,000 bed pp) is a large hotel with 19 *yotojoro* (cactus) cabins for a total capacity of 60 people. This hotel has electricity from the afternoon until dawn and has an orderly kitchen and restaurant.

Posada Pujurú (cell tel. 300/279-5048, http://posadapujuru.blogspot.com, COP$20,000 hammock, COP$50,000 bed) has 14 rooms and a space for hammocks. Pujurú is adjacent to Kite Addict Colombia kitesurfing school.

TRANSPORTATION

Shared taxis (COP$15,000) ply the hour-long route from Riohacha to Uribia. Catch one in Riohacha at the intersection of Calle 15 and Carrera 5. Ask the driver to drop you off at the spot where passenger trucks depart for Cabo de la Vela and intermediate *rancherías*. Once your taxi drops you off, take one of the **passenger trucks** (COP$20,000) from Uribia to Cabo de la Vela. The trucks depart until 2pm every day. The uncomfortable ride, on a bench in the back of the truck, can take two or more hours, depending on how many stops are made, but this may be the quintessential Guajira experience.

Punta Gallinas

Punta Gallinas is a settlement on a small peninsula jutting into the Caribbean at the very northernmost tip of the South American continent. It is home to about 100 Wayúu who claim this beautiful spot as their ancestral land. The landscape here is a symphony of oranges, ochres, and browns, dotted with cactus and shrubs. The peninsula is hemmed in to the south by Bahía Hondita, a large bay with bright aquamarine waters and thin clusters of mangroves, and to the north by the deep-blue Caribbean.

Sights in and around Punta Gallinas include the *faro* (lighthouse), which marks the northernmost tip of South America; **Bahía Hondita,** which is home to flamingos and mangroves; and the remote and unspoiled beaches at **Dunas de Taroa** (Taroa Dunes), where windswept and towering sand dunes drop abruptly some 30 meters (100 feet) into the sea, and at **Punta Aguja,** at the southwest tip of the peninsula of Punta Gallinas. These excursions are included in tour prices. If you are on your own, hotels charge around COP$20,000 per person to see the dunes (five-person minimum), COP$150,000 for a group boat ride on the Bahía Hondita to spot flamingos, and COP$20,000 per person to go to Punta Aguja (five-person minimum).

There are two good lodging options in Punta Gallinas, both with splendid views of Bahía Hondita. ★ **Hospedaje Luzmila** (Punta Gallinas, cell tel. 312/626-8121 or 312/647-9881, luzmilita10@gmail.com, COP$20,000 hammock, COP$30,000 bed pp) has 10 *cabañas* with 20 beds and is spread out alongside the bay. Breakfast (COP$5,000), lunch (COP$15,000), and dinner (COP$15,000) are served in the restaurant. Lobster dishes cost extra.

★ **Donde Alexandra** (Punta Gallinas, cell tel. 315/538-2718 or 318/500-6942, alexandra@hotmail.com, COP$15,000 hammock, COP$30,000 bed pp) has 10 rooms and 25 beds. Meals are not included in the prices but are usually around COP$6,000 for breakfast, COP$15,000 for lunch, and COP$15,000 for dinner, unless you order lobster (COP$45,000). Donde Alexandra has sweeping vistas of the bay and beyond from the restaurant area.

TRANSPORTATION

Although most travelers visit Punta Gallinas on an organized tour, it is possible to travel on your own from the Puerto de Pescadores at Puerto Bolívar on a *lancha* (boat) arranged by Hospedaje Luzmila or Donde Alexandra (COP$120,000 pp round-trip, minimum 5 passengers). In the rainy season, from September to November, this may be the only option, as overland tour companies may not be operating.

Parque Nacional Natural Macuira

The remote **Parque Nacional Natural Macuira** (PNN Macuira, 260 km northeast of Riohacha, cell tel. 311/688-2362, macuira@parquesnacionales.gov.co, 8am-6pm daily, free) covers an area of 25,000 hectares (61,780 acres) and encompasses the entire Serranía de la Macuira (Macuira mountain range), an isolated mountainous outcrop at the northeastern tip of the Guajira Peninsula. These mountains are a biological island in the middle of the surrounding desert. The Macuira range, which is 35 kilometers (22 miles) long and 864 meters (2,835 feet) in elevation at Cerro Palua, its highest point, captures moisture-laden winds from the sea that nourish a unique low-elevation tropical cloud forest teeming with ferns, orchids, bromeliads, and moss. At lower elevations, there are tropical dry forests.

The park includes 350 species of plants, 140 species of birds (17 endemic), and more than 20 species of mammals. The park is within the large Alta Guajira Wayúu Reservation. In the lower parts of the range, within the park, live many Wayúu families who raise goats and grow corn and other subsistence crops.

The gateway to the park is the Wayúu town of **Nazareth.** Visitors are required to register and participate in a brief presentation at the PNN Macuira park office, where they must also hire an authorized Wayúu guide. A few of the official independent guides are Ricardo Brito (cell tel. 312/654-5328), Pedro Quintero (cell tel. 313/648-8060), and María Eulalia Quintero (cell tel. 322/664-1319).

There are multiple hikes varying 1.5-6 hours; the cost of a guided walk ranges COP$35,000-45,000 per eight-person group. Day hikes meander along riverbeds through tropical dry forest. One leads to the **Arewolü Sand Dunes** (two hours, 1.5 kilometers/1 mile, COP$45,000), which are, surprisingly, located in the midst of the forest. Another hike takes you to the **Shipanoü pools.** A third hike goes to **Cerro Tojoro** (2.5 hours, COP$25,000), which affords beautiful views of the coast and the mountain range. The most challenging hike, **Nazareth-Siapana** (seven hours, 12 kilometers/7.5 miles, COP$120,000)

traverses the entire length of the park. Plan to hike early in the morning to increase your chances of seeing birds and other wildlife. Hiking to the Macuira's unusual cloud forest is not permitted by the Wayúu.

There are only a few lodging options in Nazareth, the town closest to the park. One suitable choice is **Hospedaje Vía Manaure** (entrance to Nazareth, cell tel. 320/310-3783 or 314/552-5513, evelasiosuarez@msn.com, COP$20,000 hammock, COP$30,000 bed pp), which can accommodate 40 people and offers Wi-Fi. It has an on-site restaurant (breakfast COP$10,000, lunch COP$15,000, dinner COP$10,000) serving regional dishes. Make arrangements in advance for meals. Another choice is **Villa Inmaculada** (cell tel. 320/504-8519, COP$20,000 pp), offering the same services as Hospedaje Vía Manaure.

TRANSPORTATION

Getting to Nazareth and PNN Macuira requires patience, money, time, and determination. If you are touring the Alta Guajira, PNN Macuira can be added to your itinerary after Punta Gallinas. Otherwise, hire a car out of Riohacha for the day (about COP$500,000, negotiable). Another option is to take public transportation from Uribia to Nazareth (Sun. only, 5-6 hours, COP$60,000). Before visiting, contact the **PNN Macuira park office** (cell tel. 311/688-2362, macuira@parquesnacionales.gov.co) for more transportation options, road conditions, and updated park information.

Western Caribbean Coast

The portion of the Caribbean coast that stretches west from Cartagena is less visited and familiar than the region to the east. That may be just the ticket for those yearning to explore the undiscovered and escape the crowds.

From Cartagena, this area extends west to the Golfo de Urabá and then juts north through the Darién Gap and the border with

Panama. The Golfo de Morrosquillo is home to the beach towns of Tolú and San Antero, as well as the inland city of Montería. Across the Golfo de Urabá, the tropical rainforests of the Darién provide an exuberant backdrop to the seaside towns of Capurganá and Sapzurro, which are accessible only by boat or plane. The diving off the coast here is superb.

What most visitors remember and cherish about a visit to this remote part of Colombia is being immersed in truly wild nature.

Safety

This region was greatly affected by violence during the worst years of the armed conflict between paramilitaries, guerrillas, and the military, with civilians often caught in the middle. This was especially so in the remote areas of the Darién, which was a major drug-trafficking route. Although drug smuggling in inland areas continues to this day, the places covered in this guide are safe. It's never a bad idea to ask locals about the security of an area, especially if you venture to parts not described in this guide.

GOLFO DE MORROSQUILLO

South of Cartagena, the Golfo de Morrosquillo is a broad, 50-kilometer-wide (31-mile-wide) inlet. Largely unknown to international visitors, the gulf's easternmost shore is home to the beach community of Tolú, which is popular with vacationing Colombian families. Off its shores are the Islas de San Bernardo, with beautiful coral reefs and the world's most densely populated island, tiny Santa Cruz del Islote.

On the southern edge of the gulf is the town of San Antero, which is home to a crocodile preserve on Bahía de Cispatá. Outside of San Antero is peaceful Río Cedro, a place to truly disconnect from the world. Inland from San Antero is the region's major city, Montería, in the heart of Colombia's cattle country.

Tolú

Balmy beachside Tolú, 160 kilometers (100 miles) southwest of Cartagena, is best described as sleepy. Here, locals get around on foot or *bici-taxi* (bicycle cab), and it's hot and humid year-round. The beaches off the mainland are pleasant, but many visitors come here in order to catch a boat to the Islas de San Bernardo.

In the evening, when the mercury has dropped a few degrees, locals congregate in the main plaza to exchange gossip and people-watch. On weekends, the town becomes more lively, with a steady influx of weekend warriors. Along the boardwalk that parallels the beach, vendors sell ceviche, bars blast music, and kids splash around in the warm water.

Tolú is home to a few decent beaches, perfect for lazing in the sun. Check out laid-back **Playa El Francés,** five kilometers (three miles) north of Tolú. Another option

rugged coast near Tolú

is **Punta Bolívar,** nearly 30 kilometers (17 miles) southwest of Tolú.

ACCOMMODATIONS

★ **Villa Babilla** (Cl. 20 No. 3-40, Tolú, tel. 5/288-6124, www.villababillahostel.com, COP$45,000 s, COP$90,000 d) is the best place to stay in Tolú by a long shot, with its garden courtyard and serene atmosphere. Rooms have no TV or air-conditioning. A kitchen is available for guest use and there is an Olímpica grocery store a couple of blocks away. Nearby roosters may disturb your sleep.

Catering mostly to Colombian families and groups, **Camino Verde** (Playa El Francés, Tolú, tel. 5/249-9464, www.vacacionescaminoverde.com, COP$270,000 d) is six kilometers (3.7 miles) east of Tolú, and is a peaceful (but not fancy) spot to relax during the week, despite its sprawling size. Room are generally set up family-style, with a double and a twin bed. Most visitors drive here.

TRANSPORTATION

There is frequent bus service from Tolú to Cartagena (3 hours, COP$30,000) and Montería (2.5 hours, COP$25,000). Buses to Cartagena and Montería are at Calle 15 where it intersects Carreteras 2A and 3A.

ADA (www.ada-aero.com) and **Satena** (www.satena.gov.co) fly from Medellín to Tolú, making this a quick, easy, and often inexpensive beach destination.

To get around Tolú, take a *bici-taxi* (bicycle cab).

Islas de San Bernardo

The easiest and least expensive way to spend some time on the turquoise waters of the Golfo de Morrosquillo and relax on a tropical white-sand beach is to visit the **Islas de San Bernardo.** These islands, located about 16 kilometers (10 miles) offshore, are part of the Parque Nacional Natural Corales del Rosario y San Bernardo, although the islands have been privately developed.

A day tour is a good way to see the islands, and generally includes a stop for a seafood lunch, snorkeling at **Isla Múcura,** and passing by a handful of the other islands, including **Santa Cruz del Islote,** the most densely populated island in the world, with one person for every 10 square meters. Book a tour of the islands with **Mundo Mar** (Av. 1 No. 14-40, Tolú, tel. 5/288-4431, www.clubnauticomundomartolu.com.co, COP$60,000 pp), a reputable tour agency. Other tour agencies are located in the hotels that line Tolú's boardwalk. Most day tours depart at 8:30am and return to Tolú by about 4:30pm each day.

FOOD AND ACCOMMODATIONS

★ **Punta Norte** (Isla Tintipán, cell tel. 310/707-4005, www.hotelpuntanorte.com, COP$195,000 pp), on Isla Tintipán in the Islas de San Bernardo, is run by a friendly Uruguayan and is most often referred to as Donde El Uruguayo, or "The Uruguayan's Place." Bring plenty of insect repellent to this remote island paradise. Accommodations are not luxurious, but it's a relaxed place. The restaurant includes all meals, and fresh lobster is part of the deal! It takes about an hour to get to the hotel from Tolú by boat (COP$40,000). When you make your reservation, inquire about transportation timing and availability.

For white-sand beaches, warm aquamarine waters, and the occasional calorie-loaded cocktail, go to the resort of **Punta Faro** (Isla Múcura, cell tel. 317/435-9594, www.puntafaro.com, COP$1,190,000 d), an island resort in the Islas de San Bernardo. There are 45 simple rooms with no hot water in the showers and unreliable Wi-Fi. All meals (included) are served buffet-style. Spend your time here lounging on the beach, discovering nearby islands, participating in various water activities, riding bikes, and taking short hikes. It's a good place to bring kids. Round-trip fast boat service from Cartagena (two hours) costs an additional COP$175,000 per person. You can also depart from Tolú. Punta Faro can assist with transportation to and from the island; inquire when you make your reservation.

For great Caribbean vibes on a floating piece of paradise, head to the ★ **Casa**

en el Agua (Isla Tintipán, cell tel. 312/756-3439, www.casaenelagua.com, COP$39,000 hammocks, COP$150,000 d), a floating solar-powered hostel near Isla Tintipán. There is a restaurant here, which serves all meals family-style. Activities include diving, island tours, and spearfishing. At night, it's possible to observe bioluminescent plankton. On nights where there's a full moon, Casa en el Agua hosts "reef raves." The quickest and easiest way to get here is via Casa en el Agua's boat service (1pm Mon., Wed., and Fri., COP$90,000 pp) from Cartagena. You must reserve a spot and confirm departure details in advance. It's also possible to get here overland, though it requires taking multiple modes of transportation. From Cartagena, take a bus to San Onofre (COP$25,000), a *mototaxi* to Rincón del Mar (COP$10,000), then a boat (COP$150,000 for four passengers) to the hostel. Or, from Tolú, it's a 45-minute trip if you hop aboard the island tour boat (8am daily, COP$35,000 pp). Check Casa en el Agua's website for specific transportation instructions.

Bahía de Cispatá

The most interesting part of this region can be found along the coastline of **Bahía de Cispatá,** a serene bay lined with undisturbed mangrove forests, near the town of San Antero. Here, an interesting project by **Asocaiman** (cell tel. 300/810-1161, www.asocaiman.org) helps in the protection and propagation of American crocodiles and turtles. These creatures were once hunted for their meat and eggs, but today, locals are trained on the importance of protecting these species. A visit to the small bayside refuge, where many species of crocodiles and turtles reside before being released back into the wild, consists of a tour led by a former hunter. There is no set price for the tour, but guides can accept tips. Asocaiman also offers boat tours (COP$15,000-50,000 pp, depending on group size) of the mangroves, during which you'll have the chance to see animals in their natural habitat. Call Asocaiman in advance to coordinate your visit.

FOOD AND ACCOMMODATIONS
Go eat at ★ **Pesecar** (Bahía de Cispatá, cell tel. 312/651-2651, 7am-9pm daily). It's worth the trip to San Antero just for lunch here—very fresh seafood with an unbeatable bayside location.

San Antero borders the water and has some nice beaches at Playa Blanca. There is a long

a young crocodile at the Asocaiman conservation center in Bahía de Cispatá

string of waterfront hotels popular with week-enders from Montería and Medellín. During the week, it's very quiet. The **Cispatá Marina Hotel** (tel. 4/811-0197 or 4/811-0887, www.cispata.com, COP$123,000 pp) has an enviable location overlooking Bahía de Cispatá and, on the other side, the beaches of Playa Blanca. The hotel comprises 16 cute red-roofed *cabañas* as well as smaller apartments. The hotel also has a large pool.

A locally run and quite friendly hotel, the **Mangle Colora'o** (Vereda Amaya, tel. 4/811-0722, cell tel. 301/203-7071, COP$35,000 pp) is just across the street from Bahía de Cispatá.

TRANSPORTATION

San Antero and Bahía de Cispatá are about 30 kilometers (18.6 miles) southwest of Tolú, on the Coveñas-Lorica highway. Regular public transportation is available for under COP$8,000 from the bus terminal along the main highway.

Río Cedro

It's hard to find a place more tranquil than Río Cedro. This community of banana and plantain farmers on a mostly undeveloped coastline in Córdoba, near San Antero, is set amid an unusual tropical dry forest that is home to sloths, howler monkeys, iguanas, and many species of birds. The gray-sand beaches are strewn with driftwood, and pelicans routinely glide by in formation above the usually calm waters.

In peaceful Río Cedro, there are paths galore that wind through the forest and excellent swimming and kayaking opportunities. But perhaps the best activity of all is lazing in a hammock, enjoying the view. Take mosquito repellent.

There are only two accommodation options here. The first, **Río Cedro Paraíso Natural** (cell tel. 313/718-4015, www.rio-cedro.com, COP$230,000 pp d, three-night min.) is a single thatched roof *cabaña* with a 12-person capacity. There are no individual rooms available—the whole cabin is rented at

once. A kitchen is available for use, but meal service is also provided.

The second option is the **Reserva Natural Viento Solar** (cell tel. 317/377-6244, www.vientosolar.org, COP$145,000 pp, all meals included), a private nature reserve with a variety of private and shared rooms. Viento Solar often hosts yoga, meditation, and indigenous healing retreats. Vegetarian meals are provided to guests.

Río Cedro is accessible from the town of Lorica, on the banks of the Río Sinú. To get to Lorica from San Antero, take one of the *busetas* (30 minutes, COP$8,000) that pass through town. From the Tolú-Montería highway in Lorica, take a shared taxi (one hour, COP$8,000) through San Bernardo del Viento to Moñitos—ask a local where to flag one down. From there, both lodges can arrange for a motorbike (45 minutes, COP$10,000) to collect you. Río Cedro Paraíso Natural will arrange from Lorica or Montería for its guests.

THE COLOMBIAN DARIÉN

The Darién Gap (Tapón del Darién) is a sparsely populated swath of land, roughly 160 kilometers (100 miles) long and 50 kilometers (30 miles) wide that straddles the border between Colombia and Panama. Its name comes from its interruption of the 48,000-kilometer (30,000-mile) Pan-American Highway, a storied road that extends from Prudhoe Bay, Alaska, to Ushuaia in Patagonia. The highway picks up again in the Colombian port town of Turbo.

The Colombian Darién is bookended by the delta of the Río Atrato that flows into the Golfo de Urabá on the east and the Serranía de Baudó mountain range on the west. This land of rivers, swamps, and rainforest-covered mountains is one of the most ecologically diverse regions of the world. Ecotourism is widely viewed as the future for this area.

The rainforests here are particularly rich in palm trees, of which 120 species have been identified, as well as cycads, ancient plants that look like palms. Notable too are more than 40 species of brightly colored poisonous frogs, known locally as *ranas kokois*. Some of these small frogs are covered with a deadly poison and have evolved stunning coloring of bright orange, red, gold, and blue. They are active in the day and therefore relatively easy to spot. Of Colombia's 1,800 species of birds, more than 1,000 have been identified in this region, including a large number of hummingbirds.

SAFETY

The absence of roads, abundance of navigable rivers, and the cover provided by the jungle's canopy have made this region into a major corridor for the trafficking of illegal drugs, which has also meant that there has been a heavy presence of both guerrillas and paramilitaries. The Colombian Darién is populated mostly by Afro-Colombian and indigenous communities that have been hard hit by violence fueled by trafficking.

Today, it is safe to visit the twin villages of Capurganá and Sapzurro, perched on idyllic crescent-shaped bays near the Panamanian border.

★ Capurganá and Sapzurro

While much of the Colombian Darién is lowland and swamp, as it is part of the Río Atrato basin, near the border with Panama, the terrain is mountainous and covered in tropical jungle. Here you'll find the twin towns of Capurganá and Sapzurro.

Capurganá is the larger village of the two, with a population of about 2,000. Many residents make their living by fishing. Tourism has increased in recent years, resulting in more guesthouses, hotels, and restaurants, many of which are run by Europeans.

Capurganá's *muelle* (port) bustles with activity during the day, with boats constantly bringing in passengers and supplies. In the evening, ramshackle bars, particularly around the town's soccer field, blast music for beer-drinking patrons. Nature is abundant here: Within minutes of leaving your hotel you'll

be surrounded by the sounds of the jungle, accompanied only by the occasional green-and-black-speckled toad and maybe a band of howler monkeys.

Sapzurro is even more laid-back than Capurganá. This village is reachable only by foot or boat. Walking here means crossing a jungle path over a mountain, which is the attraction of coming here, though it can be a strenuous journey. For a few thousand pesos, you can opt to take a boat to Sapzurro, a short 10-minute ride.

Prepare yourself for the weather here: Rain and humidity mean mud and mosquitoes, so you'll want durable shoes and layered clothing. Bring a flashlight or headlamp for walking at night. There are no cars in either village. Get around on foot, by bike, or by boat.

HIKING

There are several jungle walks to make around Capurganá. These take you through dense jungle overflowing with tropical vegetation populated by howler monkeys, birds, colorful frogs, and snakes. While the walks are short and fairly straightforward, you may want to ask at your hotel or hostel for a guide, especially for the walk between Capurganá and Sapzurro. Guides cost about COP$10,000. Wear hiking boots (waterproof if possible) and a swimsuit underneath your clothes for dips in the water off of Sapzurro or in freshwater swimming holes, and set off in the morning hours to give yourself plenty of time to get back.

An easy walk to make, without the need of a guide, is to **La Coquerita** (20-minute walk north from town, cell tel. 311/824-8022, COP$2,000), a delightfully ramshackle waterside hangout where you can have a refreshing coco-lemonade or maybe some guacamole and *patacones* (fried plantains) and take a dip in the refreshing freshwater or saltwater pools. There are also some handicrafts on sale here. To get there, walk along the Playa Caleta just north of the port, passing in front of the Hotel Almar. Continue along the jungle path that hugs the coastline. La Coquerita is less than one kilometer (0.5 mile) from town, and the path is well marked. Look out for the black and fluorescent-green frogs along the way, but don't touch them; they're poisonous.

El Cielo waterfall is a 50-minute walk (about 3 kilometers/1.8 miles) through the jungle from Capurganá. The path is flat and easy, although you'll have to make about a dozen crossings of shallow streams. Bring a bathing suit to cool off in the swimming holes you'll encounter. To get to heavenly El Cielo, set out on the road that runs parallel to the airstrip and then ask locals for directions. On the way to El Cielo, look for **El Trébol Piscina,** a pool where you can take a dip in cool waters and have lunch.

The **path to Sapzurro** leads you through the exuberant rainforest to a lookout point and then down directly to the beach. The hike takes two hours. Start at the soccer field, on the southern end of Capurganá, and ask the way. Midway up the uphill path is a shack that is the home of a man who claims to protect the jungle. Once you find him, you know you're on the right track. He expects those who pass through to pay him about COP$1,000. At the top of the mountain there is a nice overlook with views of Capurganá and the coastline. The hike is not difficult, but the path can get muddy and slippery in places. Wear hiking boots and pick up a walking stick along the way to help you manage the steep parts.

Once in Sapzurro, you're a short hike (15 minutes) from the border with **Panama** and the village of **La Miel.** This easy walk begins on the same street as Cabañas Uvali and the Reserva Natural Tacarcuna. The border crossing is at the top of a steep hill embedded with steps. You'll need to show a passport to cross over to Panama. There is not much to the community of La Miel. It has a small military outpost, many young children running around, and a pleasant beach where you can swim and have a seafood lunch or a drink.

DIVING AND SNORKELING

As you'd expect, the warm, turquoise waters off the coast of Capurganá, all the way up to San Blas in Panama, make for fantastic diving, and there are over 30 diving sites to choose from. The best time for underwater exploration is from May to November. During those months, visibility is exceptional with hardly any waves. There are coral walls, reef rocks, and caves to explore.

Dive and Green Diving Center (facing the port, cell tel. 311/578-4021 or 316/781-6255, www.diveandgreen.com, 7:30am-12:30pm

swimming hole near the El Cielo waterfall

and 2pm-6pm daily) is the best place to organize a diving trip (certified diver excursion COP$190,000) or to take a five-day PADI certification course (COP$820,000) with a bilingual instructor. For these packages it is best to pay in cash, as credit card transactions have an additional fee. For those interested in snorkeling, Dive and Green can make arrangements for you, though they don't themselves lead snorkeling trips. Dive and Green offers all the equipment you need. If you are on the fence about whether diving is for you, they offer a Discover Scuba Diving day for COP$150,000. Dive and Green has accommodations, comprising four rooms in a house adjacent to their offices. These cost COP$25,000 per person. The house faces the water, guaranteeing a pleasant evening breeze.

TOURS
Sol del Darién (cell tel. 318/633-3994) is a recommended tour agency run by a French couple. It offers an interesting menu of excursions in the region, including canoe trips, guided nature walks, and multiday adventures in the San Blas Islands. The owners also operate the hostel La Bohemia.

FOOD
Hotels are usually the best options for food in both villages. **Donde Josefina** (Playa Caleta, cell tel. 316/779-7760, noon-9pm daily, COP$30,000) remains the top restaurant for a delicious, gourmet seafood dinner, right on the beach in the heart of Capurganá. Dining on lobster in a coconut-and-garlic sauce under the swaying branches of a palm tree: That sounds like a vacation!

Hernan Patacón (no phone, hours vary, COP$18,000) is a food stand serving fresh fish and shrimp. They are located in front of the town clinic. A decent **bakery** overlooking the soccer field in the center of town serves breakfast, and is open daily.

In Sapzurro, the best places for a meal are **Doña Triny** (Hostal Doña Triny, cell tel. 312/751-8626 or 313/725-8362, noon-10pm daily, COP$20,000), a two-story brick house

facing the water, and the **Gata Negra** (cell tel. 314/725-0325, www.lagatanegra.net, open daily) for authentic home-style Italian dishes. Call in advance to let either restaurant know you're coming.

ACCOMMODATIONS
There are a surprising number of excellent and inexpensive accommodations options in both Capurganá and Sapzurro. While there are a few large, all-inclusive hotels with welcome drinks and the works, the most interesting and comfortable options are the smaller guesthouses and hostels. Nearly all hotels are owned and operated by out-of-towners.

In Capurganá, many hotels and hostels are near the *muelle* (port), the hub of activity. Many visitors stay at one of the few all-inclusive hotels in Capurganá, but those options lack charm.

One of the best "urban" lodging options in Capurganá is **Posada del Gecko** (in town, cell tel. 314/525-6037, www.posadadelgecko.com, posadadelgecko@hotmail.com, COP$20,000 dorm, COP$35,000 d), which is run by an Italian-Colombian couple and offers both dorms and private rooms spread over two houses, with a capacity of 28 people. In between the buildings is a spacious garden ideal for lounging in a hammock or the hot tub. Enjoy a good Italian dinner by candlelight at the restaurant (7:30pm-11pm daily); it's open to nonguests as well, but it's best to stop by in advance and make a reservation. The hotel can arrange three-day excursions to the San Blas Islands (Panama), in which you visit a Kuna indigenous community, frolic on pristine white-sand beaches, and snorkel.

Several excellent guesthouses reside amid the trees in the Playa Roca area, about a 15-minute walk or horse ride from Capurganá. At night you'll need no air-conditioner, and in the morning you may awake to birdsong. This is more pleasant than staying in the Centro. Some of the perks of staying at welcoming ★ **Cabañas El Tucán** (Playa Roca, www.cabanatucancapurgana.com, COP$65,000), run by a friendly Bogotana-Italian couple, are that the owners make their own pasta and are good cooks. This house in the jungle is clean and comfortable, and the prices of the four spacious rooms are reasonable.

Right across the path from El Tucán is ★ **Cabañas Darius** (Playa Roca, cell tel. 314/622-5638, www.cdarius.blogspot.com, capurga05@gmail.com, COP$85,000 pp incl. 2 meals), a very nice guesthouse among the trees. Rooms are spacious and clean, and it's cool enough at night that you won't miss air-conditioning. Balconies and hammocks provide lounging space, but the top selling points are the warm hospitality and the good food.

A third option in the same area is **Hotel Los Robles** (Playa Roca, cell tel. 314/632-8408 or 314/632-8428, COP$120,000 d incl. 2 meals). This lodge has quite the entrance—a winding path lined by bright fuchsia ginger flowers. *Caracolí* and *higuerón* trees provide shade and a home for birds. There are 12 rooms in two houses.

The most low-key place to stay in the Capurganá area is Playa Aguacate. The German owner of the ★ **Bahía Lodge** (Playa Aguacate, cell tel. 314/812-2727, www.bahia-lodge.com, COP$190,000 pp incl. 2 meals) has carved a little paradise out of the jungle—once there you won't want to leave. Its simple and comfortable cabins, each with a sea view, are popular with honeymooners and those celebrating special occasions. Over the hill from Bahía Lodge is **Hotel Las Ceibas** (Playa Aguacate, cell tel. 313/695-6392 or Medellín tel. 4/331-7440, www.hotellasceibas.com). It has three rooms in two houses set amid gardens; the rooms have pleasant balconies with hammocks for late-afternoon relaxation.

La Bohemia (south of town, no phone, www.labohemiahostal.com, COP$20,000 dorm, COP$50,000 private room) is a hostel in a cheerful wooden house with two dorm rooms and two private rooms, with a shared bath. It's a good choice thanks to the friendly, artsy atmosphere. The hostel is run by the owners of the Sol del Darién tour agency.

In Sapzurro, there are quite a few inexpensive lodging options, but fewer restaurants than in Capurganá. Most hotels offer meals, though, and are usually the best bet, as they tend to be open more frequently. **Cabañas Uvali** (in town, cell tel. 314/624-1325, COP$40,000 pp) is a friendly, clean, and straightforward little place in town. It's about a five-minute walk from the beach. **La Posada Hostal & Camping** (cell tel. 312/662-7599 or 310/410-2245, www.sapzurrolaposada.com, COP$65,000 pp d), close to the path to Capurganá, has one luxury apartment with a view, a dorm-style room, and a large space for camping under a big mango tree. They have a little tiki bar over the water, which can be set up for a romantic dinner under the stars.

The ★ **Resort Paraíso Sapzurro** (cell tel. 313/685-9862, COP$10,000 dorm, COP$50,000 pp d) has basic beachfront cabins. This hostel is more commonly known as "Donde El Chileno" (The Chilean's Place), after the Chilean owner. The hostel can organize oversea transportation directly to Cartagena. Free avocadoes and mangoes are a nice perk. It's located near the path to Capurganá and the entrance to Sapzurro.

The ★ **Sapzurro Reserva Natural Tacarcuna** (on the path to La Miel, cell tel. 314/622-3149 or 320/300-1668, COP$40,000 pp) is a special place for anyone interested in the region's flora and fauna. The two cabins are cute. The owners, Martha and Fabio, offer a botanical garden of native species with nature trails and a butterfly farm. Their other passion is birds: Go behind the house and up the mountain with a pair of binoculars to spot cuckoos, parakeets, owls, antipittas, tanagers, four different types of toucans, and many other species, along with the throngs of migratory birds that arrive between August and November each year. The owners can organize a number of hikes in the area. Don't confuse this natural reserve with the all-inclusive Tacarcuna Lodge near the Capurganá airport.

The ★ **Gata Negra** (cell tel. 314/725-0325, www.lagatanegra.net, COP$50,000) is a cozy guesthouse that also serves Italian food. It's surrounded by fruit trees and jungle.

There are two rooms with a shared bath and one with a private bath.

INFORMATION AND SERVICES

Bring extra cash to Capurganá: There are no ATMs, and credit cards are not accepted in most establishments. To avoid bringing wads of pesos, many hotels will allow (or require) you to make a *consignación* (deposit) to their bank account in advance. That can usually be done from any city in Colombia. The nearest bank, **Banco Agrario** (Cl. Las Flores with Cl. Consistorial, tel. 4/682-8229, 8am-11:30am and 2pm-4:30pm Mon.-Fri.), is in Acandí, a half-hour boat ride south from Capurganá.

TRANSPORTATION

Capurganá and Sapzurro are accessible only by plane or boat. To get here, you have to either take a flight from Medellín to either the Capurganá airport (near the town center) or the Acandí airport (10 minutes outside of Acandí) or take a *lancha* (boat) from Turbo or Acandí. Acandí is the municipality about 17 kilometers (10.5 miles) south of Capurganá. Should the seas be too rough or if a general strike shuts down all transportation options, you may be stuck in the jungle for a couple of days more.

Aerolíneas de Antioquia (www.ada-aero.com.co) serves both Capurganá and Acandí from Aeropuerto Olaya Herera in Medellín. ADA has one flight per day (Mon.-Sat., less than an hour, COP$150,000 and up each way) to Acandí from Medellín. Flights are prone to sell out on long weekends and during high season in December and January and during Semana Santa. The Capurganá airport has been closed for improvements, with an expected reopening in 2017.

To get from Acandí to Capurganá, you'll have to take a horse-drawn cart from the airport to Acandí's docks (a 15-minute trip, COP$6,000), from where you'll take a 30-minute *lancha* (boat) ride to Capurganá (COP$17,000). There is a *lancha* departure at 1pm daily. The seas can be rough at times, so try to get a seat in back to avoid too much jostling from the boat's movements. Keep your camera or other electronics in their cases so they won't be exposed to seawater. Demand a life vest. The return trip from Capurganá to Acandí generally leaves at 7:30am daily.

All boats arrive at the *muelle* (docks) in Capurganá, in the middle of town. Most hotels are within walking distance, although those on Playa Roca are a 15-minute

Boats are the main form of transportation in Capurganá.

walk away. If you have heavy luggage, ask for a horse (about COP$10,000) when you disembark.

Hotels in Playa Aguacate and Sapzurro are reachable only by taking another *lancha* from the docks in Capurganá, about a 20-minute ride. Those hotels will arrange your transportation from Capurganá in advance.

There are **buses** from Medellín (eight hours), Montería (four hours), and from cities across the Caribbean coast to the rough port city of Turbo on the Golfo de Urabá. It's then possible to take a 2.5- to 3-hour boat ride from Turbo to Capurganá or Acandí. These usually depart daily 7am-8am, costing about COP$60,000. The early-morning departure means that you will probably have to spend the previous night in Turbo. That's not ideal, but most tourists agree that **Residencias La Florida** (Cra. 13 No. 99A-56, Turbo, tel. 4/827-3531, COP$30,000 d) is an acceptable lodging option. It's close to the port, and the hotel staff is quite helpful in arranging your onward transportation.

Do not plan to take a boat from Turbo to Capurganá from December to March. The 2.5-hour journey can be awful due to high winds and unrelenting waves. This is likewise true for the trip from Acandí to Capurganá, although it is a much shorter ride.

There is also a direct **fast boat** service from the town of Necoclí (tel. 4/821-4164 or cell tel. 315/687-4284), which is a convenient option for those coming from Cartagena. It takes 1.5 hours and costs COP$120,000 round-trip (COP$70,000 one-way). In Necoclí, **Hotel Panorama Suite** (cell tel. 312/702-0813, hotelpanoramanecocli@gmail.com, COP$40,000 pp d) has 28 rooms and is run by the same people who operate boat transportation to Capurganá.

To return to the mainland from Capurganá, it's best to reserve a day in advance for *lanchas* bound for Acandí or Turbo, especially during peak tourist times. Your hotel should be able to do this for you by calling ahead to the *muelle,* where the contact is Ariel Palacios (cell tel. 312/264-5924).

To travel onward to Panama, you must go to the Colombian **Ministerio de Relaciones Exteriores** (Cl. del Comercio, Capurganá cell tel. 311/746-6234, 8am-5pm Mon.-Fri., 9am-4pm Sat.) to get an exit stamp before leaving Capurganá.

Boyacá and the Santanderes

Look for ★ to find recommended sights, activities, dining, and lodging.

Highlights

★ **Villa de Leyva:** One of Colombia's most visited and beloved colonial pueblos, relaxed Villa de Leyva is just a couple of hours away from Bogotá (page 164).

★ **Santuario Flora y Fauna Iguaque:** Hike through Andean forest and mysterious *páramo* to a sacred Muisca lake (page 170).

★ **Tunja's Historic Churches:** Glimpse the splendor of Tunja's colonial past in its beautiful churches (page 174).

★ **Parque Nacional Natural El Cocuy:** Stunning scenery greets you at every turn in this remote park of snowcapped peaks (page 186).

★ **Paragliding near San Gil:** Soar through the air with the greatest of ease in Colombia's recreational capital (page 197).

★ **Cañón del Chicamocha:** Experience the blue skies and deep canyons of this photogenic park not far from Bucaramanga and San Gil (page 200).

★ **Baricara:** Decompress and rejuvenate in one of the most beautiful pueblos in the country (page 201).

★ **Camino Real:** Follow in the footsteps of indigenous Guane traders and Spanish colonists

on this meandering path through the Santander countryside (page 202).

The mountainous departments of Boyacá, Santander, and Norte de Santander are rich in history, natural beauty, and outdoor activities.

The countryside is dotted with historic colonial towns, including two of the most beautiful and well preserved in Colombia: Villa de Leyva and Barichara. The scenery of the region runs the gamut from the desert landscape near Villa de Leyva to the bucolic rolling hills and pastures of agriculturally rich Boyacá, and from the awe-inspiring Río Chicamocha canyon to the dramatic snow-capped peaks of the Sierra Nevada del Cocuy.

Outdoor activities are the draw here, like trekking in the Sierra Nevada del Cocuy and white-water rafting, caving, and paragliding near San Gil. In most of the region, a refreshingly slow pace prevails. The pueblos of Boyacá are easily accessed from Bogotá and can even be visited on a long weekend. It will take a little more time to discover Santander, located between Bogotá and the Caribbean coast. Although most people only stop in Cúcuta on their way to Venezuela or on a visa run, the sultry city is a pleasant surprise. The historic pueblo of Pamplona is the most chilled-out place in all of Norte de Santander.

HISTORY

Before the Spanish conquest, Boyacá was part of the Muisca heartland. Hunza, where present-day Tunja is located, was the seat of the Zaque, one of the Muisca leaders. The Sun Temple, one of the Muiscas' sacred sites, was in Sogamoso, northeast of Tunja.

Boyacá and the Santanderes played a major role in the struggle for independence. In 1811, Boyacá became the seat of the Provincias Unidas de la Nueva Granada (United Provinces of New Granada), the first Republican independent government. It was in Boyacá in 1819 that the two decisive battles of independence were fought: the Batalla del Pantano de Vargas (Battle of the Vargas Swamp) and the Batalla del Puente de Boyacá (Battle of the Bridge of Boyacá). These battles marked the end of Spanish domination in Colombia.

Santander was one of the more dynamic regions in 19th-century Colombia, with an export economy based on the cultivation of quinine, coffee, cocoa, and tobacco. In the

Previous: cobblestone streets in the colonial village of Guane; Lago Tota. **Above:** waterfall near San Gil.

Boyacá and the Santanderes

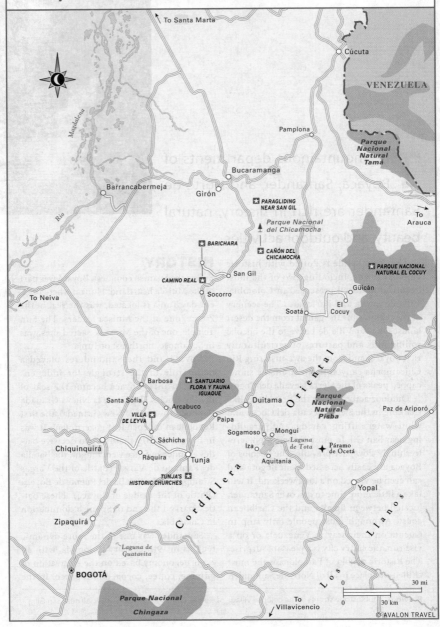

To Santa Marta

Cúcuta

VENEZUELA

Magdalena

Pamplona

Parque
Nacional
Natural
Tamá

Bucaramanga

Barrancabermeja

Girón

★ PARAGLIDING
NEAR SAN GIL

To
Arauca

Parque Nacional
del Chicamocha

Río

★ BARICHARA

★ CAÑÓN DEL
CHICAMOCHA

★ PARQUE NACIONAL
NATURAL EL COCUY

CAMINO REAL ★

San Gil

To Neiva

Socorro

Güicán

El
Cocuy

Soatá

Oriental

Barbosa

★ SANTUARIO
FLORA Y FAUNA
IGUAQUE

Santa Sofía

★ VILLA
DE LEYVA

Arcabuco

Duitama

Parque
Nacional
Natural
Pisba

Paz de Ariporó

Paipa

Sogamoso

Monguí

Sáchica

Iza

Laguna
de Tota

◆ Páramo
de Ocetá

Chiquinquirá

Ráquira

Tunja

Aquitania

Yopal

★ TUNJA'S
HISTORIC CHURCHES

Cordillera

Los

Zipaquirá

llanos

Laguna de
Guatavita

★ BOGOTÁ

0   30 mi

0   30 km

Parque Nacional

To
Villavicencio

© AVALON TRAVEL

Chingaza

early 20th century, Norte de Santander became the first major coffee-producing region in Colombia.

The mid-20th-century fighting between Liberals and Conservatives was particularly acute in Santander and Norte de Santander. In 1960, the guerrilla group Ejercito de Liberación Nacional (National Liberation Army), or ELN, was born in rural Santander.

The region has experienced steady economic growth since the early 2000s. Bucaramanga, the capital of Santander, has become a prosperous center of manufacturing and services. Cúcuta, in the neighboring Norte de Santander department, is a center of commerce whose fortunes are linked to Venezuela's.

While poverty is widespread in the Boyacá countryside, the area is an important agricultural center and supplies Bogotá with much of its food. The departmental capital of Tunja has also become a major center of learning: It is home to 10 universities.

PLANNING YOUR TIME

There are three main draws in Boyacá and Santander: the lovely colonial town of Villa de Leyva, the snowcapped wonderland of the Sierra Nevada del Cocuy, and, in Santander, the action-packed area around San Gil, including the nearby town of Barichara.

Villa de Leyva can be visited in a short two-day excursion from Bogotá, but you could easily spend a couple more relaxing days seeing all the sights, including a hike to Laguna Iguaque. Add on a day to visit the churches of Tunja. To further explore Boyacá, extend your visit for a couple of days to the area around Sogamoso, particularly the postcard-perfect Iza, Monguí, and Lago Tota. There are good public transportation links throughout Boyacá, but this is also a fairly easy place to drive.

Getting to the Sierra Nevada del Cocuy is a schlep (11 hours by bus from Bogotá), so a trip there requires a minimum of 4-5 days to make it worthwhile. To do day hikes into the park, base yourself in the gateway towns of Güicán or El Cocuy, or nearer to the park in one of

several lodges. To do the six-day circuit around the park, plan on 10 days so as to include a day or two of acclimatization before you embark. This is a remote area and there are fewer public transportation options, although buses do depart for the area from Tunja. Roads are in good shape, for the most part.

Beginning in 2013, local U'wa indigenous leaders blocked access to the park; after negotiations with the community (and with aid from the United Nations), the park service reopened the park with the blessing of the U'wa leaders. It's a good idea to contact the park service ahead of your trip and confirm that the park remains open. For the latest information, contact one of the two national park offices in the area: El Cocuy (Cl. 5 No. 4-22, tel. 8/789-0359, 7am-11:45am and 1pm-4:45pm daily) or Güicán (Transversal 4A No. 6-60, tel. 8/789-7280, 7am-11:45pm and 1pm-4:45pm daily).

In Santander, San Gil and Barichara have a lot to offer, so plan on spending at least three days in the area. Barichara is a more beautiful base for exploring the region, but San Gil is home to the main adventure sport tour operators. There are good public transportation links between Bucaramanga and San Gil and between San Gil and Barichara. However, getting from Bucaramanga and San Gil to Tunja or Villa de Leyva is slow going, as the highway is often saturated with big trucks and buses. On holidays it can be difficult to snag a seat on a bus to or from San Gil, as it's also a stop between Bogotá and Bucaramanga, in the northern part of Santander.

The bus ride between Villa de Leyva and San Gil takes 6-7 hours, with a change of bus in Barbosa and/or Tunja. Even though San Gil and the Sierra Nevada del Cocuy are only 75 kilometers (47 miles) apart as the crow flies, to get from one to the other, you must transfer buses in Tunja, requiring more than 15 hours on multiple buses.

There's frequent bus service between Bucaramanga and Pamplona and Cúcuta, the two main destinations in Norte de Santander—a day or two will suffice in these towns.

Boyacá

To the northeast of Bogotá, the department of Boyacá is a mostly rural agricultural area of bucolic highlands, home to campesinos (farmers) often dressed in *ruanas* (wool capes) as they tend to their dairy cows and potato crops. Boyacenses are known for their politeness, shyness, and honesty, and will often address you not with the formal *usted* but rather with the super-deferential *sumercé,* a term that is derived from the old Spanish *su merced* (literally, "your mercy").

Boyacá is known for its role in Colombian history: The city of Tunja was effectively the runner-up to Bogotá when the Spaniards sought a capital for their New World territory of Nueva Granada. Tunja's colonial-era importance can be seen today in the number of impressive churches that stand in its historic center. Nearby, Villa de Leyva has the perfect combination of colonial charm, good hotels and restaurants, attractions, and fantastic weather.

★ VILLA DE LEYVA

This enchanting colonial pueblo is set in an arid valley (Valle de Saquencipá) and has been a major tourist destination for decades. The population triples on weekends, when city folk from Bogotá converge on the town. The surrounding desert scenery, a palette of ever-changing pastels, is gorgeous; the typically sunny weather is never too hot nor too cool; and the town's architecture of preserved whitewashed houses along stone streets is picturesque.

The influx of visitors every weekend doesn't diminish the appeal of Villa de Leyva. A surprising number of activities and attractions are in reach, including paleontological and archaeological sites and outdoor activities such as biking and hiking. The nearby Santuario Flora y Fauna Iguaque is one of the most accessible national parks in the country, and you need only a decent pair of boots to hike to its sacred lakes. Villa de Leyva is also a good base from which to explore the Boyacá countryside and towns such as Ráquira.

Sights
PLAZA MAYOR
Villa de Leyva's **Plaza Mayor** is one of the most photographed locations in Colombia. The town's main square, the largest plaza in the country (14,000 square meters/3.5 acres), is hard to fit in one photo. In the middle of the square is a Mudejar-style well, the Ara Sagrada, that was the source of water for the townspeople in colonial times. On the western side of the square is the **Iglesia Parroquial** (Cra. 9 No. 12-68, 8am-noon and 2pm-6pm Tues.-Sat., 8am-noon Sun.), built in the 17th century from stone, adobe, and wood. It features a large golden *retablo* (altarpiece).

On the western side of the plaza is the quirky **Casa Museo Luis Alberto Acuña** (Cra. 10 No. 12-83, tel. 8/732-0422, www.museoacuna.com.co, 9am-6pm daily, COP$4,000), dedicated to obscure Colombian artist Luis Alberto Acuña. The small museum is filled with Acuña's cubist-influenced paintings of pre-Hispanic indigenous culture and his private art collection and antiques. Acuña was instrumental in the restoration and preservation of local colonial architecture.

One of the oldest and best-preserved houses in Villa de Leyva is the **Casa Juan de Castellanos** (Cra. 9 No. 13-11) on the northeast corner of the Plaza Mayor. It serves as the main office of the town government. The house belonged to Spaniard Juan de Castellanos, who came to the New World as a soldier. He was an important chronicler of the time. The house is not open to the public. Across from the Casa Juan de Castellanos is the historic **Casa del Primer Congreso de las Provincias Unidas de la Nueva Granada** (Cra. 9 No. 13-04), which was restored by artist Luis Alberto Acuña in the 1950s.

a charming cobblestone street in Villa de Leyva

The **Museo El Carmen de Arte Religioso** (Cl. 14 No. 10-04, 10:30am-1pm and 2:30pm-5pm Sat.-Sun., COP$3,000) presents paintings, crucifixes, manuscripts, and religious figures from the colonial era. The museum is on the southwest corner of the grassy **Plazoleta de la Carmen.** The complex, which dates to around 1850, also includes a monastery and convent.

The **Casa Museo Antonio Nariño** (Cra. 9 No. 10-25, tel. 8/732-0342, 9am-noon and 2pm-5pm Thurs.-Tues., free) is the house in which independence figure Antonio Nariño lived and died. It was built in the 17th century, and the museum displays some of Nariño's manuscripts as well as items from everyday life in the 19th century, such as a giant mortar used to mill corn. The small but good museum often puts on temporary art exhibits, which may have a small admission fee.

OTHER SIGHTS
On the northeastern edge of town is the **Museo Paleontológico de Villa de Leyva**

(Cra. 9 No. 11-42, tel. 8/732-0466, www.paleontologico.unal.edu.co, 9am-noon and 2pm-5pm Tues.-Sat., 9am-3pm Sun., COP$4,000). Run by the Universidad Nacional, this museum explains the fossils that have been found in the area, some as old as 130 million years. On display are ammonites, spiral-shelled marine fossils, and fossils of prehistoric animals that roamed the area. The museum has an arboretum with gardens of palms, oaks, and an Andean forest. It's about a 15-minute walk from the Plaza Mayor to the museum. It's popular with school groups on weekday mornings.

On **Plaza Ricaurte,** the 19th-century **Convento de San Agustín** houses the **Instituto Humboldt** (Cra. 8 No. 15-98, tel. 8/732-0791, www.humboldt.org.co, free), a research institute dedicated to conservation and environmental education. There are occasional exhibitions in the institute and the former convent's chapel.

The **Casa Museo Capitán Antonio Ricaurte** (Cl. 15 No. 8-17, no phone, 9am-noon and 2pm-5pm Wed.-Sun., free) is in the small house where independence figure Antonio Ricaurte was born in 1786. One room is filled with uniforms and memorabilia of the Colombian air force, of which Ricaurte was a part. Ricaurte died heroically, sacrificing his life by detonating a cache of gunpowder so that it would not fall into the hands of Spaniards.

Entertainment and Events
The most popular place in the evenings is the Plaza Mayor, where the thing to do is buy a couple of beers and hang out. But there are other watering holes in town. **La Cava de Don Fernando** (Cra. 10 No. 12-03, tel. 8/732-0073) is a spot for a cocktail where the music is often rock.

There are two weekly markets at the **Plaza de Mercado** (Clls. 12-13 and Cras. 5-6, 7am-3pm Thurs., 5am-4pm Sat.). The Thursday market is all organic fruits and vegetables, while the Saturday market is the larger of the two, during which local farmers sell produce and handicrafts. Locals and tourists alike delight in this weekly tradition.

The dark, crystal-clear skies above Villa de Leyva make for great stargazing. In February each year the town hosts the **Festival de Astronómica de Villa de Leyva** (www.astroasasac.com, Feb.), during which people are invited to view the stars from powerful telescopes in the Plaza Mayor.

During the breezy days of August, hundreds of colorful kites soar above the plaza during the **Festival del Viento y Cometas** (www.villadeleyva-boyaca.gov.co, Aug.).

Shopping

For centuries, farmers and craftspeople in Villa de Leyva have specialized in woven goods. In fact, the symbol of this part of Colombia could very well be the *ruana,* a warm, woolen cape worn by both men and women. This and other woolen goods can be found on nearly every street corner in Villa de Leyva. The town is home to many creative types; small jewelers, galleries, and handicraft shops are common throughout town.

Boyacá is known for its woven woolen scarves and *ruanas* (capes).

Alieth Tejido Artesanal (Cl. 13 No. 7-89, tel. 8/732-1672, www.alieth.8m.com) is an association of about 35 women who weave woolen sweaters, *ruanas* (wool capes), *mochilas* (handwoven purses), gloves, scarves, and colorful, psychedelic bags. A tour, the "Ruta de la Lana," can be taken to nearby farms to learn about the process from sheep to sweater. It costs COP$48,000 per person and lasts for about five hours, and snacks and a souvenir are included. Alieth Ortíz, the head of this interesting program, requests reservations be made a few days in advance so that they can organize things with the artisans.

An excellent store to browse wool items is **Creaciones Dora** (Cra. 10 No. 10-02, 9am-7pm Mon.-Fri., 9am-9pm Sat.). **La Libélula** (Cra. 9 No. 14-35, tel. 8/732-0040, 10am-7pm daily) specializes in leather: handbags, belts, and accessories.

The friendly Italian owner, Luciano, takes the mystery out of emeralds at **Misterio** (Cl. 14 No. 9-85, tel. 8/732-0418, cell tel. 313/4891-9315, 10am-8pm daily), where emeralds and quartz from mines in Boyacá are sold. He also sells handmade jewelry. Luciano enjoys educating visitors on how to choose an emerald.

Recreation

HIKING

Close to town, sporty locals regularly take a brisk morning hike up to the **Santo,** a statue on the eastern side of Villa de Leyva. The walk takes about an hour in total, and it is a steep climb. Hikers are rewarded with quite a view of the Plaza Mayor. To get to the path, walk east along Calle 11 to the tennis court and soccer field, north of the Hotel Duruelo. The path entrance is marked. It's best to make the climb early in the morning, before the midday heat envelops the valley. Although the view is nice, you'll be better off leaving your camera at your hotel—not necessarily for safety reasons, but because you may not want to be loaded down as you climb. At times you may need both hands free to scramble over rocks.

BIKE RENTAL

Renting a bike to see the sights in the valley near Villa de Leyva is a great way to spend a day and get some good exercise as you huff and puff up the hill to the Convento del Santo Ecce Homo. **Ciclotrip** (Cra. 9 No. 141-101, tel. 8/732-1485, cell tel. 317/435-5202, www.ciclotrip.com) rents mountain bikes and can organize biking tours in the area. Many hostels also have bikes for rent.

Food

COLOMBIAN

★ **MiCocina** (Cl. 13 No. 8-45, tel. 8/732-1676, cell tel. 320/488-2452, 1pm-10pm daily, COP$25,000) has earned a name for itself as a slightly upscale restaurant serving the best of Colombian cuisine. After a *calentado bogotano*, a beloved hangover cure made with fried eggs and potatoes, save room for the cheese ice cream from Paipa. They serve mostly Colombian meat-based dishes here, but there are a few vegetarian plates. There's a cooking school here as well.

Locals tend to steer clear of the overpriced restaurants on the Plaza Mayor. Close to the Terminal de Transportes, **Los Kioscos de los Caciques** (Cra. 9 No. 9-05, cell tel. 311/475-8681, noon-3pm and 6pm-8pm daily, COP$6,000) specializes in filling local dishes such as *mazamorra chiquita* (beef stew with potatoes, corn, and other vegetables) and *cuchuco con espinazo* (stew with a base of pork spine and potatoes). It's an atmospheric place where you dine in thatched kiosks.

At the Saturday market, those in the know go to **Donde Salvador** (Plaza de Mercado, Clls. 12-13 and Cras. 5-6, 5am-4pm Sat.) for *mute rostro de cordero*, a hearty corn-based soup with lamb. Salvador is well known, and he's one of the first at the marketplace on Saturdays, serving late-night carousers at 4am and more typical shoppers throughout the day. The big market takes place on Saturday, but there is also a smaller organic fruits and vegetables market on Thursdays.

Every day there is a different set lunch menu at **La Cocina de la Gata** (Cl. 11 No. 9-23, cell tel. 310/766-7980, noon-10pm daily). Vegetarian meals are served on Tuesdays and Fridays.

Popular with locals, **Donde Tere** (Cl. 10 No. 8-73, cell tel. 316/542-0387, 8am-8pm Mon. and Wed.-Sat., 8am-5pm Sun., COP$12,000), also called Tienda de Teresa, specializes in breakfast and *cazuela boyacense*, a milk-based soup.

INTERNATIONAL

★ **Mercado Municipal** (Cra. 8 No. 12-25, tel. 8/732-0229, 1pm-10pm daily, COP$22,000) has one of the coolest settings in Villa de Leyva: It's set in a courtyard (that was once part of a parsonage) overflowing with herb gardens in which a traditional Mexican barbecue wood-burning oven is built into the ground. In this oven, they slow-cook their famous barbecued goat. International dishes on the menu include pastas and several vegetarian offerings. It's open for breakfast on the weekends, and there is a nice bakery in front. The set lunch special is a good deal. For a drink and tapas, get comfortable at their adjacent swanky bar, **Bolívar Social Club,** which is open in the evenings.

French cuisine is served at **Chez Remy** (Cra. 9 No. 13-25, tel. 311/848-5000, noon-10pm Fri.-Sat., noon-4pm Sun., COP$24,000), including *quenelle de mar* (COP$28,000), which combines myriad tastes from the faraway sea: salmon, hake, shrimp, and lobster. On chilly nights, the French onion soup (COP$9,000) really hits the spot.

Casa Quintero (Cra. 9 No. 11-75, hours vary by restaurant), on the corner of the Plaza Mayor, holds several restaurants under one roof, like an upscale food hall. There is a little something for everyone here, including a Lebanese restaurant, an arepa joint, and a pizza place.

VEGETARIAN

Savia (Casa Quintero, Cra. 9 No. 11-75, cell tel. 312/435-4602, noon-9pm Thurs.-Mon., COP$25,000) has an extensive menu of both vegetarian and meaty entrées, like lentil stew, rice pilaf, and fish and chicken dishes. They also sell locally produced jams and other items in their storefront.

CAFÉS, BAKERIES, AND QUICK BITES
Flor de Maiz (Cra. 7 No. 11-83) specializes in corn arepas, tamales, and fresh juices. It's a cute hole-in-the-wall.

Panadería Astral (Cl. 12 No. 7-56, tel. 8/732-0811, 9:30am-7pm Mon.-Sat.) is the best place for fresh-baked bread and cakes.

They serve good coffee at **Sybarita Caffe** (Cra. 9 No. 11-88, cell tel. 316/481-1872, 8am-8pm daily), where the owners are on a mission to bring coffee appreciation to the masses. If you want your latte sourced from the coffee region—Quindío to be specific—then **Café Los Gallos** (Cra. 8 No. 13-55, cell tel. 300/851-4714, 9am-8pm daily) is the place.

The pizza at friendly, family-run **Gelatería Pizzería Santa Lucia** (Cra. 10 No. 10-27, cell tel. 313/880-1022, 11am-9:30pm daily) gets accolades. They also serve delicious homemade ice cream and frozen yogurt.

Accommodations
Villa de Leyva lives on tourism, so there are many accommodation options. Rates bump up on weekends and holidays like Christmas and Holy Week. During the week discounts may be possible, especially if you pay in cash.

UNDER COP$70,000
★ **Renacer** (Av. Cra. 10 No. 21, tel. 8/732-1201, www.renacerhostel.com, COP$35,000 dorm, COP$120,000 d) is the best-known hostel in town and is popular for good reason. Set at the foot of a mountain, it's about a 15-minute walk from town—but guests will be reimbursed for the initial taxi ride from the bus station. Facilities are well kept and there are ample open-air common spaces. There are seven rooms and *cabañas* for varying numbers of guests, some with private bathrooms. There is also a place for those arriving in campers or vans. The on-site restaurant has a range of comfort-food options. Through

Colombian Highlands (www.colombian-highlands.com), Renacer arranges outdoor expeditions to nearby attractions and can even assist in excursions outside of the Villa de Leyva area. They have very good information on how to hike or bike the area solo. This is an excellent place to swap travel tips with backpackers from around the world.

Run by an Austrian-Colombian couple, ★ **Casa Viena** (Cra. 10 No. 19-114, tel. 8/732-0711, cell tel. 314/370-4776, www.hostel-villadeleyva.com, COP$60,000 d) is a quiet and relaxed guesthouse on the same road as Renacer. It has just four rooms, three of which have shared baths.

A low-key hostel option is **Hostal Rana** (Cl. 10A No. 10-31, tel. 8/732-0330, cell tel. 311/464-2969, www.hostal-rana.com, COP$20,000 dorm, COP$40,000 d). It has one dorm room and four private rooms. Rooms are clean and beds are firm. There is a small kitchen for use in the back behind a pleasant patio space.

If you ask locals for a less expensive hotel option, many will tell you to check out **Hospedería Don Paulino** (Cl. 14 No. 7-46, tel. 8/732-1227, cell tel. 313/394-2507, www.donpaulino.co, COP$35,000 s, COP$65,000 d). It's not a fancy place by any means, but the price can't be beat. The 16 rooms all have wireless Internet and TV. Go for a room on the 2nd floor that has a balcony overlooking the patio. Each morning they provide coffee and a voucher for breakfast at a nearby restaurant.

COP$70,000-200,000
Family-run **Hospedería La Roca** (Cl. 13 No. 9-54, COP$90,000 d) has been a cheapie quietly overlooking the Plaza Mayor for years, but it's no longer a budget option. More than 20 rooms with high ceilings surround two interior courtyards that are filled with greenery. Try for one on the 2nd floor with a very distant view of the mountains. Around the corner is the welcoming **Posada de Los Ángeles** (Cra. 10 No. 13-94, tel. 8/732-0562, COP$110,000 d), a lovely option overlooking the Plazoleta de Carmen. Some rooms have

balconies with views of the church. Take your American-style breakfast in the cheerfully painted patio filled with potted plants and flowers. There's no wireless Internet available.

The inviting ★ **Hospedería El Marqués de San Jorge** (Cl. 14 No. 9-20, tel. 8/732-0240, www.hospederiaelmarquesdesanjorge.com, COP$130,000-200,000 d) is just a block from the Plaza Mayor, has two interior patios that are filled with greenery, and has clean and comfortable modern rooms (despite having been around since 1972). It's a bargain compared to other luxury hotels in town.

On the outskirts of town, but only about a ten-minute walk from the Plaza Mayor, is **Hotel Santa Viviana** (Diag. 8 No. 12A-76, tel. 732-0818, cell tel. 313/885-1072, www.hotelsantaviviana.com, COP$109,000 d), a spacious hotel with ample green spaces and an open-air restaurant where breakfast is served.

COP$200,000-500,000

The location of the ★ **Hotel Plaza Mayor** (Cra. 10 No. 12-31, tel. 8/732-0425, www.hotelplazamayor.com.co, COP$243,000 d), with a bird's-eye view of the Plaza Mayor from its western side, is unrivaled. The hotel's terrace is a great place to watch goings-on in the plaza and to take a photo of the cathedral bathed in a golden light in late afternoon. Rooms are spacious, some have a fireplace, and all are tastefully decorated. Breakfast is served in the pleasant courtyard.

Two other upscale options face parks. On the cute Parque Nariño, the elegant **Hotel La Posada de San Antonio** (Cra. 8 No. 11-80, tel. 8/732-0538, cell tel. 310/280-7326, www.hotellaposadadesanantonio.com, COP$238,000 d) is lavishly decorated and has spacious rooms, a pleasant restaurant, a cozy reading room, a pool, an art gallery, a billiards room, and even a small chapel. Built in 1845, it was originally home to a wealthy family. On the Plaza de Ricaurte, the ★ **Hotel Plazuela de San Agustín** (Cl. 15 No. 8-65, tel. 8/732-2175, www.hotelplazuela.com, COP$300,000 d) is a cozy hotel with fewer than a dozen enormous carpeted rooms. One room has

four beds and a fireplace. Mornings start off with breakfast served near a fountain in the lovely courtyard. The hotel is two blocks from the Plaza Mayor.

Hotel Boutique Candelaria (Cl. del Silencio 18 No. 8-12, tel. 8/732-0534, cell tel. 313/837-4230, www.hotelcandelaria.villadeleyva.com.co, COP$220,000 d) serves cheese and wine and is a very cozy option with wooden floors, antiques, and personal touches. It's next door to the **Hostería El Molino de Mesopotamia** (Cra. 8 No. 15A-265, cell tel. 311/278-8688, www.lamesopotamia.com, COP$200,000 d). Built in the 16th century, this is one of the oldest constructions in Villa de Leyva. It's set in a quiet and lush corner of the town, with babbling brooks and even a chilly pool.

Information and Services

The Villa de Leyva **tourist office** (corner Cra. 9 and Cl. 13, tel. 8/732-0232, 8am-12:30pm and 2pm-6pm Mon.-Sat., 9am-1pm and 3pm-6pm Sun.), off Plaza Mayor, has free tourist maps and brochures.

There are several **ATMs** in Villa de Leyva, particularly along the southern end of the Plaza Mayor.

An efficient and inexpensive laundry service in town near the bus terminal is **Lava Express** (Cra. 8 No. 8-21, cell tel. 320/856-1865, 8am-noon and 2pm-7pm Mon.-Fri., 8am-7pm Sat.).

Transportation

Thanks to a recently expanded four-lane highway that bypasses Tunja, Villa de Leyva is easily accessible by private car or by public bus from Bogotá, as well as from Tunja. Renting a car in Bogotá and driving to Villa de Leyva gives you a lot of flexibility to visit enchanting pueblos to your heart's content. Nearly all hotels have parking lots.

The bus terminal in Villa de Leyva is the **Terminal de Transportes** (Cra. 9 between Clls. 11-12). The bus ride from Tunja to Villa de Leyva takes about 45 minutes, and deposits riders at the bus terminal.

There are a few direct buses to Villa de Leyva (3.5 hours, COP$22,000) from both the Terminal de Transportes and the Portal del Norte in Bogotá. However, it's often quicker and easier to take a bus from the Portal del Norte to Tunja (2-2.5 hours, COP$20,000) via a bus company such as Autoboy. In Tunja, ask your bus driver where to transfer to the *buseta* (small bus) that will take you onward to Villa de Leyva. These leave roughly every 15 minutes (until 8pm). This leg takes about 45 minutes and costs COP$7,000.

Several companies offer two daily return trips to Bogotá, with buses that depart between 5am and 6am and again at around 1pm. There are many more options on Saturdays, Sundays, and Monday holidays. These tend to leave in the late afternoon at around 3pm.

To get to Villa de Leyva from Bucaramanga or San Gil in Santander, you'll have to hop on a bus to Tunja (COP$45,000). The highway that extends from Bogotá to Venezuela is a busy one, and the journey can take five or six hours.

Once in Villa de Leyva, it is easy and pleasant to walk everywhere. A few streets around the Plaza Mayor, including the main drag, Calle 13, are pedestrian-only. Even on non-pedestrian streets it's hard for vehicles to zoom along.

Santuario Flora y Fauna Iguaque

VICINITY OF VILLA DE LEYVA

The countryside near Villa de Leyva, the undulating desert of the Valle de Saquencipá, is a playground for tourists. Many of the region's sights can be visited by bike from Villa de Leyva, although the country roads are hilly.

★ Santuario Flora y Fauna Iguaque

One of the country's most accessible national parks is about 13 kilometers from Villa de Leyva. The **Santuario Flora y Fauna Iguaque** (www.parquesnacionales. gov.co, 8am-4pm daily, last entrance 10am, COP$42,000 non-Colombians, COP$16,000 Colombian residents, COP$8,500 students and children) is an excellent place to experience the unique landscape of the Andean *páramo* (highland moor) as well as dry tropical forest. The protected area extends for some 6,750 hectares. It is also a park of several *lagunas* (mountain lakes). Laguna Iguaque is known as a sacred lake for the Muisca people. They believed the goddess Bachué was born out of the blue-green waters of this lake, giving birth to humanity.

Most day-trippers based in Villa de Leyva visit the park to make the hike up to Laguna Iguaque. The climb, which takes you through three ecosystems—Andean forest, sub-*páramo*, and *páramo*—begins at the Centro Administrativo Carrizal at an elevation of 2,800 meters (9,185 feet) and ends 4.6 kilometers (2.6 miles) later at Laguna Iguaque (3,650 meters/11,975 feet). The enjoyable hike takes about 3-4 hours. Along the way you may be able to spot different species of birds and perhaps some deer or foxes. At the mist-shrouded Laguna Iguaque, you'll be surrounded by hundreds of *frailejones,* unusual cactus-like plants found only in this special ecosystem.

It is best to make the hike during the week, as the trails get crowded on weekends. You do not need a guide for the hike to Laguna Iguaque. During particularly dry spells the threat of forest fires forces the park to forbid entry to visitors. That is most likely to occur in January or August. Ask beforehand at your hostel or hotel to find out if the park is open to visitors.

If you are interested in exploring other paths in the park, consider overnighting at the **Centro de Visitantes Furachiogua,** the park's basic accommodations facility, which caters mostly to student groups. Seven rooms have 6-8 beds each (COP$39,500 pp), and the restaurant is open to day-trippers as well. The facility is about 700 meters beyond the Centro Administrativo Carrizal visitors center. There are camping facilities near the cabins (COP$10,000 pp). To inquire about accommodations or to make a reservation, contact the community organization **Naturar-Iguaque** (cell tel. 312/585-9892 or 318/595-5643, naturariguaque@yahoo.es). A guided walk to Laguna Iguaque costs COP$80,000 for a group of 1-6.

GETTING THERE

Buses bound for the town of Arcabuco leave from the bus station in Villa de Leyva and will stop at the Casa de Piedra (8 km from Villa de Leyva), a local landmark that is a house made of stone. Buses depart at 7am, 10am, and 1:30pm. It's about a 30-minute ride to the Casa de Piedra, which costs COP$5,000. From there it's about an hour-long walk (3 km/2 mi) east to the Centro Administrativo Carrizal visitors center, which is also the park entrance. This walk, along a dirt and gravel road, is an attraction in itself.

For transportation back to Villa de Leyva there are four buses each day: at 8:30am, 10:30am, 1pm, and 4:30pm, which all depart from the Casa de Piedra.

Paleontological Museums

During the Cretaceous period (66-145 million years ago), the area around Villa de Leyva was submerged in an inland sea. Some of the marine species that lived here included the pliosaurus, plesiosaurus, and ichthyosaurus.

Toward the end of this period, many species became extinct. Simultaneously the Andes mountains were created when the earth shifted. As the waters gave way to mountains, the bones of these species became embedded in rock, guaranteeing their preservation. Today this region has a handful of paleontological sites where you can view fossils of everything from parts of massive dinosaurs to small ammonites, of which there are thousands. Excavations continue throughout the valley.

In 1977, locals made a fantastic discovery: a distant relative of carnivorous marine reptiles from the pliosaurus family, to be classified as a *Kronosaurus boyacensis Hampe.* It roamed this part of the earth some 110 million years ago. The first-ever find of this species can be seen, fixed in the earth extending for about 10 meters, in the location of its discovery at the **Museo El Fósil de Monquirá** (Km. 4 Vía Santa Sofía, Vereda Monquirá, COP$6,000). Guides give a brief tour of the museum, which has hundreds of other animal and plant fossils on display. This is a major tourist sight, and there are souvenir shops and juice stands nearby.

Across the street from Museo El Fósil de Monquirá is the **Centro de Investigaciones Paleontológicas** (Km. 4 Vía Santa Sofía, Vereda Monquirá, cell tel. 314/219-2904 or 321/978-9546, 9am-noon and 2pm-5pm Mon. and Wed.-Thurs., 8am-5pm Fri.-Sun., COP$8,000). On view here are parts of a *Platypterygius boyacensis,* as well as a *Callawayasaurus colombiensis,* which were all unearthed nearby. An informative 20-minute tour (in Spanish) of the center is included.

GETTING THERE

You can visit the museums on bike, by taxi, or by public transportation. **CoomultransVilla** has hourly buses (Santa Sofía-bound, COP$2,500) in the mornings from the Terminal de Transportes in Villa de Leyva departing at 6:45am, 8am, 9am, and 10am. The driver can let you off within easy walking distance of all the museums.

There are also buses in the afternoon. The last bus departing Santa Sofía bound for Villa de Leyva leaves at around 4pm and arrives in Villa de Leyva 30 minutes later. You'll have to be on the lookout for it on the road between Santa Sofía and Villa de Leyva and flag it down. It's best to confirm all the bus schedules in advance. If you miss the bus, staff at the museums can call a taxi, which will cost about COP$15,000 to Villa de Leyva.

All hostels and hotels can arrange for a taxi to take you to the museums, wait for you, and deposit you back in town afterward. Negotiate an acceptable price for this; around COP$70,000 for two sights and round-trip travel is considered a fair price.

Convento del Santo Ecce Homo

The **Convento del Santo Ecce Homo** (8 km northwest of Villa de Leyva, tel. 1/288-6373, 9am-5pm Tues.-Sun., COP$5,000) is set idyllically atop a hill overlooking Villa de Leyva.

Dominican monks founded this monastery in 1620. The site is a delight to visit. The beautifully preserved baroque chapels and the museum, part of which is dedicated to indigenous cultures, are open to the public. A monk's cell, library, and dining hall area provide a glimpse into monastery life. Surrounded by stone columns, the courtyard is awash in a rainbow of colors, with flowers always in bloom.

GETTING THERE

You can reach the convent on bike, by taxi, or by public transportation. **CoomultransVilla** has hourly buses in the mornings from the Terminal de Transportes in Villa de Leyva, bound for Santa Sofía (COP$2,500) and departing at 6:45am, 8am, 9am, and 10am. They can let you off within walking distance of the convent.

The last bus departing Santa Sofía bound for Villa de Leyva leaves at around 4pm, and arrives in Villa de Leyva about 30 minutes later. You'll have to be on the lookout for it and flag it down on the road between these two towns. Confirm the bus schedule in advance.

All hostels and hotels can arrange for a taxi to take you to the convent (and other sights), wait for you while you visit, and then return you to town. Negotiate an acceptable

Convento del Santo Ecce Homo

RÁQUIRA

This town, 28 kilometers (17 miles) from Villa de Leyva, is synonymous with *artesanías* (handicrafts). The main drag is lined with colorful shops, and in one stop you can pick up handicrafts of every size and shape and from across the country: hammocks, *mochilas* (handbags), and row after row of trinkets.

Ráquira is the capital of Colombian **ceramics** and has been since before the arrival of the Spaniards. In fact, it is said that the name Ráquira means "city of clay pots" in the Chibcha language of the Muiscas, who lived in the area. All those reddish flowerpots and planters you may have seen in other parts of the country most likely came from here. It's estimated that some 500 families in the area make their living harvesting the clay in nearby areas or firing the pottery in their own workshops. A dwindling number of women in the area do things the old-fashioned way—with their hands. They make mostly decorative items like candlestick holders and piggybanks with imperfections—telltale signs of their artisan origins.

One large shop specializing in pottery is **Todo Ráquira** (Cra. 5 No. 3A-05, tel. 8/735-7000, www.todoraquira.com, 9am-6pm daily), about two blocks from the pleasant Parque Principal (Cras. 3-4 and Clls. 3-4). The front of the store is filled with a variety of Colombian handicrafts (but note that some are made in China). If you meander to the back, you'll see the workshop where you can check out bowls, flowerpots, and other items.

If you'd like to observe the ceramic-making process, you can visit the workshop of **Isaias Valero** (no phone, hours vary, COP$5,000 suggested donation), which is on the main road near the Casa de la Cultura. You can watch him at work, and he can show you the steps that go into creating a piece. If he is there, Isaias will gladly welcome your visit. To get to the workshop, walk up about 70 steps from the main road, just before the Casa de la Cultura.

Getting There

Buses to Ráquira (45 minutes, COP$7,000) depart from Villa de Leyva's Terminal de Transportes, leaving between 7am and 8:30am daily. Passengers are dropped off at the main plaza, in the center of town.

You may prefer to hire a cab for the day, especially if you're traveling in a small group. Cab drivers typically charge COP$80,000 to drive to Ráquira and the Convento de la Candelaria, with a couple of stops along the way. Drivers will wait for you to visit each stop. Be specific about destinations and price at the beginning (put things in writing) to avoid unpleasant surprises later.

Convento de la Candelaria

One of the oldest monasteries in Latin America, and one that is still in use today, is the **Convento de la Candelaria** (9am-noon and 2pm-5pm daily, COP$5,000), seven kilometers outside of Ráquira. A pair of Augustinian missionaries arrived in this desert area in 1588 with the mission of bringing Christianity to the native Muisca people. They lived in caves (which you can visit) until the monastery was constructed.

The complex includes two cloisters that hold a chapel and a museum. The museum is a hodgepodge of religious art and objects, examples of technological advances through the years—from a *reloj borracho* (drunken clock) to an early Apple computer—and a display on the Colombian saint Ezequiel Moreno y Díaz, who is said to have healed cancer victims.

Adjacent to the monastery is a modern hotel, **Posada San Agustín** (cell tel. 313/852-1882, vocaciones@agustinosrecoletos.com.co, COP$168,000 d), which often hosts yoga and meditation retreats. Rooms are immaculately clean and completely free from clutter. Some even have hot tubs. At night you can sit around a fire in the common area and sip hot spiced wine. Meals are served in the restaurant, and they can also prepare vegetarian food. It's a quiet and peaceful place.

A taxi ride from Ráquira to the convent will cost about COP$20,000-30,000 round-trip; it's a 15-minute drive each way. Specify if you want the driver to wait while you explore the convent. There is also a bus that runs daily from the Parque Principal in Ráquira (COP$2,500), which leaves passengers at an intersection with a dirt road that winds to the monastery.

TUNJA

This university town (pop. 178,000), home to the Universidad de Boyacá, boasts some spectacular churches. Make sure you arrive during church visiting hours, as the city does not have much else to offer. Because there are frequent bus connections with Bogotá and Santander, Tunja is a good base from which to explore Boyacá.

Sights

Everything you need to see in Tunja is in its *centro histórico,* which is between Calles 13 and 24 and Carreras 7 and 12.

★ HISTORIC CHURCHES

Tunja is a city of churches, with over a dozen that date to colonial times. Hours of visitation can be irregular, but they are always open for mass, which is a good time to take a look. Most churches celebrate mass at about 7am and 5:30pm daily, with more frequent masses on Sundays.

On the eastern side of the **Plaza de Bolívar** (Cl. 19 at Cra. 9), **Catedral Santiago de Tunja** (Cra. 9 at Cl. 19) is a 16th-century construction, originally built out of wood and earthen *tapia pisada,* which is an adobe technique. It was the first cathedral to be built in Nueva Granada. It has three naves, four side chapels, and two front chapels.

Santa Clara La Real (Cra. 7 No. 19-58, Cl. 21 No. 11-31, tel. 8/742-5659 or 8/742-3194, 8am-11:30am and 3pm-4:30pm Mon.-Fri., 8am-11:30am Sat., masses 7am and 5pm Mon.-Sat., 7am, 11am, and 5pm Sun.) was built between 1571 and 1574 and was the first Clarisa convent in Nueva Granada. It has one nave, noteworthy for the spectacular decorations adorning its presbytery including golden garlands, grapes, pineapples (which were a sacred indigenous symbol), pelicans, an anthropomorphic sun, and other symbols of nature. Also look for the seal of Tunja, the double-headed eagle, modeled on the seal of Emperor Charles V, who gave the city its charter. In the choir is the tiny cell where Madre

Plaza de Bolívar

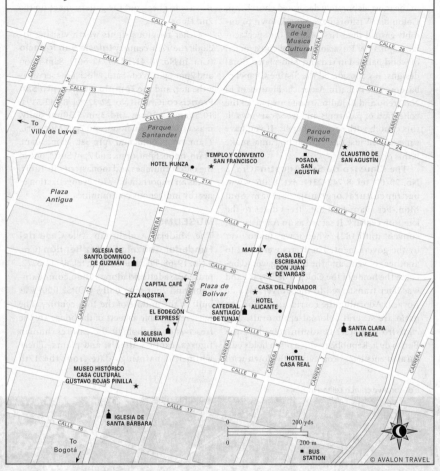

Tunja

CALLE 25

Parque de la Musica Cultural

CALLE 26

CALLE 25

CALLE 24

CALLE 23

CALLE 22

CALLE 24

CARRERA 15

CARRERA 14

CARRERA 12

CARRERA 9

CARRERA 8

CARRERA 7

← To Villa de Leyva

Parque Santander

CALLE

Parque Pinzón

CLAUSTRO DE SAN AGUSTÍN ★

HOTEL HUNZA •

TEMPLO Y CONVENTO SAN FRANCISCO

POSADA SAN AGUSTÍN

CALLE 21A

Plaza Antigua

CALLE 21

CALLE 22

CARRERA 11

MAIZAL ▼

CASA DEL ESCRIBANO DON JUAN DE VARGAS ★

IGLESIA DE SANTO DOMINGO DE GUZMÁN

CALLE 20

CARRERA 10

CAPITAL CAFÉ ▼

PIZZA NOSTRA ▼

Plaza de Bolívar

CASA DEL FUNDADOR

CARRERA 12

EL BODEGÓN EXPRESS ▼

CATEDRAL SANTIAGO DE TUNJA

HOTEL ALICANTE •

IGLESIA SAN IGNACIO

CALLE 19

SANTA CLARA LA REAL ★

CARRERA 9

CARRERA 8

CARRERA 7

CARRERA 5

CALLE 18

HOTEL CASA REAL

MUSEO HISTÓRICO CASA CULTURAL GUSTAVO ROJAS PINILLA ★

CALLE 17

IGLESIA DE SANTA BÁRBARA

CALLE 16

0 _____ 200 yds

0 _____ 200 m

■ BUS STATION

To Bogotá ↓

© AVALON TRAVEL

Josefa del Castillo lived for over 50 years in the late 17th and early 18th centuries. While there she wrote two books and several poems, with themes of sexual repression and mystical descriptions of heaven and hell. Near her cell are some frescoes made with coal, an abundant resource in the area.

The sky-blue interior of the **Iglesia de Santa Bárbara** (Cra. 11 No. 16-62, between Clls. 16-17, tel. 8/742-3021, 8:30am-12:30pm and 2pm-6pm daily, masses 5:30pm and 6pm Mon.-Fri., 7am, 9am, 10am, and 11am Sat., noon, 5pm, 6pm, and 7pm Sun.) and its Mudejar ceiling designs make this one of the prettiest churches in Tunja. The single-nave structure, with two chapels making the form of a cross, was completed in 1599. When it was built, it was raised at the edge of Tunja, near an indigenous settlement.

Built in the 1570s, the **Templo de Santo Domingo de Guzmán** (Cra. 11 No. 19-55, tel. 8/742-4725, 8am-11:30am Mon.-Fri., masses 7am and 6pm Mon.-Fri., 7am and 6pm Sat., 7am, 10am, noon, and 6pm Sun.) is one of the most elaborately decorated churches in Colombia. Visitors have been known to audibly gasp at their first sight of the spectacular Capilla del Rosario, a chapel constructed of wood painted in red and gold-plated floral designs. It's considered the Sistine Chapel of baroque art in Latin America. Figures of El Nazareno and El Judío Errante are part of the collection of paintings and woodcarvings in this church with several chapels. If you have time to visit just one church in Tunja, make it this one.

The **Claustro de San Agustín** (Cra. 8 No. 23-08, tel. 8/742-2311, ext. 8306, www.banrepcultural.org/tunja, 8:30am-6pm Mon.-Fri., 9am-1pm Sat., free) dates to the late 16th century. It served as an Augustinian convent until 1821, when it was taken over by the government. The friars were sent to another convent, and the building would become the home of the Colegio de Boyacá and was later transferred to the Universidad de Boyacá. Adorning the corridors around the patio are several colonial-era murals. The *claustro* (cloister) is administered by the Banco de la República, which often holds cultural events here. You can settle down with a book or work on your computer in the gorgeous reading rooms (free Wi-Fi is available). Be sure to check out the gallery space on the 2nd floor.

Other religious sights worth visiting include the 17th-century **Iglesia San Ignacio** (Cra. 10 No. 18-41, tel. 8/742-6611, 8am-noon and 2pm-5pm Wed.-Sat.), which now serves as a theater, and the **Templo y Convento San Francisco** (Cra. 10 No. 22-32, tel. 8/742-3194, 10:30am-12:30pm and 3pm-5:30pm daily, masses 7am, 11am, noon, and 7pm Mon.-Fri., 11am, noon, 6pm, and 7pm Sat., 8am, 10am, 11am, noon, 5pm, 6pm, and 7pm Sun.), one of the oldest churches and monasteries in Tunja. It was an important base for evangelization of nearby indigenous communities.

MUSEUMS

The Mudejar-Andalusian-style **Casa del Fundador Gonzalo Suárez Rendón** (Cra. 9 No. 19-68, Plaza de Bolívar, tel. 8/742-3272, museocasadelfundador@yahoo.com, 8am-noon and 2pm-6pm daily, COP$2,000) was built in the middle of the 16th century. The most remarkable aspects of the house are the frescoes of mythological creatures, human figures, exotic animals, and plants. These whimsical paintings date from the 17th

a decorative church ceiling in Tunja

century, although not much else is known about them. Guides will show you around.

Casa del Escribano del Rey Don Juan de Vargas (Cl. 20 No. 8-52, tel. 8/74-26611, 9am-noon and 2pm-5pm Tues.-Fri., 9am-noon and 2pm-4pm Sat.-Sun., COP$2,000) was owned by the scribe to the king, an important post in colonial Tunja. The scribe's jurisdiction covered all of present-day Boyacá, Santander, Norte de Santander, and parts of Venezuela and Cundinamarca. Student guides will give you a thorough tour of the museum. The house showcases furniture and other examples of colonial life, but the highlight of this Andalusian-style house is the unusual painted ceilings portraying exotic animals and mythological creatures, similar to the frescoes that can be found in the Casa del Fundador.

The childhood home of former president Gustavo Rojas Pinilla is now a museum: **Museo Histórico Casa Cultural Gustavo Rojas Pinilla** (Cl. 17 No. 10-63, tel. 8/742-6814, 8:30am-noon and 2pm-6pm Mon.-Fri.). Rojas, after seizing power in 1953, became the only dictator that Colombia has ever had. Upstairs are two exhibition spaces, one with memorabilia of Rojas and the other with portraits of 12 presidents that hailed from Boyacá. Despite his antidemocratic credentials, Rojas is revered in Tunja as the man who brought an end to the mid-20th-century violence between Liberals and Conservatives.

Food

Comida típica (Colombian fare) rules the day in this city lacking in restaurant options. For a really local, greasy-spoon-type experience, try **Restaurante Maizal** (Cra. 9 No. 20-30, tel. 8/742-5876, 7am-8:45pm Mon.-Sat., 9am-4:45pm Sun., COP$12,000). It has been serving *sancocho* (beef stew), *mondongo* (tripe stew), and *ajiaco* (chicken and potato soup) to Tunja for over 50 years. Another old-timer is **El Bodegón Express** (Cra. 10 No. 18-45, cell tel. 321/221-4460, 8am-4pm Mon.-Sat., COP$10,000). It's next to the Iglesia San Ignacio. It specializes in trout dishes and *cocido boyacense* (COP$6,000), which has a

variety of meats and some of the unusual tubers from the area, such as *cubios, ibias,* and *rubas.*

Pizza Nostra (Cl. 19 No. 10-36, tel. 8/740-2040, 11am-8pm daily, COP$18,000) has a few locations in and around town. The most famous one is at the Pozo de Donado (tel. 8/740-4200, 11am-11pm daily), a small park and Muisca archaeological site surrounding a lake.

It's a tradition in Tunja to while away the hours in cafés. It must be the chilly weather. While the actual coffee around town may disappoint, the atmosphere, with groups of retirees dressed in suits brushing shoulders with bevies of college students, does not. Try **Capital Café** (7am-7pm daily), which is at the entrance of the *pasaje* (passage) close to the Plaza de Bolívar.

Accommodations

Most overnight visitors stay in the decent hotels in the *centro histórico* within easy walking distance of the Plaza de Bolívar and sights of interest.

Two blocks from the Plaza de Bolívar is ★ **Hotel Casa Real** (Cl. 19 No. 7-65, tel. 8/743-1764, www.hotelcasarealtunja.com, COP$95,000 d), a colonial-style house with 10 rooms surrounding a divine courtyard. That's where a very nice breakfast is served for an additional cost. The courtyard walls feature lovely tile paintings (by artist Adriano Guio) depicting Boyacá country scenes. You can order your breakfast the night before and even request it to be delivered to your room. Rooms are tastefully decorated and comfortable, and prices here are astoundingly low. Owned by the same people, **Hotel Alicante** (Cra. 8 No. 19-15, tel. 8/744-9967, www.hotelalicantetunja.com, COP$95,000 d) caters to business clientele. This small hotel may not have the charm of Casa Real, but it's clean.

A warm and welcoming guesthouse, the ★ **Hotel Posada de San Agustín** (Cl. 23 No. 8-63, tel. 8/742-2986, www.posadadesanagustin.co, COP$100,000 d) is in a historic, wood-floored house just a few blocks from the Plaza de Bolívar.

The classy address in town is, as it has been for decades, the **Hotel Hunza** (Cl. 21A No. 10-66, tel. 8/742-4111, www.hotelhunza.com, COP$228,000 d). The hotel boasts luxurious king-size beds and card keys. Amenities include a decent-sized indoor pool and a steam room. Its neighbor is the Templo de Santo Domingo. The hotel is a popular place for wedding banquets. There is a lively bar near the entrance, but it shouldn't keep you up at night.

Transportation

Situated 150 kilometers (93 miles) northeast of Bogotá and 20 kilometers (12 miles) southeast of Villa de Leyva, Tunja is easy to get to by car or by bus. Buses to Bogotá, other towns in Boyacá, and to all major cities in Colombia depart from Tunja's **Terminal de Transportes** (Cra. 7 No. 16-40). Buses to Tunja's Terminal de Transportes from Bogotá cost about COP$18,000 and from Villa de Leyva are COP$6,000.

The best way to get around the *centro histórico* is on foot.

Puente de Boyacá

The **Puente de Boyacá war memorial** about 20 kilometers (12 miles) southwest of Tunja celebrates a decisive battle, the **Batalla del Puente de Boyacá,** which effectively ended Spanish control of Nueva Granada. At this site today there are several memorials and statues, including the Plaza de Banderas, where flags from all the departments of Colombia fly. There is also a sculpture of Gen. Francisco Paula de Santander and a large sculpture of Gen. Simón Bolívar surrounded by angels representing the South American countries that he liberated (Bolivia, Colombia, Ecuador, Peru, and Venezuela). There is a small bridge on the memorial grounds, but it dates from the 1930s; the original Puente de Boyacá is long gone.

Santander and Bolívar achieved immortality as heroes of Colombian independence for their victory here. After defeating the Spaniards at the Batalla del Pantano de Vargas

on July 25, 1819, revolutionary troops under their command marched toward Bogotá. South of Tunja, they engaged with the main Spanish army, defeating it decisively on August 7 at the Batalla del Puente de Boyacá. The engagement was a small affair with fewer than 3,000 soldiers on each side, with about 100 royalists and only 13 rebels losing their lives. Bolívar marched onward to Bogotá, which he took without a fight, ushering in independence.

At 6pm every day there is a short flag-lowering ceremony; during this time, you can have your picture taken with Colombian soldiers.

Buses passing between Bogotá and Tunja can drop you off here (COP$5,000), or you can contract a taxi (COP$12,000) from Tunja. The journey takes about 15 minutes.

SOGAMOSO AND VICINITY

Sogamoso, a city of over 100,000 inhabitants, is about 75 kilometers (46 miles) east of Tunja and is known for being an important pre-Hispanic Muisca center. It was originally known as Suamoxi. It's a city of little charm; however, the Museo Arqueológico de Sogamoso is worth a stop, and there are several worthy day-trip destinations in the area. There are a number of atmospheric haciendas in the region. Many hotels and lodges have their own restaurants.

Visit Sugamuxi (www.visitsugamuxi. com) offers information on the region and travel tips in English.

For visitors with a little time and who want more independence, it may make sense to rent a car in Bogotá, rather than rely on buses. From Bogotá to Sogamoso it's about a 2.5-hour drive.

Sogamoso

Run by the Universidad Pedagógica y Tecnológica de Colombia (UPTC) in Tunja, the **Museo Arqueológico de Sogamoso** (Cl. 9A No. 6-45, tel. 8/770-3122, 9am-noon and 2pm-5pm Mon.-Sat., 9am-3pm Sun.,

COP$5,000) has an extensive collection of artifacts of the Muisca civilization, the main indigenous group of Colombia. Muiscas lived in the area that is today the departments of Boyacá, Santander, and Cundinamarca; it was the seat of power for a confederation led by the Iraca. The most memorable sight on the museum grounds is the fantastic Templo del Sol, a re-creation of a Muisca temple that was burned to the ground by the Spaniards in the late 16th century. The museum is worth visiting, even though the exhibition spaces are drab and the sequence of exhibits does not flow very lucidly. That is a shame because there is an interesting history to tell and the collection is impressive. If you have the time and speak Spanish, hire a guide. (Inquire at the ticket office.) Look for the exhibit on *ocarinas,* which are whistles, usually ceramic, that are often zoomorphic in form. Visitors should also see the stunning black-and-white geometric designs of *torteros,* which are spindles used in spinning yarn, as well as remarkably well-preserved red-and-white ceramic vessels and urns.

FOOD AND ACCOMMODATIONS

It's said that Simón Bolívar stayed at ★ **Hacienda Suescún** (Km. 4 Vía Sogamoso-Tibasosa, cell tel. 313/853-5384 or 315/648-8985, www.hotelsuescun.com, COP$260,000 d) before he headed off to face the Spaniards at the decisive Batalla del Puente de Boyacá. This hacienda, surrounded by tall trees covered with Spanish moss, has 18 gorgeous rooms, an elegant dining area, no televisions in the rooms, and wonderful grounds you can meander about. Horses can be taken out for a spin in the countryside for an additional fee. Like many hotels in the area, the hacienda fills up on weekends with wedding parties and business groups. During the week, it's very quiet. It's about five kilometers northwest of Sogamoso.

The wonderful ★ **Hotel Finca San Pedro** (Km. 1 Vía Lago Tota, tel. 312/567-7102, www.fincasanpedro.com, COP$25,000 dorm, COP$80,000 d), which is also home to a friendly family, is a lush refuge amid lovely gardens full of fruit trees, vegetables, and flowers. It offers both private and dorm accommodations, all of which are comfortable. They also have a hammock room, a kitchen for guest use, a breakfast area where farm fresh eggs, goat's milk yogurt, and fresh juices are available for an additional cost, and common areas (both indoor and outdoor). Those traveling in motor homes are welcome too. What sets San Pedro apart is the owners: They know this region better than anyone, and they promote sustainable community-based tourism projects. It's easy to find, just off the main highway from Sogamoso to Lago Tota. A cab ride from the Sogamoso bus station costs COP$5,000.

TRANSPORTATION

Sogamoso's **Terminal de Transportes** (Cra. 17 between Clls. 11-11A, tel. 8/770-330) is downtown. Many buses connect Sogamoso with Paipa, Monguí, and Aquitania, the main town of Lago Tota.

From Bogotá to Sogamoso it's over 200 kilometers (124 miles), with regular bus service (3 hrs., COP$26,000) from the Portal del Norte bus terminal in Northern Bogotá. From Tunja the bus ride takes about one hour and costs COP$15,000.

Paipa

LOS LANCEROS MONUMENT

On the site of the **Batalla del Pantano de Vargas** (Battle of the Vargas Swamp) stands Colombia's largest sculpture, *Los Lanceros* (9 km south of Paipa on Paipa-Pantano de Vargas road, free), close to the town of Paipa. The massive monument was designed by Colombian sculptor Rodrigo Arenas Betancourt and built in commemoration of 150 years of Colombian independence. Bronze sculptures show the 14 *lanceros* (lancers on horseback) charging into battle, fists clenched in the air, with fear and defiance depicted on their faces. Above them is an odd triangular concrete slab that points into the heavens. It is 36 steps up to the platform of the monument, the age of Simón Bolívar on that fateful day.

The Batalla del Pantano de Vargas was a decisive battle during Simón Bolívar's independence march on Bogotá in 1819. After crossing the Llanos from Venezuela and climbing up the Andes via the Páramo de Pisba, the revolutionary army under Bolívar engaged a contingent of Spanish troops at the Pantano de Vargas on July 25, 1819. Exhausted after their long slog over the Cordillera Oriental mountains, the revolutionary troops were nearly defeated. However, a charge by 14 armed horsemen led by Juan José Rendón saved the day. Soldiers from the British Foreign Legion, under the command of Irishman James Rooke, also played a decisive role in this battle. The royalists lost 500 men in the battle, while 350 revolutionaries perished.

Across from the monument is the **Casa Museo Comunitario Juan Vargas** (COP$2,000), a small museum mostly about the military campaigns of Simón Bolívar. It was in this house that Juan Vargas, his wife, and their 12 children were executed by the Spaniards for supporting the rebel troops.

FOOD AND ACCOMMODATIONS

The ★ **Hacienda El Salitre** (Km. 3 Vía Paipa-Toca, tel. 8/785-1510, www.haciendadelsalitre.com, COP$350,000 d) is set in the countryside under towering eucalyptus trees, and you'll pass grazing cows to get there. At the hotel, go for one of the rooms with a thermal bathtub. You'll be treated to a thermal bath three times a day (staff come in and change the water each time). Rooms are cozy, warm, and spacious, but not quite luxurious. Here you can get a massage, or you can take a horse out for a trot to a nearby lake. From Sunday to Friday there is a 30 percent discount, so guests only pay full price for a Saturday-night stay. It's a popular location for wedding banquets and honeymoons on the weekends. The hacienda served as a barracks during the Batalla del Pantano de Vargas in 1819. The hotel has a very nice restaurant with outdoor seating, plus a café and a bar. Also open to nonguests, the restaurant, with its lovely setting, is the best around. It serves international and Colombian cuisine.

Overlooking Lago Sochagota is the **Estelar Paipa Hotel y Centro de Convenciones** (Lago Sochagota, Paipa, tel. 8/785-0944, www.hotelesestelar.com, COP$286,000 d).

the memorial of the Batalla del Pantano de Vargas, *Los Lanceros*

This upmarket chain hotel is modern, service oriented, and well maintained. The main attraction here is a spa with thermal baths, and there are other facilities on-site to keep you busy, such as a pool, tennis court, and a golf course. They also offer horseback riding. With over 100 rooms, this is a popular place for large groups.

Monguí

The chilly highland colonial village of **Monguí** was founded in 1601 and was a strategic post for the Spaniards thanks to its location between Tunja and the vast Llanos, the eastern plains. It is considered one of the most beautiful towns in Boyacá. Its narrow cobblestone streets are lined with white and green houses, many of which are multiple centuries old.

Three colonial constructions in Monguí have been declared national monuments. The stone **Basílica y Convento de Nuestra Señora de Monguí** stands on the Plaza de Bolívar. The adjacent Franciscan convent today houses the **Museo de Arte Religioso** (tel. 8/778-2050, 8am-noon and 2pm-5pm daily, free), which highlights the work of the famous 17th-century Colombian baroque painter Gregorio Vásquez de Arce y Ceballos. Other historic structures are the **Capilla de San Antonio de Padua**, which was the town's first church, and the photogenic stone bridge, the **Puente de Calicanto.**

Today Monguí is almost as famous for its soccer ball-making industry as for its colonial beauty. Around 70 percent of the town works in about 20 small factories. They churn out some 30,000 balls each month. More are produced during World Cup years. You can pick one up for about COP$25,000 at **Balones Hurtado** (Cl. 7 No. 3-60, tel. 8/778-2021, www.baloneshurtado.com, 9am-6pm Mon.-Sat.).

FOOD AND ACCOMMODATIONS

Monguí has a handful of lodging options. The reliable and comfortable choice is **La Casona de San Francisco de Asis** (Cra.

4A No. 3-41, tel. 8/778-2498, cell tel. 311/237-9823, COP$40,000 pp d). Rooms have a view over the Río Morro canyon, and the hotel is quite tidy. The restaurant, which has been in service for over two decades, is also one of the best in town, specializing in *cocido boyacense,* which has a variety of meats and some of the unusual tubers from the area, such as *cubios, ibias,* and *rubas.*

The **Calicanto Real** (Puente de Calicanto, Monguí, cell tel. 311/811-1519, calicantoreal.hostal@gmail.com, COP$25,000 pp) is an old house with five rooms overlooking the Puente de Calicanto. It was once the home of a wealthy emerald miner. Rooms are spacious with nice views and have a lot of character, but the beds are on the soft side. Within the hotel is a quirky tavern (hours vary) filled with decorations like cowboy hats, animal heads, and an homage to Monguí's most famous poet, El Indio Romulo.

TRANSPORTATION

There are two roads between Sogamoso and Monguí. The old but scenic route is partly unpaved and winds through eucalyptus forests and the pueblo of Morca. It's about 20 kilometers (12 miles) and makes for a challenging bike ride. On the new road, a bus ride to Monguí costs about COP$5,000 and takes about 45 minutes. The bus leaves from the intersection of Carrera 14 and Calle 16 in Sogamoso.

Lago Tota

One of the most popular destinations in Boyacá is **Lago Tota,** Colombia's largest lake, covering 55 square kilometers (21 square miles). The views are spectacular here, with mountains, valleys, and fields surrounding the lake. Over 145 species of birds have been seen in this area. The main town on the lake is Aquitania, and it's a rather dreary and surprisingly rough-and-tumble place. Most visitors choose to stay at one of the cozy lakeside lodges nearby.

The lake and surrounding countryside, a patchwork of fields of green onions and potatoes, is beautiful. However, the lake is in peril. The dumping of fertilizers and pesticides from lakeside farms has been the primary reason that this lake, which provides drinking water for hundreds of thousands of people, has been declared one of the top five most threatened wetlands in the world by the World Wetlands Network. There are other culprits as well, such as large caged trout farms. The threat of oil drilling in the lake was thwarted by environmental activists in 2012. Despite these environmental challenges, the lake remains a recreational draw for boaters. The water is very cold, so it's not considered a good place to swim.

Playa Blanca (COP$3,500 entry), a chilly lakeside beach, is the main draw at Lago Tota, as it's the only beach and gathering place here. At the water's edge is usually a local hawking boat rides on the lake. If you have a mountain bike, a nice ride is along the western side of the lake, along a mostly dirt road. This is also a pleasant route for a walk.

FOOD AND ACCOMMODATIONS

Along the shore of Lago Tota are many rooms with a view. Bargains can be had during the week, when you will have your lodge (if not the lake) blissfully to yourself. On long weekends,

it's especially lively with visitors from Bogotá. Most lakeside lodges offer all meals. You may feel a little stuck here, due to lack of regular public transportation.

The Decameron all-inclusive hotel chain has agreements with two hotels in the area. The nicer of the two is **Refugio Santa Inés** (Km. 29 Vía Sogamoso-Aquitania, tel. 1/628-0000, cell tel. 313/261-2429, santaineshotel@gmail.com, www.decameron.com, COP$99,000 pp d), a comfortable lodge-style hotel with 13 rooms and two cabins. Wood ceilings and floors add to the atmosphere. Set on the eastern side of the lake, the hotel has a terrace, an ideal vantage point from which to watch the sunset with a drink (also open to nonguests). Beds are very comfortable, there is wireless Internet access, and breakfast is included. The restaurant offers other meals as well. Hiking, horseback riding, and taking a boat around the lake are other activities on offer, all of which require being accompanied by a guide. The other Decameron location is **Hotel Refugio Rancho Tota** (Km. 21 Vía Sogamoso-Aquitania, cell tel. 311/273-7863, www.hotelranchotota.com, COP$80,000 pp d), with similar pricing and facilities. It also has a small spa, and some rooms have fireplaces.

Playa Blanca, Lago Tota

For charm and a view, there are two long-standing stone lodges. ★ **Pozo Azul** (Lago Tota, Bogotá tel. 1/620-6257, cell tel. 320/384-1000, www.hotelrefugiopozoazul.com, COP$196,000 d), set on an inlet, was one of the first nice hotels on the lake, and it retains its charm. You'll often see guests gathered by a circular fireplace in the lobby area. The hotel has 15 rooms and two *cabañas* (COP$340,000) that sleep four and feature their own fireplaces. Some beds are on the soft side. Getting from the parking lot to the lodge requires descending 80 steep steps, which could be difficult for those with physical limitations. The lodge can arrange a boat excursion around the lake for an additional cost. **Rocas Lindas** (Lago Tota, cell tel. 310/349-1107, www.hotelrocaslindas.wordpress.com, COP$85,000 pp d) is a cozy lodge with 10 rooms and one cabin. There's no wireless Internet here, and this hotel could use some upgrading.

TRANSPORTATION

To get to Playa Blanca from Sogamoso, there are two bus options that take different routes around the lake. Each ride takes about an hour and costs COP$5,000-6,000. One route goes through Iza and the other takes you to Aquitania, which requires transferring to a minivan at Aquitania's market, four blocks from the town's Plaza Principal. This second leg takes 10 minutes and costs COP$1,500.

Another option is to hire a car in Sogamoso for about COP$25,000 each way.

SIERRA NEVADA DEL COCUY

The Sierra Nevada del Cocuy, the highest mountains within the Cordillera Oriental (Eastern Range) of the Andes mountain chain, are 260 kilometers (162 miles) northeast of Bogotá in northern Boyacá. The entire mountain range is contained within and protected by the Parque Nacional Natural El Cocuy, the country's fifth-largest national park. With its 11 jagged snowcapped peaks, massive glacier-formed valleys, extensive *páramos* (highland moors) studded with exotic *frailejón* plants,

and stunning crystalline mountain lakes, streams, and waterfalls, it is one of the most beautiful places in Colombia. The sierra appeals to serious mountaineers and rock climbers, but it is also a place that nature lovers with little experience and no gear can explore by doing easily organized day hikes.

PLANNING YOUR TIME

Getting to the Sierra Nevada del Cocuy entails a long, grueling trip, albeit through the beautiful, verdant countryside of Boyacá. Ideally you want to spend at least four days here, taking in the spectacular mountain landscapes.

The park has three sectors: the Northern, Central, and Southern Sectors, each with many options for day hikes, more strenuous ascents to the snowcapped peaks, or highly technical rock-climbing expeditions. There is also a spectacular six-day trek along a valley between the two main ridges of the sierra. It is not a highly technical trek but requires good high-altitude conditioning. For many visitors, this is the main reason to visit the sierra.

The gateway towns of El Cocuy and Güicán are convenient arrival and departure points for visiting the area. In both you can find basic tourist services, tour operators and guides, and stores to stock up on food, though not trekking equipment (which can be rented from local tour operators). Both have a few interesting sights and are departure points for day hikes. El Cocuy is better located to access the Southern Sector of the park and Güicán the Northern Sector. However, because both these towns are around 20 kilometers (12 miles) from the park and there is limited public transportation, a good option is to base yourself nearer to the park boundary in one of several pleasant lodges or campsites. You could easily spend a few days in each one of the three sectors, setting off on beautiful day hikes from your accommodations.

The only way to do the six-day hike around the park is with an organized tour, as the trails are not marked. If you are planning to do this trek, you may want to arrive a few days earlier to do some high-altitude acclimatization hikes. Many peaks are more than 5,000 meters (16,000 feet) high.

The only dependable time to visit the Sierra Nevada del Cocuy is from December to March, during the *verano* (summer dry season) in the Cordillera Oriental. At other times, there may be permanent cloud cover and much rain. High season, when Colombian visitors flock to the mountains, is from mid-December to mid-January, and again in Holy Week (late March or April).

The best available topographical maps of the Sierra Nevada de Cocuy can be viewed and downloaded online at www.nevados.org.

GETTING THERE

The towns of El Cocuy and Güicán are served from Bogotá by three bus companies. The trip takes 11 hours; it stops at El Cocuy and terminates at Güicán. The most comfortable option is with the bus company **Libertadores** (COP$50,000), which operates a big bus that leaves Bogotá at 8:30pm. The return trip departs El Cocuy at 7:30pm. Bus line **Fundadores** (COP$45,000) has two buses; they leave Bogotá at 5am and 4:30pm, returning from El Cocuy at 7:30am and 8:30pm. **Concord** (COP$45,000) also has two services, leaving Bogotá at 3am and 5pm and leaving El Cocuy for Bogotá at 5:30am and 7:30pm.

El Cocuy

El Cocuy is a charming colonial town nestled in the lower folds of the Sierra Nevada del Cocuy at an altitude of 2,750 meters (9,022 feet). The town is meticulous, its whitewashed houses painted with a band of aquamarine. El Cocuy offers decent accommodations, a few tour operators, and some stores to stock up for a visit to the park, though no specialized mountaineering stores.

The only sight to check out is in the Parque Principal, where there is a large **diorama** of the Sierra Nevada del Cocuy. This will allow you to understand the mountain geography, with its multitude of snowcapped peaks, lakes, and valleys.

RECREATION

For a spectacular panoramic view of the entire sierra, take a hike to **Cerro Mahoma** (Mahoma Hill), to the west of town. It is a strenuous six- to seven-hour excursion often used by people who are acclimatizing before trekking in the Sierra Nevada del Cocuy. The trailhead is outside of El Cocuy on the road that leads to the town of Chita. Because the trail is not marked and splits several times, it is best to go with a guide.

For an experienced local guide, contact the local guide association, **ASEGUICOC** (Asociación de Prestadores de Servicios Ecoturísticos de Güicán y El Cocuy, cell tel. 311/557-7893, 311/236-4275, or 313/371-9735, aseguicoc@gmail.com).

FOOD AND ACCOMMODATIONS

Hotels like Casa Muñoz generally offer the best food, but don't expect to be amazed come dinnertime. Vegetarians may want to travel with a can of emergency lentils to hand over to kitchen staff to warm up for you.

Hotel la Posada del Molino (Cra. 3 No. 7-51, tel. 8/789-0377, www.elcocuycasamuseo. blogspot.com, COP$50,000 d) is a friendly guesthouse. Rooms in this old house are set around two colorful interior patios. The house has a little history to it as well. It is said that during the deadly feuds between Güicán and El Cocuy (Güicán was conservative and El Cocuy was liberal), the famous Virgen Morenita image was taken from its shrine in Güicán and hidden away in the house where the hotel is located. You can see the room that hid this secret.

Casa Muñoz (Cra. 5 No. 7-28, tel. 8/789-0328, www.hotelcasamunoz.com, COP$25,000 pp d) has a great location overlooking the main plaza in town. It offers a restaurant in the patio on the main floor. Rooms are fine, though somewhat small, with firm beds and wooden floors.

INFORMATION AND SERVICES

At the offices of the **Parque Nacional Natural El Cocuy** (Cl. 5 No. 4-22, tel.

8/789-0359, cocuy@parquesnacionales.gov. co, 7am-noon and 1pm-4:45pm daily), you can obtain a park entry permit (COP$37,500 non-Colombians, COP$14,000 residents, COP$7,500 children/students) and general information.

There is an **ATM** at the Banco Agrario at Carrera 4 and Calle 8.

Güicán

Long before its foundation in 1822, Güicán was a place of significance for the U'wa indigenous people. The U'wa fiercely resisted the Spanish conquest, and, rather than submit to domination, their chief Güicány led the people to mass suicide off a nearby cliff known as El Peñón de los Muertos.

The town, damaged by fires and civil war, is a mix of modern and old buildings, without much charm. However, it is a convenient base for visiting the Northern Sector of the park. It has good accommodations, several tour operators, and is the starting point for numerous beautiful day hikes.

Folks in Güicán resent that the national park carries the "El Cocuy" name. They feel that this natural wonder is just as much theirs as it is their rivals in the town of El Cocuy. You can score points with them by referring to the park as Parque Nacional Natural El Güicán.

SIGHTS

The main sight in town is the image of the Virgen Morenita de Güicán, located in the **Iglesia de Nuestra Señora de la Candelaria** (Parque Principal). This image of the Virgin, with strong indigenous traits, appeared to the survivors of the U'wa mass suicide and ushered in their conversion to Christianity.

At the entrance to the town on the road from El Cocuy is the **Monumento a la Dignidad de la Raza U'wa** (Monument to U'wa Dignity), a large statue that depicts the culture and history of the U'wa people. It was designed by a local artist with input from the community.

RECREATION

There are several pleasant day hikes to be done from Güicán. A mildly strenuous three-kilometer (two-mile), two-hour round-trip hike takes you to the base of **El Peñón de los Muertos** (3,800 meters/12,500 feet), site of the U'wa mass suicide. The 300-meter (985-foot) cliff is imposing, and the thought of hundreds of people jumping off in defiance is sobering. From the Parque Principal, follow the road east toward the Vereda San Juan sector of the park. Several signs for El Peñon de los Muertos indicate the way, so you will not need a guide.

A longer and more strenuous 11-kilometer (7-mile), six-hour hike leads northeast along the **Sendero del Mosco** (Mosco Trail) up the Río Cardenillo, passing sheer cliffs to a spot called Parada de Romero, which is the initial (or ending, depending on which way you go) segment of the six-day circuit around the Sierra Nevada del Cocuy. The hike ends at an altitude of 3,800 meters (12,500 feet) and is a good acclimatization walk. The trailhead is off the road that leads from Güicán to PNN El Cocuy. Because the trail is not marked, it is best to take a guide.

To book a guide, contact the association of local guides, **ASEGUICOC** (Asociación de Prestadores de Servicios Ecoturísticos de Güicán y El Cocuy, cell tel. 311/557-7893, 311/236-4275, or 313/371-9735, aseguicoc@ gmail.com).

FOOD AND ACCOMMODATIONS

The **Brisas del Nevado** (Cra. 5 No. 4-57, tel. 7/789-7028, cell tel. 310/629-9001, www.bri-sasdelnevado.com, COP$35,000 pp) has the best accommodations and restaurant in town. Four rooms in the original house sleep 2-4 people each. Outside is a nicer cabin with two rooms. The only problem is its location next to a rowdy bar. The restaurant, which serves Colombian cuisine, has varied hours, so inquire beforehand to make sure they'll be open.

El Eden (Transversal 2 No. 9-58 Urbanización Villa Nevada, cell tel. 311/808-8334, www.guicanextremo.com, COP$30,000 pp) is in a residential neighborhood about 10 minutes from the main plaza. It's a friendly place with lots of basic but clean rooms, and you can use the kitchen. Rabbits and parakeets are caged in the garden below.

Just outside of town is the **Hotel Ecológico El Nevado** (road to El Cocuy, cell tel. 320/808-5256 or 310/806-2149, www. hoteleconevado.jimdo.com, COP$60,000 d), which occupies a spacious and green setting. There are two parts to the hotel: the original quaint farmhouse with an interior patio, and a modern wing. The farmhouse has more character, but the modern wing is more comfortable.

INFORMATION AND SERVICES
At the Güicán office of the **Parque Natural Nacional El Cocuy** (Transversal 4 No. 6-60, tel. 8/789-7280, 7am-noon and 1pm-4:45pm daily), you can obtain a park entry permit (COP$55,000 non-Colombians, COP$28,000 residents, COP$13,500 children/students) and general information.

Parque Nacional Natural El Cocuy

★ Parque Nacional Natural El Cocuy
Located about 20 kilometers (12 miles) east of the towns of El Cocuy and Güicán, the **Parque Nacional Natural El Cocuy** (tel. 8/789-0359, cocuy@parquesnacionales.gov. co) covers 306,000 hectares (760,000 acres) spanning the departments of Boyacá, Arauca, and Casanare.

Entry permits (COP$55,000 non-Colombians, COP$28,000 residents, COP$13,500 children/students), which include entry fees, are required and can be easily obtained at the park offices in El Cocuy (Cl. 5 No. 4-22, tel. 8/789-0359, cocuy@parquesnacionales.gov.co, 7am-noon and 1pm-4:45pm daily) or Güicán (Transversal 4 No. 6-60, 7am-noon and 1pm-4:45pm daily). In peak season from mid-December to mid-January and during Holy Week, it is better to obtain the permit several weeks in advance through the Park Service in Bogotá. Call (tel. 1/353-2400) or email (ecoturismo@parquesnacionales.gov.co) to request a permit. You will be asked to submit the names of visitors, passport numbers, and expected dates of your arrival. The Park Service will provide instructions for paying and will send the permit by email.

The Sierra Nevada del Cocuy, consisting of two parallel ranges 30 kilometers (19 miles) long with 11 peaks higher than 5,000 meters (16,400 feet), is the centerpiece of the park. However, the park extends far north and east from the sierra and includes extensive tracts of temperate and tropical forests. It also includes 92,000 hectares (230,000 acres) of U'wa indigenous *resguardos* (reservations), which are not open to tourism.

The Sierra Nevada del Cocuy is home to the largest expanse of glaciers in Colombia, extending 16 square kilometers (6 square miles); what are usually referred to as *nevados* (snowcapped mountains) are in fact glacier-capped mountains. Unfortunately, all the glaciers in Colombia, including those of the Sierra Nevada del Cocuy, are rapidly melting due to global warming. A 2013 report by the

Parque Nacional Natural El Cocuy

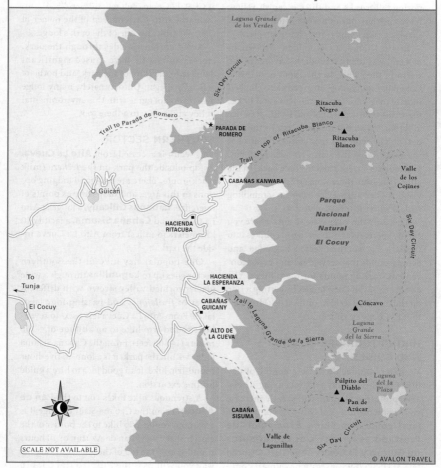

Colombian Hydrological, Meteorological, and Environmental Studies Institute (IDEAM) forecasts that, by 2030, all the glaciers in Colombia will have disappeared.

The sierra's highest peak is **Ritacuba Blanco** (5,380 meters/17,650 feet). Other notable glacier-capped peaks are **Ritacuba Negro** (5,350 meters, 17,550 feet), **San Pablín Norte** (5,200 meters, 17,060 feet), **Cóncavo** (5,200 meters/17,060 feet), and **Pan de Azúcar** (5,100 meters, 16,730 feet).

One of the most striking peaks in the Sierra Nevada del Cocuy is the **Púlpito del Diablo** or Devil's Pulpit (5,100 meters, 16,730 feet), a massive rectangular flat-topped rock formation. Ritacuba Blanco, Cóncavo, and Pan de Azúcar can be ascended by anyone in good physical shape and do not require mountain-climbing skills.

At the bases of the peaks are numerous glacier-formed valleys supporting *páramos,* unique tropical high-altitude ecosystems of the Andes. The *páramos* are covered with beautiful *frailejones,* plants that have imposing tall trunks and thick greenish-yellow leaves. Other *páramo* vegetation includes shrubs, grasses, and *cojines* (cushion plants).

Erwin Krauss, a Colombian of German descent, was the first modern explorer of the sierra in the 1930s. In the 1960s and 1970s, Colombian and European expeditions climbed most of the peaks. During the 1980s and 1990s, there was significant ELN and FARC presence and tourism all but disappeared. In the past decade, the army has reestablished control of the area around the Sierra Nevada de Cocuy, and tourists have started to come back. In the 2012-13 season, there were an estimated 9,000 visitors. The Park Service has been scrambling to deal with the influx of visitors.

There are three separate sectors where you can do spectacular one- to two-day hikes into the park. Each of these sectors has lodges and campgrounds that serve food and make convenient starting points for these hikes. You can get to any of these lodges by getting a ride on the morning *lechero* (milk truck) from either El Cocuy or Güicán.

HIKING TOUR OPERATORS AND GUIDES

Whether you decide to do a couple of day hikes or the six-day trek, securing a reliable, professional guide will greatly increase your enjoyment. For day hikes, contact the local guide association **Asociación de Prestadores de Servicios Ecoturísticos de Güicán y El Cocuy** (ASEGUICOC, cell tel. 311/557-7893, aseguicoc@gmail.com). Expect to pay about COP$80,000-100,000. If you ascend to the top of a glacier, the daily rate goes up to COP$130,000-150,000 and includes necessary gear.

One of the leading trekking operators in the Sierra Nevada del Cocuy is **Colombia Trek** (Cra. 4 No. 6-50, Güicán, cell tel. 320/339-3839, arias_rodrigo@hotmail.com, www.colombiatrek.com), run by knowledgeable veteran Rodrigo Arias. It is one of the few operators offering English-speaking guides.

Another tour company based in El Cocuy is **Servicios Ecoturísticos Güicány** (Cra. 5 at Cl. 9, El Cocuy, cell tel. 310/566-7554), run by Juan Carlos Carreño, son of the owner of Cabañas Güicány, one of the park's lodges.

Avoid horseback rides through the park. Horses and cattle have caused significant damage to the flora of the park, and both are officially illegal. Unfortunately, many lodge owners do not agree with this environmental policy and refuse to adhere to it.

SOUTHERN SECTOR

This sector is accessed from **Alto La Cueva,** a stop outside the park on the *lechero* (milk truck) route. There are two good lodging options in this area, and they serve as points of reference: **Cabañas Güicány,** a lodge at Alto La Cueva, and **Cabaña Sisuma,** a facility 10 kilometers (6 miles) from Alto La Cueva inside the park.

One popular day hike in the Southern Sector goes up to **Lagunillas** through a wide glacier-formed valley strewn with different types of *frailejones* and passing four large lakes. From Alto La Cueva it is a six- to seven-hour round-trip hike to an altitude of 4,300 meters (14,100 feet). From the Cabaña Sisuma lodge within the park, it is a four- to five-hour round-trip hike. It's a good idea to hire a guide for this excursion.

A strenuous hike takes you to the **Pan de Azúcar.** From the Cabaña Sisuma lodge it is a six-hour round-trip hike to the border of the glacier that covers Pan de Azúcar, or 10 hours round-trip to the top of the glacier. Along the way you will pass the **Púlpito del Diablo** (Devil's Pulpit). From the top of Pan de Azúcar there are spectacular views of Laguna Grande de la Sierra, Púlpito del Diablo, and Cóncavo. A guide is required for this hike.

CENTRAL SECTOR

The starting point for visits to the Central Sector is the working farm and hotel **Hacienda La Esperanza,** which is on the edge of the park and a stop on the daily *lechero* (milk truck) route. From there, it is a strenuous six-hour round-trip hike to **Laguna Grande de la Sierra,** a beautiful lake nestled between the Cóncavo and Púlpito del Diablo peaks. It's best to go with a guide on this excursion. It's possible to continue and ascend the **Cóncavo** (5,200 meters/17,060 feet), **Concavito** (5,100 meters, 16,730 feet), or **Toti** (4,900 meters/16,075 feet) peaks, though doing so requires camping a night at the lake. Each ascent involves a strenuous four- to five-hour round-trip hike and should be done with a guide. From Laguna Grande de la Sierra, it is also possible to reach Cabaña Sisuma, in the Southern Sector, in nine hours. A guide is necessary because this trail is not well marked.

NORTHERN SECTOR

The starting point for hikes in the Northern Sector is **Cabañas Kanwara,** a lodge that's about a 90-minute walk from the closest stop on the *lechero* (milk truck) route, Hacienda Ritacuba. A short and moderate three- to four-hour round-trip hike takes you to the **Alto Cimiento del Padre,** a mountain pass at 4,200 meters (13,800 feet). This hike offers spectacular views of Ritacuba Negro peak. It's a good idea to hire a guide for this hike.

Cabañas Kanwara is also the starting point for hikes to the gently sloping **Ritacuba Blanco,** the highest peak in the Sierra Nevada del Cocuy. The ascent to the top can be done in one grueling 9- to 10-hour excursion, leaving at 2am or 3am in order to reach the peak in the morning, when conditions are best for climbing on the glacier. Most people split the trek into two days, camping at the Playitas camp halfway up the mountain. A guide is necessary for this trek.

SIX-DAY CIRCUIT

An unforgettable experience is to do the six-day trek through the glacier-formed valleys lying between the two ranges of mountains. Along the entire route you will have glacier-capped mountains on both sides. There are a few mountain passes, but generally the altitude is 4,000-4,500 meters (13,100-14,800 feet). You do not need to be an expert mountaineer, but in addition to being in good physical condition, you need to be acclimatized to the altitude. You may be required to complete a few day hikes prior to this trek. Do not attempt this trek without a knowledgeable guide, as it's easy to get lost in this treacherous landscape. The basic tour, which involves carrying all your own gear, will cost on average COP$700,000 per person. Don't pay less than that because it means the operator is skimping on the guide's salary. High-end tours, with porters and a cook, will cost COP$1,500,000 per person.

ACCOMMODATIONS

While not luxurious by any means, the lodging options in and around the park are homey. The proprietors are all attentive and friendly.

The best-located accommodation in the Southern Sector is ★ **Cabaña Sisuma** (cell tel. 311/236-4275 or 311/255-1034, aseguicoc@gmail.com, COP$35,000 pp), a cozy cabin inside the park run by the local tour guide association ASEGUICOC. It has six rooms, good food, and fireplaces to keep warm. The cabin is a two-hour hike into the park from Alto La Cueva, a stop on the daily *lechero* (milk truck) route. Another pleasant and comfortable option is rustic **Cabañas Güicány** (Alto La Cueva, cell tel. 310/566-7554, cab_guaicany@yahoo.es or guaicany@hotmail.com, COP$70,000 pp with meals, COP$40,000 pp without meals, COP$10,000 pp camping), in Alto La Cueva. The *lechero* (milk truck) can drop you off at the lodge. The owner, Eudoro Carreño, is a delight to chat with over a hot drink in the kitchen.

In the Central Sector, ★ **Hacienda La Esperanza** (cell tel. 314/221-2473, haciendalaesperanza@gmail.com, COP$50,000 pp with meals, COP$35,000 pp without meals), a working farm on the edge of the park, provides accommodations in a rustic farmhouse oozing character. The family running the hotel is very hospitable, and the host is a trained chef who enjoys pampering his guests. Nothing beats hanging out by the fireplace in the late afternoon with a warm drink after a day of mountain climbing. The *lechero* (milk truck) makes a stop at the hacienda.

The most conveniently located place to stay in the Northern Sector is **Cabañas Kanwara** (cell tel. 311/231-6004 or 311/237-2260, info-kanwara@gmail.com, COP$35,000 pp). This lodge of cute wooden A-frame houses also serves good food. To get here, you must get off the *lechero* (milk truck) at the farm Hacienda Ritacuba and walk 90 minutes toward the park.

TRANSPORTATION

To get to any of the three sectors of the park from gateway towns El Cocuy and Güicán, there are three possibilities: hiking 4-5 hours uphill to the park, taking an express service (COP$80,000-100,000), or riding an early-morning *lechero* (milk truck). This is a working truck that picks up milk from farms along a set route. Merchandise and passengers share the back of the truck, which is covered with canvas. The *lechero* leaves Güicán from the intersection of Carrera 5 and Calle 6 every morning at 5:30am and stops at El Cocuy around 6am. Around 7:30am it arrives at Alto La Cueva, where you can get off to visit the Southern Sector. Around 9am it pulls up to Hacienda La Esperanza, a lodge and farm in the Central Sector. Around 10:30am it reaches Hacienda Ritacuba, from where you can walk up to Cabañas Kanwara, a lodge in the Northern Sector.

Santander

Beautiful, lush scenery, a delightful climate, well-preserved colonial pueblos, and friendly, outgoing people—this is the Santander department. Located in northeast Colombia, Santander lies to the north of Boyacá and southwest of Norte de Santander. Bucaramanga is the modern capital city, but you'll probably be drawn to the countryside. San Gil and the Cañón del Chicamocha will keep you busy with a smorgasbord of outdoor adventures, while nearby Barichara will seduce you with its tranquil ambience.

BUCARAMANGA

Known as the Ciudad Bonita (Beautiful City), Bucaramanga is a busy and growing city with a young and vibrant population and an agreeable climate that ensures the flowers are always in bloom. Its central location makes for a strategic launching point for visits to the Santander countryside, and the city is midway between Bogotá and Santa Marta on the Caribbean coast as well as Cúcuta in the far east. Including neighborhoods that are an extension of Bucaramanga (Floridablanca, Girón, and Piedecuesta), the population exceeds one million.

ORIENTATION

Most of your time will probably be spent in **Cabecera** (the upscale shopping and residential area), the **city center** (between Cras. 9-17 and Cl. 45 and Av. Quebrada Seca), and in nearby municipalities such as Girón and Floridablanca.

Carreras (avenues) run north to south, increasing in number from west to east. The main *carreras* are 15, 27, and 33. *Calles* (streets) run east to west and increase in number from north to south.

Sights

Bucaramanga's main sights are contained within the walkable city center. If you're staying in the Cabecera neighborhood it's a long, hot walk to the city center, so you're better off taking a cab.

Bucaramanga prides itself on its parks, and one of the most famous is the **Parque García Rovira** (Cras. 10-11 and Clls. 36-37). Filled with towering palms, it doesn't provide much shade, but with the pale yellow and white 19th-century **Catedral San Laureano** (Cra. 12 No. 36-08) standing prominently on the park's eastern side, it is rather photogenic.

Bucaramanga

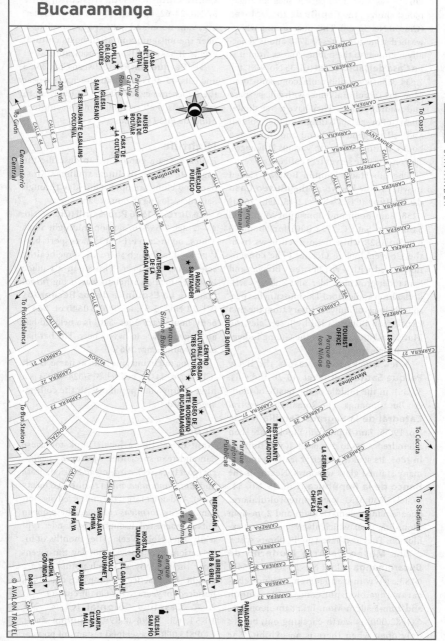

0
0   200 m
         200 yds

To Girón
To Coast
To Floridablanca
To Bus Station
To Cúcuta
To Stadium

Cementerio Central

CAPILLA DE LOS DOLORES
CASA DEL LIBRO TOTAL
Parque García Rovira
IGLESIA SAN LAUREANO
RESTAURANTE CASALINS COLONIAL
MUSEO CASA DE BOLÍVAR
CASA DE LA CULTURA

Metrolínea

CARRERA 12
CARRERA 13
CARRERA 14
CARRERA 15
CARRERA 16
CARRERA 17
CARRERA 18
CARRERA 19
CARRERA 20
CARRERA 21
CARRERA 22
CARRERA 23
CARRERA 24
CARRERA 25
CARRERA 26
CARRERA 27
CARRERA 28
CARRERA 29
CARRERA 33
CARRERA 34
CARRERA 36
CARRERA 37

SANTANDER

CALLE 44
CALLE 43
CALLE 42
CALLE 41
CALLE 45
CALLE 46
CALLE 48
CALLE 50
CALLE 51
CALLE 52
CALLE 30
CALLE 29A
CALLE 31
CALLE 33
CALLE 34
CALLE 36
CALLE 37
CALLE 35
CALLE 28A
CALLE 41
CALLE 42
CALLE 44
CALLE 45

MERCADO PÚBLICO
Parque Centenario
CATEDRAL DE LA SAGRADA FAMILIA
PARQUE SANTANDER
Parque Simón Bolívar
CIUDAD BONITA
CENTRO CULTURAL POSADA TRES CULTURAS
MUSEO DE ARTE MODERNO DE BUCARAMANGA
ROSITA
GONZÁLEZ

TOURIST OFFICE
Parque de los Niños
LA ESQUINA
Metrolínea

RESTAURANTE LOS TEJADITOS
Parque Mejoras Públicas
LA SERRANÍA
EL VIEJO CHIFLAS
TONNY'S

PAN PA YA
EMBAJADA CHINA
Parque Las Palmas
MERCAGAN
HOSTAL TAMARINDO
TAVOLO GOURMET
EL GARAJE
LA BIRRERÍA PUB & GRILL
RADHA GOVINDA'S
KIRAMA
Parque San Pío
DASH
CUARTA ETAPA MALL
IGLESIA SAN PÍO
PANADERÍA TRILLOS

© AVALON TRAVEL

On the west side of the park is Bucaramanga's oldest church, the **Capilla de los Dolores** (Cra. 10 No. 36-08). This unassuming white-washed structure dates to 1748 and is generally not open to the public. Across from it is **La Casa del Libro Total** (Cl. 35 No. 9-81, tel. 7/634-3558, www.ellibrototal.com, 8am-10pm Mon.-Fri.), a cultural center with gallery space and reading rooms. They have a free digital library of over 50,000 titles, and they publish and sell gorgeously bound and illustrated books, mostly classics in various languages. The on-site café serves free coffee.

The Libertador, Simón Bolívar, stayed in what's now known as the **Museo Casa de Bolívar** (Cl. 37 No. 12-15, tel. 7/630-4258, 8am-noon and 2pm-6pm Mon.-Fri., 8am-noon Sat., COP$2,000) for about 70 days in 1828 while he awaited news from the Convención de Ocaña. (The convention ended with a rift between Bolívar and Santander growing wider, and Bolívar's self-declaration as dictator.) The museum has personal belongs of Bolívar, a diary from the first Expedición Botánica led by José Celestino Mutis, and an exhibit on the Guane indigenous people from the area.

A few blocks to the east is the lively **Parque Santander** (Cras. 19-20 and Clls. 35-36), in the middle of the bustle of modern Bucaramanga. The Romanesque revival **Catedral de la Sagrada Familia** (Cl. 36 No. 19-56, 7am-10pm daily) took more than a hundred years to complete. It was finished in 1865. Its striking interior features include many stained glass windows. Nearby is the **Banco de la República** (Cra. 19 No. 34-47, tel. 7/630-3133, www.banrepcultural.org/bucaramanga, 8am-11:30am and 2pm-6pm Mon.-Fri., free), which always has an art exhibit on. They also have a public library space.

The **Museo de Arte Moderno de Bucaramanga** (Cl. 37 No. 26-16, tel. 7/645-0483, www.museodeartemodernodebucaramanga.blogspot.com, 8:30am-noon and 2pm-5:30pm Mon.-Fri., 8am-noon Sat., COP$2,000) is worth checking out, but it's only open when there is an exhibit. The **Centro Cultural Posada Tres Culturas** (Cl. 37 No. 24-62, tel. 7/634-4859, www.fusader. org, 9am-noon and 2pm-7pm Mon.-Sat.) is near the museum and often hosts cultural events. It has a small on-site bookstore.

The **Parque San Pío** (between Cras. 33-35 and Clls. 45-46) is a vibrant green space near the Cabecera neighborhood. At the western end stands the Fernando Botero sculpture *Mujer de Pies Desnuda*.

Nightlife

Exuberant is a good word to describe the nightlife scene in Bucaramanga. Most bars and clubs are open Thursday through Saturday, closing at 2am or 3am.

La Birrería 1516 Pub & Grill (Cra. 36 No. 43-42, tel. 7/657-7675, noon-midnight Sun.-Thurs., noon-2am Fri.-Sat.) serves sports bar-type food (although there are some healthy selections) and beer. This open-air place is where locals gather to watch big *fútbol* matches. **La Esquinita de los Recuerdos** (Cl. 22 No. 25-55, tel. 7/632-0640 or 7/645-6861, hours vary Tues.-Sat.) is a beloved bar and a good place to have a beer. The bar has been around since 1965.

As you might imagine from its name, **Dash** (Cl. 48 No. 34-12, cell tel. 315/624-6905) is a high-energy club popular with the college-aged crowd.

Food

Want to eat like a local? Look for these Santanderean specialties: *cabrito con pepitoria* (goat fricassee), *carne oreada* (dried meat), and *mute santandereano* (a corn-based meaty stew). And don't forget the ants: fried big-bottom ants or *hormigas culonas*. These queen ants are harvested throughout Santander, typically after Holy Week. After months of hibernation, on one prickly hot day, the queens leave their colony, at which point they are caught. The practice of eating ants dates back hundreds of years to the Guane culture.

★ **Casalins Colonial** (Cl. 41 No. 10-54, tel. 7/696-0539, 11am-9pm daily, COP$15,000) is a seafood restaurant popular with government bureaucrats on their lunch break. There is always a set lunch menu (plus a la carte items), and frequently you'll have to wait a bit to be seated. Tables are set around a pleasant, sunny patio. It is behind the Gobernación building.

One of Bucaramanga's favorite restaurants is ★ **El Viejo Chiflas** (Cra. 33 No. 34-10, tel. 7/632-0640, 9am-midnight Mon.-Wed., 24 hours Thurs.-Sun., COP$23,000). The atmosphere here is cowboy style with wooden tables and interiors, and the menu features local specialties, such as goat and the Santander classic *carne oreada* (dried meat). An arepa (cornmeal cake) accompanies every meal. Portions can be huge.

Los Tejaditos (Cl. 34 No. 27-82, tel. 7/634-6028, www.restaurantelostejaditos. com, 11am-10pm Tues.-Sat., 11am-5pm Sun., COP$23,000) is an old-fashioned restaurant with a popular lunch menu. **Mercagán** (Cra. 33 No. 42-12, tel. 7/632-4949, www.mercagan-parrilla.com, 11am-6pm Mon. and Thurs., 11am-11pm Tues.-Wed. and Fri.-Sat., 11am-4pm Sun., COP$25,000) is a legendary steak house in Bucaramanga that has multiple locations, but this one, with the best atmosphere, faces the Parque San Pío.

Radha Govinda's (Cra. 34 No. 51-95, tel. 7/643-3382, lunch Mon.-Sat.) is a long-running and popular vegetarian restaurant that is open only for lunch. It's on a quiet street in Cabecera.

The Chinese restaurant **Embajada China** (Cl. 49 No. 32-27, tel. 7/647-1931, 10am-10pm daily, COP$15,000) is run by a Chinese family, and they serve generous portions. It's in Cabecera near the Kasa Guane hostel.

Stir-fries, salads, and pastas are on the menu at slightly fancy **Tavolo Gourmet** (Cra. 35 No. 48-84, tel. 7/643-7461, www.tavologourmet.com, 11am-10pm Tues.-Sun., COP$18,000). It's a bright and airy place in an upscale shopping area.

★ **Toscana** (Av. Jardín Casa 1A, tel. 7/647-6666, www.toscanarestaurante.com, 11am-11pm daily, COP$24,000) is an elegant Italian restaurant with outdoor seating. It regularly receives high marks, especially for the atmosphere.

Pan Pa Ya (Cl. 49 No. 28-38, tel. 7/685-2001, 8am-10pm Mon.-Sat, 9am-noon and 5pm-8pm Sun.) is a Colombian chain that's a reliable place for a decent cup of coffee, pastries, and an inexpensive breakfast of eggs and fresh fruit.

Accommodations

Bucaramanga has a number of standard business hotels, including familiar international names like Holiday Inn and Ramada. Rates tend to dip substantially on weekends.

UNDER COP$70,000

Kasa Guane (Cl. 11 No. 26-50, tel. 7/657-6960, cell tel. 313/274-2199, www.kasaguane.com, COP$25,000 dorm, COP$80,000 d) remains the top choice of international backpackers passing through town. This busy yet friendly place has both dorms and private rooms, hosts activities, and provides insider information. The guys here will get you hooked up with paragliding and give you expert insider tips on all the Bucaramanga party spots.

COP$70,000-200,000

Antigua Belén Bed and Breakfast (Cra. 31 No. 17-22, tel. 7/634-9860, www.hotelantiquabelen.com, COP$100,000 d with a/c) has 13 rooms in a modern house full of antiques. It's located in a quiet part of town. Breakfast is served in a pleasant patio in the back.

★ **Ciudad Bonita** (Cl. 35 No. 22-01, tel. 7/635-0101, www.hotelciudadbonita.com.co, COP$174,000 d) is one of the best-known traditional hotels in the city center. It has 70 rooms, two restaurants, a café, a pool, gym, and sauna, and there's live music Thursday, Friday, and Saturday evenings. Take a cab in this area at night; the surrounding streets empty out in the evenings. There's a Pacific coast-themed seafood restaurant in the lobby.

Hotel Tamarindo (Cra. 34 No. 46-104, tel. 7/643-6502, cell tel. 316/696-5241, www.hoteltamarindobucaramanga.com, COP$195,000

d) has seven rooms, air-conditioning, private baths, and a delightful patio around a mango tree.

Located in an upscale neighborhood above the Parque San Pío, ★ **Serenity Suites Casa Boutique** (Cra. 48B No. 53A-10, cell tel. 316/875-2224, www.serenitysuitescolombia.com, COP$190,000 d) is a small, family-run hotel with 10 spacious rooms (many with balconies overlooking the city), a small pool, and a Jacuzzi. It's the calmest option in town. Although the Cabecera neighborhood is a short distance away, down the hill, it's best to take a cab to and from this hotel in the evenings.

Information and Services

The **tourist office** (Cl. 30 No. 26-117, tel. 7/634-1132) is parkside at the Parque de los Niños.

Police can be reached by dialing 123, the **Hospital Universitario González Valencia** (Cra. 33 No. 28-126, 7am-10pm daily) by calling tel. 7/634-6110.

Transportation

The **Aeropuerto Internacional de Palo Negro** (BGA, Vía Lebrija), Bucaramanga's airport, is 25 kilometers (15 miles) west of town. **Avianca** (Cl. 52 No. 35A-10, tel. 7/657-3888, www.avianca.com, 8am-6pm Mon.-Fri., 8am-1pm Sat.), **EasyFly** (tel. 7/697-0333, www.easyfly.com.co), **VivaColombia** (tel. 1/489-7989, www.vivacolombia.com.co), and **LATAM** all serve BGA. Taxis between the airport and Bucaramanga cost COP$32,000.

Frequent long-distance bus service is offered between Bucaramanga and all major Colombian cities as well as small locales in Santander. The **Terminal de Transportes** (Km. 2 Tr. Metropolitana, tel. 7/637-1000, www.terminalbucaramanga.com) is modern, clean, and open-air. It is off Calle 70 on the way toward Girón.

The **MetroLínea** (www.metrolinea.gov.co) is the Bucaramanga version of Bogotá's TransMilenio. These green buses are clean and efficient, and the system covers just about the entire city, although it can be difficult to figure out. Maps of the system are hard to come by, obligating you to ask fellow travelers for information. You can purchase cards for the regular buses (ones that do not have dedicated lanes) at kiosks on the streets.

Reliable taxi-hailing and ride-sharing companies, such as EasyTaxi, Tappsi, and Uber, operate in Bucaramanga.

The city center and Cabecera area are easily visited on foot, although the streets are often clogged with traffic.

Floridablanca

Floridablanca has evolved to become essentially a southeastern suburb of Bucaramanga, five kilometers away.

There aren't many reasons to make a special trip here, but a good one is to take a bite out of one of their famous *obleas,* crisp paper-thin wafers filled with gooey and delicious *arequipe* (caramel spread). **Obleas Floridablanca** (Cra. 7 No. 5-54, tel. 7/648-5819, 10am-8pm daily) is a famous *oblea* factory that's been around since 1949. There are around 30 types of *obleas* you can order, although the classic is an *oblea* with just *arequipe.* Two of the more popular flavors are the *amor eterno* (eternal love), which has *arequipe,* cheese, and blackberry jam, and the *noviazgo* (courtship), which has *arequipe* and cheese. They also have do-it-yourself *oblea* kits that you can take home with you.

Along the manicured lawns of the **Jardín Botánico Eloy Valenzuela** (tel. 7/634-6100, 8am-5pm daily, COP$4,000), you can wander paths that you'll share with turtles, and view enormous ceibas and other trees. If you look closely at the treetops in this botanical garden, you might even see some sloths. The small Río Frío flows through the gardens, which were revamped in 2012. It's not terribly easy, but you can get to the gardens via MetroLínea from Bucaramanga.

At the time of research, the **Museo Arqueológico Regional Guane** (Casa Paragüitas, 9am-5pm Mon.-Sat., free) was

a yellow-footed tortoise at the Jardín Botánico Eloy Valenzuela

The launch site opens each day at 10am, but winds are best in the afternoon, from noon until 4pm. A 10-minute flight costs COP$50,000, 20 minutes costs COP$90,000, and a 30-minute flight costs COP$120,000. The views are quite spectacular from above Bucaramanga, so bring your camera. At the fly site there is also a snack bar. The place gets very crowded on weekends and holidays. For a fee of COP$25,000, you can get a DVD of your flight.

The Kasa Guane hostel (Cl. 11 No. 26-50, tel. 7/657-6960, cell tel. 313/274-2199, www. kasaguane.com) can arrange transportation from Bucaramanga to the launch point.

A 10-day certification course is offered by Colombia Paragliding at the Águilas site, with additional flight time in the Chicamocha area. The course costs COP$3,200,000, including transportation, meals, and lodging.

Next door to the launch site, ★ **Nest Fly Site Hostel** (Km. 2 Vía Mesa de Ruitoque, cell tel. 312/0432-6266, www.colombiaparagliding.com, COP$25,000 dorm, COP$60,000 d) is the place to stay if you're interested in paragliding. It's a quiet and cute place, with a pool and a view, and it's only 20 minutes away from the bustle of Bucaramanga. Nest is run by the same people as Colombia Paragliding and the Kasa Guane hostel.

Girón

While Bucaramanga is a pulsating tribute to modern Colombia, nearby Girón, 12 kilometers (7 miles) west, is a living reminder of the colonial past, at least in the city's historic center. The population of Girón is around 150,000. The main plaza is a vibrant meeting place.

On weekends Girón has a festive air to it as city folk from Bucaramanga and other day-trippers stroll the town's cobblestone streets. Check out the **Parque Las Nieves** (Clls. 30-31 and Cras. 25-26), which houses the **Basílica Menor San Juan Bautista,** and walk along the *malecón* (wharf) of the town's small brook.

in the process of being moved to the Casa Parguitas, a lovely colonial construction. The collection of ceramics here is impressive and extensive.

Mesa de Ruitoque

A surprisingly quiet and rural area to the southeast of Bucaramanga and Floridablanca, Mesa de Ruitoque sits on a plateau that has perfect conditions for paragliding.

PARAGLIDING

This area is blessed with 350 flyable days per year. It's a great location to take your first tandem paragliding flight or enroll in a 10-day course.

Colombia Paragliding (cell tel. 312/432-6266, www.colombiaparagliding.com) offers tandem flights of different durations from the launch point, **Voladero Las Águilas** (Km. 2 Vía Ruitoque, tel. 7/678-6257, www. voladerolasaguilas.com.co), about 10 kilometers (6 miles) south of Bucaramanga. Instructors are all certified and speak English.

FOOD AND ACCOMMODATIONS

Girón makes a good base. It's charming and quiet, and traveling back and forth to neighboring Bucaramanga is easy. The trip takes less than 15 minutes, and a taxi ride will cost only around COP$10,000. You can also get to Girón on the MetroLínea system.

La Casona (Cl. 28 No. 28-09, tel. 7/646-7195, www.lacasona-restaurante.com, noon-8pm Tues.-Sun., COP$16,000) is a spiffy old place, and they have a fun *onces* (tea time) menu for late-afternoon tea, Colombian style: You get a tamale, cheese, bread, and hot chocolate.

In a remodeled colonial house, ★ **Girón Chill Out Hotel Boutique** (Cra. 25 No. 32-06, tel. 7/646-1119, www.gironnchillout.com, COP$144,000 d) is run by an Italian couple (hence the Italian flag). It has a quiet vibe, and they serve authentic Italian food.

Las Nieves (Cl. 30 No. 25-71, tel. 7/681-2951, www.hotellasnievesgiron.com, COP$82,000 d, COP$116,000 d with a/c) faces the plaza. The interior of the hotel is full of palm trees and greenery, and the owner's dog is friendly. There are about 30 rooms, many full of twin beds. It's a standard place.

SAN GIL AND VICINITY

Rafting, paragliding, caving, mountain biking, canyoning, hiking, birding, and rappelling are all within reach in San Gil, Colombia's outdoor adventure capital. Even if your idea of "adventurous" is merely being in Colombia, the breathtaking Santander scenery of canyons, rivers, waterfalls, and mountains is more than enough reason to warrant a visit.

During the late 19th and early 20th centuries, San Gil and nearby towns built their prosperity on quinine, coffee, cocoa, and tobacco cultivation. Today, old tile-roofed hangars to dry tobacco, known as *caneys,* still dot the landscape. It's a peaceful place to visit and a top tourist destination.

There's no need to stay in bustling San Gil in order to enjoy the many outdoor activities that the area offers. You can easily organize rafting trips or paragliding adventures from

quieter and more charming towns such as Barichara, which is 20 kilometers (12 miles) north.

San Gil

This spry city (pop. 43,000) on the steep banks of the Río Fonce is 95 kilometers (59 miles) southwest of Bucaramanga. It caters to international tourists. San Gil can feel claustrophobic, but accommodations here are plentiful, comfortable, and inexpensive.

SIGHTS

On the Río Fonce about a 15-minute walk from town is the **Jardín Botánico El Gallineral** (Cra. 11 No. 21-1, tel. 7/723-7342, 8am-5pm daily, COP$8,000). This used to be just a park, but it has been given a makeover and now it's a botanical garden. There are cute stalls selling handicrafts, sweets, and coffee along the orderly paths. It's a pretty place for a late-afternoon walk among the towering trees. The on-site restaurant is open for lunch.

RAFTING AND KAYAKING

Two rivers near San Gil offer excellent year-round rafting adventures. The **Río Fonce,** whose banks the town stands on, is the closest and one of the best suited for rafting. It's a Class II-III. A 90-minute rafting trip on the Fonce costs about COP$30,000.

The **Río Suárez** is a Class IV-V river. Between March and April and October through November, the water levels are higher, and if there have been excessive amounts of rain this river can be too dangerous to tackle. The starting point for rafting on the Suárez is about an hour's drive from San Gil toward Bogotá. The trip leaves at 10am and returns at 4pm, and costs COP$125,000. You're on the water for about two hours.

Colombia Rafting Expeditions (Cra. 10 No. 7-83, tel. 7/724-5800, www.colombiarafting.com) is considered the best rafting company in town. They focus exclusively on river activities. The walls of their small office are covered with diplomas and certificates earned by their team of experienced guides. They can organize

San Gil and Vicinity

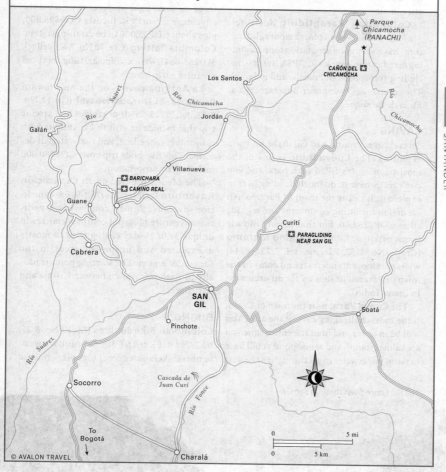

rafting trips on the region's rivers, determining which one is right for you based upon on your skill level and sense of adventure and the rivers' water levels. They also do kayaking trips. This company takes safety very seriously and conducts safety training exercises in English. Three-day kayaking courses (four hours per day, starting at 8am) cost COP$400,000 and take place on the Río Fonce. They also rent out kayaks to those with experience.

★ PARAGLIDING

There are two main paragliding areas near San Gil. One is the spectacular **Cañón del Chicamocha,** where 35-minute tandem paragliding trips over the canyon cost around COP$170,000 (including transportation). These flights take place in the mornings.

The other location for paragliding is 16 kilometers (10 miles) from San Gil at the launch site, **Las Vueltas,** in the town of Curití.

Here, 20-minute paragliding excursions cost COP$60,000. These flights are held in the afternoon.

Colombian Paragliding (cell tel. 312/432-6266, www.colombiaparagliding.com) has a very good reputation for paragliding certification courses (COP$3,200,000, including transportation, meals, and lodging). The company is based near Bucaramanga at Mesa de Ruitoque.

CAVING

Several caves around San Gil make for good exploring. The **Cueva Indio** is one of the most popular. It's filled with bats, and you don't really have to do much bending over to explore it. It's near the town of Páramo. An excursion including equipment and a guide costs COP$25,000, but that doesn't include transportation. Contact **Páramo Extremo** (Cra. 4 No. 4-57, Páramo, tel. 7/725-8944, www.paramosantanderextremo.com) in the town of Páramo to sign up for an excursion to Cueva Indio.

The **Cueva Vaca,** near the town of Curití, is the most challenging cave in the area. You will be in water and mud the entire time you are underground, and at one point you'll have to swim underwater to get through to the next cave. There are lots of stalactites and stalagmites and bats to see. It's action packed and there are some tight squeezes as well, but the adventure is worth it. It costs COP$25,000, plus about COP$3,000 in bus transportation. **Colombia Rafting** (Cra. 10 No. 7-83, cell tel. 311/283-8647, www.colombiarafting.com) can organize a trip here.

La Antigua cave is on the road toward Barichara. **El Dorado Hostel** (Cl. 12 No. 8-55, tel. 7/723-7588) organizes an extreme trip that includes a visit to La Antigua with canyoning, rappelling, and two waterfall descents. This five-hour trip costs COP$80,000 including transportation.

The Medellín-based outfit **Expedición Adventure** (cell tel. 314/258-9499, expedicionadventure@gmail.com, www.expedicionadventure.blogspot.com) specializes in unique 3- to 20-day caving trips to mostly unexplored and unspoiled areas in the Santander region. The starting point is usually in Barbosa, a town between Tunja and Barichara.

BIKING

Colombian Bike Junkies (Cl. 12 No. 8-35, tel. 7/724-1165, cell tel. 316/327-6101, www.colombianbikejunkies.com) organizes intense

The Río Fonce flows through San Gil.

downhill day-trip rides and multiday adventures. A single-day trip (COP$100,000) starts at an elevation of 2,000 meters (6,500 feet) on the top of the Cañón del Chicamocha, then goes down through beautiful countryside to the ghost town of Jordan. After a swim and lunch, there is yet one more downhill trip near the town of Curití, for a total of some 50 kilometers (30 miles) of downhill riding, on top-of-the-line mountain bikes.

To rent a cheap bike for the day, go to **Bicicletería El Ring** (Cl. 7 No. 10-14, tel. 7/724-3189, cell tel. 315/648-8543).

SWIMMING

On weekends and holidays, families head to the area's swimming holes. The atmosphere is joyous, and there's usually music and plenty of food and drink as well.

Pozo Azul (Km. 2 Vía San Gil) is a natural pool with small cascades that's surrounded by tress. From San Gil, Pozo Azul is about five minutes by bus or taxi or a 20-minute walk just off the highway. **Pescaderito** is better, with five swimming holes in which to cool off—all of them completely free. It's near the town of Curití, about a 40-minute bus ride (COP$3,000) from San Gil. Both spots are quieter during the week.

TOURS

Planeta Azul (Parque El Gallineral, Cra. 11, tel. 7/724-0000, cell tel. 310/771-7586, www.planetaazulsangil.com) is an agency that organizes rafting trips as well as a host of other activities, like bungee jumping (COP$46,000), caving (COP$40,000), rappelling (COP$40,000), paragliding (COP$60,000), and horseback riding (COP$95,000).

Aventura Total (Cl. 7 No. 10-27, tel. 7/723-8888, cell tel. 316/693-9300, www.aventuratotal.com.co) has a good reputation. They offer all-inclusive packages that include rafting, caving, and other activities as well as hotel accommodations. Aventura Total often organizes activities for large school groups. **Nativox** (Cra. 11 No. 7-14 Malecón, tel. 7/723-9999, cell. tel. 315/842-2337, www.

nativoxsangil.com) is similar to Planeta Azul and Aventura Total.

Hostels can also organize activities for guests.

FOOD

Mostly Tex-Mex ★ **Gringo Mike's** (Cl. 12 No. 8-35, tel. 7/724-1695, 8am-11:45am and 5pm-10pm daily, COP$18,000) is paradise for Americans who have been on the road awhile, with guacamole and chips, barbecue burgers, black bean burgers, Philly cheesesteaks, and even breakfast burritos.

To brush elbows with the locals, try **Rogelia** (Cra. 10 No. 8-09, tel. 7/724-0823, 7am-7:30pm daily, COP$12,000) or **Maná** (Cra. 10 No. 9-49, lunch daily, COP$12,000), the latter of which is a popular and inexpensive place for lunch. Try the grilled chicken stuffed with ham and cheese, but don't expect gourmet cuisine or charm.

The best aspect of **Gallineral Restaurante** (Parque Gallineral, Cra. 11, cell tel. 300/565-2653, 8am-5pm daily, COP$20,000) is its lush setting.

ACCOMMODATIONS

Excellent and affordable lodging options are plentiful in San Gil, but they are geared toward international backpackers. If you're looking for fresh air, more luxury, or more privacy, consider staying in nearby Barichara.

One of the first hostels in town to cater to international backpackers, ★ **Macondo Hostal** (Cra. 8 No. 10-35, tel. 7/724-8001, www.macondohostel.com, COP$30,000 dorm, COP$70,000 d w/bath) remains an excellent and reliable choice. Their clean dorm rooms (popular with backpackers) and private rooms fill quickly, so make a reservation in advance. They have a hot tub, small garden, and hammocks for post-adventure relaxing. What sets Macondo apart is its extremely knowledgeable, helpful, and friendly staff, who will organize outdoor activities in the region.

Bacaregua Hostel (Cra. 9 No. 16-77, tel. 724-2241, cell tel. 320/260-6277, COP$25,000 dorm, COP$60,000 d) is a low-key, locally operated hostel in a familial setting with hot showers, high ceilings, and ample common space. There are a couple of dormitory rooms in addition to private rooms.

Sam's VIP Hostel (Cr. 10 No. 12-33, tel. 7/724-2746, www.samshostel.com, COP$17,000 dorm, COP$70,000 d) has a fine location on the town's main plaza. It bustles with activity as international backpackers plot their travels on the sun-soaked terrace or by the small pool. The owner, Sam, has a second place with 11 rooms in an old renovated house: **La Mansion de Sam Hotel Boutique** (Cl. 12 No. 8-71, tel. 7/724-6044, www.hotelmansionsangil.com, COP$70,000-100,000 d), which is set just a block from the main plaza. Inside this hotel is an inviting pub (7:30am-10pm daily) that specializes in steaks, ribs, and beer.

If you'd like to get away from the backpacker scene but still pay backpacker prices, there are several cheap hotels in town. At ★ **Posada Familiar** (Cra. 10 No. 8-55, tel. 7/724-8136, cell tel. 301/370-1323, COP$45,000 pp high season) the name says it all—the lady of the house makes guests feel at home. The patio overflows with flowers and plants, you can cook in the kitchen, and the owner is a warm and generous person.

Almost exactly halfway between San Gil and Barichara on a quiet farm is ★ **La Pacha Hostel and Camping** (Km. 7 Vía San Gil-Barichara, cell tel. 310/221-1515, www.la-pachahostel.com, COP$60,000 d), where goats roam free, the common space is a funky old bus, and guests sleep in tents and yurts. It's run by a friendly English-Colombian couple.

To enjoy the peace of the countryside and charm of a colonial town but still be within striking distance of San Gil restaurants and activities, consider staying in the hamlet of Pinchote. ★ **Hotel Boutique Wassiki** (Km. 3 Vía San Gil-Bogotá, tel. 7/724-8386, www.wassiki.com, COP$210,000 d) is an excellent upscale hotel, offering well-appointed and airy rooms, comfortable common areas, a beautiful dining room, lots of hammocks, and a pool. It has a fine view of the valley below and is within walking distance of Pinchote's idyllic Plaza Principal.

TRANSPORTATION

San Gil's main **Terminal de Transportes** (Vía al Socorro, tel. 7/724-5858) is five minutes out of town, on the south side of the Río Fonce. Buses depart there for major cities such as Bucaramanga, Tunja, and Bogotá. Taxis to and from the Terminal de Transportes to the town center cost COP$3,200. Getting to San Gil from Bucaramanga by bus takes 2.5 hours and costs COP$15,000. Getting here from Tunja will take 3-5 hours. From Bogotá, the trip to San Gil (COP$45,000) takes seven hours. From Santa Marta or Medellín, the bus ride takes about 12 hours and costs COP$70,000. From Bucaramanga, the trip takes six hours and costs COP$15,000.

A smaller bus terminal for nearby towns is on Carrera 15 at Calle 11. It serves towns such as Barichara, Charalá, Curití, and Pescadero. It doesn't have an official name, but some refer to it as the **Mini Terminal.** Buses to Barichara depart every 30 mintues from 6am to 6:30pm.

★ Cañón del Chicamocha

The Cañón del Chicamocha is the result of eons of work by the Río Chicamocha, which carved its way through mountains to create a stunning canyon. This area is worth a visit for its breathtaking views, and is also home to an amusement park that holds a cable car offering a unique view of the canyon.

PARQUE NACIONAL DEL CHICAMOCHA

Set in a spectacular location above the Cañón del Chicamocha, the privately run **Parque Nacional del Chicamocha** (Km. 54 Vía Bucaramanga-San Gil, tel. 7/639-4444, www.parquenacionaldelchicamocha.com, 10am-6pm Wed.-Fri., 9am-7pm Sat.-Sun., COP$50,000 admission) is a cheesy amusement park geared toward Colombian families, but the views are superb. Also known as

a gondola ride across the Cañón del Chicamocha

Panachi, the park has several attractions, like an ostrich farm, areas that celebrate Santander culture and traditions, extreme sports, and a water park. The main point of interest for international travelers is the 6.3-kilometer (3.9-mile) **cable car ride** (10:30am-5:30pm Wed.-Fri., 9am-7pm Sat.-Sun., included with admission) across the canyon over the Río Chicamocha. The trip over the river takes about 12 minutes, and rather than shooting straight across the canyon, it follows the contours of the mountains. Plan to spend about an hour or two here.

Buses leaving from the Bucaramanga bus terminal bound for San Gil can drop you off at the park; this trip takes one hour and costs COP$12,000. The vistas from the road that hugs the canyon high above the Río Chicamocha make the right-hand-side window seat from Bucaramanga worth fighting for. The bus company COTRASANGIL (tel. 7/724-3562) offers regular bus service (30 minutes, COP$6,000) from San Gil's Terminal de Transportes.

MESA DE LOS SANTOS

The village of Los Santos is on the opposite side of the canyon from Parque Nacional del Chicamocha. In this area, known as **Mesa de los Santos,** there are a few places to stay. The area ranks second in the world for annual number of tremors at 390 per month (a rate of about one earthquake every two hours). The tremors are usually short in duration and not very powerful.

Refugio La Roca (Km. 22 in La Mojarra, cell tel. 312/333-1480, www.refugiolaroca.blogspot.com, COP$60,000 d shared bath) overlooks the Chicamocha canyon. Here you can camp for COP$10,000 per night (they have tents and sleeping bags for rent). In addition to private rooms, there is also one dorm room with four beds for COP$80,000.

At the other end of the spectrum from Refugio La Roca is ★ **Hotel Hacienda El Roble** (Vía Piedecuesta-Los Santos, Mesa de los Santos, tel. 1/232-8595, www.cafemesadelossantos.com, COP$325,000 d). This romantic getaway is on a large certified organic coffee farm, set underneath towering oak trees on a property teeming with over 100 species of birds. The rate includes a tour of the on-site plantation where their award-winning organic coffee is grown. The hotel is located after the Mesa toll booth.

★ Barichara

In 1975, when it was declared a national monument, Barichara (pop. 8,000) was named the most beautiful pueblo in Colombia. Despite its popularity with weekenders and a steady stream of international visitors, it hasn't lost its charm. This old tobacco town of sloping cobblestoned streets and whitewashed colonial-era homes is permanently blessed with bright blue skies and warm temperatures. Located 20 kilometers (12 miles) northwest of San Gil, the town is on a plateau that overlooks the Río Suárez. Don't skimp on your time here.

All around town are structures that utilize the technique of adobe block-making called *tapia pisada*. You'll often see a small patch of the mud interior exposed on these brilliantly white walls, purposely done to show passersby that it's authentic *tapia pisada*.

On the serene Parque Principal is the circa 1780 **Templo de la Inmaculada Concepción,** with two grandiose towers that soar 22 meters (72 feet) into the air. The sandstone church is particularly striking when lit up at night. Up picturesque Calle 6, at the top of the hill, is the **Capilla de Santa Bárbara,** a Romanesque-style church that is a popular place for weddings.

There are two other colonial churches to see: the **Capilla de Jesús** (Cra. 7 at Cl. 3), next to the cemetery, and the **Capilla de San Antonio** (Cra. 4 at Cl. 5).

Barichara is the birthplace of Aquileo Parra Gómez, who was the 11th president of the Estados Unidos de Colombia. His childhood home, **Casa Aquileo Parra Gómez** (Cl. 6 at Cra. 2), has been extremely well preserved and is an excellent example of typical 19th-century Barichara architecture. The site is also a handicraft workshop for the elderly, who weave shoulder bags and other items out of the natural fiber *fique*. They are there Monday through Thursday.

★ CAMINO REAL

A must-do activity in Barichara is to take the 5.3-kilometer (3.3-mile) **Camino Real** to the pueblo of Guane. It's a lovely path that zigzags down from the plateau of Barichara through farmland, affording nice views of the countryside. Parts of the path are lined with centuries-old stone walls.

Before the conquest, indigenous tribes throughout what is now Colombia traded crops and goods with each other, utilizing an extensive network of footpaths. These trails meandered through the countryside of present-day Santander, Boyacá, Norte de Santander, Cundinamarca, and beyond. During Spanish rule, the paths continued to be a major means of communication between colonial towns, and the networks became known as Caminos Reales. In the late 19th century, a German, Geo von Legerke,

Barichara is one of the country's most beautiful pueblos.

restored the Barichara-Guane Camino Real and built a stone bridge across the Río Suárez in order to improve transportation.

The hike to Guane takes two hours, and you don't need a guide: It's well marked, well trodden, and safe. To get to the trailhead, walk west along Carrera 10 to the Piedra de Bolívar, where you'll see the stone path leading down toward the valley.

In Guane you can check out the small **Museo Isaias Ardila Díaz** (Parque Principal, hours vary), which has three rooms: one on paleontology, with fossils; the next on archaeology, with a mummy; and a third on colonial life in rural Santander.

Sabajón, the Colombian version of eggnog, is the sweet specialty in Guane, and it is sold in various shops around Parque Principal.

If you are not up for the hike, a bus (COP$2,000) departs daily from the Parque Principal in Barichara at 6am, 9:30am, 11:30am, 2:30pm, and 5:30pm. The bus returns 30 minutes later from Guane.

FESTIVALS AND EVENTS

Little Barichara proudly hosts two annual film festivals. The **Festival Internacional de Cine de Barichara** (www.ficba.com.co) takes place in June, and the **Festival de Cine Verde** (www.festiver.org), an environmentally themed festival, is held every September in the town's churches.

SHOPPING

Barichara has always been a magnet for artists and craftspeople, many of whom have shops in town.

The **Fundación Escuela Taller Barichara** (Cra. 5 No. 4-26, tel. 7/726-7577, www.tallerdeoficiosbarichara.com, 8am-7pm Mon.-Thurs., 8am-9pm Fri.-Sat., 8am-4pm Sun.) is a gallery, museum, school, shop, and restaurant, all wrapped up in one. Occasional photography and painting exhibitions are held at this lovely cultural center, traditional decorative objects from the area are always on display, ceramics and other items made by students are for sale, and anyone can take a monthlong (or longer) course here. They offer dozens of classes for free. The on-site Restaurante y Café Las Cruces is one of the finest places to eat in town.

The **Taller de Papel de Fique** (Cl. 6 No. 2-68, no phone, 8am-3pm Mon.-Thurs.) makes for an interesting stop. At this workshop, artisans make beautiful paper out of the natural fiber of *fique*. On sale in this small store are cards, stationery, and handicrafts, all produced from *fique*. They also experiment with paper made from pineapple leaves. Short tours explaining the papermaking process are given for a small charge.

One of the best-known ceramic artists in town is **Jimena Rueda** (Cra. 5 No. 2-01, cell tel. 314/400-5071, 10am-6pm Mon.-Sat.). In addition to browsing her work, you can ask Señora Jimena if she has any pieces of the famous rustic handmade pottery of the Guane indigenous people. There is only one person who knows and uses this technique: **Ana Felisa Alquichire.** Doña Ana Felisa has been declared a living national cultural treasure by the Colombian presidency; her plates and bowls are sold in a few different shops in Barichara and Guane.

Galería Anil (Cl. 6 No. 10-46, cell tel. 311/470-1175) is the studio for local artists Jasmín and Carlos.

Formas de Luz (Cl. 10 No. 7-20, tel. 7/726-7279, cell tel. 317/438-4042, www.formasdeluz.com, 8am-noon and 2pm-6pm Mon.-Sat., 9:30am-1:30pm Sun.) is

the Camino Real between Barichara and Guane

the workshop of talented designer Muriel Garderet.

FOOD

Restaurants in Barichara gear up for the weekend crowd, but opening hours may vary during the week.

★ **Restaurante y Café Las Cruces** (Cra. 5 No. 4-26, tel. 7/726-7577, www.tallerdeoficiosbarichara.com, 6pm-9:30pm Fri., noon-9:30pm Sat., noon-4pm Sun., COP$28,000) is considered the top restaurant in Barichara for its ambience and creative dishes. It's in the beautiful patio of the Fundación Escuela Taller Barichara. Look for signature dishes such as *peril de cabro* (barbecued goat leg) with an ant sauce or *costillitas de tamarindo* (tamarind ribs). It's not open Monday through Thursday.

La Puerta (Cl. 6 No. 8-51, tel. 7/726-7649, www.baricharalapuerta.com, lunch and dinner daily high season, COP$22,000) is a beautiful place, with candlelit tables at night. They serve tasty pastas and use local, organic ingredients when possible.

Shimbala Shanti (Cra. 7 No. 6-22, cell tel. 318/391-3124) serves big stir-fries, both vegetarian and nonvegetarian, as well as salads and fresh juices.

Don Juan (Cra. 6 No. 6-13, cell tel. 318/775-5691, COP$12,000) is famous for its set lunches, but it only serves 20 each day, so arrive early. Don Juan also serves delicious Venezuelan arepas. In the evening, ask for balcony seating.

Overlooking the Parque Cementerio, **Al Cuoco** (Cra. 6A No. 2-54, cell tel. 312/527-3628, noon-9pm or 10pm daily, COP$22,000) is an authentic Italian place with a small menu of homemade pasta served up by its Roman chef. Try the parmesan ice cream.

For pizza, check out **7 Tigres Pizza & Pita** (Cl. 6 No. 10-24, cell tel. 312/521-9962), a funky favorite serving thin-crust personal pizzas and grilled meat pitas.

Locals flock to **El Balcón de Mi Pueblo** (Cl. 7 No. 5-62, cell tel. 318/280-2980, noon-5pm daily, COP$12,000) for good, meaty Colombian food like *cabro* (grilled goat), *carne oreada* (sun-dried steak), and *churrasco* (steak). It's a cute place up on the 2nd floor.

Another favorite is the lunch-only **Misifú** (Cra. 6 No. 6 31, tel. 7/726-7321, noon-6pm daily, COP$12,000). Their specialty is *carne oreada*, a dry and toothsome steak that is reminiscent of beef jerky.

For a coffee or the popular *galletas de cuajada* (cheese cookies), head to **Panadería Barichara** (Cl. 5 No. 5-33, tel. 7/726-7688, 7am-1pm and 2pm-8pm daily). They've been around since 1954.

ACCOMMODATIONS

With Barichara's growth in popularity, accommodation options to fit all budgets and styles have popped up in the town. Weeknight rates will be lower.

Backpackers and budget travelers have several options in Barichara. The ★ **Color de Hormiga Hostel** (Cl. 6 No. 5-35, cell tel. 315/297-1621, http://colordehormiga.com/hostel.html, COP$45,000 d) used to house teachers from a neighboring school. It's decorated with institutional furniture that was left behind, and it still has its original groovy tiled floors. There are seven small rooms for one or two people, each with its own private bath. The kitchen is open for use by guests.

On an old tobacco farm, the ★ **Reserva Natural** (Vereda San José Alto, cell tel. 315/297-1621, COP$70,000 pp d), from the same owner as the Color de Hormiga Hostel, is a step up, with more luxury and more solitude. Birds representing all colors of the rainbow appear like clockwork every morning to munch on pieces of banana and papaya, to the delight of guests enjoying their breakfasts. This spot is about a 10-minute walk from town. The staff is incredibly friendly. The property also has dorm rooms and campsites.

At **Tinto Hostel** (Cra. 4 No. 5-39, tel. 7/726-7725, www.tintohostel.com, COP$30,000 dorm, COP$120,000 d) there's a ton of open green space, a pool, and perfectly fine rooms, making it a backpacker favorite. Dorm rooms have either four or six beds.

On the edge of town, peaceful **Artepolis** (Cra. 2 No. 2-2, cell tel. 300/203-4531, www. artepolis.info, COP$85,000 d) has eight minimalist rooms overlooking the countryside. Artist workshops are held here occasionally. Breakfast is sold by the woman who runs the kitchen.

The peaceful **Posada Sueños de Antonio** (Cra. 9 No. 4-25, tel. 7/726-7793, www.suenosdeantonio.com, COP$135,000 d) has five spacious rooms surrounding an interior patio that attracts birds every morning.

Casa Oniri (Cl. 6 No. 7-55, tel. 7/726-7138, cell tel. 312/300-8870, www.casaoniri.com, COP$196,000 d) is one of the swankiest options around, with rooms surrounding two courtyards and an upstairs lookout to boot.

Hicasua Hotel Boutique & Centro de Convenciones (Cl. 7 No. 3-85, tel. 7/726-7700, cell tel. 312/419-7154, www.hicasua. com, COP$285,000 d) offers very comfortable medium-sized rooms, satellite TV, and an inviting pool that is perfect after a long, active day.

The wonderful ★ **Posada del Campanario** (Cl. 5 No. 7-49, tel. 7/726-7261, www.posada-campanario.com, COP$290,000 d), one of the first hotels in Barichara, has seven rooms that are comfortable, but not overly luxurious. It's surrounded by gardens, and has an open-air dining area and a divine *mirador* (lookout) with a view of the Templo de la Inmaculada Concepción. Church bells may awaken you early in the morning.

La Nube (Cl. 7 No. 7-39, tel. 7/726-7161, cell tel. 310/334-8677, www.lanubeposada. com, COP$276,000 d) was boutique before the word entered the Colombian hotel industry's lexicon. It's a comfortable choice with 11 rooms and a good restaurant (breakfast not included). The patio is a sublime place for relaxing to the soothing sound of a fountain.

GETTING THERE

Most visitors to Barichara arrive either in their own transportation or by bus. To get to Barichara from Bogotá, head to Bogotá's Portal del Norte bus terminal. The journey to Barichara takes six hours or more, and you'll have to transfer in San Gil. It costs COP$30,000.

From Bucaramanga, from the Terminal de Transportes, a CONTRASANGIL bus leaves for Barichara at 4:45pm Monday-Friday, 9:15am on Saturday, and 7:30pm on Sunday. It takes three hours and costs COP$18,000.

Busetas leave San Gil every half hour (daily) from the Terminal de Transportes starting at 5am, with the last bus departing at 6:45pm. The 20-kilometer (12-mile) journey to Barichara takes 45 minutes and costs less than COP$5,000.

Norte de Santander

This department in the northeast of the country borders Venezuela to the east and Santander to the south. The main places of interest are Pamplona and Cúcuta, two very different cities. Pamplona is a charming and cool highland town that was important during the colonial era, though much of its period architecture has disappeared due to earthquakes and the march of progress. To the north, the departmental capital of Cúcuta is a hot and busy commercial city and gateway to Venezuela. Both cities are easily accessed by road from Bucaramanga. The southernmost area of Norte de Santander and the northernmost area of Catatumbo have been plagued with guerrilla and paramilitary activity in recent years and are best avoided.

PAMPLONA

Set in a lush, agriculturally rich valley at 2,300 meters (7,500 feet), this historic colonial town is a refreshing change from the heat of Cúcuta and Bucaramanga. In addition to colonial remnants like the Casa de las

Tres Marías (now Museo de Arte Moderno Eduardo Ramírez Villamizar), Pamplona is known for being the home of abstract expressionist artist Eduardo Ramírez, and for being a surprisingly lively college town that hosts the Universidad de Pamplona and its thousands of students. Pamplona is also well known for its processions during Semana Santa (Holy Week).

Sights

Pamplona has its share of museums, all easily visited in a day on foot. During the week, when there are few visitors in town, museums may not open as their official hours suggest.

The top museum in town is the **Museo de Arte Moderno Eduardo Ramírez Villamizar** (Cl. 5 No. 5-75, tel. 7/568-2999, www.mamramirezvillamizar.com, 9am-noon and 2pm-5pm Tues.-Sun., COP$3,000), set in a lovingly restored 16th-century house. It features the work of modernist sculptor and painter Eduardo Ramírez Villamizar, and also puts on temporary shows of contemporary Colombian artists. In the courtyard, surrounding a magnolia tree, are many Ramírez sculptures.

Around the corner is the **Museo Arquidiocesano de Arte Religioso** (Cra. 5 No. 4-87, tel. 7/568-2816, 10am-noon and 3pm-5pm Wed.-Mon., COP$2,000). It houses oil paintings from masters such as Gregorio Arce y Ceballos, woodcarvings dating back to the 17th century, and silver and gold ceremonial items.

The town's most interesting churches include the imposing **Catedral Santa Clara** (Cl. 6 between Cras. 5-6, 8am-noon and 2pm-6pm daily), which dates to 1584, and the **Ermita del Señor del Humilladero** (Cl. 2 between Cras. 7-8, 6:30am-noon Mon. and Wed.-Fri., 6:30am-noon and 1:30pm-7pm Sat.-Sun.), which is next to the cemetery and filled with aboveground tombs. It is famous for its realistic carving *Cristo del Humilladero*.

The **Museo Casa Colonial** (Cl. 6 No. 2-56, tel. 7/568-2043, www.casacolonialpamplona. com, 8am-noon and 2pm-6pm Mon.-Fri.,

free) packs a punch in its 17th-century abode. It includes exhibits on some of the native cultures from the area, touches on the independence movement and struggles of the early Colombian republic, and takes the visitor through to the 20th century. It surrounds a courtyard bursting with color.

Finally, the small **Museo Casa Anzoátegui** (Cra. 6 No. 7-48, 9am-noon and 2pm-5:30pm Mon.-Sat., COP$1,000) examines the life of General José Antonio Anzoátgui and the fight for independence from Spain. It was in this house that the war hero died in 1819. He was the head of Bolívar's honor guard and was promoted to general following the Batalla del Puente de Boyacá.

The **Casa Mercado** (Cl. 6 between Cras. 4-5) stands on the previous location of a Jesuit college; this covered market, where you can buy fruit, vegetables, and much more, was built in 1920, and retains its popularity despite the arrival of supermarkets. The vendors will be happy if you buy some fruit from them.

Food and Accommodations

Pierro's Pizza (Cra. 5 No. 5B-67, tel. 7/568-0160, 5pm-11pm daily, COP$20,000) is the most popular place for pizza and pasta.

Vegetarians will want to head to **Majesvara** (Cra. 3B No. 1C-26, cell tel. 310/267-9307, noon-2pm and 7pm-8:30pm Mon.-Sat., COP$8,000), where you can eat a healthy meal for cheap. They offer a simple lunch menu with soup, a main dish with a vegetable protein and rice or potatoes, salad, and juice. The restaurant is about a 12-minute walk from Parque Águeda Gallardo.

★ **Hostal 1549** (Cl. 8B No. 8-64, Calle los Miserables, tel. 7/568-0451, cell tel. 317/699-6578, www.1549hostal.com, COP$130,000) is the cozy and comfortable option in town. Seven spacious rooms have big, comfortable beds, and many have fireplaces. The hotel has an adjacent restaurant where breakfast is served. At night locals gather to drink, but they are usually shown the door by 11pm.

The quirky **Hotel Ursua** (Cl. 5 No. 5-67, tel. 7/568-2470, cell tel. 311/847-4027,

COP$40,000 d) has a fantastic location facing the main plaza, the Parque Águeda Gallardo (Cras. 5-6 and Clls. 5-6), and rooms come in all shapes and sizes. The on-site restaurant serves inexpensive breakfasts and lunches.

Once home to a scribe to the Spanish authorities in the 18th century, ★ **El Solar** (Cl. 5 No. 8-10, tel. 7/568-2010, www.elsolarhotel.com, COP$110,000 d) is one of the most popular accommodation and restaurant options. It has 10 rooms comprising 21 beds. Breakfast at the on-site restaurant is included, as is wireless Internet. The restaurant is open to the public, and at night the bonfire in the center creates the best ambience in town.

Getting There

Pamplona is on the road between Bucaramanga and Cúcuta. Its bus station is the spick-and-span **Terminal de Transportes** (Cra. 9 No. 3-120), about a 10-minute walk from the town center.

The road between Bucaramanga and Pamplona winds through *páramo* (highlands) and meanders through mountains, so the trip between these towns can be slow going. The bus ride to Pamplona from Bucaramanga costs about COP$25,000 and takes less than five hours.

From the bus station in Cúcuta, shared taxis, *busetas,* and buses leave on a regular basis all day long. Shared taxis are quick, but less comfortable than both *busetas* and larger buses, as you're likely to be crammed into the back seat of a small car. The under two-hour trip costs about COP$10,000.

CÚCUTA

The capital of the Norte de Santander department, Cúcuta is a tree-lined, historic, and pleasant city that straddles the border with Venezuela. It's most often visited as a waypoint for travelers headed into Venezuela.

The main tourist attraction, Parque Gran Colombiano, is just outside of the city in Villa del Rosario, on the way to Venezuela. That's where General Francisco de Paula Santander was born and where the first constitution for Gran Colombia was drafted. Simón Bolívar officially became the country's president here.

In recent years, the city has seen an influx of refugees fleeing violence in other parts of Norte de Santander and Arauca. During the 1990s there was a bloody turf war between paramilitaries and leftist guerrillas. In 2008, in response to months of simmering tension with Venezuela, Colombian pop singer Juanes organized Paz sin Fronteras (Peace Without Borders), a concert on the border that attracted 300,000 delighted fans. Today, although the situation in neighboring Venezuela is uncertain, Cúcuta is a safe place to visit.

ORIENTATION

The western boundary of Cúcuta is the Avenida Libertadores. Many of the big restaurants are located here, and this is where the Ciclovía is held on Sundays. All the decent hotels and most sights in Cúcuta are in the downtown area between Avenida 0 to the east and Avenida 6 to the west and Calle 8 to the north and Calle 13 to the south. The Aeropuerto Camilo Daza is in the northwest of the city.

Sights
CITY CENTER

There are a handful of cultural sights in downtown Cúcuta that can be easily visited on foot. The small but cool **Museo de Norte de Santander** (Cl. 14 No. 1-03, tel. 7/595-8377, 8am-noon and 2pm-6pm Mon.-Fri., 9am-noon Sat., free) hosts art exhibitions and events.

The beautifully restored **Biblioteca Pública Julio Pérez Ferrero** (Av. 1 No. 12-35, Barrio La Playa, tel. 7/595-5384, www.bibliocucuta.org, 8am-noon and 2pm-6pm Mon.-Fri., 9am-noon Sat., free) served as a hospital in the 19th century. This cultural center has a reading room open to the public and there is an outdoor café (hours vary).

The **Palacio de Gobierno Departamental** (Clls. 13-14 and Avs. 4-5) is noteworthy for its Republican-era neoclassical

Cúcuta

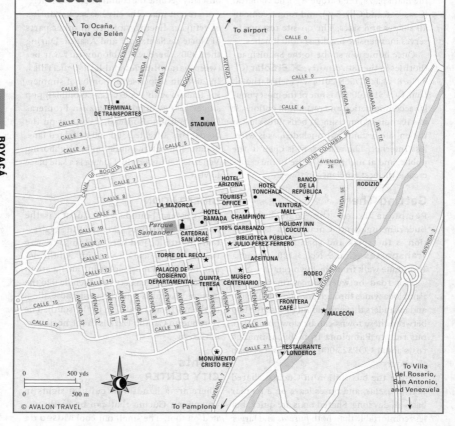

To Ocaña,
Playa de Belén

To airport

CALLE 0

CALLE 0

CALLE 0

CALLE 4

AVENIDA 7

AVENIDA 6

AVENIDA 5

BOGOTÁ

AVENIDA 8

AVENIDA 9E

GUAIMARAL

AVE 11E

CALLE 2

TERMINAL
DE TRANSPORTES

STADIUM

CALLE 4

LA GRAN COLOMBIA 9E

CALLE 3

CALLE 4

CALLE 5

AVENIDA
2E

CANAL DE BOGOTÁ

CALLE 6

CALLE 7

CALLE 8

CALLE 9

LA MAZORCA

HOTEL
ARIZONA

TOURIST
OFFICE

HOTEL
TONCHALÁ

BANCO
DE LA
REPÚBLICA

RODIZIO

AVENIDA 5E

AVENIDA 3

HOTEL
RAMADA

CHAMPIÑÓN

VENTURA
MALL

CALLE 10

Parque
Santander

100% GARBANZO

HOLIDAY INN
CÚCUTA

CALLE 11

CATEDRAL
SAN JOSÉ

BIBLIOTECA PÚBLICA
JULIO PÉREZ FERRERO

CALLE 12

TORRE DEL RELOJ

ACEITUNA

CALLE 13

PALACIO DE
GOBIERNO
DEPARTAMENTAL

QUINTA
TERESA

MUSEO
CENTENARIO

RODEO

CALLE 14

LIBERTADORES

AVENIDA 13

AVENIDA 12

AVENIDA 11

AVENIDA 10

AVENIDA 9

AVENIDA 7

AVENIDA 6

AVENIDA 5

AVENIDA 3

AVENIDA 1

FRONTERA
CAFÉ

CALLE 15

CALLE 17

CALLE 18

CALLE 19

MALECÓN

CALLE 21

RESTAURANTE
LONDEROS

MONUMENTO
CRISTO REY

0   500 yds

0   500 m

© AVALON TRAVEL

To Pamplona

To Villa
del Rosario,
San Antonio,
and Venezuela

---

architecture. It's not open to the public. The neoclassical **Catedral San José** (Av. 5 No. 10-53) faces the shady **Parque Santander** (Avs. 5-6 and Clls. 10-11).

The **Torre del Reloj** (Cl. 13 No. 3-67) stands in what is now the **Casa de la Cultura** (tel. 7/583-2215, 7:30am-noon and 2pm-6pm Mon.-Fri.). This sophisticated early 20th-century Italian-made clock tower houses bells that toll the national anthem. Inquire at the Casa de la Cultura if you want to make the climb. From the top, you can get a nice view of the city with the **Monumento Cristo Rey** (Av. 4 at Cl. 19) in the distance. The Casa de la Cultura complex also hosts art exhibitions.

The **Banco de la República** (Diag. Santander No. 3E-38, tel. 7/575-0131, www. banrepcultural.org/cucuta, 8am-11:30am and 2pm-6pm Mon.-Fri.) always has an art exhibition on view, usually featuring a Colombian artist. Concerts are also held at the facility's theater.

PARQUE GRAN COLOMBIANO
The major historical site in greater Cúcuta is seven kilometers (4.3 miles) outside the city, near the town of **Villa del Rosario** on the road toward San Antonio del Táchira, Venezuela. The **Parque Gran Colombiano** (Km. 6 Autopista Internacional, no phone,

dawn-dusk daily, free), also known as the **Templo Histórico,** is a park set in the middle of the busy highway that leads to the Venezuelan border. Much of the park, which extends for about a kilometer, is green space where couples cuddle below royal palm trees and others jog or walk their dogs.

The **Casa Natal del General Santander** (Km. 6 Autopista Internacional, tel. 7/570-0265, 8am-11am and 2pm-5pm Tues.-Sat., 9am-5pm Sun., free) is a museum that tells the story of important independence figure General Francisco de Paula Santander, known as Colombia's Thomas Jefferson. It's the westernmost structure in the park, and is set in Santander's childhood home. Guides show visitors around for free, but you may wish to give a small tip afterward. Note the brick aqueduct and the tamarind and laurel trees that have been around for centuries.

The photogenic ruins of the **Templo del Congreso** are where Gran Colombia's Constitution of 1821 was drafted and where Simón Bolívar was sworn in as president (and Santander as vice president). Congress met for over a month to draft the constitution, and on their breaks, they would rest under the shade of a huge tamarind tree. The tree is still there, in front of the church. The Templo was badly damaged in the Cúcuta Earthquake of 1875. Only the dome, in a different style altogether, was rebuilt. A marble statue of Bolívar stands amid the ruins. The Templo is within walking distance of the Casa Natal del General Santander.

Across the highway from the Templo is the **Casa de la Bagatela,** which was the seat of the executive branch of Gran Colombia. It was named in honor of independence figure Antonio Nariño, who helmed a revolutionary paper in Bogotá called *La Bagatela.* There's not much more to see up close, so there's no need to cross this busy thoroughfare.

To get to the park, you can take a shared taxi or a *buseta* (small bus) bound for San Antonio del Táchira at the Centro Comercial Ventura Plaza. These cost around COP$2,500. Ask to be dropped off at the Templo Histórico. Private taxis cost about COP$7,500 from downtown Cúcuta.

Food

The most typical food from Cúcuta includes *hayacas cucutenas,* similar to tamales; *mute,* a meaty stew; and *pastel de garbanzo,* a fried garbanzo bean pastry.

For a welcome break from meat, try **Champiñon** (Cl. 10 No. 0-05, tel.

Parque Gran Colombiano

7/571-1561, 8am-8:30pm Mon.-Sat., COP$12,000). This is Cúcuta's best exclusively vegetarian restaurant, highlighted by a generous set lunch.

★ **Aceituna** (Av. 0 No. 13-135, tel. 7/583-7464, cell tel. 320/210-2332, 10:30am-10pm daily, COP$18,000) is a long-standing restaurant run by a Lebanese-Colombian family. They specialize in shawarma and falafels.

When darkness falls in Cúcuta, especially on the weekends, the energy shifts to the *malecón* area, about a 10-minute cab ride west from downtown. That's where many of the big restaurants are located. **Londeros Sur** (Av. Libertadores No. 0E-60B, tel. 7/583-3335, www.restaurantelonderos.com, COP$25,000) is famous around town for its Argentinian steaks. **Rodizio** (Av. Libertadores No. 10-121, tel. 7/575-1719, www.rodizio.com.co, COP$30,000) is known for its Brazilian-style grilled meats. **Rodeo** (Av. Libertadores No. 16-38, www.rodeogourmet.com, COP$25,000) is another very popular option for carnivores.

For coffee prepared in one of five different ways, head to **Frontera Tienda de Café** (Av. 1E No. 16A-15, tel. 7/589-8979, 7:30am-8:30pm Mon.-Sat.) in the leafy Caobos neighborhood. Breakfast is also served.

Accommodations

There are no true backpacker hostels in Cúcuta. International brands Holiday Inn and Ramada have both set up shop in town, and they are excellent choices.

Hotel Tonchalá (Av. 0 at Cl. 10, tel. 7/575-6444, www.hoteltonchala.com, COP$340,000 d) is a classic big hotel and is popular for business meetings. The lap pool may be its major selling point. It's within a five-minute stroll of Centro Comercial Ventura Plaza. Staff at **Hotel Arizona Suites** (Av. 0 No. 7-62, tel. 7/573-1884, www.hotelarizonasuites.com, COP$148,000) are exceptionally friendly. Rooms are fine, if a little on the small side. The restaurant overlooks a small pool. The location (decent, but not great) is near two busy streets and about a 10-minute walk to downtown.

Information and Services

The **tourist office** (Cl. 10 No. 0-30, no phone, 8am-11:50am and 2pm-6pm Mon.-Fri., 8:30am-noon Sat.) has lots of brochures and maps for Cúcuta as well as the rest of the Norte de Santander department.

In case of an emergency, contact the **Policía Nacional** by dialing 123. A major hospital in town is the **Hospital Erasmo Meoz** (Av. 11E No. 5AN-71, tel. 7/574-6888).

Transportation

The **Aeropuerto Camilo Daza** (CUC, Km. 5 Autopista Panamericana) is a 15-minute cab ride (COP$22,000) from downtown. **Avianca** (Cl. 13 No. 5-22, tel. 7/571-3877, www.avianca. com, 8am-noon and 2pm-6pm Mon.-Fri., 8am-noon Sat.) flies nonstop between Cúcuta and Bogotá and Medellín. **EasyFly** (tel. 7/595-5005, www.easyfly.com.co) connects Cúcuta with Bucaramanga and Medellín. **LATAM** (Aeropuerto Camilo Daza, Km. 5 Autopista Panamericana, tel. 1/745-2020, 5:30am-9:30pm Mon.-Fri., 6:30am-10:30am and 2pm-6pm Sat., 8am-noon and 4pm-8pm Sun.) offers flights from Bogotá.

The bus ride from Bogotá to Cúcuta costs around COP$70,000 and the trip takes 14 hours. From Bucaramanga it costs COP$30,000 and takes six hours, and from San Gil it costs about COP$45,000 and takes eight hours. The **Terminal de Transportes** (Avs. 7-8 between Clls. 1-2) in Cúcuta is dirty, chaotic, and generally unpleasant. When departing from the bus terminal, try to get your ticket in advance so you don't have to be there longer than necessary. If you are waiting for a bus, it's best to wait outside on the curb, away from the claustrophobic station.

If you are staying downtown, all attractions are within relatively easy walking distance. It's always a good policy to call a cab beforehand, and always after dark. The best way to call for a cab is to use a smartphone app such as Easy Taxi or Uber.

CROSSING INTO VENEZUELA

Crossing the border from Cúcuta into San Antonio del Táchira, Venezuela, is theoretically easy. But there is always some uncertainty, depending on the political situation. *Busetas* (shared taxis) depart from in front of Centro Comercial Ventura Plaza in Cúcuta. Expect to pay about COP$2,500 for a *buseta* ticket. Taxis will cost upwards of COP$20,000. Note that there is a 30-minute time difference in Venezuela.

Be sure to get off before the bridge in order to get an exit stamp from immigration officials in your passport. (Making this stop is a standard practice for bus drivers.) Visas are not required for citizens of North America or the European Union.

Hotels in San Antonio del Táchira are dismal, so it's better to either stay in Cúcuta or continue onward in Venezuela.

For more information on visas, visit the **Consulado Venezuelano** (Venezuelan consulate, Av. Aeropuerto Camilo Daza, Sector Corral de Piedra, Zona Industrial, Cl. 17 Esquina, tel. 7/579-1954 or 7/579-1951, 8am-10am and 2pm-3pm Mon.-Thurs., 8am-10am Fri.). It's close to the airport.

Medellín and the Coffee Region

The hallmarks of Colombia's heartland are its countless coffee plantations and colorful pueblos, with Medellín as the department's proud and dynamic capital.

For many, a visit to this area is a highlight of their trip to Colombia. This region has it all: lush countryside, beautiful mountain landscapes, welcoming locals, a plethora of recreational activities, vibrant cities, and gorgeous haciendas.

Medellín, the surrounding department of Antioquia, and the coffee region departments of Caldas, Risaralda, and Quindío comprise the central, mountainous section of Colombia, covering the Cordillera Central (Central Range) and Cordillera Occidental (Western Range) north of Cali. The mountains then flatten out into the Caribbean coastal lowlands.

HISTORY

Despite its inaccessible terrain, Antioquia was an important province of colonial Nueva Granada thanks to its abundant gold deposits. It attracted settlers who panned the rivers or cultivated food for the mining camps. Santa Fe de Antioquia, founded in 1541, was the main colonial settlement.

After independence, the province continued to prosper, even attracting foreign investment in gold mining. Demographic pressure triggered a southward migration known as the *colonización antioqueña*. Waves of settlement brought Paisa families to unoccupied lands in the south of Antioquia, the coffee region, and the northern part of the Valle del Cauca.

During the early part of the 20th century, coffee was a major source of prosperity in Antioquia. Medellín grew rapidly and became the industrial powerhouse of Colombia. The last decades of the 20th century were difficult times for Antioquia, which suffered from the triple scourge of drug trafficking, paramilitary armies, and guerrillas. In the past decade, the government has made huge strides in bringing back the rule of law, and today Antioquia is one of the safest and most prosperous regions in Colombia.

PLANNING YOUR TIME

Weather-wise, any time of the year is a good time to visit Medellín and the coffee region.

Previous: colorful doors in Salento; coffee plantations near Manizales. **Above:** sunny street in Belalcázar.

Look for ★ to find recommended sights, activities, dining, and lodging.

Highlights

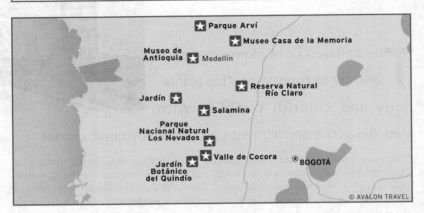

Parque Arví
Museo Casa de la Memoria
Museo de Antioquia Medellín
Reserva Natural Río Claro
Jardín
Salamina
Parque Nacional Natural Los Nevados
Jardín Botánico del Quindío
Valle de Cocora BOGOTÁ

© AVALON TRAVEL

★ **Museo de Antioquia:** The galleries of this art museum are filled with works from the best Colombian artists spanning nearly four centuries. And the terrace café has the best people-watching in the Centro (page 218).

★ **Museo Casa de la Memoria:** Go to this museum to hear the heartwrenching stories from victims—and survivors—of the country's decades-long armed conflict (page 222).

★ **Parque Arví:** Chill out in the cool climes of this park and enjoy a ride on the Metrocable, an innovative public transportation system using gondolas (page 223).

★ **Reserva Natural Río Claro:** This jungle paradise is set along a canyon that was discovered only recently. This private natural reserve offers caving, river rafting, and a surplus of peace (page 240).

★ **Jardín:** Just a few hours south of busy Medellín, life slows to a crawl in this picture-perfect town, which is surrounded by lush green mountains full of recreational opportunities (page 245).

★ **Salamina:** Life goes on much as it always has in this remote Paisa town known for its superb architecture and warm hospitality (page 261).

★ **Parque Nacional Natural Los Nevados:** Dozens of hikes leading through tropical jungles afford fantastic views of snow-capped volcanes and mountain lakes in this easily accessed national park (page 263).

★ **Jardín Botánico del Quindío:** In the best botanical garden in the region, you can take a guided tour through a tropical forest (page 271).

★ **Valle de Cocora:** One of the most dramatic and photographed scenes in Colombia is this valley filled with towering wax palms, the national tree (page 278).

Medellín and the Coffee Region

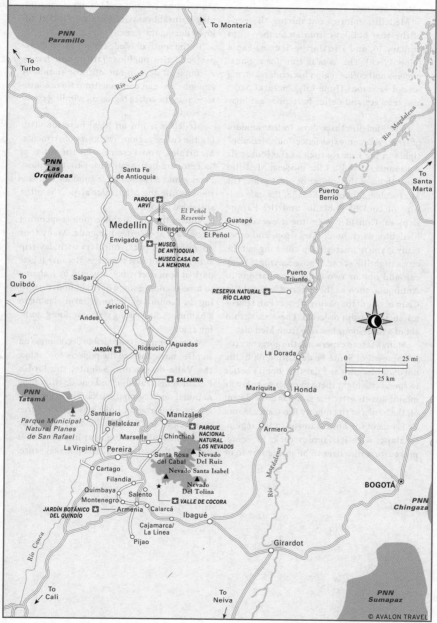

To Monteria

PNN
Paramillo

To
Turbo

Río Cauca

PNN
Las
Orquídeas

Santa Fe
de Antioquia

To
Santa
Marta

Río Magdalena

Puerto
Berrío

PARQUE
ARVÍ

El Peñol
Resevoir

Guatapé

Medellín

Rionegro

El Peñol

Envigado

MUSEO
DE ANTIOQUIA
MUSEO CASA DE
LA MEMORIA

To
Quibdó

Salgar

Puerto
Triunfo

RESERVA NATURAL
RÍO CLARO

Jericó

La Dorada

Andes

Aguadas

0   25 mi

JARDÍN

Riosucio

0   25 km

SALAMINA

Mariquita   Honda

PNN
Tatamá

Manizales

Parque Municipal
Natural Planes
de San Rafael

Santuario

Belalcázar

Chinchiná

PARQUE
NACIONAL
NATURAL
LOS NEVADOS

Armero

Marsella

La Virginia

Pereira

Santa Rosa
del Cabal

Nevado
Del Ruiz

Río Magdalena

Cartago

Filandia

Nevado Santa Isabel

BOGOTÁ

Quimbaya

Salento

Nevado
Del Tolina

PNN
Chingaza

Montenegro

JARDÍN BOTÁNICO
DEL QUINDÍO

Armenia

Calarcá

VALLE DE COCORA

Ibagué

Cajamarca/
La Línea

Pijao

Girardot

Río Cauca

To
Cali

To
Neiva

PNN
Sumapaz

© AVALON TRAVEL

The entire region has a temperate climate, which is why they call Medellín the "City of Eternal Spring."

Medellín empties out during the end-of-the-year holidays from December 15 to January 15, and also during Semana Santa (Holy Week). This is peak time for regional pueblos and coffee region haciendas. During school vacations (June-July), natural parks and reserves and coffee haciendas get busy again.

Give Medellín three days. In that amount of time, you can experience "old Medellín" sights in the Centro, such as the Museo de Antioquia, as well as the modern Medellín icons that are the subject of great pride: the Metrocable, Biblioteca España, the café culture of cool El Poblado, and the Parque Explora. Consider spending a weekend in Medellín, when hotel rates drop, and especially if you're interested in checking out the city's nightlife scene. Those staying a week can add one or two other destinations in Antioquia, such as the Reserva Natural Río Claro or one of the picture-perfect Paisa pueblos, such as Jardín or Jericó. These are within about a three-hour bus ride from Medellín.

Many visitors experience the gorgeous colonial town of Santa Fe de Antioquia to the north of Medellín as a day trip, but it's better to spend one night there in order to enjoy its quaint streets after the sun has gone down; on the banks of the mighty Río Cauca, Santa Fe is one of the hottest towns in the region. Guatapé, with its famous rock, El Peñol, makes for a nice overnight on the way to or from the Río Claro reserve, where two nights are necessary. These three destinations are popular on weekends and holidays. The stunning natural beauty of Río Claro is best enjoyed during the week.

To the south of Medellín are two picture-perfect Paisa pueblos, Jardín and Jericó. A couple of days in one of those should be enough. You can continue from there southward into the coffee region on winding country roads.

Medellín is not an ideal base for visiting the coffee region: The cities of Armenia, Manizales, and Pereira, and the town of Salento, are better suited for that purpose. Pereira and Armenia have good air connections, while the Manizales airport is often shrouded in fog.

One of the joys of this region is spending a few days at a coffee hacienda. Many tour operators will pack your days with day-trip activities, but resist this urge. Because it gets dark at 6pm every day, it would be a shame to miss spending some daylight hours strolling the grounds of the *finca* (farm), lazing in a hammock or rocking chair, or doing nothing at all.

A week or more is needed to decompress on a coffee farm and see the region's top sights: the Valle de Cocora, Salento, the Jardín Botánico del Quindío, and one or two of the national and regional parks. There are very good transportation links between the three major cities and Salento. Roads are generally excellent. While renting a car in Colombia is not often the best option, here it makes sense.

Medellín

While Medellín is the country's second city in terms of population and importance, perpetually behind Bogotá, this metropolis of around 2.7 million is truly on the move and an example of Colombia's ongoing transformation. It's the country's only city with an urban train system. It's also the first city with a gondola and modern trolley transportation network.

The first settlement in the region, near the present-day Poblado sector, was established in 1616. Medellín proper was founded in 1675, and was designated the capital of Antioquia in 1826.

In the 1980s, Pablo Escobar, born in nearby Rionegro, established a cocaine-trafficking empire based Medellín. In its heyday, the Medellín Cartel controlled 80 percent of the world's cocaine trade. When President Virgilio Barco cracked down on the cartel in the late 1980s, Escobar declared war on the government. He assassinated judges and political leaders, set off car bombs to intimidate public opinion, and paid a bounty for every policeman that was murdered in Medellín—a total of 657. In 1991, Medellín had a homicide rate of 380 per 100,000 inhabitants, the highest such rate on record anywhere in the world. In 1993, Escobar was killed while on the run from the law.

During the 1990s, leftist guerrillas gained strength in the poor *comunas,* or sectors, of Medellín, waging a vicious turf war against paramilitaries. At the turn of the century, the homicide rate was 160 per 100,000 inhabitants, making Medellín one of the most dangerous places on Earth.

Shortly after assuming power in 2002, President Álvaro Uribe launched Operación Orion to wrest the poor *comunas* of Medellín from the leftist guerrillas, and violence decreased notably. By 2005, homicides were still high by international standards but a fraction of what they had been a decade before. Under the leadership of Mayor Sergio Fajardo, elected in 2004, and his successors Alonso Salazar and Aníbal Gaviria, Medellín has undergone an extraordinary transformation. In partnership with the private sector, the city has invested heavily in public works, including a new cable car transportation system, museums, and libraries. In recent years, the city has become a major tourist destination and has attracted significant foreign investment.

Orientation

Medellín is in the Valle de Aburrá, with the trickling and polluted Río Medellín dividing the city into east and west. Both the Metro (Line A) and Avenida Regional or Autopista Sur, a busy expressway, run parallel to the river.

The main neighborhoods are **El Poblado,** including the mini-hood of Provenza; the **Centro;** and the **Carabobo Norte** area (often referred to as **Universidades**).

If you arrive in Medellín from the Rionegro airport, you will descend the hill into the valley and land more or less in El Poblado. The neighborhood is packed with great restaurants, bars, hostels, hotels, and glitzy shopping malls. It is also full of tall brick high-rise apartment buildings, home to the well-to-do. Luxury hotels and malls line Avenida El Poblado. Parque Lleras is the center of the **Provenza** neighborhood, a small, leafy, and very hip part of El Poblado on the eastern side of Avenida El Poblado. To the west, down Calle 10, is Parque del Poblado, and a few blocks farther is the El Poblado Metro station.

The Centro is between El Poblado to the south and Carabobo Norte to the north. The heart of the Centro is the Plaza Botero and Parque Berrío Metro station area. Avenida El Poblado, also known as Carrera 43A, connects El Poblado with the Centro, as does the Metro.

Across the river from El Poblado is

the Terminal del Sur bus station and the Aeropuerto Olaya Herrera. **Cerro Nutibara** (Nutibara Hill), home to the Pueblito Paisa, is north of the airport. Northwest of Cerro Nutibara is the quiet neighborhood of **Laureles,** and farther west is the **stadium area.** The B line of the Metro connects the Centro with the stadium area.

Between El Poblado and the Centro is an up-and-coming area with new hotels and high-rises being built in what is known as **Ciudad del Río,** where the Museo de Arte Moderno de Medellín is located. **Barrio Colombia** is also home to many nightspots.

In the far south of town are the municipalities of **Envigado** and **Itagüí.** Avenida El Poblado connects El Poblado with Envigado, which has some good restaurants, a busy main plaza, and the Parque El Salado. Itagüi is an industrial town with little of interest for the tourist except for bars and clubs, many of which are open until the wee hours.

Safety

The streets of the Centro should be avoided after dark, and valuables should be secured during the daytime. It is not a good idea to take a carefree stroll in the northern or western neighborhoods or, especially, in the *comunas* (city sectors) on the surrounding hills, but specific sights mentioned can be visited. The Metro, Metrocable, Metroplús, and Tranvía are not only clean and efficient, but are also safe.

It's best to avoid hailing taxis on the street, particularly at night. Instead, order a cab from a taxi app like Tappsi or EasyTaxi or a ride-sharing app like Uber. Be careful at clubs and bars, and don't accept drinks from strangers.

SIGHTS

To see Medellín in full motion, visit the Centro during the week. On Saturdays it's quieter, although the Peatonal Carabobo bustles with activity. Downtown is practically deserted on Sundays. Most visits to the Centro start from the Parque Berrío Metro station,

the Museo de Antioquia

and the main sights can easily be seen on foot in a few hours.

Centro
★ MUSEO DE ANTIOQUIA

The **Museo de Antioquia** (Cra. 52 No. 52-43, tel. 4/251-3636, www.museodeantioquia.org.co, 10am-5pm Mon.-Sat., 10am-4:30pm Sun., COP$18,000 non-Colombians) is one of the top art museums in the country, with an extensive permanent collection of works from Colombian artists from the 19th century to modern times. The building itself is an architectural gem, an art deco-style structure from the 1930s that originally served as the Palacio Municipal. Inside, look for the iconic painting *Horizontes* (*Horizons*) by Francisco Antonio Cano, a romantic 1913 work portraying the *colonización antioqueña,* the period when families from Antioquia headed south to settle in what is now known as the coffee region. In the contemporary art rooms, you'll see *Horizontes* (1997) by Carlos Uribe. This painting presents the same bucolic scene,

Centro

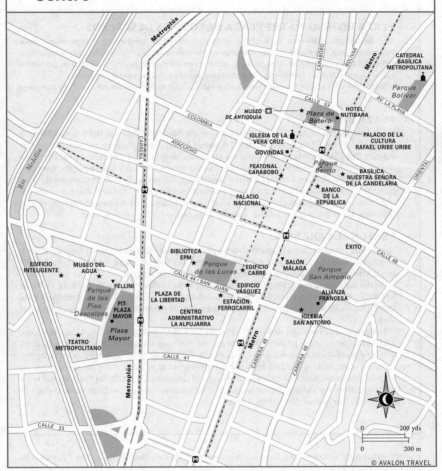

© AVALON TRAVEL

except in the background a plane sprays pesticides over the countryside to eradicate coca and marijuana crops. Native son Fernando Botero has donated several of his works, over 100 of them, to the museum. There is also a small room with a series of works, contemplations on mortality, by Luis Caballero. There is a free guided tour at 2pm every day.

Carabobo Norte

Over 37,000 students are enrolled at the **Universidad de Antioquia** (Cl. 67 No. 53-108, tel. 4/263-0011, www.udea.edu.co), one of the country's top universities. Its campus, full of plazas and public art, buzzes with vibrant student energy. In addition to a busy calendar of cultural events, the university has an excellent museum, **MUUA** (Cl. 67 No. 53-108, Bloque 15, tel. 4/219-5180, www.udea.edu.co, 8am-5:45pm Mon.-Thurs., 8am-3:45pm Fri., 9am-12:45pm Sat., free), featuring contemporary art exhibits and a permanent natural

Medellín Walking Tour

PLAZA BOTERO TO THE PLAZA DE LOS PIES DESCALZOS

Medellín's brash downtown makes for a compact history tour comprising stoic remnants from the colonial era, brick-and-mortar evidence of Medellín's reign as Colombia's most important industrial center in the early 20th century, and the vibrant public spaces, modern transportation systems, and futuristic architecture showing this proud city's 21st-century optimism.

Begin the tour at the Parque Berrío Metro station and walk five minutes north to the Plaza Botero.

PLAZA BOTERO

Most visits downtown begin under the shadow of the **Palacio de la Cultura Rafael Uribe Uribe** (Cra. 51 No. 52-03, 8am-5pm Mon.-Fri., 8am-2pm Sat., free), which occasionally hosts of art exhibits. The **Plaza Botero** (in front of the Museo de Antioquia, Cra. 52 No. 52-43) gets its name from its 23 corpulent bronze sculptures by Fernando Botero. Passersby often pose for snapshots in front of the sculptures, such as *La Mano (The Hand)* and *Eva (Eve)*. One of the most prolific, and by far the best known, of contemporary Colombian artists, Botero donated these works to his hometown of Medellín. His paintings and sculptures of rotund people often portray campesino (rural) life, but many of them are also commentaries on the violence in Colombia.

PEATONAL CARABOBO

To the south, the **Peatonal Carabobo** is a pedestrian walkway that extends for eight blocks. Lined with shoe shops, five-and-dime stores, and snack bars, it's busy, loud, and colorful. (Although there is usually a police presence, be sure to watch your stuff.)

On the right-hand side is Medellín's oldest church, the brilliantly white **Iglesia de la Vera Cruz** (Cl. 51 No. 52-38, tel. 4/512-5095), which dates to 1682. It is often filled with working-class faithful, sitting or standing in meditation and prayer. It's a refuge of quiet in this busy commercial area.

The Belgian architect who designed the grandiose **Palacio Nacional** (Cra. 52 No. 48-45, tel. 4/513-4422) in the 1920s probably never expected that it would become the domain of around 400 vendors of discount tennis shoes and jeans. Built to house governmental offices, today the corridors of this historic building are filled with the chorus of *"a la orden"* ("at your service") from hopeful shop attendants. Toward the end of Peatonal Carabobo is **Donde Ramón,** a small kiosk in the middle of the walkway that is jam-packed with antique objects like brass horse stirrups or old *carrieles* (leather handbags) from Jericó.

history exhibit. Visitors to the UA campus must show their passport at the Portería del Ferrocarril gate for entry.

Adjacent to the university near the Metro station is the photogenic **Parque Explora** (Cra. 52 No. 73-75, tel. 4/516-8300, www.parqueexplora.org, 8:30am-5:30pm Tues.-Fri., 10am-6:30pm Sat.-Sun, COP$24,500), one of the most iconic architectural landmarks of modern Medellín. It is a complex of science and natural history museums, with a highly regarded **aquarium,** one of the largest in Latin America. The ticket office closes 90 minutes before closing time. The **Planetario Medellín** (Cra. 52 No. 71-117, tel. 4/516-8300, www.planetariomedellin.org, 8am-5pm Tues.-Wed., 8am-7pm Thurs.-Fri., 10am-6pm Sat.-Sun., COP$15,000) is across the street from the Parque Explora.

Up for a walk in the park? Across from Parque Explora is the **Jardín Botánico de Medellín** (Cra. 73 No. 51D-14, tel. 4/444-5500, www.botanicomedellin.org, 9am-4:30pm daily, free), a pleasant green space in the city. The highlight here is the Orquiderama, an open-air wood lattice-like

PARQUE DE LAS LUCES

After years of abandonment and urban decay, in 2005 the artificial forest of the **Parque de las Luces** or **Plaza Cisneros** (Cl. 44 at Cra. 52) was opened in an effort to rejuvenate the area. The park, consisting of 300 illuminated posts, looks somewhat odd during the day but is spectacular at night when it shines. Check it out by car at night; it is not safe to roam about after dark. On the east side of the plaza are two historic early-20th-century brick buildings: the **Edificio Carré** and **Edificio Vásquez** (Cl. 44B No. 52-17, tel. 4/514-8200). When they were built they were the tallest buildings in Medellín. These buildings were important warehouse facilities during the industrial boom of the early 20th century. The plaza used to be the home of the main marketplace. On the western side of the plaza is the **Biblioteca EPM** (Cra. 54 No. 44-48, tel. 4/380-7516, 8:30am-5:30pm Mon.-Sat.), a stunning public library sponsored by the electric company EPM (Empresas Públicas de Medellín), built in 2005. In addition to reading rooms, there are occasional exhibitions and cultural events held at the library.

Across from the Parque de las Luces on the southern side of Calle 44 is the **Estación Ferrocarril** (Cra. 52 No. 43-31, tel. 4/381-0733), the old main train station. There's not much to see here, except for a train engine and forgotten old tracks.

PLAZA MAYOR

To the west of the Estación Ferrocarril is the **Centro Administrativo La Alpujarra** (Cl. 44 No. 52-165), which houses the Departamento de Antioquia government offices. The sculpture *Homenaje a la Raza,* by Rodrigo Arenas Betancur, stands in the middle of the large intermediary plaza. Just beyond is the **Plaza de la Libertad** (Cra. 55 between Clls. 42-44), a complex of modern office space and interesting public space complete with urban gardens.

Cross the pedestrian bridge over the lanes of the Metroplús bus station. (Opened in 2013, Metroplús is the latest addition to Medellín's transportation network.) Here is the **Plaza Mayor** (Cl. 41 No. 55-80, www.plazamayor.com.co), the city's preeminent convention and event venue; it has a fair share of nice restaurants. The **Teatro Metropolitano** (Cl. 41 No. 57-30, tel. 4/232-2858, www.teatrometropolitano.com), a 20th-century brick building, hosts concerts.

Finally, the **Plaza de los Pies Descalzos** (Cra. 58 No. 42-125) is a plaza filled with a *guadua* (Colombian bamboo) forest and fountains, where you can take off your shoes and play. It's flanked by eateries on one side and the massive **Museo del Agua** (Cra. 57 No. 42-139, tel. 4/380-6954, 8am-6pm Tues.-Fri., 10am-7pm Sat.-Sun., COP$4,000) on the other. In the distance is a longstanding Medellín architectural icon: the **Edificio Inteligente** (Cra. 58 No. 42-125). Built in the late 1950s, it has served as the headquarters of EPM, the utility company.

structure where events—even thumping raves—are held. Inside the gardens, the **In Situ restaurant** (tel. 4/460-7007, www.botanicomedellin.org, noon-3pm Mon., noon-3pm and 7pm-10pm Tues.-Sat., noon-4pm Sun., COP$35,000) boasts gorgeous views and is a posh choice for lunch. Behind the park is an overlooked homage to notable women from the area: the **Esquina de las Mujeres** (Cra. 51 at Cl. 73), a small public space with busts of accomplished women from Medellín and Antioquia from the colonial era to the present day.

Presidents, artists, and writers rest in the **Museo Cementerio de San Pedro** (Cra. 51 No. 68-68, tel. 4/516-7650, www.cementeriosanpedro.org.co, 8am-5:30pm daily, free). Marble statues and elaborate tombs pay tribute to influential Antioqueños from the 19th century onward, but the reminders of the city's turbulent past may strike you as more interesting. One plot near the tomb of Fidel Cano, founder of the *El Espectador* newspaper, contains the tombs of several of drug kingpin Pablo Escobar's associates and guards. Some tombs have stickers identifying allegiance to one of Medellín's soccer clubs; others have touching handwritten notes from children left behind. There is usually a free tour on Sunday afternoons. Check the cemetery's up-to-date website for a schedule of activities, including evening tours.

Cerro Nutibara

To see an authentic Paisa pueblo, go to Jardín, Jericó, or Salamina. They're just a couple of hours away and are as real as you can get. Can't do that? Then go to the **Pueblito Paisa** (Cl. 30A No. 55-64, tel. 4/235-6476, 5am-midnight daily, free), a Disney-esque celebration of Paisa architecture and culture, set atop Cerro Nutibara. Plenty of food (including an overpriced restaurant) and handicrafts are on sale here. On a clear day the views of Colombia's second city aren't bad. The hill is also a popular place for an early-morning jog.

Northern Medellín
★ MUSEO CASA DE LA MEMORIA

Tourism campaigns promoting Colombia highlight the country's natural beauty, welcoming people, and cultural diversity, understandably not dwelling on its sad recent history of bloody armed conflict. Opening in 2016, the **Museo Casa de la Memoria** (Cl. 51 No. 36-66, tel. 4/383-4001, www.museocasadelamemoria.gov.co, 9am-6pm Tues.-Fri., 10am-4pm Sat.-Sun., free) nudges Colombians and international visitors alike to face those dark years head-on. Dedicated to the memory of victims of the world's longest-running war, the museum documents the disappeared, the displaced, and the fallen. Exhibits (most descriptions are in Spanish) put faces to the numbers of victims, and give them—the survivors and the deceased—a chance to recount to the world their stories. Outside is a wall of memory, with names of victims etched on bricks. To get to the museum, you can take the Metro to Parque Berrío station and walk up Calle 52 and Avenida La Playa, just beyond the Teatro Pablo Tobón.

CASA MUSEO PEDRO NEL GÓMEZ

In the barrio of Aranjuez is the **Casa Museo Pedro Nel Gómez** (Cra. 51B No. 85-24, Barrio Aranjuez, tel. 4/444-2633, ext. 102, free). This delightful, small museum houses an extensive collection of the painter's works, including several murals for which he is best known. Much of his work portrays the plight of campesinos (rural peasants), workers, and indigenous people. The house, now the museum, was designed by Gómez, its location was chosen by his Italian-born wife. The hills overlooking the city here reminded her of Florence, somehow. In the new wing of the museum there is a small public library. The courtyard holds a snack bar-café. The museum is not easy to get to via public transportation, so it may be best to cab it.

BIBLIOTECA ESPAÑA

When this public library was opened in the low-income neighborhood of Santo Domingo, King Juan Carlos came from Madrid for the ceremony; as the facility's name implies, Spain helped fund the project. It's one of many newly created *biblioteca parques* (public library parks) in Medellín. More than a place for books, these library parks have become community centers and sources of pride in neighborhoods that continue to struggle with poverty and violence. Of them, the **Biblioteca España** (Cra. 33B No.107A-100, tel. 4/528-9495, www.reddebibliotecas.org. co, 8am-7pm Mon.-Sat. and 11am-5pm Sun.) boasts one of the most daring designs: It resembles giant boulders clinging to the edge of the mountainside. It was designed by architect and Barranquilla native Giancarlo Mazzanti, who won a prize for this work at the VI Bienal Iberoamericana de Arquitectura y Urbanismo in Lisbon in 2008.

Getting to Santo Domingo is an attraction in itself. The neighborhood is connected to the metropolis by the Metrocable cable car system. Take the Metro toward Niquía station and transfer to the Metrocable at Acevedo. The Santo Domingo station is the third and final stop. Many visitors are content to view the library from the Metrocable gondola as they continue onward to the Parque Arví.

When the Metrocable K line was opened in 2004, it was the first of its kind: a gondola-like public transport system with a socioeconomic purpose, connected to a metro. The system has eliminated eternal climbs up and down the mountain for low-income residents.

★ PARQUE ARVÍ

For some fresh, crisp, country air, a visit to the **Parque Arví** (Santa Elena, tel. 4/444-2979, www.parquearvi.org, 9am-5pm Tues.-Sun., free), covering 16,000 hectares (40,000 acres) of nature, hits the spot after a few days of urban exploring.

Highlights in the sprawling park include some well-marked nature paths that meander through cloud forests thick with pine and eucalyptus trees, over brooks, along ancient indigenous paths, and to mountain lakes and lookout points with fine views of the Valle de Aburrá and Medellín below. Most paths are less than three kilometers (two miles); they are not strenuous whatsoever and require no guide, although there are often free guided nature walks as well.

Other recreational activities on offer include horseback riding, zip-lining, and

visiting a butterfly farm. The park's layout, based around different *nucleos* (nuclei), is somewhat confusing, but park staff can orient you.

Many visitors enjoy the trip to the park—on the Metrocable—as much as or more than the park itself. To get there from the city, take the Metro to the Acevedo station in the north of the city (Línea A toward Niquía). From there, transfer to the Metrocable (Línea K) to the Santo Domingo station. From there you must transfer to the Línea L, an additional COP$4,850 one-way.

The temperature can drop substantially and abruptly in the park. Pack a light sweater and a lightweight rainproof jacket. Various snack bars and restaurants are located throughout the grounds. Aim for an early start in order to enjoy the park at your leisure.

Southern Medellín

One of the city's most important cultural spaces is the **Museo de Arte Moderno de Medellín** (MAMM, Cra. 44 No. 19A-100, tel. 4/444-2622, www.elmamm.org, 9am-5:30pm Tues.-Fri., 10am-5:30pm Sat., 10am-5pm Sun., COP$10,000), set in a revamped steel mill, Talleres Robledo, that began operations in the 1930s. Exhibitions (usually two at a time) are

A trip to the Parque Arví in northern Medellín is an excellent break from the city.

Getting Up the Hill

During the late 1990s to the 2000s, thousands of families from rural areas in Antioquia, Córdoba, and Chocó were forced to leave their homes due to violence. Moving to Medellín to start a new life, many arrived in the *comunas,* the low-income neighborhoods along the steep slopes of the mountains surrounding the city. But here, where many live in meager brick homes covered with corrugated zinc roofs secured only by large stones, horrific violence has followed them. First it was turf wars between guerrillas and paramilitaries in the early 2000s. Today the bloodshed is caused by drug-trafficking gangs with links to former paramilitaries. This wave of violence has given birth to a new phenomenon: intra-urban displacement, during which families have been displaced within the city due to urban violence. For many, this is the second displacement that their families have had to endure.

City leaders have sought to improve the quality of life in the *comunas* in a variety of innovative ways. Two lines of the Metrocable gondola system have made a huge difference in allowing residents to travel to work or school in the city without having to walk up and down the mountainside. Spectacular modern public libraries have been built in many low-income communities, providing a safe and pleasant space to study, read, and connect to the Internet. These have developed into important cultural centers, with an active schedule of films, children's activities, and other cultural activities. New homes have been built and donated to 200-300 displaced families, with funds from the national government under President Juan Manuel Santos.

In 2012, the city debuted its latest project, one aimed at improving life in the numerous neighborhoods making up Comuna 13, the most notorious of the city's *comunas.* The project involved the creation of open-air escalators in this neighborhood, and today a series of six dual, interconnected escalators extend down the slopes for some 384 meters (1,260 feet). The system operates from early in the morning until about 10pm. They are monitored by city employees, and their use is free. It is the first time in the world escalators have been used to improve the lives of the less fortunate.

The escalators have made a difference in the lives of the 134,000 Comuna 13 residents, although there are some who believe that the money spent on the project (around US$6 million) could have been better used otherwise. There have been alarming reports as well that some gangs have been intimidating residents by charging them to use the escalators, under the threat of dire consequences.

Despite the high levels of violence affecting residents (never foreign tourists), the escalators have become a tourist attraction, and even appear in the city's tourism-promotion materials. Celebrities and dignitaries from President Juan Manuel Santos to French fashion designer François Girbaud have taken a ride on the escalators.

It is indeed a strange kind of tourism, with which some may feel uncomfortable. However, if you would like to see this escalator project, you certainly can. Go during the day, don't wander too far away, and avoid being in the neighborhood after dark. To get there, take the Metro Línea B to San Javier station. As you depart the station, in front are *colectivos* (small buses) that regularly transport passengers to Comuna 13. It's about a 15-minute trip and costs under COP$1,500. Ask anyone which bus to take, and let the bus driver know that you'd like to go to the *escaleras eléctricas.*

From San Javier, there is also a Metrocable line (Línea J) that has three stops and travels to the top at La Aurora.

To get a local's perspective on life in Comuna 13—and take pics of cool graffiti—contact the **Grafitour** (cell tel. 4/252-0035, tel. 312/889-5564).

hit or miss, but the facilities are gorgeous and there are often film screenings in the modern auditorium. The museum store, the *tienda,* is an excellent place to pick up a whimsical Medellín souvenir.

The **Parque El Salado** (Cra. 27A No. 41S-58, Envigado, tel. 4/270-3132, www. parqueelsalado.gov.co, 9am-5pm Tues.-Sun., COP$3,000), a well-organized municipal park covering 17 hectares (42 acres) in

Envigado, has trails and activities, such as a zip line (COP$7,000) and a rock-climbing wall (COP$3,000), and makes for a relaxing excursion. On weekends it gets packed with families on a *paseo de olla*. Literally a soup-pot excursion, *paseo de olla* usually means *sancocho*, a hearty beef stew. Essential gear for a day out at the park includes giant aluminum pots for slowly heating a *sancocho* over a campfire; it can get smoky on the weekends. Getting to the park is easy using public transportation. From the Envigado Metro station look for a green bus with a sign that says Parque El Salado (COP$2,000). It's about a 20-minute ride toward the mountains; you can also cab it (COP$10,000).

ENTERTAINMENT AND EVENTS
Nightlife

Except for the very traditional music venues and bars, Facebook pages are the best resource for what's up at the clubs.

Since 1969, **El Social Tienda Mixta** (Cra. 35 No. 8A-8, tel. 4/311-5567) has been selling the basics to neighborhood residents (soap, sugar, coffee); it's only a recent phenomenon that it's the hippest place to be seen at night, when it is converted into the most popular bar in Provenza. It's so popular on weekend evenings that you can forget about finding a vacant plastic chair.

On Thursday and Friday evenings, the Medellín microbrewery **3 Cordilleras** (Cl. 30 No. 44-176, tel. 4/444-2337, 5:30pm-9pm Thurs.-Fri., COP$21,000-26,000) offers tours of its brewery, tastings of five beers, and friendly socializing. There's live music on Fridays.

Calle 9+1 (Cra. 40 No. 10-25, cell tel. 313/753-8392, 6pm-2am Mon.-Sat., cover varies) is a hipster's paradise in El Poblado. Music varies wildly from salsa to house to folk. The dim lighting and well-worn couches provide the perfect chilled-out atmosphere.

Cuchitril Club / Sala Bombay (Cl. 10 with Guayabal, cell tel. 313/745-6349, 9pm-4am Fri.-Sat.) is a happening venue that packs in exuberant crowds for live music and DJs. **Salón Amador** (Cra. 36 No. 10-38, www.salonamador.com) often hosts international DJs.

Working-class locals, intelligentsia, and students converge on the Parque del Periodista downtown to meet friends over a few beers and listen to music. It may very well be the coolest corner of Medellín. **Bar El Guanábano** (Parque del Periodista, Girardot with Maracaibo, tel. 4/216-3742) is a faithful—and funky—friend at the center of it all. Rock (like Bowie) plays on the sound system in this dark and cozy hangout, the centerpiece of which is the sacrilegious (yet good-natured) depiction of the Divino Niño made from the bizarre-looking guanabana fruit.

Short on cash? Head to the beer stalls (there are dozens) at the **Parque San Antonio** (Cra. 46 with Cl. 45). Pull up your red plastic chair and mix it up with the locals over a Poker beer.

SALSA, TANGO, AND JAZZ

Medellín is no Cali, but salsa has its aficionados here. If the musical genres *son, la charanga, el guaguanco,* and *la timba* don't mean anything to you now, they might after a night at **Son Havana** (Cra. 73 No. 44-56, tel. 4/586-9082, www.sonhavana.com, 8pm-3am Wed.-Sat., cover Sat. COP$8,000), which often has live performances. Nearby is **El Tíbiri** (Cra. 70 No. 44B-01, cell tel. 310/849-5461, hours vary Wed.-Sat.), an underground salsa and Afro-Colombian music joint on Carrera 70 that is hugely popular on the weekends. They say the walls sweat here, as after 10pm it gets packed, especially on Friday nights. El Tíbiri also regularly offers an array of dance classes.

The downtown **Salón Málaga** (Cra. 51 No. 45-80, tel. 4/231-2658, www.salonmalaga.com, 9am-11pm daily, no cover) has plenty of character. It's filled with old jukeboxes and memorabilia, and has its clientele who come in for a *tinto* (coffee) or beer during the day. The Saturday tango show at 5:30pm and oldies event on Sunday afternoons are especially popular with locals and travelers alike, but a stop here is a fine idea anytime.

Near the Parque de la Periodista, a

major weekend hangout for the grungy set, there are some small bars big on personality. Tuesday nights border on legendary at **Eslabón Prendido** (Cl. 53 No. 42-55, tel. 4/239-3400, 3pm-11pm Tues.-Sat., cover varies), a hole-in-the-wall salsa place that really packs them in. **El Acontista** (Cl. 53 No. 43-81, tel. 4/512-3052, noon-10pm Mon.-Thurs., noon-midnight Fri.-Sat.) is an excellent jazz club downtown. It has a bookstore on the 2nd floor and live music on Monday and Saturday evenings. It has great food, too, making it an excellent stop for unwinding following an arduous day of tourism.

In Envigado, **La Venta de Dulcinea Café Cultural** (Cl. 35 Sur No. 43-36, tel. 4/276-0208, www.laventadedulcinea.jimdo.com, 2pm-11pm Mon.-Sat.) is a somewhat bohemian spot where live performances (salsa, *milonga*, bossa nova, and tango) are often held. Check the venue's website or Facebook page for the latest.

DANCE CLUBS

Jesús Dulce Mío—Mi Pueblo (Cra. 42 67A-151, tel. 4/444-6022, www.fondadulcejesusmio.com, 8pm-4am Thurs.-Sat., cover varies) is a long-running and colorful nightspot that plays mostly crossover music. It's on the Autopista Sur, and there are other locations around the city, too.

There's a big electronic music scene in Medellín, but it's not obvious what's going on and where. Your best bet is to check the international website www.residentadvisor.net or the Medellín Underground Facebook page.

GAY BARS AND CLUBS

The online guide **Guia Gay Colombia** (www.guiagaycolombia.com) has a complete listing of bars.

There is a lively and youthful gay nightlife scene in Medellín. **Donde Aquellos** (Cra. 38 No. 9A-26, tel. 4/312-2041, cell tel. 313/624-1485, 4:30pm-2am daily) is an easygoing kind of place near the Parque Lleras in El Poblado. This friendly bar is a good place for a terrace drink. **Purple** (Cl. 10A No. 36-29,

COP$10,000) is where the boys (and some girls) go to dance to pop and electronica.

Theater and Cultural Centers

Intellectuals, wannabes, artists, students, and downtown purists congregate at **Ateneo** (Cl. 47 No. 42-38 Local 9901, Torres de Bomboná, tel. 4/216-0708, www.ateneomedellin.com), which has an ongoing cultural program of concerts, theater performances, and art exhibitions. At its café you can drink *micheladas* all night and listen to live music or conversation.

A cool theater with 1960s flair is the **Teatro Pablo Tobón** (Cra. 40 No. 51-24, tel. 4/239-7500, www.teatropablotobon.com). Almost every day there's something happening here—concerts, theater, yoga, lectures, parties, chess—and even when there isn't, you can just hang out in the lobby café.

Otraparte (Cra. 43A No. 27AS-11, Envigado, tel. 4/448-2404, www.otraparte.org, 8am-8pm Mon.-Fri., 9am-5pm Sat.-Sun.) is a cultural center that offers a dynamic program of free concerts, films, book launches, and even free yoga classes.

Festivals and Events

The **Festival Internacional de Tango** takes place each year during the last week of June, commemorating the anniversary of the death of Carlos Gardel. This festival, and in fact the perseverance of tango culture in Medellín, is largely due to one man's passion and efforts: Argentine Leonardo Nieto visited Medellín in the 1960s, primarily to get to know this city where tango icon Gardel died in an airplane crash. He fell in love with the city, stayed, and created the Festival Internacional de Tango. During this festival, tango concerts and events take place across the city, the culmination of which is the **World Tango Championship** (www.worldtangochampionships.co), held at the **Teatro Pablo Tobón** (Cra. 40 No. 51-24).

Since 1991, Medellín has hosted an impressive **Festival Internacional de Poesía de Medellín** (www.festivaldepoesiademedellin.org), which routinely attracts poets from dozens of countries; they share their work in more

International Day of Laziness

Paisas are known throughout Colombia to be some of the most hardworking and driven people in the country. The Medellín Metro, routine 7am business meetings, the orderly pueblos in the Antioquian countryside, and even former president Álvaro Uribe, a native Paisa, are examples of this industriousness. Uribe's famous words upon taking office in 2002 were *"trabajar, trabajar, trabajar"* ("work, work, work"). Laziness is quiet simply anathema to Paisas.

But you can't be productive *all* the time. The people of **Itagüí,** an industrial town bordering Medellín, have taken that to heart. In fact, on one day each year they not only take it easy, they embrace and celebrate the virtues of slothfulness during their **Día Internacional de la Pereza** (International Day of Laziness) celebrations. On that day in August, residents rise at the leisurely hour of 10am, put out their hammocks and beds in front of their houses, and laze the day away, sometimes still in their pajamas. The day's events include a bed (on wheels) race and general goofing off. Ironically, most of the action (or inaction) of that day takes place in the Itagüí Parque del Obrero (Worker's Park).

than 100 venues across the city. It's held in either late June or early July each year.

As the leading textile manufacturing center in Colombia, Medellín is the obvious choice for the most important fashion event in the country: **Colombiamoda** (www.inexmoda. org.co). It attracts designers and fashionistas from across the globe, and during this week, the Plaza Mayor becomes a fabulous model-fest. Taking place in late July, Colombiamoda often coincides with the Feria de las Flores.

The **Feria de las Flores** (www.feriadelasfloresmedellin.gov.co) is the most important festival of the year in Medellín, and is when the city is at its most colorful. It's a weeklong celebration of Paisa culture, with horseback parades, concerts, and the highlight, the Desfile de los Silleteros. That is when flower farmers from Santa Elena show off incredibly elaborate flower arrangements in a parade through the city streets. The festival, which includes a staggering number of events, is mostly free of charge and takes over the city for around three weeks in late July-early August each year.

At Christmastime, Medellín sparkles with light, every night. It all begins at midnight on December 1, during the **Alborada.** That's when the sights and sounds of fireworks and firecrackers envelop the entire Valle de Aburrá. On December 7, the **Alumbrado Navideño,** the city's Christmas light display, begins. The Cerro Nutibara and the Río Medellín, along with other city sites, are illuminated with 14.5 million multicolored lights. Sponsored by the electric company, it's quite a sight to behold.

SPORTS AND RECREATION
Biking

On Sundays and on holidays, Medellín residents take to the streets on their bikes and blades, or in their running shoes, during the **Ciclovía** (8am-1pm Sun.). There are several routes, including along Avenida El Poblado and along the Río Medellín. On Tuesday and Thursday evenings there is a **Ciclovía Nocturna** (8pm-10pm) on two routes: one along the river and another around the stadium.

Encicla (www.encicla.gov.co) is Medellín's free bike-share program. Visitors can check out a bike, though it will take a week for permission, which can be obtained online. Some nice bike paths are along Carreras 65 and 70 and around the universities, connecting the Estadio and Universidad Metro stations.

Bike Rent (Cra. 35 No. 7-14, cell tel. 310/448-3731, www.bikerent.com.co, 9am-7pm Mon., Wed., and Fri.-Sat., 9am-10pm Tues. and Thurs., 8am-1pm Sun., COP$25,000 half day, COP$35,000 full day) rents good bikes cheaply, and the prices decrease as the number of hours you rent them increases. It also has information on routes and suggestions at this convenient Provenza location. Bike shop **Giant** (Cra. 43A No. 10-38, tel. 4/444-3850, COP$40,000-60,000) has a few road and mountain bikes available for rent, as well as details on group rides and races in the region.

Barranquero Cicloturísmo (tel. 4/538-0699, cell tel. 314/806-5892, ciclobarranquero@gmail.com, www.barranquero.co, COP$70,000-90,000 pp) organizes interesting day-trip bike rides for all levels of cyclists in the city and beyond, such as in the nearby pueblo of Santa Elena and in Guatapé. Bikes and necessary equipment are included in the price, but transportation to the meeting point is not.

Paragliding

For incredible views of both the verdant Antioquian countryside and the metropolis in the distance, check out a paragliding adventure organized by the **Aeroclub San Felix** (Km. 6 Vía San Pedro de los Milagros, tel. 4/388-1077, www.parapenteencolombia.com, 20-min. flight COP$125,000, complete course COP$2,500,000). Bus transportation toward the town of San Felix is available from the Portal del Norte bus station, and buses can drop you off at the Estadero El Voladero. Numerous other outfits offer paragliding (*parapente* in Spanish), including **DragonFly** (Vía Sanpedro de los Milagros, cell tel. 300/333-0080, www.parapenteenmedellindragonfly.com).

Hiking

Ecoturismo Arewaro (Cra. 72A No. 30A-21, tel. 4/444-2573, cell tel. 300/652-4327, www.ecoturismoarewaro.com, COP$30,000) organizes day-trip walks and bike trips in parks and pueblos near Medellín. *Arewaro* means "gathering of friends" in the Wayúu language, and this is an interesting option for those looking to meet outdoorsy locals.

Soccer

Medellín has two professional teams, and Envigado has one. By far the most famous team, with rabid followers across the country, is **Atlético Nacional** (www.atlnacional.com.co). Nacional, wearing the green and white of the Antioquian flag, has been playing since 1947. It's one of the most successful teams in Colombia and has won the top division 11

the Estadio Atanasio Girardot complex

times. Nacional is wildly popular with young men and boys in Medellín, Antioquia, and beyond. The cheap seats at Nacional games are always packed with kids from the barrios. It's an intense affair. The other team in town is **Deportivo Independiente Medellín** (www.dalerojo.net). This is the oldest club in Colombia and was originally called Medellín Foot Ball Club when it was established in 1913. Both teams play at the **Estadio Atanasio Girardot** (Cl. 48 No. 73-10, www.inder.gov.co). Meanwhile, the new kid on the block is **Envigado FC,** a club that curiously has quite a visible following of European and North American expats ("La Familia Naranja") living here. Tickets can be purchased at **Ticket Factory Express** (tel. 4/444-4446, www.tick-etexpress.com.co).

Tours

Turibus (www.turibuscolombia.com, 9am-7:40pm daily, COP$35,000 24-hour pass) operates a hop-on, hop-off service that has seven stops in the city, including the Plaza Botero and the Cerro Nutibara/Pueblito Paisa. It also offers tours to other parts of the Antioquia department, such as to Jericó and Guatapé.

A popular walking tour catering mostly to backpackers is **Real City Tours** (www.realcitytours.com), which offers free tours twice a day Monday-Saturday, although a tip is expected. It also has an exotic fruit tour (COP$40,000) in the mornings. Book tours on the website. A five-hour bike tour (22 km) of the city is on offer from **BiciTour** (www.bicitour.co); a portion of the proceeds go to the children's nonprofit, Fundación Niños del Sol.

While some may find it unseemly to go on a tour of Pablo Escobar's Medellín, others find it fascinating. During the three-hour **Pablo Escobar Tour** (cell tel. 317/489-2629, www.paisaroad.com, 9:30am Mon.-Sat., COP$60,000) offered by Paisa Road, you'll see where the world's most notorious drug baron grew up, learn about the violent world of the cartels, and visit his tomb. The meeting point for the tours (offered in English) is at the Black Sheep and Casa Kiwi hostels in the Provenza area of El Poblado. If you'd like to visit Escobar's grave independently, you can take the Metro to the Sabaneta station. The **Parque Jardines Montesacro** (Cra. 42 No. 25-51, Autopista Sur Itagüi, tel. 4/374-1111, 9am-5pm daily, free) is within walking distance from there.

Colombian Bike Junkies (cell tel. 318/808-6769, www.colombianbiekjunkies.com) offers several exciting multiday trips in the area, including bike adventures with white-water rafting on the Río Buey (Class 3-4) and other thrills. **El Dorado Trips** (cell tel. 321/874-3440, www.eldoradotrips.com) offers more conventional day tours to coffee farms, Guatapé, and Río Claro.

SHOPPING

The Provenza neighborhood and the area around Parque Lleras are home to several boutique clothing and accessories shops. The **Milla de Oro** in El Poblado is the pride of modern Medellín: a strip of modern shopping malls, hotels, and office buildings. **Santa Fe** (Cl. 43 No. 7 Sur-107, www.centrocomercialsantafe.com) is one of the largest and flashiest of all.

FOOD

Twice a year, typically in April and in September, around 75 of the city's top restaurants participate in **Medellín Gourmet** (www.medellingourmet.com), during which they offer special prix fixe menus.

El Poblado
COLOMBIAN

Popular with a local crowd, ★ **3 Típicos** (Cl. 34 No. 7-05, www.3tipicos.com, tel. 4/322-3229, 11am-4pm Mon.-Tues., 11am-9pm Wed.-Thurs., 11am-10pm Fri.-Sat., 11am-6pm Sun., COP$23,000) is a pleasant open-air place where you order grilled meat and fish. For dessert, there's figs with *arequipe*. Vegetarians can have the beans and rice with avocado salad.

Along Avenida Las Palmas above El Poblado are several large and famous grilled

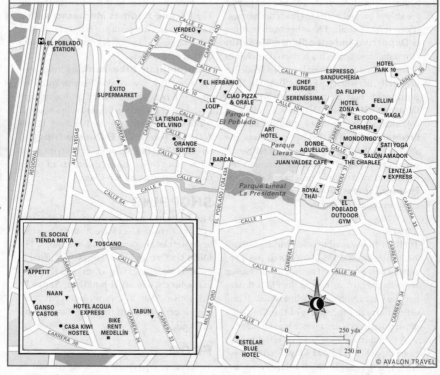

El Poblado

meat and *comida típica* restaurants. They are especially popular on weekend afternoons. Open-air and under a giant thatched roof is **Hato Viejo** (Cl. 16 No. 28-60, Av. Las Plamas, tel. 4/268-5412 or 4/268-6811, www.hatoviejo. com, noon-11pm daily, COP$25,000), a popular place for a weekend lunch with the gang. On Friday nights they have live music. **San Carbón** (Cl. 14 No. 30-10, tel. 4/444-7602, www.sancarbon.com.co, noon-10pm weekdays, noon-2am on weekends, COP$29,000) often has live music Wednesday-Sunday. Specialties include barbecue pork ribs and pepper steak.

FUSION

★ **Carmen** (Cra. 36 No. 10A-27 tel. 4/311-9625, www.carmenrestaurante.com.co,

noon-2:30pm Tues.-Fri., 7pm-10:30pm Mon.-Sat., COP$38,000) is considered one of the top restaurants in the country, and this sophisticated dining spot has a fantastic location on the fringes of El Poblado. Reservations are required. The open kitchen allows you to observe the attention to detail from your table.

★ **La Provincia** (Cra. 42 No. 3Sur-81, tel. 4/322-0192, www.laprovinciarestaurante. com, noon-3pm and 7pm-midnight Mon.-Sat., COP$35,000) is a Medellín classic, always ranked at the top of the city's restaurant list. It is a fusion of Mediterranean cuisine (lots of seafood) and Colombian flair. Try for a table on the romantic patio out back. Try the exotic grilled fish fillet in a peanut sauce with green papaya strips. At La Provincia you're guaranteed a memorable evening out. Reservations are recommended.

El Herbario (Cra. 43D No. 10-30, tel. 4/311-2537, www.elherbario.com, noon-3pm and 7pm-11pm daily, COP$24,000) has an inventive menu with items such as lemongrass tuna, turmeric prawns, and artichoke risotto. Spacious and minimalistic, it can feel a little like eating in a warehouse, though. The attached store sells exotic jams and chutneys and the like.

Feeling guilty for consuming too much fried food, carbs, and alcohol? You'll start to feel better just by stepping into slow-food believer **Appetit** (Cl. 8A No. 35-40, tel. 4/268-9901), a clean and fresh corner restaurant in in Provenza. Under the watchful eye of its German owner, Appetit specializes in organic ingredients. Mains include grilled octopus with hummus (COP$23,500) and organic lentils with shrimp (COP$26,000).

Set in a modernist house with interior gardens is sophisticated **Barcal** (Cl. 7D No. 43A-70, tel. 4/268-8714, www.restaurantebarcal.com, Mon.-Sat. noon-3pm and 7pm-10pm, COP$34,000), which specializes in Mediterranean fusion dishes. Start your meal with the octopus popcorn.

Wagon wheel lamps and antiques add to the atmosphere at long-time favorite **La Tienda del Vino** (Cl. 9 No. 43B-93, tel. 4/311-5822, www.latiendadelvino.com.co, Mon.-Sat. noon-10pm, Sun. noon-5pm), where a menu of mostly grilled meats and pastas is served in an open-air environment.

FRENCH

Stylish French bistro **Ganso & Castor** (Cra. 36 No. 7-46, tel. 4/268-9572, 8am-7:30pm Mon.-Sat., 8am-1pm Sun., COP$16,000) serves breakfast anytime and dishes up menu items such as croque monsieur, quiches, steak tartare, and escargots. There are two tables outside. It has a second location at the Museo de Arte Moderno.

Entrecôte (steak) and *pommes frites* (fries) await diners at upscale **Le Loup** (Cra. 43C No. 9-50, tel. 4/311-8986, noon-7pm Tues.-Sat.,

COP$32,000), which is set on a street full of interesting antique shops.

MIDDLE EASTERN

Tabun (Cra. 33 No. 7-99, tel. 4/311-8209, www.eltabun.com, noon-10pm Mon.-Wed., noon-11pm Thurs.-Sat., noon-5:30pm Sun., COP$22,000) serves standard Middle Eastern fare in generous portions, and they also have a few Indian dishes. Belly dancers perform on weekends.

ITALIAN

Fantastic artisanal pizzas pair with Argentinian wine at **Da Filippo** (Cra. 40 No. 10A-30, tel. 4/266-3489, noon-3pm and 6pm-midnight Tues.-Sat., noon-5pm Sun., COP$26,000). It's run by the same people as neighboring Il Castello.

There's a nice atmosphere at the small Italian restaurant **Serenissima** (Cra. 40 No. 10A-13, tel. 4/311-8593, noon-10:30pm Mon.-Sat., noon-3:30pm Sun.), which has a rustic old-world feeling about it.

Whereas most restaurants in El Poblado face rather busy and noisy streets, ★ **Toscano** (Cl. 8A No. 34-20, tel. 4/311-3094, cell tel. 314/739-6316, noon-2:30pm and 6:30pm-9:30pm Mon.-Thurs., noon-2:30pm and 6:30pm-11pm Fri.-Sat., noon-4pm Sun., COP$13,000 lunch set menu, COP$24,000) is on a quiet stretch. It's a delight to sit outside and have a pasta dish with a glass of wine.

VEGETARIAN

Most restaurants except the hard-core Colombian *parilla*-type places now offer at least one lonely vegetarian dish on their menus. In Provenza, there's no need to pity the herbivore any longer: Make a beeline for the cool atmosphere and fantastic vegetarian food at two-story ★ **Verdeo** (Cl. 12 No. 43D-77, tel. 4/444-0934, www.ricoverdeo.com, noon-10pm Mon.-Wed., noon-11pm Thurs.-Sat., noon-4pm Sun., COP$18,000). This vegetarian haven could be the best vegetarian restaurant in Colombia. Veggie burgers go down well with an artisanal beer, but there are also Asian- and Italian-inspired a la carte options. Lunch menus are inventive, and are a bargain.

Lenteja Express (Cra. 35 No. 8A-76, tel. 4/311-0186, cell tel. 310/879-9136, 11am-9pm Mon.-Sat.) specializes in veggie burgers: chickpea burgers, lentil burgers, and Mexican burgers. They have several locations in the city.

ASIAN

Authentic Asian restaurants are few and far between in Medellín. **Royal Thai** (Cra. 8A No. 37A-05, tel. 4/354-2843, www.royalthai-colombia.com, 6pm-10pm Mon.-Wed., noon-3pm and 6pm-11pm Thurs.-Fri., 1pm-4pm and 6pm-11pm Sat., 6:30pm-9:30pm Sun., COP$27,000) is a welcome change of pace serving authentic Thai cuisine.

Naan (Cra. 35 No. 7-75, tel. 4/312-6285, noon-3pm and 7pm-10pm Mon.-Wed., noon-3pm and 7pm-11pm Thurs.-Fri., noon-11pm Sat., noon-4pm Sun., COP$24,000) is a small and trendy Indian place in the Provenza area.

BURGERS AND SANDWICHES

The original ★ **Fellini** (Cra. 37 No. 10B-04, www.fellini.com.co, tel. 4/444-5064) has a gorgeous location amid gardens and trees, and it's home to a friendly cat. They serve lots of burgers here, and vegetarian dishes as well (falafel burger and portobello pesto). The owner moved to Medellín from the Netherlands years ago.

Hip, good, and popping up all over Medellín is chain **Chef Burger** (Cl. 11A No. 42-05, tel. 4/448-2378, noon-10:30pm Sun.-Wed., noon-11:30pm Thurs.-Sat.), where they stake the claim of serving the best burger in town. There are quite a few from which to choose.

Sandwiches don't have to be boring. At **Espresso Sanduchería** (Cra. 40 No. 10A-37, tel. 4/268-8300, cell tel. 318/343-6827, noon-10pm Mon.-Sat., COP$18,000) you can order a bahn mi or a blue cheese-and-beef sandwich. It's a smart little place on a pleasant side street.

CAFÉS AND QUICK BITES

The **Juan Valdez Café** (Cra. 37A No. 8A-74, 10am-9pm daily), atop the Parque Lleras, is a point of reference for the area and the place to meet up with someone for a cappuccino. It's popular with travelers and locals alike.

If you're feeling decadent, as in you'd like your latte in an actual coffee cup and served to you at a table, try **Pergamino Café** (Cra. 37 No. 8A-37, tel. 4/268-6444, 10am-9pm Mon.-Fri., 11am-9pm Sat.). It's on a relatively quiet street in the Provenza area. This could become your favorite coffee place. A few blocks from the hordes of cappuccino-seeking tourists is **Urbania Café** (Cl. 8 no. 43B-132, Mon.-Fri. 7am-8pm, Sat. noon-8pm, Sun. 10am-6pm), a cool place with organic chocolates, light pastries, and a little style.

La Maga (Cl. 10B No. 36-38, tel. 4/386-0673, 8am-7pm Mon.-Thurs., 8am-6pm Fri., 10am-5pm Sat.) may be on the nicest block in Medellín. It's tree-lined and quiet. In the front of the Perceptual interior design store is this tiny coffee and pastry stand, where you can sip coffee and savor a piece of cinnamon bread on the divine terrace.

They serve food at **El Codo de San Lorenzo** (Cra. 36 No. 10A-71, tel. 4/580-4022, noon-8pm Mon.-Tues., noon-9pm Wed., noon-11:30pm Thurs., noon-1:30am Fri.-Sat.), but the café's terrace may be nicer for a beer or two on a pleasant spring evening.

Centro

COLOMBIAN

A cheerful option downtown with a decent lunch menu is **El Tunel Café y Cocina** (Cra. 42 No. 54-62, tel. 4/239-6536, noon-10pm Mon.-Sat., COP$15,000).

FUSION

★ **In Situ** (Jardín Botánico, tel. 4/460-7007, www.botanicomedellin.org, noon-3pm Mon., noon-3pm and 7pm-10pm Tues.-Sat., noon-4pm Sun., COP$35,000) may have the nicest view of any eatery in Medellín. It's surrounded by a million shades of green on the grounds of the Jardín Botánico. It's an elegant place for a lunch, but if you've been sweating while visiting the city you may feel out of place among the sharply dressed business and society crowds. In Situ has an interesting menu with items such as apple sea bass (COP$30,000) and beef medallions in a coffee sauce with a plantain puree (COP$29,000).

Next to the Museo de Arte Moderno de Medellín is hip **Bonuar** (Cra. 44 No. 19A-100, tel. 4/235-3577, www.bonuar.com, 10am-7pm Tues.-Fri., 11am-6pm Sat., noon-4pm Sun., COP$22,000), where the burgers (including a portobello and lentil version) are famous and so is the brunch. It's a cool place with a nice outdoor seating area. During weekdays, it's better to go in the evening when the atmosphere is livelier. Try the fish in coconut creole sauce.

VEGETARIAN
Govinda's (Cl. 51 No. 52-17, tel. 4/293-2000, www.govindas.co, 11am-3pm Mon.-Sat., COP$14,000) is a Hare Krishna restaurant downtown serving delicious vegan lunches.

BURGERS
Fellini (Plaza Mayor, Cl. 41 No. 55-80, Local 105, tel. 4/444-5064, www.fellini.com.

co, noon-8pm Mon.-Fri., noon-4pm Sat., COP$15,000) specializes in burgers, but it also serves sandwiches, salads, and pastas. Plan to eat here after your long day of sightseeing downtown.

Laureles and the Stadium Area
COLOMBIAN
★ **Mondongo's** (Cra. 70 No. C3-43, tel. 4/411-3434, www.mondongos.com.co, 11:30am-9:30pm daily, COP$20,000) is a well-known and popular place for typical Colombian food and for drinks with friends. *Mondongo* is a tripe stew, a Colombian comfort food. In addition to the Carrera 70 location, there is another Mondongo's on the busy Calle 10 in El Poblado (Cl. 10 No. 38-38, tel. 4/312-2346) that is a popular drinking hole as well. They even have a location in Miami.

Another popular place on the Carrera 70 strip is **La Tienda** (Cra. 70 Circular 3-28, tel. 4/260-6783, 10am-2am daily). It's a festive restaurant that morphs into a late-night drinking place as the Medellín evenings wear on. Their *bandeja paisa* is famous. It's a signature Antioquian dish that includes beans, rice, sausages, and pork rinds.

Bandeja paisa is made of beans, rice, sausage, and pork rinds.

Maru Rico Guayabal (Cra. 51 Sur No. 6-8, tel. 4/354-5565, 11am-7pm Mon.-Sat., COP$14,000) is famous for its beans.

MIDDLE EASTERN

★ **Fenicia** (Cra. 73 No. C2-41, Av. Jardín, tel. 4/413-8566, www.feniciacomidaarabe.com, noon-8pm Mon.-Thurs., noon-9pm Fri.-Sat., noon-4pm Sun., COP$22,000) is an authentic Lebanese restaurant run by a family who immigrated to Colombia years ago. *Pastel cartageneros* (rice tamale) are served only on weekends, while delicious desserts like date pastries and fig flan with coconut are always awaiting after a delicious meal.

ITALIAN

At **Crispino** (Circular 1A No. 74-04, Laureles, tel. 4/413-3266, noon-11pm Mon.-Thurs., noon-midnight Fri.-Sat., noon-5pm Sun., COP$20,000), owner Salvatore, direct from Naples, offers authentic Italian cuisine and freshly baked bread in an agreeable atmosphere.

ASIAN

Korea House (Transversal 39B No. 77-56, tel. 4/412-1874, 11:30am-8pm Mon.-Sat.) has the bulgogi you've been craving, as well as zucchini pancakes.

CAFÉS AND QUICK BITES

Four in the morning and you've got the munchies? Join the legion of taxi drivers, college kids, and miscellaneous night owls at **Trigo Laurel** (Circula 1A No. 70-06, tel. 4/250-4943, 24 hours daily), where it never closes. They specialize in baked goods, but they also serve cheap lunches. It's on a quiet corner of Carrera 70.

Envigado
SPANISH

Cozy and chic Spanish restaurant **El Barral** (Cl. 30 Sur No. 43A-38, tel. 4/276-1212, noon-10pm Mon.-Sat., COP$30,000) specializes in paella, tapas, and sangria, and does them well in sophisticated surroundings.

STEAK

With Colombian newspapers plastered on the walls displaying headlines of yesteryear, the Argentinian steak house **Lucio Carbón y Vino** (Cra. 44A No. 30S-40, Envigado, tel. 4/334-4003, noon-midnight Mon.-Sat., COP$32,000) specializes in grilled steak, paired with a nice Malbec.

ACCOMMODATIONS

Accommodation options to fit every budget and taste are plentiful in Medellín. El Poblado has the most options, with luxury hotels along Avenida El Poblado and hostels and boutiques in the walkable Provenza area, close to a smorgasbord of restaurants and bars and close-ish to the El Poblado Metro station. Laureles is a quiet and green residential area with a growing number of fine options for those wanting an escape from the madding crowd. Some may choose to stay in the Centro, but note that it's an area of town that feels unsafe at night. As is the case in cities in the interior of the country, hotel prices fall on weekends, and vacancies increase.

El Poblado
UNDER COP$70,000

Medellin is a top destination on the international backpacker trail, and hostels geared toward that market have sprung up throughout the city. Hostels have distinct "vibes," from mild to wild, with the latter tending to be close to the action near Parque Lleras in Provenza.

Waypoint Hostel (Cra. 48B No. 10 Sur 08, cell tel. 300/671-9912, www.waypointhostel.com, COP$25,000 dorm, COP$80,000 d) is close to the EAFIT university and has friendly staff and clean facilities. A big selling point here is the pool. It's a bit of a hike to the Parque Lleras area, but the property is close to the Metro. The hostel has bikes for rent. Some dorm rooms have a lot of beds in them.

COP$70,000-200,000

Acqua Hotel Express (Cra. 35 No. 7-47, tel. 4/448-0482, cell tel. 320/788-4424, www.hotelacqua.com, COP$148,000 d) is a fairly good value, mostly because of its prime location in Provenza. There are 43 spotless rooms that are somewhat comfortable. You will be charged if you bring a guest to the room, though.

The **Hotel BH El Poblado** (Cra. 43 No. 9 Sur 35, tel. 4/604-3534, www.bhhoteles.com, COP$195,000 d) is across from the enormous Centro Comercial Santa Fe. This Colombian chain hotel with 70 rooms has huge, comfortable beds and modern rooms, and despite its location on a major street (Av. El Poblado), it's not that noisy. An included breakfast buffet is served in a pleasant open-air terrace. It also has a tiny hotel gym, with about three cardio machines.

Hotel Zona A (Cl. 10B No. 37-69, tel. 4/580-3800, www.hotelzonaa.com, COP$172,000 d) is a cute little hotel (19 rooms) with small rooms and a nice outdoor terrace where you can have breakfast. The location is perfect, in a surprisingly woodsy area of El Poblado, but that doesn't necessarily mean there will be no traffic noise.

A touch of rustic charm in happening El Poblado is on offer at **La Campana Hotel Boutique** (Cl. 11A No. 31A-70, tel. 4/312-2525, COP$180,000 d), a house with 13 rooms and pleasant common areas.

COP$200,000-500,000

Estelar Blue (Cra. 42 No. 1 Sur-74, tel. 4/369-8380, COP$245,000 d) is a Colombian business hotel chain. This location has spacious and no-surprises rooms and offers both breakfast and light dinner buffets.

For more privacy, consider an aparta-hotel such as **Orange Suites** (Cl. 8 No. 43C-37, tel. 1/216-9843, www.travelers.com.co/ciudades/medellin, COP$215,000 d). This high-rise in El Poblado has lots of space.

Yes, the ★ **Charlee Lifestyle Hotel** (Cl. 9A No. 37-16, tel. 4/444-4968, www.thecharlee.com, COP$485,000) is awesome: hot tubs on room balconies with a view to the Parque Lleras, a massive mini bar, a pool on the terrace, a spectacular gym, good food, and a disco. Polished concrete floors, a gallery space in the lobby, and a rooftop terrace make the **Art**

Hotel Boutique (Cra. 41 No. 9-31, tel. 4/369-7900, www.arthotel.com.co, COP$238,000 d) a swank choice. It's a bargain, considering how upscale it is. The gym and spa area in the basement is a little sad. This hotel is just a couple of blocks from the Parque Lleras.

OVER COP$500,000

Impeccable service awaits at **Park 10 Hotel** (Cra. 36 B No. 11-12, tel. 4/310-6060, www.hotelpark10.com.co, COP$520,000 d), located in a tree-lined area of El Poblado within walking distance of fine restaurants. Amenities include fantastic breakfasts and a small gym with modern machines and pilates studio. An English-speaking staff welcomes visitors to this classic property.

Centro
COP$70,000-COP$200,000

Hard-core city lovers will be the ones interested in staying in the Centro. The **Hotel Nutibara Conference Center** (Cl. 52A No. 50-46, tel. 4/511-5111, www.hotelnutibara.com, COP$127,000 d) is the area's best choice. It's a faded, grand old hotel located steps from the Museo de Antioquia, but the rooms are updated. With wide corridors and huge rooms with parquet floors, it retains mid-20th-century elegance and personality. There's a bar in the basement that hosts jazz performances, and there's a food court nearby. Many advise not to wander after dark in the area.

Hotel 61 Prado (Cl. 61 No. 50A-60, tel. 4/254-9743, www.61prado.com, COP$68,000 s, COP$91,000 d) is a charming guesthouse downtown, with large rooms and a rooftop terrace for breakfast at their 24-hour restaurant. Light sleepers may want to request a room in back to avoid street noise.

Laureles and the Stadium Area
UNDER COP$70,000

Located in a quiet residential neighborhood, but just behind a big Éxito department store, the ★ **Palm Tree Hostal** (Cra. 67 No. 48D-63, tel. 4/4447256, cell tel. 300/241-9209, www.

palmtreemedellin.com, COP$28,000 dorm, COP$70,000 d with shared bath) is known for its friendly staff and similiarly laid-back guests. Despite having been around a long while, it remains a favorite. It's three blocks from the Suramericana Metro station. A basic breakfast is provided.

Wandering Paisa (Cl. 44 A No. 68A-76, www.wanderingpaisahostel.com, cell tel. 320/749-2073, tel. 4/436-6759, COP$27,000 dorm, COP$70,000 d) has a social vibe, with the on-site Paisa Bar and events like karaoke taking place often. It's close to the stadium. There are four dorm rooms, two with eight beds and two with four beds; it's more comfortable to be in a room with four. A metro station is a five-minute walk from the hostel.

In between bed-and-breakfast and hostel, the ★ **Yellow House Hostel** (Cra. 81A No. 47A-48, tel. 4/411-2873, www.yellowhouse.com.co, COP$25,000 dorm, COP$80,000 d) is a laid-back option on a quiet residential street in Floresta, a 10-minute walk to the Metro station. There are five private rooms (four with en suite bath) and one dorm room with six beds. Besides the relaxing and welcoming environs, guests love the breakfasts—and the fluffy canine residents.

COP$70,000-COP$200,000

The **Casa Hotel Asturias Medellín** (Circular 4 No. 73-124, tel. 4/260-2872, COP$145,000 d) is on a delightful corner of the tree-lined and quiet Laureles neighborhood. That's the big selling point for this small hotel. Rooms are modern and comfortable, although not terribly huge. It's a good deal.

COP$200,000-500,000

Located across from the Atanasio Girardot sports complex, the **Hotel Tryp Medellín** (Cl. 50 No. 70-24, tel. 4/604-0686, www.tryphotels.com, COP$220,000 d) has 140 large, comfortable (if spartan) rooms and an excellent rooftop terrace with a whirlpool and steam room. Guests have access to an on-site gym. Restaurants are nonexistent in this area, except for street food, and hotel room

service is iffy. The area revs up when Atlético Nacional is playing.

Ciudad del Río
COP$70,000-200,000

In contrast to many Colombian cities, Medellín has a fair variety of midrange hotels. Chain hotels tend to be best, holding few surprises.

French budget chain ★ **Hotel Ibis** (Cl. 20 No. 44-16, tel.4/444-1554, www.ibis.com, COP$99,000 d) has modern rooms with comfortable beds at great rates, and is in an interesting area of the Ciudad del Río, across the street from the Museo de Arte Moderno de Medellín. There's no gym, but the neighborhood is quiet, making a morning jog a possibility. The best views are on the hotel's south side. The hotel restaurant offers buffet meals for an additional price. On the weekends it's very quiet, and room rates may slide further.

It has a boring and unattractive location, but the standard-to-the-core **GHL Comfort Hotel San Diego** (Cl. 31, No. 43-90, www.ghlhoteles.com, COP$150,000 d) offers good prices and an attentive staff. A standard Colombian breakfast is served on the top-floor terrace (featuring an excellent view), and amenities include a sauna and small gym. It's close to a couple of malls and is between the Centro and El Poblado on a main road. The Ciclovía passes by on Sundays, making it a snap to get out and move.

INFORMATION AND SERVICES
Tourist Information

Medellín produces the most comprehensive tourist information of any city in Colombia. In addition to visitor information booths at the bus terminals and airports, there is a large office at the **Plaza Mayor** (Cl. 41 No. 55-80, tel. 4/261-7277, 8am-noon and 2pm-6pm Mon.-Sat.). The tourism office website (www.medellin.travel) maintains up-to-date information on what's going on in the city.

The main newspaper in Medellín is *El Colombiano* (www.elcolombiano.com).

Another excellent resource is the website **Medellín Living** (www.medellinliving.com), which is run by expats. **Universo Centro** (www.universocentro.com) has a more urban focus: It's produced by and for folks living in Medellín's Centro.

Spanish-Language Courses

Universidad EAFIT Centro de Idiomas (Cra. 49 No. 7S-50, Bldg. 31, Of. 201, tel. 4/261-9399, www.eafit.edu.co/spanishprogram, COP$1,010,000 38-hr. course) offers intensive (20 hours per week) and semi-intensive (10 hours per week) Spanish classes.

TRANSPORTATION
Air

There are two airports serving Medellín. The main airport, with several international flights, is **Aeropuerto Internacional José María Córdova** (MDE, tel. 4/402-5110 or 4/562-2885) in the town of Rionegro, about 35 km (22 miles) from the city. Avianca, LATAM, and Viva Colombia operate domestic flights from MDE.

Taxis cost around COP$60,000 between the city and the airport; the drive takes about 45 minutes. To go to the airport in Rionegro, call the special **Rionegro airport taxi service** (tel. 4/261-1616, cell tel. 313/744-0680, http://acoataxiaeropuerto.com.co); these white cabs have a blue stripe on them.

There are also *busetas* (small buses) leaving the airport bound for the San Diego neighborhood, which is convenient to El Poblado. These can be found as you exit the terminal toward the right. Traveling to the airport from Medellin, there are buses (Conbuses, tel. 4/231-9681) that depart from a side street just behind the **Hotel Nutibara** (Cl. 52A No. 50-46, tel. 4/511-5111) in the Centro. These depart from about 4:30am until 8:30pm every day, and the trip costs COP$8,800. The buses are hard to miss: They're green and white with the word *aeropuerto* printed in all caps on the front window.

The **Aeropuerto Olaya Herrera** (EOH, Cra. 65A No. 13-157, tel. 4/403-6781, www.

aeropuertoolayaherrera.gov.co) is the super-convenient in-town airport. It's especially useful for traveling to the Pacific coast and to Capurganá/Acandí. From EOH, **Satena** serves Bogotá, Quibdó, Apartadó, Bahía Solano, and Nuquí; **ADA** (Aerolínea de Antioquia) connects the city with towns such as Bahía Solano, Acandí, and Capurganá; and **EasyFly** serves cities in eastern Colombia like Cúcuta and Bucaramanga. The Olaya Herrera terminal was built in the 1930s and is an architectural gem—you'll love it.

Intercity Buses

Medellín has two bus terminals: the Sur and the Norte. The **Terminal del Sur** (Cra. 65 No. 8B-91, tel. 4/444-8020 or 4/361-1186) is across from the Aeropuerto Olaya Herrera, and it serves destinations in southern Antioquia and the coffee region. The **Terminal del Norte** (Cra. 64C No. 78-580, tel. 4/444-8020 or 4/230-9595) is connected to the Caribe Metro station. It serves Santa Fe de Antioquia and Guatapé, the Caribbean coast, and Bogotá.

Metro

Medellín's **Metro** (tel. 4/444-9598, www.metrodemedellin.gov.co) is the only urban train system in the country. It's a safe and super-clean system of two lines: Línea A, which runs from Niquía (north) to La Estrella (south), and Línea B, from San Antonio in the Centro west to San Javier. The Metro line A is useful for traveling between El Centro, El Poblado, and Envigado. Metro line B has a stop at the stadium. The current Metro fare is COP$1,800; however, if you think you may use the Metro, Metrocable, and Metroplús system on a regular basis, consider purchasing a refillable Tarjeta Cívica card that is valid on all three transportation networks. The cost per ride with the Tarjeta Cívica modestly drops to COP$1,600. The card can be purchased at Metro ticket booths.

Metrocable

The Metrocable public transportation system, consisting of gondola (*teleférico*) lines, was inaugurated in 2004 and consists of three lines, with two under construction. It has been internationally lauded as an innovative approach to solving the unique transportation needs of the isolated and poor *comunas* (residential sectors) built on the mountainsides of the city. The three Metrocable lines are: Línea J from the San Javier Metro station to La Aurora in the west, Línea K from the Acevedo Metro station in the north to Santo Domingo, and Línea L from Santo Domingo to the Parque Arví. The Metrocable runs 9am-10pm daily. The Metrocable Línea L from Santo Domingo to the Parque Arví operates 9am-6pm Tuesday-Sunday. When Monday is a holiday, the Línea L runs that day and does not operate the next day, Tuesday.

Metroplús Rapid Bus

The first line of the **Metroplús** (www.metro-plus.gov.co) rapid bus system, with dedicated bus stops similar to those of the TransMilenio in Bogotá, debuted in 2013. There are two Metroplús lines: Línea 1 and Línea 2. Línea 1 connects the working-class neighborhood of Arjuanez in the north with the Universidad de Medellín in the southwest. Línea 2 connects the same two sectors but passes through the Centro and Plaza Mayor area. To access the system, you must use the Tarjeta Cívica, which can be purchased at any Metro station.

Taxis

Taxis are plentiful in Medellín. You can order them over the phone at 4/444-4444, or use an app like **Easy Taxi, Tappsi,** or **Uber.**

Northern and Eastern Antioquia

SANTA FE DE ANTIOQUIA

Living and breathing colonial charm, this pueblo 80 kilometers (50 miles) northwest of Medellín is the best of Antioquia. Set on the banks of the Río Cauca, Santa Fe was founded in 1541 by Jorge Robledo, a ruthless conquistador. It became an important center for gold mining, and the town was the capital of Antioquia until 1823, when it ceded that title to Medellín. Today its proximity to Medellín makes Santa Fe an easy trip for those interested in seeing a colonial-era jewel of a pueblo.

With the average temperature a sizzling 27°C (81°F), it can be a challenge to fully enjoy strolling the lovely streets of the pueblo during the heat of the day. If you can, plan to stay the night (one weekday night will do), arriving in late afternoon.

Sights

The town's narrow stone streets and compact center are adorned with charming plazas and parks and five historic churches. It's a delight to stroll the town in the late afternoon, after the heat of the day has subsided. Churches and historic buildings in Santa Fe are often built in the typical *calicanto* style, a mix of brick and stone construction materials. Historic colonial churches, with majestic facades, often face parks and are illuminated at night.

The "grandmother" of churches in Antioquia is the **Templo de Santa Bárbara** (Cl. 11 at Cra. 8, masses 7am and 6pm Mon.-Sat., 6am and 6pm Sun.). Built toward the end of the 18th century, it is characterized by its many baroque elements. Next to it, in what was a Jesuit college, is the **Museo de Arte Religioso** (Cl. 11 No. 8-12, tel. 4/311-3808, 10am-1pm and 2pm-5pm Fri.-Sun., COP$3,000), a museum that highlights paintings, sculptures, and gold and silver pieces from the Spanish New World colonies.

A nicely presented museum contained in a colonial-style house, the **Museo Juan del Corral** (Cl. 11 No. 9-77, tel. 4/853-4605, 9am-noon and 2pm-5:30pm Mon.-Tues. and Thurs.-Fri., 10am-5pm Sat.-Sun., free) has exhibits on the history of Santa Fe, including historical items from 1813 when Antioquia was

The big event in Santa Fe is the weeklong **Festival de Cine de Antioquia** (www.festi-cineantioquia.com), a film festival held each year in early December. There is usually an international director or actor who is the guest of honor. Some free showings are held outdoors in the town's plazas and parks.

Recreation
Naturaventura (Hotel Mariscal Robledo, Cl. 10 No. 9-70, tel. 4/853-1946, cell tel. 313/667-8150, naturaventura1@hotmail.com) organizes nature walks, bike trips, horseback riding, and rafting excursions.

Shopping
Spaniards were once attracted to Santa Fe because of its gold. Today it is famous for its intricate filigree jewelry. To peruse some, visit **ORFOA** (Cl. 9 No. 6-02, tel. 4/853-2880, 9am-noon and 2pm-6pm daily) or **Dulces & Artesanías Clavellina** (Hotel Mariscal Robledo, Cl. 10 No. 9-70, tel. 4/853-2195, 9am-noon and 2pm-6pm daily).

Guarnielería y Marroquinería (Cl. 10 No. 7-66, cell tel. 314/847-8354, noon-7pm Mon.-Fri., 10am-7pm Sat.-Sun.) sells authentic Jericó *carrieles* (shoulder bags used by Paisa cowhands) and other locally made leather handicrafts. **La Casa Solariega** (Cl. de la Amargura No. 8-09, tel. 4/853-1530, 9am-noon and 2pm-6pm daily) has an eclectic collection of handicrafts, paintings, and antiques in a typical Santa Fe house.

Food
There are few places in Colombia where one can dine to the soft tones of classical or jazz music. The **Restaurante Bar La Comedia** (Parque Santa Bárbara, tel. 4/853-1243, noon-3pm and 6pm-10pm Wed.-Sun., COP$18,000) is one such place. Light dishes, sandwiches, and crepes dominate the small menu, and this is also an option for late-afternoon *onces,* tea time—or maybe an iced coffee. It's diagonal to the Santa Bárbara church.

Restaurante Portón del Parque (Cl. 10 No. 11-03, tel. 4/853-3207, noon-8pm

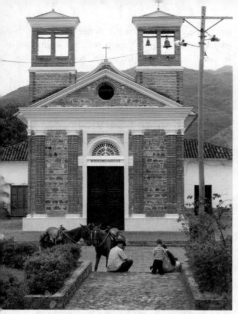
The historic town of Santa Fe de Antioquia makes for a pleasant overnight trip from Medellín.

declared free. The museum also puts on temporary exhibits of contemporary Colombian artists and hosts other cultural events.

Six kilometers (four miles) outside of town, on an old road that leads to the town of Sopetrán on the other side of the Río Cauca, is an architectural wonder: the **Puente de Occidente,** a suspension bridge made of iron and steel. It was built toward the end of the 19th century by José María Villa, an engineer who studied in New Jersey and worked on the Brooklyn Bridge. It's a narrow span and has been closed to vehicular traffic, for the most part. *Mototaxis* can take you there from town, cross the bridge, and return for COP$15,000. The bridge is easily reached by bike as well.

Festivals and Events
Semana Santa in Santa Fe (www.semanas-antafe.org) means processions along the cobblestone streets and a Festival de Música Sacra y Religiosa that features concerts. Visitors from across the region converge on the town for this religious celebration.

Sun.-Thurs., noon-9:30pm Sat.-Sun., COP$20,000) is lavishly decorated with portraits and paintings by owner Olga Cecilia. In addition to typical Paisa specialties (lunch specials during the week go for less than COP$10,000), the extensive menu offers seafood and international cuisine.

The restaurant at the **Hotel Mariscal Robledo** (Cl. 10 No. 9-70, tel. 4/853-1111, cell tel. 313/760-0099, www.hotelmariscalrobledo.com, 8am-3pm and 7pm-10pm daily, COP$25,000) is a reliable choice serving a range of cuisines, from local Paisa specialties to pasta.

Accommodations

Medellín families converge on Santa Fe en masse on weekends, and for many the draw is the opportunity to lounge by the pool at one of the hotels lining the main road leading into town. Hotels in town, however, have more charm. Hotel prices can drop substantially during the week.

In town, the ★ **Hotel Mariscal Robledo** (Cl. 10 No. 9-70, tel. 4/853-1111, cell tel. 313/760-0099, www.hotelmariscalrobledo.com, COP$120,000-170,000 d) is far and away the most comfortable hotel, and one oozing personality. Antiques, especially with a cinematic theme, decorate the lobby and common areas. Rooms on the 2nd floor, which have not been given a 21st-century makeover, are nonetheless comfortable, and have far more character. The pool area is luxurious.

On the boutique side and just two blocks from the Parque Principal, the **Hotel Casa Tenerife** (Cra. 8 No. 9-50, tel. 4/853-2261, www.hotelcasatenerife.com.co, COP$162,000 d) has 12 rooms, is tastefully decorated, and has a nice pool and interior courtyard area adorned with a soothing fountain. It often caters to couples celebrating romantic getaways, with such details as rose petals on the bed. This house is over 200 years old.

The family-run **Hotel Caserón Plaza** (Cl. 9-41, Plaza Mayor, tel. 4/853-2040, www.hotelcaseronplaza.com.co, COP$145,000-208,000 d) has an excellent location but is overpriced for what you get. Some of the 33 rooms have air-conditioning, which is a plus in Santa Fe. There is also a pool in back, another plus. The pool is the major hangout area on weekends, and the area also has a nice deck with views.

Information and Services

A **tourist information office** on the Plaza Mayor (Cra. 9 and Cl. 9, tel. 4/853-1022) has maps and hotel information.

Transportation

There is regular bus service, several times a day, from the **Terminal de Transportes del Norte** (Cra. 64 No. 78-344, Medellín, tel. 4/267-7075, www.terminalesmmedellin.com) in Medellín to Santa Fe. The two-hour journey takes you through a feat of modern engineering: the **Túnel Fernando Gómez Martínez,** the longest tunnel in South America. To return from Santa Fe, walk a couple of blocks to the Turbo-Medellín highway near the market at Carrera 10 and flag down passing buses. Most of them are going to Medellín. The trip costs about COP$14,000 each way.

MAGDALENA MEDIO
★ Reserva Natural Río Claro

A visit to the spectacular, privately run **Reserva Natural Río Claro** (Medellín office tel. 4/268-8855, cell tel. 311/354-0119, www.rioclaroreservanatural.com, 8am-6pm daily) is a highlight for anyone visiting Colombia. In the steamy and remote Magdalena Medio region of Antioquia, about 200 kilometers toward the Río Magdalena to the east, the reserve encompasses 500 hectares (1,230 acres) along the Río Claro canyon, a babbling, crystal-clear river. This reserve is a place to enjoy the unspoiled beauty of the river and its jungle and to disconnect from the hectic pace of urban life.

The story behind the park begins with an oft-repeated tale about a pesky jaguar. It seems that the cat was blamed for killing some livestock of a campesino in the area. In a quest to track down the guilty party (the jaguar got away unharmed), the farmer followed its tracks through the jungle and to a spectacular canyon. When Juan Guillermo Garcés heard about the astonishing discovery, he had to see this undiscovered territory for himself. Garcés immediately knew that this was a special place, and he made a commitment to purchase the land to protect it from development, including a highway that was to pass through this pristine land.

Río Claro receives many weekend visitors. In addition to those staying at the reserve, many day visitors spend the afternoon at Río Claro. Don't go on a Saturday, Sunday, or holiday if you seek a peaceful commune with nature. If you visit the reserve midweek, you'll most likely have the place practically to yourself, which is heavenly.

RECREATION

Guides don't speak English, generally. There are two must-do activities at the reserve. The first is an easy rafting trip down the river (COP$25,000), during which you can see the karstic jungle, in which trees grow atop rocks. This excursion takes about two hours. The second activity is a combination swim/hike trip to the **Caverna de los Guácharos** (COP$20,000 pp). This guided walk has its challenging moments: wading across the swiftly flowing river, making your way through the dark cavern, climbing out of the cavern, and then making your way back across the river. *Guácharo* birds (oilbirds), living inside the cavern, act like they own the place (the cavern is, after all, named for them). They don't like it when humans invade their space, and they'll let you know that with their screeching. The cavern is made of marble; its stalactites and stalagmites are impressive. Waterproof shoes with good traction are recommended, as you'll be wading in water most of the time. Also, it's nice to have a headlamp so that you'll have hands free. You can take your camera, but at a certain point it will need to be kept in a water-repellent bag, which the guide will have. If you're up for both trips, go on the cavern tour in the morning and go rafting in the late afternoon.

Other activities at the reserve include rock climbing, a zip line, hanging out on the marble beach, self-guided nature walks, and tubing. These are all arranged by Río Claro staff.

ACCOMMODATIONS

The reserve has a variety of accommodation options. Contact the Río Claro office (tel. 4/268-8855, cell tel. 311/354-0119, www.

Reserva Natural Río Claro

rioclaroreservanatural.com) for all reservations and information. The **Bluemorpho Ecolodge** (COP$85,000) is above the reserve's reception and dining area, boasting comfortable all-wood construction. The best and most isolated lodging is at the far end near the canyon, a 15-minute walk from the main reception area in the **Cabañas El Refugio** (COP$95,000-200,000 pp). Rooms here are open-air and quite spectacular. You'll sleep well with the sounds of the rushing water to lull you asleep. Rooms are completely open, but there are no problems with mosquitoes.

The **Hotel Río Claro** (COP$95,000 pp) is across the highway from the rest of the reserve but still along the river, and it has a big pool. These are small concrete bungalows. The hotel is popular with student groups. All meals are included in the room rates. Tell staff when you make your reservation if you have any dietary needs or special requests, like fresh fruit.

GETTING THERE

The reserve is easily reached by bus from Medellín. All buses between Medellín and Bogotá pass in front of the Río Claro entrance, where there is a small security booth. From Medellín, it takes roughly three hours and costs around COP$24,000. Be sure to tell the driver you'd like to be dropped off at the *"entrada de la Reserva Río Claro."* ("the entrance to the Río Claro Reserve").

Hacienda Napoles

The **Hacienda Napoles** (Puerto Triunfo, tel. 4/444-2975, cell tel. 318/219-4553, www.haciendanapoles.com, 9am-5pm Tues.-Sun., COP$36,000) was a vacation home for the world's most infamous drug trafficker, Pablo Escobar, complete with an airstrip and exotic animals—including quite a few hippos, who apparently adapted nicely to the muggy climes of the Río Magdalena area. Today Hacienda Napoles is a theme park with giant dinosaur sculptures, some of which were built by Escobar for his children; two water parks (additional fees); hippopotami, zebras, and ostriches; an Africa museum; the remnants of Pablo Escobar's country house (now a museum); and his private airstrip.

Avoid the oppressive heat and intense sun of midday (and the crowds on weekends) by visiting early on a weekday morning. The park can easily be visited from Río Claro, which is about an hour away. When Monday is a holiday, the park closes on Tuesday rather than on Monday.

GUATAPÉ

The stone monolith La Piedra dominates the landscape here, but the Guatapé area is more than just a big rock: It's a weekend playground chock-full of recreational activities that keep the crowds from Medellín busy. While Guatapé is doable as a day trip, plenty of outdoorsy activities could keep one blissfully occupied for a day or two.

Sights

Guatapé is a resort town. Aside from La Piedra, it's known for its *zócalos,* the colorful friezes on the lower levels of the town's houses. Many of these honor the traditions of townspeople, such as farming and fishing; others have sheep or other animals; and still others hot rods or the occasional Pink Panther. A particularly colorful street is the **Calle del Recuerdos** near the Parque Principal.

On a serene mountainside near Guatapé, beyond El Encuentro hostel on the same road, is the **Monasterio Santa María de la Epifanía** (www.monjesbenedictinosguatape.org), home to around 30 Benedictine monks. Guests, up to eight at a time, are welcome to stay at the monastery. Every day of the week at the 5:15pm *visperas* (vespers) service, the public is invited to hear the monks sing Gregorian chants.

For a day at the park, head to the **Parque Recreativo COMFAMA Guatapé** (on main road toward Medellín, tel. 4/861-0840, www.comfama.com, 9am-5pm Tues.-Fri., COP$11,500). Run by an insurance company, this private park outside of Guatapé has nature paths and a lake where you can kayak or waterbike. Picnicking makes for a fine idea here; you're allowed to bring in food (but no alcohol).

LA PIEDRA PEÑOL

Known simply as La Piedra, **La Piedra Peñol** (8am-6pm daily, COP$15,000) is a giant rock monolith that soars 200 meters (650 feet) into the sky from the scenic Embalse Peñol-Guatapé, a reservoir covering some 64 square kilometers (25 square miles) that is an important source of hydroelectric energy for the country. There's been quite a rivalry between the towns of El Peñol and Guatapé over the years, with arguments over which town can claim La Piedra as its own. (The rock is located between the two, a tad closer to the Guatapé side.) Things digressed to a point where folks from Guatapé began to paint their town's name in large letters on one prominent side of the rock. People from El Peñol were not amused, and this giant marking of territory was halted by authorities. Today all that remains of that fierce brouhaha is what appear to be the letters "GI."

In front of La Piedra, there is a statue of Luis Villegas López, the man who first climbed the monolith in 1954. Inspired by a priest, López and two friends took five days to slowly climb up cracks in the rock. They had

to deal with a beehive and a rainstorm the way, adding to the challenge.

Today the rock is one of the top tourist attractions in Antioquia. La Piedra can be visited several ways. You can walk from Guatapé, which takes 45 minutes. (Sunscreen and water are essential.) You can bike it, although the road that winds its way up to the rock entrance is quite steep. You can take a *mototaxi* from your hotel (COP$10,000), or you can hop on a Jeep from the Parque Principal (between Cras. 28-29 and Clls. 31-32) in Guatapé. Visit during the early-morning hours or late in the afternoon.

Once you're at the bottom of the rock, look up and notice the hundreds of bromeliads growing along the sides of it. Then head to the top. The 360-degree views from the top of La Piedra over the Guatapé reservoir and Antioqiuan countryside are worth the toil of climbing the more than 600 steps of the ramshackle brick and concrete stairwell that is stuck to the rock. To celebrate your feat, you can have a drink at one of the snack bars at the top.

The town of El Peñol is surrounded by the reservoir, which is operated by Medellín utility company EPM. The reservoir was built in phases during the 1970s and was not without

the great view that comes from hiking La Piedra Peñol

is the flooding of the area began ... full consent of the inhabitants. ... families were resettled by EPM ... the town of El Peñol gradually ... with rising waters, with only a ... e remaining as a reminder of the town's past.

Tours

A popular excursion is to take a **boat tour** of the reservoir (Hotel Las Araucarias, cell tel. 313/646-7946). A standard stop on the tour is to (or rather, above) the submerged town of Viejo Peñol. It was flooded during the construction of the reservoir and nearby dam in 1978, and today the only visible remnant of the town is a large cross rising out of the water. A small historical museum displays old photos and historical memorabilia from the town. These tours typically last 45 minutes to 1.5 hours.

Guatape Motos (Cl. 32 No. 22-09, cell tel. 313/788-9332, www.guatapemotos.com) does fun motorcycle and scooter tours of 1-3 days involving activities such as visits to old farms of Pablo Escobar (Hacienda Napoles and Finca Manuela), tubing, and people-watching at a refreshing waterfall; it can even throw in a paragliding adventure. Guatape Motos also rents scooters (COP$100,000 day), perfect for zipping around town and beyond.

Food

Fish such as massive carp and trout from the reservoir are the specialty in Guatapé. A reliable spot for fish and Colombian cuisine is **La Fogata** (Cra. 30 No. 31-32, tel. 4/861-1040, cell tel. 314/740-7282, 8am-8pm daily), on the waterfront.

For some healthy food, tilting toward the vegetarian persuasion, try the delightful sidewalk café ★ **Hecho con Amor Deli** (Cra. 27A No. 30-71, cell tel. 321/834-7979, noon-7pm Sat.-Tues.). The freshly baked bread is awesome, as are the desserts. The deli is across from the soccer field.

Bar Baroja (Plazoleta de Zócalos No. 30-48, cell tel. 323/523-5153) is the coolest place for a beer in Guatapé. It's run by Boris from Belgium, a fellow with a *barba roja* (red beard), hence the name: Bar Baroja. A gregarious mix of Colombians and foreigners sit on the colorful steps of Guatapé as they sip some refreshing cocktails. Twister competitions may take place.

Sometimes exceptional hospitality can give one a sugar headache. That's what happens at Gloria Elena's generous candy tastings at **Dulces de Guatapé** (Cl. 29 No. 23C-32, Barrio Villa del Carmen, tel. 4/861-0724, 7am-6pm). At this small candy factory, they make all kinds of sweets, many with *arequipe* (caramel) and some with fruits like the tart *uchuva* and guava. There are also some chocolate bonbons that have peanuts and almonds.

Accommodations

During the week, prices drop significantly at most hotels, especially if you pay in cash.

Tomate Café Hostel (Cra. 31 No. 30-41, tel. 4/861-1100, cell tel. 310/450-7981, www. tomatecafehostel.com, COP$18,000 dorm, COP$40,000 d) is run by a Paisa family and has four small private rooms and two dorm rooms in town. A strong cup of coffee is always on offer here, as well as healthy and vegetarian food in their restaurant.

At ★ **Mi Casa Guatape** (tel. 4/861-0632, cell tel. 301/457-5726, www.micasaguatape. com, COP$30,000 dorm, COP$70,000 d) guests wake up, step outside with a cup of coffee in hand, and greet their neighbor, La Piedra, with a warm *buenos días*. You can't get much closer to that big rock than from this small English-Colombian hostel. The hostel has five private rooms and one four-bed dorm as well as two kitchens for use. When not outdoors climbing La Piedra or taking the hostel's kayak for a spin, guests can laze in hammocks on the deck, watch movies, or bond with the owners' sweet dog. Mi Casa works closely with next-door neighbor **Adventure Activities** (cell tel. 301/411-4442), a group that organizes an intense-rock climbing excursion to one of dozens of routes up La Piedra (COP$90,000, 4-5 hours), as well as other outings. Owner Sean takes guests on a waterfall hike (6 km/4 miles round-trip, COP$15,000, 4 hours). It's easy to go into town from the hostel by catching a ride with a passing Jeep or with Mi Casa's preferred *mototaxi* driver. Mi Casa is about three kilometers before Guatapé on the main road (25-min. walk or COP$1,500 taxi ride) and is across the street from the landmark El Estadero La Mona.

There are a couple of upscale hotels in town. **Hotel Portobello** (Cl. 32 No. 28-29, tel. 4/861-0016, cell tel. 312/783-4050, www.hotelportobeloguatape.com, COP$215,000 d) has 16 rooms, and most of them have a view of the lake. You can obtain a 25 percent discount during the week if you pay in cash.

Transportation

There is frequent bus service from Medellín's north terminal to Guatapé. The trip takes about two hours and costs COP$13,000. Buses depart Guatapé at a waterfront bus terminal that was completed in 2013. It's just one block from the main plaza. Buses returning to Medellín often fill up in a hurry on Sundays, especially during holidays. If you are relying on public transportation, book your return bus trip early. The last bus for Medellín departs at 6:30pm.

Southern Antioquia

★ JARDÍN

Sometimes place-names fit perfectly. Such is the case with the picture-perfect Antioquian town of Jardín. The main park gushes year-round with trees and flowers that are always in bloom, and even the streets are corridors of color, lined with one brightly painted house after another.

The word is out about Jardín. Even still, if you arrive during the week, you'll feel like you've stumbled upon something special. On weekends, and especially holidays, a festive atmosphere fills the air, and the Plaza Principal buzzes with activity. The colorful town is an attraction in itself (especially for shutterbugs), but the cloud forests nearby—with caves, waterfalls, and birds aplenty—provide reasons for lacing up those hiking boots.

Sights

The **Parque Principal** is the center of life in Jardín. It's full of colorful wooden chairs, flower gardens, tall trees that provide welcome shade, and an endless cast of characters passing through, hanging out, or sipping a coffee. Prominent on the east side of the park is the neo-gothic cathedral the **Basílica Menor de la Inmaculada Concepción** (Cra. 3 No. 10-71, mass 11am daily), a 20th-century construction with a striking interior painted in shades of turquoise.

The **Museo Clara Rojas** (Cra. 5 No. 9-31, tel. 6/845-5652, http://mcrpjardin.blogspot.com, 8am-noon and 2pm-6pm daily, COP$2,000) has 19th-century period furniture and relics from the *colonización antioqueña*, as well as a small collection of religious art, including a painting of Jesus as a child surrounded by lambs with medals hanging around their necks. The town's tourism office is behind the facility, operating the same hours as the museum.

Recreation

There's almost no better Jardín plan than taking a morning walk. You'll be enchanted by the scenery, reinvigorated by the fresh air, and perhaps get the heart rate up a little as you explore the countryside. There are two fairly easy walks that can be done in a couple of hours and are manageable without a guide; if you get lost, there's always a kind local to point you in the right direction. The first is the **Camino Herrera,** which begins at the sweets shop Dulces del Jardín (Cl. 13 No. 5-47), and leads to two waterfalls—Casacada del Amor and Cascada Escondida—a swimming hole, and the Garrucha gondola. The second walk is the **Camino La Salada,** which starts at the Liceo San Antonio (Cl. 16 with Cra. 5) and takes you to the 55-meter (174-foot) Cascada Escalera waterfall and Cristo Rey hill, from where you can return via mini chairlift.

Jardín has not one, but two mini chairlifts in town. The **Cable Aéreo** (8am-6pm daily, COP$5,000 round-trip) goes up to the Cristo Rey hill. The other, more rustic **La Garrucha** (8am-6pm daily, COP$4,000) goes across town. Although these are popular with tourists, they were built so that rural farmers would have an easier way to bring their coffee and other crops to market.

BIRDING

The mountainous countryside near Jardín is a fabulous habitat for birds, including the yellow-eared parrot *(Ognorhynchus icterotis),* which makes its nest in *palma de cera* (wax palm) trees. Both of these—the birds and the trees—are threatened. Dozens of bird species have been spotted here, as well as the next-to-impossible-to-glimpse pumas and famed *oso de anteojos* (an Andean bear), which live deep in the jungle.

It's easy to view birds in the area, and you don't have to join up with a flock of other tourists to go on a bird-watching expedition. On the road toward the town of Riosucio (Caldas) to the south of Jardín is an excellent spot to view birds—as well as hike, mountain bike, or wander. This area is called **Alto de Ventanas.** Many visitors head up here early in the morning and walk along the main road to observe birds. A good place to start is just a couple of kilometers beyond the highest peak on the right-hand side at **Lucia's farm.** For a small fee, Lucia will prepare breakfast for you; as you sip your locally grown coffee, you'll be treated to visits by hummingbirds, and more than likely, flocks of yellow-eared parrots will fly by. Rufous antpittas, chestnut-naped antpittas, Munchique wood wrens, tanagers, and the critically endangered dusky starfrontlet may also make cameos. Call Lucia (cell tel. 314/683-7549) or her son Octavio (cell tel. 313/686-1631 or 312/715-4711) in advance so they'll know to expect you and how you like your eggs; they'll also give you specific directions. To get to Ventanas, there is a bus that departs Jardín at 8am, which may arrive too late for optimal bird-watching. Alternatively, you can arrange for private transportation (COP$200,000 round-trip). Note that the area's high elevation (1,900-3,000 meters) means

Jardín

Devils of Riosucio

Every two years in January, in the sleepy coffee- and plantain-growing town of Riosucio in northern Caldas near the Antioquian town of Jardín, residents (and a growing number of visitors) commune with the devil during the revelry of the **Carnaval de Riosucio.** This festival, one of the most beloved in the region, has an interesting story. It began out of a plea made by local priests for two feuding pueblos of Riosucio—the gold-mining village of Quiebralomo and La Montaña, home to a large indigenous population—to get along. In 1847 both communities were nudged to participate in that year's Three Kings Day commemoration and to set aside their differences, temporarily at least. If they didn't come together that year in peace, they would invite the wrath of the devil.

Over time, it was that last bit that resonated with the townspeople. From that 1847 onward, groups of families, friends, and neighbors would get together and create elaborate floats and costumes, seemingly in homage to the devil over this five-day celebration. The festival is run by the República del Carnaval, which reigns over the town during that time, and the culmination of the event is the ceremonial burning of an effigy of the devil. The festival gets going on the first Friday of January, with the most colorful activities taking place on Sunday.

temperatures can dip as low as 4°C (39°F). Warm clothing and layers are essential; rubber boots, not so much.

La Esperanza (cell tel. 312/837-0782, US$80 pp all meals incl.) is a nonprofit nature reserve dedicated to habitat preservation, education, and research. It's set on a mountain ridge 15 minutes from town. Sunrises, with a view to Jardín, and sunsets, looking out toward the mountains of Los Farallones de Citará, cannot be beat. The facility is run by an American, Doug Knapp. A jack of many trades, birder Knapp built four comfortable cabins for birding enthusiasts complete with

siesta-friendly decks and natural light pouring through the windows. He's also carved out some forest paths that meander through the property. Oh, and he cooks, too. At La Esperanza, you don't have to go far to catch a glimpse of some spectacular birds. Knapp's colleagues have documented the presence of eight special and endemic birds, including the Parker's antbird, whiskered wren, and Colombian chachalaca. Of the close to 400 species estimated to live in the Jardín area, this site now has registered 175. Also present are numerous mammals: the newly discovered olinguito (a big deal), the tayra, two-toed treesloth, aquatic opossum, northern tamandua (a tree anteater), and western night monkey.

Another birding option is just a five-minute walk from the Parque Principal, at a site where you can observe the Andean cock-of-the-rock (*Rupicola peruvianus*). Flocks of 5-15 of these gorgeous birds, native to the cloud forest, can be seen here. Males of this species have bright orange plumage on their heads and put on a show, usually in the early morning and early evening, at this roosting site where they compete for the attention of females (lekking). To find out how to get to the site, go to **Las Margaritas restaurant** at the park and inquire about the *gallitos de roca*, as they are called, or contact Olga or Orlando at cell tel. 312/756-2650 so that they will open the gate and let you in to the observation deck they have built; you'll have to pay a fee for this, under COP$15,000.

TOURS

One of the most popular excursions in the area is to the **Cueva El Esplendor** (Vereda La Linda, COP$7,000 entrance fee, COP$70,000 tour incl. lunch and entrance), a cave through which waters cascade into a chilly natural pool. You can walk to the cave independently, but it'll be a long day; most choose to go by horseback. Groups typically meet in the Parque Principal at around 8am, then take a Jeep Willy about 20 minutes to the Alto de la Rosa farm, where they are paired with their companion horse. There are a couple of river crossings, so rubber boots will be needed (inquire about this). A country lunch is provided, and you may visit a farm where they make *panela* (brown sugar loaf). To organize a tour, contact Bernardo López (cell tel. 314/714-2021), who offers horseback riding excursions. Alternatively, you can go with **Original Travel** (Cra. 4 No. 8-64, cell tel. 301/286-1144) or **Condor de los Andes** (tel. 4/845-5374, cell tel. 311/746-1985, condordelosandes@colombia.com).

For a taste of campesino life, take the **Finca Los Ángeles Coffee Tour** (Vereda La Casiana, cell tel. 300/774-9395, COP$30,000 pp). At this family farm outside of town, you'll take part in a standard coffee tour, and then sit down together for a delicious home-cooked meal. To participate, you must reserve at least 24 hours beforehand.

Food

At **Las Margaritas** (Cra. 3 No. 9-68, tel. 4/845-6651, 7am-9pm daily, COP$15,000), the specialty is *pollo a la Margarita* (chicken fried with a Parmesan cheese breading). This back-to-Paisa-basics place is good for a hearty breakfast. Vegetarians will appreciate a generous morning serving of *calentado* (beans and rice). If you want to add some juice (not a part of the typical Paisa breakfast), there is a juice stall two doors down from Las Margaritas, as well as fruit vendors in the park. The *tienda* (store) next door often has fresh Colombian pastries, such as *almojabanas* (cheese rolls) and *pandebonos* (delicious pastries made of yuca flour and cheese).

It's a weekend ritual in Jardín: spend the afternoon with family and friends at one of the *trucheras* (trout farms). One of the largest and best known of these is **La Truchería** (Km. 5 Vía Riosucio, tel. 4/845-5159, noon-6pm daily, COP$18,000). Trout is served infinite ways here: *a la mostaza* (mustard), with fine herbs, and stuffed with vegetables, to name a few.

Soft candlelight and a little rare ambience—along with delish pizza and wine—are served up at ★ **Café Europa** (Cl. 8 No. 4-02, cell tel. 312/230-2842, 4pm-10pm daily). You'll

want to settle in and get comfortable at this corner restaurant run by a German photographer and travel writer.

The menu at **Pastelatte** (Cra. 4 No. 8-45, cell tel. 301/482-3908, noon-8:30pm Wed.-Mon., COP$14,000) features crepes, cheesecakes, coffee, sandwiches, and pastas, and service is speedy and always with a smile. **Trigo y Centeno Crepes** (Cl. 9 No. 2-57, cell tel 315/258-3686) is a quaint café that specializes in French food—including rather massive crepes and drinks.

★ **Café Macanas** (Cra. 5 No. 9-43, cell tel. 313/657-5979) wins with its appealing decor and outdoor seating. It also has great pastries and light meals. After lunch you can buy a bag of coffee from Don Dario's farm.

Dulces del Jardín (Cl. 13 No. 5-47, tel. 4/845-6584, 8am-6pm Mon.-Sat.) is the candymaker in town. In addition to *arequipe* (caramel) sweets, they make all-natural jams and fruit spreads (COP$6,000) from pineapple, coconut, and papaya.

Accommodations

If you are planning to visit Jardín on a *puente* (long weekend) or during holidays, you will need to make a reservation at a hotel well in advance. On regular weekends, there is usually no problem in finding a hotel, although the best options do tend to fill up. During the week, the town is yours, and prices drop substantially (especially if you plan to pay in cash).

★ **Casa Selva y Café** (Cabaña La Isla-Vereda Quebrada Bonita, tel. 4/845-5430, cell tel. 318/518-7171, www.hostalselvaycafe.com, COP$40,000 dorm, COP$1000,000 d) is a cozy countryside spot, about a 30-minute walk away from the hustle and bustle of Jardín city life. Located behind a little pond surrounded by flowers and fruit trees, and with a backdrop of pastureland and mountains, it is pure peace here. This spot is simple: just a single wooden cabin with a dorm rooms (three beds) and four private rooms. Alexandra, the owner, is a yoga teacher, and when the weather cooperates, she may be up for holding a class outside. She also offers a day trip to some remote waterfalls called the Chorros de Tapartó to the northwest of town, near Andes.

Hotel Casa Grande (Cl. 8 No. 4-33, tel. 4/845-5487, cell tel. 311/340-2207, www.hotelcasagrande.co, COP$30,000 pp) features 12 rooms that have a capacity of 2-5 persons each. Most rooms have 2-4 beds to accommodate families. Breakfast is included in the price, and dinner can be arranged at the hotel as well. The friendly owner, a Jardín native, can supply tourist information for the area.

Want a front-row seat to park action? **Hotel Valdivia Plaza** (Parque Principal, next to the Museo Clara Rojas, tel. 4/845-5055, cell tel. 316/528-1047, COP$58,000 d) has 20 rooms and is clean, yet not bursting with personality. Splurge for a room with a private balcony and view. Across the park is **Hotel Jardín** (Cra. 3 No. 9-14, cell tel. 310/380-6724, COP$40,000 pp),with 11 spacious and modern apartments with a capacity of 4-8 persons each. It's a bargain. This is the most colorful house in this colorful town, with orange, yellow, red, and blue balconies, doors, and trim.

A comfortable, if conservative, choice is **Comfenalco Hotel Hacienda Balandú** (Km. 1 Vía Jardín Riosucio, tel. 4/845-5561, COP$158,000 d), a hotel with all the extras: restaurant, sauna, and heated swimming pool. It's a tranquil 15- to 20-minute walk from town.

Transportation

The bus company **Transportes Suroeste Antioqueño** (tel. 4/352-9049, COP$18,000) leaves Medellín each day bound for Jardín, leaving from the Terminal de Transportes Sur.

There is also one bus at 6:30am that departs for Manizales to the south from Jardín. This route goes through the town of Riosucio. From there you can board a *chiva* (rural bus) bound for Jardín. These depart at 8am and 3pm everyday except on Saturday, when there's one departure at noon. It's a bumpy three-hour journey from Riosucio to Jardín.

JERICÓ

Set on a gentle slope of a mountain overlooking a valley dotted with cattle ranches and coffee, tomato, plantain, and cardamom farms, Jericó is still a Paisa cowboy outpost. Colombians know Jericó for two very different reasons. The first is its unique handicraft, the *carriel*, a shoulder bag made from leather and cowhide that is a symbol of Paisa cowboy culture. The second is its homegrown saint, Laura Montoya, who was canonized in 2013. Jericó is a pleasant place to hang one's (cowboy) hat for a night or two, and its sleepy, sloping streets lined with brightly colored wooden balconies and doors are a playground for shutterbugs. Just don't visit Jericó on Wednesdays: Everything is closed.

Sights

The **Catedral de Nuestra Señora de las Mercedes** (Cl. 7 No. 4-34, Plaza de Bolívar, tel. 4/852-3494) is a brick construction that towers over the Parque Reyes. The cathedral is where Laura Montoya was officially declared a saint (Colombia's first) during a ceremony in 2013. Born into poverty in 1874 and raised by her grandmother, Montoya made her mark as a missionary to indigenous people. At the entrance to the cathedral, there is a bronze statue of the saint alongside an indigenous child, representing Montoya's devotion to assisting impoverished communities in remote areas. Locals are very proud of her, their favorite daughter.

Below the cathedral is the **Museo de Arte Religioso** (Cl. 7 No. 4-34, Plaza de Bolívar, tel. 4/852-3494, 8:30am-noon and 1:30pm-6pm Mon.-Fri., 8:30am-6pm Sat., 9am-noon and 1:30pm-5:30pm Sun., COP$2,000), in which religious art and ceremonial items from the colonial period onward are on display.

The **Museo de Jericó Antioquia** (MAJA, Cl. 7 between Cras. 5-6, tel. 4/852-4045, cell tel. 311/628-8325, 8am-noon and 1:30pm-6pm Mon.-Fri., 9am-5pm Sat.-Sun., COP$2,000) is mostly an archaeology museum, featuring ceramics and other items from the Emberá indigenous group of western Colombia, but there is also space devoted to contemporary Antioquian artists. The museum shows art films on Monday evenings and hosts occasional concerts.

The **Centro Historia de Jericó** (Cra. 4 No. 8-51, tel. 6/852-3481, www.centrodehistoriajerico.org, 8am-11am and 3pm-5pm Mon.-Tues. and Thurs.-Fri., donations accepted) has an art collection of around 130 works, along with exhibition spaces and a small library.

Shopping

To find your very own *carriel* shoulder bag or another leather souvenir from Jericó, walk down Carrera 5 around Calle 5. The classic *carriel* goes for about COP$130,000. *Carrieles* were used by *arrieros* (Paisa cowboys) for their horseback trips around Tierra Paisa. These bags are accordion-like, with several divisions in them for carrying items like money, a lock of hair, a knife, or a candle. Some suspect that the name *carriel* is derived from the English "carry all," while others say it comes from the French *cartier*, or handbag. It has been historically a masculine trade, but two young women are making names for themselves for their award-winning *carrieles* and other accessories. Their store is called **Carriel Arte**

the colorful Paisa town of Jericó

Jerico (Cra. 3 No. 7-03, tel. 4/852-4063, www. carrielarte.com).

Jericó is Colombia's cardamom capital—who knew? **Delicias del Cardamomo** (Cra. 5 No. 2-128, tel. 4/852-5289, 9am-6pm daily) pushes cardamom everything: candies, cookies, and plain old seeds.

Food

While tourist sights and most shops are closed on Wednesdays, many restaurants are open.

There are quite a few restaurant and café options along the east side of the Parque Principal. In the late afternoon, the entire length of one side of the plaza is full of folks enjoying a *tinto* (coffee) and watching the comings and goings of townspeople milling about the plaza. A meal with a view is the selling point of **El Balcón Restaurante** (Parque Principal, Cra. 4 No. 6-26, tel. 4/852-3191, cell tel. 311/784-4419, 8am-9pm daily, COP$15,000). From its perch on a balcony, you have front-row seats to the action below in the plaza and a nice vista of the mountains in the distance. The Colombian dishes are filling.

Other local favorites include **Montaña Parilla Burger** (Cra. 4 No. 6-20, 2nd Fl., tel. 4/ 852-3021) for hamburgers and grilled

meats, and **Terra Santa** (Cl. 7 No. 5-22, tel. 4/ 852-3072), which has a little of everything.

On the Calle de los Poetas, **Café Saturia** (Cl. 5 No. 4-27, cell tel. 314/815-3437) features a variety of local coffees, and you can see the beans being roasted on-site (and delight in the aroma).

For dessert, enjoy a local delicacy: *postre Jericoano*. This very sweet treat has been enjoyed by locals for a century. It's a cake of seven creamy and cookie layers, doused in rum. The real deal takes two weeks to prepare. It is sold in stalls run by local women at Calle 6 with Carrera 6.

Accommodations

As in all Colombian pueblos, room rates tend to drop during the week.

★ **Hotel El Despertar** (Cra. 6 No. 8-29, tel. 4/852-4050, www.eldespertarhotel.com, COP$150,000 pp) is a boutique-ish option in which two old houses were meticulously refurbished and joined. A hot tub and views of the Río Piedras valley are included.

The best value in town is the **Casa Grande** (Cl. 7 No. 5-54, tel. 4/852-3229, cell tel. 311/329-2144, COP$40,000 pp). It's a nicely renovated old house with 15 simple rooms. Rooms facing the street are preferable. **Hotel Portón Plaza** (Cl. 7 No. 3-25, tel. 4/852-3009, cell tel. 313/732-3568, www.hotelportonplazajerico.com, COP$35,000 pp) runs a close second, although it's much larger. It is just off the plaza. Ask for room 209 for a good view, or a 2nd-floor room with a view over the street.

Hostal las Cometas (Cra. 5 No. 10-16, cell tel. 313/233-6786, www.lascometashostal.com, COP$20,000 pp dorm), diagonal from the hospital, is one of the first hostels in town geared toward international budget travelers. The main house is over 100 years old and is made in the traditional *bareque* construction method, with wooden floors and an interior

courtyard with orange and guava trees. Some rooms are small, and decorated with kites on the walls. There are some private rooms with their own baths. It's a 10-minute walk from town.

Set in pure nature is the ★ **Centro Ecoturístic La Nohelia** (Vereda Buga, Vía Antigua Jericó, tel. 4/842-3567, cell tel. 310/384-5206, www.lanohelia.com, COP$30,000 pp), around four kilometers from town. Accommodations are generally in cabins almost entirely built with *guadua*. It offers a range of activities for guests and nonguests alike, such as a tour of a coffee farm (COP$50,000 pp), hikes to waterfalls, and Jeep trips to the Río Cauca canyon (COP$86,000 pp).

Information and Services

There is a small **tourist office** in the 1st floor of the Alcaldía Municipal building next to the cathedral. A recommended English-speaking guide is **Walter Montoya Suárez** (cell tel. 319/467-8320, walmontsur@hotmail.com). **Turísmo Jericó** (Cl. 7 No. 3-31, tel. 4/852-3065, cell tel. 314/651-4030, www.turismojerico.com) is a locally run agency specializing in outdoor adventures in and around Jericó, as well as walking tours of town.

Transportation

From Medellín, there is regular bus service (Transportes Jericó) from the Terminal del Sur (COP$25,000), starting at 5am and going until 6pm. Buses arrive and depart Jericó from the **Parque Principal.**

To get to Jardín from Jericó, you must take a *chiva* (rural bus) to the town of Andes (two buses daily) or to the town of Peñalisa and transfer there to Jardín. It's easier to go to Peñalisa (COP$6,000), because you can just hop on a bus bound for Medellín that passes through there. The ride from Peñalisa to Jardín costs about COP$12,000.

The Coffee Region

Blessed with lush, tropical vegetation, meticulously manicured countryside dotted with beautiful haciendas and towns, spring-like weather, and a backdrop of massive, snow-capped mountains, Colombia's coffee region is almost Eden. Nature here is a thousand shades of green: bright green bamboo groves, emerald-colored forests with spots of white *yarumo* trees, dark green coffee groves, and green-blue mountains in the distance punctuated by brightly colored flowers and polychromatic butterflies and birds.

Though the main cities and many towns lack charm, dozens of well-preserved villages offer colorful balcony-clad buildings. Life in most of these towns remains untouched by tourism. A visit on market day, with bustling streets jammed with Jeeps and plentiful goods, is a memorable one.

And then there is coffee. It is true that Brazil and Vietnam are the world's top coffee producers, but arabica beans are grown throughout Colombia. Coffee grown in some parts of the country (such as Cauca and Nariño) is considered superior to that from this region, but here, more than anywhere else, coffee is an inseparable part of Paisa identity. While the extent of land devoted to coffee farming is diminishing, the numbers are still impressive: The department of Caldas contains over 80,000 hectares (200,000 acres) of coffee farms; Risaralda, 52,000 hectares (128,000 acres); and Quindío, 30,000 hectares (74,000 acres). Visit a coffee farm to understand the laborious production process or—even better—stay overnight.

In pre-Columbian times, this region was inhabited by the Quimbaya people. In 1537, Spanish conquistador Sebastián de Belalcázar conquered the region as he moved north from Ecuador toward the central Muisca region. Due to the sparse indigenous population and lack of precious metals, the region, which was governed from faraway Popayán, was largely uninhabited during most of the colonial period.

Planning Your Time

It's hard to go wrong as a tourist in the coffee region. No matter your starting point or home base, an immersion in coffee culture is easy, nearby, and rewarding. If you can, plan to spend about five days in this most pleasant part of Colombia. In that time you can stay at a coffee hacienda, visit a natural park, and tour a picture-perfect pueblo.

However, if time is short, a quick visit can be equally as rewarding. With easy transportation links to the major cities of the region and excellent tourism infrastructure to meet all budget needs, Salento has the trifecta of coffee region attractions: It's a cute pueblo, coffee farms are within minutes of the main plaza, and jungle hikes that lead through tropical forest to the Valle de Cocora are easy to organize. The town gets packed with visitors on weekends and during holidays, resulting in a more festive atmosphere, but also traffic jams.

Another option is to stay a couple of days at a hacienda. You can leisurely explore the farms and countryside, relax, and possibly go for a day trip or two to a nearby attraction. Many haciendas are high-end, like Hacienda Bambusa, Finca Villa Nora, and Hacienda San José. However, budget travelers can also enjoy the unique atmosphere of hacienda life at Hacienda Guayabal outside of Manizales and Finca El Ocaso in Salento. Meanwhile, Hacienda Venecia has something for travelers of all budgets.

For birders, the lush region offers many parks and gardens to marvel at the hundreds of species in the area. The Reserva del Río Blanco near Manizales, Jardín Botánico del Quindío near Armenia, and the Santuario de Flora y Fauna Otún-Quimbaya near Pereira are within minutes of the city, guided walks

The Birth of the Coffee Economy

During the 19th century, demographic pressures spurred settlers from the northwestern province of Antioquia to migrate south, giving origin to what is known as the *colonización antioqueña*. For this reason, the coffee region is akin to Antioquia, with similar dialect, cuisine, and architecture. As the settlers made their way south, they founded towns and started farms: Salamina was established in 1825, Manizales in 1849, Filandia in 1878, and Armenia in 1889.

The region prospered enormously throughout the 20th century due to ideal conditions for producing coffee. The Colombian National Coffee Federation, owner of the Juan Valdez brand, provided technical assistance, developed infrastructure, and helped stabilize prices. High international coffee prices during the 1980s and 1990s made the region one of the most prosperous areas in the country.

The fall of global coffee prices in the past decade has forced the region to reinvent itself. Rather than produce a low-value commodity, many farmers have invested in producing high-quality strains that fetch much higher prices. Growers have also diversified, planting other crops, such as plantains, often interspersed through coffee plantations. Finally, agro- and ecotourism has provided a much-needed new source of revenue.

are regularly offered, and birdlife is abundant. Outside of metropolitan areas, the Parque Municipal Natural Planes de San Rafael, which adjoins the Parque Nacional Natural Tatamá, is less known, but is a natural paradise.

Day trips to natural parks, including the Parque Nacional Natural Los Nevados, are easily organized. PNN Los Nevados is home to *páramos* (highland moors), lunar landscapes, and snowcapped volcanoes. It can be accessed from many points, and it can even be visited by car. Multiple day treks offer challenges.

If there were a Cute Pueblo Region of Colombia, this might be it. While you'll have more flexibility driving your own vehicle, it's easy to check out a pueblo or two from the region's major cities traveling by public transportation. A night or two is enough to embrace village life.

MANIZALES

The capital of the Caldas department, pleasant and easygoing Manizales (pop. 393,200) is the region's mountain city. Instead of developing in a lowland valley like Armenia or Pereira, Manizales is set atop meandering mountain ridges. This location means that getting around town involves huffing and puffing up and down hills on foot, enduring roller coaster-like bus or taxi rides along curvy roads, or taking the scenic route on the city's expanding Cable Aéreo gondola network.

Perched above lush coffee farms below, at an altitude of 2,160 meters (7,085 feet), spectacular views abound in Manizales—but only when the sky is *despejado* (clear). On those days, you might see the peaks of the Parque Nacional Natural Los Nevados in the distance. It's easy to visit that park—as well as other natural sights—with Manizales as one's base.

Sights

The two main drags in Manizales—Avenida Santander (Carrera 23) and the Paralela (Carrera 25)—will take you to where you want to go in town. They connect the Zona Rosa/El Cable area with downtown and with Avenida 12 de October, which leads to Chipre and the Monumento a los Colonizadores.

CENTRO

Downtown Manizales is bustling with activity during weekdays but vacates in a hurry in the evenings. There aren't many sights of interest, save for some Republican-period architecture and some noteworthy churches.

Manizales

The **Plaza de Bolívar** (Cras. 21-22 and Clls. 22-23) holds an odd sculpture to honor Simón Bolívar created by Antioqueño Rodrigo Arenas Betancourt. It's known as the *Condor-Bolívar,* portraying the Liberator with a body of a condor, the national bird. On the north side of the plaza is a **tourist office.**

On the south side of the plaza, the neogothic **Catedral Basílica de Manizales** (Cra. 22 No. 22-15, tel. 6/883-1880, open until 6:30pm daily) is imposing. Construction began in the late 1920s and was completed in 1936. It replaced the previous cathedral on the same spot, which had been damaged by earthquakes and had to be demolished. For 360-degree views of Manizales and beyond, climb the 500 steps of the spiral Corredor Polaco

(the Polish corridor) in Colombia's tallest church tower. To climb the tower, a guide is required (COP$10,000), although it's hard to imagine getting lost inside. The tower is open 9am-noon and 2pm-5pm Thursday-Sunday. A cathedral café serves sadly mediocre coffee, but the view is nice.

Not as grandiose as the cathedral a couple of blocks away, the interior of the **Inmaculada Concepción** (Cl. 30 at Cra. 22, in the Parque Caldas, tel. 6/883-5474, 7am-noon and 2pm-6:30pm daily) is much more beautiful. The neo-gothic-style church, completed in 1909, was built with *bahareque* and *guadua,* natural materials used in construction across Colombia. The wooden rib vaulted ceiling is made of cedar, as are the columns and pews.

CHIPRE

This neighborhood to the west of downtown is known for its views and sunsets. Manizaleños like to boast how Chilean poet Pablo Neruda, when strolling on the promenade in Chipre along Avenida 12 de Octubre, marveled at this "sunset factory." You're guaranteed a nice vista from atop the futuristic lookout tower **La Torre al Cielo** (tel. 6/883-8311, 8am-8pm daily, COP$2,000).

At the far end of the walkway is the **Monumento a los Colonizadores** (Av. 12 de Octubre and Cra. 9, tel. 6/872-0420, ext. 22, 10am-6pm daily, free), designed by Luis Guillermo Vallejo. This monument honors the courage and sacrifice of Antioquian colonizers who settled the city. It depicts an Antioquian family on horseback and on foot forging ahead, with cattle in tow, to this part of Colombia during the *colonización antioqueña,* when hundreds of families migrated from Medellín to settle farms in the coffee region. Manizales residents played a role in building the monument by donating keys and the like to be melted and used in its construction. The sculpture stands atop 20 tons of *piedra de mani* (peanut stone), the namesake for the city. It was inaugurated in 2001. To get to this part of the city, look for a bus with a "Chipre" sign along Avenida Santander (Cra. 23).

EL CABLE

One of the city's icons is a soaring wooden tower known as **El Cable** (52 meters/171 feet tall) that once supported the unusual gondola system that transported coffee (10 tons per hour), other materials, and sometimes people from Manizales over the Central Cordillera. The system reached elevations of 3,700 meters (12,100 feet) and descended to the town of Mariquita (495 meters/1,625 feet). From there the coffee would be transported overland to Honda on the banks of the Río Magdalena. The rest of the journey in Colombia would take the coffee north to the port city of Barranquilla, where it would be transferred to big boats bound for North America and Europe. This system was developed in the 1920s and would last until the early 1960s.

Of the 376 towers that supported the line, this tower, which was in the town of Herveo, was the only one built out of wood (all the others were made of iron). They were all supposed to be made of iron, but the boat carrying one of them from Europe to Colombia was sunk by a German submarine in the Atlantic Ocean during World War I. An English engineer in Colombia, who also designed the neat **Estación del Cable,** the adjacent station for the cable transport system, designed this tower using wood found locally.

RESERVA DEL RÍO BLANCO

Nearly 400 species of birds have been spotted at the **Reserva del Río Blanco** (Vereda Las Palomas, tel. 6/887-9770, cell tel. 311/775-5159, reservarioblanco@aguasdemanizales.com.co, 6am-6pm daily, COP$20,000 entrance), only three kilometers (two miles) outside of Manizales. From August to March the area receives many migratory birds from North America. This reserve is a must-do for serious international birders visiting the country.

An *oso anteojo andino* (Andean bear) that lived in captivity for most of his life was adopted and now lives in an enclosed field in the reserve near the cabins. It was decided that he would not be able to be released back into the wild.

It's a cumbersome process to obtain permission to visit the reserve and organize a birdwatching day trip—but not impossible. Most visitors ask front desk staff at hostels or hotels to set things up for them. A half-day guided hike costs COP$45,000 per person; some guides speak English. To see birds at their most active, consider staying overnight in one of the park's two **cabins** (tel. 6/870-3810, cell tel. 310/422-1883, COP$70,000 pp). These have a total of eight rooms, and meals are available as well. Hummingbird feeders dangle along the deck, and there are nearly always customers to be seen. Taxi transportation to the reserve entrance costs COP$30,000 from Manizales.

RECINTO DEL PENSAMIENTO

For a walk in the park, the **Recinto del Pensamiento** (Km. 11 Vía al Magdalena, tel. 6/889-7073, ext. 2990, www.recintodel-pensamiento.com, 9am-4pm Tues.-Sun., COP$20,000 guided walk and chairlift) is a tranquil green space with guided nature walks, a chairlift, a two-hectare orchid forest with 12,000 orchids, a butterfly farm, and a Japanese bonsai garden. The centerpiece of the park is the **Pabellón de Madera,** a large open-air event space made of *guadua* (a type of bamboo) and built by a renowned Colombian architect. It's possible to get there by taking a blue public bus (that says Maltería) from downtown Manizales (Cra. 20) for about COP$2,000.

ECOPARQUE LOS YARUMOS

On undisturbed mountainsides throughout Colombia, you have undoubtedly noticed the silvery-white leaves of the *yarumo blanco* tree. Should you get a closer look, you'll see that the leaves of this tree are actually green; they have a fuzzy outer layer that only makes them appear white. The **Ecoparque Los Yarumos** (Cl. 61B No. 15A-01, Barrio Toscana, tel. 6/872-0420, ext. 22, 9am-6pm Tues.-Sun., free) is named for those tricky trees. A few *yarumos* can be seen in the more than 50 hectares (125 acres) of cloud forest and green space that make up this park. Geared toward families, the park has nature paths, a lookout tower, and activities such as jungle zip lines. Get there by taking a bus from the Manizales city center bound for Minitas. It's about a 7- to 10-minute walk from the bus stop to the entrance. The Cable Aéreo is scheduled to reopen its station here in 2017, which will make for the most scenic way to arrive.

HOT SPRINGS

Near Manizales are three popular *termales* (hot springs). Bring your own towel and

For a nature walk, check out the Recinto del Pensamiento outside of Manizales.

sandals and visit on a weekday if you want to avoid the crowds.

Near the river, **Tierra Viva** (Km. 2 Vía Enea-Gallinazo, tel. 6/874-3089, www.termalestierraviva.com, 9am-midnight Mon.-Thurs., 9am-1am Fri.-Sun., COP$12,000-14,000) is closest to Manizales and less expensive. It consists of one pool, some bare-bones changing rooms, and a snack bar. A Gallinazo bus along Carrera 19 drops passengers off close to the springs for COP$2,000. You can also cab it for about COP$12,000.

With superior facilities to Tierra Viva, **Termales Otoño** (Km. 5 Vía Antigua El Nevado del Ruiz, tel. 6/874-0280, www.termaleselotono.com, 7am-midnight daily, day pass COP$40,000, hotel COP$107,000-356,000 d) is a hot spring-and-hotel complex a 25-minute ride (COP$15,000 taxi) southeast of the city. It's large, with four pools (though two of these are reserved exclusively for hotel guests).

One of the area's old mountain lodges has been given a much-needed facelift. The **Termales del Ruiz** (35 km south of

Manizales, cell tel. 310/455-3588, www.termalesdelruiz.com, COP$18,000 day pass) is the most picturesque of the region's hot springs, set at 3,500 meters (11,500 feet) elevation on the edge of the Parque Nacional Natural Los Nevados, about 35 kilometers (22 miles) from Manizales and 10 kilometers (6 miles) from its source, the Nevado del Ruiz volcano. There is one large thermal pool, as well as a nature path, and many bird species can be spotted on the mountain slopes. Believe it or not, in the 1950s, this lodge was the headquarters for international ski competitions. Those days are long gone; the snow has bid *adiós*. Rooms at the hotel are chilly at night but have been completely revamped and are luxurious, and the restaurant is good too. Day-trippers to PNN Los Nevados often stop here for a soak on the way back down to Manizales. There is no public transportation here, but you can hire a taxi from Manizales (about COP$190,000) or have your hotel arrange for a hired car (about COP$165,000).

Festivals and Events

The Plaza de Toros (Cra. 27 10A-07, tel. 6/883-8124, www.cormanizales.com), or bullfighting ring, is the heart of the action during Manizales's biggest annual bacchanal, the **Feria de Manizales** (www.feriademanizales.gov.co, Jan.). The festivities also include concerts, a ballad festival (Festival de Trova), and a Miss Coffee beauty pageant. This city-wide party is held in early January.

In June each year, jazz takes center stage at the Universidad de Caldas, the main university in town, during the **Temporada Internacional de Jazz** (June). Quartets from universities in the United States are often invited to perform in this event sponsored by the Centro Colombo Americano and the U.S. Embassy.

One of the country's top theater festivals is the **Festival Internacional de Teatro de Manizales** (www.festivaldemanizales.com, early Sept.). Theater troupes from Manizales and around Colombia, the Americas, and beyond perform in theaters throughout the city,

and free performances are given in the Plaza de Bolívar, El Cable, and other public spaces.

Sports and Recreation

The **Ciclovía** in Manizales takes place every Sunday from 8am to noon along Avenida Santander (Carrera 23) and other main streets. The last Thursday evening of each month a **Ciclovía Nocturna** (7pm-10pm) is held.

Once Caldas (www.oncecaldas.com.co) is the Manizales soccer club, and their stadium, the **Estadio Palogrande** (Cra. 25 No. 65-00), is in the Zona Rosa within walking distance of many hostels and hotels. Tickets can be purchased in the Cable Plaza Mall (Cra. 23 No. 65-11, tel. 6/875-6595, 9am-9pm daily).

TOURS

Horseback riding through the countryside is what **Hato Caravana Club de Caballería** (Ecoparque Río Claro-Villamaría Occidental, cell tel. 311/739-2845, www.hatocaravana.com, COP$80,000) is all about. Excursions usually begin at around 9am and end with a hearty lunch.

A handful of recommended and professional tour agencies specialize in day trips and multiday adventures in Parque Nacional Natural Los Nevados. These are **Kumanday** (Cl. 66 No. 23B-40), **Ecosistemas** (Cra. 21 No. 20-45, tel. 6/880-8300, cell tel. 312/705-7007, www.ecosistemastravel.com.co), and **Asdeguías** (Cl. 25 No. 20-25, Of. 7, tel. 6/884-4525). Kumanday is famous for its downhill mountain bike day tours, but it also offers multiday excursions in the park out of Manizales. Ecosistemas focuses on treks to the Nevado del Ruiz and Santa Isabel (COP$170,000).

Food

For excellent down-home, regional cuisine, head to ★ **Don Juaco** (Cl. 65 No. 23A-44, tel. 6/885-0610, cell tel. 310/830-2218, noon-10pm daily, COP$15,000), which has been serving contented diners for decades. Try the Paisa hamburger: a hamburger sandwiched in between two arepas (cornmeal cakes). Enjoy it or the popular set lunch meals on the pleasant terrace.

For delectable grilled meat dishes, **Palogrande** (Cra. 23C No. 64-18, tel. 6/885-3177, 11am-10pm daily, COP$25,000) is the place you want. Located on a quiet street, it's a rather elegant, open-air place with a nice atmosphere.

For Italian fare, there are two decent options. **Spago** (Cl. 59 No. 24A-06, Local 1, tel. 6/885-3328, cell tel. 321/712-3860, noon-3pm and 6pm-10pm Mon.-Sat., noon-3pm Sun., COP$25,000), one of the upmarket restaurants in town, has tasty thin-crust pizzas. **Il Forno** (Cra. 23 No. 73-86, tel. 6/886-8515, noon-10pm Mon.-Sat., noon-3pm Sun., COP$22,000) is a family-style chain restaurant with a view of the city.

Vegetarian restaurants exist in Manizales, but it can be difficult to find them. **Orellana** (Cra. 24 No. 51-59, tel. 6/885-3907, noon-3pm Mon.-Sat., COP$10,000) serves healthy set lunches from its spot in the Versalles neighborhood. It's near the supermarket Confamiliares de la 50. Vegetarians should rush to the Palogrande area and to ★ **Rushi** (Cra. 23C No. 62-73, tel. 6/881-0326, cell tel. 310/538-8387, 11am-9pm Mon.-Sat., 11am-3pm Sun., COP$12,000), where they can find plant-based lunch specials and veggie burgers made with many organic ingredients.

A fantastic place for a late-afternoon cappuccino and snack is ★ **Juan Valdez Café** (Cra. 23B No. 64-55, tel. 6/885-9172, 10am-9pm daily). Yes, it's a chain, and there's one in any self-respecting mall in Colombia. But this one is different: Locals proudly boast that it is the largest Juan Valdez on the planet. But what truly sets this one apart is its great location, under the shadow of the huge wooden tower that once supported the coffee cable car line that ran from Manizales to Mariquita.

Tablecloths, stylish presentation, and an extensive menu of seafood dishes set **Vino y Pimienta** (Cl. 77 No. 21-74, tel. 6/886-5571) apart from the rest.

Accommodations

The El Cable area in Manizales is the best place to stay thanks to its large number of lodging options and its proximity to restaurants and shopping centers. It's a quiet neighborhood that bustles with international visitors, particularly on Calle 66.

One of the long-standing budget accommodations in Manizales is **Mountain Hostels** (Cl. 66 No. 23B-91, tel. 6/887-4736, cell tel. 300/521-6120, www.mountainhostels.com.co, COP$22,000 dorm, COP$60,000 d). Spread over two houses, it has a variety of room types and a small restaurant where you can order a healthy breakfast. It's also a fantastic source of information.

Hostal Kumanday (Cl. 66 No. 23B-40, tel. 6/887-2682, cell tel. 315/590-7294, www.kumanday.com, COP$25,000 dorm, COP$40,000 pp d) is a quiet and clean option on the same street as Mountain Hostels. There are 10 rooms and one small dorm room, and all options include breakfast. Kumanday has its own, highly recommended tour agency that specializes in hiking in and around the Parque Nacional Natural Los Nevados.

Casa Lassio Hostal (Cl. 66 No. 23B-56, tel. 6/887-6056, cell tel. 310/443-8917, COP$23,000 dorm, COP$35,000 private room pp) has six rooms, and they also organize bike tours.

The Colombian chain Estelar (www.hotelesestelar.com) has three hotels in the Manizales area. They are among the top hotels in the city, and all have spacious and clean rooms, as well as at least one room that is accessible for people with disabilities. Weekend rates tend to be significantly lower than during the week. There are few reasons for wanting to stay in downtown Manizales, but if you do, **Hotel Estelar Las Colinas** (Cra. 22 No. 20-20, tel. 6/884-2009, COP$188,080 d) is the best option (but only on weekends, when traffic, noise, and general urban stress is manageable). The hotel's 60-some rooms are large and clean, but the restaurant and bar area is a little gloomy. A breakfast buffet is available for an additional cost.

The ★ **Estelar El Cable** (Cra. 23C No. 64A-60, tel. 6/887-9690, COP$294,000 d) has 46 rooms over nine floors and is the upscale option in the El Cable/Zona Rosa area. Breakfast and a light dinner are often included in room rates. Rooms are spacious and clean, with pressed wood floors. A small gym offers modern cardio machines.

If you prefer birds and trees, check out Estelar's 32-room hotel at the **Recinto del Pensamiento** (Km. 11 Vía al Magdalena, tel. 6/889-7077, COP$210,000 d). Outside the city, surrounded by nature, this hotel feels a little isolated. It's a popular place for business conferences and events during the week. Rooms are spacious.

Information and Services

A **Punto de Información Turística** (Cra. 22 at Cl. 31, tel. 6/873-3901, 7am-7pm daily) can be of assistance in organizing excursions to parks and coffee farms throughout Caldas. A small **tourist office** is also located in the main hall of the Terminal de Transportes (Cra. 43 No. 65-100).

In case of an emergency, Manizales has a single emergency line: 123.

Transportation

Avianca and **ADA** serve **Aeropuerto La Nubia** (tel. 6/874-5451), about 10 kilometers (six miles) southeast of downtown. The runway is often shrouded in clouds; because of this, the airport is closed 35 percent of the time and always at night.

There is regular and speedy **bus service** to both Armenia (COP$17,500, 2 hours) and Pereira (COP$11,000, 70 mins.). **Empresas Arauca** (www.empresaarauca.com.co) runs buses to Pereira every 15 minutes. Buses bound for Cali and Medellín cost around COP$35,000-40,000 and take five hours each. Buses to Bogotá cost COP$50,000 and take about nine hours.

The **Terminal de Transportes** (Cra. 43 No. 65-100, tel. 6/878-5641, www.terminal-demanizales.com) is spacious, orderly, and clean. From there it is about a 15-minute taxi

ride to the Zona Rosa area. The terminal adjoins the cable car **Cable Aéreo** station. The cable car route transports passengers from the terminal (Estación Cambulos) to the Fundadores station (Cra. 23 between Clls. 31-32) in the Centro.

Buses can get you where you want to go in Manizales, but you'll likely have to ask a local which one to take and where to flag it down. To get downtown from the Zona Rosa, take a bus bound for Chipre.

COFFEE FARMS

The Caldas countryside is home to coffee haciendas large and small. Hacienda Venecia and Hacienda Guayabal are two of the most highly recommended for coffee tours, as well as overnight stays. They are located near Chinchiná, only a 30-minute drive from Manizales. Many travelers comment that a day or two at one of these is the highlight of their trip to Colombia.

Hacienda Venecia

One of the most well-known, organized, and most visited coffee farms is **Hacienda Venecia** (Vereda El Rosario, Vía a Chinchiná, cell tel. 320/636-5719, www.haciendavenecia.com, coffee tour COP$50,000). This large working coffee plantation has been in the same family for four generations, and their coffee was the first in Colombia to receive UTZ certification for sustainable farming, in 2002. The farm is set far from the highway, providing a peaceful atmosphere; you're surrounded by coffee plants growing everywhere you look.

If you are day-tripping, organizing an excursion to the farm for a coffee tour is easy from Manizales. In fact, you won't have to do much at all except inform the hostel or hotel where you are staying that you'd like to go. The Hacienda Venecia makes a daily pickup at the main hostels in town at around 9am. Tours are given daily at 9:30am. The 2.5-hour tour begins with a comprehensive presentation of coffee-growing in Colombia and in the world, the many different aromas of coffee, and how to differentiate between a good bean and a bad bean. (And you'll be offered a knock-your-socks-off espresso to boot.) Later, the tour heads outside through the plantation, where you'll see coffee plants at all stages in the growing process. You'll also be able to observe the soaking and drying process. At the end, in the lovely original hacienda house, it's time to roast some beans and drink another freshly roasted cup of Venecia coffee. A typical and delicious lunch, such as *ajiaco* (chicken and potato soup), is offered as well (COP$15,000) at the end of the tour. A farm tour by Jeep and private tours can also be arranged, if requested in advance.

There are lodging options suitable for all budgets at Venecia: It's a big operation, attracting a United Nations of visitors every day. A hostel (COP$35,000 dorm), in the former quarters of coffee pickers, has three rooms, a social area, and a kitchen. Hostel guests can prepare their own breakfasts (ingredients provided) as well as other meals, or dine in the Casa de Huéspedes for an additional cost. In the Casa de Huéspedes (COP$135,000 d), which is the hub of activity at the farm, there are seven basic rooms, some with a private bath. And for those in search of charm, there is the Casa Principal (COP$400,000 d), the original house, dating back at least a century. It has six rooms, some with private bath, lovely common areas, and a beautiful *comedor* (dining room). It's not uncommon to see overlanding travelers drive up in their buses and campers. And, no matter where you stay, there's coffee on the house, all the time, and usually a hammock to sink into.

For those staying overnight, other activities at the farm include horseback riding (for an additional fee) or walks around the plantation on your own. A particularly pleasant activity in the early morning is to go on a self-guided birding walk, using the Venecia birding checklist. More than 117 species have been documented here. Guests are permitted to wander at their leisure on six trails.

Hacienda Guayabal

Hacienda Guayabal (Km. 3 Vía Chinchiná-Pereira, cell tel. 314/772-4856 or 315/540-7639,

lush countryside near Hacienda Guayabal

www.haciendaguayabal.com, tour COP$35,000, lodging COP$65,000 pp incl. breakfast) has a jaw-dropping setting, with mountains and valleys covered in coffee crops and *guadua* (bamboo) completely enveloping the hacienda. This hacienda has been in Doña María Teresa's family for over 50 years. This is a working coffee farm, and one of the pioneers in coffee farm tourism, but it's equally interesting to take a nature walk through the *guaduales* (forests of Colombia's bamboo) that tend to spring up along water sources.

If you come, you might as well stay, so that you can enjoy the peace and warm hospitality of this special place. While accommodations in the handful of rooms are not luxurious, they are more than adequate. There is a small cabin available as well, in the middle of nature. Meals are delicious, one of the things for which Guayabal is known. Tours around the *finca* (farm) take about two hours, and you learn about the coffee process as you maneuver along the orderly rows of coffee plants. In addition, you can hike up to a spectacular lookout on a mountainside for breathtaking views of the hills, the valleys, the forests, and the farms all around. Near the guesthouse just past the pool is a hut made from *guadua* with recycled floor tiles; it houses a small coffee bar where you can have a cup of coffee and wait for birds of every color and shape to fly up to nibble on a piece of banana. Tranquility is the watchword here, and it's no wonder Guayabal is occasionally host to meditation retreats. Ask about visiting the pueblo of Marsella from here; it makes a nice day trip.

To get to Guayabal, take an Autolujo bus (COP$3,000) or a shared taxi from Manizales to Chinchiná. From Chinchiná it's about COP$9,000 for a taxi to the hacienda. Regular cabs from Manizales are also an option.

★ SALAMINA

Designated as one of Colombia's most beautiful pueblos, Salamina features history, beauty, personality, and spectacular countryside; yet, for the most part, it remains off most tourists' radars. When you visit this historic town, you'll feel as if you have stumbled upon a hidden gem. The historic center of Salamina is marked by colorful and well-preserved two-story houses with their stunning woodwork, doors, and balconies. Salamina is often called the *pueblo madre* (mother town), as it was one of the first settlements of the Antioquian colonization. It's older than Manizales.

Sights

The **Plaza de Bolívar** (Clls. 4-5 between Cras. 6-7) is the center of activity in Salamina. It's an attractive plaza with a gazebo and large fountain brought over from Germany. Carried by mules over the mountains from the coast, it took a year to arrive, in several pieces, to its destination. The **Basílica Menor de la Inmaculada Concepción** (Cl. 4 between Cras. 6-7) has an unusual architecture. The single-nave worship hall is rectangular and flat with wooden beams and no columns. The church was designed by an English architect, who is said to have been inspired by the First Temple in ancient Jerusalem.

The **Casa Rodrigo Jiménez Mejía** (Cl. 4 and Cra. 6) is the most photographed house in Salamina. The colors of this exceptionally preserved structure were chosen in an interesting way. An owner of the house called kids from the town to gather in the plaza and to give the owner their proposal on what colors to use for the house's exterior. The winner was a four-year-old girl, who chose bright orange, yellow, and green.

The **Casa de la Cultura** (Cra. 6 No. 6-06, tel. 6/859-5016, 8am-noon and 2pm-5pm Mon.-Fri., free) displays photos of old Salamina. It's often a hub of activity. It's also known as the Casa del Diablo, for the wood-carving of a jovial devil above the door that greets visitors as they enter.

For decades, the **Cementerio San Esteban** (Cra. 3 between Clls. 2-4, no phone), the town cemetery, was divided into three sections: one for the rich, one for the poor, and another for so-called "N.N." bodies (nonidentified corpses, or "no names"). A wall was built to divide the rich from the poor, but it was knocked down at the behest of a priest in 1976. A skull and crossbones is displayed over the cemetery entrance. There is a small neo-gothic-style chapel (open occasionally) on the grounds.

In the village of **San Félix,** 30 kilometers (19 miles) east of Salamina, you can hike through serene countryside and admire a forest of 300-year-old *palmas de cera* (wax palms) from the hills above. It's as impressive as the Valle de Cocora, and without the crowds. Afterward, on the village plaza, ask at the stores for a refreshing *helado de salpicón* (ice cream made from chunks of fresh fruit in frozen watermelon juice). A bus makes the round-trip (COP$10,000 each way) to San Felix twice a day, once in the early morning and again in the afternoon. It leaves from the Plaza de Bolívar in Salamina.

Festivals and Events

Salamina's **Semana Santa** (Holy Week) celebrations, which fall in either March or April, are not that well known, but it is nonetheless a great time to get to know this cute town. Orchids and other flowers adorn the balconies of houses, adding even more color. In addition, free classical, religious, and jazz music concerts are held in churches, plazas, and even the cemetery.

San Felix is known for its **Exposición de Ganado Normando** in May, when local farmers show off their best Norman cows, with various competitions. It's an important event for ranchers throughout the region, and a chance to see an authentic display of Paisa culture.

Halloween is a big deal in Salamina. Here it's called the **Tarde de María La Parda,** named after a local woman who is said to have sold her soul to the devil to obtain riches. Her ghost supposedly causes mischief in the countryside every now and then. Events for Tarde de María La Parda take place in Plaza de Bolívar, and there are costume parties at night.

December 7 is a special day—or rather, night—to be in Salamina. That's when the lights are turned off in town, and the streets and balconies are illuminated with handmade lanterns made by locals. This beautiful celebration is called the **Noche de las Luces,** a night to stroll the streets and enjoy the special atmosphere. Locals greet each other serving sweets, snacks, or drinks. Music fills the air and the evening culminates in a fireworks show.

Food

One of the town's culinary specialties is *macana,* a hot drink made of milk, ground-up cookies, cinnamon, and sugar. The other is *huevos al vapor,* a boiled egg that is methodically steamed using giant coffee urns and served in a coffee cup.

Popular and atmospheric **Tierra Paisa** (no phone, 8am-9pm daily, COP$10,000), below the Hotel Colonial on the park, serves typical Colombian food, like *bandeja paisa* (a quintessential Paisa dish of beans, various meats, yuca, and potatoes), at incredibly low prices.

Accommodations

The best place to stay in Salamina by a long shot is the ★ **Casa de Lola Garcia** (Cl. 6 No. 7-54, tel. 6/859-5919, www.lacasadelolagarcia.com, COP$221,000 d, COP$84,000 dorm with breakfast), which opened its doors in 2012. The dream of a native Salamineño, musician Mauricio Cardona García, the carefully restored house was once the home of his

a friendly devil in Salamina

grandmother, Lola García. Rooms are spacious and on the luxurious side. If you provide Mauricio with some notice, meals at the hotel can be arranged. Mauricio and his staff are the best resource there is on Salamina and things to do in the area, and the hotel can arrange a day trip to another beautiful town, Aguadas, known for its handicrafts. It's just a couple hours away to the north.

There are two other traditional hotels in town, that, while not fancy, will do the trick if you're sticking to a budget. Breakfast isn't included at these two. **Hospedaje Casa Real** (Cra. 6A No. 5-33, tel. 6/859-6355, cell tel. 311/784-2364, www.hospedajecasareal.wix.com, COP$70,000 d) has 24 rooms and is around the corner from the Plaza de Bolívar on a fairly busy street. The owners also have a *finca* with lodging facilities in the countryside. **Hotel Colonial** (Cl. 5 No. 6-74, tel. 6/859-5078, cell tel. 314/627-9124, hotelcolonial2011@hotmail.com, COP$55,000-95,000 d) is right on the square and has a variety of room options. In both hotels, ask to see the rooms before you check in, as their characteristics vary.

Want some cultural immersion? Manizales-based travel agency **Rosa de los Vientos** (Centro Comercial Parque Caldas Nivel 2, Local PB45, tel. 6/883-5940, www.turismorosadelosvientos.com) can set up a home stay (COP$35,000-50,000 pp) in one of the many historic homes in Salamina.

Transportation

There is frequent **shared taxi service** to Salamina from Manizales, costing COP$20,000. Taxis depart from the Terminal de Transportes (Cra. 43 No. 65-100) in Manizales.

One **bus** leaves Medellín at 7am daily bound for Salamina and other communities in the area. It departs from the **Terminal del Sur** (Cra. 65 No. 8B-91, tel. 4/444-8020 or 4/361-1186). The trip takes 4-6 hours on rural roads. The operator **T.P. Adventours** (cell tel. 312/864-1571) offers transportation from both Medellín and Manizales to Salamina.

★ PARQUE NACIONAL NATURAL LOS NEVADOS

This national park covers 583 square kilometers (225 miles) of rugged terrain along the Central Cordillera between the cities of Manizales to the north, Ibagué to the southeast, and Pereira to the northwest. Whether you do a day trip or a multiday trek, a visit to **Parque Nacional Natural Los Nevados** (www.parquesnacionales.gov.co) allows you to enjoy firsthand the stark beauty and intriguing flora and fauna of the upper reaches of the Andes, far above the forest line. Within the park are three snowcapped volcanoes: **Nevado del Ruiz** (5,325 meters/17,470 feet), **Nevado del Tolima** (5,215 meters/17,110 feet), and **Nevado Santa Isabel** (4,950 meters/16,240 feet), as well as myriad lakes, such as **Laguna del Otún.**

This rugged landscape was formed by volcanic activity and later sculpted by huge masses of glaciers. At their maximum extension, these glaciers covered an area of 860 square kilometers (332 square miles). They began to recede 14,000 years ago and, according to a 2013 study by the Colombian Institute of Hydrology, Meteorology, and Environmental Studies (IDEAM), will completely disappear by 2030.

Most of the park consists of *páramo,* a unique tropical high-altitude ecosystem, and super *páramo,* rocky terrain above the *páramo* and below the snow line. *Páramo* is a highland tropical ecosystem that thrives where UV radiation is higher, oxygen is scarcer, and where temperatures vary considerably from daytime to nighttime, when the mercury falls below freezing. It is the kingdom of the eerily beautiful *frailejones,* plants with statuesque tall trunks and thick greenish-yellow leaves. Other *páramo* vegetation includes shrubs, grasses, and cushion plants (*cojines*). The super *páramo* has a stark, moonlike landscape, with occasional dunes of volcanic ash. Though it's largely denuded of vegetation, bright yellow plants called *litamo real* and orange moss provide splashes of color. On a

Parque Nacional Natural Los Nevados

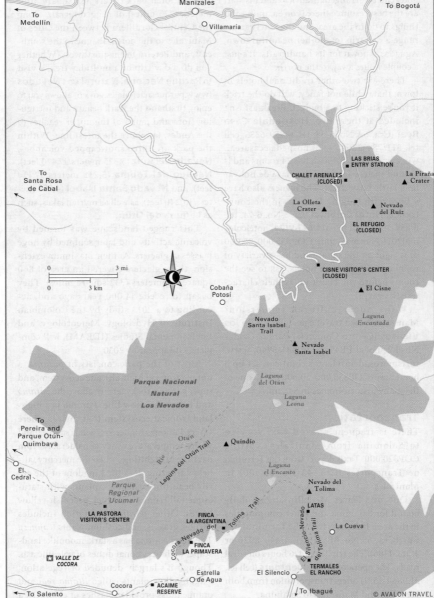

To Medellín ←

To Bogotá ↗

Manizales

Villamaría

← To
Santa Rosa
de Cabal

LAS BRISAS
ENTRY STATION

CHALET ARENALES
(CLOSED)

La Piraña
Crater

La Olleta
Crater

Nevado
del Ruiz

EL REFUGIO
(CLOSED)

0   3 mi
0   3 km

CISNE VISITOR'S CENTER
(CLOSED)

Cobaña
Potosí

El Cisne

Laguna
Encantada

Nevado
Santa Isabel
Trail

Nevado
Santa Isabel

Parque Nacional
Natural
Los Nevados

Laguna
del Otún

Laguna
Leona

To
Pereira and
Parque Otún-
Quimbaya

Otún

Río

Quindío

Laguna del Otún Trail

El
Cedral

Laguna
el Encanto

Parque
Regional
Ucumari

Nevado del
Tolima

LATAS

LA PASTORA
VISITOR'S CENTER

La Cueva

FINCA
LA ARGENTINA

del

Tolima Trail

El Silencio-Nevado

del Tolima Trail

Cocora-Nevado

FINCA
LA PRIMAVERA

★ VALLE DE
COCORA

Estrella
de Agua

El Silencio

TERMALES
EL RANCHO

← To Salento

Cocora

ACAIME
RESERVE

To Ibagué ↓

© AVALON TRAVEL

the lunar-like landscape of the Parque Nacional Natural Los Nevados

The Nevado del Tolima and Nevado del Ruiz volcanoes are considered active, with the Ruiz presenting more activity. In 1985 it erupted, melting the glacier, which in turn created a massive mudslide that engulfed the town of Armero, burying an estimated 20,000 of the town's 29,000 residents.

Parques Nacionales has an office in Manizales (Cl. 69 No. 24-69, tel. 6/887-1611 or 6/887-2273, 8:30am-4pm Mon.-Fri.) for updated information on park conditions.

ORIENTATION

The Northern Sector of the park includes the Nevado del Ruiz, with its three craters (Arenales, La Piraña, and La Olleta), and extends south to the extinct Cisne volcano and Laguna Verde. Much of this sector can be accessed by vehicle.

The Southern Sector includes everything from the Nevado Santa Isabel south to the Quindío peak, as well as Nevado del Tolima, with Pereira, Salento, and Ibagué being the main points of entry into the park.

Northern Sector

The **Northern Sector** (turnoff to Las Brisas entry point at Km. 43 Vía Manizales-Honda, tel. 6/887-1611, www.parquesnacionales. gov.co, 8am-2pm daily, non-Colombians COP$38,000) is the most visited part of the park. Until relatively recently, day-trippers could drive from Manizales directly to El Refugio, a camp at the base of the Ruiz, and climb up to the main Arenales crater (5,325 meters/17,470 feet) in a strenuous three-hour hike. The Cisne visitors center provided lodging in this sector of the park and allowed easy access to the Nevado Santa Isabel and Laguna Verde. However, due to heightened volcanic activity at Ruiz, only a small section of the Northern Sector is open. A small area, from the **Las Brisas entry station** to the beautiful and eerie landscape of the **Valle de las Tumbas** (also known as Valle del Silencio), is open to visitors in organized tours and private vehicles. For current conditions at the Ruiz volcano, check

clear day, the views from the *páramo* or super *páramo* of the snowcapped volcanoes and lakes are simply stunning.

The black-and-white Andean condor, *vultur gryphus,* with its wingspan of up to three meters (10 feet), can sometimes be spotted gliding along the high cliffs in the park. While it is estimated that there are over 10,000 of the birds on the continent (mostly in Argentina), there are few remaining in Colombia. Some estimates report that by the mid-1980s, there were no more than 15 left in Colombia, due in large part to poaching by cattle ranchers. To boost their numbers in Colombia, a reintroduction program was initiated in the park (and in other parts of the country) in the 1990s in conjunction with the San Diego Zoo, where newborns were hatched. Today it is estimated that there are 200-300 condors soaring above Colombia's Andean highlands. Numbers of the endangered birds in Los Nevados range 8-15. Other fauna includes spectacled bears *(oso de anteojos),* tapirs, weasels, squirrels, bats, and many species of birds.

the Colombian Geological Service website (www.sgc.gov.co/Manizales.aspx).

If you don't have a vehicle, the only way to visit this part of the park is on an organized day tour from Manizales. These tours leave early in the morning, drive to Las Brisas park entry station, and continue to the Valle de las Tumbas, making stops along the way to gaze at the landscape, particularly the Nevado del Ruiz and La Olleta crater (weather permitting), and to view birds and vegetation. On the way back to Manizales, the tour stops for an hour at some hot springs (often Termales de Otoño). You're back in Manizales by 5pm. This experience will be unsatisfying for people who want to move their legs, as you'll be in the car most of the day. **Asdeguias** (Cl. 25 No. 20-25, tel. 6/884-4525, cell tel. 314/507-4735, www.asdeguiascaldas.com) and **Ecosistemas** (Cra. 21 No. 23-21, tel. 6/880-8300, cell tel. 312/705-7007, www.ecosistemastravel.com.co) offer this day tour for around COP$140,000 for nonresidents. This excursion usually covers pickup in Manizales, transportation, meals, the park entrance fee, and a stop at hot springs.

If you have a vehicle (a car with 4WD is not necessary) you can drive the Brisas-Valle de las Tumbas segments but you will be required to take a guide in your vehicle and participate in a *charla* (chat) at the park entrance. The cost is COP$27,000 for nonresidents or COP$5,000 for students with valid student ID, COP$11,000 for obligatory guided tour per group, and COP$5,500 for the vehicle entry.

Nevado Santa Isabel Trek

A spectacular day trek from Manizales is up to the snow line of the **Nevado Santa Isabel.** It is a long day trip, starting with a bumpy 50-kilometer (31-mile) drive to the border of the park at Conejeras and then a three-hour (5.5-kilometer/3.4-mile) hike up the canyon of the Río Campo Alegre and then to the snow line. This hike requires good physical condition; it takes you from an elevation of 4,000 meters (13,100 feet) up to 4,750 meters (15,600 feet) through *páramo* and super *páramo*.

More serious mountaineers can extend the trek to the summit of the Nevado Santa Isabel (4,950 meters/16,240 feet) by camping past Conejeras and doing an early-morning ascent to the top. At sunrise, the views onto the surrounding high mountain landscape, with the Nevado del Ruiz and Nevado del Tolima in the background, are magnificent. The ascent to the top requires specialized gear.

Asdeguias (Cl. 25 No. 20-25, tel. 6/884-4525, cell tel. 314/507-4735, www.asdeguias-caldas.com), **Ecosistemas** (Cra. 21 No. 23-21, tel. 6/880-8300, cell tel. 312/705-7007, www.ecosistemastravel.com.co), and **Kumanday** (Cl. 66 No. 23B-40, tel. 6/887-2682, www.kumanday.com) each offer this tour out of Manizales. You'll have to get up with the chickens though: You'll be leaving town at 4am.

Laguna del Otún Trek

A popular three-day trek from Pereira is to the **Laguna del Otún.** The starting point is El Cedral, a *vereda* (settlement) 21 kilometers (13 miles) east of Pereira at an altitude of 2,100 meters (6,900 feet). The trek terminates at the lake at 3,950 meters (13,000 feet). This 19-kilometer (12-mile) hike provides an incredible close-up view of the transitions from humid tropical forest to higher-altitude tropical forests and the *páramo*. The trek follows the valley of the crystalline Río Otún, first through the Parque Regional Natural Ucumarí and then into the Parque Nacional Natural Los Nevados. It's not too strenuous. Most trekkers split the climb into two segments, camping at El Bosque or Jordín on the way up and spending one night at the Laguna del Otún. The return hike can be done in one day. The path is easy to follow, though quite rocky and muddy. A guide is not necessary.

The only accommodation along this route is at the **Centro de Visitantes La Pastora** (6 km/4 mi from El Cedral toward Laguna del Otún, no phone, cell tel. 312/200-7711, COP$22,000 pp) in the Parque Regional Natural Ucumarí. The dormitory-style rooms are clean and comfortable in this cozy lodge.

Meals (COP$6,000-9,000) by the fireplace are excellent. It is possible to buy snacks along the way, but there is no food at the *laguna,* so bring cooking equipment and food along with tents and sleeping bags.

To get to El Cedral from Pereira, take a *chiva* (rural bus) offered by **Transportes Florida** (tel. 6/331-0488, COP$5,000, 2 hrs.), which departs from Calle 12 and Carrera 9 in Pereira. On weekdays, the bus departs at 7am, 9am, and 3pm. On weekends there is an additional bus at noon. The buses return from El Cedral approximately at 11am, 2pm, and 5pm.

The Laguna del Otún can also be visited on an organized tour in a long day trip from Pereira. This involves leaving Pereira at 5am and driving 88 kilometers (55 miles) to Potosí (3,930 meters/12,895 feet) near the park border and then hiking two hours to the lake. This is not a strenuous walk. A recommended tour operator in Pereira for this excursion is **Ecoturismo Risaralda-Cattleya S.E.R.** (Cl. 99 No. 14-78, La Florida, tel. 6/314-4162, cell tel. 313/695-4305, grupocattleya@gmail.com, www.cattleyaser.com). The **Kolibrí Hostel** (tel. 6/331-3955, cell tel. 321/646-9275, www.kolibrihostel.com) in Pereira also offers guided treks to the laguna.

Nevado del Tolima and Paramillo del Quindío Treks

There are two ways to reach the classically cone-shaped Nevado del Tolima (5,215 meters/17,110 feet). The somewhat easier and more scenic route is from Vereda del Cocora near Salento, which takes four days. A more strenuous route is from Ibagué, which can be done in two days.

From **Vereda del Cocora** (2,200 meters/7,215 feet), you hike 7-8 hours (13.5 kilometers/8.4 miles) through the Valle del Cocora, up the Río Quindío canyon, and through the Páramo Romerales to the Finca La Primavera at 3,680 meters (12,075 feet). There you spend the night (COP$10,000 pp) and take a simple meal. On the second day you hike 6-7 hours (12 kilometers/7.5 miles) to a campsite at 4,400 meters (14,450 feet) near the

edge of the super *páramo.* On the third day, you depart the campsite at 2am and climb 8 kilometers (5 miles) to reach the rim of the Tolima crater at 7am or 8am, when there are incredible views to the Quindío, Santa Isabel, Cisne, and Ruiz peaks. That evening you sleep again at the Finca La Primavera and return to Vereda del Cocora the following day. The path is not clearly marked and it is easy to lose your way (there's a reason why one part is called the Valle de los Perdidos, or Valley of the Lost), so it is best go with a guide. The ascent to the glacier requires specialized gear.

From Ibagué the starting point for the trek to Nevado del Tolima is **Juntas** (17 km/10.6 miles from Ibagué) in the beautiful Cañón de Combeima river canyon. There are two options for overnighting: a campground called **Finca Las Nieves,** which requires six hours of hiking on the first day, or the campground known as **Escuela El Salto/El Vergel,** which requires eight hours. On the second day, hikers arrive at **Termales de Cañón** (4,000m/13,123 ft.) after about four hours of hiking. There are again two options to reach the Tolima summit: via the **Ingeominas weather station,** leaving at 2am, or the **Helipuerto route,** which requires an additional overnight at 4,600 m (15,091 ft); the latter is the preferred route for those with less experience in high mountain climbing. Guide **Truman David Alfonso Bejarano** in Ibagué (cell tel. 315/292-7395, trumandavid01@gmail.com, www.truman.com.co) can organize excursions from Salento or Ibagué. His blog (www.truman-adventure.blogspot.com) has detailed information about the various routes up to Nevado del Tolima.

Another less traveled but beautiful hike is to the **Paramillo del Quindío** (4,750 meters/15,585 feet), an extinct volcano that once was covered by a glacier. The 17-kilometer (10.5-mile) ascent from Finca La Primavera takes eight hours and can be done in one long day. Alternatively, you can split the hike in two, camping so as to arrive at the top of the crater in the early morning when visibility is best. There are spectacular views of the

Tolima, Santa Isabel, and Ruiz volcanoes. This is a strenuous but not technically difficult climb.

Recommended guides for the Tolima and Quindío treks are **Salento Trekking** (Cl. 4 No. 6-09, cell tel. 313/654-1619, www.salentotrekking.com) and **Páramo Trek** (Cl. 5 No. 1-37, cell tel. 311/745-3761, www.paramotrek. com). Salento Trekking often prefers to stay at Finca La Argentina, which is less crowded with hikers than Finca La Primavera.

ARMENIA

The defining moment for Colombia's Ciudad Milagro (Miracle City) arrived uninvited on the afternoon of January 25, 1999, when an earthquake registering 6.4 on the Richter scale shook the city. One thousand people lost their lives, nearly half the city became instantly displaced, and thousands of nearby coffee farms were destroyed. The miracle of this coffee region city can be seen in how it rapidly rebuilt and began to thrive once more.

As is the case with sister cities Pereira and Manizales, Armenia was settled in the late 19th century by Antioquian colonizers. The city is not a tourist destination in itself, but you'll be astonished to see, within just a few blocks of the city center, a sea of green coffee farms. That lush countryside is the real attraction.

The city was founded in 1889 and initially named Villa Holguín to honor then-president Carlos Holguín Mallarino. It is widely believed that the city was renamed Armenia to honor victims of the 1894-1896 Hamidian massacres of ethnic Armenians living in the Ottoman Empire.

Armenia is a small city by Colombian standards, home to 294,000 residents. The downtown is compact and easy to traverse on foot. The northern areas of the city are where the hotels, malls, and restaurants are found. That part of town, around the Hotel Armenia, is also walkable.

Carreras run north-south and *calles* east-west. Main drags include Carreras 14 (Avenida Bolívar), 18, and 19, as well as Avenida Centenario, which runs parallel to the Río Quindío on the eastern side of the city. Carrera 14 is pedestrian-only downtown.

Sights

Standing in downtown Armenia's **Plaza de Bolívar** (between Cras. 12-13 and Clls. 20-21) is a sculpture of Simón Bolívar (northern side of the plaza) and the love-it-or-hate-it **Monumento Al Esfuerzo,** designed by Rodrigo Arenas Betancourt and built in the 1960s. This sculpture stands in remembrance of the sacrifices made and hardships faced by Antioquian settlers who arrived in the area seeking opportunity. The modern, triangular-shaped **Catedral de la Inmaculada Concepción** (Cra. 12 between Clls. 20-21, hours vary) is located on the plaza, which is on the stark side.

A stroll down the **pedestrian street** from the Plaza de Bolívar to the Parque Sucre is a pleasant way to see the modern downtown at its busiest.

MUSEO DEL ORO QUIMBAYA

Even if you have visited the world-famous Museo del Oro in Bogotá, it is worth the trek to Armenia just to visit the **Museo del Oro Quimbaya** (Av. Bolívar No. 40N-80, tel. 6/749-8433, www.banrepcultural.org, 10am-5pm Tues.-Sun., free) on the outskirts of town. In contrast to the Gold Museum in Bogotá, this museum, designed by famed architect Rogelio Salmona, focuses exclusively on the Quimbaya nation, which predominated in the coffee region before the Spanish conquest. Much of the museum is devoted to ceramic and gold decorative and ceremonial items that were found in the area. Excellent explanations in English provide interesting background information on the history, ways of life, and traditions of the Quimbaya people.

Festivals and Events

Armenios celebrate their city's founding in October with the **Fiestas Cuyabras.** City parks and plazas are the stages for cultural events, a beauty pageant, and a fun Yipao

Armenia

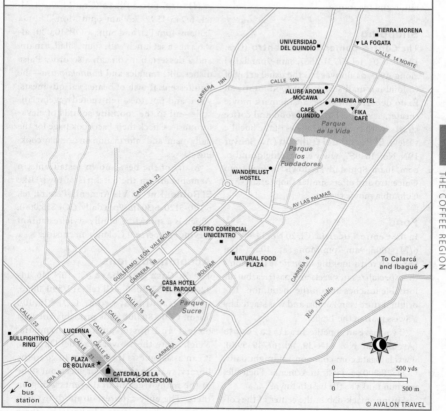

(Jeep) parade. These U.S. military Jeeps (called Jeep Willys), a symbol of the region, began arriving in Colombia around 1946, after World War II.

Recreation

Several city parks and plazas are great places to enjoy the wonderful Armenia climate. These include the **Parque de la Vida** (Cra. 13 at Cl. 8N) and the **Parque Sucre** (Cra. 13 at Cl. 13) downtown, the latter of which is adjacent to a delightful pedestrian street. Locals and visitors gather in the late afternoon at the **Café Quindío** in the park for *onces* (tea time).

The **Parque El Bosque** (Cl. 21 No. 22-23)

is a green space that has a bust of Abraham Lincoln that was donated to the city by the Armenian community of Fresno, California, to express their gratitude for naming the city in solidarity with the decimated Armenian nation in the early 20th century. The bullfighting ring is adjacent to the park.

Globos Colombia (cell tel. 320/667-7818, www.globoscolombia.com, COP$475,000) offers commanding views of the endless fields of coffee of this fertile region from a hot-air balloon. Flights (shared or private) usually lift off at 6am-6:30am and last 45 minutes, and breakfast is typically included. To paraglide over coffee fields, contact **Parapente**

Quindío Calarcá (cell tel. 320/775-9888, COP$100,000). The price includes transportation and insurance.

Shopping

The **Centro Comercial Unicentro** (Cra. 14 No. 6-02, tel. 6/731-2667, 8am-9pm daily) along Avenida Bolívar has the usual array of Colombian mall stores, fast-food joints, an Éxito department store, a Cinemark movie theater, several ATMs, and food and coffee courts (with spectacular views of the bucolic valley). **El Portal del Quindío** (Av. Bolívar 19N No. 46-057, www.elportaldelquindio.com, 10am-8pm daily) is down the road from Unicentro and offers similar shops and a Cine Colombia movie theater.

Food

In the Centro, **Lucerna** (Cl. 20 No. 14-40, tel. 6/741-1005, 9am-7pm Mon.-Sat., 10am-7pm Sun.) is a retro-looking *salón de té* (tearoom) that specializes in sweets and pastries, but affordable lunches are on the menu, too. The original store is in Pereira and was started by a Swiss man in the 1950s.

If you have an appetite, head to **La Fogata** (Av. Bolívar No. 14N-39, tel. 6/749-5980, www.lafogata.com.co, noon-midnight daily, COP$28,000), a classic in Armenia. Their filet mignon ranks as the best in town.

Sitting smack-dab in the center of the coffee universe, you wouldn't think that finding a nice, hot brew in Armenia would have ever been a challenge. But it's a relatively recent phenomenon that fancy coffees and cafés have made it to the streets. **Café Quindío Gourmet** (Parque de la Vida, Cra. 14/Av. Bolívar 7N, tel. 6/745-4478, www.cafequindio.com.co, 11am-9:30pm Mon.-Sat., noon-4:30pm Sun.) is the most famous (and most commercial) of coffees around here, and this location has a very nice restaurant as well, with baby coffee plants on each table. Those in the know, however, will head to other cafés, appropriately hidden on back streets. Look for **Fika Café** (Cra. 13 No. 8N-16 #104, cell tel. 320/524-0373, 9am-12:30pm and 3pm-9pm

daily), which is a pleasant spot to settle into on a late afternoon.

Natural Food Plaza (Cra. 14 No. 4-51, tel. 6/745-1597, 7:30am-6pm Mon.-Thurs., 7:30am-4pm Fri. and Sun., COP$10,000) always has a set lunch with soup, salad, a main, and a dessert, but you can also order Paisa dishes, like tamales and *bandeja paisa*—the quintessential dish of beans, various meats, yuca, and potatoes, reinvented vegetarian-style—all to the soothing sounds of elevator music. Check their Facebook page for the daily menu and information on one-day cooking classes.

Many of the best-known restaurants in Armenia are on the outskirts of town, like **El Roble** (Km. 12 Vía Armenia-Pereira, tel. 6/740-5120, 6:30am-9pm daily, COP$15,000), which is a sprawling family-style restaurant serving 100 percent Colombian cuisine.

Accommodations

The ★ **Casa Quimbaya** (Cl. 16N No. 14-92, tel. 6/732-3086, cell tel. 312/590-0066, www.casaquimbaya.com, COP$25,000 dorm, COP$80,000 d) is probably the best budget and hostel option in Armenia. Neighbor to the Universidad del Quindío, it can assist guests if they want to go to the library, swim in the pool, or check out some of the many free cultural events going on there. The busy café/restaurant draws students as well as tourists. The hostel has three dorm rooms with 4-5 beds each and three private rooms. It's in an ordinary-looking house on a quiet street, very close to the action of Carrera 14.

A midrange option downtown is **Casa Hotel del Parque** (Cra. 14 No. 12-26, tel. 6/731-3166, www.casahoteldelparque.com, COP$99,000 d). It has just five rooms and a great location on the Parque Sucre and a pedestrian street.

Isa Victory Hotel Boutique (Av. Bolívar No. 21N-47, cell tel. 320/770-7079, www.isavictoryhotelboutique.com, COP$150,000 d) lacks charm, but is a good midrange option along Avenida Bolívar. This modern business hotel has a terrace with hot tub on the top floor.

The top-end address in town is ★ **Allure Aroma Mocawa** (Cra. 14 No. 9N-00, tel. 6/735-9599, www.allurearomamocawahotel. com.co, COP$196,000 d), a 16-story high-rise with nearly 100 rooms, an awesome rooftop pool on the 17th floor with a view of the countryside, an ample breakfast buffet, and free parking. It's on Avenida Bolívar (Carrera 14) close to shopping malls.

The **Armenia Hotel** (Av. Bolívar and Cl. 8N, tel. 6/746-0099, cell tel. 320/696-9111, www.armeniahotel.com.co, COP$183,000 d) may have lost some of its allure to nearby Mocawa, but it remains a popular address, especially with Colombian business travelers. It has 129 rooms on nine floors, and a big atrium smells of eucalyptus emanating from the steam room. Rooms are furnished with locally made *guadua* bamboo furniture and have been updated. A spa, pool, and small gym are available on the premises, and guests also have privileges at a gym four blocks away.

Information and Services

Tourist offices are located at the bus station (Cl. 35 No. 20-68) and in the Edificio de la Gobernación (Plaza de Bolívar, tel. 6/741-7700, 8am-noon and 2pm-6pm Mon.-Sat.).

Transportation

There are few domestic flight options from **Aeropuerto Internacional El Eden** (Km. 10 Vía La Tebaida, tel. 6/747-9400). **Avianca** flies to Bogotá, while **Aerolíneas de Antioquia (ADA)** and **Air Panama** fly into Medellín. The airport is about 20 kilometers from town, and a taxi costs around COP$30,000. **Milano Rent A Car** (www.milanocar.com, cell tel. 300/800-1180) can set you up with wheels in Armenia. Before driving into Armenia, find out the days for *pico y placa*—vehicle restrictions in place during the workweek and based on the last digit of the license plate—in order to avoid fines.

The bus terminal, the **Terminal de Transportes** (Cl. 35 No. 20-68, tel.

6/747-3355, www.terminalarmenia.com) is just south of downtown, about 13 blocks from the Plaza de Bolívar. There is frequent service to Pereira (1 hour, COP$8,000), Salento (1 hour, COP$4,000), and Manizales (4 hours, COP$17,000). Buses bound for Medellín (6.5 hours, COP$38,000) leave all day from before dawn to around midnight. While short-distance buses depart until about 10pm or later, it's better to travel earlier if possible—for both safety reasons and so you can enjoy the scenery along the way.

The rapid bus system in Armenia is called the **Tinto** (www.tinto.com.co). A line on Avenida Bolívar connects the northern part of the city with downtown. The website can be confusing, so it's best to ask someone how to get around.

VICINITY OF ARMENIA
★ **Jardín Botánico del Quindío**
Just 10 minutes outside of town, the well-run **Jardín Botánico del Quindío** (Km. 3 Vía al Valle, tel. 6/742-7254, cell tel. 310/404-5223, www.jardinbotanicoquindio.org, 9am-4pm daily, English tour COP$30,000) is home to hundreds of tree and plant species, many of which are threatened. Knowledgeable volunteer guides, who are usually college students, lead visitors on a mandatory 2.5-hour tour along jungle paths, stopping every so often to point out flora that you would have overlooked had you walked through on your own. That might strike you as a major time commitment, but it really doesn't seem like it. In addition to palms (which aren't technically trees) and *guadua* (which is actually related to grass), look out for *matapalos*, a tree that wraps itself around other trees, strangling them as they fight for sunlight. It's been lovingly nicknamed the *abrazo de la suegra* (mother-in-law's hug).

In Colombia where there is tropical forest, there will be birds. The gardens are no exception, and they are home to at least 119 species. The birds are at their most active early in the morning. Some of the commonly seen species include tanagers, toucans, owls, woodpeckers, the multicolored *torito cabecirrojo* (red-headed barbet), and iconic *barranqueros* or *barranquillos* (blue-crowned motmots). These birds make their nests in the earth. Rodent residents who frequently make cameo appearances are *ardillas* (squirrels) and cute *guatines* (Central American agoutis). By far the most photographed sector of the park is the *mariposario* (enclosed butterfly garden) in the shape of a giant butterfly; it is home to thousands of the insects. The butterflies are livelier when the sun is out.

Guides are volunteers, and although the entry price is steep, it's good form to tip the guides after the tour. Call in advance to inquire about English-speaking tours. It's easy to get to the park using public transportation from Armenia. Just look for a bus from the Plaza de Bolívar or along Avenida Bolívar that says "Jardín Botánico."

Theme Parks

These parks are mobbed with families on weekends and holidays.

RECUCA (Km. 5 Vía La Y-Barcelona, Vereda Callelarga, tel. 6/749-8525, www.re-cuca.com, 9am-3pm daily, tour with lunch COP$30,000) is a theme park, but one without roller coasters or water rides. RECUCA stands for Recorrido de la Cultura Cafetera (Coffee Culture Experience). Upon arrival at the *finca* (farm), you'll be greeted by smiling employees dressed in traditional bean-picking garb. Then you'll explore a coffee farm, lend a hand by picking some ripe beans, and learn about the entire process. After that, you'll enjoy a big Paisa lunch (beans and rice for herbivores). If you prefer, you can just take part in a coffee-tasting session (COP$14,000). You can get to RECUCA by taking a bus bound for Barcelona from the Terminal de Transportes in Armenia (Cl. 35 No. 20-68). The bus drops you off at the park entrance. From there it is a 30-minute walk, or the guard at the entrance can order a Jeep for you (COP$5,000).

The **Parque Nacional del Café** (Km. 6 Vía Montenegro-Pueblo Tapao, tel. 6/741-7417, www.parquedelcafe.co, 8am-6pm daily, COP$25,000-59,000) is near the town of **Montenegro,** 12.5 kilometers (8 miles) west of Armenia. While part of the park is devoted to telling the story of coffee production in Colombia, it's mostly an amusement park with roller coasters, a chairlift, horseback rides, a coffee show, a water park, and other attractions.

PANACA (Km. 7 Vía Vereda Kerman, tel. 6/758-2830, cell tel. 313/721-9211,

Jardín Botánico del Quindío

www.panaca.com.co, 9am-6pm daily, COP$45,000-62,000) is an agriculture-themed amusement park near the town of **Quimbaya,** where visitors can see and interact with all types of farm animals and watch the occasional pig race.

Festivals and Events

In June or sometimes July, **Calarcá** puts on an event to honor what made the coffee region what it is today. A number of the usual festival events take place during the **Fiesta Nacional del Café** (www.calarca.net), but it's the **Desfile de Yipao** that steals the show. That's when Jeep Willys—U.S. military Jeeps from World War II and the Korean War that were sold to farmers in the coffee region—are filled with people, animals, and furniture, and go on parade. There are competitions (essentially Willy beauty pageants) and a contest in which the Jeep Willys are loaded down with 1,800 kilos of cargo and race forward on two wheels only.

Accommodations

With more than a century's experience growing coffee, the **Hacienda Combia** (Km. 4 Vía al Valle-Vereda La Bella, tel. 6/746-8472, cell tel. 314/850-5695, www.combia.com.co, COP$152,000 d) has 33 rooms and an infinity pool that has a fantastic view, and there are coffee tours available through the nearby fields. This hotel is not far from a highway, but you can easily block out reminders of suburbia by focusing on the fertile lands that surround you and are home to colorful birds. Its proximity to the airport (airport pickups can be arranged) and easy access make it a popular event space for Colombian businesses. It also attracts foreign embassy staff living in Bogotá.

Surrounded by 160 hectares of pineapple, cacao, banana, and citrus crops, it's hard to imagine a more relaxing place than ★ **Hacienda Bambusa** (off Vía Calarcá-Caicedonia south of Armenia, tel. 6/740-4935, cell tel. 300/778-8897 reservations, www.haciendabambusa.com, COP$490,000 d). Its isolation is a selling point, providing the perfect environment to disconnec[t] house and much of the furniture are mad[e] *guadua* and other traditional materials, an[d] its seven rooms are luxurious and tastefully decorated, each with its own private balcony or terrace. The views from those balconies are spectacular, with endless farms punctuated by *guadua* forests and mountains in the distance. There are cacao tours to take, horses to ride, birds to watch, and massages to be enjoyed. The Armenia airport is about 40 minutes away; taking a cab from there costs COP$45,000, although the hotel can arrange all your transportation. Bambusa offers a range of packages, some including activities and excursions, transportation to and from the airport, and all meals.

Near the town of Quimbaya and off the road 800 meters past some ordinary-looking houses and apartments, a well-maintained hacienda awaits: ★ **Finca Villa Nora** (tel. 6/741-5472, cell tel. 310/422-6335, www.quindiofincavillanora.com, COP$180,000 d with two meals). It's a 120-year-old red-and-white house that is charming and full of character. It's built in the typical Paisa style. Amid fruit trees, flowers, coffee fields, and a huge ficus tree, at Villa Nora the air is pure, sunsets are lovely, and drinks on the veranda is not a bad idea. There are only six rooms at this quiet refuge.

SALENTO

On the western edge of the Parque Nacional Natural Los Nevados, Salento (pop. 7,000) is one-stop shopping for those seeking a quintessential coffee region experience. The town, an enchanting pueblo that is home to coffee growers and cowboys, is adorned with the trademark colorful balconies and facades of Paisa architecture. It was one of the first settlements in the region during the 19th-century Antioquian colonization. In the nearby countryside, coffee farms dominate the landscape. Here you can be a Juan Valdez, the iconic personification of Colombian coffee, during a coffee tour in which you harvest coffee beans, learn about the bean-to-bag sip the freshest coffee you've

...utes of town, to the east, is the ...a, where you can play tree tag ...*alma de cera* (wax palm, the ...ional tree), the skyscrapers of ....*y*. Some of these can reach up to 60 meters (200 feet) high. For a more challenging hike, continue to the Reserva Acaime, a private nature reserve of tropical forest, babbling brooks, and not a few hummingbirds. From here adventurers can ascend into the *páramos* (highland moors) and, eventually, the snowcapped peaks of the Parque Natural Nacional Los Nevados.

Salento is easily accessed from between both Armenia and Pereira, and has become a destination for international backpackers. The town is loaded with hostels, hotels, and restaurants catering to visitors. To experience Salento with fewer crowds, go during the week. During high tourist season, such as around New Year's and during Semana Santa, it can be a nightmare with long traffic jams on the road into town. At times, authorities close the roads, not allowing any visitors into town.

Sights

The **Parque Bolívar,** or **Plaza Principal,** is the center of town and center of activity. The festive pedestrian **Calle Real** (between Cl. 1 and Cl. 5), lined by restaurants and shops painted in a rainbow of colors, is the most photogenic street in town. It starts at the Plaza Principal and leads up to the **Alto de la Cruz Mirador,** a scenic lookout atop the Calle Real from where you can catch a nice view of Salento. Farther on is another lookout with views over the surrounding jungles and valleys.

About a 10-minute walk southwest from the town center, near the cemetery, is the **Aldea Artesano** (cell tel. 315/436-6850 or 312/868-8633), a funky artists' commune where jewelers, weavers, painters, and musicians live and work. Browse their workshops and participate in a class. The artists enjoy

sharing their craftsmanship with visitors. Aldea Artesano is in a peaceful setting, with a short nature path and a community garden.

Coffee Tours

In the outskirts of Salento are two very popular coffee tours. Your individual experience may vary, particularly depending on your guide and his or her English abilities (or your adeptness in Spanish). Tours typically last 1-1.5 hours. Tack on an hour or so if you plan on walking from Salento.

Finca El Ocaso (Km. 3.8, Vía Salento-Vereda Palestina, cell tel. 310/451-7329, cafeelocaso@hotmail.com, www.fincaelocasosalento.com, five tours in English 9am-4pm daily, tour COP$10,000) is a family-run farm with some 12 hectares (30 acres) of coffee crops. It produces coffee that has several international certifications, such as the German UTZ and the Rainforest Alliance. Elevation here is around 1,780 meters (5,800 feet), a good altitude for growing coffee. If you're doing the tour as a day trip and plan to walk, you can do a full loop, starting from the Puente Amarillo in Salento and returning along a river to Boquía, then taking a bus back to Salento. In addition, visitors can spend a night or two here in one of four cozy rooms.

The **Finca Don Eduardo coffee tour** (Plantation House, Alto de Coronel, Cl. 7 No. 1-04, cell tel. 316/285-2603, www.theplantationhousesalento.com, COP$20,000) is the most fun of the three tours (and the longest at more than two hours), and, being a London transplant, Tim's English isn't bad. He almost always gives the tours and, along with his Colombian partner, Cristina, runs the Don Eduardo coffee farm. This gorgeous land has been a working coffee farm for over 80 years. The farm grows four subvarieties of arabica coffee.

Recreation

For the real Paisa experience, **horseback riding** is a good way to enjoy the fresh air and birdsong of the hilly back roads near Salento and Boquía. In the Parque Bolívar there are usually horses at the ready, especially on weekends. **Don Álvaro** (cell tel. 311/375-1534, 3-hr. trip COP$40,000 pp) treats his horses well and is considered the best guide for this activity.

Most hostels can arrange bike rental. Additionally, **CicloSalento** (near Plantation Hostel, Alto de Coronel, Cl. 7 No. 1-04, cell tel. 318/872-9714, COP$10,000/hr., COP$35,000/day) rents out good-quality mountain bikes with helmets. Caution: The winding road leading into town from the Valle de Cocora does not have a shoulder for bikes. Vehicles tend to speed along this road, making this a dangerous stretch for cyclists and pedestrians. Another **bike place** is at Cra. 5N No. 9-06 (cell tel. 313/653-7622, COP$30,000 day).

A popular **day hike** takes you to **Cascada Santa Rita,** a 15-meter (50-foot) waterfall and swimming hole in the tropical jungles north of Salento. The starting point is near the Monteroca camping site in Boquía. There's a small fee to visit the waterfalls, as they are on the Santa Rita farm property. This could be done without a guide, if you get specific instructions, but it's best to contract an experienced local guide such as **Blaney Arisizabal of UMAYAKU** (cell tel. 314/885-3326, theblaney@gmail.com). Another option is **Salentour** (salentourcafetero@gmail.com). The cost of this guided day hike is around COP$80,000-100,000.

Food

With a fantastic location on the Parque Bolívar, ★ **Juan Esteban Parrilla y Vinos** (Cra. 7 No. 5-45, cell tel. 315/410-1059, 8am-11am and noon-3pm daily) is a popular place, with beautiful photography of the local scenery on its walls and a big menu of traditional Colombian dishes. It's a grilled meat place but it happily accommodates vegetarians.

It's a real treat to discover a restaurant like ★ **Casa La Eliana** (Cra. 2 No. 6-45, cell tel. 314/660-5987, http://casalaeliana.com, 10am-9pm daily, COP$20,000), where great service, a cozy atmosphere, and fantastic food are the norm. This Spanish-run spot a few blocks from the center of town is the only place in this part of the woods where you can find curry dishes and gourmet pizzas on the menu. And try as they might, the friendly cocker spaniels aren't allowed to mingle with diners.

The best place in town for pizzas is **Pizzería Piccola** (Cra. 6 No. 1-10, cell tel. 315/410-1059). Under the guidance of its Italian owner, it has a nice atmosphere with

Horseback-riding is popular in Colombia's cowboy country.

open-air seating. It also has a small attached guesthouse.

Brunch (Cl. 6 No. 3-25, cell tel. 311/757-8082, 6:30am-9:30pm daily, COP$15,000), a hip little joint with graffiti and messages from hundreds of visitors from around the globe decorating the walls, is another restaurant that operates with the international traveler in mind. They do serve brunch, but also breakfast, lunch, and dinner. The menu seems aimed squarely at Americans: hot wings, Philly cheesesteaks, black bean burgers, and peanut butter brownies.

On a quiet side street, **Café Bernabe** (Cl. 3 No. 6-3, cell tel. 318/393-3278) is the gourmet address in Salento, serving delicious coffee and desserts but also interesting main dishes like filet mignon with blackberry and coffee sauce. The outdoor terrace is perfect for a sunny Salento afternoon.

Swanky, with great views, fine drinks, and comfort food is ★ **Luciernaga** (Cra. 3 No. 9-19, cell tel. 310/425-0197, 7am-11:30pm daily). Sometimes it has live music, and this is the best place in Salento for a sundowner cocktail. **Mojitería** (Cl. 4 No. 5-54, cell tel. 310/409-2331, 2pm-11pm daily, COP$18,000) is a lively spot where you can grab a quick bite (appetizers, salads, soups, and pastas) or try one or two of the many mojitos on offer. At night it takes on a bar atmosphere, often with live music on the weekends and, of course, big, satisfying mojitos.

Hands down, the finest and fanciest café in this coffee region pueblo is ★ **Café Jésus Martín** (Cra. 6 No. 6-14, tel. 6/759-3282, www.cafejesusmartin.com, 8am-8pm daily), a family-run coffee producer. In addition, it runs excellent coffee tours, with transportation included, to the Finca Santana near the town of Quimbaya.

Ice cream, fruit salads, and the like draw visitors to **Sueño de Fresas** (Cl. 5 No. 6-35, cell tel. 310/892-6624, www.fresas.salento.com.co, noon-9pm daily).

Cheap local eats are on the menu at **Rincón de Lucy** (Cl. 4 with Cra. 6, 11am-2pm Mon.-Sat.), where the set lunch deal goes for a pittance: COP$6,000. Meanwhile, if you're hankering for a buttery arepa, look for **Luz Dary's stall** at the corner of Carrera 5 and Calle 7, near the bridge and a laundry place. She's usually up for a chat.

Accommodations

One of the best hostels in the area is ★ **Tralala** (Cra. 7 No. 6-45, cell tel. 314/850-5543, www.hostaltralalasalento.com, COP$18,000 dorm, COP$45,000 d). It's hard to miss this in-town option: It's a two-story white house with bright orange wooden trim, and the owner is from the Netherlands. At Tralala there are only seven rooms, including a dormitory that sleeps six, making for a chilled-out environment for guests. The hostel is spick-and-span and tastefully decorated. Its minimalist style provides a nice vacation for the eyes. Staff are friendly and knowledgeable, and the kitchen is a pleasant area to hang out and chitchat with others. There's a sundeck and garden area in case relaxation is needed. **Casa La Eliana** (Cra. 2 No. 6-45, cell tel. 314/660-5987, http://laelianasalento.com, COP$70,000 d) is more than just delicious food; it has nine comfortable, no-nonsense rooms as well.

Centrally located **Hostal Ciudad de Segorbe** (Cl. 5 No. 4-06, tel. 6/759-3794, www.hostalciudaddesegorbe.com, COP$145,000 d, COP$40,000 dorm) is a bed-and-breakfast-slash-hostel set in a nicely preserved centuries-old Paisa house. The hostel's seven rooms have high wooden ceilings with gorgeous original geometric designs and small balconies. One room is equipped for physically challenged visitors.

La Moraleja (Cra. 5 No. 7-4, cell tel. 321/632-8409, COP$65,000 pp) has 10 rooms, including two larger suites. It's an old house with antique furnishings and a pleasant garden.

Beta Town (Cl. 7 No. 3-45, cell tel. 321/218-7043, www.beta.com.co, COP$150,000 d) is a small hotel in town that boasts its own tejo court and even a small football field. It's one of the friendliest spots in town—and that also goes for its restaurant, which serves great breakfasts.

★ **Terrazas de Salento** (Cra. 4 No. 1-30, cell tel. 317/430-4637, COP$185,000-235,000) has seven rooms in gorgeous, understated Scandinavian style, a beautiful backyard garden area, and views of the pueblo. It's quiet, with tons of natural light, and furnishings are made of natural materials.

Londoner Tim was one of the first to help transform Salento from a sleepy Paisa pueblo into one of Colombia's top tourist destinations. His **Plantation House** (Alto de Coronel, Cl. 7 No. 1-04, cell tel. 316/285-2603, www.theplantationhousesalento.com, COP$22,000 dorm, COP$55,000 d), with 24 rooms total, remains one of the top places to get to know Salento and the surrounding areas. Catering to international visitors, this hostel has two houses, one of which is over 100 years old. It's quiet and green around the hostel, and, though you'll be bound to meet other travelers like yourself, there is plenty of space to find a little solitude. Plantation House can organize bike excursions, horseback riding, hikes to the Valle de Cocora, and more. Making life easier, it can also take care of airport transfer to Armenia and Pereira. It is an environmentally friendly hostel: Solar panels enable guests to have a hot shower, and a rainwater collection system provides water. Tim also runs coffee farm **Finca Don Eduardo.**

Another excellent hostel-type option is **La Serrana Eco-farm and Hostel** (Km. 1.5 Vía Palestina Finca, cell tel. 316/296-1890, www.laserrana.com.co, COP$22,000 dorm, COP$55,000 d). It's situated on a bluff with lovely views of coffee farms in every direction. The nine rooms, of various types and sizes, are comfortable, and there is also a women-only dorm room. Camping is also available for COP$12,000. It's a peaceful place where you can enjoy sunrises and sunsets, go for a walk into town, or just hang out. La Serrana is best known for its delicious (and nutritious) family-style dinners and other meals. Vegetarians always have options, and the cooks make an effort to buy local, fresh food.

La Serrana has another, smaller lodging option, ★ **Las Camelias** (Km. 1.5 Vía Palestina Finca, cell tel. 316/296-1890, www.laserrana.com.co, COP$70,000 d), a colonial-style house you can see from the hostel. This is geared toward couples who want a little more privacy—there are only three rooms. Rooms, drenched with natural light, are spacious, with hardwood floors and fireplaces. Common space is ample with large windows, and there is a kitchen for guest use.

Between the Valle de Cocora and Salento is the fabulous ★ **Reserva El Cairo** (Km. 3 Vía Cocora, cell tel. 321/649-3439, www.reservaelcairo.com, COP$220,000 d), a meticulously maintained old farm with six rooms. Its almost 100 acres of cloud forest is now a nature reserve, and paths lead into the forests and mountains behind the house; you can even go to a swimming hole. A half-day bird-watching walk with an English-speaking guide can be arranged (COP$100,000, 4-person max.), or overnight guests can independently set out and take their bird checklist with them; about 100 bird species have been identified in the reserve. There are mammals in the reserve, as well, not to mention amphibians and reptiles: They can be spotted on a nighttime tour. Meals here use local organic ingredients, and the sitting area, full of books on birds and the natural world, is an inviting place to linger after dinner. Bikes are also available for use.

Kasaguadua (2.5 km south of town, cell tel. 313/889-8273, www.kasaguaduanaturalreserve.org, COP$38,000 dorm, COP$90,000 d) is a 12-hectare Andean rainforest nature reserve outside of town that has several trails that can be visited by nonguests for interesting guided walks. But the true Kasaguadua experience is to stay a few nights in one of the geodesic pods, called EcoHabs, that owners Nick and Carlos built themselves. There are private rooms and a dorm-style room. Meals are communal, taken with staff and fellow travelers. The very popular tours (requested donation COP$20,000-50,000), which generally last 3-3.5 hours, begin promptly at 9am. Over 82 species of birds inhabit the area, and birders will want to rise early to spot them. A Jeep Willy to Kasaguadua from the Parque Bolívar in Salento costs about COP$12,000. This reserve is on the road that leads to Palestina.

Located on the old Camino Nacional high up in the mountains is the lodge **El Rocio Eagle Nest** (Km. 16 Vía Toche, cell tel. 317/717-5714, www.elrocioeaglenest.com, COP$20,000 dorm, COP$50,000 d). There's just one private room and one dorm for eight sleepers. Without much nightlife around, activity centers on the warmth of the fireplace. Run by a community group, El Rocio offers day excursions including hikes to the cloud forest, reforestation activities, mountain biking, and birdwatching.

Four kilometers outside of Salento, on the banks of the Río Quindío, is **Camping Monteroca** (Valle del Río Quindío, cell tel. 315/413-6862, www.campingmonteroca. com, COP$70,000 cabin, COP$15,000 tent), a sprawling campground catering mostly to Colombian weekenders. The camp has 11 cabins, one of which is called the Hippie Hilton, and several of them have awesome waterbeds. There is a lot of space for tents here as well. Monteroca has a restaurant and two bars. Recreational activities such as horseback riding (COP$12,000 per hour), a three-hour hike to nearby waterfalls (COP$25,000), and yoga classes are on offer. To get there from Salento, take a Jeep bound for Las Veredas. They leave every 15 minutes from the Parque Bolívar during weekends.

Information and Services

Hostels usually provide the best tourist information, and most all have maps, but there is also a good city-run tourist kiosk, the **Punto de Información Turística** (10am-5pm Wed.-Mon.), in front of the Alcaldía (city offices) in the Parque Bolívar.

Transportation

There is frequent bus service from Pereira and Armenia to Salento. The last bus (COTRACIR) from Armenia leaves at 9pm (COP$4,000). From Pereira, there are four direct buses each weekday, costing under COP$6,500. There is more frequent service on weekends. Because Salento is well established on the tourist route, thieves are known to prey on foreigners on late-evening buses traveling from Pereira to Salento. Keep a vigilant eye on your possessions.

Buses to Armenia (every 20 mins. from 6am to 9pm, COP$4,000) depart from the Parque Bolívar. Buses to Pereira (COP$6,500) depart from the intersection of Carrera 2 and Calles 4-5, near the fire station, at 7:50am, 10am, 12:50pm, 2:50pm, and 5:50pm, with the last departure at 7:50pm daily. For Filandia you must first go to Armenia. Bus service to Medellín departs at 9:30am and at 4pm on Flota Occidental (call cell tel. 321/848-4158 to reserve, COP$44,000).

★ VALLE DE COCORA

The main attraction for most visitors to Salento is seeing the *palmas de cera* (wax palms) that shoot up toward the sky in the Valle de Cocora. These are some of the tallest palms in the world, reaching 50-60 meters high (200 feet), and they can live over 100 years. They have beautiful, smooth, cylindrical trunks with dark rings. In 1985, the species was declared the national tree of Colombia. **Día del Arbol Nacional** (National Tree Day) is celebrated on September 16 with gusto, with seed planting in the valleys and other events.

The Valle de Cocora is a 15-kilometer (9-mile) section of the lower Río Quindío valley. Much of it has been turned into pastureland, but, thankfully, the palms have been preserved. The palms look particularly stunning in the denuded landscape.

The gateway to the valley is the **Vereda de Cocora,** a stretch of restaurants specializing in trout. Most Colombian tourists come for a late lunch and take a stroll along the main road behind the *vereda* to view the palms.

From December until February, you'll get the best views, but it may be dusty, and there will be less likelihood of seeing wildlife. High season is in early January. March and November tend to be wet months.

A 2016 census of endangered condors, symbols of Colombia, found seven of the birds living in the park. They, along with eagles, may be spotted with some luck, particularly near the area called Chispas. Pumas and *osos anteojos* (bears) also call the park home.

Hiking

If you have the time and energy, you can make a large loop of the valley on a four- to five-hour hike. The route goes up through the cloud forest and Reserva Acaime, backtracks a little, and then goes up to La Montaña—a ranger station for the local environment agency—before heading down through the main attraction: the palms.

The starting point for the loop is the blue gate after the last building in the Vereda de Cocora. There may be a sign for Acaime, which is what you want. After walking about four kilometers (2.5 miles) through pasture, you'll enter the dense cloud forest. The path crisscrosses the trickling Río Quindío. After three kilometers (two miles) you reach the **Reserva Acaime** (cell tel. 321/636-2818 or 320/788-1981, COP$5,000), a private reserve created to preserve the surrounding cloud forest. With the entrance fee, you can enjoy a complimentary cup of hot chocolate, *agua de panela* (a hot sugary drink), or coffee and watch throngs of hummingbirds of several varieties fly up to feeders. It's quite a show. You can also stay at Acaime, either in private rooms or a large dormitory (COP$40,000 pp including all meals).

After energizing and warming up a little at Acaime, backtrack a kilometer and then climb a steep path to **La Montaña** (about 3,000 meters/9,800 feet). Now for the delicious dessert: the valley of wax palms. You'll descend from La Montaña back to Vereda del Cocora through hills and valleys adorned with the trees.

Rubber or at least waterproof boots are recommended, as the path along the Río Quindío is muddy. Although authorities have been considering regulating visitors, at this point you do not need a guide for this wonderful hike.

TREK TO FINCA LA PRIMAVERA

If you would like to do a longer expedition, you can extend the Valle de Cocora hike beyond Reserva Acaime to the **Páramo de Romerales** on the border of the Parque Nacional Natural Los Nevados and to **Finca La Primavera,** a working farm located at an altitude of 3,680 meters (12,075 feet). All tour

the picturesque Valle de Cocora and its famous wax palms

outfitters in Salento offer this trek, and typically this is accomplished in two days, with an overnight at Primavera. This excursion allows you to enjoy the transition from cloud forest to *páramo* (highland moor), the latter of which is dotted with the unusual Andean *frailejón* plants. The path from Acaime continues to **Estrella de Agua,** a research station, through the Páramo de Romerales and finally Finca La Primavera. The entire hike from Vereda de Cocora to Primavera is 16 kilometers (10 miles) and takes nine hours. On the way back, you'll pass through **Finca Argentina** (3,400 meters/11,155 feet) before descending to the Valle de Cocora. This family farm is cozy, and there are lots of birds flying around, including many varieties of hummingbirds and toucans. For a slower pace, this trek can be done in three days, with the first night spent at Finca Argentina and the second at Primavera.

From Finca La Primavera, you can continue into the **Parque Nacional Natural Los Nevados,** hiking to snowcapped volcano **Nevado del Tolima** (5,215 meters/17,110 feet). For this, hikers will need four days. Another option is the less visited **Paramillo del Quindío** (4,750 meters/15,585 feet), which no longer has snow. From here you can take in the views of the Nevado del Tolima, Santa Isabel, and Ruiz peaks. This trek requires three days.

Salento Trekking (Cl. 4 between Cras. 6-7, cell tel. 313/654-1619, www.salentotrekking.com) may be the most professional trekking outfit around, as the multilingual owners lead every hike. The company offers multiday hiking trips (2-5 days) for all fitness levels and takes care of everything. A three-day trek goes for COP$550,000 per person. **Páramo Trek** (cell tel. 311/745-3761, www.paramotrek.com) is also recommended.

Getting There

To get to Vereda de Cocora from Salento, take a Jeep Willy (COP$3,800), which leaves the Parque Bolívar at 6:10am, 7:30am, 9:30am, 11:30am, 2pm, and 4pm each day. More Willys ply the route on weekends. The last Willy back to town departs at about 5pm.

FILANDIA

As far as cute Paisa pueblos go, word among those in the know in the coffee region is that Filandia is the new Salento. This town, set halfway between Armenia and Pereira, offers charming coffee culture atmosphere and, although it attracts fewer visitors than Salento, has a burgeoning tourism infrastructure.

The focal point of the **Parque Central** (between Cras. 4-5 and Clls. 6-7) is the church, the **Templo María Inmaculada** (Cra. 7), which was built in the early 20th century. From the plaza you can branch out to explore the charming streets of the town, including the **Calle del Tiempo Detenido** (Cl. 7 between Cras. 5-6) and the **Calle del Empedrado,** two streets of two-story houses made of *bahareque* (a natural material) adorned by colorful doors and windows. Stop by the town's oldest construction, the **Droguería Bristol** (Cra. 6 No. 5-63), along the way. A nice view of the countryside can be had near the *clínica mental* (mental hospital; Cra. 8 No. 7-55).

Festivals and Events

The third Saturday of every month sees a **market** in the main square, with handicrafts—including the Filandia specialty of baskets, *cestería del bejuco*—fresh produce, and food.

Food and Accommodations

Accommodations and restaurants in Filandia are limited. In a traditional Paisa house, the **Hostal La Posada del Compadre** (Cra. 6 No. 8-06, tel. 6/758-3054, cell tel. 313/335-9771, www.laposadadelcompadre.com, COP$60,000 d) offers a handful of rooms and ample outdoor hangout space. Rooms are large, beds are adequate, breakfast is included, and the prices are reasonable.

The ★ **Hostal Colina de Lluvia** (Cl. 5 No. 4-08, COP$25,000 dorm, COP$60,000 d private) is a very friendly guesthouse with a home to the **Hostal de Jahn** (cell tel. 317/435-3732, www.jahnquindio.com, COP$50,000d), a comfortable and colorful little guesthouse.

Orale's (Cl. 7 No. 7-58, cell tel. 311/795-0320, Mon.-Fri. 5pm-10pm, Sat. 2pm-10pm, Sun. noon-10pm) is a tiny spot serving authentic Mexican flavors, with fresh ingredients.

Information and Services

The Filandia tourist office is in the **Casa del Artesano** (Cra. 5 at Cl. 7, 2nd floor, tel. 6/758-2172, 7am-noon and 1:30pm-4:30pm Mon.-Fri.).

Transportation

Buses to Filandia leave from Armenia (COP$4,500, every 20 minutes) and Pereira (COP$5,600, hourly) all day long until around 8pm. These circulate the town picking up passengers, especially on Carrera 7. Travel to or from Salento involves a transfer at Las Flores.

PEREIRA AND VICINITY

Close to so much in the coffee region, Pereira (pop. 465,000), the capital of the Risaralda department, also makes a strong case for being the capital of the entire region, second only to Medellín in importance. Luring visitors just beyond the city are gorgeous hacienda hotels and natural parks such as Santuario de Flora y Fauna Otún-Quimbaya, and Pereira is also less than an hour's drive from Salento and other impossibly cute pueblos. A wide array of lodging, dining, and shopping options are here, but Pereira also has more to offer, including an abundant cultural life and a gritty-yet-not-unappealing old downtown area that feels like a step back in time.

Sights

The pulsing heart of the city is downtown, at the palm-lined **Plaza de Bolívar** (Clls. 19-20 and Cras. 7-8), where there stands a bronze sculpture by Rodrigo Arenas Betancourt depicting Simón Bolívar on horseback charging ahead to fight the Spaniards—naked. Facing the plaza is the beautiful **Catedral de Nuestra Señora de la Pobreza** (Cl. 20

Nuestra Señora de la Pobreza Catedral

range of options. Tastefully decorated rooms are spick-and-span with comfortable beds, and there is a small garden patio and several hammocks for late-afternoon snoozes.

Candlelit tables, lounge music, and art on the walls—you won't believe your eyes when you see ★ **Helena Adentro** (Cra. 7 No. 8-01, cell tel. 312/873-9825, noon-2am Sat.-Sun.). Started by a New Zealander and a Paisa, it's by far the coolest spot in Filandia, Quindío, and perhaps this side of Medellín. Cured meats and goat cheeses come from local farmers, as does the coffee. They have their own brand but also serve coffee from other regions of Colombia, using different brewing techniques. Locals keep coming back for the inventive libations here, such as the house cocktail, the Adentro Helena (aguardiente, *lulo* juice, and lime).

The popular place for a cappuccino is **Jahn Café** (Cl. 6A No. 5-45, 7:30am-midnight Mon.-Fri., 7:30am-2am Sat.-Sun.). For tea, go to its **Salón de Té** (Cl. 6 with Cra. 6), on the 2nd floor on the corner, which is also

Pereira

No. 7-30, tel. 6/335-6545, masses every hour 6am-noon and 5pm Mon.-Sat., 6am-noon and 5pm-8pm Sun.). The cathedral was built in 1890 using industrial-era building techniques; it was later damaged by an earthquake, needing to be almost completely reconstructed. It was rebuilt with a wooden ceiling and supports made from cumin laurel, a tree native to Colombia that is now endangered. The branch of **Banco de la República** (8:30am-6pm Mon.-Fri., 9am-1pm Sat., free) in Pereira, which has a public library and exhibition spaces with ever-changing shows, is located nearby. As interesting as these downtown highlights is the chance to brush shoulders

with the locals and observe them going about their daily lives; the stretch between the Plaza de Bolívar and the **Parque El Lago** (Cl. 24 with Cra. 8) is particularly lively, with a couple of charming pedestrian alleys on Calles 18 and 22 between Carreras 7 and 8.

The **Museo de Arte de Pereira** (Av. Las Américas No. 19-88, tel. 6/317-2828, www.museoartepereira.org, 10am-7pm Tues.-Fri., 10am-5pm Sat.-Sun., COP$3,000) is one of the best art museums in the region, and deserving of a visit. It features temporary exhibitions of contemporary Latin American artists. There are often film showings on weekend evenings. It's south of downtown.

In the **Parque Olaya Herrera** (between Cras. 13-14 and Clls. 19-21) is the well-preserved **Antigua Estación del Tren,** a photogenic old train station. There is a Megabus station in the park, and the park is a nice place for a morning jog.

Amble along 11 paths lined by local plants and, of course, *guadua* bamboo, at the impressive **Jardín Botánico de la Universidad Tecnológica de Pereira** (Vereda La Julita, Vía Mundo Nuevo, tel. 6/321-2523, www.utp.edu.co/jardin, 8am-6pm Mon.-Fri., 9am-1pm Sat.-Sun., COP$20,000 1-3 persons). Residents in these 13 hectares of jungle include butterflies, tortoises, and 168 species of birds. This campus is south of the city, past the bus station.

Entertainment and Events

The city's website (www.pereiraculturay-turismo.gov.co) is a resource for finding out what's happening in Pereira. If you're visiting on a **first Thursday,** then head to **La Cuadra** (Cra. 12 Bis with Cl. 12, 7pm-11pm first Thurs. of the month, free), a long-running open-air cultural space that hosts concerts, art exhibitions, theater performances, and more. The centrally located **Centro Cultural Lucy Tejada** (Cra. 10A No. 16-60, tel. 6/324-8749) is the city's major venue for concerts and events.

Recreation

For bike tours and rentals, contact **RetroCiclas Tours** (cell tel. 310/540-7327, www.retrociclas.co). One of the more popular tours is a trip to the village of Estación Pereira (COP$86,000), where in the town you'll take two different and exciting means of transportation: a *brujita,* a motorcycle-powered cart that zooms along old train tracks, and later a *garrucha,* which is a gondola-like metallic basket that transports passengers over the Río Cauca. Another trip on offer is along the Río Otún (COP$80,000) to the Santuario de Flora y Fauna Otún-Quimbaya.

On Sundays (8am-noon) Pereira celebrates the **Ciclovía,** during which the road from the Viaducto César Gaviria Trujillo to the Villa Olímpica is closed to traffic and open only to cyclists, joggers and walkers. Free bikes are available for rent at the Parque Olaya Herrera (between Cras. 13-14 and Clls. 19-21), but you'll need to leave ID (like a passport).

Food

★ **Ambar Diego Panesso** (Cra. 17 No. 9-50, tel. 6/344-7444, noon-3pm and 6pm-10pm Mon.-Sat., COP$30,000) serves the Pereira elite elaborate dishes like portobello mushrooms stuffed with apple puree and bacon bits. While vegetarian dishes are mostly nonexistent on the menu, the kitchen will gladly take on the challenge and whip up a pasta dish for you. It's in the upscale Pinares neighborhood. Another restaurant on the elegant side is **El Mirador** (Av. Circunvalar at Cl. 4, Colina, tel. 6/331-2141, noon-2am Mon.-Sat., COP$30,000), a steak house that has an incredible view of the city. There's an extensive list of Argentinian wines.

The menu at **El Meson Español** (Cl. 14 No. 25-57, tel. 6/321-5636, noon-3pm and 7pm-midnight daily, COP$22,000) runs the gamut from paella (the house specialty) to pad Thai.

For a hearty Colombian meal, like a big bowl of *ajiaco* (a filling potato-based stew), or to hang out and have a couple of beers at night, **La Ruana** (Av. Circunvalar No. 12-08, tel. 6/325-0115, 8am-2am Mon.-Sat., 8am-10pm Sun., COP$20,000) is the place to go on Avenida Circunvalar.

★ **Aly Torres** (Cl. 4 No. 16-45, tel. 6/331-3955, 8am-10:30pm daily, COP$20,000) is a cheerful restaurant at the Kolibrí Hostel, and it serves typical Colombian meals as well as backpacker favorites. It's worth a trip even if you're not staying at the hostel.

For a hamburger made from lentils, amaranth, cauliflower, or chicken, head to **Burger Green** (Cra. 12 No. 3-22, tel. 6/331-3236, www.burgergreen.co, 11am-10pm Tues.-Sun., COP$12,000).

Archie's (Centro Comercial Parque Arboleda, Circunvalar No. 5-20, tel.

6/317-0600, www.archiespizza.com, 8am-11pm daily, COP$22,000) has great pizzas (try the thin-crust *pizzas rústicas*) and salads. Its location on the top floor, with a breezy terrace, is a cool one. They also deliver.

Downtown, check out **Urbano** (C.C. Bolívar Plaza, Cra. 8 No. 19-41), a restaurant on the 2nd floor with a view to the Plaza de Bolívar. It has an extensive menu of international cuisine and happy hour specials. You may forget you're in a mall. On a quiet corner in the Centro, directly across from the Banco de la República library and cultural center is **Café Kahlua** (Cl. 18 Bis Peatonal with Cra. 9A, tel. 6/344-2144, 8am-8pm Mon.-Sat.). This open-air place on a pedestrian alley serves snacks, coffee, and beer.

Accommodations

Most visitors gravitate toward the Circunvalar area in Pereira, with malls and restaurants within walking distance. Otherwise, live it up at a nearby hacienda. The Centro has options, but prices are comparable to hotels on the Circunvalar, where you can walk without much concern at night.

Way better than any tourist information office is ★ **Kolibrí Hostel** (Cl. No. 16-35, tel. 6/331-3955, cell tel. 321/646-9275, www.kolibrihostel.com, COP$25,000 dorm, COP$85,000 d), the first hostel to take hold in the city, run by a Dutch-Colombian couple who have traveled extensively in the region. The owners will keep you busy with loads of activity options including coffee, paragliding, and biking tours. The hostel is located just off the Circunvalar, within walking distance of the Arboleda mall and several restaurants. In addition to a mix of private rooms and dorms, Kolibrí has two extended-stay apartments that go for around COP$150,000 a night.

The **Hotel Movich** (Cra. 13 No. 15-73, tel. 6/311-3300, COP$333,000 d) is a good option if you like comfort and don't desire any surprises, yet want to be close to it all. The pool (usually open until 9pm) and gym (open 24

hours) are quite nice. A massive breakfast buffet is included in the room rate. It's across the street from the imposing neo-gothic Iglesia de Carmen.

The classic 77-room **Hotel Soratama** (Cra. 7 No. 19-20, COP$146,000 d) is right in the thick of things on the Plaza de Bolívar. It has a nice rooftop terrace area with a dipping pool, and the restaurant is all right.

Outside of town is the upscale **Sonesta Hotel** (Km. 7 Vía Cerritos, tel. 6/311-3600, www.sonesta.com, COP$260,000 d), with over 160 spacious rooms, good restaurants, and a huge outdoor pool area. It's particularly popular for business meetings during the workweek.

A restful sleep is assured at the **Hotel Don Alfonso** (Cra. 13 No. 12-37, tel. 6/333-0909, www.donalfonsohotel.com, COP$264,000 d), a small boutique-style hotel on the main nightlife and shopping drag of Avenida Circunvalar. It has 11 comfortable air-conditioned rooms, each with inviting beds covered by quilts.

Castilla Real Hotel (Cl. 15 No. 12B-15, tel. 6/333-2192, www.hotelcastillareal.com, COP$170,000 d) has 24 comfortable rooms and is located on a side street near the Circunvalar area.

HACIENDAS

Within minutes of Pereira's bright lights are some gorgeous and luxurious hacienda hotels. Some of them are popular places for special events, such as weekend weddings and corporate seminars during the week.

Hacienda Malabar (Km. 7 Vía a Cerritos, Entrada 6, tel. 6/337-9206, www.hotelmalabar.com, COP$257,500 d) is an authentic hacienda with seven rooms, ample gardens to wander, and a pool. The wooden ceilings with their geometric designs and tile floors with Spanish Mudejar designs throughout the house are spectacular.

★ **Castilla Casa de Huespedes** (Km. 10 Vía a Cerritos, tel. 6/337-9045, cell tel. 315/499-9545, www.haciendacastilla.com, COP$281,000 d), built in the 19th century, is set amid fruit trees and has a pool to boot. The nine rooms are lovely, and staff are friendly. They make their own jam at this serene spot, and a majestic cedar tree near the pool area looks even more regal when illuminated at night.

The **Hacienda San José** (Km. 4 Vía Pereira-Cerritos, Entrada 16, Cadena El Tigre, tel. 6/313-2612, www.haciendahotelsanjose. com, COP$275,000-310,000 d) was built in 1888 and has been in the Jaramillo family for generations. It's in the countryside, and the entrance to it, lined with palms, is a dramatic one. The home, with 11 rooms, is spectacular, and the lovely wooden floors make a satisfying creak when you step on the planks. Service is impeccable and the restaurant is excellent. The grounds make for a nice late-afternoon stroll, and you can admire an enormous and regal old *samán* tree, well into its second century of life, as you dine alfresco. Living Trips (www.livingtrips.com) manages this hotel, and they can arrange day-trip excursions for you. The restaurant is open to the public, and members of the public can also come for the day and enjoy the pool. The airport is only 10 minutes away.

Luxury hotel **Sazagua** (Km. 7 Vía Cerritos, Entrada 4, tel. 6/337-9895, www. sazagua.com, COP$446,000 d) is not technically a hacienda, as it is in a country club-type environment. But there's no need to be put off by that. Here attention to detail reigns. The 10 rooms are impeccable, the common space is inviting, the gardens are perfectly manicured (surrounded by elegant heliconia flowers, birds, and the occasional iguana), and you can lounge by the pool or enjoy a massage at the spa. Nonguests can enjoy the spa facilities for a separate charge.

Information and Services

There is a small **tourist information booth** in the lobby of the Centro Cultural Lucy Tejada (Cl. 10 No. 16-60, tel. 6/311-6544, www. pereiraculturayturismo.gov.co, 8am-noon and 2pm-6pm Mon.-Fri.).

Call 123 for any type of emergency.

Transportation

Excellent bus connections are available between Pereira and most major cities. The **Terminal de Transportes de Pereira** (Cl. 17 No. 23-157, tel. 6/315-2323, www.terminaldepereira.com) is relatively close to the Avenida Circunvalar area. It is clean.

The articulated bus rapid transit system, the **Megabus** (tel. 6/335-1010), has three routes and connects with 28 intracity buses. It's not terribly convenient for those staying near Avenida Circunvalar, unfortunately.

The **Aeropuerto Matecaña** (Av. 30 de Agosto, tel. 6/314-2765) is pint-sized and in need of some love, but it's only about a 10-minute ride east of the city. **Avianca, LATAM,** and **Viva Colombia** fly to Bogotá; **Viva Colombia** flies to Cartagena; **EasyFly** and **ADA** will take you to the heart of Medellín and the Olaya Herrera Airport; and **ADA** also serves Quibdó.

For those looking to rent a car, **Hertz** (airport tel. 6/314-2678, www.hertz.com, 8am-6pm Mon.-Fri., 8am-noon Sat.) has an office at the airport. **Milano Rent A Car** (cell tel. 300/800-1180, www.milanocar.com) is an alternative. Its office is nearby, but staff will meet you at the airport. If you do rent a car, find out the *pico y placa* days and hours (www. transitopereira.gov.co) before putting the key into the ignition; these are vehicle restrictions during the workweek based on the last digit of the license plate.

VALLE DEL RÍO OTÚN

A visit to the Valle del Río Otún between Pereira and the Laguna del Otún (located within Parque Nacional Natural Los Nevados) is an interesting, highly enjoyable, and easy-to-organize introduction to Andean cloud forests. There are many possibilities for visiting the valley, from day trips out of Pereira to multiday excursions utilizing some very pleasant lodging facilities in the Santuario de Flora y Fauna Otún-Quimbaya and Parque Regional Natural Ucumarí.

The Río Otún flows 78 kilometers (48 miles) from the Laguna del Otún to the Río

Cauca and is the main source of water for Pereira. The conservation of the upper segment of the river, from Pereira to the Laguna del Otún, has been a success story, thanks to reforestation and land-protection efforts.

PLANNING YOUR TIME

The Santuario de Flora y Fauna Otún-Quimbaya is 14.4 kilometers (9 miles) southeast of Pereira along the Río Otún. The Parque Regional Natural Ucumarí is 6.6 kilometers (4 miles) upriver.

You can do day trips out of Pereira to either, but don't try to do both in one day. Santuario de Flora y Fauna Otún-Quimbaya is easily accessible by public transportation, and the main nature trails can be visited in one day. However, getting to Parque Regional Natural Ucumarí involves public transportation and a two-hour hike. It can be visited on a long day trip but it is much preferable to spend a night or two at the comfortable Pastora visitors center in the midst of the Andean forest. You can combine a visit to both, visiting Santuario de Flora y Fauna Otún-Quimbaya and then spending a day or two in Parque Regional Natural Ucumarí.

December and July-August are drier months, and are considered the best time for a hike to the Laguna del Otún. However, during mid-December through mid-January and Semana Santa (Holy Week) in March or April the trails can be packed with hikers, as this is high season for Colombians. The hike through Parque Regional Natural Ucumarí to the Laguna del Otún is very popular then, and there can be over a hundred hikers camping each night at that mountain lake.

Santuario de Fauna y Flora Otún-Quimbaya

It's a snap to trade the concrete jungle of Pereira for the real thing: make your way to the **Santuario de Fauna y Flora Otún-Quimbaya** (Km. 4.5 Vía Florida-El Cedral, Vereda La Suiza, cell tel. 313/695-4305, www.parquesnacionales.gov.co, COP$5,000) outside of town. Part of the national park system,

the Río Otún

Otún-Quimbaya covers 489 hectares (1,208 acres) of highly biodiverse Andean tropical forest at altitudes between 1,750 and 2,250 meters (5,740 and 7,380 feet). The vegetation is exuberant, and there are animal-viewing opportunities. The park is home to more than 200 species of birds, including endangered multicolored tanagers and the large *pava caucana* (Cauca guan). And, although you may not see them, you'll definitely hear the *mono aulladores* (howler monkeys). They make quite a brouhaha.

The main activities at the park are guided walks along three nature paths led by knowledgeable and enthusiastic guides from a local community ecotourism organization, the **Asociación Comunitaria Yarumo Blanco** (cell tel. 310/363-5001, www.yarumoblanco.co, reservas@yarumoblanco.co). Costs for the fairly easy walks (you must go with a guide) are around COP$50,000 per group, and generally take 1.5 hours.

Visitors can also bike along the main road that borders the crystalline Río Otún.

Yarumo Blanco rents mountain bikes (COP$10,000 all day). The visitors center offers simple but comfortable lodging (COP$32,000-42,000 pp) and meals (COP$6,000-9,000).

To get to Otún-Quimbaya from Pereira, take a bus operated by **Transportes Florida** (tel. 6/331-0488, COP$4,000, 90 mins.) from Calle 12 and Carrera 9 in Pereira. On weekdays, the bus departs at 7am, 9am, and 3pm. On weekends there is an additional bus at noon.

Parque Regional Natural Ucumarí

The **Parque Regional Natural Ucumarí** is 6.6 kilometers (4 miles) southwest of Santuario Flora y Fauna Otún-Quimbaya. This regional park covers an area of 3,986 hectares (9,850 acres) of Andean tropical forest at altitudes between 1,800 and 2,600 meters (5,900 and 8,500 feet). The main path follows the Río Otún through lush cloud forests, with waterfalls feeding into the river. The park is a wonderful place to view nature, with more than 185 species of birds.

The starting point of the main path is **El Cedral**, a small *vereda* (settlement) southwest of Santuario Flora y Fauna Otún-Quimbaya. The path is a well-trod one (by humans and horses) and is often muddy and rocky. It is best to take rubber or waterproof boots. It takes about 2.5 hours to climb to the main La Pastora visitors center, six kilometers (3.73 miles) from El Cedral.

Day-trippers from Pereira can lunch at the **visitors center** (COP$7,000-10,000 pp) and set off independently on one of three nature hikes before returning to El Cedral to catch the last bus at 5pm. Better yet, consider overnighting in the clean and cozy **dormitory-style rooms** (COP$25,000 pp, COP$8,000 camping) there. That way, as the mercury begins to fall in the late afternoon, you'll be able to relax by the lodge's fireplace and sip hot chocolate and eat cheese (that's how they do it in Colombia). There is no electricity, making a stay at **La Pastora** truly restful. To make a

reservation, contact the ecotourism organization **FECOMAR** (cell tel. 312/200-7711, fecomar.anp@hotmail.com). It can also arrange horses, if you would rather ride than hike up.

Beyond La Pastora, the path continues 13 kilometers (8 miles) to the Laguna del Otún in the Parque Nacional Natural Los Nevados.

To get to El Cedral, take the **Transportes Florida** bus (tel. 6/331-0488, COP$5,500, 2 hrs.) from Calle 12 and Carrera 9 in Pereira. On weekdays, the bus departs at 7am, 9am, and 3pm. On weekends there is an additional bus at noon. The buses return from El Cedral at noon and 6pm on weekdays and noon, 3pm, and 6pm on Sundays.

SANTA ROSA DE CABAL

Ready to soak up some atmosphere? Do as the Colombians do, and head to the hot springs of Santa Rosa de Cabal, near Pereira. To get there, you'll most likely pass through the town of Santa Rosa de Cabal. Start at the **Parque las Araucarias** (between Cras. 14-15 and Clls. 12-13), the main square, where there are juices to be drunk, *chorizo santarosano* sausages to be devoured (a specialty here), handicrafts to be bought, and people to be watched. Other points of interest are the **Santuario La Milagrosa** (Cl. 7 at Cra. 14, tel. 6/368-5201 or 6/368-5168), a modern church with fantastic stained glass windows, and the **Monumento al Machete** (Parque Gonzalo Echeverry, Cra. 16N No. 12-77, www.monumentoalmachete. blogspot.com.co), a small plaza with what are assumed to be the largest machetes in the world, at 4.5 meters (15 feet) long. There's food, beer, and souvenir stalls at this quirky homage to Paisa masculinity.

Hot Springs

There are two *termales* (hot springs) near Santa Rosa de Cabal: **Termales de Santa Rosa de Cabal** (Km. 9 Vía Termales, tel. 6/364-5500, www.termales.com.co, 9am-11:30pm daily, COP$22,000 in Feb. and Sep. and during the workweek, COP$36,000 weekends and high season) and **Termales San Vicente** (18 km east of Santa Rosa de Cabal, tel. 6/333-3433, www.sanvicente.com.co, 8am-midnight daily, COP$75,000 incl. transportation). Both can get packed with Colombian families on weekends and holidays. Go during the workweek, when it's less a scene and prices dip, too. Both springs offer bus transportation from Pereira, but it's ideal to have your own transportation so that you can take off when you wish.

Built in 1945, the Termales de Santa Rosa de Cabal hot springs are closer to Santa Rosa de Cabal. There are two areas in the complex. The first area, on the left as you enter the park, was recently built and is called the **Termales Balneario.** These consist of three large pools for adults and one for children. This area is the most popular for day-trip visitors, though it lacks natural beauty. The oldest part of the complex, called **Termales de Hotel** (COP$32,000 in Feb. and Sept. and during the workweek; COP$50,000 weekends and high season), is farther on at the base of some spectacular waterfalls of cool and pure mountain waters. The highest waterfall drops some 175 meters (575 feet). If you choose to stay the night, there are three options. **La Cabaña** (COP$360,000 d) is the newest and most comfortable place to stay and has 17 rooms. La Cabaña guests are allowed entry to the Termales Balneario, the Termales de Hotel, and their own small private pool. The advantage of staying at one of the hotels is that you can enjoy full use of the pools from 6am on, before the day-trip crowd begins arriving at 9am; the drawback is that the rooms are not luxurious, and the food doesn't receive raves either. At both Termales Balneario and Termales de Hotel, there are additional activities on offer, such as a guided nature walk (COP$14,000) to some waterfalls—wear shoes with traction for this, as the path is slippery—and spa treatments such as massages (COP$50,000, 30 mins.) and other services in a shabby-looking spa area.

The San Vicente hot springs are more remote, but the scenery of rolling hills, mountains in the distance, and farms is enchanting. Particularly scenic are the *pozos de amor,* small natural pools the size of whirlpools that perfectly fit two. Buses leave Pereira at 8am, returning at 5pm. San Vicente also offers various accommodation options, mostly cabins. A cabin for two people costs around COP$160,000 per person without meals.

Food and Accommodations

The bucolic countryside outside of Santa Rosa is home to many roadside, family-style restaurants and lodging facilities, good alternatives for hot springs day-trippers. The best two are run by the same owner. On the road toward the Termales de Santa Rosa, **Mamatina** (Km. 1 Vía Termales, La Leona, cell tel. 311/762-7624 or 314/767-2519, www.mamatinahotel.com, 9am-10pm daily, COP$18,000) specializes in trout covered with sausage, *sancocho* (a meaty stew), grilled meats, and beans and rice. Adjoining the restaurant is a hotel by the same name, which offers clean and comfortable rooms ranging in price from COP$40,000 per person to COP$140,000 for the suite with a hot tub. Horseback riding and walks through the countryside can be arranged here.

On the way toward Termales de San Vicente is the Mamatina owner's other, newer hotel. The ★ **Hospedaje Don Lolo** (Km. 5 Vía Termales San Vicente, cell tel. 316/698-6797, COP$50,000 pp d) is on a farm with cows, pigs, fish, horses, and dogs. If you're interested, you can lend a hand milking a cow or two. Some walks through the countryside are options as well, such as to an old Indian cemetery, to a big waterfall, and through jungle to see birds and butterflies. The countryside views and fresh air are delightful. If you're lucky, you may be able to see the Nevado del Ruiz in the distance in the early morning. The **Don Lolo** (Km. 5 Vía Termales San Vicente, cell tel. 316/698-6797) restaurant just down the road has a lot of personality and is a popular stop for those going to or returning from the Termales de San Vicente.

BELALCÁZAR

The coffee and plantain town of Belalcázar rests impossibly on a ridge, with fantastic views of the Valle de Cauca on one side and the Valle del Río Risaralda on the other. Besides the incredible views, Belalcázar, an agricultural town off the tourist map, offers the visitor pure coffee country authenticity. Belalcázar boasts distinct architecture, with its houses covered with colorful zinc sheets to protect against whipping winds.

Built in 1954 in hopes of preventing further bloodshed during the bloody Violencia period, the 45.5-meter-high (149-foot-high) **Monumento a Cristo Rey** (Km. 1 Vía Pereira-Belalcázar, COP$3,000) has become the symbol of this town. To get to the top of the statue of Jesus, you'll have to climb 154 steps. From atop, on a clear day, you can see six Colombian departments: Caldas, Risaralda, Quindío, Valle del Cauca, Tolima, and Chocó; and both the Central and Occidental mountain ranges. The other attraction in town is the **Eco Parque La Estampilla hike** (1.5 km, open daylight hours, free). It's on the northeast side of town, a 10-minute walk from the **Parque Bolívar** (Clls. 15-16 and Cras. 4-5), in which you can wander a winding path through forests of *guadua* (bamboo).

The best time to check out Belalcázar life at its most vibrant is on market day—Saturday—when farmers from the countryside converge on the town to sell coffee beans, plantains, pineapples, and other crops. The Parque Bolívar buzzes with activity as Jeep Willys, packed with farmers and marketgoers, come and go all day long. It's quite a carnival atmosphere.

The best hotel in town is the **Hotel Balcón Colonial** (Cra. 4A No. 12-10, tel. 6/860-2433, cell tel. 313/552-4652, COP$35,000 d). It's clean, cool, and basic, having just nine rooms.

Getting There

It is 54 kilometers from Pereira to Belalcázar. Buses depart from the Pereira Terminal de Transportes (Cl. 17 No. 23-157, Pereira, tel. 6/315-2323). **Flota Occidental** (tel. 6/321-1655, www.flotaoccidental.com) is the bus company that serves Belalcázar (COP$8,000,

2 hrs.) on an hourly basis from 6am until 6:30pm.

SANTUARIO

It's worth the arduous journey to this remote village on a mountaintop in the Cordillera Occidental (Western Mountains) just to take a photo of its famous **Calle Real,** dotted with stately Paisa houses that have been done up in a rainbow of colors. Calle Real is one of the most photographed streets in Colombia.

On Saturdays, campesinos converge on the town to sell their coffee, cacao, sugarcane, and other crops. There is so much activity on market day in the **Plaza de Bolívar** (between Clls. 6-7 and Cras. 5-6) that you'll be tempted to find a front-row seat in a café and take it all in: produce and coffee being unloaded and loaded, Jeep Willys filled with standing-room-only passengers arriving and departing, farmers drinking beer in taverns, women selling sweets in the park, and children being children. Many farmers, money in hand, whoop it up in town and stay the night.

Although Santuario is picture-perfect, it's far better to continue to the **Parque Nacional Natural Tatamá** than to spend the night in Santuario, even if you are not interested in doing any hiking: Hotels in town are not recommended.

There is regular bus transportation from the Terminal de Transportes de Pereira (Cl. 17 No. 23-157, Pereira, tel. 6/315-2323) to Santuario. **Flota Occidental** (tel. 6/321-1655, www.flotaoccidental.com) makes this two-hour trip (COP$8,000) three times a day: 6:55am, 11:45am, and 5:20pm.

PARQUE MUNICIPAL NATURAL PLANES DE SAN RAFAEL

Located in the remote, little visited Cordillera Occidental (Western Mountains), the Tatamá Massif contains one of the world's few remaining pristine *páramos* (highland moors). The topography of the mountain range is very broken, especially the jagged **Cerro Tatamá** (4,250 meters/13,945 feet), which is the highest point in the Cordillera Occidental. The range is highly biodiverse, with an estimated 564 species of orchids and 402 species of birds. It is also home to pumas, jaguars, and *osos anteojos,* the only breed of bear in Colombia. The central part of the massif is protected by the 15,900-hectare (39,300-acre) Parque Nacional Natural Tatamá.

Access to PNN Tatamá is through the Parque Municipal Natural Planes de San Rafael, which not only acts as a buffer zone on the eastern side of the national park near the town of Santuario, but is an attraction in itself. The **Parque Municipal Natural Planes de San Rafael** (10 km from Santuario, cell tel. 311/719-1717, www.planesdesanrafael. blogspot.com, amorosa_santuario@hotmail. com) covers 11,796 hectares (29,149 acres) of cloud forest between the altitudes of 2,000 and 2,600 meters (6,562 and 8,530 feet), with significant patches of old-growth forest. Nature walks are conducted by friendly and knowledgeable guides from a local community organization, the **Asociación de Guías e Interpretes Ambientales (GAIA),** many of whom got their start through participation in groups of youth bird-watchers.

Within the park there are four paths. The shortest, called the **Lluvia de Semillas** (Rainfall of Seeds), allows visitors to see a forest in recuperation. It is a one-kilometer (0.6-mile) loop through land that was once used for cattle grazing and, over the past 15 years, has been slowly returning to a forest. The 9.6-kilometer (6-mile) round-trip **Cascadas** trail is a strenuous path to the border of the Parque Nacional Natural Tatamá at an elevation of 2,600 meters (8,530 feet). It crisscrosses the Río San Rafael and culminates at a group of waterfalls. Along the way you can see a great variety of birds and large patches of primary forest. The hike takes 3.5 hours up and 2.5 hours down. The 12-kilometer (7.5-mile) **Quebrada Risaralda** hike takes six hours and can be combined into a loop with the Laguna Encantada hike. The **Laguna Encantada** path is a nine-kilometer (5.5-mile) circuit that takes five hours and

is especially good for bird-watching, with the possibility of viewing many hummingbirds. The best time for these hikes is early in the morning. Costs for these excursions are COP$25,000-50,000 per group of any size.

Parque Nacional Natural Tatamá

From Parque Municipal Natural Planes de San Rafael it is also possible to organize excursions into the **Parque Nacional Natural Tatamá** (tel. 6/368-7964, www.parquesnacionales.gov.co), located at the highest point of the Cordillera Occidental between the departments of Chocó, Risaralda, and Valle del Cauca. Though the park is not officially open to ecotourism, the folks at GAIA can organize an excursion that requires at least two nights of camping. The first day involves a 12-kilometer (7.5-mile), eight-hour hike to a campground at 3,200 meters (10,500 feet). The following day you explore the upper reaches of the Tatamá, with the unusual shrub-covered *páramo* (high tropical mountain ecosystem), craggy outcrops, and deep gorges. From the top you can see the Chocó lowlands. You return by nightfall to camp and return to Parque Municipal Natural Planes de San Rafael the following day. Contact **Parque Municipal Natural Planes de San Rafael** (cell tel. 311/719-1717) to organize.

Accommodations

The clean, comfortable, and cozy **lodge** (COP$25,000 pp or COP$52,000 with three meals) at the Parque Municipal Natural Planes de San Rafael visitors center accommodates 40 people. Meals (COP$7,000-10,000) are nothing short of delicious. To reserve lodging, contact the ecotourism organization **FECOMAR** (cell tel. 312/200-7711, fecomar.anp@hotmail. com) or call the park administrator (cell tel. 311/719-1717, amorosa_santuario@hotmail. com).

Bird-watching brings visitors to the **Rainforest Montezuma Ecolodge** (cell tel. 317/684-1034, www.montezuma-ecolodge.blogspot.com.co, COP$130,000 pp incl. all meals) at the fringes of the Tatamá park and the Cordillera Occidental near the town of Pueblo Rico (Risaralda). This lodge is a favorite among Colombian birding fanatics. There's a basic lodge, run by Leopoldina, which can accommodate 10. Visitors must contract a local guide to enter the national park (COP$80,000). Hiring a Jeep for the day to explore the area costs COP$300,000, although that is not essential.

Getting There

To get to the Parque Municipal Natural Planes de San Rafael visitors center and lodge, board one of the Jeeps that leave from the main square in Santuario each weekday at 7am and 3pm, or on Saturdays at 2pm and 5pm. If you miss those, no worries: You can take a *servicio express* (private car) for COP$35,000. To get to Pueblo Rico (Rainforest Montezuma Ecolodge) from Pereira there are about 15 buses daily on Flota Occidental (COP$18,000, 3.5 hrs.), but any bus destined for Quibdó will also get you there. From Pueblo Rico to Montezuma hiring a Jeep costs COP$70,000.

IBAGUÉ

The bustling capital city of the Tolima department, Ibagué (pop. 600,000) is Colombia's "City of Music," hosting several music festivals each year. It's hard to believe, but just to the west of this tropical-fruit-producing region, and beyond the green folds of mountains and valleys, looms the snowy peak of the Nevado del Tolima in the Parque Nacional Natural Los Nevados. Ibagué is a great launch pad for the challenge of ascending to that mountain.

Sights

Should you have some time to spend in Ibagué, a handful of sights are worth a look. Shade is not an issue at the **Plaza de Bolívar** (between Cras. 2-3 and Clls. 9-10): The square is full of majestic, centuries-old trees, but it is the **Catedral Inmaculada Concepción** (Cl. 10 No. 1-129, tel. 8/263-3451, 7am-noon and 2:30pm-7:30pm daily) that steals attention.

The **Banco de la República** (Cra. 3A No. 11-26, tel. 8/263-0721, www.banrepcultural. org, 8:30am-6pm Mon.-Fri., 8:30am-1pm Sat., free) always has an exhibit in its 2nd-floor exhibition hall. It's close to the **Calle Peatonal** (Cra. 3 between Clls. 10-15), which is refreshingly free from cars and motorbikes.

The **Conservatorio del Tolima** (Cra. 1 between Clls. 9-10, tel. 8/826-1852, www. conservatoriodeltolima.edu.co, open only for concerts) is one of the reasons Ibagué prides itself the "Capital Musical de Colombia." A few bars from the Colombian national anthem are painted on the exterior of the yellow Republican-era building.

Music festivals take place in the city year-round, including the **Festival Nacional de la Música Colombiana** (www.fundacion-musicaldecolombia.com, Mar.) and **Festival Folclórico Colombiano** (www.festivalfolclorico.com, June or July).

The **Museo de Arte del Tolima** (Cra. 7 No. 5-93, tel. 8/273-2840, www.museodeartedeltolima.org, 10am-12:30pm and 2pm-6:30pm daily, COP$3,500) is a small museum with a permanent collection and temporary exhibition space dedicated to contemporary Colombian artists. A leafy park in this pleasant part of town is the **Parque Centenario** (Cra. 6 between Clls. 8-10). Along with usual park goings-on, cultural events are often held in an amphitheater.

Food and Accommodations

The trendy dining and drinking spot in Ibagué is 15 stories high, with a superb bird's-eye view of the city and the Parque Nacional Natural Los Nevados. **Altavista** (Cra. 2 at Cl. 11, tel. 8/277-1381, noon-midnight Mon.-Wed., noon-3am Thurs.-Sat., noon-4pm Sun., COP$25,000) has a little bit of everything: Asian-inspired dishes, tapas, and vegetarian options. At night on weekends it becomes more of a lounge atmosphere, often with live shows.

The most luxurious hotel in town is the Colombian chain **Hotel Estelar Altamira** (Cra. 1A No. 45-50, tel. 8/266-6111,

COP$203,000 d), located outside of the city center. In town choose the century-old **Hotel Lusitania** (Cra. 2 No. 15-55, tel. 8/261-9166, www.hotellusitania.com), a classic with comfortable rooms surrounding a nice-sized swimming pool.

For fresh air and birdsong galore, the welcoming ★ **Ukuku Rural Lodge** (www.ukuku.co, COP$42,000 dorm, COP$142,000 d) is the place to be. It's located in the beautiful Cañón del Combeima gorge, about 17 kilometers (10.6 miles) from Ibagué, and only about a 1.5-kilometer (0.9-mile) hike into the mountains. The ecolodge offers various types of rooms and specializes in a wealth of natural pursuits: bird-watching, canyoning, rock climbing, and especially trekking, to the Nevado del Tolima and a hike the lodge dubs the "Ruta de la Palma de Cera," which follows the path taken by European explorers and naturalists Alexander von Humboldt and Aimé Bonpland.

Transportation

The **Terminal de Transportes** (Cra. 2 No. 20-86, tel. 8/261-8122, www.terminalibague.com) is in a rough part of town, so you should take a cab to and from the bus station. For the most part, Ibagué is not a walkable city, except in the center of town. From the Ibagué airport there are nonstop flights to Bogotá and Medellín.

Cali and Southwest Colombia

Highlights

★ **Salsa in Cali:** There is no better place to practice your moves than at one of Cali's count-less *salsotecas* (salsa clubs). But even if you have two left feet, you can still get into the spirit by taking in a salsa show (page 303).

★ **Centro Histórico in Popayán:** Explore the region's volcanoes, coffee farms, indigenous markets, or hot springs by day, but save some energy to amble the streets of the White City's beautiful historic center after the sun goes down (page 318).

★ **Tierradentro:** Dozens of elaborate burial chambers lie beneath the hilltops at this impor-tant archaeological site in Cauca (page 323).

★ **San Agustín:** This incredible archaeological site, with access to nature hikes and rafting adven-tures, is Colombia's Easter Island (page 326).

★ **Laguna La Cocha:** Take a boat ride from the colorful fishing village of Encano to the tiny tropical rainforest on Isla de la Corota, home to Colombia's smallest national park (page 337).

★ **Laguna Verde:** The emerald-green waters of this crater lake in the Nudo de los Pastos moun-tains are a fantastic sight to behold (page 337).

Hiking boots and dancing shoes are essential in southwestern Colombia, an unsung destination chock full of natural adventures.

The distances between the cities in the southwest of Colombia are not great as the crow (or in this case, the condor) flies. However, Cali, Popayán, Pasto, and their environs are worlds apart. Cali, Colombia's third-largest city, is best known for its warm people and its hot salsa dancing. In Pasto, a volcano looms in the distance. Popayán is the White City, home of presidents and poets.

As you set off from Cali, the flat countryside of the Valle de Cauca is dominated by fields of sugarcane, interrupted by occasional umbrella-shaped *samán* trees. Buga, a Catholic pilgrimage site, is perfectly situated near the weekend playground of Lago Calima. In the north of the department is the sleepy town of Roldanillo, which was put on the map thanks to its famous son, abstract expressionist artist Omar Rayo. For adventurous types, this cute town is all about paragliding.

Many travelers make a quick detour on their way to or from Ecuador to admire the neo-gothic gem of Las Lajas church, set impossibly in a narrow canyon near Ipiales. But it's worth spending more time to get to know the department of Nariño. Jagged mountains, turquoise lakes, and sleeping volcanoes provide dramatic backdrops to the neat patchwork of potato crops that sustain many families in this agricultural region.

Upstream along the Río Cauca is the "White City" of Popayán, home to the Universidad del Cauca. Students fill the city's cafés, bars, and its stately main plaza, the Parque Caldas. Nearby are several interesting day-trip destinations, from organic coffee farms to hot springs to indigenous markets. In Parque Nacional Natural Puracé, intrepid hikers trek to the rim of a snow-covered active volcano. Farther on are two of Colombia's most important and beautiful archaeological sites: Tierradentro, where dozens of ancient underground burial chambers are preserved, and San Agustín, where hundreds of well-preserved stone statues of deities and animals stand.

Previous: *Chontaduro* (peach palm) for sale in Cali; fishing community at Laguna La Cocha. **Above:** a statue at archaeological site San Agustín.

Cali and Southwest Colombia

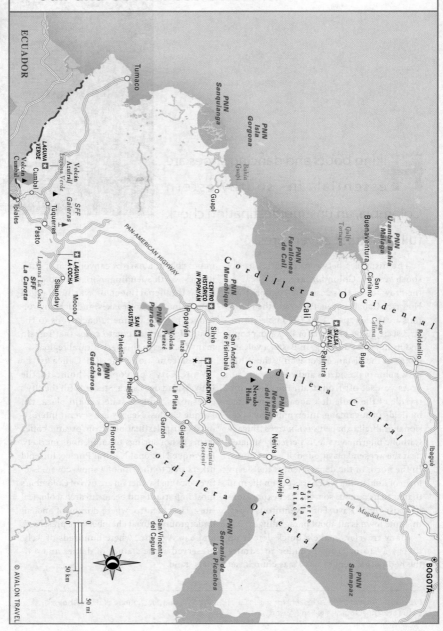

ECUADOR

Tumaco

PNN
Sanquianga

PNN
Isla
Gorgona

Bahía
Guapi

LAGUNA
VERDE
Volcán
Cumbal

Cumbal

Laguna Verde

Guapi

Ipiales

Volcán
Azufral/
Laguna Verde

SFF
Galeras

Tuquerres

Pasto

Laguna La Cocha
La Carota
SFF

LAGUNA
LA COCHA

PNN
Uramba Bahía
Málaga

Buenaventura

PNN
Farallones
de Cali

San
Cipriano

Golfo
Tortugas

PAN-AMERICAN HIGHWAY

Sibundoy

Mocoa

PNN
Munchique

CENTRO
HISTÓRICO
IN POPAYÁN

Cordillera   Occidental

Lago
Calima

Palestina

SAN
AGUSTÍN

PNN
Puracé

Isnos

Volcán
Puracé

Popayán
Inzá

Silvia

San Andrés
de Pisimbalá

SALSA
IN CALI

Palmira

Roldanillo

Buga

Ibagué

PNN
Los
Guácharos

Pitalito

La Plata

TIERRADENTRO

Nevado
del Huila

Nevado
Huila

PNN
Nevado
del Huila

Cordillera   Central

Florencia

Garzón

Gigante

Betania
Reservoir

Neiva

Villavieja

Desierto
de la
Tatacoa

Río Magdalena

Cordillera   Oriental

San Vicente
del Caguán

PNN
Serranía de
Los Picachos

PNN
Sumapaz

BOGOTÁ

0   0

50 km

50 mi

© AVALON TRAVEL

PLANNING YOUR TIME

Three days is just enough time to get a feel for the Cali way. Try visiting the city over part of the weekend so that you can check out a salsa show or visit a *salsoteca* (salsa club). Other sights of interest in the Valle de Cauca can be visited out of Cali or perhaps from Buga. Roldanillo makes a nice side trip between Cali and the coffee region near Armenia.

It's an easy trip between Cali and Popayán, about three hours by minivan on a good road. If you'd like to check out sights near Popayán, such as the Guambiano town of Silvia, or hike to the Puracé volcano, plan for at least 3-4 days in the capital of Cauca. A circuit tour of the sights of Tierradentro, the Tatacoa desert,

and San Agustín can be done out of Popayán. For that you'll need five days.

It is often slow going on the Pan-American Highway from Ipiales through Pasto to Popayán. But the scenery is simply incredible. While Ipiales is not a great base for sightseeing, the larger city of Pasto is. You can happily spend a few days seeing the city and taking some day trips, such as those to La Cocha or the Laguna Verde. The strenuous climb up Volcán Cumbal takes planning but is worth it.

Some of the big goings-on in the region are the Semana Santa (Holy Week) processions in Popayán, the Feria de Cali (late December), and the Carnaval de Negros y Blancos (early January) in Pasto.

Cali

Cali's relaxed pace is evident everywhere you go in this diverse city of 2.4 million. Just sip a *lulada* (a refreshing, fruity drink), listen to some salsa, and wait until sundown. Here in the Valle del Cauca, where sugarcane fields go on forever, you're far removed from uptight Bogotá and overambitious Medellín. In a swipe at those two cities, locals like to say, *"Cali es Cali y lo demás es loma"* ("Cali is Cali but those other cities are just hills").

While the colonial churches of the Centro are lovely and the Museo La Tertulia top-notch, Cali is not a city packed with must-see sights; its main attraction is its atmosphere. Tourists keep falling in love with the "Sultan of the Valley." Is it that refreshing late-afternoon breeze? The Pacific cuisine? The people? Or is it the salsa?

Cali is the world's salsa capital. Incorporating a little salsa into your visit to Cali is a necessity if you want to get to know this seductive city, its people, and their ways.

History

Present-day Valle del Cauca was settled by the Calima people as early as 1200 BC. The first Europeans to arrive were soldiers under the

command of Spanish conquistador Sebastián de Belalcázar, known today for conquering most of present-day Ecuador and southwestern Colombia. In 1536, he founded Santiago de Cali, slightly north of the city's current location. During the colonial period and most of the 19th century, Cali was a small agricultural settlement, surrounded by haciendas, with a significant slave population. To this day, Afro-Colombians make up a large part of the Cali population, with over 25 percent belonging to this ethnic group.

In the 20th century, Cali developed rapidly, becoming a center of manufacturing. In 1971, the city hosted the Pan-American Games. That was probably Cali's heyday. During the 1980s and 1990s, Cali became a global drug-trafficking center and the seat of the eponymous drug cartel. For a time in the 1990s, the Cali Cartel ruled the global cocaine business unchallenged.

As a result of drug-related violence, Cali's civic leaders fled, taking investment and business elsewhere. During the 1990s and early 21st century, the city suffered from the double scourge of urban violence and guerrilla intimidation. The FARC (Fuerzas Armadas

Cali

Parque del Acueducto

Parque del Periodista

MUSEO LA TERTULIA
ALDIA, CALATHEA
BARIKHA

Parque San Antonio

IGLESIA DE SAN ANTONIO

SEE DETAIL

AVENIDA 4N
AVENIDA 4A

Parque Artesanal Loma de la Cruz
LA LOMA DE LA CRUZ
LA TOPA TOLONDRA
PUNTO BARÉ
LA TABERNA

CENTRO CULTURAL DE CALI
ENRIQUE BUENAVENTURA
TEATRO MUNICIPAL
ASOMUCA
LA MERCED COMPLEX
NUTRI CENTRO
LA GUACHARACA CAFÉ

BANCO DE LA REPÚBLICA/ MUSEO DEL ORO CALIMA
BOCADOS
DA GUSTO
IGLESIA SAN FRANCISCO
GOBERNACIÓN BUILDING
TORRE MUDÉJAR
CATEDRAL SAN PEDRO
PALACIO NACIONAL
PLAZA Caycedo
RIKUS
TEATRO JORGE ISAACS
IGLESIA LA ERMITA
PUENTE ORTIZ
JAIRO VARELA
PLAZOLETA DE LA CALIDAD
CAM
Parque de los Poetas

CASTELLON JUANAMBÚ
CENTENARIO
PLATILLOS VOLADORES
HOTEL MS CENTENARIO
SHOPPING MALL
TEATRO DEL PRESAGIO
NOW HOTEL
MARRIOTT
CARAMBOLO
QUEENS BAR
RINGLETE
LITANY LEBANESE RESTUARANT
BENDITO COFFEE
HOTEL EL PORTÓN DE GRANDA
LUGAR A DUDAS
ZAPEROCO BAR
JUAN VALDEZ
D'TOLUCA
LARRY'S
PELICAN
HOSTAL CASA DEL GATO

AVENIDA 6N
AVENIDA 6B

Parque Jorge Isaacs
La Ermita
San Pedro
Torre de Cali
HOTEL PLAZA
TORRE DE CALI
Versalles
Las Américas
San Nicolás

Parque Principal
Parque Panamericana

INTERCONTINENTAL CALI/ LA PIZZERIA

Cemetery

AVENIDA DE LAS

Fray Damián
San Pascual

CARRERA 14
CARRERA 13
CARRERA 12
CARRERA 11
CARRERA 10
CARRERA 9
CARRERA 8
CARRERA 7
CARRERA 6
CARRERA 5
CARRERA 4
CARRERA 3N
CARRERA 2N
CARRERA 1N

CALLE 5
CALLE 6
CALLE 7
CALLE 8
CALLE 9
CALLE 10
CALLE 11
CALLE 12
CALLE 13
CALLE 14
CALLE 15
CALLE 18
CALLE 19
CALLE 21
CALLE 22
CALLE 23
CALLE 24
CALLE 25
CALLE 26

Santa Rosa
Petecuy
Centro

0 400 yds
0 400 m

Detail:

ATHAUALPA
IGLESIA DE SAN ANTONIO
Parque San Antonio
EL ENCUENTRO
HOTEL
MALECÓN CUBAR
LA COLINA
HOTEL DANN CARLTON
OJO DE CAFÉ
SAN ANTONIO
HOTEL BOUTIQUE
LA CASA
EL PARGO ROJO
RUTA SUR
ANTIGUA CONTEMPORANEA
MACONDO POSTRES Y CAFÉ
AZUL
VALLE PACIFICO
BUEN ALIMENTO
PITA MAJITA
GRECO BAR
EL VIAJERO
HOTEL EL PEÑÓN

CALLE 1 OESTE
CALLE 2
CALLE 3
CALLE 4
CALLE 5
CALLE 6
CARRERA 1
CARRERA 2
CARRERA 3
CARRERA 4
CARRERA 5
CARRERA 6
CARRERA 10
CARRERA 9

© AVALON TRAVEL

Revolucionarias de Colombia; Revolutionary Armed Forces of Colombia) occupied much of the surrounding mountainous areas. In 2002, FARC was responsible for the audacious kidnapping of 12 *deputados* (assemblypersons) from downtown Cali, 11 of whom were eventually killed—an event that shook Colombia to its core.

Cali has since turned over a new leaf, undertaking major infrastructure projects, such as the MIO (Masivo Integrado de Occidente) mass transit system, and is beginning to attract new investments. In 2013, Cali was the proud host of the World Games, an international sports competition.

Orientation

Nearly all of the city's tourist attractions are in the **Centro,** in three areas in particular: **La Merced, La Ermita,** and **Plaza Cayzedo/ Iglesia San Francisco.** You can visit all these areas on foot in one day. The Centro is brimming with activity during weekdays. Avoid the midday heat by planning your visit for the morning or late afternoon. Avoid lingering downtown after dark.

Inviting neighborhoods such as **San Antonio, Granada,** and **El Peñon** lack attractions but are a delight to get to know.

Within a 10- to 15-minute cab ride from the Centro, these tree-lined barrios are filled with restaurants, shops, and hotels. Late-night activity on weekends tends to shift to northern areas (not far from Granada) such as Menga and Yumbo.

You may have difficulty figuring out the lay of the land in Cali, as it is not as straightforward as other cities in Colombia. The Río Cali (actually more of a stream), the Tres Cruces hill, the Torre de Cali, and the Intercontinental Cali are well-known points of reference.

Climate

The average temperature in Cali is about 24°C (75°F); however, the average daily high is a sizzling 30°C (86°F). But between 4:30pm and 6:30pm, as the sun begins its descent over the Cordillera Occidental into the Pacific, the drop in temperature (to around 19°C/66°F) and a gentle breeze combine to make the weather absolutely *delicioso*. During this most pleasant time of day, head to the Parque de San Antonio, Parque Artesanal Loma de la Cruz, or anywhere outdoors.

Safety

Strolling the Centro is fine during daylight hours, but be alert near sights such as Iglesia

the towering palms of the Plaza Cayzedo

La Ermita. Walking within and between neighborhoods such as Centro, Granada, and San Antonio is safe, but you'll probably want to avoid this in the evenings. Hostels in Cali provide useful maps with go and no-go areas. As in most Colombian cities, there are community police stations (Centros de Atención Inmediata, or CAI) in every neighborhood and often in parks, such as the Parque de San Antonio.

Follow the general precautions of any large Colombian city, especially regarding the use of taxis and precautions to take in nightspots, and you'll be fine. The national toll-free hotline for any emergency is 123. The police have an additional number, 112.

SIGHTS

The easily walkable main points of interest in the Centro are clustered near Iglesia La Merced and Plaza Cayzedo. You'll need just a few hours to see everything.

Colombia Walking Tours (cell tel. 318/318-4551) organizes occasional thematic tours (COP$10,000) in the area, usually in both English and Spanish, on culture, religion, and history. Groups usually set off in the late afternoon.

La Merced Complex

On June 25, 1536, the city of Santiago de Cali was founded by Sebastián de Belalcázar. He changed his mind about the location and moved the city shortly thereafter to its present location, and a mass was held to celebrate the foundation of the city. It was on this site that the Iglesia La Merced (Cra. 4 at Cl. 7, tel. 2/889-2309, 6:30am-10am and 4pm-7pm daily, masses 7am and 6pm Mon.-Sat., 9am and 6pm Sun.) was built, sometime around 1545. The oldest church in Cali, it is a lovely example of typical colonial construction of the time, with its thick, whitewashed walls. The church, in the shape of a cross, has a single nave with red wooden beams. The only extravagance to be seen is the golden baroque altar with a statue of the Virgen de las Mercedes, who is the patron saint of Cali.

Housed in the church's chapels of the Virgen de la Merced and Virgen de los Remedios, the **Museo de Arte Colonial y Religioso La Merced** (Cra. 4 No. 6-117, tel. 2/888-0646, cell tel. 312/731-5948, 9am-noon and 2pm-5pm Mon.-Fri., 9am-noon Sat., COP$4,000 adults, COP$3,000 students, COP$2,000 children) is a small museum containing Quiteño school paintings, silver objects, statues, and religious items from the colonial period. Student guides will be happy to show you around for a small fee.

The **Museo Arqueológico La Merced—MUSA** (Cra. 4 No. 6-59, tel. 2/885-4665, 9am-1pm and 2pm-6pm Mon.-Sat., COP$4,000 adults, COP$2,000 children) is in the same complex, in part of the Augustinian convent, and has two exhibition rooms highlighting ceramics from native cultures of the region: Tolima, Quimbaya, Calima, Tierradentro, San Agustín, Tumaco, and Nariño.

MUSEO DEL ORO CALIMA

Within the Banco de la República building across the street from Iglesia La Merced is the excellent **Museo del Oro Calima** (Cl. 7 No. 4-69, tel. 2/684-7754, www.banrepcultural.org/cali, 9am-5pm Tues.-Fri., 10am-5pm Sat., free). Cali's gold museum has a collection of more than 600 ornamental gold and utilitarian ceramics, attributed to the ancient Calima people, that have been unearthed northwest of present-day Cali.

The **Sala de Exposiciones** (Cl. 7 No. 4-69, tel. 2/684-7751, 9am-5:30pm Mon.-Fri., free) is in the same building as the Museo del Oro, and often hosts temporary exhibits from the Banco de la República art collection. It's worth a peek.

CENTRO CULTURAL DE CALI

There are always art exhibitions on in the basement galleries of the **Centro Cultural de Cali** (Cra. 5 No. 6-05, tel. 2/885-8859, ext. 109, www.cali.gov.co/cultura, www.funhi.org, 8am-noon and 2pm-5pm Mon.-Fri., free), a building that also houses the tourist information offices.

the Torre Mudéjar in downtown Cali

a large outdoor cultural space to be used for concerts and other events. Along the river, the pedestrian walkway Bulevar del Río extends from Calle 5 to La Ermita. On Sunday mornings there are free aerobics classes. These new projects provide an exciting contrast to some of the grandiose relics of the 19th century, such as the **Teatro Jorge Isaacs** (Cra. 3 at Cl. 12) and **Puente Ortiz** (Cra. 1 at Cl. 12).

PLAZA CAYZEDO AND AROUND
The dozens of majestic wax palms in the **Plaza Cayzedo** (Cras. 4-5 between Clls. 11-12) create a green oasis in the middle of gritty downtown Cali. Plaza Cayzedo was known as the Plaza Mayor during the colonial era, but in 1913 it was renamed to honor the most famous independence figure from Cali, Joaquín de Cayzedo y Cuero. When passing through the park on the brick walkways you'll encounter a colorful cross-section of Caleños, from university students to shoe shiners to dapper older men watching the world go by from the comfort of a park bench.

Dating to the turn of the 19th century, the brilliant-white neoclassical **Catedral San Pedro** (Cl. 11 No. 5-35, tel. 2/881-1378, masses 9am, 10am, 11am, and noon Mon.-Sat., 9am and 5pm Sun.) on the southern corner of the Plaza Cayzedo has been rebuilt several times due to destruction caused by earthquakes. The most stunning building on the plaza is the French neoclassical gem the **Palacio Nacional** (Cra. 4 No. 12-04), also known as the Palacio de Justicia. Completed in the early 1930s, it houses various judicial bodies of the Valle de Cauca departmental government. The Palacio Nacional is not open to the public.

Nearby the plaza are some small and very lively pedestrian streets leading to the Bulevar del Río (Calle 12), where vendors sell their wares.

The distinctive redbrick church complex of the **Iglesia San Francisco** (Cl. 10 No. 6-00, tel. 2/884-2457, masses 7am and 5pm Mon.-Sat., 9am and 6pm Sun.) includes the **Capilla de la Inmaculada,** the **Convento de San Joaquín,** and the **Torre Mudéjar,**

IGLESIA LA ERMITA
Near the Río Cali is one of the city's most iconic landmarks: the miniature, neo-gothic **Iglesia La Ermita** (Cra. 13 at Cl. 1, no phone, masses 7am and 5pm Mon.-Fri., 10am and 5pm Sat.-Sun.). Originally built in the 16th century, the church was nearly destroyed by earthquakes in 1787 and in 1925; not much was left after the 18th-century tremor, except for the painting of the Señor de la Caña (Lord of the Sugarcane). Its survival was attributed to a miracle. The three-nave church has an Italian marble altar and many stained-glass windows. The current building was completed in the 1940s.

PLAZOLETA JAIRO VARELA AND BULEVAR DEL RÍO
In 2013 the **Plazoleta Jairo Varela** (Av. 2N between Clls. 10-11) and **Bulevar del Río** (Calle 12), megaprojects to revitalize the deteriorating downtown, were completed. The Plazoleta Jairo Varela pays homage to a beloved salsa singer and founder of the Grupo Niche who passed away in Cali in 2012. It's

all built between the 17th and 19th centuries by Franciscans. The architectural star here is the Torre Mudéjar, a four-story bell tower 23 meters (75 feet) high. It is divided into four redbrick sections, with each level displaying a different geometric design. It is considered a good example of neo-Mudéjar design in the New World. The architect of the tower was supposedly a Moor who had fled Spanish authorities, seeking refuge in the convent. In return for shelter, he designed the bell tower.

Beyond the Centro
MUSEO LA TERTULIA

One of the best art museums in the country is Cali's **Museo La Tertulia** (Av. Colombia No. 5 Oeste-105, tel. 2/893-2939, www.muse-olatertulia.com, 10am-6pm Tues.-Sat., 2pm-6pm Sun., COP$10,000 adults, COP$7,000 students, free Sun.). Museum galleries highlight contemporary Colombian artists such as Beatriz González, Hugo Zapata, Omar Rayo, and others. Built in the 1960s, Museo La Tertulia is perhaps the most important cultural center in Cali. The word *tertulia* refers to a social gathering for talking and sharing ideas about culture, art, and other themes. The *cinemateca* shows art films in the evenings and hosts festivals such as EuroCine. A concert hall offers chamber music concerts and poetry readings, and the lush grounds house an amphitheater as well as yoga on Wednesday evenings. A deli/café on the terrace is a popular meeting place in the evenings.

ZOOLÓGICO DE CALI

The **Zoológico de Cali** (Cra. 2 Oeste and Cl. 14, tel. 2/488-0888, 9am-4:30pm daily, COP$18,000 adults, COP$12,000 children) is considered the best zoo in the country, although that may not say very much. Straddling the Río Cali and full of trees and flowers, this is a pleasant place to spend a weekday afternoon. Most of the zoo is dedicated to Colombian species. Beware of swarms of families on weekends. The zoo is accessible by MIO by taking the A02 bus from the San Bosco station.

IGLESIA AND PARQUE DE SAN ANTONIO

Built in the mid-18th century, the small, white **Iglesia de San Antonio** (Cl. 1 Oeste at Cra. 10, tel. 2/893-7185) is beautiful in its simplicity, with whitewashed adobe walls and wooden beams. If the main doors are closed (which is often the case, as the church is only open for mass), head to the back left of the church and ring (once) at the door. Clarisa nuns from the convent there may give you a quick tour.

The **Parque de San Antonio** is the place to experience San Antonio life. You'll see a vibrant mix of Caleños (and their canine companions) here, especially in the late afternoon and on weekends. Lining one side of the sloping park are fast-food joints, bars, and ice cream shops.

PARQUE ARTESANAL LOMA DE LA CRUZ

While technically it's known as an *artesanías* (handicrafts) market, **Parque Artesanal Loma de la Cruz** (Cl. 5 between Cras. 14-16, 9am-10pm daily) has such a pleasant atmosphere, especially in the early evening Thursday-Sunday, that it's worth a visit even if you're not in the mood for shopping—plus, it's free. Handicrafts, such as *mochilas* (shoulder bags) created by indigenous weavers and leather goods, are for sale, and you may stumble upon concerts featuring Andean music, poetry readings, dance performances, or open-air films in the small amphitheater. From San Antonio, the market is a short walk up through the adjacent San Cayetano neighborhood. The entrance at the bottom of the *loma* (hill), is hard to miss, with a waterfall cascading down and a sign that reads "Loma de la Cruz."

EL CERRO DE CRISTO REY

The statue of Christ on **El Cerro de Cristo Rey** (south of the Cerro de las Tres Cruces in Los Andes neighborhood) stands 26 meters (85 feet). It was created by an Italian sculptor to celebrate 50 years of peace following the

Guerra de Mil Días (the Thousand Days' War) over the turn of the 20th century. That civil war claimed around 100,000 lives in Colombia and Panama. While there is a path to the top, it is best to take a taxi (COP$45,000). Along the way you can check out the sculpture on the side of the mountain called *El Lamento de la Pacha Mama,* which is a tribute to indigenous peoples, and munch on an empanada at a roadside stall. Don't make the Cristo Rey excursion after dark.

UNIVERSIDAD DEL VALLE MUSEO ARQUEOLÓGICO

The dynamic **Museo Arqueológico** (Biblioteca Mario Carvajal, tel. 2/321-2975, museo.arqueologico@correounivalle.edu.co, Mon.-Fri. 9am-noon and 2pm-5pm, Sat. 10am-1pm, free) has a massive archaeological collection and changing exhibits. It's located in one of the main libraries on the expansive grounds of the **Universidad del Valle,** one of Columbia's largest campuses, in the south of the city. The museum marks its 50th year in 2017. The campus itself is interesting to visit— it won a national architectural prize when it was built in the early 1970s—and makes an important contribution to the city's cultural fabric, with around 30,000 students.

ENTERTAINMENT AND EVENTS
★ **Salsa**

In Cali, there are many ways you can experience (and very likely get hooked on) salsa.

SALSA AL PARQUE

On the first Saturday night of the month, go to **Salsa al Parque** (fculturalatina@gmail.com, 4pm-midnight, free). This friendly and open-air freebie, held in different areas of the city, is known as an *audición,* which is a chance for *coleccionistas,* enthusiasts who collect salsa albums, to play their favorites for the crowd. People young and old, and visitors and locals from all walks of life, gather for these events, with the common denominator being a love of salsa. The event is organized by the Fundación

Cultural Nuestra Cosa Latina; check its Facebook page to see what it has planned.

SALSOTECAS

No matter where you go on a Saturday night, there's a good chance that you'll hear some salsa. But there are some places—*salsotecas*—where it's all about salsa and nothing more. Most are open from Wednesday until Sunday, closing at around 2am. Big *salsotecas,* like Tin Tin Deo, will have a cover. Many of the famous spots are in the south of the city, clustered along Calle 5. While two women dancing together is generally accepted, two men may not be; however, some places, such as La Topa Tolondra, are pretty open-minded.

Within walking distance of the San Antonio neighborhood, **La Topa Tolondra** (Cl. 5 No. 13-27, cell tel. 314/664-1470, 6pm-1am Wed.-Thurs., 6pm-3am Fri.-Sat., COP$10,000) is a cool little spot near Parque Artesanal Loma de la Cruz, packing them in every night. It often has special live international acts. La Topa is next door to **Punto Baré** (Cl. 5 No. 13-15, cell tel. 316/446-4544, www.puntobare.com, 9pm-2am Wed.-Thurs. and Sun., 9pm-4am Fri.-Sat.), an awesome hole-in-the-wall that is full of an older clientele and has an active calendar of events.

Zaperoco Bar (Av. 5N No. 16-46, tel. 2/661-2040, www.zaperocobar.com, 8pm-3am Thurs.-Sat., cover COP$20,000) confidently calls itself the best rumba spot in Cali. It regularly hosts live acts featuring salsa, music from the Pacific, and Cuban *son* music.

Cuba Libre, the house band at **Rincón Don Heberth** (Cra. 24 No. 5-32 Local 6, cell tel. 310/409-7229) keeps the party going—even spilling out on to the street. This bar is called "the most Caleño corner in the city," as it's a favorite among locals.

The **Casa Latina** (Cl. 7 No. 27-38, tel. 2/556-6549, cell tel. 316/555-0412, garylatina1@gmail.com, no cover) is a welcoming bar with tons of personality that draws in the salsa aficionados of Cali. Owner Gary Domínguez has theme nights, usually on

Saturdays, celebrating a star salsa performer. Salsa memorabilia is plastered on the walls, and the DJ booth that Gary mans is jam-packed with records.

In San Fernando, **Tin Tin Deo** (Cl. 5 No. 38-71, tel. 2/514-1537, www.tintindeo.com, 8pm-3am Thurs.-Sat., cover COP$15,000, with ladies usually getting a discount) is a requirement on a Thursday night. At Tin Tin Deo, people also dance *chichoky,* which is a style of Cali salsa that incorporates African rhythms. Saturday night is also big here, when the music is *pachanguero,* which is sort of "party music," Cali style. Tin Tin Deo is the new *chico* on the block—it's only been around since 1985, started by some friends from the Universidad del Valle, and it's generally a good bet.

SALSA SHOWS

A number of flashy (and pricey) salsa shows take place in Cali, during which you can sit back in amazement (and vicarious exhaustion) at the fast and fancy footwork of the salsa dance troupes. The talented and high-energy dancers range in age from 4 to 40. Shows sell out quickly, so reserve a week or two in advance.

Delirio (Centro de Eventos Valle de Pacífico, Cra. 26 No. 12-328, tel. 2/893-7680, www.delirio.com.co, COP$180,000) is a sort of Cirque du Soleil—a la Cali—that combines dance, music, and circus, and it has delighted audiences all over the world. The group is constantly updating its shows, creating segments on different themes that inspire them (for instance, a Michael Jackson tribute). During intermission, audience members are invited to dance on stage. Performances go from about 8pm to well after midnight, and are generally held Fridays between April and December. Minors under the age of 18 are not allowed inside the big tent.

Another popular ongoing show is **Ensálsate** (cell tel. 313/585-7616, www.en-salsate.co, COP$120,000), which takes place the second Friday of each month and during the Feria de Cali at the Salón Ritz of the Hotel Dann Carlton (Cra. 2 No. 1-60, tel. 2/893-3000). It's a three-act show with a mix of music and dance, with salsa, music from the Caribbean, tango, and even some hip-hop added to the mix. Tickets can be obtained at Tu Boleta (www.tuboleta.com).

Other Nightlife
BARS AND LOUNGES

Mikasa Bar (Cl. 26N No. 5AN-15, tel. 2/374-7301, cell tel. 310/535-9181, 8pm-3am Thurs.-Sat., COP$12,000) is a funky place serving up all kinds of tunes—from "Latin urban music" to house—to which you can dance under a mango tree. **Aurora** (Cl. 13N No. 8N-14, www.auroradiscoymordisco.com.co, cell tel. 304/612-3952) is a restaurant and watering hole that turns into a full-on party spot with guest DJs spinning in the outdoor terrace on weekends. Both spots are in Granada.

The pub **Martyn's** (Av. 6AN No. 24N-22, tel. 2/667-3296, 8pm-3am Wed.-Sat.) is a rock-and-roll institution in Cali. For over 30 years Martyn, originally from Wales, has been serving tequila shots and playing the rock classics to a devoted clientele.

The jet set of Cali hangs out in El Peñon on Avenida 2 Oeste, a strip of fashionable restaurant/bars popular with the after-work crowd. Terrace seating is hard to come by on Thursday and Friday evenings. In the same area but with a much more relaxed atmosphere is **Malecón Cubar** (Cl. 1 Oeste No. 1-32, tel. 2/892-2977, www.maleconrestauran-tebar.com, 3pm-2am Tues.-Sat.). Here you can groove to Caribbean sounds, drink a mojito or two, and have a meal.

On the cusp of San Antonio, **Greco Bar** (Cra. 4 No. 2-116, cell tel. 312/854-0151, 5pm-midnight Wed.-Sat.) is in an old wooden house that appears abandoned but has music, drinks, and pizza. Lounge in a hammock out front or sink into a sofa inside. **La Colina** (Cl. 1 No. 4-83B, no phone, open daily) is an old San Antonio *tienda* where you can chat up the locals. It's been around for over seven decades, and is a perfect spot to start out the evening.

LGBT

Gay clubs in Cali are friendly and mixed with women and men. In Granada, **Queens Bar** (Av. 9AN No. 15N-07, tel. 2/373-9778, www.queenscali.co, cover COP$15,000) has three different dance floors, each with its own type of music. Before last call, at around 3am, ask around for the best after-party recommendation—if you still have the stamina.

TANGO

Tango lovers may feel outnumbered in this salsa town, but not at **La Matraca** (Cra. 11 No. 22-80, tel. 2/668-6783, www.lamatraca-cali.com, 6pm-2:30am Fri.-Sat., 3pm-11pm Sun.), a Cali institution that has been around for over 50 years. On the Parque Obrero, La Matraca used to be a corner shop where you could buy staples like rice and potatoes and hear tango from the owner's collection. There are no more potatoes here; today it's just music, dancing, and drinks. It tends to be happening on Sundays after 3pm.

CULTURAL CENTERS

Alternative cultural space **Lugar a Dudas** (Cl. 15 Norte No. 8N-41, tel. 2/668-2335, www.lugaradudas.org) puts on edgy video art installations, photography exhibits, and occasional films in its space in Granada.

Teatro de Presagio (Av. 9A Norte No. 10N-50, tel. 2/487-6432, cell tel. 301/485-8228, www.teatrodelpresagio.com) often has theater or dance performances on the weekends in its Granada space. On Tuesday evenings, it's free art house cinema night.

The **Biblioteca Departmental** (Cl. 5 No. 24A-91, tel. 2/620-0400, www.bibliovalle.gov.co, 8am-5pm Mon.-Sat.) is both a quiet place for work or study and host to cultural events. It's located near San Fernando.

Festivals and Events

During the last week of June is the **Festival de Macetas,** taking place primarily in Parque San Antonio. This is a very Cali celebration during which locals create elaborate and colorful sweets and pinwheels. There are also concerts, storytelling events, and other activities going on.

A celebration of Afro-Colombian and Pacific coast culture, the **Festival Petronio Álvarez** (www.festivalpetronioalvarez.com, mid-Aug., free) is a series of competitive outdoor concerts mostly held at the Canchas Panamericanas sports complex. It's fast becoming Cali's premier and most beloved annual event. The vibrations of the drums and good vibe of the crowd at this annual festival may intoxicate you!

The **Festival Mundial de Salsa** (www.cali.gov.co, mid-Sept.) began in 2006. It is a fiercely competitive dance contest, attracting thousands of salsa dancers of all ages from around the world. The finals are usually held in the Plaza de Toros. For tickets go to www.colboletos.com.

The **Media Maratón,** a half-marathon, is held in late May (www.juanchocorrelon.com).

Two lesser-known arts festivals take place in October. The **Festival Internacional de Ballet** (www.festivalinternacionaldeballet.com) happens early in the month, with performances in some of Cali's iconic theaters, such as the Teatro Jorge Isaacs downtown. The **Cali International Film Festival** (www.festivaldecinecali.gov.co) is held toward the end of the month, with showings at various theaters in the city, including at the Chipichape mall.

During the last week of the year when other Colombian cities become virtual ghost towns, the opposite occurs in Cali. It becomes Colombia's party central with parades, concerts, beauty pageants, and plenty of drinking and dancing during the beloved **Feria de Cali** (www.feriadecali.com). Occurring between Christmas and New Year's, the *feria* is a celebration that crosses barriers of class and age; it's like a big homecoming celebration.

SHOPPING

Malls and more malls: That's how Cali shops. There's open-air **Chipichape** (Cl. 38N 6N-35, tel. 2/659-2199, www.chipichape.com.co, 9am-midnight daily), not far from Granada, as well as smaller **Centenario** (Av. 4N No.

7N-46, tel. 2/683-9604, www.centenariocc.com, 8am-11:45pm daily), between Centro and San Antonio. To the south are newer malls like **Jardín Plaza** (Cra. 98 No. 16-200, tel. 2/324-7222, www.jardinplaza.com, 8am-11:30pm daily), which is also open-air; it's near the Universidades MIO station. Food courts dish out traditional Colombian food, fast food, and reliable coffee. Plus, seeing a matinee movie to beat the heat is never a bad idea.

SPORTS AND RECREATION
El Cerro de las Tres Cruces

A weekend ritual for many Caleños is to hike up **El Cerro de las Tres Cruces** (Three Crosses Hill), west of the Santa Monica neighborhood and not far from Granada. The climb will get your blood pumping, and at the top and along the way you'll have some good, albeit hazy, views of Cali, especially early in the day. The ascent will take about an hour. At the top, if you still feel energetic, you can join Cali's fitness peacocks and work out in the *Flintstones*-esque outdoor gym next to the hill's crosses. Bring some cash to enjoy a freshly squeezed orange juice.

The hardest part about the walk is figuring out where to start it. Various paths lead to the top; their trailheads are not far from Granada in the Altos de Normandía neighborhood or in Juanambú. If you can find your way to Avenida 10 Oeste at Calle 12N, you will be close to the path and can ask anyone you come across for directions. If you're not going with someone who knows how to get there, take a cab and request to be dropped off close to the *sendero al Cerro de las Tres Cruces* (path to Three Crosses Hill).

Parts of the path are quite steep, and you may need to climb up on all fours at some points. Therefore, don't bring items that you don't need, so you can have your hands free. And bring water.

Bird-Watching

To get a glimpse of Colombia's celebrated bird diversity, check out a bird-watching excursion offered by **Mapalina** (cell tel. 318/627-7062 or 316/805-2117, www.mapalina.com). Associated with the American Birding Association, the group organizes birding field trips year-round to locations near Cali, from tropical San Cipriano to the west to the Laguna Sonso in the northeast near Buga, one of the only remaining wetlands in the Valle del Cauca. Some of the

making the hike to the top of El Cerro de las Tres Cruces

The Little Witches of San Cipriano

A popular day trip from Cali is to take a ride on the *brujitas,* literally "little witches," of San Cipriano. Train tracks run through the villages of Córdoba and San Cipriano, although trains are rare nowadays. Local entrepreneurs saw an opportunity here in providing a quick transportation alternative to walking the train tracks for residents to get from one village to the other. They created a wooden cart transportation system that was set upon the rails. It was originally propelled manually using long sticks. The drivers resembled witches on broomsticks flying by, hence the name *brujitas.* Nowadays, passengers—up to about 10—zip by, as the *brujitas* are powered by motorbikes (less charming but more adventurous). The teenage drivers like to go fast, so hold on and, if you see a train coming toward you, get ready to jump off. It's about a 30-minute journey from Córdoba to San Cipriano.

Upon arrival in San Cipriano, you can have a hearty seafood lunch or continue just beyond the village to a protected area (admission COP$2,000), where you can wander down a path that leads to a refreshing swimming hole in the Río San Cipriano. Inner tubes can be rented for about COP$5,000, and you can opt to float back to Córdoba.

A spin on the *brujita* costs about COP$8,500 round-trip for tourists, less for locals. However, if you go on your own, aggressive touts may try to charge you up to 10 times that amount. Pay for the trip only after you have returned to Córdoba.

The experience is best enjoyed in a group. These are often organized by hostels in Cali or by **Valleytours** (Cl. 2 No. 22-39, cell tel. 301/754-9188, www.valleyadventours.com/tours), an agency that offers this excursion several times per week. If you would like to go on your own, though, you can take any bus bound for Buenaventura and ask the driver to let you off at Córdoba. Buses depart Cali from the Terminal para Buenaventura in the southwest of the city. Look for the metallic black sculpture of the *maríamulata* bird (the local name for a great-tailed grackle) by renowned artist Enrique Grau (Cl. 7 Oeste No. 3-03). The ride costs about COP$18,000. Be sure to make a pineapple pit stop at **Piñas del 44.** It's at kilometer 44 on the highway, and buses will often take a break here.

San Cipriano isn't the only place in Colombia with *brujitas.* Visitors to the coffee region can take a ride in the village of Estación Pereira along the Río Cauca near Pereira.

---

birds you might see include several endemic tanagers, chachalacas, and apical flycatchers. Trips, almost always with an English-speaking guide, are tailored according to the wishes of the visitors, and can be arranged for groups of 1-10. Each year in December the organization participates in a daylong bird census in a cloud forest area near Kilometer 18, west of Cali, in collaboration with the Red Nacional de Observadores de Aves de Colombia bird-watching network. No prior experience is required to participate in the census.

The **Colombia Bird Fair** (www.colombia-birdfair.org) is an annual birding event held at the Cali Country Club in March, during which there are a number of birding excursions in the area, all open to the public.

Biking

On Sundays and holidays, many streets are closed to traffic, open only to cyclists, joggers, and pedestrians during the **Ciclovida** (8am-1pm Sun.). The main route extends from Calle 9 at Carretera 66 Sur (near the Canchas Panamericanas) to Calle 70 at Carretera 1N. **River Bike Colombia** (Av. 4N No. 9N-47, cell tel. 314/814-1081) is one of the only agencies around that rents bikes for the Ciclovida (COP$25,000 for the day). If you can't find a bike, you can always jog or walk the route, plus there are free open-air Zumba classes at various points in the city, such as along the river near downtown.

Spectator Sports

There are two professional soccer teams in Cali: **Deportivo** (www.deportivocali.com.co), which plays at the **Estadio Deportivo Cali** (Km. 8 Vía Cali-Palmira, tel. 2/688-0808), and **América** (www.america.com.co). América plays at the **Pascual Guerrero Stadium** (Cra. 36 No. 5B-32, tel. 2/556-6678), which is where the 1971 Pan American Games were held. For ticket information, go to www.tuboleta.com or the teams' websites.

FOOD

Cali lacks the international cuisine options that are found in Bogotá, but a handful of creative fusion restaurants help to fill that void. Granada and San Antonio are full of good options; the Centro has numerous options for lunch, but it gets quiet after dark.

Nothing accompanies a hearty meal in this hot city like a cool *lulada* drink, made from *lulo,* a tangy fruit.

Centro

Reasonable lunch options abound in the Centro. On weekends and evenings, options are fewer and less popular.

COLOMBIAN AND FUSION

Despite its location in a parking lot, **Da'Gusto** (Cra. 4 No. 9-49, tel. 2/881-8697, 6am-5pm daily, COP$8,000) packs in the crowds at lunchtime. Service is quick and the action in the kitchen is fast yet friendly. *Sancocho,* a meaty stew, is a favorite, as is fried fish. Set lunches are served with juice, salad, and lots of carbs: potatoes, yuca, plantains, and rice. They can do rice and beans for vegetarians.

At the lunch counter at tidy **Rikus** (Cra. 4 No. 12-56, tel. 2/896-0795, 7am-5pm Mon.-Sat., COP$8,000) you can feast on freshly prepared Colombian fare and watch the kitchen staff furiously stir, mix, pour, and serve. For a hearty breakfast, look no further.

La Guacharaca Café (Cra. 6 No. 7-12, www.laguacharaca.co, noon-3pm Mon.-Thurs., noon-3pm and 7pm-10pm Fri.-Sat., COP$20,000) is a refreshing gourmet oasis in downtown Cali. Ring the doorbell to enter, and you'll be ushered into a lovely interior patio filled with plants. Try the seafood *buñuelos,* akin to southern hush puppies, as a starter.

CAFÉS, BAKERIES, AND QUICK BITES

For healthy brunches (think granola and fresh fruit) and light meals, head to **Bocados** (Cl. 7 No. 1-08, tel. 2/881-1666, 7am-7pm Mon.-Wed., 7am-8:30pm Thurs.-Sat.), a refreshing addition to the Bulevar del Río.

For a pastry and a coffee or, better yet, an inexpensive and delicious vegetarian buffet lunch (with a devoted clientele), check out ★ **Nutricentro** (Cra. 5 No. 7-34, tel. 2/895-9777, 10am-6pm Mon.-Sat.). It's a cheerful place near the museums in the Centro.

Granada
COLOMBIAN AND FUSION

Ringlete (Cl. 15A Norte No. 9N-31, tel. 2/660-1540, www.ringlete.com, noon-3pm and 6:30pm-10pm Mon.-Sat., noon-4:30pm Sun., COP$24,000) features *nueva cocina Vallecaucana* (new Valle de Cauca cuisine) in a cheerfully decorated restaurant. Check out the pork chops, shrimp ceviche, or seafood *cazuela* (stew).

★ **Carambolo** (Cl. 14N No. 9N-18, tel. 2/667-5656, noon-midnight Mon.-Sat., noon-5pm Sun., COP$30,000) has a creative menu combining Mediterranean and Colombian flavors. Many dishes in this restaurant are whimsically named, such as the Shakira (stuffed eggplant combining Middle Eastern and Caribbean flavors) and the Celia Cruz—shrimp coated in coconut and *chontaduro* (fruit from a type of palm tree) and served in a *maracuya* (passion fruit) sauce. It's a popular place with Cali society and out-of-towners.

Platillos Voladores (Av. 3N No. 7-19, tel. 2/668-7750, www.platillosvoladores.

a café in Granada

15A Norte No. 9N-35, tel. 2/661-3736, cell tel. 316/449-9843, www.restaurantelitany.com, COP$26,000), one of the best Middle Eastern cuisine restaurants in the country.

CAFÉS, BAKERIES, AND QUICK BITES

A top contender in the city for the crown of best *pandebono*, a delicious pastry made of yuca flour and cheese, is **Kuty Panadería** (Av. 6N No. 27N-03, tel. 2/661-1465, www.panaderiakuty.com, 6am-9pm daily). Kuty also serves other fast-food fare all day long.

At **Bendito Coffee Shop** (Av. 9N No. 12-05 tel. 2/372-0101), there's more to the place than cups of joe: Beer, cocktails, and light bites are on the menu as well.

Although it's a chain, café **Juan Valdez** (Av. 9N No. 17-11, tel. 2/660-7337, www.juan-valdezcoffee.com, 10am-9pm Mon.-Thurs., 10am-midnight Fri.-Sat., 11am-9pm Sun.), with its outdoor terrace under the trees, is one of the best options for a cup of coffee in Cali.

El Peñón
CAFÉS, BAKERIES, AND QUICK BITES

In addition to delicious bread and baked goods, **Barakha Panadería Ancestral** (Cra. 1 Oeste No. 1-109, 2nd Fl., tel. 2/892-0135, 8am-9pm Mon.-Sat., COP$12,000) is a place to spend a leisurely afternoon enjoying sandwiches, salads, desserts, and coffee.

Delicious homemade ice cream awaits you at **Calathea** (Cl. 4 Oeste No. 3A-50, tel. 2/371-0188, 11am-7pm Mon.-Sat., noon-6pm Sun.). Exotic flavors are constantly being invented, like coconut-lemon, strawberries with red wine, and the native fruit *arazá* with mint.

San Antonio
COLOMBIAN AND FUSION

Local favorite ★ **El Pargo Rojo** (Cra. 9 No. 2-09, tel. 2/893-6987, noon-3pm daily, COP$18,000), or the Red Snapper, offers fresh fried sea bass and *cazuelas* (seafood stews) from the waters of the Pacific. El Pargo Rojo is open for lunch only.

com, noon-3pm and 7pm-11pm Mon.-Sat., COP$35,000) is consistently rated as one of Cali's top restaurants. Fusion is the watchword here: Thailand, Lebanon, Italy, France, and the Colombian Pacific all make appearances on the menu. Favorites include a fresh fillet of fish from the Pacific in a caramelized *chontaduro* (a starchy fruit that grows on a variety of palm) and garlic sauce (COP$43,000), quinoa stir-fry (COP$26,000), and an exotic and spicy ostrich carpaccio (COP$23,000). Reservations are recommended.

TEX-MEX

D'Toluca (Cl. 17N No. 8N-46, tel. 2/668-9372, 11:30am-3pm and 5:30pm-11:30pm Sun.-Thurs., 11:30am-3pm and 5:30pm-1am Fri.-Sat., COP$15,000) serves up reliable Tex-Mex cuisine and often has lunch or drink specials, including massive margaritas.

LEBANESE

Authentic and delicious Lebanese cuisine is at your reach at **Litany Comida Arabe** (Cl.

Coconut milk is a regular ingredient in the seafood dishes at **Valle Pacífico** (Cl. 2 No. 4-52, cell tel. 300/245-2827, restaurantevallepacifico@hotmail.com, 12:30pm-3pm and 6:30pm-10pm Mon.-Sat., COP$25,000), which features food from the Guapi area on the Cauca coast.

Azul (Cra. 9A No. 4-02, tel. 2/893-6057, noon-3pm and 6pm-11pm Mon.-Fri., 6pm-11pm Sat., COP$25,000) is a fusion-style restaurant, with Mediterranean, Colombian, Middle Eastern, and Asian flavors represented on the menu. Ask for the *clandestinos*—dishes that don't appear on the menu.

An upscale addition to the San Antonio culinary scene is **Antigua Contemporánea** (Cl. 2 No. 9-08B, tel. 2/893-6809 or 2/893-6813, noon-11pm Mon.-Sat., COP$32,000), which features items such as seafood pasta (COP$39,000) and Vietnamese curry (COP$32,000) in an elegant antiques and interior design store. Ample outdoor seating under the stars with live music on weekends makes this a favorite choice for a night out. Try the *uchuva* (cape gooseberry) margarita.

VEGETARIAN
★ **El Buen Alimento** (Cl. 2 No. 4-53, tel. 2/375-5738, 11:30am-10pm Tues.-Thurs., 11:30am-11pm Fri.-Sat., 11:30am-5pm Sun., COP$15,000) always has a set menu option for lunch, including fresh juice, soup, and the main course, but you can also order a la carte. Veggie burgers, pastas, and vegetarian tamales are plentiful. This cheerful spot with bright decor is even popular with devout meat eaters.

CAFÉS, BAKERIES, AND QUICK BITES
Weary travelers and San Antonians alike flock to ★ **Macondo Postres y Café** (Cra. 6 No. 3-03, tel. 2/893-1570, www.macondocafe.blogspot.com, 11am-11pm Mon.-Thurs., 11am-midnight Fri.-Sat., 4:30pm-11pm Sun.) at all hours of the day. It's one of the best places to hang out in San Antonio, and is known for its sandwiches, coffee, and beer as well as its busy calendar of cultural events, such as films and jazz evenings.

ACCOMMODATIONS
Cali has no shortage of sound accommodation options for all types of travelers. Granada and San Antonio are considered the best neighborhoods to stay during a visit. These areas are safe, walkable, and offer diverse dining options. There are numerous hotels in the Centro within a few blocks of the main tourists sights, but it's not a desirable place to be at night.

In charming San Antonio, many hostels have taken root, making this neighborhood the favorite choice for international budget travelers. Air-conditioning and hot water are not standard at hostels; if these amenities are important for you, double-check with the hostel before booking. Salsa and Spanish classes are commonly offered at hostels.

Granada can feel somewhat dull during the week. Wi-Fi is standard in most accommodations, as is breakfast.

Granada
Proximity to restaurants and nightspots draws visitors to Granada, although during the week it feels deserted.

UNDER COP$70,000
The ★ **Iguana Hostel** (Av./Cl. 9N No. 22N-22, tel. 2/660-8937, www.iguana.com.co, COP$18,000 dorm, COP$45,000 d w/bath) is a long-time favorite in Cali for budget travelers. The hostel is located on a steep, quiet street within easy walking distance to restaurants. Those driving campers can park on the street nearby in exchange for a small fee collected by informal parking attendants. The staff can answer questions and give recommendations. Salsa classes are held in the garden. An alternative to Iguana—with a pool—can be found around the corner at **Casa del Gato** (Av. 9 Norte No. 21N-30, tel. 2/384-8435, www.hostalcasadelgatocali.com). It's friendly and has big rooms, but note that people do enjoy their poolside socializing, sometimes until late. Private rooms have en suite baths, but no hot water.

COP$70,000-200,000

With just eight rooms, the **Hotel Portón Granada** (Av. 9 Norte N. 13-19, tel. 2/379-9595, cell. tel. 318/696-6117, www.hotelportondegranada.com.co, COP$110,000 d), in an old converted home with high ceilings, offers what few others do in trendy Granada: a dose of charm.

Part of a midrange Colombian business hotel chain, **MS Centenario** (Av. 3 Norte No. 7N-20, tel. 2-660-6778, www.hotelesms.com, COP$105,000 d) has a fine location between the Centro and San Antonio—and across the street from the famous restaurant Platillos Voladores. It's not an exciting choice, but this 26-room hotel offers spacious and clean rooms and amenities such as air-conditioning and TV.

For more independence, more space, balconies with views, and proximity to Granada, **Castellón de Juanambú** (Av. 9 Norte No. 4N-120, www.travelers.com.co, COP$232,000 d) is a fine option. These 15 apartments are spacious with full kitchens, and there's a pool.

COP$200,000-500,000

A dose of South Beach in the middle of Granada, ★ **NOW Hotel** (Av. 9A Norte No. 10N-74, tel. 2/488-9797, www.nowhotel.com.co, COP$297,000 d) has 19 industrial-chic, high-tech bedrooms, and there are balconies and DirecTV. Two restaurants are in the hotel, and there are certainly worse places to be at sunset than the rooftop terrace bar, which is sometimes host to weekend parties.

El Peñón

This upscale neighborhood, with the Parque El Peñón as its main landmark, hugs the Río Cali and is home to restaurants and hotels. It's close to San Antonio and Centenario.

COP$70,000-200,000

Hotel Peñón (Cl. 1 Oeste No. 2-61, tel. 2/893-3625, www.hotelelpenon.com, COP$136,000 d) has large rooms near the river in El Peñón. Much of this hotel, built in the 1980s, has been given a needed facelift.

Aloja (Cl. 4 Oeste No. 3A-50, cell tel. 310/831-0288, www.aloja.com.co, COP$120,000) offers only five *apartamentos amoblados* (furnished apartments) for rent, but if one is available, it's a great bargain. The three-story building on a sublime tree-lined street is directly above an excellent ice cream shop and is a two-minute walk from restaurants.

San Antonio is Cali's most charming neighborhood.

San Antonio

Colorful hostels, guesthouses, and restaurants line the streets of this, perhaps the most charming neighborhood in Cali. This neighborhood of artists and hipsters has options for all budgets. The action is centered on Parque San Antonio, which is one of the best places in Cali to be when the sun sets. It's possible to walk from San Antonio to the Centro in about 20 minutes, but it's only advisable in the daytime.

UNDER COP$70,000

In two adjoining houses, ★ **La Casa Café** (Cra. 6 No. 2-13, tel. 2/893-7011, www.lacasacafecali.blogspot.com, COP$25,000 dorm, COP$70,000 d) is a welcoming spot to hang one's hat, with an ideal location just below the Parque San Antonio. In the main house with creaky wooden floors and high ceilings, there is a café, a kitchen, and reading areas, with one dorm and private rooms (shared bath, one with hot water) upstairs. The second house has four small private rooms with their own baths and fans.

El Encuentro (Cl. 2 Oeste 4-16, tel. 2/890-2464, www.hostalencuentro.com, COP$30,000 dorm, COP$80,000 d shared bath) is surrounded by greenery and flowers, has a terrace with views toward downtown, and is in one of the most peaceful corners of San Antonio. You'll feel at home here. There are hot showers.

COP$70,000-200,000

The ★ **San Antonio Hotel Boutique** (Cra. 6 No. 2-51, tel. 2/524-6364, cell tel. 317/404-6647, www.hotelboutiquesananto-nio.com, COP$179,000 d) is a high-end choice if personalized attention and comfort are your priorities. Two of the hotel's 10 rooms have their own terrace, but anyone can enjoy the rooftop patio. Rooms have air-conditioning, comfortable beds, and DirectTV.

The **Posada San Antonio** (Cra. 5 No. 3-37, tel. 5/893-7413, www.posadadesananto-nio.com, COP$116,000 d) is in an old restored home in San Antonio. With 14 rooms, it offers a family-oriented and rustic environment. There's no air-conditioning here, but fans and a fountain in the interior courtyard provide relief.

Comfy ★ **Ruta Sur** (Cra. 9 No. 2-41, tel. 2/893-6946, www.hostalrutasur.com, COP$98,000 d) has 10 private rooms—including some with three beds—that each have their own private bath, fan, and TV. Breakfast and laundry cost extra. At night you can laze in a hammock under the stars in an open-air interior patio. It's all about comfort and rest at this guesthouse.

INFORMATION AND SERVICES
Tourist Information

If you are downtown, stop by the **Punto de Información Turístico de Cali** (Cra. 4 No. 6-05, Oficina 102, tel. 2/885-8855, ext. 122, 8am-noon and 2pm-5pm Mon.-Fri., 10am-2pm Sat.) for maps and brochures on Cali and the surrounding region.

Money

ATMs are not as easy to come by in San Antonio compared to other neighborhoods in the city, but if you are in a bind, there is an ATM at the Dann Hotel casino nearby. Otherwise head to a shopping mall.

To receive a wire transfer, **Western Union** (www.westernunion.com) has several offices in Cali. Check the website for locations. **Titan Intercontinental** (Cl. 11 No. 4-48, tel. 2/898-0898, www.titan.com.co, 8am-5pm Mon.-Fri., 9am-1pm Sat.), a currency exchange office, is located in the Centro.

Spanish-Language Classes

All the major universities in Cali offer Spanish programs for those learning Spanish as a second language; however, these require a commitment of several months. Many hostels offer Spanish instruction on-site or can put you in contact with a tutor. An alternative is the language school **Lingua Viva** (Cl. 2 Oeste No. 26-43, cell tel. 316/442-8158, www.eslinguaviva.com), which offers group classes, private classes, and interpreter services.

Internet and Telephone

Wireless Internet availability is more the norm than the exception at restaurants, cafés, and big shopping malls. **Juan Valdez** (Av. 9N No. 17-11, tel. 2/660-7337, www.juan-valdezcoffee.com, 10am-9pm Mon.-Thurs., 10am-midnight Fri.-Sat., 11am-9pm Sun.) in Granada is a good place to get connected. Small Internet cafés, open until about 8pm, are plentiful too.

To report any emergency, dial 123. The city telephone code for Cali is 2, but you'll only need to use it if you're calling Cali from a different part of the country, or from abroad. It's generally easy to find people selling use of their cell phones, called *minutos* (minutes), for cheap on the street downtown and in *tiendas* (stores) elsewhere. Cell phone numbers must have 10 digits.

Newspapers

Cali does not have any English-language newspapers. The main daily newspaper in town is *El País* (www.elpais.com.co), although the national newspaper *El Tiempo* (www.eltiempo.com) is also available in drugstores, bookstores, and malls.

The free monthly *Cali Cultural* (www.calicultural.net) has an extensive listing of cultural events in the city. Snag a copy of *ADN* (www.diarioadn.co/cali), a daily free newspaper, at traffic lights on weekday mornings.

Health

The **Fundación Valle del Lili** (Av. Simón Bolívar Cra. 98 No. 18-49, tel. 2/331-9090, appointments tel. 2/680-5757, www.valledellili.org, 8am-10pm daily) and the **Centro Médico Imbanaco** (Cra. 38A No. 5A-100, tel. 2/682-1000, appointments tel. 2/685-1000, www.imbanaco.com, 8am-9pm daily) are two of the top hospitals in the country, both of which offer emergency care.

TRANSPORTATION
Getting There
AIR

The Cali airport, the **Aeropuerto Internacional Alfonso Bonilla Aragón** (CLO, tel. 2/280-1515, www.aerocali.com.co) is about 20 kilometers (12 miles) northeast of Centro, less than an hour's drive. A taxi ride from the airport to the San Antonio neighborhood will cost around COP$50,000. Minibuses from the airport to the city are usually at the ready just outside of the departure hall. They cost about COP$12,000 and take you to the main bus station, the **Terminal de Transportes** (Cl. 30N 2AN-29). From there, the most convenient way to get to San Antonio or Granada is to take a cab from the official taxi area. A cab to these neighborhoods costs about COP$8,000.

All major Colombian airlines and some international carriers serve Cali. **Avianca** (Cl. 38 No. 6AN-35, tel. 2/398-2000, www.avianca.com, 9am-9pm Mon.-Fri., 9am-8pm Sat., 9am-7pm Sun.) flies between Cali and Bogotá, Medellín, Cartagena, Barranquilla, Pasto, and Tumaco. Internationally, Avianca flies nonstop between Cali and Madrid and between Cali and Miami.

American Airlines (Cra. 1 No. 2-72, tel. 2/892-7256, www.aa.com, 9am-6pm Mon.-Fri.) is the only U.S.-based airline with service to Cali out of Miami.

LATAM (Cl. 25N No. 6 Bis-36, tel. 1/745-2020, www.latam.com, 8am-6pm Mon.-Fri., 9am-1pm Sat.) flies nonstop to Bogotá, Medellín, and San Andrés, and to Quito, Ecuador. Discount airliner **Viva Colombia** (tel. 2/485-6666, www.vivacolombia.co) offers daily flights between Cali and Bogotá, Medellín, Cartagena, and San Andrés. **Copa Airlines** (tel. 1/800-011-2600, www.copaair.com) flies from Cali to Panama City, Panama.

BUS

Cali's organized and bustling **Terminal de Transportes** (Cl. 30N No. 2AN-29, tel. 2/668-3655, www.terminalcali.com) is a 15-minute taxi ride (COP$7,000) from Granada. A small information booth is in the center of the terminal, and attendants will be able to give you a rough idea of bus fares and provide bus company suggestions. There is an efficient taxi stand at the main entrance (Puerta 3). Food options are dismal at the bus station.

Getting to Cali from Buga will cost COP$7,000 (1 hr.). From Popayán it's COP$15,000 (3 hrs.) and from Medellín it costs COP$55,000 (9 hrs.). From faraway Bogotá, the ride will set you back COP$70,000 (12 hrs.).

If you are taking a MIO bus to the terminal, the nearest station is Las Américas, about two blocks away.

Getting Around
TAXI
Yellow taxis are plentiful in Cali, and you will need to travel by cab often to get around, especially at night. It's always advisable to order a cab from a company like Taxi Express (tel. 2/555-5555) over the phone or by using the smartphone app Tappsi or Easy Taxi, or use a ride-sharing service like Uber. From Granada, expect to pay about COP$7,000 to get to the bus terminal and about COP$6,000 to get to San Antonio.

BUS
The Masivo Integrado de Occidente, or MIO (www.mio.com.co), is Cali's public transport system. It comprises several dedicated bus rapid transit lanes with stations, as well as alimentadores—feeder buses that connect with the articulated MIO network at various points. MIO is mildly useful if you are staying in or near Granada and plan to visit the Centro or sights in the south. The bright blue buses are immaculately maintained and considered safe. Note that if you would like to ride one of the alimentadores you must present a MIO card on board. Those must be purchased at MIO stations such as Versailles (Av. 3 with Cl. 21) or Cayzedo (Cl. 13 with Cra. 4). MIO runs 5am-11pm Monday-Saturday and 6am-10pm Sundays and holidays. The fare for a single trip is COP$1,800.

CAR AND MOTORCYCLE
The roads in the Valle de Cauca region are generally of high quality and the terrain is flat. Renting a car or motorbike for excursions outside of Cali (to the valley's haciendas, Buga, Lago Calima, and Roldanillo) may be a good option. Driving to Popayán or to Pasto along the Pan-American Highway is more taxing because of its winding two-lane roadway.

Hertz (Av. Colombia No. 1-14, El Peñon, tel. 2/892-0437, www.rentacarcolombia.co, 8am-noon and 2pm-6pm Mon.-Fri., 8am-3pm Sat.; airport tel. 2/666-3283, 7am-5pm Mon.-Sat.) has two offices in Cali. For motorcycle rental and tours, get in touch with Motolombia (Av. 6N No. 48N-48, tel. 2/396-3949, www.motolombia.com, 8am-6pm Mon.-Fri., 8am-2pm Sat.).

VICINITY OF CALI
Pance
Cali residents seeking relief from urban fatigue don't have to go far. About 25 kilometers (15 miles) southwest of the city is the town of Pance, set along the Río Pance and nestled next to jagged mountains. It offers outdoorsy options from the challenging to the relaxing. The area revs up with locals on the weekends, but during the week, it's peaceful.

RESERVA NATURAL ANAHUAC
The Reserva Natural Anahuac (1 km before Pance on the Cali-Pance road, tel. 2/331-4828, www.reservanaturalanahuac.com, 7:30am-9:30pm daily, COP$6,000) is a well-maintained private nature reserve along the Río Pance. It has a pleasant path that meanders through guadua (bamboo) forests, a fishing pond, a restaurant, and a camping area. Easily undertaken independently, this excursion may be just the ticket on a hot Cali day.

GETTING THERE
A taxi to Pance from the San Antonio and Granada neighborhoods of Cali will cost around COP$50,000 and take about 45 minutes.

If you have time and want to save cash,

there are buses that regularly make the trip to Pance from Cali. There are two options. The first takes around two hours and costs COP$1,800. It requires taking a MIO bus to the Universidades station in the south of Cali, then transferring to an *alimentador* (feeder) MIO bus, the A-19, toward Pueblo Pance. The second option takes about 1.5 hours and costs COP$2,500. This route requires taking a Recreativo bus from the bus station bound for Pueblo Pance. These buses depart starting at around 5:15am. Both options will stop at Reserva Natural Anahuac (Entrada 5, or the fifth stop), but you must tell the driver your destination is Anahuac as you board. Take care crossing the street here, as traffic tends to zoom by. On weekends, try to beat the crowds by returning to Cali during the early afternoon, as finding transportation can be difficult later in the day.

Buga

Founded in 1555, Buga (pop. 115,000) was one of the first cities established by the Spaniards in New Granada. It is best known as a place of pilgrimage; more than a million Colombian faithful come each year seeking miracles at the Basílica Señor de los Milagros. Buga may not be chock-full of attractions, but it is an excellent launching point from which to discover many lesser-known towns and recreational areas of the Valle de Cauca, and there is some beautiful colonial and Republican-period architecture in town.

SIGHTS

The pink 20th-century **Basílica Señor de los Milagros** (Cra. 14 No. 3-62, tel. 2/228-2823, www.milagrosdebuga.com, 5:30am-7:30pm daily) is not of architectural significance, but it is heavily visited by Colombian Catholics hoping for miracles from the "Cristo Negro" or Señor de los Milagros—a charred woodcarving of Christ that is displayed in a chapel behind the altar.

Praying to the "Black Christ" is believed to provide miracles, and the story behind this icon is one of generosity and devotion.

Buga is a popular pilgrimage site.

In colonial times an indigenous woman who had converted to Christianity saved for years to purchase a crucifix. One day she met a man who was crying because he'd go to jail if he didn't pay a debt. The woman showed her generosity by giving him all the money she had saved. Months later, she noticed a small crucifix floating down the river toward her. She picked it up and made an altar to pray to it. The crucifix grew, prompting her and others to believe it had miraculous powers. After years of deterioration, the church decided to burn it and replace it with another, but it never burned, remaining charred and black—another miracle.

The **Parque Cabal** (between Clls. 6-7 and Cras. 14-15) is the center of this slow-paced city. Old-timers drink their *tinto* (small cups of black coffee) in corner cafés in the late afternoon, engrossed in political conversations with their friends, while lottery vendors circulate among the tables hoping to sell a couple of tickets. On the corner of Calle 6 and Carrera 15 is the **Catedral de San Pedro** (8am-noon and 2pm-6pm Mon.-Fri.), a beautifully preserved three-nave church that was built in the 16th century. It is a couple of blocks west of the park.

FOOD AND ACCOMMODATIONS

The best part of the small ★ **Buga Hostel** (Cra. 13 No. 4-83, tel. 2/236-7752, www.buga-hostel.com, COP$16,000 dorm, COP$35,000-COP$45,000 d) is its **Holy Water Ale Café** (lunch and dinner daily), where you can sidle up to the bar, try one of the house brews on tap, and chow down on sourdough pizza or a black bean burger. It's a popular university student hangout. The hostel has one large dorm room and two private rooms. Hostel staff can recommend day trips to nearby nature reserves.

The **Hotel Guadalajara** (Cl. 1 No. 13-33, tel. 2/236-2611, www.hotelguadalajara.com.co, COP$200,000 d) is a large, old-fashioned hotel of long, wide corridors and comfortable rooms, with a fantastic pool in which you can get an excellent lap workout. Its main business these days is from weekend wedding parties and weekday business groups.

GETTING THERE

Buses depart Cali for Buga all day long. Tickets cost around COP$8,500, and the journey through the sugarcane plantations of the valley takes less than two hours. Buga's pleasant open-air **Terminal de Transportes** (Cl. 7 No. 17-17, tel. 2/238-9318), modern and clean, is a straightforward 15-minute walk from town, and on the way you can look out for the old abandoned train station. Cabs are also always at the ready to meet arriving buses. A cab ride into town costs about COP$2,500.

LAGO CALIMA

Lago Calima, 25 kilometers west of Buga, is the largest artificial lake in Colombia. The area is a preferred weekend party spot for Cali residents. With winds reaching 43 knots (46 mph), it's known for its kitesurfing and windsurfing. Also available are waterskiing, boating, and swimming, for those who don't mind the chilly water.

Most of the action at the lake takes place on the west side of the lake at Entrada 5, where the popular **Arriero Paisa** (cell tel. 315/439-5939) restaurant is located.

Darién is the uninspiring town on the northern banks of Lago Calima, and the only sight is its small **Museo Arqueológico Calima** (Cl. 10 No. 12-50, tel. 2/253-3121, www.calimadarien.com, 8am-noon and 1pm-5pm Tues.-Fri., 10am-6pm Sat.-Sun., COP$3,000). The museum has a collection of ceramics dating to 8000 BC, and it includes artifacts from the Ilama, Yotoco, and Sonso indigenous cultures.

Kite Colombia (cell tel. 317/821-4889, www.kitecolombia.com, 5-day course w/lodging US$500, 1-day intro course US$55) offers a range of kitesurfing courses and can also arrange accommodations in its lakeside hostel (US$15 dorm, US$22 d).

The **Museo Rayo** (Cl. 8 No. 8-53, tel. 2/229-8623, www.museorayo.co, 9am-6pm daily, COP$5,000) is the only sight in town, and it is well worth a visit. Omar Rayo, who was part of the Op Art, or Optical Art, movement, is known for bold and abstract paintings that often appear three-dimensional. Dedicated mostly to Rayo's paintings, drawings, and sculptures, the museum comprises five octagonal exhibition spaces, each one with a different theme. Temporary exhibits showcase other renowned Colombian artists.

Want to soar like a condor above the sugarcane fields in the valley? **Cloudbase Colombia** (Cra. 9 No. 8-65, tel. 2/229-9106, cell tel. 312/808-8841, www.cloudbasecolombia.com) can make that happen. Started by a pair of European paragliding fanatics, Cloudbase offers both paragliding and hang gliding lessons and excursions. The optimal time to fly is between late December and late March, although any time is fine. Roldanillo regularly hosts big-time international paragliding competitions.

The best lodging option in town is **Hotel Cloudbase** (Cra. 9 No. 8-65, tel. 2/229-9106, cell tel. 312/808-8841, COP$35,000 s, COP$50,000 d), a small guesthouse with a pleasant garden complete with a Jacuzzi and bar. It has 13 rooms. You don't have to be a flier to spend a couple of enjoyable days here.

a paragliding excursion with Cloudbase Colombia

ROLDANILLO

Against a backdrop of mountains and the vast valley to its east, Roldanillo (pop. 35,000) is on the map for two reasons: It was the home of modernist artist Omar Rayo, and boasts of being Colombia's paragliding capital. This town is about 80 kilometers (50 miles) north of Buga (just two hours by bus), far from the well-trodden tourist route.

Popayán

The temperate capital of the Cauca department, Popayán is known as the White City. It is located along the banks of the Río Cauca between the Cordilleras Central and Occidental (Central and Western Mountain Ranges). It is a dignified city, proud of its place in history as the home of presidents, poets, and priests. It retains some colonial charm despite earthquakes and modernization. Religion retains its importance in the lives of its people; during the annual Holy Week celebrations the entire city takes part in solemn processions through the streets. Idyllic churches and museums are the main places of interest in Popayán, but lingering in the Parque Caldas on a sunny afternoon or strolling the lonely streets on a Sunday evening may be what you remember most.

Popayán is also a great base from which to explore sights nearby. Just outside of

Popayán

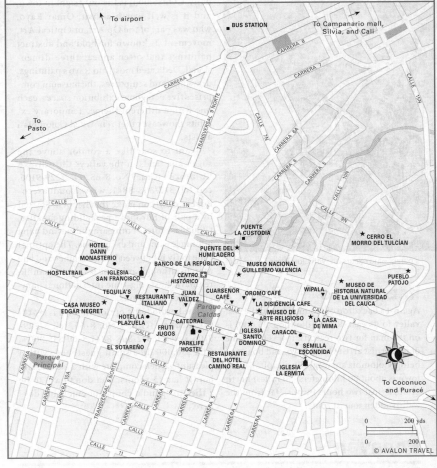

↑ To airport

■ BUS STATION

To Campanario mall,
Silvia, and Cali →

CARRERA 8

CARRERA 9

CARRERA 7

CALLE 15N

TRANSVERSAL 9 NORTE

CALLE 7N

CARRERA 6A

CARRERA 6

CARRERA 5

CALLE 10N

To
Pasto
↙

CALLE 1

CALLE 1N

CALLE 9N

CALLE 3

CALLE 2

PUENTE
LA CUSTODIA ★

CALLE 1N

★ CERRO EL
MORRO DEL TULCÍAN

HOTEL
DANN
MONASTERIO ●

PUENTE DEL ★
HUMILADERO

BANCO DE LA REPÚBLICA ■

MUSEO NACIONAL
GUILLERMO VALENCIA

PUEBLO ●
PATOJO

HOSTELTRAIL ●

IGLESIA
SAN FRANCISCO ✝

CENTRO ✚
HISTÓRICO

CUARSENOR
CAFÉ ▼

OROMO CAFÉ ▼

WIPALA ★

★ MUSEO DE
HISTORIA NATURAL
DE LA UNIVERSIDAD
DEL CAUCA

TEQUILA'S ▼

RESTAURANTE
ITALIANO ▼

JUAN
VALDEZ ▼

★ LA DISIDENCIA CAFÉ

CASA MUSEO ★
EDGAR NEGRET

Parque
Caldas

CALLE

▼ MUSEO DE
ARTE RELIGIOSO

★ LA CASA
DE MIMA

3

HOTEL LA
PLAZUELA ●

CATEDRAL ✝

CALLE

IGLESIA
SANTO
DOMINGO ✝

CARACOL ▼

FRUTI
JUGOS ▼

CALLE

6

EL SOTAREÑO ▼

PARKLIFE
HOSTEL

▼ SEMILLA
ESCONDIDA

Parque
Principal

CARRERA 12

CARRERA 11

CARRERA 10A

TRANSVERSAL 9 NORTE

CARRERA 8

CALLE

CALLE 7

RESTAURANTE
DEL HOTEL
CAMINO REAL

IGLESIA
LA ERMITA ✝

To Coconuco
and Puracé →

CALLE

CALLE 6

CARRERA 5

CARRERA 4

CARRERA 3

CALLE

CALLE 10

CALLE 11

0   200 yds

0   200 m

© AVALON TRAVEL

town is the Guambarino indigenous town of Silvia, famous for its colorful Tuesday market. In Coconuco, you can take a dip in the hot springs, and Parque Nacional Natural Puracé is a nearby national park where you can hike to the rim of a volcano, the Volcán Puracé.

Farther afield in Cauca is the archaeological site of Tierradentro, and beyond that, in the Huila department, is San Agustín. These sights can be combined in a circuit trip in three or four days from Popayán, although many tourists choose one or the other.

SIGHTS
★ Centro Histórico

The **Parque Caldas** (Clls. 4-5 and Cras. 6-7) in the center of Popayán is a shade-filled pedestrian square and the city's main point of reference. It's a fantastic place to have a coffee (there's a Juan Valdez Café) or just hang out, day or night.

an 18th-century house near the Puente del Humilladero that was the home of Popayán poet Guillermo Valencia.

The **Museo de Arte Religioso** (Cl. 4 No. 4-56, tel. 2/824-2759, 8am-noon and 2pm-6pm Mon.-Fri., 9am-2pm Sat., COP$6,000) has 10 rooms of religious art from the colonial era in an 18th-century neoclassical house covering Quiteño, Popayán, and Spanish styles. You'll probably be guided through by a friendly police cadet.

CHURCHES

There are several colonial churches dating from the 17th to 18th centuries to visit in Popayán. Most of them have been restored following earthquakes over the years. The **Iglesia San Francisco** (Cl. 4 and Cra. 9, tel. 2/824-0160) is one of the most beautiful churches and dates to the late 18th century. You can ask at the church to see the mummies that were found here following the earthquake. The **Iglesia La Ermita** (Cl. 5 and Cra. 2, tel. 2/820-9725) is older, dating to the 16th century. It has some fine woodcarvings and paintings. The **Iglesia Santo Domingo** (Cl. 4 and Cra. 5, tel. 2/824-0536) is where the Good Friday procession begins every year.

The neoclassical **cathedral** (Cl. 5 and Cra. 6, tel. 2/824-1710) on the Parque Caldas was completed in the early 20th century. The cathedral's official name is **Catedral Basílica de Nuestra Señora de la Asunción de Popayán,** but it is always referred to as "*la catedral.*"

Cerro El Morro del Tulcán

For a quick early-morning or afternoon walk and some nice views of the city, check out the **Cerro El Morro del Tulcán,** a hill to the northeast of Popayán. A statue of the city's founder, Sebastián de Belalcázar, stands on horseback on top of the hill. It is thought that this hill is actually a man-made pyramid built by pre-Columbian peoples. Don't take valuables with you if you make this walk, as there have been some isolated cases of theft here.

A cheesy handicraft market celebrating all

the White City of Popayán

MUSEUMS

The **Casa Museo Edgar Negret and Museo Iberoamericano de Arte Moderno de Popayán—MIAMP** (Cl. 5 No. 10-23, tel. 2/824-4546, www.museonegret.wordpress. com, 8am-noon and 2pm-6pm Wed.-Mon., COP$2,500) is in the home of Edgar Negret, a Colombian artist best known for massive abstract iron sculptures that adorn public spaces in cities throughout Colombia and museums throughout the world. Negret donated this 18th-century house to the city to promote its rebirth following a devastating earthquake in 1983.

The **Museo de Historia Natural de la Universidad del Cauca** (Cra. 2 No. 1A-25, tel. 2/820-9861, 9am-noon and 2pm-5pm daily, COP$2,000) was founded in 1936. The museum highlights the astounding variety of species, both plant and animal, that are found in Colombia. A guide will show you through.

Museo Nacional Guillermo Valencia (Cra. 6 No. 2-69, tel. 2/820-6160, 10am-noon and 2pm-5pm Tues.-Sun., COP$2,000) is things Popayán, the **Pueblito Patojo** (9am-6pm daily) adjoins the Cerro El Morro.

ENTERTAINMENT AND EVENTS
Nightlife

For unsurpassed old-school atmosphere, **El Sotareño** (Cra. 6 No. 8-05, no phone, 8pm-midnight daily) can't be beat. It's a cozy mom-and-pop place where the pop plays old vinyl tunes (lots of tango) from his collection and patrons of all ages settle in to the comfortable booths.

For nightlife of a different sort, head to the drinking hall alongside university students at the **Campanario shopping mall** (Cra. 9 No. 24AN-21, 5pm-9pm daily), on the outskirts of town.

Festivals and Events

The most important religious site in Colombia during **Semana Santa** (Holy Week) is Popayán. During Easter week, solemn processions take place on the streets of the center, a tradition that has been fulfilled every year in the White City since 1566. This is also the only time of the year that the mummies discovered in the Iglesia San Francisco are displayed. The **Festival de Música de Popayán** (www.fespo.co) also takes place during the week, with mostly classical and religious music performances each day, some of which are free to attend.

Congreso Nacional Gastronómico (www.gastronomicopopayan.org) is an annual food festival held in early September, mostly at the Hotel Dann Monasterio. To attend, you must make a bank transfer in advance for the hefty sum of COP$350,000, which gives you access to several days of food and drink.

RECREATION
Guided Tours

The staff at **Hosteltrail** (Cra. 11 No. 4-16, tel. 2/831-7871, www.hosteltrailpopayan.com) and **Hostel Caracol** (Cl. 4 No. 2-21, tel. 2/820-7335, www.hostelcaracol.com)

can arrange outings, such as a wildly popular day trip to the Coconuco hot springs with an exhilarating bike ride back (COP$55,000); a trip to Parque Nacional Natural Puracé (COP$85,000 pp, 4-person minimum); or a trip to the market at Silvia.

FOOD

Five-course meals are standard at the **Restaurante del Hotel Camino Real** (Cl. 5 No. 5-59, tel. 2/824-3595, www.hotelcaminoreal.com.co, noon-3pm and 6pm-9:30pm daily, COP$25,000). The cuisine is mostly French, but also on the menu are Colombian specialties.

Mora Castilla (Cl. 2 No. 4-44, tel. 2/824-1513, www.moracastilla.com, 10am-7pm Mon.-Sat., 3pm-8pm Sun.) packs a punch with its local specialties, such as the famous *empanada de pipian,* an empanada filled with mashed potatoes and peanuts.

La Semilla Escondida (Cl. 9N No. 10-29, cell tel. 310/823-0313, noon-3pm and 6pm-10pm Mon.-Sat.) serves healthy lunches and an economical set lunch. Go for the crepes—the owner is French, after all.

Wipala (Cra. 2 No. 2-38, tel. 2/823-3141, 3pm-9pm daily, COP$15,000) is a live music venue/gallery/restaurant surrounding a verdant patio. In the evenings it's a cool place to visit and mingle with locals as well as visitors and expats. Wipala serves unique juices, some with coca leaf. They also serve light meals.

Tequila's (Cl. 5 No. 9-25, tel. 2/822-2150, 5pm-9pm Wed.-Sun., COP$15,000) serves fantastic Tex-Mex food, and is the perfect spot to delight in the dynamic duo of enchiladas and *micheladas* (a beer cocktail). The Mexican and Colombian owners are friendly and lived in Long Island for many years.

The ★ **Restaurante Italiano** (Cl. 4 No. 8-83, tel. 2/824-0607, 11am-10pm daily, COP$20,000) is a reliable choice. Run by a Swiss woman, it's been in Popayán for years, stays open late, and serves large portions of pasta and pizzas. During the day the set lunch—usually Colombian fare—is hard to beat.

Cuarsenor Café (Cra. 6 No. 3-85, tel. 2/834-4040, COP$6,000) is hopping all day long, packed mainly with local workers. It's a bargain breakfast spot, but it also serves hearty lunches with trout or grilled chicken. There's an adjoining bakery.

For coffee from the region prepared in any number of fancy ways, try **Oromo** (Cra. 5 No. 3-34, cell tel. 310/257-1219, 9am-8pm Mon.-Sat.). **Café Disidencia** (Cra. 5 No. 3-48, cell tel. 311/367-0457, 8:30am-10pm Mon.-Sat.) caters to university students. In addition to serving light bites and drinks, it is also a cultural space.

ACCOMMODATIONS

Popayán has a fair number of accommodation options, and its hostels are some of the country's better ones. Colombian visitors snatch up rooms during Semana Santa and during the annual food festival, Congreso Nacional Gastronómico.

UNDER COP$70,000

Relaxed is the best word to describe the ★ **Hostel Caracol** (Cl. 4 No. 2-21, tel. 2/820-7335, www.hostelcaracol.com, COP$48,000 d with shared bath). The atmosphere has a lot to do with its easygoing staff, who are full of great suggestions on how to make the most of your visit. If you feel like mingling with other travelers or locals, check out their small café. ★ **Hosteltrail** (Cra. 11 No. 4-16, tel. 2/831-7871, www.hosteltrailpopayan.com, COP$25,000 dorm, COP$70,000 d private bath), owned by the same Scottish couple, is a sociable place, with 14 rooms. Hosteltrail is about a 15-minute walk from the bus station.

Parklife (Cl. 5 No. 6-19, cell tel. 300/249-6240, www.parklifehostel.com, COP$25,000 dorm, COP$70,000 d) takes the prize for best location in Popayán. Right next to *la catedral* and overlooking Parque Caldas, it can't get much better. This is a lively and bright hostel, with a pair of spacious and private "rooms with a view" that overlook the park, as well as two dorm rooms with 8-10 beds each.

COP$70,000-200,000

La Casa de Mima (Cl. 3 No. 2-37, cell tel. 310/494-4082, www.lacasademima.com, COP$150,000 d) is a quiet and cozy bed-and-breakfast a few blocks from Parque Caldas. Seven rooms overlook three courtyards. The owner, Doña Olga, lives here as well, and will make you feel right at home. **Hotel La Plazuela** (Cl. 5 No. 8-13, tel. 2/824-1084, www.hotellaplazuela.com.co, COP$110,000 d) is a colonial-style house with a lovely large interior courtyard. The rooms are not as great as the setting, which is hard to beat.

COP$200,000-500,000

The finest option in town, although falling short of five stars, is the classic ★ **Hotel Dann Monasterio** (Cl. 4 No. 10-14, tel. 2/824-2191, www.hotelesdann.com, COP$252,000 d). It's housed in an old monastery overlooking a serene interior courtyard where you can have a coffee. It has a pool amid spacious, well-kept grounds.

TRANSPORTATION

The **Aeropuerto Guillermo Leon Valencia** (PPN) is only one kilometer north of the Centro Histórico. The airport is served by **Avianca** (Cra. 5 No. 3-85, tel. 2/824-4505, www.avianca.com, 8am-noon and 2pm-6pm Mon.-Fri., 9am-1pm Sat.) and offers several daily flights from Bogotá.

There are frequent buses from Cali (3-4 hrs., COP$17,000) and Pasto (5 hrs., COP$35,000), arriving at the **Terminal de Transportes** (Transversal 9 No. 4N-125, Oficina 201, tel. 2/823-1817, www.terminalpopayan.com), a modern bus station within walking distance of the airport. It's about a 15-minute walk south to downtown.

VICINITY OF POPAYÁN
Market at Silvia

The **Market at Silvia** (town of Silvia, 5am-2pm Tues.) is a popular day trip from Popayán. It is about 60 kilometers (37 miles) away. On market days starting at dawn, Guambiano indigenous people converge on the market from nearby communities to buy and sell fruit, vegetables, and textiles. There are few handicrafts to purchase. The market and the people are photogenic; however, if you would like to take photos of people, request permission first. The market occurs rain or shine.

To get to the market, take a bus bound for Silvia from Popayán's Terminal de Transportes. They leave every 20 minutes or so, and the trip takes about an hour (COP$6,000).

Termales de Coconuco

For a dip in some *termales* (hot springs), there are two possibilities near the town of Coconuco and the Parque Nacional Natural Puracé. The **Termales Aguatibia** (Km. 4 Vía Coconuco, cell tel. 310/543-7172, www.termalesaguatibia.com, 8am-6pm daily, COP$16,000 adults) is nestled among the hills. Here, there are six pools, the temperatures of which vary between 80 and 104 degrees F. There is also a waterslide, making it a popular destination for families on the weekends.

Termales Agua Hirviendo (Vía Comfandi, cell tel. 321/934-1746, adults COP$7,000), three kilometers from the town of Coconuco, is another option, promising hotter water in its pools and 24-hour service. These springs are run by a local Coconuco indigenous community.

To get to these hot springs, take a cab from Popayán, but expect to pay around COP$50,000 each way. Alternatively, there are buses departing from Popayán's **Terminal de Transportes** (Trans. 9 No. 4N-125) to the town of Coconuco about 30 kilometers (19 miles) away. This trip takes about an hour, costing COP$4,000. From town, you can either walk about four kilometers (2.5 miles) along a well-marked road to the springs, or take a *mototaxi* (COP$2,500). The last bus from Coconuco to Popayán departs at 6pm.

Parque Nacional Natural Puracé

The **Parque Nacional Natural Puracé** (main ranger station: 44 kilometers east of Popayán, COP$20,000 non-Colombians, COP$8,500 Colombian residents, COP$4,000 children) is a national park covering some 83,000 hectares (205,100 acres) that includes two important mountainous formations within the Cordillera Central: the Serranía de los Coconucos and the Masizo Colombiano. It is a region of immense environmental importance that was declared a UNESCO Biosphere Reserve in 1979.

The Serranía de los Coconucos is a six-kilometer chain of volcanoes, including the snow-covered Pan de Azúcar (5,000 meters/16,400 feet), Coconuco (4,600 meters/15,100 feet), Puracé (4,580 meters/15,000 feet), and Sotará (4,400 meters/14,400 feet). Puracé and Sotará are currently active. The Masizo Colombiano is a mountainous formation where five major Colombian rivers originate: Río Magdalena and Río Cauca, which flow into the Caribbean Sea; the Río Patía, which flows into the Pacific Ocean; and the Río Caquetá and Río Putumayo, which are tributaries of the Amazon.

The park includes more than 30 mountain lakes, including Laguna del Magdalena, which is the source of the Río Magdalena. Most of the park lies at an altitude greater than 2,600 meters (8,500 feet).

PRACTICALITIES

High season in the park is from mid-December to mid-January, as well as during Semana Santa (Easter week) and school vacations from mid-June to mid-July.

The main ranger station and main entrance is called **Pilimbalá**. It's 44 kilometers (27 miles) east of Popayán.

Near Pilimbalá, the park has **cabins** (COP$25,500-35,000 pp high season), and **camping** is also available (COP$9,500 pp). To make a reservation, contact the Pilimbalá ranger station (tel. 8/521-2578 or 8/521-2579, cell tel. 313/680-0051).

A **restaurant** at Pilimbalá serves three meals a day for under COP$5,000 each.

Note that most of the park is under the jurisdiction of an indigenous *resguardo* (reservation), and its leaders have the final word on whether visitors will be permitted in the park. There is often a difficult relationship between the parks service and indigenous tribes, not only in Purace, but in many of Colombia's most spectacular natural areas.

VOLCANO TREK

The primary attraction at this park is the fairly strenuous climb to the summit of the **Volcán Puracé** (7 km/4.3 mi) in the northern part of the park. The trek, which requires about five hours up and three down, takes you through high mountain tropical jungle and then *páramo,* a unique high-elevation Andean ecosystem.

It's a very good idea to hire a guide for this trek. Contact the Popayán branch of the Parques Nacionales (Cra. 9 No. 25N-6, tel. 2/823-1279, purace@parquesnacionales. gov.co) or the **Pilimbalá ranger station** (tel. 8/521-2578 or 8/521-2579) in advance to arrange for a guide. Guides usually charge around COP$35,000 for the hike up to the crater. The highly recommended outfitter **Popayan Tours** (www.popayantours.com) works with the community and offers two tours to Puracé. One is a trek to the Volcán Puracé (COP$85,000 pp) and another is a condor-feeding excursion (COP$75,000 pp). Transportation and a guide are included.

GETTING THERE

The main entrance of the park, Pilimbalá, is 45 kilometers (28 miles) east of Popayán. From Popayán, buses depart the **Terminal de Transportes** (COP$5,000) bound for the community of La Plata. The company Sotracauca runs buses that leave at 4:30am and 6:45am (COP$5,000), but there are often delays. The trip takes approximately 1.5 hours. Get off at the Cruce de la Mina, also known as El Crucero, and from there walk about 800 meters (0.5 mile) toward the left to the Pilimbalá ranger station. There are return buses heading back to Popayán until around 5:30pm. You can find a return bus at Cruce de la Mina/El Crucero.

★ TIERRADENTRO

From AD 500 to AD 900, the area of Tierradentro was settled by an agricultural society that dug magnificent decorated underground tombs, produced large stone statues, and built oval buildings on artificial terraces. These people disappeared without a trace. We do not even know what they called themselves. By the time of the Spanish conquest, the area was inhabited by the Nasa-Paez, a Chibcha-speaking people who still inhabit the area and who are organized in *cabildos* (indigenous ruling bodies) that are recognized by the Colombian government.

Tierradentro is the site of a major indigenous necropolis that includes monumental funeral statues and hypogea (underground burial chambers). These chambers, some 12 meters wide, are decorated with intricate red and black anthropomorphic and zoomorphic geometric designs, some of which are in relief. They were first excavated and studied in the 1930s. This archaeological park was declared a UNESCO World Heritage Site in 1995.

These awe-inspiring burial chambers, believed to have been built between AD 600 and AD 900, reveal the existence of a rich and complex society that devoted significant time and effort to preparing the way to the afterlife. There is also an intriguing symmetry to be found between these ornate underground chambers and the houses of the living aboveground.

PRACTICALITIES

A high-quality flashlight is a must for getting a good look at the interior paintings of the tombs and some of the elaborate artwork decorating them. Rubber boots could be useful during the rainy months of March-June and September-November. Also, be sure to bring water and snacks. It's a tough six-hour walk from La Portada to Alto de San Andrés, Alto del Aguacate, and down to the museum and park entrance. And that's just a little more than halfway.

Near the museums you can buy juice,

water, or homemade ice cream at one of the little shops or nearby hostels.

At Alto de Segovia and Alto del Duende, a park guard will open some of the tombs and let you in and out. The steps can be quite steep and dark, so watch your footing.

Tierradentro Archaeological Park

Tierradentro Archaeological Park (91 km east of Popayán, www.icanh.gov.co, 8am-4pm daily, COP$20,000) comprises five sites spread across four hills, straddling Vía San Andrés de Pisimbalá-El Crucero.

It's possible to visit all the archaeological sites in one circuit for a total of about 14 kilometers (8.5 miles) in one long day. Many people visit the museums and the three sites on the eastern side of Vía San Andrés de Pisimbalá-El Crucero, take a break for lunch in San Andrés de Pisimbalá, then continue onward to the two sites on the western side of the road. It's also possible to go at a slower pace, as your admission ticket is good for two consecutive days. If you are in a hurry, prioritize a visit to Alto de Segovia, the first stop on the circuit and the easiest to access. Expect to spend about 15-20 minutes at each site.

Begin your visit at the museums, located at the park entrance and start of the circuit. The two small museums provide a good introduction to the park and are across the street from one another. On the western side of the road is the **archaeological museum,** featuring artifacts found in Tierradentro's tombs. On the opposite side of the road, across from the ticket booth, is the **ethnographic museum,** which focuses on the Paez indigenous communities who live in the area. Plan to spend around 15-20 minutes in each museum.

The first site to visit is on the eastern side of Vía San Andrés de Pisimbalá-El Crucero, about a 20-minute walk from the park entrance: **Alto de Segovia,** which has some of the most impressive burial chambers. Some of the 25 tombs open to the public are as much as six meters (20 feet) deep, with central columns and multiple chambers. Walls are decorated with elaborate geometric designs in red, black, and yellow. They are extraordinarily well preserved.

Alto del Duende, a 15-minute walk beyond Alto de Segovia, has five tombs, including one that resembles a dwelling. The third site on the circuit is **El Tablón,** a 30-minute walk from Alto del Duende. It features nine large stone statues. Follow Vía Santa Rosa-San Andrés de Pisimbalá to get there.

the well-preserved burial chambers of Tierradentro Archaeological Park

stone carving at Tierradentro Archaeological Park

Accommodations

Basic accommodations are plentiful near the official park entrance and museums, and are all located on the same main road that leads to San Andrés de Pisimbalá. **Hospedaje Pisimbalá** (cell tel. 311/605-4835 or 321/263-2334, COP$20,000 pp) is a neat and comfortable option, with a cool thatched-roof gazebo in front. It also has a restaurant.

El Refugio (tel. 2/825-2904, hotelalbergueelrefugio@gmail.com, COP$60,000 d) is the largest and most luxurious option. It even has a pool.

★ **La Portada** (cell tel. 311/601-7884, laportadatierradentro@hotmail.com, www.laportadahotel.com, COP$40,000 d w/private bath, COP$25,000 s) is the best option. In the town of San Andrés de Pisimbalá, it's well run and orderly, and the structure is made from *guadua,* a type of bamboo. Leonardo, the owner, is friendly and full of good information. His wife is an excellent cook, too. Nonguests can dine at the restaurant. La Portada is close to the center of San Andrés de Pisimbalá.

Next, you'll cross through the town of San Andrés de Pisimbalá. Just next to the hotel La Portada is the path to the **Alto de San Andrés.** Parts of the trail—especially between Alto de San Andrés and the next site, Alto de Aguacate—are poorly marked. When in doubt, keep going left and upward. You will eventually reach the top of the mountain ridge. Along the way you may run across campesinos (farmers) tending to their coffee and banana plantations who can point you in the right direction. The Alto de San Andrés has seven open tombs, each decorated with red-and-black murals and central columns. One tomb, named SA5, is distinguished by its representation of human faces.

Getting to the **Alto de Aguacate** is a steep climb, but the views of the countryside are breathtaking. At this site are 42 open tombs, which have been deteriorated by vandalism and erosion.

From here, it's a 1.5-hour walk downhill to return to the museums and the park entrance.

Getting There

The 100-plus kilometer trip to Tierradentro from Popayán will take you through gorgeous countryside of farms, villages, and gentle mountains shrouded in mist. One bus a day leaves from Popayán directly to San Andrés de Pisimbalá, the closest town to the park. It leaves at 10:30am and takes 4-5 hours, costing around COP$25,000. From San Andrés de Pisimbalá back to Popayán there is one direct bus that departs at 6am.

Another option from Popayán is to take a bus bound for Inzá and get off at El Cruce (the name of a junction), which is a short walk from the museum area. These buses leave at 5:30am, 8:30am, 10:30am, 1pm, and 3pm. It is a five-hour trip and costs COP$25,000. Return buses from El Cruce depart at 9am, 11am, and 1pm. From El Cruce, a *mototaxi* can take you into San Andrés de Pisimbalá for COP$3,000 or directly to the park for COP$2,000.

Public transportation between San Agustín and Tierradentro requires multiple transfers. From San Agustín you can take the 6am bus bound for Bogotá, then transfer in Garzón (COP$15,000) to the bus toward La Plata (COP$7,000). From there you can take the 10:30am bus to San Andrés de Pisimbalá. That trip takes about three hours and costs COP$12,000. To return to San Agustín, you can take a bus at 6am. It arrives in the early afternoon.

★ SAN AGUSTÍN

The small colonial town of San Agustín, nestled within the folds of the southern Colombian Andes and west of the Río Magdalena, would probably be an attractive destination in its own right. At an elevation of 1,800 meters (5,900 feet), it is set in a place of enormous natural beauty and has wonderful springlike weather. However, its fame comes from its location near the largest pre-Columbian archaeological site south of Central America and north of Perú. From approximately AD 100 to AD 800, this region was home to an indigenous culture that produced spectacular monumental funeral statues hewn out of volcanic rock. Researchers do not know what these people called themselves, and so, lacking a better name, they have been labeled the San Agustín Culture.

To visit the main archaeological sites near San Agustín, you will need about two days. However, don't rush your stay here, as it is a pleasant and peaceful place to visit, with several options for hiking and rafting amid spectacular mountain landscapes. This little town has surprisingly good restaurants and accommodations.

HISTORY

The area around San Agustín was occupied as early as 3300 BC. Starting in the 1st century AD, the people of San Agustín created hundreds of monumental funeral stone statues set on large platforms. Very little is known about these people, except that they were agrarian and formed compact settlements. By AD

800, this society had mysteriously vanished and other indigenous peoples coming from the Amazon basin occupied the area. Today, the inhabitants are predominantly mestizo.

Spanish chroniclers of the 16th century mention the statues, as did Colombian naturalist Francisco José de Caldas in the early 19th century. However, it was not until 1913 that German ethnographer Konrad Theodor Preuss conducted the first systematic excavation. When he was finished, he carted off (probably illegally) 35 large statues that are now at the Ethnographic Museum in Dahlem on the outskirts of Berlin. David Dellenback, an American-born researcher and long-time resident of San Agustín, discovered on a 1992 trip to Berlin that only three of these statues were on exhibit, while the rest were piled away haphazardly in a storehouse. He found no trace of the numerous ceramic pieces that Preuss took and which were probably destroyed during the Allied bombings of World War II. Dellenback and his wife, Martha Gil, have promoted a petition, signed by more than 1,800 residents of San Agustín and nearby towns, for the German authorities to return the statues to their rightful home. Dellenback and Gil coauthored a comprehensive guide to San Agustín called *The Statues of the Pueblo Escultor,* which is available in shops in San Agustín.

PRACTICALITIES

Armed with a map and a willingness to ask directions, it's possible to visit the Parque Arqueológico de San Agustín on foot. This can make for a wonderful escape. However, many tourists opt for half-day or full-day **horseback tours,** which can also cover sites like the Parque Arqueológico Alto de Ídolos. It usually costs about COP$35,000 for a horse and guide; a local guide is **Parmenidez Martínez** (Cra. 7 No. 17-50, cell tel. 312/477-7878). The **tourism information office** (Cra. 11 No. 3-61, cell tel. 320/486-3896, 8am-noon and 2pm-6pm Mon.-Fri.) can also assist with this, or you can ask your hotel to recommend a guide.

Visiting the sites near the town of Isnos (the other archaeological parks, El Estrecho, and the waterfalls) by public transportation can be difficult; most people opt for daylong Jeep tours that cover the Parque Arqueológico Alto de los Ídolos, Parque Alto de Las Piedras, El Estrecho, and the waterfalls. A recommended tour agency affiliated is **Chaska Tours** (tel. 8/837-3437, www.chaskatours.net); however, any hotel can organize this, or you can stop by the **tourism information office** (Cra. 11 No. 3-61, cell tel. 320/486-3896, 8am-noon and 2pm-5pm Mon.-Fri.).

Parque Arqueológico de San Agustín

The excellent **Parque Arqueológico de San Agustín** (San Agustín Archaeological Park, 8am-4pm daily, COP$20,000) covers 80 hectares (200 acres) of what was one of the most important ritual areas of the San Agustín culture. Some 130 kilometers (80 miles) southeast of Popayán, it was established in 1937 and declared a UNESCO World Heritage Site in 1995. The park contains over 130 statues with striking human and animal-like features, as well as carved tombs and monumental stone tables, or dolmens. The park is easy to navigate: Plan on a couple of hours to stroll it at leisure and absorb the beauty. The park is two kilometers (1.25 miles) west of the town of San Agustín and can be reached on foot or by bus. A ticket here is also valid at the Parque Arqueológico Alto de los Ídolos.

Near the entrance to the park is the highly recommended **Museo Arqueológico** (free). It contains pottery, tools, jewelry, and some smaller-scale statues. It's a good educational stop to learn more about the San Agustín culture before visiting the sites themselves.

As you enter the park, you'll walk along the lovely 800-meter Bosque de las Estatuas, a meandering shady path lined with statues. Many of these statues were recovered from other locations in the region. Most of the park's monumental stone objects are concentrated on four funeral hills, designated Mesitas A, B, C, and D. The first stops in the park are Mesitas B and A. Mesita B, atop a hill, has some of the most well-known statues. Mesita A was the first area open to the public and holds some of the largest funerary mounds ever excavated, at 30 meters in diameter and four meters high. Mesita C has one burial mound with 15 statues and 49 simple tombs. Statues here tend to be more abstract, with less detail.

The unusual **Fuente de Lavapiés** contains bas-reliefs of human and animal figures

horses at the ready, San Agustín

sculpted on the rocky bed of a stream. This is the only non-funeral site in the park. On a hill, at the highest point of the park, behind the *fuente* is the **Alto de Lavapiés,** where excavations have shown human presence dating back to 3300 BC.

Other Archaeological Parks

Five kilometers (three miles) southwest of the town of Isnos on the other side of the Río Magdalena, and about 25 kilometers (16 miles) northeast of the town of San Agustín, the **Parque Arqueológico Alto de los Ídolos** (8am-5pm daily, COP$20,000) is the second-largest archaeological park. It includes an anthropomorphic statue that measures 4.3 meters (14 feet), along with large sarcophagi. A ticket here is also valid for Parque Arqueológico Nacional de San Agustín. To get here, take a public bus toward Isnos (COP$2,500) or call a cab (COP$10,000).

The much smaller **Parque Arqueológico Alto de Las Piedras** (8am-5pm daily, entrance included with admission to Parque Arqueológico de San Agustín) is six kilometers (3.7 miles) north of Isnos on the road that leads to the Salto de Borodones waterfall. It has statues and tombs with original pigments, including the Doble Yo—a statue that is half man, half animal. It's not easy to get here using public transportation, so it's best to take a cab from San Agustín (COP$10,000).

Recreation

Several natural sights are near San Agustín. The entire upper gorge of the Río Magdalena is majestic. About 15 kilometers (9 miles) north of San Agustín, at **El Estrecho,** the river spurts through a 2.2-meter (7-foot) rocky funnel. To get here, you'll need to take a bus headed toward Obando, and ask to be let off at the river. The trip costs about COP$5,500.

Less than 10 kilometers (6 miles) north of the town of Isnos are two waterfalls, the 400-meter (1,300-foot) **Salto de Borodones** and 200-meter (650-foot) **Salto de Mortiño.** To get here, take a bus to El Cruce de Isnos (COP$2,000), then a shared taxi to Isnos

(COP$4,000), and finally, a *mototaxi* (COP$3,000) to the waterfalls.

About an hour from the town of San Agustín, the upper Río Magdalena offers some of the best white-water river rafting in Colombia, set within spectacular mountain landscapes. **Magdalena Rafting** (cell tel. 311/271-5333, www.viajes-colombia.com) offers rafting, rappelling, and hiking tours for people of all abilities, ranging from 90-minute excursions to daylong trips.

Food

Most restaurants are on the main drag in town, Calle 5.

Both **Donde Richar** (Cl. 5 No. 23-45, cell tel. 312/432-6399, noon-7pm daily, COP$23,000) and **Andrés a la Parrilla** (Cl. 5 No. 15-67, cell tel. 311/858-4451) are known for their *asado huilense,* a plate of grilled meats that's a regional specialty.

Tomate (Cl. 5 No. 16-02, cell tel. 314/265-5527, 8am-3pm Thurs.-Mon., COP$8,000) is San Agustín's veggie headquarters, serving breakfast and a daily special. This is the best place in town for fresh vegetables, and the menu changes each day.

Restaurante Italiano da Ugo (Vereda El Tablón San Agustín, cell tel. 314/375-8086, 6pm-9:30pm Thurs.-Sun., COP$15,000) is helmed by an Italian chef and is a nice place to cap off the day. The tiramisu is outstanding. It's a bit outside of town.

For a cup of coffee or a small meal on the main square, head to **Macivo Coffee** (Cl. 2 No. 13-17, 8:30am-8pm daily).

Accommodations

There are a surprising number of cozy and friendly accommodations options in San Agustín, many run by European expats. Staff at these spots can provide expert advice on the area, arrange recreational activities such as horseback riding and rafting, and assist with travel needs.

A perennial favorite of international travelers is Swiss-run ★ **El Maco** (tel. 8/837-3437, cell tel. 311/271-4802, www.elmaco.

ch, COP$16,000-50,000 pp), nestled in the hills about a 20-minute walk from town. Accommodations consist of small cabins, a tepee, a chalet, and an indigenous-style *maloca* (cabin) distributed among pleasant gardens that are home to dogs and chickens. Staff can organize great horseback-riding trips to nearby archaeological spots.

La Casa de Francois (tel. 8/837-3847, cell tel. 314/358-2930, www.lacasadefrancois.com, COP$25,000 dorm, COP$50,000 d) offers cabins, two dorm rooms with 10 beds total, and lots of hammocks to laze about after a hard day's archaeological exploration. The on-site restaurant is quite good and is reasonably priced, and they bake their own bread. It's a 10-minute walk north of town, past the brick factory.

Colombian-run **Huaka Yo** (Bogotá tel. 1/489-9269, cell tel. 320/846-9763, www.huakayo.com, COP$116,000 d high season) is just 200 meters from the archaeological park. It consists of a large house that has 12 rooms and 6 loft spaces, each with its own private bath. Huaka Yo is a 5-minute bus ride (or a 20-minute walk) east from town.

Bursting with flowers and vegetation, **Casa de Nelly** (Vía Vereda La Estrella, cell tel. 310/215-9067 or 311/535/0412, www.hotelcasadenelly.co, COP$25,000 dorm, COP$40,000 d) is just two kilometers from the park and on a hill overlooking town. Guests love hanging out in Nelly's gardens after a day in the park.

Information and Services

The **tourist information office** (Cl. 3 and Cra. 12, cell tel. 320/486-3896, 8am-noon and 2pm-6pm Mon.-Fri.) can assist with transportation and activities in the area.

Transportation
FROM BOGOTÁ

It's easy to visit San Agustín from Bogotá by flying into **Aeropuerto Benito Salas** (NVA) in Neiva. **Avianca** (tel. 1/401-3434, www.avianca.com) and **Easy Fly** (tel. 1/414-8111, www.easyfly.com.co) operate several of the one-hour flights daily.

Next, take a bus (4 hours, COP$30,000) from Neiva to the town of Pitalito, about 30 kilometers east of San Agustín. It's a beautiful drive along the Río Magdalena. Shared taxis (45 minutes, COP$5,000) take you from there to San Agustín. Private taxis can also be contracted from Neiva to San Agustin, but you'll have to negotiate a price—expect to pay at least COP$150,000.

FROM POPAYÁN

From Popayán there are about four buses per day bound for Pitalito (5 hours, COP$35,000); you'll have to get off at the intersection called Cruce de Isnos, where minivans await to take you the last leg into San Agustín (10 minutes, COP$2,000). Be sure to tell the bus driver that you're headed to the town of Isnos. This journey takes you through the spectacular scenery of Parque Nacional Natural Puracé. It's often slow going.

Tatacoa Desert

The 330-square-kilometer (127-square-mile) **Desierto de Tatacoa** makes for an unusual overnight stop on the way to San Agustín from Bogotá. It's not technically a desert, but rather a semiarid zone with dry tropical forest. It feels and looks like a desert, though, with temperatures regularly soaring above 90 degrees Fahrenheit. It's a popular party place on weekends and holidays.

A visit to Tatacoa includes a stop at the historic town of **Villavieja,** with its 17th-century **Capilla de Santa Barbara** (Plaza Principal Villavieja), a church founded by the Jesuits in honor of the indigenous cacique Tocaya, who was killed by the Spaniards. The **Museo Paleontológico** (Cl. 3 No. 3-05, 7:30am-1pm Mon.-Fri., 7am-6pm Sat.-Sun., COP$2,000) provides a sample of the many fossils, dating from 3.8 million years ago, that have been found in the Tatacoa Desert.

The dry conditions at Tatacoa make for ideal stargazing. The **Observatorio Astronómico Tatacoa** (Vereda El Cuzco, tel. 8/879-7584, cell tel. 310/465-6765, www.tatacoa-astronomia.com, COP$5,000), near town, provides telescopes for visitors to scan the sky in the evening hours. Each year, usually over a long weekend in June or July, hard-core and novice astronomers alike head to Tatacoa for the annual Star Party event. A restaurant next to the observatory serves mostly grilled goat and mutton.

ACCOMMODATIONS

Hostal Noches de Saturno (400 meters past the observatory, cell tel. 313/305-5898 or 314/288-3337, moisestatacoa@yahoo.es, COP$50,000 d) has five rooms, along with a pool and restaurant. This is a very social spot. Nonguests can use the property's pool for COP$4,000.

Within walking distance of the Observatorio Astronómico Tatacoa, **Posada Elvira Clever** (Vereda El Cusco, cell tel. 312/559-8576, COP$20,000 pp) has two rooms available in a small and simple zinc-roof house. There is no electricity.

In Villavieja, **La Casona** (Cl. 3 No. 3-60, tel. 8/879-7636, cell tel. 320/243-9705, http://hotel-lacasonavillavieja.blogspot.com, COP$50,000 d) is a small hotel in an old house on Parque Principal, overseen by friendly owners. Simón Bolívar is said to have stayed here.

TRANSPORTATION

To get to Tatacoa from Bogotá, it's a five- to six-hour bus ride (COP$45,000) to Neiva, then another hour to the desert.

From Villavieja, *mototaxis* regularly transport visitors to the Tatacoa Desert. These cost about COP$15,000 per person. This is the way to go, as the scenery and desert light are gorgeous.

Neiva

Many people pass through Neiva (pop. 340,000), the capital of the Huila department,

on the way to Bogotá from San Agustín. It also has easy air and bus connections to Bogotá.

Neiva has few attractions for tourists. However, if you do happen to stop here, a nice place for a stroll is the **Malecón Río Magdalena.** This boardwalk along the Río Magdalena follows Avenida Circunvalar, spanning the Cacica Gaitana monument to the Caracoli docks.

The town really gets going during the **Fiestas de San Juan y San Pablo** (June 15-June 30). The highlight is the Reinado del Bambuco, a beauty pageant named after *bambuco,* a traditional music of the Colombian Andes. Entrants, in flowery and frilly costumes, must dance the Sanjuanero, a famous *bambuco,* and other folk songs.

ACCOMMODATIONS

Catering to business clientele, the **Hotel Neiva Plaza** (Cl. 7 No. 4-62, tel. 8/871-0806, www.hotelneivaplaza.com, COP$189,000 s, COP$243,000 d) has 86 spacious rooms, a rooftop gym, and a pool. It's the reliable (if overpriced) choice in Neiva.

TRANSPORTATION

Neiva's airport is the **Aeropuerto Benito Salas** (NVA, Cra. 6 No. 32-45, tel. 8/875-8198). It's in the north of the city on the road to the Tatacoa Desert.

Neiva's bus station is the **Terminal de Transportes** (Transversal 5 No. 53-12, tel. 8/873-1232), in the south of the city. From San Agustín, the bus ride to Neiva is four hours and costs COP$30,000.

If you'd like to explore the region with your own wheels, you can rent a vehicle at **ANT Rent A Car** (Av. 26 No. 5-12, tel. 8/872-2859, ant.rentacar@hotmail.com). They also have chauffeured cars available.

Pasto

With church steeples rising from its colonial center, the city of Pasto (pop. 446,000) lies in the verdant Valle de Atriz with the deceivingly gentle Volcán Galeras watching over it. This rich agricultural region where potatoes are king even has a potato named after it—the *papa pastusa*—that is sold in every supermarket in Colombia. Pasto, the "Ciudad Sorpresa," indeed may surprise you with its museums and sights that will keep you intellectually stimulated for more than a couple of days. Of particular interest is the extraordinary handicraft technique called *barniz de Pasto,* as well as some incredible woodcarvings, a remnant of Quiteño culture.

Wonderful day trips can be made from the city to Laguna La Cocha and to Laguna Verde to the south, or to Volcán Cumbal, along the Ecuador border; one of the highest peaks in the Nudo de los Pastos mountain range, it's where the Andes split into the Cordilleras Occidentales y Centrales (Western and Central Ranges).

Due to its rugged terrain and poorly patrolled border with Ecuador, Nariño, the department of which Pasto is capital, became a major corridor for drug and guerrilla activity. The areas described in this guide are safe, however.

SIGHTS
Historic Churches
The most important and only colonial-era church in the city is the baroque **Iglesia de San Juan Bautista** (Cl. 18A No. 25-17, tel. 2/723-5440, 7:30am-11am Sun.-Fri., 3:30pm-6:30pm Sat.), in the heart of the Centro on the **Plaza Nariño.** The original construction was built in the 16th century, but an earthquake demolished that, and in 1669 the current church was built. The interior has outstanding geometric Mudéjar designs on the ceiling and around the presbytery.

Statues of angels set atop the twin towers of the **Iglesia de Cristo Rey** (corner Cl. 20 and Cra. 24) beckon from blocks away. This is a stunning gothic revival church. The sanctuary is lined by 19 woodcarvings created by famous local sculptor Alfonso Zambrano and Ecuadorian craftspersons. Above, light

Plaza Nariño, Pasto's main plaza

Pasto

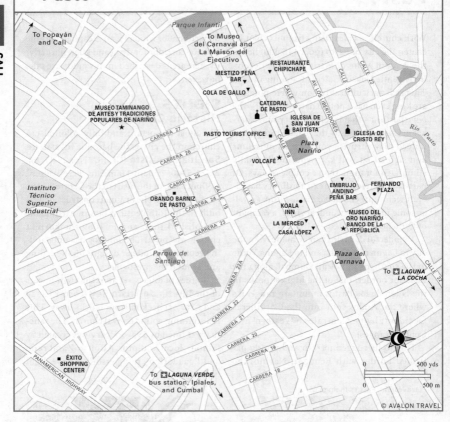

To Popayán
and Cali

Parque Infantil

To Museo
del Carnaval and
La Maison del
Ejecutivo

RESTAURANTE
CHIPICHAPE

MESTIZO PEÑA
BAR

COLA DE GALLO

CATEDRAL
DE PASTO

MUSEO TAMINANGO
DE ARTES Y TRADICIONES
POPULARES DE NARIÑO

IGLESIA DE
SAN JUAN
BAUTISTA

IGLESIA DE
CRISTO REY

Río Pasto

CARRERA 27

PASTO TOURIST OFFICE

*Plaza
Nariño*

CARRERA 26

VOLCAFÉ

CALLE 19

CALLE 21

CALLE 22

AV. LOS LIBERTADORES

CARRERA 25

EMBRUJO
ANDINO
PEÑA BAR

FERNANDO
PLAZA

*Instituto
Técnico
Superior
Industrial*

OBANDO BARNIZ
DE PASTO

CARRERA 24

KOALA
INN

MUSEO DEL
ORO NARIÑO/
BANCO DE LA
REPÚBLICA

CALLE 16

CALLE 17

CARRERA 23

LA MERCED

CASA LÓPEZ

CALLE 15

CALLE 13

CALLE 12

CALLE 11

CALLE 10

*Parque de
Santiago*

CARRERA 22A

*Plaza del
Carnaval*

To LAGUNA
LA COCHA

CALLE 22

PANAMERICAN HIGHWAY

ÉXITO
SHOPPING
CENTER

CARRERA 22

CARRERA 21

CARRERA 20

CARRERA 19

CARRERA 18

To LAGUNA VERDE,
bus station, Ipiales,
and Cumbal

0   500 yds

0   500 m

© AVALON TRAVEL

streams through enormous stained glass windows, creating a mystical environment.

Built in 1920, the **Catedral de Pasto** (Cra. 26 No. 17-23, tel. 2/723-3328, 7am-11am Sun.-Fri., 3pm-7pm Sat.) was recently renovated.

Museo Taller Alfonso Zambrano Payán

The **Museo Taller Alfonso Zambrano Payán** (Cl. 20 No. 29-78, tel. 2/731-2837, hernandozambrano@gmail.com, 9am-11am and 2pm-5pm Mon.-Sat., free) is a tribute to Alfonso Zambrano, one of Pasto's most famous sons. Zambrano was an accomplished woodcarver, and year after year he won awards for his work on carnival floats. Both woodcarving and painting continue to take place at this workshop/museum, where Zambrano's children and grandchildren keep the family craft alive. There is also a small collection of pre-Columbian ceramics and Quiteño school paintings on view.

Museo Taminango de Artes y Tradiciones Populares de Nariño

Set in a colonial house built in the early 17th century (said to be the oldest house still standing in Pasto), the **Museo Taminango de Artes y Tradiciones Populares de Nariño**

(Cl. 13 No. 27-67, tel. 2/723-5539, 8am-noon and 2pm-6pm Mon.-Fri., 9am-1pm Sat., COP$2,000) is a museum dedicated to handicrafts. Catalina Morgan, an American missionary who arrived in Pasto in 1934, set out to preserve the house, which had fallen into disrepair. She raised enough money to restore it and to convert it, eventually, into a cultural center. It was opened as a museum in 1989. The museum presents traditional handicrafts from Nariño, including explanations of the *barniz de Pasto* technique. This technique, developed by indigenous groups, uses the leaves and fruits of the *mopa mopa* bush, from which a resin is extracted. It is dyed in different colors using vegetable dyes, and thin sheets of it are applied to decorate wooden boxes and other objects. Adjacent to the museum is a small handicrafts store.

Museo del Oro Nariño

The **Museo del Oro Nariño** (Cl. 19 No. 21-27, tel. 2/721-9100, ext. 2624, www.banrepcultural.org/pasto, 10am-5pm Tues.-Sat., free) is on the 3rd floor of the Banco de la República building facing the Plaza Carnaval. It has a small but good collection of pre-Columbian ceramics from the Nariño *altiplano* (high plains) and Pacific coast. The Pasto indigenous group populated the area around Pasto and Ipiales (south of Pasto) and parts of Ecuador. The predominant group in the area was the Quillacingas, who had arrived from the Caribbean region and who were fierce warriors.

Of particular interest in the museum are the stunning *discos giratorios* (metallic discs plated with gold and copper designs) that were presumed to have been used—specifically, spun—in hypnotic religious ceremonies. In the same building you can often find temporary exhibits featuring Colombian artists.

Also in the **Banco de la República** (8:30am-6pm Mon.-Fri., 9am-1pm Sat., free) is a public library and a *sala de exposiciones* that nearly always has an interesting art exhibit on display. Sometimes there are concerts of touring international classical musicians.

Museo del Carnaval

For information on the city's Carnaval celebration, head forthwith to the **Museo del Carnaval** (Cl. 19 at Cra. 42, tel. 2/731-4598, 8am-11:30am and 2pm-5:30pm Mon.-Fri., free). This museum, located in a former slaughterhouse, shows off what Pastuosos are most proud of: their famous Carnaval de Negros y Blancos in early January. A guide will show you the colorful floats, costumes, and masks from the annual celebration.

ENTERTAINMENT AND EVENTS
Nightlife

Pasto isn't much of a party town, but there are a few watering holes to check out. Try some *hervidos* (hot alcoholic fruit drinks) at **Embrujo Andino Peña Bar** (Cra. 23 No. 19-58, cell tel. 313/604-4935). Sometimes there's live music.

Volcafé (Cl. 18 No. 24-29, tel. 2/722-4301, 8am-1am Mon.-Sat.) is a decent perch for a late-afternoon cappuccino or beer. **Cola de Gallo** (Cl. 18 No. 27-47, tel. 2/722-6194, 3pm-1am Mon.-Sat.) serves its own coffee and is a relaxed place for a drink later in the evening.

Festivals and Events
CARNAVAL DE NEGROS Y BLANCOS

Every January the population of sleepy Pasto explodes as up to 300,000 visitors from Colombia and beyond converge on the city during the **Carnaval de Negros y Blancos** (www.carnavaldepasto.org, Jan. 2-6), which is recognized as a world heritage tradition by UNESCO. The celebration actually gets going on December 28, the "day of the innocents." That's a day of purification and celebration of the natural beauty of the area; many hop on their bikes on this day, cruising down the main parade route. On December 31 a parade pokes fun at politicians and other unpopular figures from the previous year (and sometimes effigies of them are burned).

On January 2 the parade of the colonies takes place, a celebration of cultures from the

Nariño department, which includes a horse-back procession. January 3 is a day of celebration just for children.

January 4 celebrates the arrival of the Castaneda family, who arrived in Pasto (from the Putumayo department), were welcomed with open arms, and worked to help the city grow. This marks the symbolic beginning of the *negros y blancos.* January 5 is the day of the *negros,* when revelers paint themselves or others black. This day is a celebration of diversity. Finally the festival concludes with the day of the *blancos,* when fantastic floats slowly make their way along the city streets, and hundreds of thousands of onlookers pelt each other with white powder (a Colombian version of Holi, the Indian festival of colors).

In addition to the parades, there are concerts featuring Andean and other styles of music, and presentations of elaborately costumed stilt walkers and dancers. The Carnaval spills over one more day to January 7, when the Cuy Festival is held, but you have to be fond of roasted guinea pig to truly enjoy this event. The main parade route departs the stadium and ends in the Plaza de Carnaval in the Centro.

For the Carnaval, locals strategically seek out the best spot to watch the parades, with some getting out as early as 6am. The parades—and the drinking—start at 9am on the dot. Airlines add dozens of flights to Pasto during this time, but it's still best to make plans several months in advance if you want to be a part of the fun.

SHOPPING

Fine handicrafts from the region can be picked up at **Obando Barniz de Pasto** (Cra. 25 No. 13-4, tel. 2/722-0363, 9am-12:30pm and 2:30pm-6pm Mon.-Fri., 9am-12:30pm and 3pm-7pm Sat.), a family business that has been in existence since 1850. It specializes in *barniz de Pasto,* also known as *mopa mopa,* after the jungle plant that grows in the neighboring department of Putumayo and produces the resin utilized in this handicraft technique.

FOOD

Pasto is Colombia's *cuy* capital. *Cuy* is guinea pig, which is prepared by slowly barbecuing the meat for about an hour. The delicacy appears on many menus around town, but it's more of a weekend or special-occasion dish, so you may have to seek it out. A popular chain of restaurants specializing in Pasto cuisine such as *cuy* and *lapingacho* (a type of cheese-filled potato cake), **Cuyquer** (Cra. 40 with Cl. 19, tel. 2/731-5533, www.cuyquer.com, COP$15,000), has a location in Palermo.

Cafeteria, bakery, and pizzeria **La Merced** (Cra. 22 No. 17-37, tel. 2/723-8830, 7am-10pm daily) has something for everyone, from typical Colombian fare to seafood to pizzas. It also has an array of sweets and baked goods.

Near and along the Avenida Los Estudiantes are several good restaurants, mostly serving international fare. For a veggie take on Colombian favorites, such as the potato stew from Bogotá (*ajiaco*) and *bandeja paisa* from Medellín, try **Huerta del Chef** (Cra. 36 No. 18-114, cell tel. 301/447-0350, 7am-2:30pm Mon.-Fri., 7am-1pm Sun., COP$12,000). At colorful **AvLîlâh** (Cl. 20 No. 34A-45 Av. Los Estudiantes, tel. 2/720-8840, COP$20,000) customers design their own meal, choosing each ingredient at the counter (which can be somewhat confusing). Many healthy and vegetarian options are here.

Considered the best pizza place in town, **Alina Pizza Gourmet** (Cl. 20 No. 38-70, tel. 2/731-3565, 6pm-10pm daily, COP$25,000) is a hip and overpriced joint on the Avenida Los Estudiantes. It serves only pizza—including many vegetarian options—and drinks. The walls are decorated with thousands of photos and the atmosphere is friendly.

For a coffee or a light meal, the **Café La Catedral** (Av. Los Estudiantes, Cl. 20 No. 34-34, tel. 2/729-8584, www.cafelacatedral. com, 8:30am-12:30pm and 3pm-8:30pm Mon.-Fri., 10am-12:30pm and 3pm-8:30pm Sat, COP$22,000) is a good bet. Look for local favorites such as *empanadas de añejo* (corn flour empanadas filled with a meat and egg sauce) and some *lapingachos.* This restaurant has three locations, and this one has pleasant outdoor seating. It's a shame it isn't open on Sunday morning, though, as it's nearly impossible to find a decent cup of coffee at that time.

Elegant-ish **Portón Veinte** (Cl. 20 No. 30-05, tel. 2/731-2940, noon-10pm Mon.-Sat., COP$25,000) is a traditional restaurant specializing in Italian and French cuisine. Waiters are very formal here, and the walls are adorned with old photos. Some Colombian dishes are on the menu, and Sunday afternoon means *ajiaco* (potato and chicken stew).

ACCOMMODATIONS

★ **La Maison del Ejecutivo** (Cl. 19 No. 37-16, tel. 2/731-0043, www.lamaisondelejecutivo.com, COP$185,000 d) is a cozy place to stay in the peaceful and green residential neighborhood of Palermo, a short taxi ride from the Plaza Nariño and within walking distance to restaurants on the Avenida los Estudiantes. The 12 rooms are quite comfortable, and cheerfully decorated. What sets this place apart, though, is the excellent service. The French owner, Patrice, has lived in Pasto with his Colombian wife for many years. He is quite knowledgeable about tourist attractions and can give some expert travel tips, and the staff is attentive. Breakfasts are generous and healthy, a rarity for hotels in Colombia. Dinner is also served for those who wish. **Hotel Palermo Suites** (Cl. 19A No. 39-10, tel. 2/731-3104, COP$190,000 d) is a second choice in the same pleasant neighborhood. It's friendly and has 12 clean rooms.

A couple of blocks from the neo-gothic Iglesia de Cristo Rey is **Fernando Plaza** (Cl. 20 No. 21B-16, tel. 2/729-1432, www.hotelfernandoplaza.com, COP$153,000 d), a business hotel in a quiet part of the Centro. It offers 34 immaculate and comfortable rooms. On weekends it often hosts wedding parties and events, so it might be a little noisy; but, this being Pasto, things generally simmer down by 1am.

★ **Hotel Casa López** (Cl. 18 No. 21B-11, tel. 2/720-8172, COP$150,000 d) is truly a diamond in the rough in these parts. It's set in a large old colonial house with an interior patio, and its refurbished rooms are charming. It's a place you'll want to hang out in. The owners are *muy queridos* (very nice).

Started by an Australian many years ago (hence the name) but under other management for quite some time, the **Koala Inn** (Cl. 18 No. 22-37, tel. 2/722-1101, COP$30,000 s, COP$45,000 d) remains the only true backpacker hostel in Pasto, and just barely cuts it.

INFORMATION AND SERVICES

The **Pasto tourist office** (Cl. 18 No. 25-25, tel. 2/723-4962, 8am-noon and 2pm-6pm Mon.-Sat.) is across from the Iglesia de San Juan Bautista. Here you can purchase a city map (COP$2,000), pick up materials on nearby attractions, and purchase some *artesanías*. The timid staff may not volunteer information: Be persistent. A recommended Pasto-based tour agency for outdoor adventures throughout the Nariño department, including Laguna Telpis (Galeras), Laguna Verde, Laguna La Cocha and others, is **Ríos y Aventura** (Cl. 20 No. 25-19, 2nd fl., tel. 2/729-8072, cell tel. 311/705-8836, riosdeaventurasur@gmail.com).

TRANSPORTATION

The **bus terminal** (Cra. 6 No. 16D-50, tel. 2/730-8955, www.terminaldepasto.com.co), about a 10-minute taxi ride from the Centro, is well organized, with shops, cafeterias, and ATMs. From the bus terminal, *colectivos* (small, fast buses) make the journey to and from Ipiales all day long and cost around COP$7,000 (1.5 hrs.). Grab a window seat if you make this trip along the Pan-American Highway: The scenery is breathtaking and the hairpin curves thrilling. Buses going to Bogotá take around 20 hours and cost COP$90,000, while buses from Popayán take about six hours, costing COP$30,000.

Avianca serves the **Aeropuerto Antonio Nariño** (Chachaguí, tel. 2/232-8141 or 2/732-8064), which is about 35 kilometers (22 miles) north of the city. The landing strip is dramatically set upon a plateau 50 meters (164 feet) above rich agricultural land, with mountains all around. Landing here in August when the winds blow can be alternately exciting and terrifying. There is regular flight service to Bogotá and Cali on Avianca and Satena. A taxi into town will cost around COP$40,000. Shared *colectivos* can sometimes be found for less.

Taxis cost about COP$3,500 to anywhere in the city. As a matter of precaution, after dark order taxis by phone, or better yet, use an app like Easy Taxi. The **SIT** public bus system is good, but it's a little confusing to figure out on one's own. The vast majority of tourist sights are in the Centro, and are best visited on foot.

SANTUARIO DE FAUNA Y FLORA GALERAS

The Quillacinga people called it Urcunina, the Mountain of Fire. The Spaniards renamed it **Volcán Galeras,** because the gently sloping volcano reminded them of the sails of ships in the Mediterranean Sea. Today, Pasto residents call it a menace, as this volcano sits right above the city, only eight kilometers (five miles) away on its western side. Galeras has been one of the most active volcanoes in Colombia, and indeed the world, in recent years. There have been minor eruptions almost every year over the past decade, with the last reported in 2013. In 1993, during an international meeting of volcanologists, six scientists in the crater of the volcano were killed when it erupted.

The **Santuario de Fauna y Flora Galeras** (El Doral, Cra. 41 No. 16B-17, tel. 2/732-0493, galeras@parquesnacionales.gov.co, COP$2,000) is part of the national park system, but much of the park has been closed for many years due to the volcano's activity; the only authorized persons allowed to go to the volcano's crater are researchers and park staff.

San Felipe-Laguna Telpis Hike

A highly recommended hike that is open to the public is the 5.7-kilometer (3.5-mile) hike from the town of San Felipe up the northern side of the volcano to Laguna Telpis, a mountain lake that's often shrouded in fog. The hike takes about 3 hours up and 1.5 hours down. It meanders from the serene farming village of San Felipe to *páramos* (Andean highland moors), where sentries of *frailejones*, unusual cactus-like plants, stand at attention. Birds and tiny chirping frogs make the only sounds here.

The park service recommends going with a guide from the village of San Felipe, part of an initiative to support rural tourism. Guides charge around COP$30,000 per group. To reserve a guide, contact the national parks office in Pasto (tel. 2/732-0493).

It's easy to make this excursion as a day trip from Pasto. However, the community of San Felipe is hoping tourists will want to stay a night or two. There are several families that, through the association **Bio-Telpis** (cell tel. 314/796-4085, sanfelipeturismo99@gmail.com), offer lodging in their homes (COP$30,000 pp plus meals) and provide delicious home-cooked meals utilizing organic ingredients fresh from their own farm plots.

Pay the entry fee at the ranger station near Laguna Telpis. Hiking boots, a lightweight sweatshirt or sweater, a hooded waterproof jacket, drinking water, and sunblock are needed for this excursion. Limited supplies can be purchased at one of the few general stores in San Felipe. Ideal times of the year for the hike are between January and February and June and September, when the skies are generally clear.

Getting There

To get to San Felipe from Pasto, you'll first need to travel via cab (COP$4,000) to Yacuanquer, which is 25 kilometers (15.5 miles) southwest of Pasto on the Pan-American Highway. From Yacanquer to San Felipe, a journey of 10 kilometers (6.2 miles), a *mototaxi* will cost COP$2,000.

The starting point of the hike is another four kilometers (2.5 miles) from the center of San Felipe.

★ LAGUNA LA COCHA

Only about 45 minutes outside of Pasto is **Laguna La Cocha** and the smallest park in the national park system, the **Santuario de Fauna y Flora Isla de la Corota** (corota@parquesnacionales.gov.co). This excursion is a delight.

The lakeside fishing village of Encano, on the shores of Laguna La Cocha, is home to about 200 families who mostly make their living as trout farmers. The cheerfully painted wooden A-frames, the flower boxes, and the colorful *lanchas* (wooden boats) waiting at the ready will remind you of someplace—but probably not Colombia! There are many simple restaurants in Encano, all specializing in La Cocha trout, served in a multitude of ways.

From Encano, you can hire a boat to take you to the sanctuary on tiny **Isla de la Corota**, not far away (about a 10-minute ride). It's a lovely excursion, one that won't take long: The island covers only about 16 hectares (40 acres) of land. This excursion costs about COP$25,000 per boat; the boat's owner will wait for you and take you back to the mainland. On the island, you'll have to pay an entry fee (COP$1,000) and sign in at the ranger station. From there you'll walk through the virgin rainforest on a wooden walkway. Although the vegetation is tropical, with 500 species of plants including ferns, bromeliads, orchids, lichen, and *siete cueros* trees, the climate is actually quite cool. It's about 2,800 meters (9,200 feet) above sea level. The highest points on the island have similar vegetation to that of *páramos* (highland moors). It's nice to go on a weekday when there are few visitors, so that you can enjoy the wonderful peace that the island brings.

Surrounding the lake are more than 50 private natural reserves managed by local farmers through the Asociación de Desarollo Campesino (www.adc.org.co). Many of these offer accommodations for visitors. One such reserve is **El Encanto Andino** (Vereda Santa Teresita, cell tel. 321/263-2663 or 311/634-7635, COP$65,000 pp including meals; transportation COP$70,000 per group). Here you can take walks through the jungle, visit an orchid farm, and do some bird-watching, among other activities. Food is produced at the reserve, and it is all organic. To get to this peaceful spot, you'll have to take a boat across the lake, but the reserve will make those arrangements for you. You can also visit as a day trip.

The **Hotel Sindamonoy** (tel. 2/721-8222, cell tel. 314/863-5186, www.hotelsindamanoy.com, COP$176,000 d) is a large hotel with spectacular lake views. It has 23 large rooms. If coming for the day, you can take a boat from El Encano to the hotel and have lunch at the restaurant, which is the best on the lake.

Getting There

To get to Encano, take a *colectivo* (a small minivan) from Pasto. They leave from in front of the hospital (along Avenida Colombia) facing the big Alkosto store (not from the bus terminal). Expect to wait about 20 minutes for the vehicle to fill up with passengers. It is a 45-minute drive and costs COP$4,000.

★ LAGUNA VERDE

The hike up to the sulfurous **Laguna Verde** (3,800 meters/12,500 feet), a dazzling, emerald-green crater lake on the north side of the dormant **Volcán Azufral,** is easy to make from Pasto. Laguna Negra is a smaller neighboring lake. A sacred site for the Pasto indigenous people, the volcano is part of the Nudo de los Pastos mountain range, which serves as a natural border between Colombia and Ecuador. The vegetation in the *páramo* (highland moor) is sparse, with low shrubs, wildflowers, moss, and lichen. There is little fauna to be seen, except for the occasional *gavilan* (vulture) gliding through the air. From here on a clear day you can see as far as the Galeras volcano in Pasto.

The Nudo de los Pastos is where the great Andes mountain range coming north from Ecuador splits into two ranges in Colombia: the Cordillera Central (Central Mountain Range) and the Cordillera Occidental (Western Mountain Range). The Cordillera Central continues northward through Pasto,

Cali, much of the coffee region, Medellín, and eventually into the Bolívar department near the Caribbean. The Cordillera Occidental rises between the Pacific Ocean and the Río Cauca and continues through the departments of Chocó and Antioquia to the Gulf of Urabá on the Caribbean coast.

The **Reserva Natural Azufral** is managed by a community organization, the **Asociación Azufral los Andariegos Túquerres** (Cra. 6A No. 16D-50, tel. 2/730-8955, cell tel. 316/713-3823). From the park's ranger cabin, it is a six-kilometer (3.7-mile) hike to Laguna Verde and Laguna Negra. Hikers are requested to register at the cabin and pay a small entry fee (COP\$2,000). It is an easy, gradual ascent as the path follows a dirt road all the way up the mountain. This can take 3-5 hours. It is hard to get lost, especially on weekends and holidays when there are many fellow hikers.

Weather can change on a dime, temperatures can dramatically drop, and the winds can be fierce. Wear warm clothing, bring along a waterproof windbreaker and drinking water, and pick up some fruit from the Túquerres market to keep you going. Economical breakfasts, lunches, and a hot *agua de panela* (hot drink made from raw brown sugar) or *tinto* (black coffee) can be had at the ranger cabin. Call in advance (cell tel. 316/713-3823) to arrange for meals. The best time to make the trek is July-October or January-April when the weather is drier.

Túquerres, the nearest town to the hike's starting point, is not beautiful, but if you make the hike on a Thursday, be sure to catch the open-air **Santamaría Market** (6am-2pm). There's the usual cornucopia of fruits and vegetables, including some wacky-looking potatoes. Stray dogs tend to hang out in the section containing freshly slaughtered meat. The call of *"a mil, a mil, a mil"* ("for one thousand, for one thousand") rings across the market, as increasingly anxious vendors try to sell their vegetables (and rabbits and chickens) to a dwindling number of potential customers.

Getting There

If you are making this trip independently, there is regular *colectivo* service from the Pasto bus terminal (Cra. 6A No.16D-50, tel. 2/730-8955) bound for Túquerres starting at 5am. The trip will cost about COP\$8,000 and takes two hours. Plan to leave Pasto no later than 8am, however. Laguna Verde is 72 kilometers (45 miles) south of Pasto.

view from the path to Laguna Verde

From Túquerres it is about 15 kilometers (9.3 miles) to the hike's starting point (the ranger cabin), just past the San Roque village. *Colectivos* (COP$1,000) leave from the Parque Bolívar in the morning to San Roque. (The ranger cabin is 500 meters/0.3 mile from there.) This is the cheapest option. However, this service is infrequent (ask a local about the bus upon arrival). Private taxis (COP$50,000 round-trip) can be contracted from Túquerres to take you all the way to the ranger cabin and pick you up at a designated time afterwards, but it is recommended to contact **Asociación Azufral los Andariegos Túquerres** (cell tel. 316/713-3823) in advance to coordinate this transportation, as this group is always an honest broker. The trip up takes you past idyllic farmhouses and fields of potato crops.

VOLCÁN CUMBAL

At 4,764 meters (15,630 feet) high, the snow-dusted **Volcán Cumbal** is the highest volcano in the Nudo de los Pastos mountain range in southern Colombia. It is 15 kilometers (9.3 miles) northwest of Cumbal (pop. 20,000), a peaceful town of broad streets.

The volcano has not seen any activity since 1930, but the Colombian Geological Service upped its level of threat from green to yellow in 2012. Indigenous people used to extract sulphur rock and snow and ice for sale in the market at Ipiales, and to make *helado de paila*, an ice cream made in large copper bowls.

To hike to the top of Volcán Cumbal, it's ideal to spend the previous night in the town of Cumbal and get an early-morning start. It is a strenuous hike: five to six hours up and three down. The volcano has two peaks; most visitors climb the southern one. There are two paths to the top: **Las Fumarolas** and **La Nieve.** From the top, there are spectacular views of the mountainous surrounding countryside extending into Ecuador.

The path to the volcano begins in the settlement called La Origa, which is 20 minutes from town (guides will take you in a truck up to that point). The paths are not clearly marked, and it could be easy to get lost,

particularly when the fog rolls in. Contact Fidencio Cuaical of **Turicumbes** (cell tel. 310/513-7234, turicumbes@hotmail.com, COP$80,000 per group of up to 9), a community association of guides, to organize your hike. Turicumbes can also assist with transportation from Pasto and from Ipiales, as well as lodging.

The best time of year to make the climb is during the dry months between July and September.

Accommodations

Turicumbes (cell tel. 310/513-7234, turicumbes@hotmail.com) can assist with lodging, including arranging farm stays in the countryside.

The **Hotel Paraíso Real** (Cl. 17 at Cra. 9, cell tel. 314/640-6046, COP$25,000 d) is really the only lodging available in Cumbal. Rooms are clean but quite basic. Surprisingly, there is wireless Internet, and the hotel adjoins a small bakery. Adjacent to the hotel is a basic restaurant serving trout fished from the sacred Laguna Cumbal, about six kilometers (3.7 miles) from town.

Getting There

To get to Cumbal from Pasto, you must take a bus to Ipiales first. This costs around COP$10,000, and the trip takes two hours. At the Ipiales terminal, transfer to a minivan bound for Cumbal; the trip takes about an hour (COP$6,000).

IPIALES

Border towns are rarely beauties, and Ipiales, on the Pan-American Highway across the border from Ecuador, is no exception. However, Ipiales is home to the stunning neo-gothic Santuario Nuestra Señora de las Lajas, a major pilgrimage site that is worth a look. It's best to visit as a day trip and return to Pasto, which is more tourist friendly, for the night.

Las Lajas

The neo-gothic **Santuario Nuestra Señora de las Lajas** (tel. 2/775-4462,

7am-6pm daily), seven kilometers (4.3 miles) from the city, surpasses all other churches of the world in terms of beauty, according to many Colombians. What is most striking is its location, sandwiched impossibly in the middle of a river gorge. Las Lajas is swarmed with Colombian and Ecuadorean tourists on Sundays and religious holidays and, to a lesser extent, on Saturdays. You can admire the church from inside and out, and visit its small museum inside (COP$2,000). For much of its history, the cathedral has been under construction. Originally built as a small chapel in the 18th century, its latest incarnation took about 33 years (until 1949) to complete. It was designed by an architect from Pasto and built by an Ecuadorean.

The stone path leading to the church is lined with souvenir shops and diners where you can grab a *quimbolito* pastry and a sweet coffee to warm up, usually served by a woman in a *ruana* (poncho). For something a little more adventurous, go for roasted *cuy* (guinea pig). Along the walkway you'll notice thousands of plaques of prayers and thanksgiving. Families often bring picnic lunches and watch their kids run around by the river, the trickling Río Guáitara. The bridge leading to the cathedral is a favorite spot for photos.

The sanctuary is a place of miracles, according to believers. It is said that an indigenous girl and her mother were traveling home and, during a storm, sought refuge from the rain under the protection of rocks. The girl, Rosa, who was deaf and mute, discovered the illuminated image of Mary on the side of the canyon after a lightning bolt struck, and she astonished her mother by later uttering her first words: *"Mamita, la mestiza me llama"* ("Mommy, she is calling me").

Food

For meals, the area around the Plaza La Pola is where to go. Overlooking the plaza is the

Santuario Nuestra Señora de Las Lajas

restaurant **La Terraza** (Cra. 6 No. 13-17, tel. 2/775-7677, 10am-9pm Mon.-Sat., 10am-3pm Sun., COP$18,000), which serves burritos and pasta.

Getting There
IPIALES

There is frequent *colectivo* (small bus) service between Pasto and Ipiales along the Pan-American Highway. It's a beautiful, if slow-going, ride, with awe-inspiring scenery of mountains, valleys, and rivers on both sides. The road is two-lane and traffic is heavy, especially with big trucks. If there is a wreck on this route, the 2.5-hour journey can take much longer. The trip costs about COP$8,000.

Buses from Popayán take about eight hours and cost COP$32,000; from Cali the journey takes 11 hours and costs COP$46,000. You can take a 23-hour bus ride from Bogotá for COP$107,000, but Satena has a morning flight to the capital a few times a week from the tiny Ipiales airport if you want to cut 22 hours off the trip.

LAS LAJAS

A recently opened *teleférico* (cable tramway, tel. 2/725-6090, www.telefericodelaslajas.com, COP$16,000-20,000 adults, COP$7,000 seniors) departs from kilometer 4 on the Ipiales-Las Lajas road, and is the scenic way to get to Las Lajas. The trip, over valleys of crops and the Río Guaítara, takes about 20 minutes. There is a still a hike to the church, once the tram drops you off in Las Lajas.

Alternatively, you can take a minibus (COP$2,000) from Ipiales (Cra. 6 with Cl. 4)

or a cab (COP$10,000). Either way, there is about a 20-minute walk down to the church from town.

CROSSING THE BORDER

The border with Ecuador is at the town of **Rumichaca,** about three kilometers (1.9 miles) south of the center of Ipiales. Minibuses depart from the center all day long and from the bus terminal as well. These cost about COP$1,700, or you can take a cab, which will cost COP$8,000. Leaving Colombia, you will need to fill out an entry form at the Ecuadorean side of the bridge and request either a 30- or 90-day-long permission. The border is open 5am-10pm.

The Pacific Coast

Colombia is the only country in South America with coastline on both the Pacific Ocean and the Caribbean Sea.

Colombia's Pacific coast is wild, remote, and mysterious. For the few who venture to this little-visited area, the vast sandy beaches, tropical jungles, and people are simply unforgettable.

The Pacific coast of Colombia extends for 1,392 kilometers (865 miles), just under the length of the California coast. The departments of Chocó, Valle de Cauca, Cauca, and Nariño each have real estate on the Pacific, with Chocó boasting the largest stretch of coast. The tiny islands of Gorgona and Malpelo, both national parks, are 35 kilometers (22 miles) off the coast of Guapi and 490 kilometers (305 miles) from Buenaventura, respectively.

The Pacific coast is populated by indigenous peoples, primarily the Emberá, who live mainly in small riverside settlements in the interior of Chocó; *colonos,* or "colonists" who have arrived from Antioquia for generations; and Afro-Colombians, descendants of African slaves who make up the majority of the population (over 80 percent).

It is a sparsely populated region, but there are a few large cities, including Buenaventura (pop. 363,000), Colombia's most important port. Of far more interest to tourists are the coastal towns of Nuquí and Bahía Solano, where both sea and land provide countless opportunities to appreciate the natural world.

National parks and protected areas on the Pacific coast include the Parque Nacional Natural (PNN) Utría, halfway between Bahía Solano and Nuquí; the PNN Isla Gorgona, an island park that's currently only accessible via diving tours; and the Santuario de Flora y Fauna (SFF) Malpelo, an internationally known wildlife preserve that offers superb diving.

HISTORY

In pre-Columbian times, the region was inhabited by indigenous groups, notably the Tumaco-La Tolita people, who produced stunning goldwork. During the colonial era and into the early 20th century, the entire Pacific coast corridor was governed (or rather, not

Previous: breadfruit; boats loaded down with plantains in Guapi. **Above:** a fern's coil.

Look for ★ to find recommended sights, activities, dining, and lodging.

Highlights

★ **Sportfishing in Bahía Solano:** This town's coastal waters are a huge draw for sport fishers (page 349).

★ **Estación Septiembre Sea Turtle Hatchery and Release Program:** Witnessing valiant baby sea turtles fearlessly scampering across the sands into the crashing waves is an unforgettable experience (page 351).

★ **Parque Nacional Natural Utría:** Jungle walks, swimming, and whale-watching are the order of the day at this beautiful national park (page 353).

★ **Santuario de Flora y Fauna Malpelo:** There's incredible diving among hammerhead sharks around this tiny rocky island (page 358).

PANAMA

Sportfishing in Bahía Solano ★ Bahía Solano

Estación Septiembre Sea Turtle Hatchery and Release Program ★

Nuquí ★

Parque Nacional Natural Utría

PNN URAMBA ▲

Santuario de Flora y Fauna Malpelo ★ Bahía Málaga

0   50 mi
0   50 km

ECUADOR   © AVALON TRAVEL

The Pacific Coast

Cartagena and were immediately separated from their families, sold, and transported across the colony. Some slaves revolted or escaped from their owners and established communities in inaccessible areas. After the abolition of slavery in 1851, many former slaves migrated and settled along the rivers and coast of the Pacific. These communities survived intact through the 20th century but, in recent years, have been severely affected by Colombia's internal conflict. Many displaced Afro-Colombians from the Pacific region have resettled in cities such as Cali.

Due to a lack of transportation links, the Pacific region has always been isolated from the rest of Colombia. While rich in biodiversity and cultural identity, cities such as Buenaventura, Quibdó, and Tumaco are underdeveloped; they are plagued with inadequate government services, poor infrastructure, and lack of economic opportunity. Poverty rates in urban areas often exceed 70 percent. Outside the cities, inhabitants subsist on small-scale farming, fishing, and illegal gold mining and forestry.

Initiatives such as Invest in Chocó (www.investinchoco.com) are seeking to stimulate growth in the region with the help of the United States Agency for International Development (USAID) and other international agencies. Another emerging bright spot is ecotourism, especially around Bahía Solano and Nuquí, where many enterprising Paisas from Antioquia and a trickle of expats have started tourist-related businesses. A more recent development has been the strengthening of local organizations, which are making strides in sharing the tourism *peso* with the broader community. The government has been heavily promoting the region, especially for whale-watching.

SAFETY

Coastal settlements of interest to tourists are quite safe, but parts of the Pacific, especially in the Nariño department bordering Ecuador and the Chocó department bordering Panama, remain major drug-trafficking

governed at all) from the city of Popayán. The main economic activity was gold mining, mostly in the Patía river valley in Nariño and the Chocó region. Afro-Colombian people, now comprising more than 80 percent of the region's population, are descendants of slaves who were forced to work in these mines and in the haciendas of the Cauca river valley.

These slaves began arriving in New Granada from different parts of Africa starting in the 17th century. Most arrived in corridors. The abrupt geography, dense jungle, easy water transportation routes, and lack of government border control have attracted drug traffickers, paramilitaries, and FARC guerrillas alike. With a strong and visible police and military presence, the Bahía Solano-Nuquí area is considered safe. Those towns are OK to walk around at night. The interior jungles of the Pacific provide cover for drug traffickers and illegal groups. Ask hotel staff for updated security tips.

PLANNING YOUR TIME

It requires more effort (and more money) to visit the Pacific coast than other parts of Colombia, so it would be a shame to spend just a couple of days there. Plan for about five days, perhaps split across two locations. If you visit between July and October, you'll catch humpback whale season, when these majestic mammals travel 8,000 kilometers (5,000 miles) from Antarctica to give birth to their young in the warm waters off the Colombian coast.

Many visitors fly into Bahía Solano and out of Nuquí (or vice versa), spending two or three days in each area. Time here can be complete beach relaxation, a more active vacation filled with activities such as jungle hikes and canoe trips, or a combination of both. Activities can be arranged independently, but it's easier to let hotels take care of it all.

There is little activity at night, save for some excellent stargazing on the beach, at least in northern coastal communities. Thus it's an excellent place to decompress and rest.

Tourism picks up during humpback whale-watching season, especially during Colombian school vacations in August. The end-of-year holiday season is also a popular time, especially for Colombian families. Reserve far in advance to stay at some of the higher-end hotels during the holidays. Other times of the year are quiet.

Regardless of where you go, it will rain during your stay, maybe once or twice a day. Chocó is one of the rainiest places on the planet.

Bahía Solano

What to Pack

Hot and humid weather is the norm (the average temperature is 28°C/82°F), so plan on getting wet each day—either on purpose or by accident. Daytime activities nearly always involve water. For walks along rivers, sandals with traction or rubber boots are very useful (flip-flops not so much). Clothes and towels take days to dry, sometimes refusing to dry altogether. Bring only lightweight clothing, packing a few more T-shirts than you usually would. And have them ready to throw in the nearest washing machine when you arrive in the city.

Bug repellent is a good idea, although, thanks to a pleasant breeze most evenings, mosquitoes are not usually a problem. There's no need to take malaria pills or any extraordinary precautions. All hotels provide mosquito netting, usually covering all windows in addition to a mosquito net over your bed.

Waste management is an issue for towns, hotels, and restaurants along the coast. Beer and soda in bottles is preferable to aluminum cans, as the glass is returnable. However, hydration is very important. Tap water isn't safe; hotels all provide filtered or boiled drinking water for guests. Bring a heavy-duty water bottle that can be refilled again and again. If you don't see filtered water readily available for guest use, don't be shy to ask kitchen staff to refill your bottle with *agua filtrada* (filtered water). Bags *(bolsas)* of water are usually sold in corner stores and are preferable to plastic bottles. There is an expanding landfill in the jungle between El Valle and Bahía Solano; however, you may want to spare the rainforest by taking accumulated plastic back with you for recycling in Medellín or another large city.

Binoculars are good for jungle outings and excellent for whale-watching. Take along only the most necessary electronics with you to the jungle. Extreme humidity, river crossings, sudden rain showers, and bumpy boat rides are not kind to laptops and cameras. Waterproof bags for cameras are essential, as well as sachets of silica gel to throw in camera cases.

Here on the equator, it gets dark at around 6pm every evening year-round. There is limited electricity in this part of Colombia, with generators usually cranking on for only a few hours at night. A flashlight is necessary for strolls on the beach or about town. A lack of nighttime entertainment makes this a great time for reading. Pack books and magazines rather than relying on electronic gadgets. A deck of cards can also provide some evening entertainment.

Bring cash. Credit cards are not accepted at hotels. At some of the top-end places, you can make a deposit into the hotel's bank account before arriving, limiting the amount of cash you carry.

Chocó

You fly into the department of Chocó over green mountains, part of the Cordillera Occidental, punctuated by orderly Antioquian pueblos and pastureland. But then, the jungle begins: thick, impenetrable tropical forest, of a thousand shades of green. This lowland tropical forest, with vegetation not unlike that found in the Amazon, begins to rise with undulating forested hills as you pass over the smaller Serranía del Baudó mountain range, one of the rainiest places on Earth. If you look down you will notice the tops of these low mountains shrouded in clouds. Every once in a while a milk-chocolate-brown river meanders its way through the jungle westward, and tiny Afro-Colombian and Emberá communities of thatched or zinc-topped roofs spring up alongside it. Here rivers and streams are the only means of transportation, just as it has been for centuries. Just after the captain announces the initial descent, you'll find yourself above the turquoise coastal waters of the Pacific.

Along the Pacific coast of the Chocó department are four general areas that have decent tourism infrastructure: Bahía Solano, El Valle, the Parque Nacional Natural Utría, and Nuquí.

Do not expect wireless Internet, regular cell phone service, or 24-hour electricity at your hotel along the coast. There are Internet cafés in the towns, such as Bahía Net in Bahía Solano, but connection speed is very slow.

A recommended tour agency, affiliated with the Humpback Turtle hostel in El Valle, is **Pacífico Tours** (www.pacificotours.com). This outfit prides itself on its commitment to the environment and community and specializes in surfing (COP$1,300,000 pp), fishing, and jungle adventures (COP$350,000 pp).

BAHÍA SOLANO

When many visitors arrive at the tiny Bahía Solano airport, after they collect their bags they head straight to the village of El Valle about 22 kilometers (14 miles) away and to the

Biodiversity in Chocó

This region is part of the **Chocó Biogeográfico,** one of the most biodiverse regions in the world. It comprises a wide swath of rainforest extending from Panama to Ecuador, hemmed in by the Pacific Ocean to the west and the Andes to the east. The Colombian part of this region includes an amazing 8,000 plant species, of which 2,000 are endemic. (In comparison, all of Canada, which is hundreds of times larger, has 3,270 plant species, of which 140 are endemic.) In addition, there are 838 bird species, 261 amphibian species, 188 reptile species, and 180 mammal species. Some creatures calling the region home include leatherback turtles, colorful poison dart frogs, red-capped manakin birds (the moonwalking birds), and basilisk lizards (called the Jesus lizard for its impressive running-on-water skill). The relative isolation of this region has resulted in a high level of endemism of about 25 percent. It is one of the wettest places on Earth, with annual rainfall of 10,000 millimeters (33 feet), with some places registering up to 20,000 millimeters (66 feet). Due to the high rainfall, this biodiversity hot spot boasts one of the densest river networks in the world, with dozens of major arteries, such as the Baudó, San Juan, and Patía. The Colombia Pacific is quite well preserved: An estimated 75 percent of the region is still covered with rainforest, and there are significant areas of mangroves. However, its future is far from certain. Colombia has the most mangroves in the hemisphere after Brazil and Mexico, but has lost over 57 percent of its mangroves since 1960. The illegal felling of trees and export of lumber, controlled by illegal groups that have traditionally relied upon drug trafficking, is also a troubling trend; it's estimated that over 40 percent of lumber exported from the Bahía Solano area in 2015, for example, was illegally harvested.

hotels on the beaches of Playa Almejal. But Ciudad Mutis, as Bahía Solano is officially named (after the famed botanist), is actually a good base for your visit—there's no need to rush off. It is one of Colombia's sportfishing capitals, and excellent diving and whalewatching excursions can be arranged from here. The town, although the largest one in the Chocó Pacific coast, is small, and everywhere is accessible on foot.

Nice jungle walks to swimming holes fed by crystalline freshwater waterfalls are within walking distance from the town, and depending on the tides, you can also walk to the beaches of **Punta Huína** and **Playa Mecana.** These can also be easily reached by boat. During low tide, the bay becomes a soccer field; when the tide comes in, it's a place to cool off.

Recreation
HIKING
There are three easily done walks in or around Bahía Solano. **Punta Huína, Playa Mecana,** and the **Cascadas Cocacola** can also be reached on foot, and are all under two hours walking from town. You may want to go with a guide (hotels can arrange this) at least the first time, and find out the day's tide information before heading out. If the tide has come in, you'll have to take a boat back to the town.

The **Virgen de la Loma** path is an easy 30-minute climb through lush vegetation to the top of a hill with a nice view of the bay. The entrance to the trail is well marked and is only 20 meters (66 feet) from the Hostal del Mar. For this you'll need no guide. About two blocks from there on the west side of town is the trail to the **Cascada Chocólatal,** which takes you along a river to a roaring waterfall. Taking about 40 minutes or so, this hike may not necessarily require a local guide, but it may be helpful, especially so you'll have someone with trained eyes to point out the occasional colorful frog, lizard, bird, or humongous spider to you. (They are otherwise quite tricky to spot.) You will crisscross the narrow, shallow creek several times, which can be treacherous because the rocks are slippery. You'll need to have both hands free.

Wear a bathing suit so you can frolic in the cool waters of the swimming hole at the five-meter (16-foot) waterfall.

The third hike is called the **Cascada del Aeropuerto.** This hike is right across the street from the airport and leads to a towering jungle waterfall. You probably won't need a guide, but it is not impossible to become lost. Follow the stream and note that it will eventually veer to the left. It's about a 30-minute walk. All three paths are maintained by a group of community members with the help of high school students who have posted signs to point the way.

★ SPORTFISHING

The waters off the Chocó coast are excellent for sportfishing. The **Posada Turística Rocas de Cabo Marzo** (tel. 4/682-7525, cell tel. 313/681-4001, bahiatebada@hotmail.com, www.posadaturisticarocasdecabomarzo.com) regularly organizes fishing adventures in the area. Species that can be found in the waters here include marlins (blue, black, and striped) and sailfish. These are considered endangered and are caught and then released. Yellowfin tuna, red snapper, wahoo, and sierra are other fish that are caught and eaten. The best time of the year for fishing is March-June.

October-December is also a good time to fish (catch-and-release) for marlin and sailfish, but this is a rainy season and the waters are rough. Rental of a boat and an eight-hour day excursion costs around COP$1,500,000, with a maximum of four fishers. Much of the Chocó coast, especially around the Cabo Marzo area, is protected as a Zona Exclusiva de Pesca Artesanal del Chocó (ZEPA). That means it is limited to only local fishers using their traditional fishing methods. This initiative is supported by Conservation International (www.conservation.org.co).

DIVING

Moray eels (*morenas*), grouper (*mero*), sharks (*tiburones*), whale sharks (*tiburón ballena*), snapper (*pargo*), and pompano are some of the species divers may view in the waters off the Colombian Pacific coast. You'll likely spot larger species than the colorful tropical fish often observed in the Caribbean. Both **Posada Turística Hostal del Mar** (tel. 4/682-7415, cell tel. 314/630-6723, hostaldelmarbahiasolano@yahoo.com) and **Posada Turística Rocas de Cabo Marzo** (tel. 4/682-7525, cell tel. 313/681-4001, bahiatebada@hotmail.com, www.posadaturisticarocasdecabomarzo.com) offer diving excursions. A

the port of Bahía Solano

popular trip is to the shipwrecked Colombian navy vessel, the *Sebastián de Belalcázar*, to the northeast of Bahía Solano. Note that diving in the Pacific may be more expensive due to the higher price of gasoline.

Food and Accommodations

There are a handful of good accommodation options located near the bay, each of which can organize whale-watching and other excursions. ★ **Posada Turística Hostal del Mar** (Cra. 3 with Cl. 1, tel. 4/682-7415, cell tel. 314/630-6723, hostaldelmarbahiasolano@yahoo.com, COP$50,000 pp) is run by Rodrigo Fajardo and Estrella Rojas. They are pioneers in the area in terms of community organizing and ecotourism. The property has four comfortable cabins tucked amid gardens filled with orchids, vegetation, chickens, and a lazy cat named Julia. Meals, often served with homemade *ají* (hot sauce), are taken on a picnic table in the middle of this miniature tropical paradise. Rodrigo is a certified diving instructor, and you can learn that sport in the waters of the Pacific with him or arrange a diving trip if you already know what you're doing. A nearby shipwreck is a popular place for underwater exploration. Both he and Estrella know the area exceptionally well and can give you pointers on how to make the most of your stay and can coordinate day trips. Estrella has a small *tienda* in the arrivals area of the airport, where she sells handicrafts made by locals.

★ **Posada Turística Rocas de Cabo Marzo** (Cra. 1 with Cl. 2, tel. 4/682-7525, cell tel. 313/681-4001, bahiatebada@hotmail.com, www.posadaturisticarocasdecabomarzo.com, COP$200,000 pp d, all meals and activities incl., 3 nights) is a cozy lodge-like guesthouse with five rooms. Room rates include airport pickup and drop-off, all meals, and excursions such as jungle hikes and walks to nearby beaches. The small hotel restaurant might be the only place in the jungle where you'll find homemade pizza. It's open daily, but just for guests. In addition to fishing and diving expeditions, Rocas de Cabo Marzo organizes

visits to the Estación Septiembre turtle hatchery program (COP$60,000), a walk to the Playa and Río Mecana (COP$110,000 for 2 people) with return in a boat, and a specialized expedition to see poisonous frogs (as well as howler monkeys and sloths) in the jungle with an indigenous (Emberá) guide. A day trip with two dives costs COP$230,000, while a day of sportfishing (catch-and-release) costs COP$1,500,000, including all equipment.

Choibaná Casa (Playa Huína, cell tel. 310/878-1214 or 312/548-2969, www.choibana.com, COP$150,000 d incl. breakfast) is a cute and colorfully painted wooden house on the beach two kilometers from lively Punta Huína. There are just five rooms, including one spectacular hut majestically set atop a rock. It's a 20-minute boat ride from Bahía Solano, and the property can take care of airport pickup for COP$50,000.

Information and Services

There is an **ATM** at the **Banco Agrario.** You can access the Internet at **Bahía Net,** but the connection is very slow.

There is a **hospital** in Bahía Solano as well as a **pharmacy.**

Getting There

Military-owned **Satena** has flights between the convenient Aeropuerto Olaya Herrera in Medellín and Bahía Solano's airport, **Aeropuerto José Celestino Mutis** (BSC), which is about three kilometers southwest of town. **Aerolínea de Antioquia** (www.ada-aero.com) offers service to Bahía Solano from Aeropuerto Olaya Herrera as well. Two small charter airlines also serve the region: **TAC** (tel. 4/361-0945 or 1/413-5819, www.taccolombia.com) and **Selvazul** (tel. 4/362-2590 or 4/352-8560, www.selvazul.net) both fly from Aeropuerto Olaya Herrera in Medellín. For information and reservations on the charters, you'll need to call.

If you have a reservation at a hotel, most properties will arrange to pick you up at the airport upon your arrival. This is the worry-free, recommended way to go. Otherwise, it costs just COP$3,000 via *mototaxi* to get to Bahía Solano from the airport, which is only two kilometers from the town.

EL VALLE

This fishing community to the south of Bahía Solano is authentic if grubby, with wooden houses lining unpaved (often muddy) streets. Just outside of town, about a 15-minute walk north, is **Playa Almejal,** a broad beach with hotels set back against the jungle. The beach is home to thousands of *cangrejos fantasmas* (ghost crabs) scurrying about—at a speed of up to 20 kilometers (12 miles) per hour. The gray-sand beaches are often covered with driftwood, but during the spectacular sunsets, the pastels of the sky are perfectly reflected on the wet sands. The water is great for jumping in the waves, bodysurfing, and surfing.

★ Estación Septiembre Sea Turtle Hatchery and Release Program

From August until December, female olive ridley sea turtles return to the beaches of the area (to the same spot where they were born) to lay up to 80 eggs. Around 40-60 days later, these eggs hatch, and baby turtles are welcomed to the world. At the **Estación Septiembre Sea Turtle Hatchery and Release Program** (Playa La Cuevita, 5 km south of El Valle, contact Fundacion Natura in Bogotá: tel. 1/245-5700, csolano@natura. org.co or sgalan@natura.org.co), turtle eggs are collected from the beaches and protected from stray dogs, birds, and humans. They remain protected in the sand until the turtles are born, after which the baby turtles are released into the ocean; witnessing one of these releases, which are most common during the month of September, can be the highlight of a visit to the Pacific coast. Run by the Fundación Natura, the program is administered by the community-based **Fundación Caguama.** (*Caguama* means sea turtle in the Emberá language.)

The Estación Septiembre can be visited for the day at any time of year, but it's best to contact them in advance so they can coordinate your visit. A small donation may be requested. Or you can stay in one of the three simple rooms at the Estación Septiembre (contact Fundación Natura, Bogotá, tel. 1/245-5700, csolano@natura.org.co or sgalan@natura.org. co, COP$50,000 pp, additional COP$50,000 pp for meals).

To get to the Estación Septiembre, take a *mototaxi* along the beach (COP$6,000) from

Playa Almejal

El Valle. There is also a fairly well-marked path, which takes about 1.5-2 hours to walk, from El Valle to the PNN Utría. Estación Septiembre is located at Kilómetro 4 of the path.

Recreation

There are some pleasant excursions to make nearby Playa Almejal. The **Cascada El Tigre** can be reached by boat or by walking (4 hrs. one-way, COP$55,000 guide), and this cascade of cool water right on a secluded cove makes for an unforgettable shower/massage. The **Río Tundó** just outside of El Valle is a great place for a jungle canoe or kayak trip. This excursion, which usually includes a two-hour hike in the verdant jungle, costs about COP$50,000 per person.

Food and Accommodations

Posada Don Ai and El Almejal both serve delicious seafood meals. At most guesthouses in the region, don't expect hot showers, except perhaps at the higher-end places. And air-conditioning—forget about it! There may be limited electricity as well.

Home-cooked meals are on offer in the small but immaculate *casa* of **Doña Rosalía** (El Valle, past the Internet café, no phone). If you can't find it, just ask anybody around; everybody knows Rosalía. If you have a special request—if you'd like lentils or beans instead of fish, for instance—let her know by dropping by beforehand.

As for drinking spots, shops in El Valle sell snacks and usually have seating if you want a cold drink or beer among locals. Besides these, the best option by far is **El Mirador.** Hard to miss, it's the only multicolored bar set on a boulder on the beach. It's between Humpback Turtle and El Almejal, and only open on Sunday afternoons, when it gets packed with mostly locals—but visitors are more than welcome.

On Playa Almejal, the **Posada Don Ai** (Playa Almejal, cell tel. 314/651-1160 or 320/662-7014, COP$120,000 pp incl. meals) is a relaxed place with nine small cabins each with a porch and requisite hammock. Meals, usually fried fish, *patacones,* rice, and salad, are included in the price of your stay and served under a breezy thatched-roof dining area overlooking the Pacific. It's quite a good value. Even if you are not staying there, you can stop by for a meal.

Just beyond Posada Don Ai on the beach is ★ **El Almejal** (tel. 4/412-5050, www.almejal. com.co, COP$200,000 pp incl. meals). This eco-conscious, award-winning lodge and nature reserve, with airy, tastefully done cabins, is a consistent favorite for those who want a little more comfort. One of the pioneers of ecotourism in the region, El Almejal has been around since the 1980s. Today there are 10 cabins, plus two in the jungle situated along a bird-watching trail (organized early-morning bird-watching walks are available). El Amejal has its own organic garden, and the restaurant is probably the best in the area. Electricity is available 24 hours a day, and some cabins have hot water. Staff can arrange many different excursions and activities for guests. This lodge is also the best place to stay for birders, as staff are knowledgeable and can organize bird-watching itineraries. Some of the 800 species to be found in the area include the rare harpy eagle, snowy cotinga, endangered and endemic Baudó oropendola, toucans, and tanagers. In May and June, it's dolphin time, and El Almejal can take guests to spot them frolicking in the Pacific.

When you first walk up from the beach, barefoot and backpack on, you'll pass through several enormous boulders, and then the ★ **Humpback Turtle** (Playa Almejal, tel. 314/766-8708, cell tel. 312/756-3439, www. humpbackturtle.com, thehumpbackturtle@ gmail.com, COP$20,000 camping/hammock pp, COP$35,000 dorm bed, COP$120,000 d) suddenly appears. Nestled at the edge of the jungle, this colorful beachside hostel, started by an American, has a dorm room with six beds and four private rooms as well as a campsite. With an organic garden, composting, water conservation measures such as dry toilets, and reuse of plastic water bottles as

Hang loose and kick back at the Humpback Turtle hostel.

construction material, this is by far the most environmentally minded option in the area. But it's also a fun place to hang out. Staff are loaded with ideas on adventurous area excursions and can assist with arrangements. Options include trips to the Cascada El Tigre waterfall (COP$55,000), crystalline rivers (COP$50,000), and indigenous Emberá communities. Sportfishing (COP$150,000) trips and, of course, outings to observe humpback whales—one of the main draws to the region—can also be arranged.

Between Playa Almejal and the town of El Valle are other options, including Villa Maga and El Nativo. **El Nativo** (Playa Almejal, cell tel. 311/639-1015, nativo58@hotmail.com, COP$60,000 d incl. meals) has two simple cabins (four rooms in total) made from natural materials such as *guadua* (bamboo) and palm leaves. They can organize day-trip excursions for you. Nearby is **Villa Maga** (Playa Almejal, no phone, COP$45,000 pp), with a setup similar to El Nativo, although with more natural light in the A-framed cabins

and a little more comfort. Just across from Playa Almejal, El Nativo and Villa Maga are both run by *nativos,* as local Afro-Colombians identify themselves.

Information and Services

There is no ATM in El Valle. There is a **pharmacy** in El Valle.

Getting There

To get to El Valle and Playa Almejal on your own from the Bahía Solano airport you can take a *mototaxi* or truck (starting at COP$20,000 pp). Much of the road to El Valle, through the jungle, has been paved. The 18-kilometer (11-mile) trip takes about 45 minutes.

★ PARQUE NACIONAL NATURAL UTRÍA

Halfway between Bahía Solano and Nuquí, the **Parque Nacional Natural Utría** (www. parquesnacionales.gov.co, 8am-5pm daily, COP$42,000 non-Colombians, COP$16,000 Colombians and residents, COP$8,500 students with ID) has a spectacular location on the edge of the jungle but close to some great beaches. It encompasses over 54,000 hectares (135,000 acres) of tropical forest, mangroves, and waters. Several nature paths await exploration, and you can also walk to a secluded beach nearby with a guide and arrange to be picked up later.

PLANNING YOUR TIME

High season in the park is late December to early January, Semana Santa, and during school holidays from June to August. A few days in the park during the week or in the off-season can be wonderfully relaxing. If the park is crowded, however, it could become quite a social scene, especially during the long evenings. Playa Blanca is a party place for locals on weekends and holidays.

If you are not staying at the park, it can be visited on a day trip from El Valle, Bahía Solano, or Nuquí. But that excursion gets a failing grade from some due to its high cost (upwards of COP$125,000 per person). The standard day-trip visit includes a short walk, snorkeling in the lagoon in front of the Centro de Visitantes, and a boat ride to Playa Blanca, where you can snorkel and have lunch.

Hiking

Most excursions require a guide. However, there are some short walks you can make near the **Centro de Visitantes.** One of the more unusual activities at the park is searching for bioluminescent mushrooms in the evening along the **nature trail.** Another is a pleasant walk above the mangroves on an **elevated wooden walkway.**

Other Recreation

Some excursion options include a nature hike to Playa Cocalito (COP$62,500), a visit to Playa Blanca for snorkeling (COP$50,000), a trip to the colorful fishing village of Jurubirá and its saltwater springs (COP$121,300), and whale-watching expeditions (COP$110,000). Contact park staff to arrange any of these excursions. Kayaks are available for free to those staying at the park.

During whale-watching season (July-Oct.), humpbacks have been known to swim into the narrow lagoon in front of the park cabins, providing exclusive shows for park guests. The park puts on the **Festival de la Migración** during this time.

Practicalities

Park facilities are managed by the local community organization **Mano Cambiada** (cell tel. 310/793-7664, corporacionmanocambiada@yahoo.es). There is no ATM in the park.

The park has three beautiful wooden cabins that are each separated into three inviting private rooms (COP$190,000-225,000 pp incl. meals), each with its own bathroom, with a total capacity of just over 30. One cabin has dormitory-style accommodations. There's an open-air **restaurant** near the cabins.

Transportation

You can reach the park through the jungle or by water. The jungle option involves a moderately difficult 3-4-hour hike from the fishing community of El Valle to the northern section of the park. Guides can be contracted for this journey via Mano Cambiada (cell tel. 310/793-7664, corporacionmanocambiada@yahoo.es) and cost about COP$50,000. From there, a *lancha* (boat) picks up hikers for COP$15,000 and takes them across a lagoon to the Centro de Visitantes (visitors center).

Parque Nacional Natural Utría

It's also possible to take a boat from either Nuquí or El Valle to the park. This service costs about COP$60,000. Figuring out schedules will require some assistance from hotel staff.

Another option is to hire a private boat from El Valle or Nuquí for your party, which will cost about COP$300,000 to get to the park.

NUQUÍ

Rough-around-the-edges Nuquí makes a good base for exploring the jungles and beaches of Chocó. The town doesn't have much to offer save for basic services and the airport, but nearby beaches and eco-lodges are wonderful.

Here you can hike into the jungle in search of colorful frogs, go on a whale-watching expedition, try your luck surfing, and row in dugout canoes along serpentine rivers that serve as highways between communities. Or you can blissfully relax in a hammock and while away the hours to the sound of crashing waves.

Accommodations

From locally owned accommodations in typical wooden Chocó houses to cabins on the beach to luxurious secluded resorts, the beaches near Nuquí have options for every budget. All hotels can organize hikes, whale-watching trips, diving excursions, and other activities. There are also a number of locally run *posadas* (guesthouses) in communities such as Joví, Coqui, and Termales. **Palenque Tours** (www.palenque-tours-colombia.com), based in Medellín, specializes in community-based tourism and can assist with stays in these Afro-Colombian communities.

★ **El Cantíl** (tel. 4/448-0767, www.el-cantil.com, from COP$700,000-1,000,000 pp for 2 nights, all meals and transportation incl.) is perhaps the most widely known eco-lodge in the area. Run by a couple from Medellín, El Cantíl is composed of small but comfortable cabins nestled on the edge of the jungle—views of the ocean included. It is about a 35-minute boat ride from Nuquí.

Whale-watching, diving, and surfing can be arranged. In the dense jungles behind El Cantíl, you can take a hike and go on an exotic frog safari. Beautiful nearby beaches can be explored on your own, and you'll likely be alone on the sand. The fresh seafood at the hotel restaurant is both abundant and delicious. Electricity is supplied by the lodge's own hydroelectric plant.

In solitary splendor, ★ **Morromico** (45 mins. north of Nuquí, tel. 8/521-4172 or 8/522-4653, www.morromico.com, COP$250,000-380,000 pp incl. meals) has only five rooms—along with a private beach, free sunsets, and just-caught red snapper cooked in fresh coconut milk for lunch. This hotel is close to the Parque Nacional Natural Utría. There is no Internet or other distractions here.

Guachalito is another favorite beach near Nuquí, and the village of Jovi. Check out **Joviseña** (Guachalito, Medellín office tel. 4/363-1655, cell tel. 315/510-8216, www.lajovisena.com, COP$250,000 d incl. meals), composed of simple thatched-roof *cabañas*, with 10 rooms total, on the beach. The couple who run it are locals; they are extremely friendly, grow vegetables and fruit in their garden, and will happily arrange excursions for guests. It's about three kilometers into the town.

Information and Services

There is no ATM in Nuquí, although there are two banks: **Banco Agrario** and **Bancolombia. Super Giros** (tel. 4/683-6067) can wire money.

There is a **hospital** in Nuquí as well as a **pharmacy.**

Getting There

Military-owned **Satena** has flights between Aeropuerto Olaya Herrera in Medellín and Nuquí's airport, **Aeropuerto Reyes Murillo** (NQU), which is near the center of town, by the water. Two small charter airlines also serve the region: **TAC** (tel. 4/361-0945, 1/413-5819, www.taccolombia.com) and **Selvazul** (tel. 4/362-2590 or 4/352-8560, www.selvazul.net) also fly from Aeropuerto

Olaya Herrera in Medellín. For information and reservations on the charters, you'll need to call.

If you have a reservation at a hotel, most properties will arrange to pick you up at the airport upon your arrival. This is the most efficient and easiest method of getting to your hotel.

It's possible to get to Nuquí from Bahía Solano and El Valle. Because gasoline costs about three times as much as it does in the rest of Colombia, boat trips will seem expensive, costing about COP$80,000 to get to Nuquí. You can try to negotiate a better price, especially if you have a group going with you. There is usually public boat service on Monday and Friday mornings. Otherwise private boats can be rented.

South Pacific Coast

The beaches of the South Pacific coast of Colombia in and around the port of Buenaventura have not been on the radar of many international visitors, but they have drawn Colombian tourists for decades. Off the coast, you'll find the island oases of Parque National Natural Isla Gorgona and the Santuario de Flora y Fauna Malpelo, where nature rules the day.

Safety

Both Buenaventura and Tumaco have been severely affected by turf battles involving rival drug trafficking gangs over the past few years. The beaches, however, are secluded and safe, and tourists are always welcomed with open arms. But do avoid the interior of the cities.

BUENAVENTURA

Buenaventura is the largest city on the coast, with a population of over 300,000, and it is Colombia's busiest port. It is home to one of the most vibrant Afro-Colombian communities in the country. Most visitors pass through Buenaventura on their way to the coastal communities of Juanchaco and Ladrilleros.

The area around the **Muelle Turístico**, the tourist port, hums with activity and is safe to meander about.

Food and Accommodations

Leños y Mariscos (Cl. 1 No. 5-08, tel. 2/241-7000) is a recommended seafood place. Also look for **La Escuela** (Cl. 2 No. 1A-07, Escuela Taller de Buenaventura, Antigua Estación del Ferrocarril, tel. 2/297-8948, lunch Mon.-Sat.), a restaurant in the old train station that has been beautifully refurbished. La Escuela is, as the name suggests, a culinary school. It specializes in local seafood.

The golden years of Buenaventura are long gone, but one of the remnants of its heyday is the elegant ★ **Hotel Tequendama Estación** (Cl. 2 No. 6-8, tel. 2/241-9512, COP$175,000 d) near the busy Muelle Turístico (tourist port). Adjacent is the very posh **Cosmos Pacifico Hotel** (Cl. 3 No. 1A-57, COP$269,000 d), with a fabulous pool and 150 rooms.

Getting There

Most travelers get to Buenaventura by land from Cali. It's a four-hour trip and the bus fare to Buenaventura from Cali's Terminal de Transportes costs about COP$23,000.

Satena (tel. 1/605-2222, www.satena. gov.co) offers a daily flight from Bogotá to Buenaventura's **Aeropuerto Gerardo Tovar López** (BUN), which is about four kilometers (2.5 miles) south of town.

Juanchaco and Ladrilleros

From Buenaventura's Muelle Turístico, you can catch a boat to the nearby gray-sand beaches of **Juanchaco** and **Ladrilleros**, which have their charm (and the surf's often up in Ladrilleros). From the beachside bluffs, during whale-watching season

45-minute ride to Juanchaco. Ladrilleros is a half-hour walk from Juanchaco.

PARQUE NACIONAL NATURAL ISLA GORGONA

A visit to **Parque Nacional Natural Isla Gorgona** (www.parquesnacionales.gov.co) is an unforgettable one, no matter the time of year. This 9-by-2.6-kilometer (5.6-by-1.6-mile) island about 35 kilometers (20 miles) off the coast was thought to have been originally settled by Kuna indigenous peoples who lived near present-day Panama. Spanish conquistador Francisco Pizarro landed on the island in 1527. He and his crew didn't stay long: Too many men were getting bitten by snakes. The Spaniards named it after the mythical female Greek monster, Gorgon, who, among other things, wore a belt made of snakes and even had them coming out of her hair. Following Pizarro's visit, the island was mostly uninhabited.

Surrounded by sharks and crawling with snakes, the island served as a prison starting in 1959, primarily for those accused of atrocities during La Violencia, when Liberals and Conservatives fought each other in cities and towns across Colombia. Many say that the prison was modeled after the Alcatraz penitentiary in California. Once the prison was closed in 1984, the island was converted into a national park.

Water—in the form of babbling brooks, trickling streams, roaring waterfalls, dewdrops on leaves, crashing waves, and gentle rain storms—is the proof that this island is very much alive. Because of the 90 percent humidity, mist is often seen rising from the thick tropical jungle. It has its own permanent cloud lingering above its highest points.

SAFETY

In 2014, there was a FARC attack on the small police station on the island, resulting in the deaths of three people. Since that time, the park's concessionaire, Aviatur, has suspended

Parque Nacional Natural Isla Gorgona

(June-November) you can spot humpbacks frolicking in the waters.

A popular hotel on a cliff in Ladrilleros, with a spectacular view of the infinite Pacific, is the ★ **Reserva Aguamarina** (Playa de Ladrilleros, tel. 2/246-0285, cell tel. 311/728-3213 or 321/768-0539, www.reservaaguamarina.com, COP$130,000 d incl. meals), which has more traditional hotel rooms as well as *cabañas*. The pool is a popular gathering place, and there is a lot of green space. From here you can also take a walk to waterfalls and discover other remote beaches. To get there, take a *mototaxi* (COP$2,000) from Juanchaco's port, a trip of about 20 minutes.

Lanchas (boats) make the trip to Ladrilleros from the Muelle Turístico in Buenaventura several times a day. **Asturías** (Muelle Turístico Local No. 2, tel. 2/240-4048, www.buceaencolombia.com) is one company that provides this service, with boats at 10am, 1pm, and 4pm. Round-trip fares are around COP$55,000. It's a operations, leaving the park without services or overnight accommodations.

Access to the park is indefinitely limited to those visiting on day trips and boat tours. The park is not expected to reopen services until a new concessionaire is secured. Check the website of the National Parks of Colombia (www.parquesnacionales.gov.co) to see the most current information on the park.

Diving Tours

Isla Gorgona is an excellent place for diving. You can contract a diving trip from an independent dive company. These depart from either Buenaventura or Guapi. **Arrecifes del Pacífico** (Cra. 38 No. 8A-17, Cali, tel. 2/514-1691, cell tel. 321/642-6015, www.arrecifesdelpacifico.com, viajes@arrecifesdelpacifico.com) organizes four-day/three-night trips to Gorgona throughout the year. These typically depart by boat from Buenaventura. It's about an 11-hour trip to Isla Gorgona from there, and accommodations are on board the boat, which has a capacity of about 25 passengers. This trip, including six dives and one night dive with transportation, meals, and accommodations, costs around COP$1,390,000 per person (not including equipment). Diving spots include Tiburonera, Plaza de Toros, Montañita 1, Cazuelam, Parguera, El Viudo, and Remanso de la Parguera. For beginners, they recommend a short course in Cali before departing to Gorgona, where certification can be obtained.

★ SANTUARIO DE FLORA Y FAUNA MALPELO

Covering around 900,000 hectares (2.2 million acres) of protected Pacific Ocean waters and the tiny **Isla Malpelo,** the **Santuario de Flora y Fauna Malpelo** (www.parquesnacionales.gov.co, COP$97,000) was established in 1995. The area was declared a Particularly Sensitive Sea Area by the International Maritime Organization in 2002 and a UNESCO World Heritage Site in 2006. The steep volcanic rock of Isla Malpelo is nearly 500 kilometers (310 miles) from the coast of Colombia. It is administered by **Parques Nacionales** (tel. 1/353-2400, ext. 138, www.parquesnacionales.gov.co).

The sanctuary is the largest no-fishing zone in the Eastern Tropical Pacific, thus making it one of the top places for diving in the world. There are 11 main dive sites, including the most important site, **La Nevera,** where it is common to see scores of hammerhead sharks.

Isla Malpelo

The deep waters surrounding Isla Malpelo are home to some of the most important coral formations in the Colombian Pacific. Mollusks and crustaceans, fish such as snapper, endangered *mero* (grouper), hammerhead sharks, whale sharks, sun ray sharks, and manta rays are found in abundance in the sanctuary. It is one of the few places in the world where the short-nosed ragged-toothed shark, a deepwater shark, has been spotted. Inhospitable to much animal life, the island is home to crabs, lizards, and geckos. Among birds, the world's largest colony of the Nazca booby is found on Malpelo.

Malpelo is for experienced divers only. To get there you must coordinate with one of the following authorized diving tour groups:

- Out of Buenaventura: **Embarcaciones Asturías** (tel. 2/242-4620, cell tel. 313/767-2864 and 313/767-4076, barcoasturias@yahoo.com)

- From Cali: **Pacific Diving** (tel. 2/558-3903, info@cascoantiguocolombia.com, seawolfaboard@gmail.com) and **Arrecifes del Pacífico** (tel. 2/514-1691, cell tel. 321/642-6015, www.arrecifesdelpacifico.com)

- Out of Panama City: **Coiba Dive Expeditions** (tel. 507/232-0216, www.coibadiveexpeditions.com) and the German group **Inula UAA Adventures** (tel. 507/667-95620, inuladiving@gmail.com, www.inula-diving.de)

The **Fundación Malpelo** (www.fundacionmalpelo.org) is a nonprofit organization working to protect this sanctuary. The island is under constant threat from illegal fishing, particularly of hammerhead sharks. In 2012 it was estimated that 200 tons of fish were illegally caught in the Colombian Pacific, mostly by boats hailing from Costa Rica, Ecuador, and from Asian countries. During Semana Santa, shark fin stew is sold in Buenaventura.

San Andrés and Providencia

The beaches of San Andrés and Providencia are pristine and secluded. The waters here are an inviting turquoise.

Seafood, particularly fresh crab, is always on the menu, accompanied by cold beer. The San Andrés Archipelago is made up of seven atolls and three major islands: San Andrés, Providencia, and Santa Catalina. San Andrés is 775 kilometers (492 miles) northeast of the Colombian mainland and only 191 kilometers (119 miles) east of Nicaragua. The islands are small: San Andrés, the largest island, has an area of 26 square kilometers (10 square miles), Providencia just 17 square kilometers (6.5 square miles), and Santa Catalina, attached to Providencia by a photogenic pedestrian bridge, is 1 square kilometer (247 acres) in size.

San Andrés is popular with rowdy Colombian vacationers escaping the chilly climes of the Andes. Here, sunbathing, snorkeling, diving, and relaxing are always the order of the day.

Once serving as a base for notorious English pirate Henry Morgan, less developed Providencia—or Old Providence, as English-speaking locals call it—and its tiny tagalong neighbor of Santa Catalina are places to experience how the Caribbean used to be. Here you'll enjoy small bungalow-style hotels, home-cooked creole food, and picturesque palm-lined beaches.

On both islands English and a creole patois are spoken, although Spanish is rapidly taking over in San Andrés and the tourism sector.

HISTORY

Little is known of the early history of San Andrés, Providencia, and Santa Catalina. In pre-Columbian times, the Miskito people of Central America visited the islands but never settled there.

In 1631, 100 Puritans from England founded a colony on Providence Island (the English name for Providencia). Rather than establishing a self-sustaining agricultural community, the colonists imported slaves and established a plantation-based economy. Spaniards attacked the islands in 1641 and put an end to the Puritan experiment. Over the

Previous: iguana in San Andrés; sailboat race at Bahía Manzanillo. **Above:** the *coco loco*, the official cocktail of San Andrés.

Highlights

★ **Jardín Botánico:** This well-tended botanical garden sits on a bluff overlooking the turquoise sea. A walk among the native trees, plants, and flowers provides a pleasant break from the beach (page 366).

★ **Snorkeling and Diving off of San Andrés:** Dozens of dive sites among thriving coral formations and steep ocean walls keep divers blissfully busy (page 368).

★ **Parque Nacional Natural Old Providence McBean Lagoon:** Paddle through the mangrove lagoons and snorkel offshore among tropical fish at this small national park (page 376).

★ **Beaches on Providencia:** Undertake the tough fieldwork of determining your favorite palm-lined Providencia beach. Your investigations could take several days (page 378).

★ **The Peak:** From the highest point on Providencia, hikers enjoy 360-degree vistas from the jungle toward the deep-blue sea (page 379).

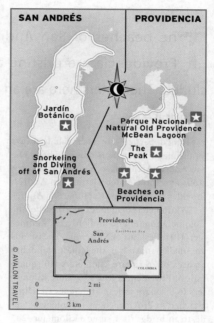

San Andrés and Providencia

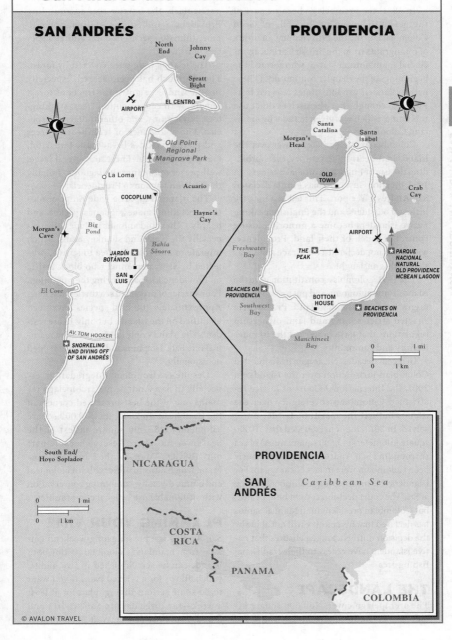

SAN ANDRÉS

North End
Johnny Cay
Spratt Bight
AIRPORT
EL CENTRO
Old Point Regional Mangrove Park
La Loma
Acuario
COCOPLUM
Hayne's Cay
Morgan's Cave
Big Pond
Bahía Sónora
JARDÍN BOTÁNICO
SAN LUIS
El Cove
AV. TOM HOOKER
SNORKELING AND DIVING OFF OF SAN ANDRÉS
South End/ Hoyo Soplador

0   1 mi
0   1 km

PROVIDENCIA

Santa Catalina
Morgan's Head
Santa Isabel
OLD TOWN
Crab Cay
Freshwater Bay
AIRPORT
THE PEAK
PARQUE NACIONAL NATURAL OLD PROVIDENCE MCBEAN LAGOON
BEACHES ON PROVIDENCIA
BOTTOM HOUSE
BEACHES ON PROVIDENCIA
Southwest Bay
Manchineel Bay

0   1 mi
0   1 km

PROVIDENCIA
SAN ANDRÉS
Caribbean Sea
NICARAGUA
COSTA RICA
PANAMA
COLOMBIA

next 50 years, the island was fought over by Spain and England.

In 1821, the archipelago became part of the newly independent Republic of Gran Colombia. During the 19th century, an influx of immigrants from the British Caribbean included many former slaves, who formed the beginnings of the islander community. (These native islanders are sometimes referred to as Raizales, though they themselves don't use this name, which was given to them by mainland Colombians.)

Colombia exerted greater power over the islands in the early 20th century, even forbidding the use of English in official business. In 1953, dictator Gustavo Rojas Pinilla declared San Andrés a free port. This led to a massive influx of outsiders, and the English-speaking native islanders became a minority, losing control of much of their land. Providence, which was not declared a free-trade zone, was spared this onslaught.

The 1991 Colombian constitution gave the islands some autonomy and put an end to immigration from the mainland. Providencia enacted strict zoning and land-ownership regulations that have preserved the islander identity and community.

In recent decades, Nicaragua has contested Colombian jurisdiction over the islands. In 2001, the International Court of Justice reaffirmed Colombian sovereignty over the islands but left the maritime border unresolved. In 2012, the court decided that 70,000 square kilometers (43,500 square miles) of sea surrounding San Andrés that had previously been Colombian were in fact Nicaraguan. For islanders this meant losing traditional fishing areas. The court decision cannot be appealed, but Colombian president Juan Manuel Santos has declared that his country will not abide by the decision until Nicaragua ensures that native islanders have access to their traditional fishing areas.

THE LANDSCAPE

The archipelago covers 280,000 square kilometers (174,000 square miles) of marine area. It includes three major islands, seven atolls, and some well-preserved coral reefs, particularly the barrier reef surrounding Providencia and Santa Catalina, home to more than 80 species of coral and 200 species of fish.

The islands were once covered by forest. Though much has been cleared, especially in San Andrés, significant tracts of forest remain, with cedars, cotton trees, stinkingtoes, birch gums, and other indigenous species. The abundance of fruit-bearing trees and plants includes breadfruit, tamarind, mango, and guava. There are several large, well-preserved mangrove lagoons, notably the McBean Lagoon in Providencia.

The islands support a wide range of reptiles, including snakes, iguanas, geckos, and lizards. Other land animals include crabs, especially the black and shankey crabs, which migrate to and from the sea to spawn, protected by army personnel who block traffic on Providencia's roads during the migration. Four species of protected sea turtles nest here. Approximately 100 bird species have been identified on the islands, but only 18 are resident. The island's only nonhuman land mammals are bats. Dolphins and whales are sighted occasionally.

Despite environmental degradation, especially in San Andrés, the archipelago remains one of the best-preserved corners of the Caribbean. In 2000, the 300,000 square kilometers (186,400 square miles) of the Seaflower Biosphere Reserve became part of UNESCO's "Man and the Biosphere" program, which aims to preserve both biological and ethnic diversity, combining conservation with sustainable use by local communities.

PLANNING YOUR TIME

San Andrés is a possible long-weekend getaway from mainland Colombia; visiting both islands can be accomplished in five nights, which allows for a relaxed pace. If you want to do some serious diving, plan for at least a week—say three days in San Andrés and four days in Providencia. Wait 24 hours after

breadfruit, Jardín Botánico

an extra flight, and hotels and restaurants are generally more expensive than in San Andrés (which itself is more expensive than the mainland).

High tourist seasons on both islands are during Christmas and New Year's. It may be hard to find a hotel from mid-December until mid-January. During this time, throngs of Colombian families and a growing number of Brazilians and Argentinians take over San Andrés. Also popular are Semana Santa (Holy Week) and school vacations, which fall between mid-June and August. May and September are quiet. Because it's more difficult to reach, Providencia rarely feels crowded.

The average daily temperature is 27°C (81°F). During the dry season (January-April), water rationing can be necessary, especially in Providencia, where it rains as little as five days per month. The rainy season extends from June until November, when it can rain 20-24 days per month. October is the rainiest month and is also when hurricanes occasionally churn up the warm Caribbean waters. March and April are the best months for snorkeling and diving because the waters are calm. December and January are windy, making snorkeling and diving challenging. Strong winds can prompt airlines to cancel flights into and out of Providencia.

diving to get in an airplane, due to pressurization concerns.

A visit to Providencia from San Andrés can be a budget buster, but it is well worth the expense if you are interested in getting away from it all. Getting to Providencia involves

San Andrés

Surrounded by a large barrier reef, San Andrés is Colombia's Caribbean playground. Here the waters are seven shades of blue, the sandy beaches are white, and *coco locos*, the official island cocktail, are always served. Days here are spent lazing on the beach, island-hopping, snorkeling and diving, and enjoying fresh seafood. For many Colombians, the deals at the many duty-free stores are too good to pass up—and one reason why they visit the island in the first place.

San Andrés has a population of about 75,000, about two-thirds of whom are of mainland Colombian origin. The rest are English- and creole-speaking native islanders, many of whom are descended from Jamaican slaves. There is also a community of "Turcos" or "Arabes," whose roots can be traced to mostly Lebanon and Syria. Their presence on the island is not an insignificant one, as demonstrated by a brilliantly white modern mosque that stands prominently in the commercial center.

Orientation

The island of San Andrés resembles a seahorse

floating gently eastward in the western Caribbean Sea. It is only about 13 kilometers (8 miles) long from top to bottom and 3 kilometers (2 miles) wide, and has a total area of 26 square kilometers (10 square miles). The Circunvalar ring road more or less circles the entire island.

The "town" of San Andrés is usually called the **Centro** or the **North End.** It is in the snout of the seahorse, in the northeast. This is the center of activity and where the majority of the island's restaurants, hotels, and shops (nearly all of which are owned and operated by mainland Colombians) are found. About 1.6 kilometers (1 mile) of the main drag here, Avenida Colombia, is the *paseo peatonal* or *malecón*. Officially known as the Spratt Bight Pathway, it's a delightful pedestrian promenade along the Spratt Bight beach. About two kilometers (1.25 miles) northwest of the Centro is the airport. The west side is quieter, with a handful of points of interest, hotels, and restaurants. The coastline on the west side is all coral; there are no beaches. At the southernmost point of the island is the Hoyo Soplador blowhole. Continuing counterclockwise, the town of **San Luis** extends along the southeastern edge of the island. This area has some good beaches, hotels, and restaurants, and is much more laid-back than the Centro.

The middle part of the island, called **La Loma** (The Hill), is the highest point on the island. The main point of reference here is the stately white First Baptist Church. This area is home to the largest community of native islanders.

SIGHTS

Other than the botanical gardens, the majority of sights in San Andrés are tourist traps. The attractions here are the island's innate pleasures—sun, sand, water, seafood, and tropical drinks.

Spratt Bight Pathway

For many, the first stop in San Andrés is the **Spratt Bight Pathway** (Centro). This pedestrian walkway is the liveliest stretch on the island. It's lined with restaurants, hotels, and souvenir shops on one side and the island's most popular beach, **Spratt Bight,** on the other. In the distance you can spot the palm trees on Johnny Cay.

★ Jardín Botánico

Extending over eight hectares (20 acres) of wilderness, the **Jardín Botánico** (Vía Harmony Hill in front of Hotel Sol Caribe Campo, tel. 8/513-3390, 8:30am-5pm Mon.-Fri., 10am-4pm Sat.-Sun., COP$5,000) is easily the most peaceful place on San Andrés. In this lovely botanical garden run by the Universidad Nacional, you can stroll along several paths and view trees and plants that grow in San Andrés. Of particular interest are the many fruit trees, which include breadfruit, and a section on medicinal plants. From the five-story lookout tower, you can take in an impressive view of the island and its barrier reefs. Guided tours, included in the price of admission, are available (but not required), and take about an hour.

Casa Museo Isleña

Casa Museo Isleña (Km. 5 Av. Circunvalar, tel. 8/512-3419, 8:30am-5pm daily, COP$8,000) is a reconstruction of a typical island wooden house that provides a glimpse into island life in the 19th century. After a required guided tour (15 minutes), your cheerful young guide will tell you "now let's dance!" Reggae dancing is a rather strange component of the museum experience, but then again, it's hard to say no. Those smiling guides are a persuasive lot.

Cueva de Morgan (Morgan's Cave)

It would seem that all caves hidden along the coasts of San Andrés and Providencia are reputed to hold hidden treasures stashed away by notorious pirates. On the western side of San Andrés is **Cueva de Morgan** (Morgan's Cave, tel. 8/513-2946, 9am-6pm daily, COP$10,000), a sort of theme park where Welsh privateer/pirate Captain Henry Morgan allegedly stored some of his loot (but there's no evidence to prove this). There isn't much to see at the cave itself. That's why the park owners added on some reconstructions of traditional wooden island cabins that serve as mini-museums on island culture and ways of life. You visit these on a guided tour that is included in the cost. One is an art gallery where local dancers often perform to calypso beats. Also on the premises is the Coconut Museum, which is a house made out of coconuts. All in all, it's a tourist trap.

Hoyo Soplador

At **Hoyo Soplador** on the island's southern tip, the attraction is a blowhole in the coral where, when the tide and winds are right, water sprays up, reaching heights of more than 10 meters. It can't compare to Old Faithful, but then again, can you order a *coco loco* in Yellowstone? There is no fee to see the hole, but vendors will strongly encourage visitors to purchase something.

First Baptist Church

The white, clapboard **First Baptist Church** (La Loma, no phone, services 7:30pm Thurs. and 10:30am Sun., COP$3,000 donation requested) was built in 1844 and rebuilt before the turn of the 20th century using wood imported from Alabama. It was the first Baptist church established on the island. A guide will tell you the history of the church and allow you to climb up to the bell tower for a commanding view of the island. The Sunday worship service can last several hours. Church members dress up for services, and you'll often see a smattering of tourists in the balcony on Sundays. The church is an excellent place to hear gospel music.

Paradise Farm

Job Saas, a native islander, operates **Paradise Farm** (Cove Seaside, Km. 11 Polly Higgs Rd., tel. 8/513-0798 or cell tel. 315/770-3904, donations accepted). Saas decided to transform the former standard family farm into one with a focus on conservation and the environment. Here you can see animals, such as iguanas and turtles, and plants that are threatened due to overdevelopment on San Andrés. Saas uses the same farming techniques that his family has applied for decades. It is a great initiative on an island where environmental awareness is lacking. Saas welcomes visitors to the farm, and, if you are lucky, you can hear his band play.

First Baptist Church

Big Pond

Managed by a Rastafarian community, the **Big Pond** (La Loma, no phone, no set visiting hours, donations requested) is a pond on the top of La Loma, home to a few domesticated alligators. When called, they will swim close to the shore, where they are fed a diet of white bread. The alligators live in harmony with turtles, and herons watch the action from a tree nearby. You can order a beer at the bar where reggae music blares from speakers. There is no set entry fee, but young men hanging out at the entrance (who are not associated with Big Pond) will insist on a payment. It's expected that you'll pay, but you can negotiate—don't pay more than COP$10,000 per person.

ENTERTAINMENT AND EVENTS
Nightlife

The nightlife scene on San Andrés is big and brash. The most popular nightspots, near Spratt Bight, cater to visiting Colombians. Clubs generally are open from Thursday to Saturday during off-season but every night during high season. Things get cranking around 10pm. The perennial top discos are **Coco Loco** (Av. Colombia, tel. 8/513-1047), **Extasis** (Hotel Sol Caribe, Av. Colón No. 2-77, tel. 8/512-3043), and **Blue Deep** (Sunrise Hotel).

A relaxing alternative to the club scene is stargazing with beer in hand at **Bar de Kela** (San Luis, no phone, 3pm-midnight daily), a rustic but charming bar that plays reggae, in front of the San Luis Village hotel.

SHOPPING

Ask any Colombian about San Andrés and they will tell you that one of the top things to do here is to go shopping for cheap and duty-free goods. (In fact, Bogotá's shopping district known for its affordable wares, San Andresito, is named in honor of the island.) There are numerous duty-free shops in the Centro, where deals can be had on booze, perfume, watches, and the like. **La Riviera** is the best known of

these. It has multiple locations close to the Spratt Bight walkway.

Casa BazArte (San Luis, cell tel. 317/375-4779, 9am-6pm daily) has local handicrafts like papier-mâché (a typical island handicraft), paintings, and wallets made of coconut fiber, among more common Colombian wares. Luly, the owner, can hook you up with local artisans if you're interested. The shop is located in a protected heritage house that's over 90 years old; its cheerful paint job makes it hard to miss.

RECREATION
★ Snorkeling and Diving

San Andrés is surrounded by a well-preserved coral reef teeming with marine life that makes it a diver's and snorkeler's paradise. On the eastern edge is the windward barrier, 15 kilometers (9.3 miles) long and 60-80 meters (200-260 feet) wide, with significant live coral communities. Beyond the reef, the shelf ends abruptly with a vertical wall that drops hundreds of meters. To the west, the windward barrier protects a large marine lagoon that has sea grass cover. The reef on the western, leeward side is a bit less well preserved due to tourism and boat traffic, but it also has beautiful patches of coral and significant marine life. In all, the waters surrounding San Andrés include more than 40 species of corals and 131 species of fish. It is common to see large schools of brightly colored jacks, tangs, grunts, and snapper, as well as barracudas, groupers, and parrot fish. Other marine creatures include turtles, stingrays, moray eels, octopus, squid, and lobster.

A unique feature of San Andrés is that the dives are very close to shore, which means a 10- to 30-minute boat ride maximum. The water is warm and has excellent visibility year-round. The best conditions for diving occur January to May, with stronger winds in June and July. Popular dive sites are The Pyramids, a shallow 4-meter (13-foot) dive with striking anemones and fish; Nirvana, a reef at about 15 meters (50 feet) that is teeming with marine life; Trampa Tortuga, a reef at about 15 meters

(50 feet) with great visibility; and Blue Wall, on the eastern edge of the windward barrier, which starts at 6 meters (20 feet) and drops to 60 meters (200 feet). It contains magnificent corals and large tube sponges.

Most dive operators also offer short (three-hour) introductory courses for beginners, costing around COP$155,000 per person, which allow you to do an easy dive without being certified. There are also many opportunities to do full introductory and advanced courses with certification. A three-day open-water certification course typically costs around COP$800,000.

Highly recommended diving operators on San Andrés include **Banda** (Hotel Lord Pierre, tel. 8/513-1080, www.bandadiveshop. com, two dives COP$185,000, open-water course COP$900,000), where the friendly owner Gloria will help with everything, and German-run **Karibik** (Av. Newball 1-248, Edificio Galeón, tel. 8/512-0101 or cell tel. 318/863-9352, www.karibikdiver.com, two dives COP$170,000), which prides itself on its dive safety. **Sharky Surf Shop** (Sunset Hotel, Km. 13 Carretera Circunvalar, tel. 8/512-0651, www.sharkydiveshop.com) is another reputable agency, whose offerings include a four- to five-day open-water course (COP$800,000) and a mini-course for beginners (COP$140,000). Night diving trips can be arranged by most dive shops for experienced divers.

Other Water Sports

Samuel Raigosa, better known as Chamey, is the kitesurfing guru of San Andrés, and the staff at **Chamey's Náutica** (Km. 4 Vía San Luis, tel. 8/513-2077, cell tel. 317/752-4965) are experts on kitesurfing. A one-hour class costs COP$70,000.

Supported by environmental agencies, **Ecofiwi Turismo Ecológico** (Vía San Luis, Mango Tree sector, cell tel. 316/567-4988 or 316/624-3396, www.sanandresecotourism. com, ecofiwi@gmail.com, 9am-4pm daily, COP$70,000 pp) offers two-hour **kayak tours** of the mangroves in the Old Point Regional Mangrove Park led by local guides. The kayaks are completely transparent, providing kayakers with up-close views of sealife such as upside-down jellyfish, sea cucumbers, sea grass beds, and also birds such as frigate birds, pelicans, herons, and migratory birds. Snorkeling is also part of the tour (equipment included).

Spectacular diving awaits at numerous sites off of San Andrés.

Beaches

Some of the best beaches on the island include **Spratt Bight,** near the Centro in front of the pedestrian walkway; **San Luis,** near Chammey Marina; **Cocoplum; Bahía Sonora** (near Rocky Cay) beaches; and the **Parque Regional Johnny Cay.** Out of all of these, the beaches on Johnny Cay, the island off Spratt Bight, are some of the most popular. During peak tourist seasons, on weekends, and on holidays, they get very crowded.

To get to Johnny Cay, you must take a *lancha* (boat) from Spratt Bight on a quick 15-minute ride. There are always boats (owned by individuals, not organized tour companies) at the ready at Spratt Bight. To arrange a trip, your negotiating skills will be put to the test. Hiring an individual boat can cost up to COP$200,000. The inexpensive option is to take a day tour (COP$20,000). These leave from Spratt Bight by 9:30am every day of the year, returning at around 4pm. In the late afternoon, Johnny Cay clears out, but you can stay until almost 6pm when the last boats leave. It's nice to be one of the last visitors on the island as the sun begins its descent. There are no accommodation options on the island, but there are *coco loco* stands aplenty and some restaurants serving the usual fried fish fare. While there, take a walk around the entire island, where flocks of birds are likely the only company you'll have. It takes about 15 minutes.

On the eastern side of San Andrés, the beaches at **San Luis** and **Rocky Cay** have easy access and great food options. It's possible to wade through the shallow waters to Rocky Cay.

Tours

A popular activity in San Andrés is to take a day tour of some swimming spots just off of the mainland. A standard day tour costs COP$20,000 and leaves at around 9am daily (with return trips departing at 1:30pm and 3:30pm). Tours include a 1.5-hour stop at **El Acuario/La Piscina/Haynes Cay,** where you can wade and swim in waters described

The beach at Spratt Bight is full of activity during holidays.

as "seven shades of blue." Here, a common attraction is swimming with manta rays, though it's best to avoid participating. On busy days, the rays are handled constantly, being lifted out of the water for snapshots with smiling tourists. They are fed a steady diet of white sandwich bread. The rest of the day is spent on **Johnny Cay,** where you can buy lunch and drinks, and rent snorkeling equipment. There is no need for a guide here, so resist offers to pay for one. **Coonative Brothers** (Spratt Bight Beach, tel. 8/512-3522) offers these tours, as do many of the larger hotels.

Local boaters affiliated with Coonative Brothers also offer day tours with more stops, including a visit to the **San Andrés mangroves** for COP$60,000 per person. There is a minimum of 10 passengers for these tours. Private tours can cost up to COP$200,000, depending on your negotiating skills. Inquire at the Coonative Brothers' beach kiosk.

To swim with sharks and manta rays in unbelievable crystalline waters, you can

Sustainable Seafood

To protect their sustainability, some seafood should be avoided during certain times of the year, and some should be avoided completely.

Langosta (lobster), pargo (snapper), and caracol pala (conch) are the three most fished species around San Andrés and Providencia, and are very often found on restaurant menus. It is recommended to avoid ordering conch from June to October (but due to overfishing it's wise to avoid conch entirely), lobster from April until June, and cangrejo negro (black crab) from April to July.

Other threatened species include Atlantic bluefin tuna, tarpon, Lebranche mullet, robalo blanco (white sea bass), mero guasa (goliath grouper), cherna (Nassau grouper), and the masked hamlet, which is only found in the waters off Providencia.

take a day tour to the exotic **Cayo Bolívar** (COP\$170,000), which is about an hour by boat from San Andrés. The tour leaves at 8am and returns at 5pm. Lunch and drinks are provided. Coonative Brothers also organizes this trip, which, due to the relatively steep cost, attracts fewer customers.

Another option to get out on the water is to take a glass-bottom boat tour with **San Andrés Unlimited** (Tom Hooker Rd. No. 8-75, South End, tel. 8/513-0035 or 8/513-0129, cell tel. 316/889-8701 or 310/625-2938, www.sanandresultd.com). During this tour, the boat makes several stops at coral reefs, sunken ships, and exotic islands. You'll be able to get in the water and snorkel several times to observe sealife. The nearly two-hour tour costs around COP\$45,000 per person.

FOOD

Seafood is on every menu in every restaurant in San Andrés. Fish, lobster, crab, and conch are likely to come from the waters off of San Andrés and Providencia. However, langostinos (prawns) and camarones (shrimp) often come from either the Pacific or from the Cartagena area on the mainland. A Caribbean specialty you'll likely find only on San Andrés, Providencia, and Jamaica is rondón (rundown). It is a filling stew that has fish or conch, pig's tail, dumplings, yuca, and other ingredients slow-cooked in coconut milk. All restaurants are beach casual, and most of the larger ones accept credit cards. Service is often laid-back. On Sundays, local women sell food, like fried fish cakes, on the beach in San Luis.

Seafood

North of downtown, the blue-collar **Fisherman's Place** (Cra. 9 No. 1-10 Spratt Bight, tel. 8/512-2774, noon-4pm daily, COP\$20,000) is a restaurant run by a cooperative of local fishers. Overlooking the water, it's also close to the airport runway. Try the rondón or the lobster.

Ask anyone in town to recommend the best seafood place on the island and a solid majority will mention ★ **La Regatta** (tel. 8/512-0437, www.restaurantelaregatta.com, noon-11pm daily, COP\$40,000), next to the Club Náutico. It is open-air and juts out onto the water. For a sampling of the finest of San Andrés seafood, try their Fiesta Náutica, which includes lobster tails, prawns, and crab, or go for the tesoros del mar, a filling seafood stew. The restaurant is festively decorated. Reservations are a good idea.

Just far enough from the Centro for a little peace and quiet, **Niko's Seafood Restaurant** (Av. Colombia No. 1-93, tel. 8/512-7535, 11am-11pm daily, COP\$30,000) is what a family-run seafood place should be: over the water, not fancy-schmancy, and no lounge music. The house specialties are lobster and coconut lemonade.

The Grog (Rocky Cay, Cocoplum Hotel, tel. 8/513-3244 or cell tel. 311/232-3247, 10am-6pm Wed.-Sun., COP\$25,000) is everything you'd expect in a Caribbean seafood restaurant. In an idyllic location on the beach and steps from the water, this is a great spot for a grilled fish lunch on a lazy afternoon.

Although the namesake for **Miss Celia** (Av. Newball and Av. Raizal, tel. 8/513-1062 or 8/512-6495, restaurantemisscelia@gmail.com, noon-10pm daily, COP$30,000) passed away, the restaurant continues on in this colorful spot. Located in front of the Club Náutico, Miss Celia is surrounded by flower gardens, and the sounds of local music add to the atmosphere. The restaurant recommends ordering *rondón* (seafood, pig tail, and yam stew) only at lunchtime, as it's a heavy dish. There are also various rice dishes, some with shrimp, some vegetarian; for dessert there's homemade ice cream.

From its simple beachside *cabañas*, it might surprise you that ★ **Donde Francesca** (El Pirata Beach, San Luis, tel. 8/513-0163, cell tel. 318/616-8547, restaurantedondefrancesca@gmail.com, 10am-6pm daily, COP$35,000) serves gourmet food. The varied menu includes *langosta tempura* (tempura lobster, COP$50,000) and *pulpo reducción al balsámico* (balsamic octopus, COP$34,000). The drinks are good, too, like gin cocktails and margaritas, all made from non-bottled ingredients. This may explain why folks arrive for lunch at 11am and don't leave until sundown.

In-the-know locals make a weekly visit to ★ **Restaurante Lidia** (Ground Rd. No. 64-65, San Luis, tel. 8/513-2192) a ritual. It's only open on Sundays and on holiday Mondays. This place gets great reviews from local foodies. Lidia's crab empanadas are recommended.

The **Restaurante Punta Sur** (Km. 15.8, South End, tel. 8/513-0003, cell tel. 312/449-0301, 10am-6pm daily, COP$30,000) is close to the Hoyo Soplador. Sitting on the terrace when the waves come crashing in, it feels like you might be taken out to sea. Bring a bathing suit and chill out in their small pool overlooking the sea. *Arroz con camarones* (rice with shrimp) and grilled lobster are the most popular menu items at this well-liked spot on the southern tip of the island.

International

Mr. Panino (Edificio Bread Fruit Local 106-7, tel. 8/512-3481 or 8/512-0549, 10:30am-10pm Mon.-Sat., 11am-4pm Sun., COP$30,000) is a reliable, somewhat upscale Italian restaurant, popular at both lunch and dinner, but more pleasant in the evening. There is typically a set lunch menu of Colombian fare. It's nice to sit on the high wooden tables in the back. Try their *risotto con langostinos*, a prawn risotto that's a generous plate to share. Service can be chilly.

★ **Gourmet Shop** (Av. Newball in front of Parque de la Barracuda, tel. 8/512-9843, cell tel. 315/770-0140, noon-11pm Mon.-Sat., 6pm-11pm Sun., COP$30,000) is an excellent choice for a break from seafood. The salads, pasta, and other dishes are good, and on every table there is a big bottle of imported spicy chili sauce. With gourmet food items and wine for sale along the walls, and thousands of empty wine bottles decorating the ceiling, it's a cozy place. For something quick, like a slice of pizza, you can try the hole-in-the-wall **Gourmet Shop To Go** (Av. Newball in front of Parque de la Barracuda, tel. 8/512-9843, 11am-3pm daily, COP$15,000) around the corner in the same building.

Margherita e Carbonara (Av. Colombia No. 1-93, tel. 8/512-1050, 11am-11pm daily, COP$30,000) gets packed at night during high season due to its prized location near the big hotels and nightclubs. Stick with the pasta and pizza at this boisterous family-style place.

It's a rarity to find vegetarian options in San Andrés, but **New Dawn Paradise** (Vía Tom Hooker No. 1-107, tel. 8/513-0015, cell tel. 314/444-9418, 11am-3pm Sun.-Fri., COP$15,000) delivers. This simple restaurant is in the modest home of super-friendly Enaida Veloza, who serves vegetarian hamburgers, salads, and the like, as well as baked goods. Many of the vegetables come from her prosperous organic garden.

Cafés, Bakeries, and Quick Bites

Part of the Casablanca Hotel, the groovy turquoise **Sea Watch Caffé** (Av. Colombia, 7am-11pm daily, COP$18,000) is as close as it comes in Colombia to a New York-style coffee shop. Here you can have a leisurely breakfast as you watch the tourists file by on the walkway out front. They also offer pizza, hamburgers, ceviche, pasta, and desserts.

From the outside, ★ **Coffee Break** (Av. Colombia No. 3-59, in front of Parque de la Barracuda, tel. 8/512-1275, 7am-11pm daily) often appears empty or even closed. But when you go inside, it's almost always packed with visitors and locals alike sipping on Vietnamese coffee, munching on nachos, or smearing cream cheese on their toasted bagels. Customers here take their time (likely because of the air-conditioning).

A bakery/café popular with locals and visitors alike is **Bread Fruit** (Av. Francisco Newball No. 4-169, outside the Sunrise Hotel, tel. 8/512-6044, 7:30am-8:30pm Mon.-Sat.), named after the breadfruit tree, which is typical to the area. This solid breakfast spot offers outdoor seating and table service.

Miss Carmen is a familiar face on the Spratt Bight walkway, where she has been selling her homemade empanadas, ceviche, and cakes for years. Her stand doesn't really have a name, but you can call it **La Mesa Grande de Carmen** (Av. Colombia pathway).

ACCOMMODATIONS

On this island where tourism is king, lodging options are plentiful, except during high season (mid-December to mid-January, Holy Week, and, to a lesser extent, during school vacations from June to July). Top-end hotels and low-end hostels are not as common as mid- to upper-range all-inclusive hotels.

Most visitors stay on or near the beach on the eastern side of the island, including in quiet San Luis. From here, you can hop on public transportation or hail a cab if you want to go to town, or rent a motorbike, golf cart, Jeep (*mulita*), or bicycle. The busy downtown (Centro) of San Andrés can feel claustrophobic, but you'll always be within walking distance of restaurants and services, and you can often find some good deals in this area. Waterfront hotels here have pools, not beaches. Stay in the north beyond the airport

if you prefer more seclusion but still want to be close to the action in the city center.

The western side of the island has coral coastline instead of beaches, and the few hotels cater mostly to divers, so this side feels more isolated.

In the interior of the island are numerous *posadas nativas* (native guesthouses), owned and operated by locals, many of whom have deep roots on the island. Staying at a *posada nativa* is the best way to get to know the local culture. Don't expect fancy amenities.

Renting an apartment offers advantages for those looking for more space, privacy, or the use of a kitchen. **Sol & Mar** (tel. 8/512-5834 or cell tel. 317/665-0273, www.solymarislas.com, two-bedroom apartment COP$450,000 per night) has several fully furnished two- and three-bedroom options, including in quiet Sarie Bay, near the airport. Some of the apartments are in large complexes with access to a swimming pool.

Centro

The Colombian all-inclusive chain Decameron has several properties on the island. Decameron offers optional transportation to the island. Guests can dine at other Decameron locations on the island, but may have to make reservations in advance, which can be a hassle. Wi-Fi is available at an additional cost. The newest, largest, and arguably best Decameron property is the **Royal Decameron Isleño** (Av. Colón Cl. 3 No. 6-106, tel. 8/513-4343, www.decameron.co, COP$660,000 d), with a fantastic location on a quiet stretch along Spratt Bight. During high season, it gets crowded here, but during the off-season, you may just have the facilities, with open-air dining and a pool, practically to yourself.

Decameron Los Delfines (Av. Colombia No. 1B-86, tel. 8/512-7816 or Bogotá tel. 1/628-0000, www.decameron.co, COP$600,000 d), located in town and on the water, is a hotel geared toward couples. It has 39 comfortable rooms and a pool. This is the "boutique"

Decameron hotel, but that may be a generous description of this property.

Although it may look retro, blindingly white **Hotel Casablanca** (Av. Colombia No. 3-59, tel. 8/512-4115, www.hotelcasablan-casanandres.com, COP$480,000 d) is a large hotel facing the Spratt Bight Parkway. Of the 91 rooms it offers, 10 are *cabañas*. There is a small pool and, more importantly, a pool bar, Coco's. The hotel has three on-site restaurants. Casablanca gets mixed reviews, but is one of the better options along Spratt Bight.

In the North End, boutique hotel ★ **Casa Harb** (Cl. 11 No. 10-83, tel. 8/512-6348, www.casaharb.com, COP$880,000 d) is by far the most luxurious place to stay in San Andrés. The six suites, lobby, dining area, and spa are thoughtfully decorated with fantastic art and furniture from Morocco to Malaysia, personally chosen by owner Jak Harb. The fabulous on-site restaurant is open to the public (but call first).

On an unassuming street in a quiet neighborhood two blocks from the beach, ★ **Hostal Mar y Mar** (Av. Colombia No. 1-32, Sarie Bay, cell tel. 317/783-6420, www.hostalmarymar.com, COP$190,000 d) offers 10 clean and comfortable rooms. Noise from airplanes may be a nuisance in the mornings for some.

The small hotels in the busy downtown are far more reasonably priced than those with a view to the sea and are just a few blocks away. The most popular choice for backpackers is the five-floor **El Viajero** (Av. 20 de Julio No. 3A-122, tel. 8/512-7497, www.elviajerohostels.com, COP$60,000 dorm, COP$250,000 d), which is part of an Uruguayan chain. It has several air-conditioned gender-separated dorms, as well as private rooms. The top-floor bar serves cold beer and assorted rum drinks, and there are several common areas with wireless Internet and computers. A small breakfast is included, and a kitchen is provided for guest use. Staff aren't overly friendly, but they can arrange excursions.

It's surprising just how peaceful the **Posada Mary May** (Av. 20 de Julio No. 3-74, tel. 8/512-5669, COP$60,000-110,000 d) is. Every morning you can pick up a cup of coffee in the lovely courtyard that is shaded by a huge avocado tree. On the downside, beds (usually three per room) are on the soft side in the spacious rooms, wireless Internet is sporadic, and in general the place could use an update. Around the corner, **Cli's Place** (Av. 20 de Julio No. 3-47, tel. 8/512-0591, luciamhj@hotmail.com, COP$160,000 d), owned by Cleotilde Henry, has four double rooms in the main house as well as a *cabaña* that accommodates seven people. You will feel at home here.

San Luis

Brightly colored **Cocoplum Hotel** (Vía San Luis No. 43-49, tel. 8/513-2121, www.cocoplumhotel.com, COP$350,000 d) in the San Luis area has the most important feature for a beach hotel: It's actually on the beach, with rooms that are steps from the water. The rooms are generally fine, the food is OK, and service can be chilly.

★ **Ground Road Native Place** (Circunvalar No. 54-88, before the health clinic, tel. 8/513-3887 or cell tel. 313/776-6036, edupeterson1@hotmail.com, COP$50,000 pp) is a comfortable *posada nativa* with five spacious rooms and some large apartments, with air-conditioning and wireless Internet. The *posada* is in the home of friendly Edula and George Peterson and is just a three-minute walk to the beach. The neighborhood is not close to many tourist amenities, but there are always public buses on the main road out front.

Tucked away on a quiet lane is ★ **Villa Verde** (Vía Tom Hooker 1A-24, cell tel. 315/770-0785, temporadasanandres@yahoo.es), a charming guesthouse that offers rooms in the owner's home, an inviting pool surrounded by trees, and camping on the lush grass.

About five minutes to the beach, **Posada Buganvilla** (Vía Tom Hooker No. 3-41, cell tel. 315/303-5474 or 317/804-1952, posadabuganvilla@gmail.com, COP$170,000 d) is a cheerfully colored house in a quiet location, with four air-conditioned rooms, tile floors, and shared bathrooms. The guesthouse offers bikes for rent.

La Loma

This neighborhood, home to the island's highest point—hence the name La Loma (The Hill)—is situated in the interior of the island and is almost completely inhabited by English-speaking native islanders, some of whom run *posadas nativas*. A fine option is ★ **Coconut Paradise Lodge** (Vía La Loma, Claymount No. 50-05, tel. 8/513-2926 or cell tel. 301/543-2344, oldm26@hotmail.com, COP$55,000 pp with breakfast), a beautiful turn-of-the-20th-century wooden home with just four rooms. It's close to the botanical gardens and the San Luis beaches. Try for the top-floor room, which has great views and a refreshing breeze. Across the street is **Caribbean Refuge** (Vía La Loma, tel. 8/523-2878 or cell tel. 313/823-3587, COP$50,000 pp), run by Clemencia Livingston. It's a spotless, modern house (though lacking in charm), and Clemencia is a very gracious host.

West

For those interested in diving, ★ **Sunset Hotel** (Km. 13 Circunvalar, cell tel. 318/523-2286, www.sunsethotelspa.com, COP$300,000 d), on the quiet west side of the island, is a great option. It has 16 bright and basic rooms that surround a small pool. While there is no beach, the hotel's dive shop, Sharky's, offers diving lessons and organizes diving excursions. You can go snorkeling in the waters across the street. Weeklong diving packages are a good option. Great sunsets are included at no extra cost. You can also rent bikes here.

INFORMATION AND SERVICES

A **tourist office** (Av. Newball, tel. 8/513-0801, 8am-noon and 2pm-6pm daily) is located between downtown and San Luis, across from Club Náutico. Tourism bureau staff are on hand at a **tourist information kiosk** (intersection of Av. Colombia and Av. 20 de Julio, 8am-7pm daily).

There is a small branch of **Universidad Nacional** (National University, San Luis, tel. 8/513-3310 or 8/513-3311, 8am-noon and 2pm-6pm Mon.-Fri.) here, where the library is open to the public. Anyone is welcome to work or read there.

TRANSPORTATION

San Andrés's **Aeropuerto Gustavo Rojas Pinilla** (ADZ) is very close to many hotels. Cabs to the airport cost COP$10,000. San Andrés is served by all the major Colombian airlines, with most options from Bogotá and Medellín. There are nonstop flights from Cartagena on **VivaColombia** (www.vivacolombia.co) and **Copa** (www.copaair.com); Copa also offers a nonstop flight from Barranquilla. **Air Transat** (www.airtransat.com) operates charter flights between Canada and San Andrés on a seasonal basis.

Public buses serve the entire island; rides cost about COP$2,000 each way. To get to San Luis, flag down a bus from the Parque de la Barracuda just south of the Centro.

Renting a car is possible, but parking is scarce, distances are not far, and, more importantly, there are more fun options than driving a car. Most visitors rent heavy-duty, gas-powered golf carts referred to as *mulas* (literally, mules). **Millennium Rent A Car** (Av. Newball, Parque de la Barracuda, tel. 8/512-3114, 10am-6pm daily) rents standard golf carts (COP$70,000 day) and *mulas* (COP$150,000 day). **Rent A Car Esmeralda** (Av. Colombia, in front of Buxo del Caribe, tel. 8/513-1170 or cell tel. 315/303-7037, 10am-6pm daily) offers similar prices. Although you can rent both golf carts and *mulas* for multiple days, their use is prohibited after 6pm.

Rent a bike at **Bicycle Rental Shop** (Cra. 1B, Sector Punta Hansa, in front of Edificio Hansa Reef, cell tel. 318/328-1790 or 321/242-9328, 8am-6pm daily, COP$45,000/day).

Providencia and Santa Catalina

Secluded palm-lined beaches, gorgeous turquoise Caribbean waters, mellow locals, fresh seafood, and rum drinks make it easy to become smitten with Providencia.

Located about 90 kilometers (56 miles) north of San Andrés, these islands are the easygoing cousins of that hyperactive island. Of volcanic origin, Providencia and Santa Catalina are older islands than San Andrés, and are smaller in area and population than it, having a total area of about 18 square kilometers (7 square miles) and a population of only 5,000. Only 300 people live on minuscule Santa Catalina, an island known as the "Island of Treasures" and which was once home to an English fort.

Orientation

The two islands of Providencia and Santa Catalina combined are about seven kilometers long and four kilometers wide (4 miles by 2.5 miles). A ring road encircles the entire island of Providencia. The harbor/downtown area of Providencia is called **Santa Isabel** and is the center of island activity. Adjacent to this is **Santa Catalina.**

Other settlements on the island are usually referred to by the names of their beaches or bays. The main ones are on the western side of the island: **Manchineel Bay (Bahía Manzanillo),** on the southern end, which has some excellent beaches; **Southwest Bay (Bahía Suroeste);** and **Freshwater Bay (Bahía Aguadulce),** home to most of the island's hotels and restaurants. **Smoothwater Bay (Bahía Aguamansa),** on the southeastern edge of the island, is more remote. Smoothwater is adjacent to **Bottom House (Casa Baja),** which is more residential. **Maracaibo** is on the northeast part of the island, between Santa Isabel and the airport. In the middle of the island is its highest point, **The Peak.**

★ PARQUE NACIONAL NATURAL OLD PROVIDENCE MCBEAN LAGOON

The **Parque Nacional Natural Old Providence McBean Lagoon** (office Jones Point, east of airport, tel. 8/514-8885 or 8/514-9003, www.parquesnacionales.gov.co, oldprovidence@parquesnacionales.gov.co, 9am-5pm daily, COP$16,000 non-Colombians, COP$9,500 Colombians, COP$4,500 students) is a small national park on the northeast coast of the island. It occupies about 1,485 hectares/3,670 acres (1,390 hectares/3,435 acres of that is in the sea). Here you can observe five different ecosystems: coral reefs, sea grass beds, mangroves, dry tropical forests, and volcanic keys.

Crab Cay (Cayo Cangrejo) is one of the main attractions of the park, and it's a convenient spot for some splashing about in the incredibly clear, warm waters. This is a great place for some easy snorkeling, and, in addition to tropical fish, you may see manta rays or sea turtles. A short five-minute nature path takes you to the top of the island. A snack bar on Crab Cay sells water and snacks like ceviche. It is open every day until around 1pm.

Boat tours, organized by all hotels and dive shops, motor around the coast of Providencia, stopping at beaches and at Crab Cay for snorkeling or swimming. These tours depart the hotels at around 9am each morning and cost about COP$35,000 per person. Once you disembark at Crab Cay, you'll have to pay the park entry fee of COP$14,000. Following the stop at Crab Cay, the boats go to Southwest Bay for a seafood lunch, not included in the price of the tour.

Otherwise you can hire a boat for yourself at around COP$350,000 total. Upon arrival at the island, you'll be required to pay the park entry fee. All hotels can arrange this more exclusive option.

The park's **Iron Wood Hill Trail** is a three-kilometer (1.8-mile) round-trip nature trail along which you can explore the tropical dry forest landscape and see different types of lizards, birds, and flora. There are nice views from here of the coastline. This path is less popular than the hike to The Peak, but many find it more beautiful. Tourists are encouraged to go with a local guide arranged by the **park's office** (Jones Point, east of airport, tel. 8/514-8885, 8/514-9003, www.parquesnacionales.gov.co, 8am-12:30pm and 2pm-6pm daily, COP$25,000 pp plus park entry fee). But the trail is straightforward, and most visitors simply head off on their own. Be sure to pay the park entry fee before leaving.

An additional activity is to hire a **kayak** and paddle to Crab Cay or through the park's McBean Lagoon mangroves. Passing through the mangroves you'll enter the **Oyster's Creek Lagoon,** where you'll see several species of birds, like blue and white herons and pelicans, as well as crabs, fish, and some unusual jellyfish. This is an interesting trip. Try to go early in the morning or late in the afternoon, as the sun can be brutal. Kayaks can be rented at the **Posada Coco Bay** (Maracaibo sector on the northeastern side of the island, tel. 8/514-8226, cell tel. 311/804-0373, www.posadacocobay.com, COP$30,000). A kayak with a guide costs COP$50,000, and for snorkeling equipment tack on another COP$10,000.

LIGHTHOUSE PROVIDENCIA

Lighthouse Providencia (Hoy's Hill, cell tel. 313/380-5866 or 318/758-1804, www.lighthouseprovidencia.com, 5pm-9pm Mon.-Sat.) is a cultural center/café that's worth a stop. They host a range of cultural activities, including art exhibitions and film showings, all with an environmental bent, including a film on the famous black crab migration that brings the island to a virtual standstill.

ENTERTAINMENT AND EVENTS
Nightlife

Bob Marley never seems to fall out of fashion at **Roland Roots Bar** (Manchineel Bay, tel. 8/514-8417, hours vary). This spot beneath the coconut palms is the perfect place to spend a lazy, sunny day in Providencia. Or go at night, when you can order your rum drink to go and walk to the beach and stargaze, or

kayaking through the mangroves at Old Providence McBean Lagoon

hang out by a bonfire. On Sunday afternoons, it's a popular spot for locals. Roland's competition is **Richard's Place** on the beach in Southwest Bay. You can broaden your Caribbean music horizons here with reggae roots, rocksteady, ska calypso, ragamuffin, and soca dub—but more often than not, it's Marley on the sound system. Both bars serve fried fish during the day.

Festivals and Events

In early January of each year (usually a Saturday), the Parque Nacional Natural Old Providence McBean Lagoon organizes the colorful **Festival del Chub** (tel. 8/514-8885 or 8/514-9003, Jan.). Chub is a plentiful but not very popular fish (it can have a strong aroma). The purpose of the festival is to encourage fishers and consumers to choose chub instead of other fish like red snapper, the stocks of which have been depleted throughout the Caribbean. The festival is held at Rocky Point (Punta Rocosa), where chub is widely eaten. In addition to serving dishes like chub burgers and chub ceviche, there is also a sailing race from Southwest Bay to Manzanillo. It's fun to hang out at **Roland Roots Bar** (Manchineel Bay, tel. 8/514-8417) in the morning to watch the sailors ready their boats for the race.

Between April and August each year is when the **black crab migration** takes place. This species of crab lives in the mountainous interior of the island for most of the year, but as the rainy season begins (usually April or May), thousands of the female crabs, carrying up to 120,000 eggs each, make an arduous journey to the sea to deposit their eggs. The migration peaks during nighttime hours, so watch your step. More crabs can be seen on the western side of the island. A second migration occurs a few weeks later, when the young crabs make their trip from the sea up to the mountain. During both migrations, the main road on the island may be closed—enforced by military personnel—as a means of protecting the crabs from vehicles.

SHOPPING

Kalaloo Point Café-Boutique (near Halley View lookout, eastern side of the island, tel. 8/514-8592 or cell tel. 317/387-6448, 10am-8pm Mon.-Sat.) is a cute shop and café in a wooden house that sells tropical dresses by a Colombian designer and various knickknacks. There's also a small library.

RECREATION
★ Beaches

The best beaches on Providencia can be found generally on the western side of the island. From Manchineel Bay (Bahía Manzanillo) on the southern end to Allan or Almond Bay in the northwest, they are each worth exploring, if you have the time. On these beaches, the waters are calm, the sand golden, and there's always a refreshing breeze.

Manchineel Bay (Bahía Manzanillo), home to Roland Roots Bar, is an exotic beach where you can relax under the shade of a palm tree. (Be careful of falling coconuts.) In **Southwest Bay (Bahía Suroeste)**, there are a couple of hotels and restaurants nearby, and you can sometimes see horses cooling off in the water or people riding them along the shoreline. The beaches of **Freshwater Bay** are very convenient to several hotels and restaurants.

The beach at **Allan Bay** (or **Almond Bay**) is more remote. It's notable for its large octopus sculpture on the side of the road (can't miss it) and nicely done walkway down to the beach from the ring road. The beach area is a public park, and there is a snack bar and stand where you can purchase handicrafts. You'll have to either drive to this beach or hitch a ride from a taxi.

A couple of coves on Santa Catalina have some secluded beaches on the path to Morgan's Head, and they offer snorkeling opportunities as well.

Snorkeling and Diving

Providencia, which is surrounded by a 32-kilometer-long (20-mile-long) barrier reef, is a fantastic place to dive or to learn to dive. The water temperature is always warm, and water visibility is usually 25-35 meters (82-115 feet). The best time of year to dive is between June and October. In January, the water can be particularly rough.

Popular diving sites are **Felipe's Place,** made up of several ledges with significant coral and marine life; **Turtle Rock,** a large rock at 20 meters (66 feet) covered with black coral; **Tete's Place,** teeming with fish; **Confusion,** with corals and sponges at 20-40 meters (66-131 feet); and **Nick's Place,** a deep crack in the island's shelf that starts at 18 meters (60 feet) and drops to 40 meters (131 feet). Good snorkeling can be done near **Cayo Cangrejo,** at the small islands of **Basalt** and **Palm Cays,** and around **Morgan's Head** in Santa Catalina, among other places.

The **Hotel Sirius** (Southwest Bay, tel. 8/514-8213, www.siriushotel.net) is serious about diving and offers a PADI certification (COP$850,000) that includes four immersions over open water during a period of five days. They also offer a mini-course (COP$185,000), which includes a double-immersion excursion. Hotel Sirius's diving courses have an excellent reputation.

Felipe Diving (Freshwater Bay, cell tel. 316/628-6664 or 317/805-8684, www.

felipediving.com) is also highly recommended. They offer an open-water course (COP$800,000) and rent out snorkeling equipment as well.

Kayaking

For kayak rentals and mangrove tours, contact guide **Israel Livingston Archbold** (cell tel. 318/587-7898). A two-hour tour for two people costs COP$130,000. Israel's tours depart from Posada Coco Bay in Maracaibo.

Hiking
★ THE PEAK

The Peak (El Pico) is the highest point (360 meters/1,181 feet) on Providencia, and from this mountaintop the 360-degree views are impressive. This hike takes about 1.5 hours to the top and less than an hour down. The path to The Peak begins in the middle of the island and meanders along relatively well-marked trails through tropical rainforest and tropical dry forest. You'll likely come across lizards, cotton trees, and maybe a friendly dog who will follow you up to the top and back.

From the top you'll be able to see the barrier reef that extends for 32 kilometers (20 miles) off of the east coast of the island. This reef is the second longest in the Caribbean

horses cooling off at Southwest Bay

and is part of the Parque Nacional Natural Old Providence McBean Lagoon.

To get to the starting point, go to the Bottom House (Casa Baja) neighborhood in the southeastern corner of the island just to the east of Manchineel Bay. Although you may come across a sign pointing toward The Peak, roads are not well marked. Ask at your hotel for directions to the starting point.

At the beginning of the walk, follow a path straight ahead, veering to the right. Five minutes later, go right, before a two-story house. You'll then go left (not to the right of the concrete well). From here, you will pass a small garden, then follow a rocky creek, fording it back and forth several times. You'll go through a gate and eventually veer left as you begin climbing up the hill. After you cross over a wooden bridge, the path becomes steep; hold on to the wooden handrails. Occasional signs identify some of the trees or fauna you might see along the way.

During rainy seasons, the path can become muddy and slippery. Make sure to bring a bottle of water with you. Guides are not necessary for this walk, but it's not impossible to get lost. All hotels can contract a guide for you, and this usually costs around COP$50,000.

Be careful of thorny cockspur trees along the route, which also harbor ferocious ants.

SANTA CATALINA

From atop Santa Catalina island, English colonists and privateers once ruled, keeping their eyes peeled for potential enemies—usually the Spanish Armada or competing Dutch pirates. Today you can see some remains from 17th-century English rule at **Fort Warwick.** It is adjacent to a big rock called **Morgan's Head.** If you squint hard enough, it resembles the head of Henry Morgan, the notorious Welsh pirate and admiral of the Royal Navy who marauded the Spanish New World colonies during the mid-17th century; Morgan captured Santa Catalina from the Spaniards in 1670. Morgan's Head is next to **Morgan's Cave,** where the pirate supposedly hid his loot. You can go snorkeling inside the cave, where you

may encounter the occasional shark. Start this hike at the colorful pedestrian bridge that connects Providencia with Santa Catalina in the Santa Isabel area. When crossing the bridge, particularly in the evening, you may be able to spot graceful manta rays in the water. Once on Santa Catalina, take a left and follow the path.

Tours

Paradise Tours (Freshwater Bay, tel. 8/514-8283, cell tel. 311/605-0750, paradisetourscontact@gmail.com) is your one-stop shop, offering tours around the island and snorkeling, diving, and fishing excursions. One of their popular options is the Reefs and Snorkeling Tour (3-4 hours, 4-person min., COP$85,000), during which you boat to coral reefs around the island, exploring the underwater cities that exist just below the surface. Snorkeling equipment on this tour is extra. A full-day trip to idyllic **El Faro Island** and reef, nine kilometers (5.6 miles) off of Providencia, costs COP$110,000. It's an excellent place for snorkeling in warm, crystalline waters.

On land, Paradise Tours offers several hiking options, such as to The Peak, where you can see coral reefs in the distance; to Manchineel Hill, where you might see wild orchids on your way; and to Iron Wood Hill in the Parque Nacional Natural Old Providence McBean Lagoon. These cost COP$85,000.

A popular excursion is to take a **boat tour** around the island. The tours, departing at around 9am and returning at 3pm, make several stops, including Crab Cay and Santa Catalina. Any hotel can assist you in arranging a tour; boats make the rounds to pick up tourists at various hotels. These tours cost around COP$35,000 per person and usually leave from Freshwater Bay. If you prefer, you can rent a boat for just yourself and your crew; that will cost up to COP$350,000.

Discover Old Providence (Bottom House, cell tel. 318/587-7898 or 316/761-5770, enjoyprovidence.pespo@gmail.com) offers fishing, hiking, and kayak tours in and around Providencia.

lunch with a view at Miss Mary Hotel

with pastas, interesting seafood dishes, and salads. An awesome blues soundtrack plays in the background. It's run by a local and his Canadian wife.

The **Miss Mary Hotel** (tel. 8/514-8454, noon-3pm and 6pm-9pm daily, COP$20,000) has an open-air restaurant overlooking the beach. It's one of the most reliable spots for lunch. On the beach nearby is **Restaurante Arturo** (cell tel. 317/620-0814, 11am-5pm daily, COP$22,000), where the specialty is *rondón* (regional seafood stew). It's open-air and has a relaxed atmosphere.

Freshwater Bay (Bahía Aguadulce)

★ **Caribbean Place** (tel. 8/514-8698, noon-3pm and 6pm-10pm Mon.-Sat., COP$25,000) is one of the best seafood spots in Providencia. Try the fish in ginger-butter sauce or the coconut shrimp, and for dessert, the coconut pie. Cheerfully decorated, it's a great choice for both lunch and dinner.

For a pizza night, try **Blue Coral** (tel. 8/514-8718, 11am-3pm and 6pm-9pm Mon.-Sat., COP$20,000). Though not out of this world, the pizzas and pastas here can taste exotic after several days of seafood. Service is lackluster.

Morgan's Market (8am-noon and 3pm-8pm Mon.-Fri., 9am-noon and 4pm-8pm Sat.-Sun.) is one of the main grocery stores on the island. It's hard to miss, as it's a hub of activity. There's a sandwich and juice stand inside as well.

Santa Catalina and Santa Isabel

For an evening out in Santa Catalina, try ★ **Sea Star Gourmet** (Santa Catalina, cell tel. 316/824-0451, noon-4pm and 6:30pm-9pm Mon.-Fri., noon-4pm Sun., COP$25,000), an open-air restaurant with fine service where you can feast on fish fillets, lobster bathed in a coconut-ginger sauce, or *arroz con cangrejo* (crab stir-fry).

A quirky option is **Don Olivo** (Santa Catalina, cell tel. 310/230-5260), which is

A recommended guide who can assist with transportation on the island is **Bernardo "Big Boy" Henry** (cell tel. 313/811-0121 or 311/853-5166, bbernardhenry@gmail.com). It generally costs about COP$25,000 to get from one part of the island to the other.

FOOD

Providencia is synonymous with fresh Caribbean seafood. Many restaurants in Providencia do not accept credit cards. Hotel restaurants are open every day, while others often close on Sundays.

Southwest Bay (Bahía Suroeste)

★ **Café Studio** (on ring road, tel. 8/514-9076, 11am-10pm Mon.-Sat., COP$25,000), on the side of the road near Southwest Bay, is a favorite among visitors—and not just because of their trademark cappuccino pie. Everything is good here, it's open for both lunch and dinner, and it's the best spot for afternoon coffee and dessert. Café Studio has a varied menu made up of a few small tables in front of a wooden house. Monsieur Olivier and his Colombian wife, Amparo, serve Caribbean dishes with a French flair. You have to ring the bell for service, and it's best to call first. Expect to be regaled by stories.

Old Providence Taste (Old Town Bay, to the west of Santa Isabel, tel. 8/514-9028, 11:30am-3pm Mon.-Sat., COP$18,000), on the beach to the west of Santa Isabel, is run by a local sustainable seafood and farming co-op. Each day they offer a different menu, depending on what fishers and farmers bring in. It's the best deal on the island. They can also organize visits to farms and excursions with local fishers.

Maracaibo

The ★ **Deep Blue Hotel Restaurant** (Maracaibo Bay, tel. 8/514-8423, noon-3pm and 6pm-10pm daily, COP$35,000) is the most elegant and pricey restaurant on the island. Menu items are innovative and beautifully presented, and the service is excellent. An impossibly beautiful setting under the stars makes this the perfect place for a special dinner.

ACCOMMODATIONS

Providencia and Santa Catalina offer an array of interesting and comfortable accommodations. Most options are in Freshwater Bay, but each area on this enchanting island has its charms. Note that Internet service is unreliable, and it's best to communicate with hotels via phone call or text message (rather than email) for reservations and inquiries.

Freshwater Bay (Bahía Aguadulce)

There are three affiliated locations of the all-inclusive Decameron chain in Freshwater Bay, but they are locally operated. The least expensive option is **Relax** (Freshwater Bay, tel. 8/514-8087, COP$100,000 pp). It has a small pool, hot water, and eight rooms, and is near a couple of restaurants and stores. It is across the road from the beach. **Miss Elma** (Freshwater Bay, tel. 8/514-8229 or 8/514-8854, cell tel. 310/566-3773, COP$170,000 d) has just

six rooms, all of which overlook the sea, and a restaurant on the beach. **Hotel Posada del Mar** (Freshwater Bay, tel. 8/514-8052, www.posadadelmarprovidencia.com, COP$220,000 pp d) is a 24-room hotel with air-conditioning and a pool. Instead of a beach, a grassy lawn overlooks the water.

Sol Caribe Solar (tel. 8/514-8230, www.solarhoteles.com, COP$175,000 pp) is a chain hotel with around 35 rooms and a pool, with breakfast and dinner buffets included in the cost. There are four rooms with high ceilings and balconies overlooking the water.

Somewhat far from everything is the ★ **Posada Refugio de la Luna** (Bluff, tel. 8/514-8460, providenciarefugiodelaluna@gmail.com, COP$170,000 d), a guesthouse with just one comfortable and spacious room. Carmeni, the owner, is a papier-mâché artist; her studio is upstairs.

Southwest Bay (Bahía Suroeste)

★ **Hotel Sirius** (tel. 8/514-8213 or cell tel. 318/743-5367, www.siriushotel.net, COP$290,000 d) is a beachside hotel that specializes in diving and snorkeling excursions—but you don't have to be a diver to enjoy your stay here. It offers some huge rooms, and the friendly manager will make every effort to ensure you have a pleasant stay in Providencia.

Cabañas Miss Mary (tel. 8/514-8454, hotelmissmary@yahoo.com, COP$180,000 d) is just steps away from the beach in the southwest part of the island. It has eight rooms, five of which have beach views.

Smoothwater Bay (Bahía Aguamansa)

English writer Sam Cuming (author of *A Short History of Providence and San Andrés*) owns ★ **Windy View Guesthouse** (Bottom House, tel. 8/514-8750 or cell tel. 310/589-4888, www.windyviewprovidence.blogspot.com or www.providencewindyview.com, COP$120,000 d). This gorgeous spot with two rooms and a nautical feel is brimming with books.

Casa Posada Angels (Smoothwater Bay, cell tel. 321/414-5241, COP$50,000 pp) is a guesthouse managed by Anni, an expat journalist from New Zealand who has lived in the islands for many years. There is one small cabin and a room in the main house. Across the street is a rickety pier and water access that nobody else seems to know about.

For cute accommodations in an A-frame house next to a big mango tree, hang your hat at **Miss Rossi** (Almond Bay, tel. 8/514-8327 or cell tel. 316/315-2350, COP$85,000 pp). There is one room with a double bed and a room with two twins, perfect for a small group.

Maracaibo

By far the most luxurious option on Providencia is ★ **Deep Blue** (Maracaibo Bay, tel. 8/514-8423, www.hoteldeepblue. com, COP$600,000 d). It has 13 rooms of various types, each with a view, and some with Jacuzzis. A deck with a small pool provides spectacular views of the water. There is no beach, and unless you plan on dining exclusively at their elegant restaurant, you will need to find transportation to get to other restaurants and beaches on the island. The friendly and professional staff can organize interesting day trips to nearby islands.

Located directly over the lapping waters on the eastern side of Providencia, **Posada Coco Bay** (Maracaibo, tel. 8/514-8903 or 8/514-8226, posadacocobay@gmail.com, www.posadacocobay.com, COP$180,000 d) is a small guesthouse with five comfortable rooms, three of which are on the water side. The other two (more spacious) options are across the street. You can go snorkeling just outside the hotel, and you can rent kayaks here, but there is no beach. You will have to rent a golf cart or *mula* to get to island restaurants and beaches.

Santa Isabel and Santa Catalina

Providencia is a mostly quiet and relaxed place, but Santa Catalina, a tiny island without

any motorized vehicles and just a handful of residents, is exponentially more so.

Posada Santa Catalina (tel. 8/514-8392 or cell tel. 310/842-3278, www.posadasanta-catalina.blogspot.com, COP$50,000 pp) uses solar panels for electricity, a rarity in the islands. This guesthouse offers five large rooms, with good beds, set amid fruit trees. The friendly owners grow the medicinal noni fruit here, as well as unusual herbs for teas; you might be able to try some.

Posada Villa Santa Catalina (tel. 8/514-8398 or cell tel. 311/257-3054, www.villa-santacatalina.com, COP$50,000 pp d) is a comfortable and clean option with air-conditioning, but it doesn't exude much charm. This guesthouse is next to the Sea Star restaurant.

★ **Posada Sunshine Paradise** (tel. 8/514-8208 or cell tel. 311/227-0333, COP$180,000 d) is a charming guesthouse surrounded by flower gardens, and has four clean rooms. A major selling point is the warm hospitality of the owner, Francisca.

The **Hotel Old Providence** (Santa Isabel, tel. 8/514-8691 or 8/514-8094, COP$100,000 d) is the only option in the "town" area of Santa Isabel. It's close to Santa Catalina and offers basic, comfortable rooms with air-conditioning. Breakfast is not provided.

INFORMATION AND SERVICES

There is a **tourist office** (Santa Isabel, tel. 8/514-8054, ext. 12, www.providencia.gov.co, 8am-noon and 2pm-6pm Mon.-Fri.) in the town area near the port. They may be able to assist with accommodations, including *posadas nativas* (guesthouses owned and operated by locals), and give you some maps. The town has a bank, an ATM, and an Internet café.

In case of an emergency the police can be reached at 112 or 8/514-8000. For medical emergencies, call 125.

Many hotels on the island sell *A Short History of Providence and San Andrés* (COP$30,000), by resident author Sam

Cuming. It's a good read for those interested in the mostly forgotten history of these tiny islands.

TRANSPORTATION

There are two ways to travel to Providencia: by plane or by fast catamaran boat service from San Andrés.

Satena (Centro Comercial New Point, Local 206, San Andrés, tel. 8/512-1403 or 8/514-9257, www.satena.com) offers two daily flights—one early-morning flight and one in the late afternoon—to Providencia's **Aeropuerto El Embrujo** (PVA), which is near the Parque Nacional Natural Old Providence McBean Lagoon. Charter flights are usually organized by **Decameron** (Colombian toll-free tel. 01/800-051-0765, www.decameron.co) from San Andrés to Providencia. All flights are on small propeller planes, and there are strict weight limitations. Passengers are only allowed 10 kilograms (22 pounds) in their checked baggage, and each passenger is required to be weighed upon check-in along with their carry-on bag, which makes for an amusing photo op. The average weight per passenger cannot exceed 80 kilograms (176 pounds), including luggage. The flight takes about 35 minutes.

The **Catamaran Sensation** (tel. 8/512-3675 or cell tel. 318/347-2336, www.catamaransanandresyprovidencia.com, COP$170,000 one-way, COP$300,000 round-trip) provides **fast boat service** between San Andrés and Providencia. The trip takes approximately four hours from San Andrés to Providencia (and three hours in the other direction). It provides service Sunday-Monday and Wednesday-Friday during low season. There is greater frequency during high season. Boats leave San Andrés at 8am from the Muelle Toninos and depart Providencia from the docks in Santa Isabel at 2:30pm. The catamaran service, while cheaper than air travel, often gets ghastly reviews due to the rough seas and resulting seasickness among the passengers. When the winds are strong and the waters are choppy between the two islands, especially between June and July and again in December and January, the ride can be extremely rough, requiring boat attendants to constantly circulate among the passengers to distribute seasickness bags. This is especially true on the San Andrés-to-Providencia leg. Waters are normally calmer traveling the other direction.

Taxis are expensive in Providencia, costing around COP$20,000 no matter where you go. *Mototaxis* (motorcycle taxis) are much cheaper and you can find them almost anywhere. You can also flag down passing vehicles and hitchhike (expect to pay a small fee). You can rent *mulas* (gasoline-powered golf carts) and motorbikes in Providencia. All hotels can arrange this. They cost around COP$120,000 for one day. Reputable rental agencies include **Renta Car y Motos Old Providence** (Santa Isabel, tel. 8/514-8369 or cell tel. 313/450-4833, 9am-6pm Mon.-Sat.) and **B&Q Providence Center Hans Bush Felipe** (cell tel. 311/561-1537, hours vary).

The Amazon and Los Llanos

Highlights

★ **San Martín de Amacayacu:** Experience life in this Ticuna village in the brimming-with-vitality Parque National Natural Amacayacu (page 403).

★ **Puerto Nariño:** No freeways, no traffic jams, no honking horns: In this eco-minded indigenous town overlooking the Río Loretoyacú, life is peaceful and the air is always pure (page 404).

★ **Lago Tarapoto:** Pink dolphins perform for you in their natural habitat, and you can finally overcome your long-held piranha-phobia by taking a dip in this serene lake surrounded by lush jungle near Puerto Nariño (page 405).

★ **Río Javari:** Spend a few days under the immense Amazon rainforest canopy at a spectacular eco-lodge (page 406).

★ **Caño Cristales:** Nature shows its psychedelic side at this stream of vibrant colors in the vast Llanos (page 411).

★ **Hacienda La Aurora:** Take a safari on horseback through this enormous cattle ranch-cum-nature reserve and be astounded by the abundant wildlife. If you're lucky, you may even come across an anaconda (page 413).

The Amazon and Los Llanos cover the eastern two-thirds of the country, a vast territory with very little population.

Topographically they are the same: low-lying undulating terrain that is periodically flooded. But because of soil and climate, they have evolved different vegetation: dense rainforest in the Amazon and lush tropical savannas in Los Llanos. The main draws in both the Amazon and Los Llanos are the unique natural landscapes and the magnificent wildlife inhabiting them.

A trip to the Amazon is a highlight not only of any visit to Colombia, but a highlight in any person's life. The survival of this vast ecosystem, the preservation of which is by no means assured, is of great importance to humanity. Learning about its variety of plants and animals, how it acts to stabilize the world's climate, how indigenous people managed to make a home there for thousands of years without disturbing its balance, and how modern civilization is threatening to destroy it is fascinating. Long after an introduction to Amazonia, one can't help reflecting on its significance for all of humanity.

This vast terrain of undulating hills and savannas, with large patches of forest, abounds with wildlife: *chigüiros* (capybaras), deer, armadillos, sloths, anteaters, monkeys, anacondas, and an infinity of birds. Sadly, advancing human settlement and hunting have decimated much of the animal population, but at places like Hacienda La Aurora you can view this wondrous fauna in all its glory.

The Llanos is synonymous with cattle ranching and the cowboy way of life. If you are not squeamish, viewing traditional cattle-ranching activities as they have been done for centuries by *llaneros* (plainsmen), such as herding and branding calves, is an essential Llanos experience. Finally, the Llanos is home to a natural wonder not to be found anywhere else in the world: the vivid red, purple, yellow, and green streams of Caño Cristales in the southern extreme of the remote Serranía de la Macarena.

PLANNING YOUR TIME

Traversing the Amazon and Los Llanos entails long-distance travel, mostly point to point

---

Previous: cattle in Los Llanos; San Martín de Amacayacu. **Above:** capybaras.

The Amazon and Los Llanos

MAP AREA

COLOMBIA

PERU

Bogotá

Sogamoso
Paz de Ariporo
Arauca
Yopal
Puerto Casanare
Montañas del Totumo
Villavicencio
HACIENDA LA AURORA
Los Llanos

Rio Meta
Rio Casanare
Rio Arauca

PNN La Macarena
La Macarena
CAÑO CRISTALES
Guaviare
PNN El Tuparro

Rio Guayabero
Rio Guaviare
Rio Ariari
Rio Vichada

Mitú
Rio Inírida
Puerto Inírida

Rio Caquetá
Rio Apaporis
Rio Guaviare

Rio Orinoco

Puerto Carreño

VENEZUELA

BRAZIL

Rio Putumayo

PNN Amacayacu
Leticia

Rio Amazonas

To Iquitos

RÍO JAVARI

Reserva Natural Heliconia

Reserva Natural Palmari

BRAZIL.

PERU

COLOMBIA

Caballococha

Puerto Nariño
Lago Tarapoto
LAGO TARAPOTO
PUERTO NARIÑO
Rio Loretoyacu

Rio Amazonas

Rio Amacayacu

Parque Nacional Natural Amacayacu
SAN MARTÍN DE AMACAYACU

Mocagua
Calanoa
Macedonia

Rio Purité

Santa Sofía
Isla de los Micos
Marashá
Puerto Alegría

Nazareth

Rio Amazonas

Benjamin Constant

Santa Rosa Isla (Peru)
Leticia
Victoria Regia
Tabatinga (Brazil)

BRAZIL.

To Manaus

0   10 km
0   10 mi

© AVALON TRAVEL

from Bogotá by airplane, and is therefore more expensive. To visit the Amazon, at least five days are required, and more if you want to spend some time in a nature reserve in the rainforest. The destinations in Los Llanos—Caño Cristales and Hacienda La Aurora—could be done in three days, though ideally you would want to spend more time there.

Though the Amazon rainforest covers about one-third of the country east of the Andes and south of the Río Guaviare, the most practical way to visit it is from the Amazon port city of Leticia, which has a multitude of options and ecotourism operators. From Leticia to the southeast are jungle lodges in Brazil along the Río Javari, and toward the northwest there are many easy-to-access points of interest up to the town of Puerto Nariño. For the time being, the rest of the Colombian Amazon simply does not have even the minimum infrastructure to accommodate an independent traveler, and the region may be unsafe.

The great eastern plains of Colombia, Los Llanos and the Orinoquía region, which comprise a further third of the country east of the Andes and north of the Río Guaviare, are the least explored region of the country. The reason is simply a lack of infrastructure, along with, until recently, security concerns.

The Amazon

Covering an expanse of 8.2 million square kilometers (3.2 million square miles), the Amazon rainforest is the largest humid tropical forest in the world. Rainforests are important because of the enormous biodiversity they sustain. And among rainforests, the New World rainforests are the most biodiverse. In fact, the Amazon jungle is home to one-tenth of all species on Earth, though it occupies only 1.6 percent of the world's surface. It holds more than 40,000 plant species, 3,000 fish species, 1,300 bird species, 428 mammal species, and 380 reptile species. By contrast, all of Canada, which occupies a surface larger than the Amazon rainforest, has 3,270 plant species, 1,100 fish species, 838 bird species, 188 reptile species, and 180 mammal species. Rainforests are also important as the world's main "lungs," sucking in vast amounts of carbon dioxide through photosynthesis. Their ongoing destruction means the loss of invaluable biodiversity and increased warming.

The formation of the Amazon basin started about 180 million years ago, in the Jurassic era, when the westerly drifting American Continental Plate (South America) collided with the Nazca Plate (under the Pacific Ocean), forming the Andes. Water flowing eastward down the mountains accumulated in a vast freshwater lake that was hemmed in on the east by old mountainous formations (now the Guyana and Brazilian highlands). Large amounts of sediments were deposited, forming the basis for the Amazon's undulated topography. Around 28 million years ago, the water broke through the eastern mountain barrier and started flowing east into the Atlantic, forming the Amazon drainage basin.

The Amazon River (Río Amazonas), which measures about 6,400 kilometers (4,000 miles) in length, is fed by more than 1,000 tributaries. Though Colombia only has 180 kilometers (112 miles) on the Amazon River itself, several of its major rivers originate and flow through the Colombian Amazon region into the mighty river, including the Putumayo and the Caquetá. It is estimated that one-fifth of all the water that runs off the Earth's surface flows through this basin. The gradient is very slight: Leticia, which is more than 2,000 kilometers (1,200 miles) from the mouth of the river, stands at an elevation of 96 meters (315 feet). During the annual flood, lasting from November to April, the river can rise as much as 16 meters (53 feet), submerging large sections of the jungle. Average river velocity is

1.5 kilometers per hour (0.9 miles per hour), though it increases slightly with the flooding.

The topography of the Amazon basin consists of two distinct but intermingled areas: *terra firme,* the undulated lands that are above the highest flood point (which comprise two-thirds of the surface of the basin), and *varzea,* floodplains along the main rivers, which can extend up to 50 kilometers (30 miles) from the river. *Varzea,* rich in sediments transported by the rivers, is where most human activity is concentrated.

There are two distinct types of rivers in the Amazon region: the predominant white rivers, which carry sediments down from the Andes, and the black rivers, which originate in the Guyanese and Brazilian highlands that were long ago denuded of soil due to erosion. As these waters travel through the flooded forest, they pick up pigments that give them their characteristic black color. *Igapó* is the name given to jungles flooded by blackwater rivers. The largest of the black rivers, and the largest tributary of the Amazon, is the Río Negro, called *Río Guainía* in Colombia. It flows into the Amazon at Manaus, Brazil, creating the extraordinary *encontro das aguas,* where white and black waters flow side by side for several kilometers until they mix.

The forest itself has a complex, layered structure. Towering trees, held up by complex buttresses at the base of the trunks, soar 40 meters (130 feet) high, forming the jungle's canopy. Occasionally, trees known as *emergentes* rise above the canopy to a height of 60 meters (200 feet). (According to a Ticuna myth, a giant fallen ceiba tree is the origin of the Río Amazonas.) The canopy, flooded by sunlight, is full of plant and animal life; if you don't suffer from vertigo, a climb up to the canopy is an unforgettable experience. Below the canopy, shade-tolerant species of trees and plants comprise the underbrush (*sotobosque*) and support many epiphytes (plants that live on others), such as orchids and bromeliads. Large networks of vines entangle the growth.

The waters of the Amazon are home to more than 1,500 species of fish, including the endangered pirarucu, one of the largest freshwater fishes on Earth, and notorious meat-eating piranha. They are also home to dolphins, both pink and gray. Pink dolphins evolved separately and have horizontal neck mobility that allows them to navigate the flooded forest easily, while gray dolphins are distant relations of the seafaring kind. Other aquatic mammals include manatees and *nutrias* (otters). There are dozens of species of

a rainy trip on the Amazon

Explorers in the Amazon

The first Europeans to travel to the Amazon were Spanish conquistadors Gonzalo Pizarro (half-brother of Francisco Pizarro, the infamous conqueror of Peru) and Francisco de Orellana. In 1541 they headed down the Río Napo in present-day Ecuador to search for the mythical "Land of Cinnamon." Pizarro, frustrated, turned back after one year. Orellana followed the course of the Napo, eventually floating down the entire course of the Amazon to its mouth at the Atlantic. Reportedly, he was attacked by women warriors and hence the region came to be named after the Amazons of Greek mythology.

During the colonial period, the Spaniards largely ignored the region because there were no ready sources of riches. French naturalist Charles Marie de la Condamine was the first European scientific explorer to visit the region. In 1743, he traversed the entire basin, discovering, among other things, quinine and latex (for rubber). Another notable explorer was Alexander von Humboldt, who visited the Casiquiare Canal, which links the Río Orinoco and Río Negro, in 1800. It is in southern Venezuela.

turtles, alligators, lizards, snakes, and frogs. Land-faring mammals include deer, ant-eaters, armadillos, tapirs, jaguars, ocelots, and pumas, though sightings of these large cats are quite rare. The trees support sloths, squirrels, and many species of monkeys and bats. With more than 3,000 species of birds, the Amazon is truly a bird-watcher's paradise. During the floods, a canoe ride through the partially submerged trees will allow you to spot a variety of birds, including herons, kingfishers, ducks, woodpeckers, oropendolas, kiskadees, and hawks. Finally, there are innumerable insects, including giant leaf-cutting ants, as well as centipedes and scorpions.

To truly get a sense of the place, you need to get into the jungle, either by doing a trek or taking canoe rides in the flooded jungle. Then, the small details that make up this wonderland will come into focus: a ray of sun shining through the canopy; a massive, 40-meter-high ceiba tree; a vine that has wound itself around a tree like a boa constrictor; an orange mushroom popping up from a fallen tree, accelerating its final stage of decay; a single bright blue butterfly that crosses your path momentarily and then flutters away; a leaf as big as your head floating down to the ground; a whimsical song from a bird somewhere above in the canopy.

History

During the 20th century, settlement was mostly limited to a swath of jungle in the Caquetá and Putumayo departments near the Andes. There, oil and plentiful land attracted settlers from the interior of the country. However, the sheer inaccessibility of most of the Colombian jungle has spared the type of development seen in Brazil. During the drug wars of the 1990s and early 2000s, coca cultivation spread deeper into the jungle in the departments of Caquetá, Putumayo, Guaviare, and Vaupés, bringing along the FARC, and Leticia became a center for drug trafficking. At present much of the Amazonian drug business appears to have shifted to the Peruvian side of the river.

Climate

It is always muggy in the Amazon, and rarely is there a breeze to provide some relief to the heat. The border town of Leticia reports an average 85 percent humidity year-round with an average temperature of 25.8°C (78.4°F). The region has one dry season, which used to run June-August but, due to climate change, now extends into September or even October, and one rainy season, January-May. In August it can rain as little as 10 days per month. During the dry season, rivers shrink, creating beaches, and trees and shrubs appear in

The Peruvian Amazon Company

The Colombian section of the Amazon was largely untouched until the mid-19th century, when quinine and then rubber extraction attracted Colombian and Peruvian adventurers. Vast tracts of land with rubber trees and plentiful indigenous labor seemed like a perfect combination to make a fortune. In 1901, Julio César Arana, a Peruvian *cauchero* (rubber baron), founded the Casa Arana, a company that operated a ruthless system of rubber extraction based on torture and slavery. The company, later known as the Peruvian Amazon Company and headquartered in London, operated out of La Chorrera on the Río Putumayo. A visiting American, W. E. Hardenburg, witnessed the horrors and in 1909 published a damning article in the British magazine *Truth*. This prompted the British government to order an inquiry, which uncovered the terrible conditions. In 1912, Parliament opened an investigation, which cleared the company's British board of directors of all responsibility in the atrocities. At the same time they determined that over 32,000 Huitoto people had been murdered or worked to death during a five-year period. Huitoto leaders estimate that over 80,000 were killed between 1912 and 1929.

The Peruvian Amazon Company was liquidated in 1916, but, incredibly, Arana continued operations through the 1930s. It was not until 2012 that the Colombian government formally apologized to the indigenous people for these atrocities in a letter by President Santos at a ceremony in La Chorrera commemorating the 100th anniversary of the genocide.

parts of the jungle that during the rainy season are hidden under water.

During the rainy season, water falls from the skies and pours down from the Andes into the mighty river, and canoes become the only means of getting from point A to point B in the jungle. You can glide in canoes through the treetops, an unforgettable experience. Ponchos, rubber boots, and insect repellent are especially critical during the rainy season.

Environmental Threats

Unfortunately, this diverse ecosystem is under severe threat. Over the past 40 years, 20 percent of the Amazon jungle has been destroyed. If strong measures are not taken, half of what remains could be destroyed within the next few decades. The main causes of the destruction (in order of importance) are cattle ranching, agriculture, dams, and illegal mining. The main means for its destruction are roads. Without these, human encroachment is limited to the borders of navigable rivers. Voracious, short-sighted development in Brazil, where road development has been greatest, is the main cause of the destruction of this wonderland. Though the Brazilian authorities tout decreasing levels of deforestation, the roads crisscrossing the jungle have made irreparable damage inevitable. Significant deforestation has also occurred along the Andes piedmont, especially in the headwaters of the Caquetá and Putumayo Rivers in Colombia, where illegal coca cultivation has been one of the main culprits.

There is alarming evidence that, as deforestation progresses, the Amazon ecosystem is breaking down and will be unable to sustain itself. With deforestation comes lower evaporation and rainfall. As the forest dries up, it may become prone to fires (which it is not currently), changing the overall dynamics. The Amazon has not yet reached that scary "tipping point" after which it cannot sustain itself, but vastly reduced measured rainfall points in that direction.

Though the Colombian section of the Amazon rainforest represents only 10 percent of the total, it is the best preserved, due to a dearth of roads, and it's the most likely to be preserved thanks to enlightened policies. From 1986 to 1990, President Virgilio Barco transferred 163,000 square kilometers (63,000 square miles—twice the surface of Austria or 15 percent of Colombia) to national parks and indigenous *resguardos* (land

Border Disputes

During the 19th and early 20th centuries, the border between Ecuador, Peru, and Colombia was a matter of dispute. In 1922, Colombia and Peru signed the Salomón-Lozano Treaty, settling their common border at the expense of Ecuador. In 1932, a group of Peruvian civilians and some soldiers occupied Leticia. It is not clear whether the Peruvian government supported this attack. The occupation of Leticia led to a war in which both countries scrambled to get troops to this remote area. In 1932, Peru took the remote town of Tarapacá. In 1933, Colombia sent a fleet up the Amazon (including two new warships purchased from France), retook Tarapacá, and captured the Peruvian town of Güeppi. As troops from both countries were preparing for a major confrontation, the League of Nations brokered a truce on May 24, 1932. This was the first time that the League, precursor to the United Nations, actively intervened in a dispute between two countries. On June 19, Peru returned Leticia to Colombia.

collectively owned by indigenous groups) and protected areas. Predio Putumayo, the largest *resguardo*, measures 59,000 square kilometers (23,000 square miles), the size of Costa Rica. Subsequent governments have continued to expand the protected areas, and now at least 65 percent of all the Colombian Amazon is a protected area, either through the system of national parks or through indigenous *resguardos*.

The 1991 constitution enshrined significant rights for Colombia's indigenous peoples, adding further protections. Though the threat of illegal logging and mining is ever present, particularly due to the presence of valuable rare earth minerals, Colombia seems to have taken successful steps to preserve a large section of one of the world's most important ecosystems.

In 2013, the Colombian government took a positive step by more than doubling the size of its Parque Nacional Natural Serranía de Chiribiquete, in the Amazon departments of Caquetá and Guaviare, to over 28,000 square kilometers (11,000 square miles). It is the largest national park in Colombia.

LETICIA

Leticia, the capital city of the Amazonas department, is the southernmost city in Colombia, and it sits on the northern side of the Río Amazonas at the convergence of Colombia with Brazil and Peru. It is 1,100 kilometers (700 miles) southeast of Bogotá. The closest Colombian town of any significance is Puerto Nariño, 87 kilometers (54 miles) to the northwest.

Visitors come to Leticia to experience the jungle. This border town of 40,000 doesn't have much in the way of charm, and it's clogged with buzzing motorbikes. Ecotourism is the future for Leticia, and more Colombians and visitors from abroad are discovering the area.

A handful of sights in town and along Carretera Los Kilómetros will keep you occupied for a couple of days, and there are comfortable accommodations options. But best of all, the jungle is at Leticia's doorstep, and the Río Amazonas—a busy waterway serving hamlets, jungle lodges, indigenous reservations, and rough-and-tumble towns—is always at the ready to take you there. Within minutes of arriving, you can climb up to your treehouse lodging, slide on a pair of black rubber boots for your first jungle hike, or sit down with Huitoto indigenous people in their *maloca* (community house).

ORIENTATION

Leticia borders the Brazilian town of Tabatinga to the east. Isla de Santa Rosa, Peru, is an island in the river to Leticia's south. Just to the north of the city the town abruptly ends and the rainforest takes over.

Leticia is laid out on a grid that is easy to

figure out. The airport is north of town on Avenida Vásquez Cobo, which turns into Carrera 10, one of the main drags in town. *Carreras* run north-south with *calles* going from east to west. The *malecón* (also known as the Muelle Turístico), from where all boats depart, is on the eastern side of town at the end of Calle 8. Carretera Los Kilómetros, also called Vía a Tarapaca, leads to the nature preserves of Mundo Amazónico, Tanimboca, and Cerca Viva. There are some Huitoto settlements close to those attractions, and then the road abruptly stops, surrendering to the jungle.

Sights

The best sights in Leticia are free. Occupying just one room in the bright pink **Banco de la República** building, the **Museo Etnográfico de Leticia** (Cra. 11 No. 9-43, tel. 8/592-7783, 8:30am-6pm Mon.-Fri., 9am-1pm Sat., www.banrepcultural.org/leticia, free) provides a good introduction to the ways of life of some of the main indigenous people who inhabit the Colombian Amazon region, including the Ticunas, the Huitotos, and the Yukunas. Colorful feather crowns made of *guacamaya* (macaw) feathers and descriptions of *chagras* (islands of small vegetable plots in the middle of the jungle) and *malocas* (community houses) are part of the exhibit. Explanations are provided in both Spanish and English. Sometimes art exhibits and other events are held in the building as well. A small **public library** is also in the building, and it is a quiet place to work, read, or check email; it operates the same hours as the museum.

The **Parque Santander** (between Cras. 10-11 and Clls. 10-11), better known as **Parque de los Loros,** is a quiet place where unoccupied locals go for a brief reprieve from the intense midday sun. That is, it's quiet until around 5:30pm each evening, at which time thousands of *loros* (parrots) gather in the trees, creating a cacophonous racket. Then, at precisely 6pm, the Colombian national anthem blares from loudspeakers from the military base facing the park, and people stop what they are doing and stand at attention. The birds, however, have no such respect. They won't quiet down for anyone. The *loros* have not always been here and are not native to the area.

The **Muelle Turístico** (Cra. 11 at Cl. 8), also known as the *malecón,* is a busy port. During dry season, the channel becomes too shallow for the express boats (bound for points on the Río Amazonas) to navigate, and passengers must take a *peque-peque* (motorized dugout canoe) to a *balsa* (floating dock) in the river to embark. At this port, tourists await their river tours while villagers, hailing from the very places the tourists will visit, arrive in the city to stock up on supplies. For any trip along the Amazon, including to the Peruvian town of Santa Rosa, you'll leave from here.

To learn about some of the medicinal plants, fruits, and trees you will see in the Amazon, a visit to the **Mundo Amazónico** (Km. 7 Vía a Tarapacá/Carretera Los Kilómetros, tel. 8/592-6087, cell tel. 321/472-4346, www.mundoamazonico.com, 8am-3pm daily, COP$10,000-36,000) is a must. In the park you can take a walk among exotic fruit trees (like *copoazú*) found in the area, learn about indigenous farming techniques, see some medicinal plants found in the rainforest, and observe unusual fish, reptiles, and amphibians in the aquarium and terrarium area. Taking public transportation to the park is easy. Look for a green Kilometer 11 bus (not headed toward Lagos) departing from Parque Orellana (Cra. 11 between Clls. 7-8). Tell the bus driver you'd like to be dropped off at Mundo Amazónico. From where the bus lets you off, it's a 10- to 15-minute walk to the park entrance. The ride costs COP$2,000 by bus; via *mototaxi* it costs COP$15,000.

Reserva Natural Cerca Viva (Km. 10.7 Vía a Tarapaca/Carretera Los Kilómetros, cell tel. 310/814-9908, 310/814-9907, or 311/564-6062, oatamayos@hotmail.com, 8am-4pm daily, COP$51,000 pp for groups of up to three people, COP$15,000 pp for groups over three people) is a nature preserve and community of Colombians from different parts of the country that comprises 30 hectares of jungle and river where visitors can take a 1.5-hour guided nature walk on various paths through the jungle. The preserve originated with Valeria Guarnizo, an Englishwoman who arrived in Colombia as a traveler and never left. She is also a licensed Reiki practitioner, a therapy available to visitors (COP$50,000). Contact the reserve at least a day or so in advance to coordinate a visit.

Near Leticia are the **Lagos Yahuarcaca,** a group of some 22 lakes. A community group called **Painü** (Km. 4 Vía Los Lagos, cell tel. 314/460-2422 or 314/493-3863, www.painu-amazon.wordpress.com, painuamazon@gmail.com, COP$100,000 half day for two people), made up of young people from the indigenous community of San Sebastián, organizes canoe excursions through the lakes, with the possibility of other activities such as piranha fishing and swimming. Painü will assist with transportation to the lakes from Leticia, but be sure to contact them in advance to arrange this.

The **Reserva Natural Tanimboca** (Vía a Tarapaca/Carretera Los Kilómetros, office Cra. 10 No. 11-69, tel. 8/592-7679, www.tanimboca.com) is a nature reserve and the best place to gain a real appreciation for the Amazonian jungle. Once there you can marvel at the stunning *maloca* (community house), take a jungle walk, kayak, and experience the jungle from above by canopying. Tanimboca also organizes excellent multiday tours of the Amazon region.

Festivals and Events

In terms of exuberant Brazilian parties, the **Boi Bumba Festival,** which takes place in Tabatinga and other Amazonian towns in June each year, is considered second only to Rio's Carnaval. This festival is mostly a spirited samba competition between two groups, one clad in blue and the other in red.

The **Festival de Confraternidad Amazónica** has been going strong since 1987 and is a celebration of Amazonian culture and friendship between the neighboring countries of Colombia, Brazil, and Peru. It usually takes place July 15-20 in Leticia.

The **Festival Pirarucú de Oro** takes place over three days at the end of November and beginning of December. Named in honor of the enormous pirarucu river fish, this is a cultural festival with numerous musical and dance performances at the amphitheater in Parque Orellana (Cra. 11 between Clls. 7-8) in Leticia.

Shopping

The **Mercado Municipal** (Cl. 8 at Cra. 12, 7am-3pm daily) has many food and handicraft stalls.

The **Museo Uirapuru** (Cl. 8 No. 10-35, tel. 8/592-7056, 9am-noon and 3pm-7pm Mon.-Sat., 9am-noon Sun.) is more handicraft store than museum, although you can look at various river creatures in aquariums in the back. Traditional medicines are also sold here.

Recreation

TOURS

Tour companies based in Leticia or Bogotá offer a wide range of packages, from day trips to multiday jungle excursions. Some hotels and hostels can also offer these tourism activities, but they should be a registered travel agency to do so legally—ask to see their certificate.

Ecodestinos (Cl. 8 No. 7-99, Local 2, tel. 8/592-4816; Cra. 70H No. 127A-72, Bogotá, tel. 1/608-8031, www.ecodestinos.com.co) is affiliated with Aviatur, one of the top travel agencies in Colombia and popular with Colombian tourists. It offers various package tours of the Amazon, including the Amazonas Selva y Río tour, which starts at COP$598,000 per person and includes two nights' accommodation in Leticia, all meals, and tours to Puerto Nariño, Lago Tarapoto, Parque Amacayacu, and Ticuna villages. The website has an extensive listing of options, which can be booked online. There are also some day-trip excursions, such as kayak tours (COP$75,000 pp) near Leticia.

Tanimboca (tel. 8/592-7679, www.tanimboca.org) is affiliated with the Reserva Natural Tanimboca in the jungle just outside of Leticia. Package tours with Tanimboca include jungle walks, a couple of nights in its fabulous treehouses or tree tents at the reserve, and overnight visits to Puerto Nariño and to Reserva Natural Marashá in Peru. Tanimboca offers mostly private or small group tours. For a stay of five days and four nights, including activities, expect to pay around COP$1,300,000 per person. Tanimboca can also arrange private one-day tours on the river. This is a highly recommended and reputable agency.

Selvaventura (Cra. 9 No. 6-85, tel. 8/592-3977, cell tel. 311/287-1307, www.selvaventura.org) is a reputable tour operator that offers several different excursions, all highlighted on its website, including a three-night trip through the jungle that visits an indigenous village and includes a kayak tour. You'll sleep on a platform in a tree, in a tent in the jungle, and in an indigenous *maloca*. Selvaventura is affiliated with the hostel La Casa del Kurupira and shouldn't be confused with Selva Tours, which is from the Colombian all-inclusive mega hotel On Vacation.

Food

Leticia is the place to sample some unusual Amazonian dishes. The standard Amazon meal includes fried fish, cassava, rice, *patacones* (fried plantains), and perhaps a small salad. Pirarucu is the king of fish around here. It is one of the largest fish in the world, reaching up to three meters (10 feet) long and weighing 350 kilograms (770 pounds). This fish is threatened, and regional governments have banned its fishing and consumption from November to March. You may not see it in the wild, although it does pop up to the surface to breathe every 45 minutes. You have a reasonably good chance, however, of hearing it: It makes a deep bellowing sound that echoes across the river. A popular dish here is the *patarasca*, which is two types of fish,

usually *dorado* and *pintado*, grilled with herbs and vegetables in banana leaves. This is accompanied by a juice such as *copoazú*, acai, or the ever-popular Brazilian beer.

Amazon fusion is on the menu at **El Cielo** (Cl. 7 No. 6-50, cell tel. 312/351-0427, 6pm-11pm Mon., Wed., and Fri., 11am-5pm Sun., COP$20,000), the most ambitious restaurant in town. Here the specialty is pizza made from cassava flour, served to your candlelit table. Cocktails are fine, too.

The **Decameron Decalodge Tikuna** (Cra. 11 No. 6-11, www.decameron.com, daily) is the best culinary option in town. Here you'll dine under a gigantic green anaconda-like snake with eyes that light up. There's even a vegetarian menu.

With dusty Amazonian handicrafts adorning its walls, **Tierras Amazónicas** (Cl. 8 No. 7-50, hours vary Tues.-Sun., COP$20,000) is a required stop for most hungry travelers. Some of the unusual dishes you can order here include *chicharrón de pirarucú,* which are sort of like fish nuggets, and pirarucu steamed in banana leaf. Big lemonades (to complement the big food portions) here hit the spot.

El Abuelo (Cra. 11 at Cl. 7, no phone, set lunches COP$12,000) is a popular place with locals and those on a budget. There is usually a buffet, offering a variety of dishes. The upstairs turns into a rocking watering hole at night.

Facing the Parque Santander, **Casa del Pan** (Cl. 11 No. 10-20, 6:30am-11pm Mon.-Sat.) is a place for a carb fix before or after a day in the jungle. It also serves refreshing lemonades and juices.

Accommodations

Very good accommodations options for all budgets are available in and around Leticia. Staff are generally quite helpful, and can suggest (if not organize) a jungle adventure. Many travelers arrive in Leticia and leave a bag with the hotel in order to lighten their load as they explore the region, picking it up before leaving Leticia. Staff can also assist with making reservations for river travel, from the express boat to Puerto Nariño to longer journeys such as the famous slow-boat trip to Manaus.

Run by the same folks as tour operator Selvaventura, **La Casa del Kurupira** (Cra. 9 No. 6-100, 2nd fl., cell tel. 311/287-1307, www.casadelkurupira.com, COP$25,00 dorm, COP$70,000 d) offers clean and comfortable rooms (some private) and spacious dormitory rooms for budget travelers. It's a laid-back place.

A welcome budget addition is **Leticia's Guest House** (Cra. 11 No. 4-06, COP$25,000 dorm, COP$50,000 d), which is located past the Decameron Decalodge Tikuna on the road to Tabatinga. It's a quiet place with about six rooms, a small but refreshing pool, and ample outdoor space.

The **Hotel Anaconda** (Cra. 15 No. 93-75, tel. 8/218-0125, www.hotelanaconda.com.co, COP$160,000 pp) was one of the first hotels in Leticia and has been in operation for years. The 50 air-conditioned rooms are large, there is wireless Internet in the lobby, and a restaurant is on-site. It's in the heart of town and it has a big pool and a poolside bar. If you're not staying here and want to cool off at the pool, you can get a day pass (COP$12,000). Note that per-person room rates decrease as the number of guests increases.

An excellent choice in Leticia is the friendly and professionally run ★ **Amazon B&B** (Cl. 12 No. 9-30, tel. 8/592-4981, www.theamazonbb.com, COP$210,000 d). It's on a quiet street away from the bustle of the city but is still within easy walking distance to restaurants and services. It's a popular place for a good rest before or after a few days in the jungle. There's no air-conditioning in the six *cabañas* (they have fans), but they are modern and tastefully decorated. Breakfast is included, and quite good. The bed-and-breakfast also offers Spanish classes and can arrange all sorts of excursions.

The crème de la crème of hotels in Leticia is the all-inclusive ★ **Decameron Decalodge Tikuna** (Cra. 11 No. 6-11, tel. 8/592-6600, www.decameron.com, COP$520,000 d). It's a spacious place with a very good open-air restaurant. Facilities are nice: a swimming pool, a *maloca* (community house), and tasteful *cabañas* complete with comfy beds and hammocks. The hotel organizes excursions and activities, so you don't have to plan anything. Internet access is expensive here.

At the ★ **Reserva Natural Tanimboca** (Vía a Tarapaca/Carretera Los Kilómetros, office Cra. 10 No. 11-69, tel. 8/592-7679, www.tanimboca.com, COP$220,000 d), you can spend the night 12 meters (40 feet) high in a treehouse in the canopy, where it's just you and thousands of chatty jungle creatures. These small thatched houses are comfortable and come equipped with a toilet. You can also sleep in a hammock in the nature reserve's *maloca* (community house), or spend the night in a tree tent hovering aboveground. Included in your stay is a nocturnal jungle walk. Local cuisine, mostly grilled fish, is served at the restaurant. Tanimboca also organizes a variety of tours.

The **Omshanty Jungle Lodge** (Vía a Tarapaca/Carretera Los Kilómetros, cell tel. 311/489-8985, www.omshanty.com, COP$15,000 dorm, COP$55,000 d) is north of Leticia and offers clean dorm-style accommodations as well as private rooms. You can cook meals in the kitchen. The lodge can also organize stays in nearby indigenous communities. There is a locally run restaurant and traditional handicraft store, Las Aranas, across the street that sells interesting and authentic handicrafts made from *chambira* and *chambecua,* typical natural fibers. Efficient and inexpensive bus transportation is available.

Information and Services
SUPPLIES
Supermercado Hiper Kosto (Cl. 8 No. 9-31, tel. 8/592-8067, 9am-8pm daily) is a basic grocery store where you can stock up on jungle provisions and pick up bags of filtered drinking water that use less plastic than bottles.

Although many hotels and reserves will loan you a pair of rubber boots for your jungle trip, if you want to pick up some of your own you can do so at **Mercado Municipal** (Cl. 8 at Cra. 12, 7am-3pm daily).

VISAS AND OFFICIALDOM

To travel to Tabatinga, Brazil; Isla de Santa Rosa, Peru; or for stops at Peruvian villages on the way to Puerto Nariño, there is no need for immigration formalities, but carry your passport just in case. If traveling to destinations in the interior of Brazil or Peru from Leticia, you must obtain an exit stamp at **Migración Colombia** (3 km north of town, tel. 8/592-4562) at the airport.

Once you get your passport stamped at the airport, if you're continuing to Manaus, Brazil, you will need to present your papers at the Brazilian **Policía Federal** (650 Av. da Amizade, Tabatinga, 7am-noon and 2pm-6pm Mon.-Fri.), near the Tabatinga hospital. If continuing to Peru, get your Peruvian entry stamp at the police office in Isla de Santa Rosa, which is on the main path through town.

At the **Brazilian Consulate** (Cra. 9 No. 9-73, Leticia, tel. 8/592-7530, 8am-noon Mon.-Fri.), you can obtain a visa for Brazil, which is necessary for U.S. and Canadian citizens planning an overnight stay in that country. You must present a yellow fever vaccination card and an onward airline ticket. Processing time is 2-3 days. For U.S. citizens, the visa costs around US$160. It may be easier to obtain the visa at the consulate in Bogotá (Cl. 93 No. 14-20, 8th fl., tel. 1/635-1694, 9am-noon Mon.-Fri.). No visa is required to visit Peru for less than 90 days. The **Peruvian Consulate** (Cl. 11 No. 5-32, Leticia, tel. 8/592-3947, 8am-2pm Mon.-Fri.) in Leticia can assist with further information.

HEALTH AND MEDICAL SERVICES

Colombian health authorities recommend yellow fever vaccination at least 10 days before arriving in the area. Malaria is very rare, but some visitors opt to take antimalarial pills before arrival and up until four weeks after departure from the region. These can be purchased in pharmacies across Colombia without a prescription. Wear light-colored, long-sleeved shirts, pants, and socks, especially during dawn and dusk, to prevent mosquito bites, and insist on mosquito nets if you are staying in the jungle.

The hospital in town is the **Hospital San Rafael** (Cra. 10 No. 13-78, tel. 8/592-7074). Report emergencies to the local **Policía Nacional** (Cra. 12-30, emergency line 112 or tel. 8/892-5060).

TOURIST INFORMATION

The **Fondo de Promoción Ecoturística del Amazonas** (Cl. 8 No. 9-75, tel. 8/592-4162, www.fondodepromocionamazonas.com, 8am-noon and 2pm-5pm Mon.-Fri., 8am-1pm Sat.) is the tourism office, and may be of help, especially with recommendations for certified guides.

MONEY

There are several Colombian banks in Leticia with **ATMs,** especially on Carrera 10 between Calles 7 and 10. This is the best (if not only) place in the region to get cash. Farther from Leticia, credit cards are rarely accepted and ATMs are nonexistent. Colombian currency is accepted in the entire Amazon region near Leticia, including in Brazil and Peru.

INTERNET ACCESS

Internet cafés can be found around town, and you will have no problem with access at hotels and hostels in Leticia—but don't expect to find Internet in lodges outside of town. In Leticia and throughout the region, smartphones seem to operate more slowly than simple cell phones. It may be difficult to get in touch with hotels or guides in the region, especially in the jungle communities along the river. Often the best means of communication is via Whatsapp, a commonly used smartphone messaging app.

Transportation
AIR

The Leticia airport is **Aeropuerto Internacional General Alfredo Vásquez Cobo** (LET, 3 km north of town). **Avianca** (tel. 1/401-3434, www.avianca.com), **LATAM** (tel. 745-2020, www.latam.com), and **VivaColombia** (tel. 1/743-3999, www.vivacolombia.co) fly here from Bogotá. **Satena** (tel. 1/605-2222, www.satena.gov.co) offers limited flights from Leticia to Amazonian locations La Chorrera, La Pedrera, and Tarapaca. **LCPerú** (Cra. 11 No. 6-106, tel. 8/592-5111, cell tel. 313/392-8950, www.lcperu.pe, gerencia@paraísoecologico.com.pe) has an evening flight to and from Iquitos, Peru, on Tuesdays and Saturdays. A decent restaurant is in the small airport.

Upon arrival in Leticia, you may be required to pay a tourism fee of around COP$21,000, for which you should receive a receipt. Taxis between town and the airport should cost about COP$10,000.

BOAT

All river transportation to **Puerto Nariño** departs from the **Muelle Turístico** (Tourist Wharf), the port in Leticia. There are daily boats to Puerto Nariño at 8am, 10am, and 2pm. The trip takes about 2.5 hours and costs COP$29,000 per person. Tickets for these boats can be obtained at the port in the Malecón Plaza Local 101, a shopping corridor facing the port. There are three agencies with offices there, and they take turns providing the Expresso service to Puerto Nariño: **Transportes Amazónicos** (tel. 8/592-5999, cell tel. 313/347-8091), **Líneas Amazonas II** (tel. 8/592-6711, cell tel. 311/532-0633), and **Expreso Unidos Tres Fronteras** (tel. 8/592-4687, cell tel. 311/452-6809). It's best to go in person to the offices the day before your trip. Alternatively, your hotel can make a reservation for you by phone or purchase the tickets on your behalf.

The **slow boats** to and from **Manaus,** Brazil, depart from the main port in **Tabatinga,** Brazil, at around 2pm on Wednesdays and Saturdays. The journey takes three days, and costs COP$210,000 for a hammock (which you must purchase in town beforehand) or COP$1,200,000 for a two-person cabin with air-conditioning. These prices include food on board. If you plan to sleep in

a hammock, try to board early to stake out a good place: Think ventilation. You may be allowed to board the boat up to a night before departure. Stock up on snacks and water, as the food is not great. The reverse journey upstream (from Manaus to Leticia) can also be made, but it takes six days. Weekly **fast boats** (30 hours) depart on Tuesdays and Fridays and cost COP$430,000. Be sure to obtain a departure stamp at the Leticia airport.

For travel to Iquitos, Peru, the boat operator companies **Transtur** (Rua Marechal Mallet No. 349, Tabatinga, tel. 97/8113-5239, www.transtursa.com, iquitostours@hotmail.com, 9am-noon and 2pm-6pm Mon.-Fri., 9am-1pm Sat.) and **Golfinho** (Av. Marechal Mallet No. 306, Tabatinga, tel. 97/3412-3186, 8:30am-12:30pm and 2:30-5:30pm Mon.-Fri., 10am-1pm Sat.) have offices in Tabatinga. Boats leave six days a week from Tabatinga, stopping at the Peruvian town of Isla de Santa Rosa, across from Leticia, for immigration purposes. The trip to Iquitos takes nine hours and costs COP$140,000. Departure time is 3:30am or 5:30am, depending on the boat company.

GETTING AROUND

Leticia is a small town; you can walk everywhere you'd like to go. Some hotels have rental bikes to explore the town and beyond. *Mototaxis* (motorcycle taxis) and *tuk-tuks* (three-wheeled *mototaxis*) are plentiful.

Sights along Vía a Tarapaca/Carretera Los Kilómetros can be reached by public buses (COP$3,000) that depart from Parque Orellana (Cra. 11 and Cl. 7).

ALONG THE RÍO AMAZONAS

Most visitors to the Colombian Amazon region travel on the great river northwest from Leticia, stopping at indigenous communities or nature reserves along the way, with many continuing onward to Puerto Nariño. About 84 percent of the Amazonas department consists of 22 *resguardos indígenas* (indigenous reservations); these reservations have been in existence since the colonial era, though it wasn't until the latter half of the 20th century that they would be formally recognized by Colombia. Along the Río Amazonas are several indigenous communities, with the Ticuna group predominant.

PRACTICALITIES

All travel agencies in Leticia can organize river excursions as a day trip or multiday guided adventure, but you can also travel on your own if you have minimal Spanish skills and some patience. This usually means taking the **Expresso boat** (8am, 10am, and 2pm daily, 2.5 hours, COP$29,000 pp), which operates between Leticia and Puerto Nariño three times every day. Buy tickets at the Malecón Plaza Local 101, a shopping corridor facing the port, also known as the Muelle Turístico (Tourist Wharf). There are three agencies with offices there, and they take turns providing the Expresso service: **Transportes Amazónicos** (tel. 8/592-5999, cell tel. 313/347-8091), **Líneas Amazonas II** (tel. 8/592-6711, cell tel. 311/532-0633), and **Expreso Unidos Tres Fronteras** (tel. 8/592-4687, cell tel. 311/452-6809). It's best to go in person to the offices the day before your trip.

You can also contract your own boat by going to Leticia's port; expect to pay up to COP$300,000 per boat. Before agreeing to a trip or activity, be sure to come to an agreement with your guide or boat captain on how much you are expected to pay, and what the price will include (stops to be made and duration of those stops). Note that high gasoline prices will make motorized water travel quite expensive. To keep expenses down, you can try to round up more people to go with you.

Tourists are often herded to a circuit of river stops, some of which are low on authenticity and responsibility.

The river is more scenic during the **rainy season** (Nov.-Mar.), as water levels climb to the tops of some trees, though in the **dry months** (Apr.-Oct.) you'll be astonished to see islands of beaches appear under blue skies in the middle of the Río Amazonas. Keep your eyes peeled for dolphins, both gray and pink, usually spotted in the early morning or late afternoon. Every once in a while, you'll pass a fisherman in a *peque-peque* (a type of dugout canoe) loaded down with bananas.

Reserva Natural Victoria Regia

Seven kilometers (four miles) and about a 15-minute boat ride west from Leticia,

lily pads at Reserva Natural Victoria Regia

Reserva Natural Victoria Regia

(COP$5,000) is a private reserve that is usually the first stop on the river. You can view large circular *Victoria amazonica* lily pads and their lovely white lotus flowers floating atop the water. These are some of the largest water plants in the world, and the leaves can measure up to 1.5 meters (5 feet) in diameter, with roots extending 7 meters (23 feet) below the water's surface. It's said that these plants are so strong they can support the weight of a small child (but don't test this theory out on your offspring). You can also marvel at a magnificent old ceiba tree farther along on the park walkway.

Puerto Alegría

Farther west, on the Peruvian side of the river, is the community of **Puerto Alegría** (10 km/6 miles west of Leticia). Here the attraction is exotic animals. When tourist boats show up at the community dozens of times each day, local women and children greet the visitors with all sorts of animals in hand: alligators, sloths, turtles. For a contribution you can be photographed holding several of the animals. Tourists are told that the animals are released into the wild after a period of time, but that seems hard to believe. Even if that is the case, they must have a hard time adjusting to their natural habitat after years in captivity, being held by humans day in and day out. You may find it disturbing how these creatures are used for human entertainment here. If you're on an organized tour but don't want to visit Puerto Alegría, you may wait on the boat while others visit the attraction.

Isla de los Micos

The **Isla de los Micos** (Monkey Island, COP$30,000) is the most popular tourist attraction on the river. It's about 40 kilometers (25 miles) west of Leticia. At this island, owned by the Colombian hotel chain Decameron, elevated walkways meander through the jungle, and with just a morsel of fruit in your hand, you'll make the monkeys go bananas. They'll proceed to climb all over you in hopes of a snack. The monkeys are not native to the island; they were brought here by controversial hotel owner and entrepreneur Mike Tsalickis in the 1970s. Up to 12,000 monkeys supposedly lived here at one point. It is a tourist trap, but it's hard to deny that kids love it.

Macedonia

The Ticuna village of **Macedonia** (COP$2,500) is a regular stop for tourist boats. As each boatload of visitors arrive, they are invited in to the *maloca* (community house), where a ceremonial dance is performed. Tourists are led onto the middle of the dance floor to the beat of a turtle shell drum. Around the *maloca* you can peruse an array of handicrafts at stalls set up by local women. A specialty is *palo de sangre* (bloodwood) carvings. Although touristy, it is nice that the community manages all the activities here, and all the income goes directly to them.

Reserva Calanoa

The jungle lodge ★ **Reserva Natural Calanoa** (Río Amazonas, 60 km/37 miles west of Leticia, cell tel. 311/842-4392, www.calanoaamazonas.com, COP$230,000 pp) offers understated Amazonian luxury at its finest. Guests stay in one of a handful of gorgeous cabins scattered amid the trees with views to the water and are served delicious food in the dining room. Activities offered include day- and nighttime canoe trips, bird- and dolphin-watching, and visits to local communities. Most activities are included in the price. Stopping here is generally for people who will be overnighting here, unless you contact the reserve in advance to organize a particular activity.

Fundación Maikuchiga

Fundación Maikuchiga (cell tel. 313/819-3461 or 313/397-1981, http://maikuchiga.blogspot.com, fundacionmaikuchiga@gmail.com) is a group that rescues and cares for dozens of primates, such as *churucos* (woolly monkeys), which are the largest monkeys in South America; red howlers; and brown capuchins. These animals have been injured, orphaned, or rescued from poor conditions in captivity in the Colombian Amazon, with the eventual goal that they will live freely in the jungle. Sara Bennett, a zoologist from New England, founded the group, and has since earned the title of "mother of the monkeys" along the Colombian Amazon. With involvement and support from the local Ticuna community, Bennett and her team have helped to protect the monkeys. The center comprises a solitary wooden house in the jungle, part of the Mocagua community's indigenous reservation on the banks of the Quebrada Matamata, a serpentine stream that forms part of the eastern boundary of the Parque Nacional Natural Amacayacu. Fundación Maikuchiga is a serious conservation and research center and is not especially geared toward tourists. However, they are usually happy to receive small groups of visitors (COP$120,000 required contribution). This must be arranged in advance, and it may be easier to coordinate this with the lodge Reserva Calanoa than with Fundación Maikuchiga directly. In addition, they are now offering visitors

the chance to participate in research activities (COP$2,000,000 for three-person group) over the course of three nights deep in the jungle.

Parque Nacional Natural Amacayacu

The prime, unspoiled plot of land known as **Parque Nacional Natural Amacayacu** (70 km/43 miles west of Leticia, tel. 1/353-2400, www.parquesnacionales.gov.co) covers some 300,000 hectares (740,000 acres). Its southern border is on the banks of the Amazon between the Río Amacayacu (River of Hammocks) and the Quebrada Matamata stream and extends north to the Río Cotuhe. It was declared a national park in 1975. The park is characterized by undulating hills, swamps, and an intricate network of streams. The highest point in the park reaches 200 meters (650 feet) above sea level. It is estimated that in the park are more than 5,000 plant species, 150 mammal species (including pink dolphins, tapirs, jaguars, manatees, and numerous primates), 500 species of birds, about 100 species of fish, and so on. Resident animals such as squirrel monkeys, sloths, wild boars, and jaguars are hard to spot in the park, and in the jungle in general.

Life abounds in the Parque Nacional Natural Amacayacu.

an artisan at the Ticuna community of San Martín de Amacayacu

If you are traveling by boat up the spectacular and serpentine Río Amacayacu, ask the captain to completely cut the engine at least once or twice during the journey, so that you can enjoy the incredible sounds of the jungle. When you float along in silence, hearing nothing but the calls of distant monkeys, shrieks of birds, or the constant hum of legions of frogs and insects, it is a magical experience. Boat drivers are usually in a hurry, so you'll have to ask them something like: *"Podemos parar aquí sin motor un minutico por favor?"* ("Would it be possible to stop here without the motor for a moment, please?").

Note: Each year much of the park is flooded during the rainy months of April and May. In 2012 it was a particularly wet season, resulting in extensive damage to park structures. The park has not since offered tourism services, but there are hopes it will once again open in the coming years. The Ticuna settlements of San Martín and Mocagua that lie within the boundaries of the park are still open and welcoming to visitors.

★ SAN MARTÍN DE AMACAYACU

Up the Río Amacayacu, within PNN Amacayacu, is the Ticuna community of **San Martín de Amacayacu** (70 km/43 miles northeast of Leticia, COP$5,000). The community has organized itself to receive tourists and offers jungle walks, canoe rides, and other activities such as handicrafts workshops in the community. The money from the entrance fee is used to pay for a kindergarten and other services. One of over 20 indigenous communities in and around Puerto Nariño, San Martín is considered one of the most traditional, and community members are committed to preserving their cultural identity. Plans were established by the Puerto Nariño municipal government to create a nine-kilometer (5.5-mile) wooden walkway, the **Sendero Turístico Ecovía,** to connect San Martín with Puerto Nariño. It is expected to be completed by mid-2017 and remains to be seen what the effect will be on the undisturbed jungle between the settlements and on the San Martin indigenous community.

Activities in San Martín include a visit to a *chagra* (traditional farm), visits with local artisans to observe how they make ceramics and woven handicrafts, and a jungle walk. Contact community elder Victor Ángel Pereira (cell tel. 310/911-9725) for assistance with accommodations, food, and activities. These activities can also be arranged with the lodge **Casa de Gregorio** (cell tel. 310/279-8147 or 311/201-8222, casagregorio@outlook.com). To get to San Martín directly, take the Expreso boat service from Leticia or Puerto Nariño to the Bocana Amacayacu settlement.

The ★ **Casa de Gregorio** (cell tel. 310/279-8147 or 311/201-8222, casagregorio@outlook.com, COP$180,000 pp) is a lodge run by a Ticuna-Dutch couple, Heike and José Gregorio. Heike arrived in San Martín as a doctoral student in agriculture sciences in 2004, and José is a Ticuna community leader. A stay at Casa de Gregorio provides visitors with a unique opportunity to discover the jungle and get to know Ticuna culture. They offer three basic yet comfortable rooms, and a deluxe cabin that costs COP$120,000. There are additional costs for meals (usually prepared by Heike) and guides. Although it is possible to come for a day trip, it's far better to stay at least 2-3 days. To get here, you can take a boat from Leticia (1.5 hours) for COP$24,000. These depart at 8am, 10am, and 1:30pm. Ask to be dropped off at the Bocana Amacayacu stop (not PNN Amacayacu). The return trip to Leticia costs COP$29,000. To get from Bocana Amacayacu to San Martín, you will need to arrange transportation with Casa de Gregorio (included in rate).

Another, more economical option in the community is the **Amacayacu Lodge** (cell tel. 311/251-3841 or 320/481-5817, COP$25,000). Its restaurant is open to all.

★ PUERTO NARIÑO

Upon arriving at the village of Puerto Nariño, atop a sloping hill overlooking the Río Loretoyacú, you'll wonder: Where are the motorbikes? Here in idyllic Puerto Nariño, there are no roads and no motorized vehicles. Environmentally minded town council members decided many years ago that they wanted Puerto Nariño to chart a different path than almost all other towns in Colombia, and for their efforts, this town was named the first tourism-sustainable town in the country by the Colombian government. Here, roads are palm-lined sidewalks that connect all the neighborhoods of this community. Puerto Nariño is so peaceful, you'll probably want to linger awhile.

Sights

To get a bird's-eye view of Puerto Nariño and the rivers and jungle beyond, climb the steps to the **Mirador Nai-pata** (until 6pm daily, COP$3,000). This tall treehouse (what *nai-pata* means in Ticuna) is the perfect place to be at dusk. Pick up an entry ticket in the adjacent house.

The **Centro de Interpretación Ambiental Natütama** (cell tel. 312/410-1925, www.natutama.org, 9am-5pm, donations encouraged) is run by the conservation and education nonprofit Natütama. (Natütama means, in Ticuna, the "world below the water.") Here, you can watch some excellent videos about two important river species: the pink dolphin and the manatee. While the pink dolphin is celebrated in indigenous mythology, the manatee is not and has been hunted to the brink of extinction. The focus of this organization is conservation awareness among the community. In large

a bird's-eye view of Puerto Nariño

part due to their educational outreach activities, the number of manatees in the Puerto Nariño area has grown from 11 in 2002 to 24 in 2012. The group also sells handicrafts and T-shirts, the proceeds of which help them carry out their activities.

Festivals and Events

The **Festival Autóctono de Danza, Murga y Cuento** takes place at the end of December through early January each year, and is a celebration of indigenous culture and identity. Each night the town gathers around the basketball court for evenings of storytelling, dance, and the requisite beauty pageant. Interestingly, an important component of the pageant is a demonstration of the girls' knowledge of their native tongue.

Recreation

★ LAGO TARAPOTO

Lago Tarapoto, at 37 square kilometers (14 square miles), is much larger than the adjacent **Lago El Correo,** which is closer to Puerto Nariño. These lakes are about a 20-minute boat ride from Puerto Nariño, and this area is a good place for dolphin spotting, swimming, piranha fishing, and nature hikes. Lago Tarapoto connects to the Amazon, so by swimming in its serene waters you can truthfully say that you swam in the Amazon. There are several spots in this area where you can see *renacos,* also known as *el arbol que camina* (the tree that walks), a tree with a jumble of aboveground roots.

To get to the lake you'll have to go with a guide on a boat. The tourist office in Puerto Nariño or any hotel can help organize a visit to these lakes and surrounding flooded jungles. This excursion, pleasant to make in the late afternoon, will cost COP$50,000 per person.

Food and Accommodations

Restaurant options in Puerto Nariño are few, and in high season they can get swamped with visitors on day tours. Pretty much all the choices are on the same stretch: Calle 6.

Restaurante Las Margaritas (Cl. 6 No. 6-80, hours and days vary) specializes in the usual fish dishes and can also whip up vegetarian fare, but they aren't reliably open. **Restaurante Doña Luz** (Cl. 6 with Cra. 2, cell tel. 321/248-8401) is about the same but a little more average. The most popular nighttime joints are the grilled meat and fish stalls along the same path.

Hospedaje Wone (Cra. 1 No. 4-14, cell tel. 314/266-5496 or 320/878-5785, COP$20,000 d) is a pleasant and inexpensive place, with potted plants and flowers throughout, and has just three rooms. It's near the port. A bathroom is outside in the back—meaning there's no indoor plumbing.

Set amid a garden of fruit trees higher up in Puerto Nariño is ★ **Malocas Napü** (Cl. 4 No. 5-72, cell. tel. 314/437-6075 or 315/607-4044, www.malocanapu.com, COP$35,000 pp), a popular choice among international travelers. There are eight rooms here, some with private baths, in two chalet-style houses. In addition to a trip to Lago Tarapoto, the staff here can organize several lesser-known excursions in the area, such as a walk to a nearby indigenous community and visits to a fishpond and a small refuge for alligators. Napü is owned by the same knowledgeable people who operate Ecodestinos in Leticia.

Friendly **Hotel Lomas del Paiyü** (Cl. 7 No. 2-26, cell tel. 313/268-4400, www.hotellomasdelpaiyu.turismo.co, COP$50,000-80,000 d) offers 22 clean, if a little stuffy, rooms.

The top-end option in town is the 12-room ★ **Hotel Waira Selva** (Cra. 2 No. 6-72, tel. 8/592-4428, cell tel. 312/448-7511, www.wairahotel.com.co, COP$150,000 d), where rooms are immaculate and quite comfortable. The quiet restaurant here is probably the best choice in Puerto Nariño, serving typical Amazonian food as well as pasta and the like. Stop by beforehand to inquire about opening hours.

If you'd like to get away from the hustle and bustle of Puerto Nariño but still be within walking distance of it, the **Alto del Águila Cabañas del Fraile** (cell tel. 311/502-8592, altodelaguila@hotmail.com, COP$25,000 pp with private bath) is your best bet. Cabins are clean and cheerful, the kitchen area is a comfortable place to hang out, and you can take a kayak out for a spin on the river for free. To get there, you'll have to walk about 20 minutes from town and cut across the boarding school grounds.

Information and Services
The **tourist office** (Cra. 1 at Cl. 5, Palacio Municipal, no phone, 7am-noon and 2pm-5:45pm Mon.-Fri.) can assist you with finding official tour guides.

There are no ATMs in Puerto Nariño. There are a couple of Internet cafés, but the connections are very slow.

Transportation
It takes just under two hours on a public boat to make the 87-kilometer (54-mile) river journey from Leticia to Puerto Nariño without stopping. Tickets (COP$30,000 one-way) for this trip can be purchased at the Leticia *malecón,* also known as the port or the Muelle Turístico (Tourist Wharf). Look for the office at Malecón Plaza Local 101. Three companies provide this service: **Transportes Amazónicos** (tel. 8/592-5999), **Líneas Amazonas II** (tel. 8/592-6711), and **Expresos Unidos Tres Fronteras** (tel. 8/592-4687). There are usually three boats per day, departing at 8am, 10am, and 2pm.

When leaving Puerto Nariño bound for Leticia, make sure you reserve your spot a day or more in advance. You can do this at the office along the walkway to the docks. Boats leave Puerto Nariño at 7:30am, 11am, 2pm, and 4pm.

★ RÍO JAVARI
The **Río Javari** (Río Yavarí in Spanish) begins in Peru and serves as a border between Brazil and Peru. Its waters flow some 1,050 kilometers (650 miles) before meeting the Amazon in Brazil. About a six-hour journey from Leticia by boat (three hours when the jungle is flooded), this part of the Amazon basin is unspoiled, isolated, and home to two excellent private natural reserves where you will be immersed in the jungle. Spend at least three days or up to a week at one of the Javari nature reserves (they are both excellent) to gain a real appreciation for jungle life. The longer you stay the more wildlife you are apt to see: pink dolphins, alligators, snakes, and dozens of birds. Although this region is technically in Brazil, it very well may be one of the highlights of your trip to Colombia.

Reserva Natural Palmarí
Located on a bluff overlooking the river, the **Reserva Natural Palmarí** (office Cra. 10 No. 93-72, Apt. 602, Bogotá, tel. 1/610-3514, www.palmari.org or www.travesiassas.com, COP$280,000 pp) is a pioneer in ecotourism in this part of the Amazon. Once you arrive, you will be paired with a guide who will accompany you throughout your stay. You won't be grouped together with others. Activities offered include jungle walks (including nighttime), treks, canopying, kayaking, canoe rides, and visits to nearby indigenous communities. Usually guests spend one night in the jungle. Near Reserva Natural Palmarí you can admire massive ceiba trees, also called *lupuna* trees. These noble giants reach up to 70 meters (230 feet) high and have witnessed a lot in their over 400 years of life. Ticuna Indians believe that these trees are what started life and created the river.

The reserve, first and foremost, has a strong commitment to the environment and community. The rooftops are made from a durable, recycled material imported from Canada. (That is because of the growing scarcity of the native palm trees.) Palmarí works with local communities on sustainable agriculture and ecotourism projects as well as environmental education, and has been instrumental in the construction of schools in several villages. *Mucho* credit is due to gregarious Axel, the German-Colombian owner of the reserve, for being a forward-thinking eco-example. Some of the proceeds from Palmarí go toward a conservation nonprofit it set up, the Instituto De

Desenvolvimento Socioambiental Do Vale Do Javari (www.idsavj.org).

Palmarí has a range of accommodations, and if you are traveling in a group, this is an excellent choice. You can sleep in a hammock, in a communal lodge, or in private rooms. Food is delicious and varied, and, yes, there is cold beer: It's all included in the price. You can also get online as well, although this might be the perfect time for an Internet diet. There are two great places at Palmarí to spend the late-afternoon hours as you watch the sun go down: the lookout tower and the swing set. Although it is possible (and adventurous) to get to Palmarí on your own, they will arrange your transportation directly from Leticia.

To get to Palmari from Leticia, you can take public transportation along the river, which will require multiple transfers, or you can let Palmarí take care of everything and go direct (COP$150,000 pp one-way).

Reserva Natural Heliconia

In Brazil, 109 kilometers (68 miles) southeast of Leticia, the **Reserva Natural Heliconia** (office Cl. 13 No. 11-74, Leticia, tel. 8/592-5773, cell tel. 311/508-5666, www.amazonheliconia.com, COP$1,600,000 pp d for 4 days/3 nights incl. transportation) is a fantastic

lodge and nature reserve hidden in the dense Amazonian jungle on a tributary of the Río Javari, which flows into the Río Amazonas. And that makes it all the more exotic, like a bird of paradise flower (for which it is named) growing in the middle of a sea of green in the jungle. Ideally, plan on spending at least three nights here, as anything less than that will feel rushed.

Activities (included in the price except for canopying) include nature walks, bird-watching, pink dolphin-watching, canoeing above the inundated forest, fishing, and canopying. You'll usually have two outings each day, and sometimes in the evenings you can explore the jungle at night, panning the darkness with your flashlight as you look for red eyes of jungle beasts looking back at you. It's an unsettling feeling to be immersed in the pitch-black jungle against a backdrop of chirping insects, frogs, and birds. Another nocturnal activity is to take a canoe ride in search of alligators (or, if there are no gators, simply enjoying the sounds of the jungle and the millions of stars above).

The comfortable cabins at this reserve are made of all-natural materials. Cabins come in different sizes, such as for two guests or families, and they have an area for larger groups.

view from Reserva Natural Palmarí

At night you don't even realize there are others around, such is the privacy.

A hospitable local Brazilian family takes care of all the day-to-day details. There's no Internet access or cell phone coverage, and electricity comes on only for a few hours in the evening. Meals are taken in an open-air thatched-roof *maloca* in the center. Food does not vary much, usually fried fish, rice, and plantains. The friendly kitchen staff can, however, accommodate vegetarians if provided with some notice.

Los Llanos

The vast plains of eastern Colombia known as Los Llanos or Llanos Orientales (Eastern Plains) are lush tropical grasslands teeming with wildlife. They comprise the lands west of the Andes and north of the Amazon rainforest, and extend well into Venezuela. While this part of Colombia comprises around 25 percent of the total area in the country, it is home to only about 3 percent of the population. The border between the Amazon and the Llanos is roughly at the Río Guaviare, a tributary of the Río Orinoco, but the transition is gradual.

Elevations in the Llanos rarely exceed 300 meters (1,000 feet), and the land gradually descends from the Andes piedmont in the west toward the Río Orinoco to the east. The plains are drained by a multitude of large rivers, such as the Guaviare, Vichada, and Meta Rivers, that flow down from the Andes. The savannas are covered with long-stemmed and carpet grasses in the drier areas and swamp grasses in low-lying humid areas. There are also thick patches of forest throughout the plains and along the rivers (known as gallery forests).

The climate is marked by two clear seasons: the *invierno*, or rainy season, which lasts from April to November, and the *verano*, or dry season, from December to March. During the rainy season, the rivers overflow and large parts of the Llanos are flooded. During the dry season, the land becomes parched.

The Llanos are full of wildlife, with more than 100 species of mammals and 1,300 species of birds, including many migratory birds. Mammals include several species of deer and rabbit, anteaters, armadillos, tapirs, otters, jaguars, pumas, and *chigüiros* (capybaras), the world's largest rodent. The plains are also home to the giant anaconda and to one of the most endangered species in the world, the Orinoco crocodile, which reaches up to seven meters (23 feet) long. Unfortunately, human settlement and hunting have vastly decreased the animal populations.

History

At the time of the Spanish conquest, the Llanos were inhabited by several indigenous people, including the Guahibos, Achaguas, and Jiraras. The first European to explore the region was German conquistador Nikolaus Federmann, who set off in 1538 from Venezuela and crossed these plains on his way to the Muisca highlands of El Dorado in the Cordillera Oriental (Eastern Range of the Andes). Gonzalo Jiménez de Quesada, the founder of Bogotá, was granted dominion over a large part of the Llanos but took little interest due to the apparent lack of treasures and the sparse population. Starting in the second half of the 16th century, Jesuits set up missions to convert the indigenous people and established large cattle ranches. During the wars of independence, Venezuelan *llaneros* (plainsmen) were an important element in Bolívar's army and played a key role in the expedition that crossed the plains, climbed the Andes, and finally defeated the Spanish army at the Batalla de Puente de Boyacá on August 7, 1819.

Thanks to their lush grasslands, historically the Llanos have been an important

Los Llanos for Beginners

For a taste of the Llanos, head eastward from Villavicencio to **Lagos de Menegua** (17 km east of Puerto López, cell tel. 315/326-6068, tel. 1/616-0439, www.lagosdemenegua.com, COP$160,000 pp d). This family-friendly resort set in the grassy hills of the Llanos has 24 rooms and a large swimming pool. Here you can take a horseback ride through the ranch, enjoy a jungle walk, and see some of the wildlife that is abundant here: alligators, cute *chigüiros* (capybaras), monkeys, and many varieties of birds. While there are some walks you can make on your own, the resort offers guided tours on horseback (COP$35,000 pp), Jeep tours of the savanna (COP$25,000), and nighttime excursions to see alligators (COP$50,000 pp). *Colectivos* bound for Puerto Gaitán leave from the bus stations in both Bogotá (COP$37,000) and Villavicencio (COP$15,000). Tell the driver you'd like to be dropped off at kilometer 17 between Puerto López and Puerto Gaitán; it's just past Puerto López, where an obelisk marks the geographic center of Colombia, and the Río Meta.

cattle-ranching region in Colombia. To this day, the Llanos are synonymous with cowboy culture. Most human habitation takes place along a narrow fringe of land bordering the Andes, in cities such as Villavicencio and Yopal.

In the 1980s oil was discovered, first in the far eastern department of Arauca and then in Casanare, and today, the area is Colombia's most important oil-producing region, with several pipelines linking the oil fields to the Caribbean port of Coveñas, from where it is exported. The lucrative oil industry became a tempting target for guerrilla insurgencies operating in the area. In the 1980s, the guerrilla group ELN (the National Liberation Army) extorted large amounts of money from the oil companies and their contractors and launched a bombing campaign against the pipelines. The 780-kilometer (485-mile) Caño Limón-Coveñas pipeline, which transports petroleum from oil fields in Arauca owned by California-based Occidental Oil, was bombed an incredible 170 times in 2001 alone. With Plan Colombia came money to defend this infrastructure, and bombings had dropped to only 17 by 2004.

The FARC (Fuerzas Armadas Revolucionarias de Colombia; Revolutionary Armed Forces of Colombia) has been present in the region since the 1960s. From 1998 to 2002 their position was strengthened when President Pastrana granted them as part of a peace process a large demilitarized zone the size of Switzerland in the Meta and Caquetá departments. The FARC managed this zone like a mini-state, using it to grow and process coca, smuggle arms, and hold kidnap victims. They even built roads and a recreation center for FARC commanders.

As a result of the guerrilla presence, agricultural output from the Llanos was depressed for many years. With increased security in the mid-2000s, the Llanos emerged as an important region for big agriculture, with large multinationals such as Cargill setting up massive plantations of African palm, soy, maize, and rubber, especially in the northeast Vichada region. A source of concern to environmentalists is the fact that the Llanos, unlike the Amazon, does not have many protected areas and could succumb to unchecked development.

Security has improved dramatically in the region; however, illegal groups still have a presence in remote areas of Arauca and parts of Caquetá.

VILLAVICENCIO

The capital of the department of Meta is only 80 kilometers (50 miles) southeast of Bogotá and is a gateway to the vast Llanos. Villavicencio does not have much in the way of tourist attractions; it does, however, attract

Bogotanos en masse in search of sun and a swimming pool. It's also a base from which to visit Caño Cristales.

Centers of activity (aside from shopping malls) in Villavicencio are parks like **Parque los Fundadores** (Av. 40 and Vía a Bogotá), which has an enormous sculpture by Rodrigo Arenas Betancourt, and the **Plaza Los Libertadores** (Cl. 39 between Cras. 32-33), over which the cathedral, the late-19th-century **Catedral Metropolitana Nuestra Señora del Carmen,** stands. Near the Plaza Los Libertadores are some pleasant pedestrian side streets, the result of an urban renewal project.

Festivals and Events

Joropo is the music and dance of the Llanos. With European origins (it is said that it is related to Spanish flamenco), it's a dance of fast and fancy footwork, accompanied by folk music that utilizes the harp and guitar and other instruments. The **Torneo Internacional del Joropo** is a showcase of this particularly Llanos art form, and the festival has taken place in Villavicencio since 1960. Over a thousand dance pairs bedecked in traditional costume, including many children, participate. In addition to the dancing, there are rodeo events and a requisite beauty pageant. It's held over four days in late June.

Cowboy culture in the Llanos is not limited to men. Proof of that is the **Concurso Mundial de la Mujer Vaquera** (www. mundialmujervaquera.com), a competition in which cowgirls show their skills in a series of events held at the Parque Las Malocas in Villavicencio in late March every year. The **Encuentro Mundial del Coleo** (www.mundialcoleo.com.co) is for men, and participants demonstrate their *coleo* skills. *Coleo* is a *llanero* cowboy technique for recapturing stray bulls so they can be branded. The cowboys do this by galloping on horseback and thrusting the bulls to the ground by pulling their tails. (It's not for those concerned about animal welfare.) The competition also takes place at the Parque Las Malocas, in October of every year.

Food and Accommodations

When it comes to local cuisine, *llaneros* like their beef, and open-air steak houses are, have always been, and always will be the rage in Villavo. The specialty here is *mamona,* which is grilled veal. Ingredients of this dish aren't complex: a one-year-old calf, salt, and beer. **El Amarradero del Mico** (Vía Vanguardia Restrepo, cell tel. 313/829-6228, noon-midnight daily, COP$22,000) is a popular open-air restaurant on the outskirts of town featuring something for all manner of carnivores.

For a departure from local specialties, try **Pizza Nostra** (Av. 40 No. 25A-47, tel. 8/668-4000, noon-11pm daily, COP$18,000) for pizzas, pastas, and hamburgers. **Oliva Mediterranea** (Unicentro shopping mall, Av. 40 No. 26C-10, 3rd fl., tel. 8/668-2020, noon-9pm daily, COP$18,000) makes a noble effort to make you think you're not in a shopping mall food court. On the menu are Italian dishes, pizzas, and salads.

Those en route to Caño Cristales in La Macarena may need to spend a night in Villavo, as locals call it. One of the best hotels in town is the national chain ★ **GHL Hotel Grande Villavicencio** (Cra. 39C No. 19C-15, www.ghlhoteles.com, COP$182,000 d). It is on the back side of a small shopping mall (Villa Centro) that has a supermarket. Rooms are spacious, the restaurant is pretty good, and on the top floor is a pool with a fantastic view of the Llanos.

The backpacker option is ★ **Mochilero's Hostel** (Cl. 18 No. 39bis-10, tel. 8/667-6723, cell tel. 320/153-2829 or 321/237-2511, COP$24,000 dorm, COP$50,000 d). It has six rooms (with fans) and is close to shopping malls and restaurants. Mochilero's offers tours as well. In addition to a three-night jaunt to Caño Cristales (around COP$1,300,000 pp including airfare from Villavicencio), it offers an interesting, off-the-beaten-path trip by Jeep to San José de Guaviare. There you'll see interesting rock formations (Ciudad de Piedra) and some extraordinarily well-preserved petroglyphs

the colorful pools of Caño Cristales

frustrating hour in Bogotá traffic during much of the day. *Colectivos* going to Puerto López cost about COP$18,000. It's a good road.

Airlines **LATAM** (tel. 1/745-2020, www. latam.com) and **Satena** (tel. 1/605-2222, www.satena.gov.co) operate flights to the **Aeropuerto Vanguardia** (VVC, Vereda Vanguardia Vía Restrepo, tel. 8/670-9610) in Villavicencio from Bogotá. It's about a 45-minute flight. There are connection flights to La Macarena, usually via small charter planes.

★ CAÑO CRISTALES

Taking a flight (or two) to a remote corner of Colombia with a troubled past just to see some river algae may not, on the surface, sound like a wise investment of precious vacation time. But, here in the remote Llanos, you'll be rewarded as you trek through the stark lowland hills of the Serranía de la Macarena, with its unusual dry tropical vegetation, and behold the vibrant purple, fuchsia, goldenrod, and green *Macarenia clavigera* plants swaying in the gushing streams of **Caño Cristales.**

The Serranía de la Macarena (Macarena Range) is a 120-kilometer-long, 30-kilometer-wide (75-mile-long, 19-mile wide) mountain range 70 kilometers (43 miles) south of Villavicencio and 45 kilometers (28 miles) east of the Andes. The range, which is entirely contained within the 629,280-hectare (1.6 million-acre) **Parque Nacional Natural Sierra de la Macarena,** is the highly eroded remnant of mountains that once towered on the supercontinent of Pangaea, before the South American plate separated from the African plate and drifted westward to its present location, crashing into the Nazca plate and creating the Andes. These ancient outcrops, which form the Guyana Shield, dot the northwest Amazon basin in Colombia, Venezuela, and Guyana.

The Macarena is also unique in that it is at the confluence of three highly distinct ecosystems: the Amazon to the south, the Llanos to the north, and the Andes mountain

(over 3,500 years old), in addition to Caño Cristales (3 nights, COP$700,000 pp, 4-person min.).

Information and Services
There are **tourist information stands** at the airport (Vereda Vanguardia vía Restrepo) and at the bus terminal (Cra. 1 No. 15-05) and one at Llanocentro shopping mall. They generally keep the hours of 8am-5pm daily.

Transportation
There's really no need to fly to Villavicencio from Bogotá, unless you seek comfort, are averse to the assertive motoring style of Colombian bus drivers, or are in a hurry: There are **buses** (Flota la Macarena, tel. 1/421-5556, www.flotalamacarena.com, 2 hrs., COP$24,000) between the two cities practically 24 hours a day. From Villavicencio's **Terminal de Transportes de Villavicencio** (Cra. 1 No. 15-05, Anillo Vial, no phone) there's no shortage of *colectivo* (smaller bus) service to Bogotá, but expect at least another

rainforests to the west. A large number of endemic plants evolved in this isolated mountain range, including the striking *Macarenia clavigera,* which draws tourists from all over Colombia and from abroad.

Caño Cristales is a stream that flows from west to east in the very southern part of the sierra and flows into the Río Guayabero, a tributary of the Río Guaviare. In its upper reaches, it has three branches that join to form the Caño Cristales stream proper. The surrounding landscape is quite dry and rocky, covered with unusual *Vellozia macarenensis* plants, which have evolved to survive the dry climate and brushfires. These plants produce beautiful white flowers that add to the beauty of the stark environs.

The small town of **La Macarena** on the Río Guayabero is the gateway to Caño Cristales. It was part of the demilitarized zone granted to the FARC as part of the 1998-2002 peace process. Evincing little respect for nature, the FARC destroyed the park facilities, chased away the staff, and built a road right through the park, sparking squatters to take illegal possession of lands within the park. The town of La Macarena is now home to a 4,000-strong army base, one of the largest in Colombia. The vicinity of the town, including all the sights described in this section, is safe to visit, and tourism has given this isolated community new life. A highly successful nature guide training program for high school students has given youths in the town the opportunity to gain a living through ecotourism.

To visit Caño Cristales, you need a minimum of one full day and two nights, but staying a day or two longer is definitely worthwhile. The best time of the year to visit is during the rainy season, from May until November, when you can marvel at the *Macarenia clavigera* in bloom.

Recreation
HIKING
All excursions require a guide. Visitors are asked to avoid using sunscreen or mosquito repellent, as it can damage the *Macarenia*

clavigera. Therefore, make sure to bring a wide-brimmed sun hat and wear lightweight, long-sleeve shirts and pants to protect your skin. Wear shoes that have good traction on slippery rocks and that you don't mind getting wet.

The most popular trek is a half-day excursion that involves a pleasant 20-minute boat ride up the Río Guayabero from the town of La Macarena, a six-kilometer (3.7-mile) truck ride, and a two-kilometer (1.2 mile) hike to Caño Cristales. There, you'll admire the multicolored stream as it gushes through pools and waterfalls. At the end you get to cool off in the Piscina del Turista, a natural pool, and have a waterside lunch.

Another longer, all-day excursion takes you to the upper part of Caño Cristales, where you'll visit the three different branches of the river. The vegetation here is much denser, and the *Macarenia clavigera* also take on yellow and green hues. This excursion involves wading across the stream numerous times. If it has been raining, the level and force of the water increases considerably, making for an exhilarating experience. Depending on the level of the water and physical conditions during the trip, you may visit one, two, or all three of the branches.

Two other half-day excursions also involve a ride up the Río Guayabero to visit **Cristalitos,** a smaller stream that is Caño Cristales in miniature, or to **El Mirador,** a hike to the top of a hill that offers sweeping views of the Río Guayabero and surrounding countryside.

Another excursion, which can only be done in the dry months of December through April, is 20 kilometers (12 miles) up to the **Raudal del Guayabero** to admire the white-water rapids, ancient indigenous petroglyphs, and interesting rock formations known as **Ciudad de Piedra.**

TOURS
Visiting Caño Cristales with a tour is not imperative, as flights from Bogotá and hotels can be booked independently, with tours

easily arranged upon arrival. However, if you'd like to let someone else make those arrangements, including obtaining permission to enter the park, there are several agencies in the area and throughout the country that will be able to do that legwork for you. Two reputable local operators, **Ecoturismo Sierra de la Macarena** (Av. Alfonso López No. 40-28, Villavicencio, tel. 8/664-3364, cell tel. 314/325-3522, www.ecoturismomacarena.com) and **Cristales Aventura Tours** (Cl. 5 No. 7-35, La Macarena, cell tel. 321/842-2728, www.cano-cristales.com) offer two- to five-night packages from Villavicencio. Expect to pay around COP$1,300,000 per person for a four-day trip. This includes air transportation out of Villavicencio, local transportation, food, accommodations in La Macarena, and tours to Caño Cristales. These operators hire guides from UNIGMA, an association of young local guides that have received specialized training since high school. You can also buy these tours from tourist operators elsewhere in the country, but these will simply take a margin and send you with the two local operators.

It is quite feasible, and cheaper, to organize your Caño Cristales trip on your own by arranging air transportation, local transportation, accommodations, and food. For all hikes in and around Caño Cristales you are required to hire a guide from **UNIGMA** (cell tel. 320/856-7571, guiasunigma@hotmail.com, COP$100,000 per day for a group of up to 7 people).

Food and Accommodations

Hotels and restaurants in La Macarena, all economically priced, are nothing special. ★ **Centro Vacacional Punto Verde** (Cra. 9 No. 4-12, cell tel. 314/325-3522 or 310/341-8899, COP$40,000 pp incl. all meals) is the best option by far, with nine rooms spread out behind an ample and leafy common area, including a small pool. Breakfast is included, and the restaurant, the **Punta Verde,** is the best in town. It's open to hotel guests and non-guests. Let them know ahead of time if you require vegetarian meals.

Casa Hotel (Parque Principal, cell tel. 313/292-9925 or 314/279-2764, COP$35,000 pp) has 21 rooms, some with air-conditioning. **La Cascada** (Cl. 5 No. 7-35, tel. 8/560-3132, cell tel. 313/294-9452, cristalesaventuratours@hotmail.com, COP$80,000 d) has 32 smallish rooms over two floors.

Information

The group of local guides, UNIGMA, operates a **tourist information office** at the tiny Aeropuerto Javier Noreña Valencia (5-min. walk from Parque Principal). It's the most buzzing place in La Macarena and is open every day 8am-5pm.

Transportation

La Macarena Airport (LMC), located in town, typically has service to and from Bogotá via **Satena** (tel. 1/605-2222, www.satena.gov.co) on Sundays, Wednesdays, Fridays, and some Mondays. There are charter flights from Villavicencio on small charter planes (and, on occasion, old DC-3s). Contact **Ecoturismo Sierra de la Macarena** (Av. Alfonso López No. 40-28, Villavicencio, tel. 8/665-3870, cell tel. 314/325-3522, www.ecoturismomacarena.com) or **Cristales Aventura Tours** (Cl. 5 No. 7-35, La Macarena, cell tel. 321/842-2728, www.cano-cristales.com) to buy a seat on these flights. Travel by land to La Macarena, while possible, is not common and is difficult to arrange.

La Macarena is a small town and you can get everywhere on foot—but don't wander too far from town on your own in order to stay safe. Boats up the Río Guayabero to Caño Cristales, Cristalitos, and El Mirador will cost COP$60,000-70,000 per group of up to 10 people.

★ HACIENDA LA AURORA

Hacienda La Aurora (near the town of Paz de Ariporo, Casanare, cell tel. 310/580-5395, www.juansolito.com), 180 kilometers (112 miles) northwest of Yopal in the department of Casanare and about double that from

Villavicencio, is in many ways a typical cattle ranch of the Llanos. It was once part of the immense 430,000-hectare (1.1 million-acre) Jesuit hacienda that was subdivided over time. Today the hacienda measures 17,000 hectares (42,000 acres) and has 6,000 head of cattle. However, in one aspect it differs radically from other haciendas in the Llanos: Since the Barragán family, the current owners, purchased it in the 1970s, they have not allowed any hunting of animals, even in cases of cattle predation by jaguars and pumas. This prohibition on hunting comes from the family's deep-seated conviction that cattle ranching must be a sustainable activity and that it must coexist peacefully with the Llanos's abundant biodiversity.

Because of this ethos, the hacienda abounds with wildlife that mixes with cattle herds and is not afraid of humans. As you travel through the farm on the back of a specially outfitted safari truck, on horseback, or on foot, there is wildlife everywhere you look: herds of absurdly cute *chigüiros* (the world's largest rodents, also known as capybaras), deer, foxes, anteaters, armadillos, sloths, monkeys, tortoises, and caimans. Even non-birders will be amazed by what they see: huge ungainly *garzón soldados* (jabirus), bright red ibises, families of burrowing owls, incredibly exotic plumed hoatzins, parakeets, macaws, and toucans. In the dry season, it is not unusual to see anacondas on the banks of the Río Ariporo or in watering holes. There are also water buffalo and herds of wild horses roaming about. Finally, pumas and jaguars can also be spotted (albeit through wildlife cameras installed at strategic points on the farm). There is most definitely nowhere in Colombia where you can see this much wildlife in its natural setting.

Hacienda La Aurora is also very much a working cattle farm. The herds are spread out throughout the hacienda. There is a main hacienda house, which is the center of operations. When cattle-ranching activities need to be done, such as taming horses, branding calves, or rounding up cattle for sale, *vaqueros* (cowboys) move to one of several smaller peripheral camps called *fundos* to do these activities. Viewing the traditional cattle-ranching ways of the Llanos is a fascinating part of a visit to La Aurora.

Haciendas such as this used to be the norm in the Llanos. However, many have been subdivided into smaller, more modern ranches with fenced pastures. Others have been converted into large African palm, corn, soy, or

vaqueros (cowboys) rounding up the cattle at Hacienda La Aurora

rubber plantations. La Aurora's administrators complain that it is increasingly difficult to find personnel willing to do what they call the "work of the Llano"—cattle ranching the traditional way—as wages in the oil industry are much better and the work is less taxing.

To fully enjoy a visit to Hacienda La Aurora, stay at least two full days. Accommodations at La Aurora are at the Ecolodge Juan Solito, which borders the ranch. Visits are easier in the dry season (Nov.-Mar.), when getting around the farm is not difficult and wildlife congregates around the water holes. However, a visit in the rainy season is also interesting. The ground often gets drenched, but it is not impossible to visit the ranch and spot animals. Also, in the rainy season it is possible to do boat excursions.

Recreation

All visitors pay a fixed price of COP$150,000 per person per day for all activities on the ranch. In return, all activities are tailored to your wishes and you are accompanied by a dedicated guide. Easily arranged activities include photo safaris on the back of a truck specially outfitted with benches, visits to view the traditional cattle-ranching activities of the hacienda, excursions on horseback, nature hikes, and canoe trips up the Río Ariporo (only in the rainy season). You can also swim in the Ariporo, though you must be careful of stingrays, electric eels, piranhas (a minor threat), and anacondas (on the riverbank). If you have a particular interest, such as specialized bird-watching or photographing specific wildlife, these activities can be arranged at no additional cost.

Food and Accommodations

Lodging and food is provided at the **Ecolodge Juan Solito** (near Paz de Ariporo, Casanare, cell tel. 320/342-6409, www.juansolito.com, COP$180,000 pp including all meals) just across the Río Ariporo on the south side of Hacienda La Aurora. Juan Solito is owned by the incredibly friendly and attentive Nelson

Barragán, of the family that owns the hacienda. There are seven simple and comfortable rooms at the lodge. Meals are taken with the lodge staff on long benches in a thatched-roof dining room overlooking the river. Vegetarian fare can be arranged with advance notice. Sometimes, when there is a large group of guests, local musicians and dancers perform traditional *joropo* music and dance, with Nelson playing the harp.

Getting There

This Llanos adventure begins in **Yopal**, the orderly and pleasant capital city of Casanare. Due to the presence of large multinational oil companies in the area, there are several flights every day between Bogotá and the Yopal airport, **Aeropuerto Alcaravan** (EYP, Cl. 40 No. 19-20, tel. 8/635-8352). **LATAM** (tel. 1/745-2020, www.latam.com) and **Avianca** (tel. 1/401-3434, www.avianca.com) offer various nonstops between the two cities. **EasyFly** (www.easyfly.com.co) serves both Bogotá and Bucaramanga from Yopal.

From Yopal, the easiest way to get to Hacienda La Aurora is by contracting transportation directly with them. For COP$400,000 (each way) they will pick you up (maximum four passengers) at the Yopal airport or bus station and take you directly to the farm.

If you'd like to save some money and don't mind a little adventure, you can take public transportation to the farm entrance. From the **Terminal de Transportes de Yopal** (Cra. 23 between Clls. 25-26), take a bus to Paz de Ariparo (COP$17,000, 1.25 hours, frequent departures). From there, take a slow bus to Montañas de Totumo (COP$22,000, 6am, 12:30pm, and 3pm). The 12:30 bus continues along a road that passes in front of the entrance of Ecolodge Juan Solito. Tell the bus driver to leave you at "Finca La Vigia," where there is a sign that says "Reserva Casanare." Confirm with the ecolodge for a pickup at Montañas de Totumo (the 6am and 3pm buses) or at the entrance to the farm (12:30pm bus).

Background

The Landscape

Colombia covers a land area of 1.14 million square kilometers (440,000 square miles), roughly the size of Texas and California combined, making it the fourth-largest South American country in area after Brazil, Argentina, and Peru. It is located in the northwest corner of South America, with seacoast on both the Pacific and the Atlantic, and it borders Venezuela, Brazil, Peru, Ecuador, and Panama. The Amazonian departments of Putumayo, Caquetá, Amazonas, and Vaupés in the south of the country straddle the equator.

For a country of its size, Colombia has an astonishing variety of landscapes, including the dense rainforests of the Amazon and the Pacific coast, the vast grassland plains of the Llanos, the lofty Andes Mountains, and the Caribbean islands of San Andrés and Providencia. Colombia's mountainous regions themselves hold a succession of vertically layered landscapes: tropical rainforests at their base, followed by cloud forests at higher elevations, topped by the unique tropical high mountain *páramo* (highland moor) above 3,500 meters (11,480 feet). The country boasts several peaks higher than 5,000 meters (16,400 feet), including Nevado del Ruiz (5,325 meters/17,470 feet) and Pico Cristóbal Colón (5,776 meters/18,950 feet).

GEOGRAPHY
Región Andina
This central part of Colombia is dominated by the Andes mountain range. This region, which is referred to as the Región Andina or simply *el interior* (the interior) is the heartland of the country. It covers roughly 25 percent of the surface of the country and is home to 60 percent of the Colombian population.

The Andes mountain range, 8,000 kilometers (5,000 miles) long, runs the entire length of South America. The Andes are relatively young mountains, and some of the loftiest in the world after the Himalayas, resulting from the collision of the westward-moving South American plate with the Nazca and Antarctic plates starting 145 million years ago. The heavier Nazca and Antarctic plates to the west subducted under the lighter and more rigid South American plate, propelling it upwards and forming the Andes. In Colombia, as a result of a complex pattern of tectonic collisions, three parallel ranges were formed. At the Masizo Colombiano (Colombian Massif), a mountain range 175 kilometers north of the border with Ecuador, the Andes split into the Cordillera Occidental (Western Range), Cordillera Central (Central Range), and Cordillera Oriental (Eastern Range).

The Cordillera Occidental is the lowest and least populated of the three ranges. It runs roughly 750 kilometers parallel to the Pacific coast and ends 150 kilometers from the Caribbean Sea. Its highest point is the Cerro de Tatamá (4,250 meters/13,945 feet). Of Colombia's three ranges, it has the least human intervention and is home to some of the world's only pristine high mountain *páramos* ecosystems, notably that covering the Cerro de Tatamá.

The Central Cordillera is the highest of the three ranges and is the continuation in Colombia of the main Andes range. It runs roughly 800 kilometers and tapers off in the northern Caribbean plains, 200 kilometers from the Caribbean coast. Like the Andes in Ecuador, it is dotted with volcanoes. North of the Masizo Colombiano is the Serranía de los Coconucos (Coconucos Range), a range of

---

Previous: a protest for peace in Bogotá; countryside in the department of Nariño.

15 volcanoes including the Volcán del Puracé (Puracé Volcano, 4,580 meters/15,025 feet). Farther north, the Cordillera Central reaches its maximum elevation at the massive Nevado del Huila (5,750 meters/15,585 feet). Farther north is a large complex formed by the Nevado del Tolima (5,215 meters/17,110 feet), Nevado Santa Isabel (4,950 meters/16,240 feet), and Nevado del Ruiz (5,325 meters/17,470 feet). In its northern part, the Cordillera Central broadens to form the uneven highland that comprises the mountainous heartland of Antioquia with Medellín as its capital.

Several of the volcanoes of the Cordillera Central have seen recent activity, notably Volcán Galeras (4,276 meters/14,029 feet), near the southern city of Pasto, which last erupted in 2005, forcing evacuation of nearby settlements. Volcán Galeras is currently closed to visitors because of the threat of volcanic activity. In 1985, the Nevado del Ruiz erupted unexpectedly, creating a landslide that engulfed the town of Armero, killing more than 20,000 people. Since 2012, the Nevado del Ruiz has seen some activity, which has restricted access to the northern part of the Parque Nacional Natural Los Nevados.

The Cordillera Oriental, which like the Cordillera Occidental is non-volcanic, extends more than 1,100 kilometers to the border with Venezuela. The range broadens to form a broad high plateau called the Altiplano Cundiboyacense, which extends 200 kilometers north of Bogotá. This is an area of broad valleys with the extremely rich soil of sedimentary deposits. The Sabana de Bogotá, or Bogotá High Plateau, where Bogotá is located, is one particularly broad valley. North of the altiplano is the soaring Sierra Nevada del Cocuy, a mountain range with 11 glacier-covered peaks, including Ritacuba Blanco (5,380 meters/17,650 feet). North of El Cocuy, the Cordillera Oriental loses altitude and splits in two: A smaller western segment forms the Serranía de Perijá on the border between Colombia and Venezuela, and a larger branch continues into Venezuela to form the Venezuelan Andes.

The 1,500-kilometer-long Río Magdalena flows along a broad valley that separates the Cordillera Central and the Cordillera Oriental, making it the main commercial waterway of Colombia. Due to heavy sedimentation, it is now only navigable when waters rise during the rainy seasons in the central part of the country (Apr.-May and Oct.-Nov.). The Río Cauca, which flows parallel to the Magdalena along the much narrower valley between the Cordillera Central and the Cordillera Occidental, is the main tributary of the Magdalena. They join in northern Colombia and flow into the Caribbean.

Andean Colombia is a seismically volatile area, and the country has suffered some major earthquakes in the past. The most deadly measured 7.5 on the Richter Scale and occurred in Cúcuta in 1875. It killed 10,000 and completely destroyed the city. In recent years, around 600 were killed in the Pacific port city of Tumaco during a quake and tsunami in 1979; 300 perished in the 1983 Holy Week earthquake in Popayán; and over 1,100 died in the Armenia quake of 1999.

Caribe

Colombia's Caribbean coast runs 1,760 kilometers (1,100 miles) from the border of Panama to Venezuela, just longer than the California coast. However, the term "Caribe" or "Región Caribe" refers to much more than the narrow strip of coast; it encompasses basically all of Colombia north of the Andes, including a vast area of plains. This region covers 15 percent of the surface of Colombia and is home to 20 percent of the population.

The terrain is mostly low-lying and undulating. Near the border with Panama, the land is covered by dense tropical forests, similar to those on the Pacific coast. Farther east is the Golfo de Urabá, a large, shallow bay. Between the Golfo de Urabá and Cartagena is the Golfo de Morrosquillo, a broad inlet that is 50 kilometers (31 miles) wide. Off the shore of the Golfo de Morrosquillo are two small archipelagos, the Islas de San Bernardo and the Islas del Rosario, with beautiful coral reefs. Inland to the south is a large savanna in the departments of Córdoba and Sucre largely devoted to cattle ranching. This area was once covered by dry tropical forests, which have been largely felled.

Bahía de Cartagena, farther east, is a magnificent deep bay that caught the attention of the early Spanish explorers. To the southeast of Cartagena is the lower valley of the Magdalena and Cauca Rivers, a vast expanse of low-lying lagoons and lands prone to seasonal flooding. The Río Magdalena flows into the Caribbean east of Cartagena at the port city of Barranquilla. Farther to the east along the coast is a major mountain range, the Sierra Nevada de Santa Marta. It was formed by the collision of the South American plate and the Caribbean plate to the north and is entirely independent of the Andes. This range is home to Colombia's two highest peaks, the twin Pico Cristóbal Colón and Pico Bolívar (5,776 meters/18,950 feet), and is considered the highest coastal mountain range in the world. The Sierra Nevada de Santa Marta contains the same range of vertically layered landscapes as the Andes, from low-lying tropical forest through cloud forest, Andean forests, *páramo*, and glaciers. There are eight peaks with elevations greater than 5,000 meters (16,400 feet).

Northeast of the Sierra Nevada de Santa Marta is La Guajira, an arid peninsula jutting into the Caribbean. Punta Gallinas, at the tip of La Guajira, is the northernmost point in South America. There are a few low-lying mountain ranges in La Guajira, such as the Serranía de la Macuira (864 meters/2,835 feet), which is covered with rainforest. The Sierra Nevada de Santa Marta and Serranía de la Macuira are biological islands, and their upper reaches are home to numerous endemic species that evolved in isolation.

Pacífico

The Pacific coast of Colombia extends 1,329 kilometers from Ecuador to Panama, about the same length as the coast of California. The term Pacífico, as it relates to Colombia, designates all the land—jungle to be more accurate—that lies between the Pacific Ocean and the Cordillera Occidental. This region covers 6 percent of Colombia and is home to about 2 percent of the population.

The topography of this region is mostly flat, with the low-lying coastal Serranía del Baudó (1,810 meters/5,940 feet) providing a mountainous backdrop to the coastal plain and forming an inland basin that is drained by the mighty Río Atrato, which

beach on the Pacific coast of Colombia

flows northwards into the Caribbean Sea. The coast has a number of bays and inlets, notably the Ensenada de Utría (Utría Inlet), visited by humpback whales traveling every winter from the Antarctic Sea to give birth in the warm waters of the Colombian Pacific. South of Buenaventura, the coast has extensive mangroves, much of which are well-preserved. Offshore are two islands: Isla Gorgona is 35 kilometers off the coast on the continental shelf, and tiny Malpelo is 490 kilometers off the coast. Both of these islands are likely of volcanic origin.

The Colombian Pacific region is one of the wettest places on Earth, with average annual rainfall of 10,000 millimeters (33 feet). Due to the enormous amount of precipitation, the region has a dense river network with dozens of major arteries, such as the Río Baudó, Río San Juan, and Río Patía.

Amazon

The Amazon region of Colombia comprises 400,000 million kilometers, or roughly 35 percent of Colombia's territory, including all the territory east of the Andes and south of the Río Guaviare. The Colombian portion covers only 10 percent of the entire Amazon drainage basin. Total population in the Amazon region is 1.1 million, or 2 percent of the country's population. It is the most sparsely populated area in the country.

Like the Llanos, the Amazon has an undulating terrain, interrupted occasionally with ancient, low-lying mountainous formations of the Guyana Shield, such as the Serranía de Chiribiquete, a series of highly eroded tabletop mountains. The Amazon consists of two distinct but intermingled areas: *terra firme*, the undulated lands that are above the highest flood point, and *varzea*, floodplains along the main rivers, which can extend 50 kilometers from the river.

There are two types of rivers in the Amazon: the predominant white rivers, which carry sediments down from the Andes; and the black rivers, which originate within the rainforest in the Guyana

Shield formations that were long ago denuded of soil due to erosion. As these waters travel though the flooded forest, they pick up pigments that give them their characteristic black color. *Igapo* is the name given to jungles flooded by black water rivers. Most of the rivers of the Colombian Amazon are white, such as the massive Río Putumayo, Río Caquetá, Río Apaporis, and Río Vaupés, all of which are more than 1,000 kilometers long. The main black river in Colombia is the Río Guainía, which does originate in the Andes, and which is the headwater of the largest black river of the Amazon—the Río Negro—which flows into the milky Amazon at Manaus, in Brazil.

Los Llanos

The Llanos, Colombia's vast eastern plains, cover an area of 250,000 square kilometers, roughly 25 percent of Colombia's territory. The plains are hemmed in to the west by Cordillera Oriental and to the south by the Amazon rainforest, and extend far into Venezuela. Though the transition between the Amazon and the Llanos is gradual, the Río Guaviare, which flows from west to east at a longitude that is roughly midway between the northern and southern tips of Colombia, is considered the demarcation line between these two areas. The Llanos are home to about 1.5 million inhabitants, or about 3 percent of the population, making it the region with the second lowest population density—after the Amazon region—in the country.

After the genesis of the Andes, water flowing eastward down the mountains accumulated in a vast freshwater lake that was confined on the east by old mountainous formations (now the Guyana and Brazilian highlands). Large amounts of sediments were deposited, forming the basis for the Llanos' undulating topography. Near the Andes, elevations can reach 300 meters and, moving east, slowly decrease in altitude until they reach the north-flowing Río Orinoco, which forms the border between Colombia and Venezuela.

Colombia's National Parks

From undisturbed coral reefs to the Amazonian jungle to snow-covered mountain ranges, Colombia's national park system is a treasure, and making the effort to visit them is worthwhile for any visitor. The country's system of natural parks and protected areas covers more than 14 million hectares (34.6 million acres), around 13.4 percent of the country. It includes 43 Parques Nacionales Naturales (National Natural Parks), which are areas of major ecological interest that have remained largely untouched by human intervention, and 12 Santuarios de Flora y Fauna (Flora and Fauna Sanctuaries), areas that are devoted to the preservation of specific ecosystems. Of the 43 parks, 24 are open for tourism. The rest are officially off-limits, due to lack of infrastructure, security concerns, or in order to respect the territory of indigenous communities.

In 1960, PNN Cueva de los Guácharos, in the southwest, was the first park to be established. The number of parks steadily increased, especially from 1986 to 1990 when President Virgilio Barco doubled the park holdings from roughly 5 million hectares to 10 million hectares (12 million to 24 million acres). In the past few years, the government has again been increasing the number and extension of parks. In 2013 President Juan Manuel Santos doubled the size of the PNN Serranía de Chiribiquete to its present 2.8 million hectares (7 million acres), or three times the size of Yellowstone National Park.

Charged with the considerable task of administering this huge system are a mere 430 rangers—roughly one person for every 33,000 hectares (82,000 acres). Rangers face a great challenge in protecting the parks against threats related to human encroachment, particularly cattle ranching and the planting of illicit crops. There are other threats as well, such as illegal mining and logging. Paradoxically, what has preserved many of the parks until now has been the lack of security due to Colombia's internal conflict. As security conditions improve, there will be increasing pressure on these natural habitats. The Parks Service is actively engaging with the communities that live near the parks and is transferring the operation of much of the ecotourism infrastructure to community-based organizations as part of an effort to enlist local communities in the preservation of the land.

Entry permits and entry fees are only required in a handful of highly visited parks, such as PNN Tayrona, PNN Gorgona, PNN Cocuy, and PNN Los Nevados. At these, you will automatically be charged if you book lodging in advance, or if not, upon arrival. If you want to be meticulous, you can obtain the entry permit and pay entry fees in advance by contacting the **Parques Nacionales** (tel. 1/353-2400, www.parquesnacionales.gov.co) in Bogotá.

The only significant mountain range in Los Llanos is the Serranía de la Macarena (Macarena Range), a 120-kilometer-long, 30-kilometer-wide range that is 45 kilometers east of the Andes just of the Río Guayabero, a tributary of the Río Guaviare. This range is part of the Guyana Shield complex of ancient, highly eroded remnants of mountains that existed long before the formation of the Andes.

The Llanos are drained by a multitude of large rivers, such as the Río Guaviare, Río Vichada, and Río Meta, which flow down from the Andes and meander east. All the rivers of the Llanos are tributaries of the Orinoco—for this reason, this region is also often called La Orinoquía.

CLIMATE

Colombia has a typically tropical climate, with no change of seasons. Climate is related primarily to elevation, and there are defined annual precipitation patterns.

In the mountainous areas, temperature decreases approximately six degrees Celsius per every 1,000 meters (3,280 feet) of elevation (or three degrees Fahrenheit per every 1,000 feet). The common designations for the altitudinal zones are as follows: *tierra caliente* (hot lands) is anywhere below 1,000 meters of elevation; *tierra templada* (temperate lands) is anywhere between 1,000 and 2,000 meters; and *tierra fría* (cold land) is anywhere above 2,000 meters. Roughly 80 percent of the country is *tierra caliente*, 10 percent is *tierra templada*, and 7 percent is *tierra fría*.

Cartagena, which is at sea level, has an average temperature of 27.5°C (81.5°F); Medellín, which is at 1,600 meters (5,250 feet), has an average temperature of 22°C (71.5°F); and the capital city of Bogotá, which is built at 2,625 meters (8,612 feet), has an average temperature of 13.5°C (56°F).

Precipitation patterns vary throughout the country. In the Andean region, there are generally two periods of *verano* (dry season, literally "summer"), from December to March and from June to September, and two periods of *invierno* (rainy season, literally "winter"), in April and May and from October to November. On the Caribbean coast, the dry period is from December to April and the

rainy season is from May to November. In the Pacific it rains almost the entire year, but there is a slight dry spell from December to March. In the Llanos, there are two very marked seasons: a very dry *verano* from November to March and a very wet *invierno* from April to October. In the Amazon, it rains almost the entire year, but there is a slight dry spell from August to October.

Extreme weather in Colombia is rare, but the country is susceptible to weather phenomena such as El Niño or La Niña, when temperatures in the Pacific Ocean rise or fall, respectively. In 2015-2016, the country was affected by a strong El Niño, which brought prolonged drought.

San Andrés and Providencia are occasionally, and the Caribbean mainland of Colombia rarely, in the path of Atlantic hurricanes from August through October. The last storm of significance was Hurricane Beta in 2005. It caused considerable damage in Providencia.

Plants and Animals

When it comes to biodiversity, Colombia is a place of superlatives. Though representing only 0.2 percent of the planet's surface, it is home to about 10 percent of all the species in the world. The country has an estimated 55,000 plant species, including 3,500 species of orchids. Only Brazil, with seven times the land surface, has as many plant species. Colombia is the country with the greatest number of bird species in the world—about 1,800. It's also home to about 3,200 fish, 750 amphibian species, 500 reptile species, and 450 mammal species. No wonder Colombia was designated as one of 17 so-called megadiverse countries, a select club of countries that are home to an outsized proportion of the world's biodiversity. Other megadiverse countries include Australia, Brazil, China, Democratic Republic of Congo, Indonesia, Madagascar, Mexico, the United States, and South Africa.

This enormous biodiversity is the result of Colombia's location in the tropics, where year-round sunlight and high precipitation are conducive to plant growth, plus the country's mountainous topography with numerous climatic zones and microclimates that have created biological islands where species have evolved in relative isolation. Furthermore, the recent ice ages were not as severe in this part of the world, and as a result many ancient species were preserved. Finally, Colombia's location at the crossroads of Central and South America has further enriched the country's biodiversity.

RAINFOREST

Rainforests are among the most complex ecosystems on Earth. They have a layered structure with towering trees that soar 30-40 meters high (100-130 feet) to form the forest's canopy. Some of the most common rainforest

Colombian Fruits

Colombia is a land bursting with exotic fruit. Sold from the back of pickup trucks by farmers on the roadside, overflowing at stalls in colorful markets in every town and village, lined up in neat rows in the produce section at fancy grocery stores and at juice stands—just about anywhere you go, delicious fruit is in reach.

You know pineapple, papaya, mangoes, and bananas, but be sure to try these tropical delights that you may not have encountered outside of Colombia.

· **Pitahaya (dragon fruit):** Looking like a yellow grenade, *pitahayas* have a sweet white meat inside.

· **Guanábana (soursop):** By far the strangest-looking fruit, soursop resemble prehistoric dinosaur eggs. Inside the large green spiky fruit is a milky and slimy flesh. *Guanábana* is great in juices and desserts.

· **Granadilla:** Crack open this orangey-yellow fruit and slurp down the slimy gray contents, seeds and all. It's delicious.

· **Higo (prickly pear):** This green fruit comes from cactus plants and has sweet, if tough, orange-colored meat.

· **Chirimoya (cherimoya):** This green fruit that resembles a smooth artichoke is covered with a smooth, silky skin and filled with delectable, sweet pulp.

· **Níspero (sapodilla):** A fruit with a deep brown color that tastes like a prepared sweet.

· **Mangostino (mangosteen):** Crack open a deep-purple mangosteen and enjoy the sweet segments inside. They're full of antioxidants.

· **Uchuva (Cape gooseberry):** Known in English as Cape gooseberries, these tart yellow berries are a cousin of the tomato and are tasty on their own or in salads, but are often used in jams and sweets.

· **Mamoncillo:** Tough-skinned grapes (don't eat the skin), *mamoncillos* are usually sold only at street markets.

---

trees are the ceiba, mahogany, myrtle, laurel, acacia, and rubber trees. Occasionally, particularly high trees known as *emergentes* pierce the canopy, reaching as high up as 60 meters (200 feet). Below the canopy is the *sotobosque*, a middle layer of smaller trees and palms that vie for the sunlight filtering in through the canopy. In the canopy and *sotobosque* there are many epiphytes (plants such as orchids and bromeliads) that have adapted to live on top of trees so as to be nearer to the sunlight. Near the ground live plants that require little sunlight, including ferns, grasses, and many types of fungi. The two main rainforests in Colombia, the Amazon and the Chocó, have the same layered structure, though they have some differences in their flora and fauna.

The Amazon rainforest is home to an impressive array of vertebrates. Over millennia, a large number of canopy-dwelling species evolved. Monkeys, such as the large and extremely agile spider monkey, the woolly monkey, and the howler monkey, evolved prehensile tails that allowed them to move easily from branch to branch. Anteaters, such as the tamandua and the *oso mielero* (giant anteater) and the incredibly cute *kinkajú* (kinkajou), also developed prehensile tails. Other inhabitants of the canopy include sloths, such as the adorable three-toed sloth, whose strategy is not agility but passivity: It eats tree vegetation and is covered with algae that gradually turns the animal green to allow for good camouflage. The canopy is also home to myriad bats and many birds, including exotic eagles, curassows, toucans, woodpeckers, cotingas, and macaws.

Notable is the majestic harpy eagle, with powerful claws and the ability to fly unencumbered through the canopy. It preys on monkeys and sloths, which it kills with the force of its claws. The *tigrillo* (tiger cat) is a small and extremely endangered species. It has a long tail that helps with its balance as it moves from tree to tree.

On the ground, large vertebrates include the extremely endangered tapir, an ancient mammal species that can grow two meters long (over six feet) and weigh 300 kilograms (660 pounds). It is equally at ease on land as in the water. Other land mammals include the giant armadillo, giant anteater, deer, and boars, such as the *saíno* and *pecarí*. Smaller mammals include the *guatín* and *borugo,* both rodents. These animals are often prey to the puma and jaguar, both of which inhabit the Amazon but are difficult to observe in the wild.

The rivers of the Amazon are home to more than 1,500 species of fish, including endangered pirarucu, one of the largest freshwater fishes on Earth. There are also dolphins, both pink and gray. The former evolved separately from the oceangoing dolphins when the Amazon was an inland sea. The Amazonian gray dolphins are sea dolphins that adapted to living in freshwater. Other aquatic mammals include the highly endangered manatee and otters.

The Chocó Rainforest is particularly rich in palms, of which 120 species have been identified. In fact, it is sometimes referred to as the "Land of the Palms." The forest also abounds in cycads, ancient plants that have a stout trunk and crowns of hard, stiff leaves. Chocó is also notable for more than 40 species of brightly colored poisonous frogs, known locally as *ranas kokois*. These small frogs are covered with a deadly poison and have evolved stunning coloration, from bright orange to red, gold, and blue. They are active in the day and therefore relatively easy to spot.

Of Colombia's 1,800 species of birds, more than 1,000 have been identified in the Chocó, including a large number of hummingbirds.

Offshore, the Pacific Ocean welcomes the annual migration of Antarctic humpback whales. The beaches of the Pacific coast are popular nesting areas for sea turtles, in particular the *tortuga golfina* (olive ridley) and *tortuga carey* (hawksbill) sea turtles.

CLOUD FOREST

Rainforests that grow at higher altitudes on the flanks of the Andes are known as montane rainforests or cloud forests because they are often enveloped in mist that results from the condensation of warm air against chillier mountain currents. Unlike the lowland rainforest, cloud forests only have two layers, the canopy and ground layer. Generally, the vegetation is less dense than that in the lowland rainforest. However, it is home to many palms, ferns, and epiphytes, particularly orchids.

The type of cloud forest vegetation is dictated by altitude. *Selva subandina* (sub-Andean forest) vegetation grows between the altitudes of 1,000 and 2,300 meters (3,300-7,500 feet), where temperature varies 16-23°C (61-73°F). Plant species include the distinctive Seussian white *yarumo* with its oversized leaves, as well as cedar, oak, and mahogany trees. Many palms grow here, including the svelte wax palm and *tagua*, which produces a nut that resembles ivory. Ferns include the striking *palma boba* or tree fern. Colombia's premier crop, coffee, is grown at this elevation.

At elevations between 2,300 and 3,600 meters (7,500-12,000 feet), the vegetation is described as *selva Andina* (Andean forest). This vegetation is even less dense and at higher elevations the trees are smaller. *Selva Andina* includes many oak, *encenillo, sietecuero* (glory bush), and pine trees.

Mammals include the spectacled or Andean bear, the only species of bear in South America, the mountain (or woolly) tapir, anteaters, armadillos, sloths, boars, foxes, and *olingos,* small arboreal carnivores of the raccoon family. In 2013, the *olinguito* (small *olingo*), an incredibly cute animal, was declared a new species. Other unusual animals include the slow-moving *guagua loba* and *guatín,* both of which are rodents. In addition, numerous species of monkeys inhabit the cloud forest, including noisy troops of howler monkeys. Birds include many types of *barranqueros* (motmots), including the spectacular blue-crowned motmot. Other common birds include *tángaras* (tanagers), woodpeckers, warblers, parrots, owls, and ducks, including the beautiful white-and-black torrent duck.

PÁRAMOS

Páramos are unique tropical highland ecosystems that thrive above 3,500 meters (11,500 feet), where UV radiation is higher, oxygen is scarcer, and where temperatures vary from minus-2 to 10 degrees Celsius (28-50°F). Due to frequent mist and precipitation, *páramos* are often saturated with water and have many lakes. They are true "water factories" that provide water to many of Colombia's cities, notably Bogotá. Though *páramos* exist throughout the New World tropics, most are located in Colombia. The Parque Nacional Natural Sumapaz, south of Bogotá, is the world's largest *páramo.*

Páramo vegetation includes more than 50 species of *frailejón* (genus *Espeletia*), eerily beautiful plants that have imposing tall trunks and thick yellow-greenish leaves. Other *páramo* vegetation includes shrubs, grasses, and *cojines* (cushion plants). Mammals include the spectacled bear, *páramo* tapir, weasels, squirrels, and bats. The *páramo* is the realm of the majestic black-and-white Andean condor, which has a wingspan of up to three meters (10 feet). The condor, whose numbers had declined almost to the point of extinction, is found in the national parks of the Sierra Nevada de Santa Marta, Sierra Nevada del Cocuy, and Los Nevados. The *páramo* lakes welcome many types of ducks, including the Andean duck, as well as smaller birds.

TROPICAL DRY FORESTS

Tropical dry forests exist in areas where there is a prolonged dry season. The vegetation includes deciduous trees that lose their leaves during the dry season, allowing them to conserve water. Trees on moister sites and those with access to groundwater tend to be evergreen. Before Columbus, this ecosystem covered much of the Colombian Caribbean coast. However, much of it has since been cut down

The *frailejón* grows in Colombia's *páramos* (highlands).

for cattle ranching. Pockets still exist east of the Golfo de Morrosquillo and at the base of the Sierra Nevada de Santa Marta. Tropical dry forests are the most endangered tropical ecosystem in the world.

Though less biologically diverse than rainforests, tropical dry forests are home to a wide variety of wildlife. They were once the stomping ground of the now highly endangered *marimonda*, or white-fronted spider monkey.

TROPICAL GRASSLANDS

Los Llanos (The Plains) of Colombia are covered with lush tropical grasslands.

Vegetation includes long-stemmed and carpet grasses in the drier areas and swamp grasses in low-lying humid areas. There are also thick patches of forest throughout the plains and along the rivers (known as gallery forests). These plains are teeming with wildlife, including deer, anteaters, armadillos, tapirs, otters, jaguars, pumas, and *chigüiros* (also known as capybaras), the world's largest rodent. The Llanos are also home to the giant anaconda and to one of the most endangered species on Earth, the Orinoco crocodile, which reaches up to seven meters (23 feet) long.

History

BEFORE COLUMBUS

Located at the juncture of Central and South America, what is now Colombia was a necessary transit point for the migration of people who settled South America. However, because these peoples left few physical traces of their passage, little is known of them. The oldest human objects found in Colombia, utensils discovered near Bogotá, are dated from 14,000 BC. With the expansion of agriculture and sedentary life throughout the territory of present-day Colombia around 1000 BC, various indigenous cultures started producing stunning ceramic and gold work, as well as some monumental remains. These remains provide rich material evidence of their development. Nonetheless, there are significant gaps in the understanding of the history of these early peoples.

From around 700 BC, the area of San Agustín, near the origin of the Río Magdalena in southern Colombia, was settled by people who practiced agriculture and produced pottery. Starting in the 1st century AD, the people of San Agustín created hundreds of monumental stone statues set on large platforms, which comprise the largest pre-Columbian archaeological site extant between Mesoamerica and Peru. By AD 800, this society had disappeared.

In the northwestern plains of Colombia, south of present-day Cartagena, starting in the 1st century AD, the Sinú people constructed a large complex of mounds in the shape of fish bones. These mounds regulated flooding, allowing cultivation in both rainy and dry seasons. During rainy seasons, the water flooded the lower cavities, allowing for cultivation on the mounds; during dry season, cultivation took place in the cavities that had been enriched by the flood waters. These monumental formations are still visible from overhead. By the time of the Spanish conquest, these people no longer inhabited the area.

From AD 500 to 900, the area of Tierradentro, west of San Agustín, was settled by an agricultural society that dug magnificent decorated underground tombs, produced large stone statues, and built oval-shaped buildings on artificial terraces. As in the case of the San Agustín and the Sinú people, it is not known what happened to these people.

At the time of the conquest, present-day Colombia was populated by a large number of distinct agricultural societies that often maintained peaceful trading relations among themselves. The two largest groups were the Muisca people, who lived in the altiplano (highlands) of the Cordillera Oriental, and the Tayrona, who lived on the slopes of the Sierra Nevada de Santa Marta. Other groups included the Quimbaya, who settled the area of the present-day Coffee Region; the Calima, in present-day Valle del Cauca; and the Nariños, in the mountainous areas of southwest Colombia.

These indigenous societies were mostly organized at the village level with loose association with other villages. Only the Muisca and the Tayrona had a more developed political organization. Though these were all agricultural societies, they also engaged in hunting, fishing, and mining and produced sophisticated ceramics and goldwork. Each group specialized in what their environment had to offer and engaged in overland trade. For example, the Muiscas produced textiles and salt, which they traded for gold, cotton, tobacco, and shells from other groups.

The Muiscas, a Chibcha-speaking people, were the largest group, with an estimated 600,000 inhabitants at the time of the Spanish conquest. They settled the Cordillera Oriental in AD 300 and occupied a large territory that comprises most of the highland areas of the present-day departments of Cundinamarca and Boyacá. At the time of the conquest, they were organized into two large confederations: one in the south headed by the Zipa, whose capital was Bacatá near present-day Bogotá, and another headed by the Zaque, whose capital was at Hunza, the location of present-day Tunja. The Muiscas had a highly homogeneous culture, and were skilled in weaving, ceramics, and goldwork. Their cosmography placed significant importance on high Andean lakes, several of which were sacred, including Guatavita, Siecha, and Iguaque.

The Tayrona, who settled the slopes of the Sierra Nevada de Santa Marta, were also a Chibcha-speaking people. They had a more urban society, with towns that included temples and ceremonial plazas built on stone terraces, and practiced farming on terraces carved out of the mountains. There are an estimated 200 Tayrona sites, of which Ciudad Perdida (Lost City), built at 1,100 meters (3,600 feet) in the Sierra Nevada de Santa Marta, is the largest and best known. Many of these towns, including El Pueblito in the Parque Nacional Natural Tayrona, were occupied at the time of the Spanish conquest. The Kogis, Arhuacos, Kankuamos, and Wiwas, current inhabitants of the sierra, are their descendants and consider many places in the sierra sacred.

THE SPANISH CONQUEST (1499-1550)

As elsewhere in the New World, the arrival of Europeans was an unmitigated disaster for the Native American societies. Though there were pockets of resistance, on the whole the indigenous people were unable to push back the small number of armed Spanish conquistadores. Harsh conditions after the conquest and the spread of European diseases, such as measles and smallpox, to which the indigenous people had no immunity, killed off millions of natives. The Spanish conquest of present-day Colombia took about 50 years and was largely completed by the 1550s.

In 1499, the first European set foot on present-day Colombia in the northern Guajira Peninsula. In 1510, a first, unsuccessful colony was established in the Golfo de Urabá near the current border with Panama. In 1526, the Spanish established Santa Marta, their first permanent foothold, from where they tried, unsuccessfully, to subdue the Tayronas. In 1533, they established Cartagena, which was to become a major colonial port.

In 1536, Gonzalo Jiménez de Quesada set off south from Santa Marta to conquer the fabled lands of El Dorado in the Andean heartland. After a year of grueling travel up the swampy Río Magdalena valley, 200 surviving members of Jiménez de Quesada's 800 original troops arrived in the Muisca lands near present-day Bogotá. After a short interlude of courteous relations, the Spaniards' greed led them to obliterate the Muisca towns and temples. They found significant amounts of gold, especially in the town of Hunza, but they were, by and large, disappointed. In

428

1538, Jiménez de Quesada founded Santa Fe de Bogotá as the capital of this new territory, which he called Nueva Granada—New Granada—after his birthplace.

Sebastián de Belalcázar, a lieutenant of Francisco Pizarro, led a second major expedition that arrived in the Muisca lands from the south. Having conquered the Inca city of Quito, Belalcázar and his army traveled north, conquering a vast swath of land from present-day Ecuador to the *sábana* (high plateau) of Bogotá. Along the way, he founded several cities, including Popayán and Cali in 1536. He arrived shortly after Quesada had founded Bogotá. Incredibly, a third conquistador, the German Nikolaus Federmann, arrived in Bogotá at the same time, having traveled from Venezuela via the Llanos. Rather than fight for supremacy, the three conquistadores decided to take their rival claims to arbitration at the Spanish court. In an unexpected turn of events, none of the three obtained title to the Muisca lands: When Bogotá became the administrative capital of New Granada, they came under the sway of the Spanish crown. Other expeditions swept across the Caribbean coast, through current-day Antioquia and the Santanderes.

COLONIAL NUEVA GRANADA (1550-1810)

For most of its colonial history, Nueva Granada, as colonial Colombia was called, was an appendage of the Viceroyalty of Peru. In 1717, Spain decided to establish a viceroyalty in Nueva Granada but changed its mind six years later because the benefits did not justify the cost. In 1739, the viceroyalty was reestablished, with Santa Fe de Bogotá as its capital. It was an unwieldy territory, encompassing present-day Colombia, Venezuela, Ecuador, and Panama. To make it more manageable, Venezuela and Panama were ruled by captain-generals and Ecuador by a president. At the local level, the viceroyalty was divided into *provincias* (provinces), each with a local assembly called a *cabildo*.

Settlement in Nueva Granada occurred primarily in three areas: where there were significant indigenous populations to exploit, as in the case of Tunja in the former Muisca territory; where there were gold deposits, as in Cauca, Antioquia, and Santander; and along trade routes, for example at Honda and Mompox on the Río Magdalena. Cartagena was the main port of call for the biennial convoys of gold and silver sent to Spain. Bogotá lived off of the official bureaucracy and sustained a fair number of artisans. Present-day Antioquia and Santander supported small-scale farming to provide provisions to the gold mining camps. Nueva Granada was one of the least economically dynamic of Spain's New World possessions. The mountainous topography and high transportation costs meant that agricultural production was primarily for local consumption and gold was the only significant export.

Colonial society was composed of a small Spanish and Creole (descendants of Spanish settlers) elite class that governed a large mestizo (mixed indigenous-white) population. The Spanish had initially preserved indigenous communal lands known as *resguardos*, but the demographic collapse of the native population and intermarriage meant that, unlike in Peru or Mexico, there were relatively few people who were fully indigenous. There were also black slaves who were forced mostly to work in the mines and haciendas (plantations). Society was overwhelmingly Catholic and Spanish-speaking.

Culturally, Nueva Granada was also somewhat of a backwater. Though there was a modest flourishing of the arts, Bogotá could not compete with the magnificent architectural and artistic production of Quito, Lima, or Mexico City. The only truly notable event of learning that took place was the late 18th-century Expedición Botánica (Botanical Expedition), headed by Spanish naturalist José Celestino Mutis, the personal doctor to one of the viceroys. The aim of the expedition was to survey all the species of Nueva Granada—a rather tall order given that Colombia is home to 10 percent of the world's species. However, the expedition did some remarkable research and produced beautiful prints of the fauna and flora.

The late colonial period saw unrest in Nueva Granada. Starting in 1781, a revolt known as the Rebelión de los Comuneros took place in the province of Socorro (north of Bogotá) in present-day Santander as a result of an attempt by colonial authorities to levy higher taxes. It was not an antiroyalist movement, however, as its slogan indicates: *¡Viva el Rey, Muera el Mal Gobierno!* ("Long live the king, down with bad government!"). Rather it was a protest against unfair taxes, not much different from the Boston Tea Party. However, it gave the Spanish government a fright. A rebel army, led by José Antonio Galán, marched on Bogotá. Negotiations put an end to the assault, and later the authorities ruthlessly persecuted the leaders of the revolt.

STRUGGLE FOR INDEPENDENCE (1810-1821)

Though there was some ill feeling against the colonial government, as the Rebelión de los Comuneros attests, as well as rivalry between the Spanish- and American-born elites, it was an external event, the Napoleonic invasion of Spain, that set off the chain of events that led to independence of Nueva Granada and the rest of the Spanish dominion in the New World.

In 1808, Napoleon invaded Spain, took King Ferdinand VII prisoner, and tried to impose his own brother, Joseph, as king of Spain. The Spaniards revolted, establishing a Central Junta in Seville to govern during the king's temporary absence from power. Faced with the issue of whether to recognize the new Central Junta in Spain, the colonial elites decided to take matters in their own hands and establish juntas of their own. The first such junta in Nueva Granada was established in Caracas in April 1810. Cartagena followed suit in May and Bogotá on July 20, 1810. According to popular myth, the revolt in Bogotá was the result of the failure of a prominent Spaniard merchant to lend a flower vase to a pair of Creoles.

Though they pledged alliance to Ferdinand VII, once the local elites had tasted power, there was no going back. Spanish authorities were expelled, and in 1811, a government of sorts, under the loose mantle of the Provincias Unidas de Nueva Granada (United Provinces of New Granada), was established with its capital at Tunja. Bogotá and the adjoining province of Cundinamarca stayed aloof from the confederation, arguing that it was too weak to resist the Spanish. Subsequently, various provinces of Nueva Granada declared outright independence, starting with Venezuela and Cartagena in 1811 and Cundinamarca in 1813.

Several cities remained loyal to the crown, namely Santa Marta and deeply conservative Pasto in the south. From 1812 to 1814 there was a senseless civil war between the Provincias Unidas and Cundinamarca—that is why this period is called the Patria Boba, or Foolish Fatherland. Ultimately, the Provincias Unidas prevailed with the help of a young Venezuelan captain by the name of Simón Bolívar.

After the restoration of Ferdinand VII, Spain attempted to retake its wayward colonies, with a military expedition and reign of terror known as the Reconquista—the Reconquest. The Spanish forces took Cartagena by siege in 1815 and took control of Bogotá in May 1816. However, in 1819, a revolutionary army composed of Venezuelans, Nueva Granadans, and European mercenaries headed by Bolívar arrived across the Llanos from Venezuela and decisively defeated the Spanish army in the Batalla del Puente de Boyacá—the Battle of the Boyacá Bridge—on August 7, near Tunja. The rest of the country fell quickly to the revolutionary army. With support from Nueva Granada, Bolívar defeated the Spanish in Venezuela in 1821. Panama, which had remained under Spanish control, declared independence in 1821. Finally, Bolívar dispatched Antonio José de Sucre to take Quito in 1822, bringing an end to the Spanish rule of Nueva Granada.

GRAN COLOMBIA: A FLAWED UNION (1821-1830)

Shortly after the Battle of Boyacá, the Congress of Angostura, a city on the Río Orinoco in Venezuela, proclaimed the union of Nueva Granada, Venezuela, and Ecuador under the name of the República de Colombia. Historians refer to this entity as Gran Colombia. In 1821, while the fight for independence was still raging in parts of Venezuela and Ecuador, a constitutional congress met in Cúcuta. An ongoing debate about whether a centralist or federalist scheme was preferable resulted in a curious compromise: the República de Colombia assumed a highly centralist form, considered necessary to finish the battle for independence, but left the issue of federalism open to review after 10 years. The document was generally liberal, enshrining individual liberties and providing for the manumission of slaves, meaning that the children of slaves were born free.

Bolívar, who was born in Venezuela, was named president. Francisco de Paula Santander, who was born near Cúcuta in Nueva Granada, was named vice president. Santander had fought alongside Bolívar in the battles for independence of Nueva Granada and was seen as an able administrator. While Bolívar continued south to liberate Ecuador and Peru, Santander assumed the reins of power in Bogotá. He charted a generally liberal course, instituting public education and a curriculum that included avant-garde thinkers such as Jeremy Bentham. However, the highly centralist structure was unsavory to elites in Venezuela and Ecuador, who disliked rule from Bogotá. Shortly after the Congress of Cúcuta, revolt broke out in Venezuela and Ecuador. In 1826, Bolívar returned from Bolivia and Peru, hoping for the adoption in Gran Colombia of the Bolivian Constitution, an unusual document he drafted that called for a presidency for life.

There had been a growing distance between Bolívar and Santander: Bolívar saw Santander as an overzealous liberal reformer while Santander disliked Bolívar's authoritarian tendencies. In 1828, after a failed constitutional congress that met in Ocaña in eastern Colombia, Bolívar assumed dictatorial powers. He rolled back many of Santander's liberal reforms. In September 1828 there was an attempt on Bolívar's life in Bogotá. This was famously foiled by his companion, Manuela Sáenz. The last years of Gran Colombia were marked by revolts in various parts of the

a plaque in Mompox, denoting Simón Bolívar's presence

AQUÍ HOSPEDOSE **BOLIVAR** EN 1827 y 1830

2·44

country and a war with Peru. In 1830, a further constitutional assembly was convened in Bogotá, but by that point Gran Colombia had ceased to exist: Venezuela and Ecuador had seceded. In March 1830, a physically ill Bolívar decided to leave for voluntary exile in Europe and died on his way in Santa Marta.

CIVIL WARS AND CONSTITUTIONS (1830-1902)

After the separation of Venezuela and Ecuador, what is now Colombia adopted the name República de Nueva Granada. In 1832, it adopted a new constitution that corrected many of the errors of the excessively centralist constitution of Gran Colombia. There was a semblance of stability with the orderly succession of elected presidents. The elimination of some monasteries in Pasto sparked a short civil conflict known as the Guerra de los Supremos, which lasted 1839-1842. During this war, Conservative and Liberal factions coalesced for the first time, establishing the foundation of Colombia's two-party system. Generally, the Conservative Party supported the Catholic Church, favored centralization, and followed the ideas of Bolívar. The Liberal Party supported federalism and free trade and identified with the ideas of Santander.

The country's rugged topography meant that Nueva Granada was not very integrated into the world economy. Gold, extracted mostly in Antioquia, was the main export. Most of the country eked out its subsistence from agriculture, with trade restricted within regions. This period saw some economic development, such as steam navigation on the Magdalena and Cauca Rivers, and a contract for the construction of the trans-isthmian railroad in Panama, which had yet to secede.

Midcentury saw the rise of a new class of leaders who had grown up wholly under Republican governments. They ushered in a period of liberal reform. In 1851, Congress abolished slavery. In 1853, a new constitution established universal male suffrage, religious tolerance, and direct election of provincial governors. The government reduced tariffs and Nueva Granada experienced a short export-oriented tobacco boom.

Conflicts between radical reformers within the Liberal Party, moderates, and Conservatives led to unrest in various provinces. In 1859, discontented Liberals under Tomás Cipriano de Mosquera revolted, leading to generalized civil war in which the Liberals were ultimately victorious. Once in power, they pushed radical reform. Mosquera expropriated all nonreligious church property, partly in vengeance for church support of the Conservatives in the previous civil war.

The 1863 constitution was one of the world's most audacious federalist experiments. The country was renamed the Estados Unidos de Colombia (United States of Colombia), comprising nine states. The president had a two-year term and was not immediately reelectable. All powers that were not explicitly assigned to the central government were the responsibility of the states. Many of the states engaged in true progressive policies, such as establishing public education and promoting the construction of railroads. This period coincided with agricultural booms in quinine, cotton, and indigo that, for the first time, brought limited prosperity. This period saw the establishment of the Universidad Nacional (National University) and the country's first bank.

In 1880 and then in 1884, a coalition of Conservatives and moderate Liberals, who were dissatisfied with radical policies, elected Rafael Núñez as president. Núñez tried to strengthen the power of the central government, sparking a Liberal revolt. The Conservatives were ultimately victorious and, in 1886, enacted a new centralist constitution that lasted through most of the 20th century. The country was rechristened República de Colombia, the name it has conserved since then. During the period from 1886 through 1904, known as the Regeneración, the Conservative Party held sway, rolling back many of the previous reforms, especially anticlerical measures and unrestricted male suffrage. The Liberal Party, excluded from power, revolted in 1899. The ensuing Guerra de los Mil Días (Thousand Days' War), which raged through 1902, was a terribly bloody conflict. It is not clear how many died in the war, but some historians put the figure as high as 100,000, or an incredible 2.5 percent of the country's population of four million at the time.

One year after the end of the war, Panama seceded. During the late 19th century, there had been resentment in Panama about the distribution of revenues from the transit trade that mostly were sent to Bogotá. However, in 1902 the local Panamanian elites had become alarmed at the lackadaisical attitude of the government in Bogotá regarding the construction of an interoceanic canal. After the failure of the French to build a canal, Colombia had entered into negotiations with the United States. In the closing days of the Guerra de los Mil Días, Colombia and the United States signed the Hay-Terran Treaty, which called for the construction of the canal, surrendering control over a strip of land on either side of the canal to the United States. The Americans threatened that if the treaty were not ratified, they would dig the canal in Nicaragua. Arguing that the treaty undermined Colombian sovereignty, the congress in Bogotá unanimously rejected it in August 1903. That was a big mistake: A few months later, Panama seceded with the support of the United States.

PEACE AND REFORM (1902-1946)

Under the leadership of moderate Conservative Rafael Reyes, who was president 1904-1909, Colombia entered a period of peace and stability. Reyes focused on creating a professional, nonpartisan army. He gave representation to Liberals in government, enacted a protective tariff to spur domestic industry, and pushed public works. During his administration, Bogotá was finally connected by railway to the Río Magdalena. He reestablished relations with the United States, signing

a treaty that provided Colombia with an indemnity for the loss of Panama. During the 1920s and 1930s, Colombia was governed by a succession of Conservative Party presidents. Though there was often electoral fraud, constitutional reform that guaranteed minority representation ensured peace.

Expanding world demand for coffee spurred production across Colombia, especially in southern Antioquia and what is now known as the Coffee Region, creating a new class of independent farmers. Improved transportation, especially the completion of the railways from Cali to Buenaventura on the Pacific coast and from Medellín to the Río Magdalena, was key to the growth of coffee exports. In the Magdalena Medio region and in Norte de Santander, U.S. companies explored and started producing petroleum. Medellín became a center of textile manufacturing. With the country's broken geography, air transportation developed rapidly. The Sociedad Colombo Alemana de Transportes Aéreos (Colombian German Air Transportation Society) or SCADTA, the predecessor of Avianca, was founded in Barranquilla in 1919, and is reputedly the second-oldest commercial aviation company in the world (the oldest is KLM).

In 1930, a split Conservative ticket allowed the Liberals to win the elections. After being out of power for 50 years, the Liberal Party was happy to regain control of the state apparatus. This led to strife with Conservatives long accustomed to power—presaging the intense interparty violence that was to erupt 14 years later.

From 1932 to 1933, Colombia and Peru fought a brief war in the Amazon over the control of the port city of Leticia. The League of Nations brokered a truce, the first time that this body, which was a precursor to the United Nations, actively intervened in a dispute between two countries.

Starting in 1934, Liberal president Alfonso López Pumarejo undertook major social and labor reforms, with some similarities to Roosevelt's New Deal. His policies included agrarian reform, encouragement and protection of labor unions, and increased spending on education. He reduced the Catholic Church's sway over education and eliminated the literacy requirement for male voters. Many of these reforms simply returned the country to policies that had been enacted by Liberals in the 1850s, 80 years prior. In opposition to these policies, a new radical right, with a confrontational style and strains of fascism and anti-Semitism, arose under the leadership of Laureano Gómez.

During World War II, Colombia closely allied itself with the United States and eventually declared war on the Axis powers in retaliation for German attacks on Colombian merchant ships in the Caribbean Sea. The government concentrated those of German descent in a hotel in Fusagasugá near Bogotá and removed all German influence from SCADTA.

LA VIOLENCIA (1946-1953)

In the 1946 elections, the Liberal Party split its ticket between establishment-backed Gabriel Turbay and newcomer Jorge Eliécer Gaitán. Gaitán was a self-made man who had scaled the ladders of power within the Liberal Party despite the opposition of the traditional Liberal elite. He had a vaguely populist platform and much charisma. The moderate Conservative Mariano Ospina won a plurality of votes and was elected to the presidency. As in 1930, the transfer of power from Liberals to Conservatives and bureaucratic reaccommodation led to outbursts of violence.

On April 9, 1948, a deranged youth killed former presidential candidate Gaitán as he left his office in downtown Bogotá. His assassination sparked riots and bloodshed throughout the country, with severe destruction in the capital. The disturbance in Bogotá, known as El Bogotazo, occurred during the 9th Inter-American Conference, which had brought together leaders from all over the hemisphere. Young Fidel Castro happened to

be in Bogotá that day, though he had no part in the upheaval.

The assassination of Gaitán further incited the violence that had started in 1946. Over the course of 10 years, an estimated 100,000-200,000 people died in what was laconically labeled La Violencia (The Violence). This conflict was comparable in destruction of human life with the Guerra de los Mil Días, the last civil war of the 19th century. The killing took place throughout the country, often in small towns and rural areas. Mostly it involved loyalists of the predominant party settling scores or intimidating members of the opposite party in order to extract land or secure economic gain. In some cases, the violence was sheer banditry. Numerous, horrific mass murders took place. The police often took sides with the Conservatives or simply turned a blind eye. In response, some Liberals resorted to armed resistance, giving birth to Colombia's first guerrilla armies. The Liberal Party boycotted the 1950 elections, and radical Conservative Laureano Gómez was elected president. His government pursued authoritarian and highly partisan policies, further exacerbating the violence.

DICTATORSHIP (1953-1957)

In 1953, with the purported aim of bringing an end to fighting between Liberals and Conservatives, the Colombian army, under the command of General Gustavo Rojas Pinilla, staged a coup. Rojas was able to reduce, but not halt, the violence, by curtailing police support of the Conservatives and by negotiating an amnesty with Liberal guerrillas. In 1954, Rojas was elected for a four-term period by a handpicked assembly. Incidentally, it was this, nondemocratically elected assembly that finally got around to extending suffrage to women, making Colombia one of the last countries in Latin America to do so. Rojas tried to build a populist regime with the support of organized labor, modeled after Perón in Argentina. His daughter, María Eugenia Rojas, though no Evita, was put in charge of social welfare programs. Though a majority of Colombians supported Rojas at first, his repressive policies and press censorship ended up alienating the political elites.

THE NATIONAL FRONT (1957-1974)

In May 1957, under the leadership of a coalition of Liberals and Conservatives, the country went on an extended general strike to oppose the dictatorship. Remarkably, Rojas voluntarily surrendered power and went into exile in Spain. As a way to put an end to La Violencia, Liberal and Conservative Party leaders proposed alternating presidential power for four consecutive terms while divvying up the bureaucracy on a 50-50 basis. The proposal, labeled the National Front, was ratified by a nationwide referendum and was in effect 1958-1974.

The National Front dramatically reduced the level of violence. After years of fighting, both factions were ready to give up their arms. During this period, thanks to competent economic management, the economy prospered and incomes rose. The government adopted import substitution policies that gave rise to a number of new industries, including automobiles.

By institutionalizing the power of the two traditional parties, the National Front had the unintended consequence of squeezing out other political movements, especially from the left. As a result, during the 1960s a number of leftist guerrilla groups appeared. Some were simply the continuation, under a new name, of the guerrilla groups formed during La Violencia. The Fuerzas Armadas Revolucionarias de Colombia (FARC) was a rural, peasant-based group espousing Soviet Marxism. The Ejército de Liberación Nacional (ELN) was a smaller group inspired by the Cuban revolution. The even smaller Ejército Popular de Liberación (EPL) was a Maoist-inspired group. The Movimiento 19 de Abril (M-19) was a more urban group formed by middle-class intellectuals after alleged electoral fraud deprived the populist ANAPO

Party (Alianza Nacional Popular; created by ex-dictator Rojas) of power. During the 1970s and 1980s, the M-19 staged flashy coups, such as stealing Bolívar's sword (and promising to return it once the revolution had been achieved) in 1974 and seizing control of the embassy of the Dominican Republic in Bogotá in 1980.

UNDER SIEGE (1974-1991)
The Drug Trade and the Rise of Illegal Armed Groups

Due to its relative proximity to the United States, treacherous geography, and weak government institutions, Colombia has been an ideal place for cultivation, production, and shipment of illegal drugs, primarily to the United States. During the 1970s, Colombia experienced a short-lived marijuana boom centered on the Sierra Nevada de Santa Marta. Eradication efforts by Colombian authorities and competition from homegrown marijuana produced in the United States quickly brought this boom to an end.

During the late 1970s, cocaine replaced marijuana as the main illegal drug. Though most of the coca cultivation at the time was in Peru and Bolivia, Colombian drug dealers based in Medellín started the business of picking up coca paste in Peru and Bolivia, processing it into cocaine in Colombia, and exporting the drug to the United States, where they even controlled some distribution at the local level. At its heyday in the mid-1980s, Pablo Escobar's Medellín Cartel controlled 80 percent of the world's cocaine trade. The rival Cali Cartel, controlled by the Rodríguez brothers, emerged in the 1980s and started to contest the supremacy of the Medellín Cartel, leading to a bloody feud.

During the 1980s and 1990s, coca cultivation shifted from Peru and Bolivia to Colombia, mainly to the Amazon regions of Putumayo, Caquetá, Meta, and Guaviare. Initially, leftist guerrillas such as the FARC protected the fields from the authorities in return for payment from the cartels. Eventually, they started processing and trafficking the drugs themselves. Though the guerrillas had other sources of income, such as kidnapping and extortion, especially of oil companies operating in the Llanos, the drug trade was a key factor in their growth. With these sources of income, they no longer needed popular support and morphed into criminal organizations. By the mid-1980s, the FARC had grown into a 4,000-person-strong army that controlled large portions of territory, especially in the south of the country.

During the 1980s and 1990s, the price of land was depressed as a result of the threat posed by the guerrillas. Using their vast wealth and power of intimidation, drug traffickers purchased vast swaths of land, mostly along the Caribbean coast of Colombia, at bargain prices. To defend their properties from extortion, they allied themselves with traditional landowners to create paramilitary groups. These groups often operated with the direct or tacit support of the army.

Colombian campesinos (small farmers), caught in the middle of the conflict between guerrillas and paramilitaries, suffered disproportionately. They were accused by both guerrillas and paramilitaries of sympathizing with the enemy, and the government was not there to protect them. The paramilitaries were particularly ruthless, often ordering entire villages to abandon their lands or massacring the population. The conflict between guerrillas and paramilitaries is at the source of the mass displacement of people in Colombia. According to the Office of the United Nations High Commissioner for Refugees, the number of displaced people in Colombia ranges 3.9-5.3 million, making it the country with the most internal refugees in the world.

Peace Negotiations with the FARC and M-19

In 1982, President Belisario Betancur was elected with the promise of negotiating peace with the guerrillas. The negotiations with the guerrillas got nowhere, but the FARC did establish a political party, the Unión Patriótica (UP), which successfully participated in the 1986 presidential elections and 1988 local elections, managing to win some mayoralties. The paramilitaries and local elites did not want the political arm of the FARC to wield local power. As a result, the UP was subjected to a brutal persecution by the paramilitaries, who killed more than 1,000 party members. In the midst of this violence, Colombia suffered one of its worst natural disasters: the eruption of the Nevado del Ruiz in November 1985, which produced a massive mudslide that engulfed the town of Armero, killing more than 20,000 people.

In 1985, the M-19 brazenly seized the Palacio de Justicia in Bogotá. The Colombian army responded with a heavy hand, and in the ensuing battle, half of Colombia's Supreme Court justices were killed. Many people, including many cafeteria employees, disappeared in the army takeover, and there is speculation that they were executed and buried in a mass grave in the south of Bogotá. Weakened by this fiasco, leaders of the M-19 took up President Virgilio Barco's offer to negotiate peace. The government set down clear rules, including a cease-fire on the part of the M-19, before talks could proceed. Unlike the FARC, the M-19 was still an ideological movement. The leaders of the M-19 saw that by participating in civil life they could probably gain more than by fighting. And they were right: In 2011 the people of Bogotá elected Gustavo Petro, a former M-19 guerrilla, as their mayor. On March 19, 1990, Barco and the M-19's young leader, Carlos Pizarro, signed a peace agreement, the only major successful peace agreement to date between the authorities and a major guerrilla group.

The Rise and Fall of the Medellín Cartel

Initially, the Colombian establishment turned a blind eye to the rise of the drug cartels and even took a favorable view of the paramilitaries, who were seen as an antidote to the scourge of the guerrillas. For a time, Escobar was active in politics and cultivated a Robin Hood image, funding public works such as parks and housing projects. Rather than stick to his business, as the Cali Cartel did, Escobar started to threaten any official who tried to check his power. In 1984, he had Rodrigo Lara Bonilla, the minister of justice, assassinated. When the government subsequently cracked down, Escobar declared outright war. He assassinated judges and political leaders, set off car bombs to intimidate public opinion, and paid a reward for every policeman that was murdered in Medellín—a total of 657. To take out an enemy, he planted a bomb in an Avianca flight from Bogotá to Cali, killing all passengers on board. The Medellín Cartel planted dozens of massive bombs in Bogotá and throughout the country, terrorizing the country's population. The cartel is allegedly responsible for the assassination of three presidential candidates in 1990: Luis Carlos Galán, the staunchly antimafia candidate of the Liberal Party; Carlos Pizarro, the candidate of the newly demobilized M-19; and Bernardo Jaramillo, candidate of the Unión Patriótica.

There was really only one thing that Escobar feared—extradition to the United States. Through bribery and intimidation, he managed to get extradition outlawed, and he negotiated a lopsided deal with the government of César Gaviria: In return for his surrender, he was allowed to control the jail where he was locked up. From the luxurious confines of La Catedral, as the prison was named, he continued to run his empire. In 1992 there was an outcry when it became known that he had interrogated and executed enemies within the jail. When he got wind that the government planned to transfer him to another prison, he fled. In December 1993, government intelligence intercepted a phone call he made to his family, located him in Medellín, and killed him on a rooftop as he attempted to flee. It is widely believed that the Cali Cartel actively aided the authorities in the manhunt.

A New Constitution
The 1990s started on a positive footing with the enactment of a new constitution in 1991.

The Constitutional Assembly that drafted the charter was drawn from all segments of the political spectrum, including the recently demobilized M-19. The new constitution was very progressive, devolving considerable power to local communities and recognizing the rights of indigenous and Afro-Colombian communities to govern their communities and ancestral lands. The charter created a powerful new Constitutional Court, which has become a stalwart defender of basic rights, as well as an independent accusatory justice system, headed by a powerful attorney general, which was created to reduce impunity.

COLOMBIA ON THE BRINK (1992-2002)
New Cartels, Paramilitaries, and Guerrillas
Drug cultivation and production increased significantly during the 1990s. The overall land dedicated to coca cultivation rose from 60,000 hectares (148,300 acres) in 1992 to 165,000 hectares (407,700 acres) in 2002. As a result of the government's successful crackdown first on the Medellín Cartel and then on the Cali Cartel, drug production split into smaller, more nimble criminal organizations. During the 1990s, the paramilitaries became stand-alone organizations that engaged in drug trafficking, expanding to more than 30,000 men in 2002. They created a national structure called the Autodefensas Unidas de Colombia, or AUC, under the leadership of Carlos Castaño. The AUC coordinated activities with local military commanders and committed atrocious crimes, often massacring scores of so-called sympathizers of guerrillas.

At the same time, the guerrillas expanded significantly during the 1990s. Strengthened by hefty revenues from kidnapping, extortion, and drug trafficking, they grew to more than 50,000 mostly peasant fighters in 2002. Their strategy was dictated primarily by military and economic considerations and they had little to no public support. At their heyday, the FARC covered the entire country, attacking military garrisons and even threatening major urban centers such as Cali. They performed increasingly large operations, such as attacking Mitú, the capital of the department of Vaupés, in 1998 or kidnapping 12 members of the Assembly of Valle del Cauca in Cali in 2002. The FARC commanders moved around the countryside unchecked. In the territories they controlled, they ruled over civilians, often committing heinous crimes. In 2002, they attacked a church in the town of Bojayá in Chocó, killing more than 100 unarmed civilians, including many children, who had sought refuge there.

Plan Colombia

The increasing growth of drug exports from Colombia to the United States in the 1990s became a source of concern for the U.S. government. From 1994 to 1998, the United States was reluctant to provide support to Colombia because the president at the time, Ernesto Samper, was tainted by accusations of having received campaign money from drug traffickers and because of evidence about human rights abuses by the Colombian army. When Andrés Pastrana was elected president in 1998, the Colombian and U.S. administrations designed a strategy to curb drug production and counteract the insurgency called Plan Colombia. This strategy had both military and social components, and was to be financed jointly by the United States and Colombia. Ultimately, the United States provided Colombia, which was becoming one of its strongest and most loyal allies in Latin America, with more than US$7 billion, heavily weighted toward military aid, especially for training and for providing aerial mobility to Colombian troops. While the impact of Plan Colombia was not immediately visible, over time it changed the balance of power in favor of the government, allowing the Colombian army to regain the upper hand in the following years.

Flawed Peace Negotiations with the FARC

President Pastrana embarked on what is now widely believed to have been an ill-conceived, hurried peace process with the FARC. He had met Manuel Marulanda, the head of the FARC, before his inauguration in 1998 and was convinced that he could bring about a quick peace. Without a clear framework, in November 1998 he acceded to the FARC's request to grant them a demilitarized zone the size of Switzerland in the eastern departments of Meta and Caquetá. In hindsight, it seems clear that the FARC had no interest or need to negotiate as they were at the peak of their military power. Rather, the FARC commanders saw the grant of the demilitarized zone as an opportunity to strengthen their organization.

From the beginning, it became clear that the FARC did not take the peace process seriously. Marulanda failed to show up at the inaugural ceremony of the peace process, leaving a forlorn Pastrana sitting alone on the stage next to a now famous *silla vacilla* (empty seat). They ran the demilitarized zone as a mini-state, nicknamed Farclandia, using it to smuggle arms, hold kidnapped prisoners, and process cocaine. During the peace negotiations, the FARC continued their attacks on the military and civilians. In February 2002, after the FARC kidnapped Eduardo Gechem, senator and president of the Senate Peace Commission, Pastrana declared the end of this ill-advised demilitarized zone and sent in the Colombian army.

A Failed State?

In 2002, the Colombian army was battling more than 50,000 guerrillas and 30,000 paramilitaries, with an estimated 6,000 child soldiers among those groups. The insurgents controlled approximately 75 percent of the country's territory. An estimated 100,000 antipersonnel mines covered 30 of 32 departments. More than 2.5 million people had been internally displaced between 1985 and 2003, with 300,000 people displaced in 2002 alone. Not surprisingly, prestigious publications such as *Foreign Policy* described Colombia at the time as failed state.

REGAINING ITS FOOTING (2002-PRESENT)
Álvaro Uribe's Assault on the Guerrillas

In the 2002 elections, fed-up Colombians overwhelmingly elected Álvaro Uribe, a former governor of Antioquia who promised to take the fight to the guerrillas. Uribe had a real grudge against the FARC, who had assassinated his father. The FARC were not fans of his, either. In a brazen show of defiance, during Uribe's inauguration ceremony in Bogotá on August 7, 2002, the guerrilla group fired various rockets aimed at the presidential palace during a post-swearing-in reception. Several rockets struck the exterior of the palace, causing minor damage (attendees were unaware of the attack), but many more fell on the humble dwellings in barrios nearby, killing 21.

During his first term, Uribe embarked on a policy of Seguridad Democrática, or Democratic Security, based on strengthening the army, eradicating illicit crops to deprive the guerrillas of revenues, and creating a controversial network of civilian collaborators who were paid for providing tips that led to successful operations against the insurgents. The government increased military expenditure and decreed taxes on the rich totaling US$4 billion to finance the cost of the war. Colombian military personnel grew from 300,000 in 2002 to 400,000 in 2007.

From 2002 to 2003, the army evicted the FARC from the central part of the country around Bogotá and Medellín, although that did not prevent them from causing terror in the cities. In February 2003, a car bomb attributed to the FARC exploded in the parking lot of the exclusive social club El Nogal, killing more than 30 people—mostly employees. From 2004 to 2006, the army pressed the FARC in its stronghold in the southern part of the country. Aerial spraying of coca crops brought down cultivated areas from 165,000 hectares (407,700 acres) in 2002 to 76,000 hectares (187,800 acres) in 2006.

In 2006, Uribe was reelected by a landslide, after Congress amended the constitution to allow for immediate presidential reelection. There is clear evidence that the government effectively bribed two congressmen whose votes were necessary for passage of the measure. Uribe interpreted the election results as a mandate to continue single-mindedly pursuing the guerrillas. The FARC came under severe stress, with thousands of guerrillas deserting, and for the first time, the FARC was subjected to effective strikes against top commanders. No longer safe in their traditional jungle strongholds in Colombia, many FARC operatives crossed the border into Venezuela and Ecuador, causing tension between Colombia and the governments of those countries.

In early 2008, the Colombian military bombed and killed leading FARC commander Raúl Reyes in a camp in Ecuador, causing a diplomatic crisis with that country. Later that year, the military executed Operación Jaque (Operation Checkmate), a dramatic rescue operation in which they duped the FARC into handing over their most important hostages. The hostages released included three U.S. defense contractors and Ingrid Betancur, a French-Colombian independent presidential candidate who was kidnapped by the FARC during the 2002 presidential election as she proceeded by land, against the advice of the military, toward the capital of the former FARC demilitarized zone. In 2008, Manuel Marulanda, founder of the FARC, died a natural death. At that time, it was estimated that the FARC forces had plummeted to about 9,000 fighters, half of what they had been eight years before.

The Colombian army has been implicated in serious human rights abuses. Pressure from top brass to show results in the war against the guerrillas and the possibility of obtaining extended vacation time led several garrisons to execute civilians and present them as guerrillas killed in combat. In 2008, it was discovered that numerous young poor men from the city of Soacha, duped by false promises of work, had been taken to rural areas, assassinated by the army, and presented as guerrillas killed in anti-insurgency operations. This macabre episode—referred to as the scandal of *falsos positives* (false positives)—was done under the watch of Minister of Defense Juan Manuel Santos, who was later elected president of Colombia.

Peace Process with the AUC

From 2003 to 2008, the Uribe government pursued a controversial peace process with the right-wing paramilitaries, the Autodefensas Unidas de Colombia. As part of that process, an estimated 28,000 paramilitary fighters demobilized, including most of the high-level commanders. In 2005, the Colombian Congress passed the Justice and Peace Law to provide a legal framework for the process. Unlike previous peace laws that simply granted an amnesty to the insurgents, this law provided for reduced sentences for paramilitaries who had committed serious crimes in exchange for full confessions and reparation of victims. Domestic and international observers were extremely skeptical about the process, worrying that the paramilitaries would use their power to pressure for lenient terms. These misgivings were justified by evidence that they used their power of coercion to influence the results of the 2006 parliamentary elections, a scandal referred to as *parapolítica*. Many congresspersons, including a first cousin of Uribe, ended up in prison.

It soon became clear that the paramilitary commanders were not sincere in their commitment to peace. Many refused to confess crimes and transferred their assets to front men. Covertly, they continued their drug-trafficking operations. The government placed scant importance on the truth and reparation elements of the Justice and Peace Law, severely underfunding the effort to redress crimes committed against more than 150,000 victims who had signed up as part of the process. Through 2008, the paramilitaries had confessed to a mere 2,700 crimes, a fraction of the estimated total, and refused to hand over assets. Fed up with their lack of cooperation, in 2008 Uribe extradited 14 top-ranking paramilitary commanders to the United States, where they were likely to face long sentences. However, the extradition severely hampered the effort to obtain truth and reparation for the victims of their crimes.

The difficulty in redressing the crimes against victims has been further troubled by the growth of the dozens of small *bacrim* (*bandas criminals,* or illegal armed groups) who have taken territorial control of former paramilitary areas, intimidating victims who have returned to their rightful lands under the peace process. Many of these *bacrim* inherited the structures of the former AUC groups and employed former paramilitaries.

Social and Economic Transformation

During the past decade, Colombia has made some remarkable strides in improving social and economic conditions. Due to improved security conditions, investment, both domestic and international, has boomed, totaling almost US$80 billion from 2003 to 2012. Economic growth averaged 4.8 percent 2010-2014, a significant increase over the prior decades. The number of people below poverty, as measured by the ability to buy a wide basket of basic goods and services, has declined from 59.7 percent in 2002 to 27.8 percent in 2015. In Colombia's 13 largest cities, which represent 45 percent of the population, poverty has fallen to 18.9 percent. In terms of basic needs, most urban areas are well served in terms of education, health, electricity, water, and sewage. However, there is a wide gap between the cities and rural areas, where 30 percent of the country's population lives. As of 2013, rural poverty stood at 43 percent. Though income inequality has been slowly falling, Colombia still has one of the most unequal distributions of income in the world.

Peace with the FARC

In the 2010 elections, Uribe's former minister of defense, Juan Manuel Santos, was elected president by a large majority. Santos continued to pursue an aggressive strategy against the FARC. Army operations killed Alfonso Cano, the new leader of the FARC, as well as Víctor Julio Suárez Rojas, the guerrillas' military strategist. As evidenced in the diary of Dutch FARC member Tanya Nijmeijer, found by the Colombian army after an attack on a rebel camp, morale within the FARC had sunk to an all-time low.

At the same time, Santos recognized the need to address nonmilitary facets of the violence. In 2011, Congress passed the comprehensive Victims and Land Restitutions Law, meant to rectify Uribe's Justice and Peace Law. This law provides a framework to redress the crimes committed against all victims of violence since 1985.

After a year of secret negotiations, Santos announced the start of peace dialogues with the FARC in October 2012, first in Oslo, Norway, and then in Havana, Cuba. These have proceeded at a slow pace and have covered a large number of topics, including agrarian development and drug trafficking. Former president Uribe and his allies are against this initiative, claiming that a military defeat of the FARC is the best path forward.

In 2016, after four years of arduous negotiations, the government and the FARC agreed to comprehensive terms, which covered rural development, political participation, illegal drugs, justice for victims, and ending the armed conflict, among other topics. On September 26, 2016, the government and the FARC signed the agreement, only to have it rejected by a slim majority in a national vote. The government and the guerillas renegotiated the agreement, which was ratified on November 30, 2016, by Congress. Demobilization began in December 2016 and the guerillas are expected to hand over their weapons to the UN during the first half of 2017. President Juan Manuel Santos won the 2016 Nobel Peace Prize in honor of his efforts.

people protesting the defeat of a referendum for peace with FARC in 2016

Government and Economy

Under the 1991 constitution, Colombia is organized as a republic, with three branches of power—the executive, the legislative, and the judicial. The country is divided into 32 *departamentos* (departments or provinces) and the Distrito Capital (Capital District), where Bogotá is located. The departments are in turn divided into *municipios* (municipalities). These *municipios* include towns and rural areas.

The president of the republic, who is both head of state and head of government, is elected for a four-year term. With the exception of the military dictatorship of Gen. Gustavo Rojas Pinilla from 1953 to 1957, presidents have been elected by the people since 1914. In 2005, then-president Álvaro Uribe succeeded in changing the constitution to allow for one immediate presidential reelection. In 2009, he attempted to get the constitution changed once more to allow for a second reelection but was thwarted by the powerful Constitutional Court, which decreed that this change would break the necessary checks and balances of the constitutional framework.

Presidential elections are held every four years in May. If no candidate receives more than 50 percent of the votes, there will be a runoff election. Inauguration of the president takes place on August 7, the anniversary of the Batalla del Puente de Boyacá, which sealed Colombia's independence from Spain.

The legislative branch is made up of a bicameral legislature: the Senado (102 members) and the Cámara de Representantes (162 members). These representatives are elected every four years. Senators are voted for on a nationwide basis, while representatives are chosen for each department and the Distrito Capital. In addition, two seats in the Senate are reserved for indigenous representation. In the Cámara de Representantes, there are seats reserved for indigenous and Afro-Colombian communities as well as for Colombians who live abroad. As negotiated in 2016, the FARC will be assured 10 seats in Congress until 2022: 5 in the Senado and 5 in the Cámara de Representantes.

All Colombians over the age of 18—with the exception of active-duty military and police as well as those who are incarcerated—have the right to vote in all elections. Women only gained the right to vote in 1954.

POLITICAL PARTIES

Historically Colombia has had a two-party system: the Conservative Party and the Liberal Party. The Conservative Party has traditionally been aligned with the Catholic Church and has favored a more centralized government, and followed the ideas of Simón Bolívar. The Liberal Party favored a federal system of governing, has opposed church intervention in government affairs, and was aligned with the ideas of Gen. Francisco Paula Santander.

The hegemony of the two largest political parties came to a halt in the 2002 presidential election of rightist candidate Álvaro Uribe, who registered his own independent movement and then established a new party called El Partido de la Unidad. Since then, traditional parties have lost some influence. A third party, the Polo Democrático, became a relatively strong force in the early 2000s, capturing the mayorship of Bogotá, but has since faded, leaving no clear representative of the left.

Political parties today have become personality-oriented, and many candidates have been known to shop around for a party—or create their own—rather than adhere to the traditional parties. In 2014, President Juan Manuel Santos won a second term representing the Partido de la Unidad (known as La U), defeating a candidate allied with the founder of La U, former president Álvaro Uribe.

ECONOMY

Colombia has a thriving market economy based primarily on oil, mining, agriculture, and manufacturing. The country's GDP in 2015 was US$274 billion and per capita GDP was US$5,800, placing it as a middle-income country. Growth over the past decade has been a robust 3.29 percent. Inflation has averaged 3.8 percent in the past five years and unemployment has hovered around 10 percent.

During the colonial period and up until the early 20th century, small-scale gold mining and subsistence agriculture were the mainstays of Colombia's economy. Starting in the 1920s, coffee production spread throughout the country and rapidly became Colombia's major export good. Coffee production is of the mild arabica variety and is produced at elevations of 1,000 to 1,900 meters (roughly 3,000-6,000 feet), mostly by small farmers. During most of the 20th century, Colombia emphasized increasing the volume of production, using the Café de Colombia name and mythical coffee farmer Juan Valdez and his donkey Paquita to brand it. A severe global slump in coffee prices during the past decade has led to a reassessment of this strategy and an increasing focus on specialty coffees. Today, coffee represents only 3 percent of all Colombian exports.

Colombia is known for its coffee production.

Colombia's wide range of climates, from hot on the coast to temperate in the mountains, means that the country produces a wide range of products. Until recently, sugarcane production, fresh flowers, and bananas were the only major export-driven agribusiness. However, improvements in security in recent years have resulted in a boom in large-scale agricultural projects in palm oil, rubber, and soy. Cattle ranching occupies an estimated 25 percent of the country's land. Commercial forestry is relatively underdeveloped, though there is considerable illegal logging, especially on the Pacific coast.

In recent decades, oil production and mining have become major economic activities. The main center of oil production is the Llanos, the eastern plains of Colombia,

with oil pipelines extending from there over the Cordillera Oriental to Caribbean ports. Oil currently represents roughly half of all Colombian exports. There are also significant natural gas deposits, mostly dedicated to residential use. Large-scale mining has been focused on coal and nickel, with large deposits in the Caribbean coastal region. With the improvement of security conditions in the past decade, many international firms, such as Anglogold Ashanti, have requested concessions for large-scale gold mining, often with opposition from the community. Illegal gold mining, often conducted with large machinery, is a severe threat to fragile ecosystems, especially in the Pacific coast rainforest.

During the postwar period, Colombia pursued an import substitution policy, fostering the growth of domestic industries such as automobiles, appliances, and petrochemical goods. Since the early 1990s, the government has been gradually opening the economy to foreign competition and tearing down tariffs. In recent years, the country has signed free-trade agreements with the United States and the European Union. Today, the country has a fairly diversified industrial sector. The country is self-sufficient in energy, with hydropower supplying the bulk of electricity needs.

Until recently, tourism was minimal because of widespread insecurity and a negative image. Things started to change in the mid-2000s, and the annual number of international visitors has increased from 600,000 in 2000 to 2.3 million in 2015. While Bogotá and Cartagena still receive the bulk of visitors, almost the entire country has opened up for tourism, though there are still pockets of no-go zones. This boom in tourism has fostered a growth of community and ecotourism options, often with the support from government. The network of *posadas nativas* (guesthouses owned and operated by locals) is one initiative to foment tourism at the community level, particularly among Afro-Colombians. In recent years, Parques Nacionales has transferred local operation of ecotourism facilities in the parks to community-based associations.

People and Culture

DEMOGRAPHY

Colombia was estimated to have had a population of a little over 48.7 million in 2016 and has the third-highest population in Latin America, behind Brazil and Mexico and slightly higher than Argentina. Around four million Colombians live outside of Colombia, mostly in the United States, Venezuela, Spain, and Ecuador. The population growth rate has fallen significantly in the past two decades and was estimated at 1.01 percent in 2016. The population of the country is relatively young, with a median age of 29.3 years. Average life expectancy is 75.5 years.

Sixty percent of the Colombian population lives in the highland Andean interior of the country, where the largest metropolitan areas are located: Bogotá (9.8 million), Medellín (3.9 million), and Cali (2.6 million). On the Caribbean coast, Barranquilla is the largest metropolitan area (2 million), followed by Cartagena (1.1 million).

It is increasingly an urban country, with around 76 percent of the population living in urban areas. This trend began during La Violencia and accelerated in the 1970s and 1980s. At least 3.9 million persons have been internally displaced due to the armed conflict in Colombia, leaving their homes in rural areas and seeking safety and economic opportunity in large cities.

Most of the population (over 84 percent) is either mestizo (having both Amerindian and white ancestry) or white. People of African (10.4 percent) and indigenous or Amerindian (over 3.4 percent) origin make up the rest of the Colombian population. There is a tiny Romani or Roma population of well under 1 percent of the population, but nonetheless they are a protected group according to the constitution.

There are more than 80 indigenous groups, with some of the largest being the Wayúu, who make up the majority in La Guajira department; the Nasa, from Cauca; the Emberá, who live in the isolated jungles of the Chocó department, and the Pastos, in Nariño. Departments in the Amazon region have the highest percentages of indigenous residents. In Vaupés, for example, 66 percent of the population is of indigenous background. Many indigenous people live on *resguardos*, areas that are collectively owned and administered by the communities.

Afro-Colombians, descendants of slaves who arrived primarily via Spanish slave trade centers in the Caribbean, mostly live along both Pacific and Caribbean coasts and in the San Andrés Archipelago. Chocó has

Happy Monday!

Colombians enjoy a long list of holidays (over 20). With a few exceptions, such as the independence celebrations on July 20 and August 7, Christmas, and New Year's Day, holidays are celebrated on the following Monday, creating a *puente* (literally bridge, or three-day weekend).

During Semana Santa and between Christmas Day and New Year's, interior cities such as Bogotá and Medellín become ghost towns as locals head to the nearest beach or to the countryside. Conversely, beach resorts, natural reserves and parks, and pueblos fill up. Along with that, room rates and airfare can increase substantially.

The following is a list of Colombian holidays, but be sure to check a Colombian calendar for precise dates. Holidays marked with an asterisk are always celebrated on the Monday following the date of the holiday.

- Año Nuevo (New Year's Day): January 1
- Día de los Reyes Magos (Epiphany)*: January 6
- Día de San José (Saint Joseph's Day)*: March 19
- Jueves Santo (Maundy Thursday): Thursday before Easter Sunday
- Viernes Santo (Good Friday): Friday before Easter Sunday
- Día de Trabajo (International Workers' Day): May 1
- Ascensión (Ascension)*: Six weeks and one day after Easter Sunday
- Corpus Christi*: Nine weeks and one day after Easter Sunday
- Sagrado Corazón (Sacred Heart)*: Ten weeks and one day after Easter Sunday
- San Pedro y San Pablo (Saint Peter and Saint Paul)*: June 29
- Día de la Independencia (Independence Day): July 20
- Batalla de Boyacá (Battle of Boyacá): August 7
- La Asunción (Assumption of Mary)*: August 15
- Día de la Raza (equivalent of Columbus Day)*: October 12
- Todos Los Santos (All Saint's Day)*: November 1
- Día de la Independencia de Cartagena (Cartagena Independence Day)*: November 11
- La Inmaculada Concepción (Immaculate Conception): December 8
- Navidad (Christmas): December 25

the highest percentage of Afro-Colombians (83 percent), followed by San Andrés and Providencia (57 percent), Bolívar (28 percent), Valle del Cauca (22 percent), and Cauca (22 percent). Cali, Cartagena, and Buenaventura have particularly large Afro-Colombian populations. In the Americas, Colombia has the third-highest number of citizens of African origin, behind Brazil and the United States.

While Colombia has not attracted large numbers of immigrants, there have been periods in which the country opened its doors to newcomers. In the early 20th century, immigrants from the Middle East—specifically from Lebanon, Syria, and Palestine—arrived, settling mostly along the Caribbean coast, especially in the cities of Barranquilla, Santa Marta, Cartagena, and Maicao in La

Gay Rights in Colombia

In a country still struggling with armed conflict and basic human rights, it might come as a surprise that gay and lesbian rights have not been pushed aside. Colombia has some of the most progressive laws regarding the rights of LGBT people in the western hemisphere. Since 2007, same-sex partners have enjoyed full civil union rights with a wide range of benefits, such as immigration, inheritance, and social security rights.

However, when it comes to marriage, it's a little more complicated. In 2016, the top judicial body, the Colombian Constitutional Court, legalized marriage and adoption by same-sex couples. These rulings created a backlash with conservative politicians, who have vowed to hold a referendum to block the marriage and adoption rights.

Guajira. From 1920 to 1950, a sizable number of Sephardic and Ashkenazi Jews immigrated. Colombia has not had a large immigration from Asia, although in the early 20th century there was a small immigration of Japanese to the Cali area.

RELIGION

Over 90 percent of Colombians identify as Roman Catholics, and it has been the dominant religion since the arrival of the Spaniards. The numbers of evangelical Christians, called simply *cristianos*, continue to grow, and there are other Christian congregations, including Mormons and Jehovah's Witnesses, but their numbers are small. In San Andrés and Providencia, the native Raizal population—of African descent—is mostly Baptist.

The Jewish community—estimated at around 5,000 families—is concentrated in the large cities, such as Bogotá, Medellín, Cali, and Barranquilla. There are significant Muslim communities, especially along the Caribbean coast, and there are mosques in Barranquilla, Santa Marta, Valledupar, Maicao (La Guajira), San Andrés, and Bogotá.

Semana Santa—Holy or Easter Week—is the most important religious festival in the country, and Catholics in every village, town, and city commemorate the week with a series of processions and masses. The colonial cities of Popayán, Mompox, Tunja, and Pamplona are known for their elaborate Semana Santa processions. Popayán and Mompox in particular attract pilgrims and tourists from Colombia and beyond. In cities such as Bogotá, Cali, and Cartagena, there are multitudinous processions to mountaintop religious sites, such as Monserrate, the Cerro de la Cruz, and El Monasterio de la Popa, respectively.

LANGUAGE

Spanish is the official language in Colombia. In the San Andrés Archipelago, English is still spoken by native islanders who arrived from former English colonies after the abolition of slavery, but Spanish has gained prominence.

According to the Ministry of Culture, there are at least 68 native languages, which are spoken by around 850,000 people. These include 65 indigenous languages, two Afro-Colombian languages, and Romani, which is spoken by the small Roma population.

Three indigenous languages have over 50,000 speakers: Wayúu, primarily spoken in La Guajira; Páez, primarily spoken in Cauca; and Emberá, primarily spoken in Chocó.

Essentials

Getting There

AIR

Most visitors to Colombia arrive by air at the **Aeropuerto Internacional El Dorado** in Bogotá, with some carrying on from there to other destinations in the country. There are also nonstop international flights to the **Aeropuerto Internacional José María Córdova** in Medellín and to the airports in Cali, Cartagena, Barranquilla, and Armenia.

From North America

Avianca (www.avianca.com) has nonstop flights between Bogotá and Miami, Fort Lauderdale, Orlando, Washington, Los Angeles, and New York-JFK. From Miami there are also nonstops to Medellín, Cali, Barranquilla, and Cartagena.

American (www.american.com) flies between Miami and Dallas and Bogotá; Miami and Medellín; and Cali and Medellín. **Delta** (www.delta.com) flies from Atlanta and New York-JFK to Bogotá; they also fly between Atlanta and Cartagena. **United** (www.united.com) has flights from Newark and Houston to Bogotá.

JetBlue (www.jetblue.com) has nonstop service to Bogotá from Orlando and Fort Lauderdale; to Cartagena from New York and Fort Lauderdale; and to Medellín from Fort Lauderdale. **Spirit** (www.spirit.com) has flights from Fort Lauderdale to Bogotá, Medellín, Cartagena, and Armenia.

Air Canada (www.aircanada.com) operates nonstop flights from Toronto to Bogotá. **Air Transat** (www.airtransat.com) provides seasonal service to Cartagena and San Andrés from Montreal.

From Europe

Avianca (www.avianca.com) has service to Bogotá and Medellín from Madrid and Barcelona, and between Bogotá and London. **Air France** (www.airfrance.com) flies from Paris to Bogotá. **Iberia** (www.iberia.com) serves Bogotá from Madrid, as does **Air Europa** (www.aireuropa.com). **Lufthansa** (www.lufthansa.com) offers service between Bogotá and Frankfurt. **Turkish Airlines** (www.turkishairlines.com) flies between Bogotá and Istanbul. **KLM** (www.klm.com) serves Amsterdam from Bogotá with a stopover in Cali.

From Latin America

Avianca (www.avianca.com) flies to Bogotá from many capitals in Latin America, including Buenos Aires, São Paulo, Rio de Janeiro, Valencia, Caracas, Lima, Santiago, and La Paz in South America; Cancún, Guatemala City, Mexico City, San José, San Juan, San Salvador, and Panama City in Central America; and Havana, Santo Domingo, Punta Cana, Aruba, and Curaçao in the Caribbean. Aerolíneas Argentinas, AeroGal, Aeromexico, Air Insel, Conviasa, Copa, Cubana, LATAM, Gol, TACA, and Tiara Air Aruba also have connections to Colombia.

CAR OR MOTORCYCLE

A growing number of travelers drive into Colombia in their own car or with a rented vehicle. The most common point of entry is at the city of Ipiales on the Pan-American Highway, the site of the Rumichaca border crossing with Ecuador at Ipiales (Tulcán on the Ecuador side). This entry point is open 5am-10pm daily.

On the Venezuelan side, the border at Cúcuta and San Antonio del Táchira is open 24 hours a day. Although there are other border crossings with Venezuela, this is the recommended overland point of entry.

Previous: country road; the airport shuttle in Acandí—a horse-drawn carriage.

For those taking the Pan-American Highway southbound, note that you will run out of pavement in Panama. In the Darién Gap, the road is interrupted by the Darién mountain range. The road picks up again in the town of Turbo on the Golfo de Urabá. Many travelers ship their vehicle from Panama City to Cartagena, which is not difficult to arrange, and will set you back about $1,000 USD. It takes about 10 days to be able to retrieve your vehicle in Cartagena.

BUS

Frequent buses depart Quito bound for Cali (20 hours) or Bogotá (30 hours). You can also take a taxi from the town of Tulcán to the border at Ipiales and from there take an onward bus to Pasto, Popayán, Cali, or beyond. In Quito contact **Líneas de los Andes** (www.lineasdelosandes.com.co).

BOAT

It is possible to enter the country from Panama, usually via the San Blas Islands.

Blue Sailing (U.S. tel. 203/660-8654, www.bluesailing.net) offers sailboat trips between various points in Panama to Cartagena. The trip usually takes about 45 hours and costs around US$500. Sometimes, particularly during the windy season between November and March, boats stop in Sapzurro, Colombia, near the border. **San Blas Adventures** (www.sanblasadventures.com, contact@sanblasadventures.com) offers multiday sailboat tours to the San Blas Islands that usually depart from Cartí and end up in the Panamanian border village of La Miel. From there you can walk over the border to Sapzurro and take a *lancha* (boat) from there to Capurganá. There are regular morning boats from Capurganá to both Acandí and Turbo. During the windy season, especially between December and February, this trip can be quite rough.

It is also possible to hitch a ride on a cargo boat from Ecuador to Tumaco or Buenaventura; however, service is irregular.

Getting Around

AIR

Air travel is an excellent, quick, and, thanks to discount airlines such as VivaColombia, economical way to travel within Colombia. Flying is the best option for those looking to avoid spending double-digit hours in a bus or for those with a short amount of time—and sometimes it's cheaper than taking a bus, as well. Airlines have excellent track records and maintain modern fleets.

Bogotá is the major hub in the country, with the majority of domestic **Avianca** (tel. 1/401-3434, www.avianca.com) flights departing from the Puente Aéreo terminal (not the main terminal of the adjacent international airport). Other domestic carriers **LATAM Airlines** (Colombian toll-free tel. 01/800-094-9490, www.latam.com), **VivaColombia** (tel. 1/489-7989, www.vivacolombia.co), **EasyFly** (tel. 1/414-8111, www.easyfly.com.co), **Satena** (Colombian toll-free tel. 01/800-091-2034, www.satena.com), and **Copa** (Colombian toll-free tel. 01/800-011-0808, www.copaair.com) fly out of the new domestic wing of the international airport.

For Leticia in the Amazon, the Pacific coast destinations of Bahía Solano and Nuquí, La Macarena (Caño Cristales) in Los Llanos, and San Andrés and Providencia in the Caribbean, the only viable way to get there is by air.

If you plan to fly to Caribbean destinations such as Cartagena, San Andrés, Providencia, and Santa Marta during high tourist season, be sure to purchase your ticket well in advance, as seats quickly sell out and prices go through the roof. If your destination is Cartagena or Santa Marta, be sure to check fares to Barranquilla. These may be less expensive, and that city is only about an hour away. Similarly, if you plan to go to the Carnaval de Barranquilla in February, check fares to both Cartagena and Santa Marta. If you are flying to the Coffee Region, inquire about flights to Pereira, Armenia, and Manizales, as the distances between these cities are short. The Manizales airport, however, is often closed due to inclement weather.

Medellín has two airports: **Aeropuerto Internacional José María Córdova** (in Rionegro) and **Aeropuerto Olaya Herrera.** All international flights and most large airplane flights depart from Rionegro, a town about an hour away from Medellín. The airport is simply referred to as "Rionegro." **Satena** (Colombian toll-free tel. 01/800-091-2034, www.satena.com) and **Aerolíneas de Antioquia-ADA** (Colombian toll-free tel. 01/800-051-4232, www.ada-aero.com) use the Olaya Herrera airport, which is conveniently located in town. This is a hub for flights to remote communities in the western and Pacific region, including Acandí and Capurganá near the Panamanian border.

There are strict weight restrictions for flights to Providencia from San Andrés, which are generally on small planes such as those used by the military-owned Satena airline. These island flights sell out fast.

LONG-DISTANCE BUS

In order to thoroughly cover the country, you will have to hop on a bus at some point—just like the vast majority of Colombians. This is the money-saving choice and often the only option for getting to smaller communities. There are different types of buses, from large coaches for long-distance travel to *colectivos* for shorter distances. *Colectivos* (minivans) are often much quicker, although you won't have much legroom. There are also shared taxis that run between towns, a cramped but quick option. During major holidays, purchase bus tickets in advance if you can, as buses can quickly fill up.

When you arrive at a bus station with guidebook in hand and backpack on, you will be swarmed by touts barking out city names to you, desperately seeking your business on their bus. You can go with the flow and follow them, or, if you prefer a little more control and calm, you can instead walk past them to the ticket booths. Forge ahead and shake your head while saying *gracias*. You can try to negotiate better fares at the ticket booths, as there are often various options for traveling the same route. Find out what time the bus is leaving, if the vehicle is a big bus, a *buseta,* or minivan, and where your seat is located (try not to get stuck in the last row).

Be alert and aware of your surroundings and of your possessions when you arrive at bus stations, are waiting in the bus terminal, and are on board buses. Try to avoid flashing around expensive gadgets and cameras while on board. If you check luggage, request a receipt. During pit stops along the way, be sure to keep your valuables with you at all times.

During most bus rides of more than a few hours' length, you will be subjected to loud and/or violent films. Earplugs, eye masks, and even sleeping pills available at most pharmacies for those long journeys may come in handy, but make sure your possessions are well guarded. Expect the air-conditioning to be cranked to full blast, so have a layer or two at the ready. Pick up some provisions like apples or nuts before departing, because food options are generally unhealthy.

Bus drivers like to drive as fast as possible, and generally have few qualms about overtaking cars even on hairpin curves. Large buses tend to be safer than smaller ones, if only because they can't go as fast.

Buses may be stopped by police, and you may be required to show or temporarily hand over your passport (keep it handy). Sometimes passengers may be asked to disembark from the bus so that the police can search it for illegal drugs or other contraband. Young males may be given a pat-down. Even if it annoys you, it is always best to keep cool and remain courteous with police officers who are just doing their job.

PUBLIC TRANSPORTATION

For visitors, public transportation networks are most useful in Bogotá, Medellín, and Cali. Many cities, such as Medellín, Cali, Armenia, Bucaramanga, Pereira, Barranquilla, and Cartagena have adopted the Bogotá rapid bus system (BRT) model of the TransMilenio.

Today, buses, such as the SITP bus network in Bogotá, are clean, safe, and only pick up passengers at designated stops. In large cities, you will need to purchase an electronic refillable bus card. These can be purchased at *papelerías* (stationery shops), which are often close to bus stops and stations.

The free app **Moovit** provides route information for public transportation options in many Colombian cities.

CAR, MOTORCYCLE, OR BICYCLE

Although conditions are improving, driving in Colombia is generally a poor idea for international tourists. Roads are often in a poor state and are almost always just two lanes, speed limits and basic driving norms are not respected, driving through large towns and cities can be supremely stressful, signage is poor, sudden mudslides can close roads for hours on end during rainy seasons, and roads can be unsafe at night.

One exception is the Coffee Region. Here the roads are excellent and often four lanes, distances are short, and traffic is manageable. If you are planning on spending some time visiting coffee farms and idyllic towns, this might be a good option.

Another region where renting a car may make sense is in Boyacá. Here the countryside is beautiful and traffic is manageable.

There are car rental offices in all the major airports in the country. **Hertz** (tel. 1/756-0600, www.rentacarcolombia.co) and the national **Colombia Car Rental** (U.S. tel. 913/368-0091, www.colombiacarsrental.com) are two with various offices nationwide.

Touring Colombia on motorcycle is an increasingly popular option. One of the best motorcycle travel agencies in the country is **Motolombia** (tel. 2/665-9548, www.motolombia.com), based in Cali. A growing number of travelers are motoring the Pan-American Highway, shipping their bikes from Panama or the United States to Cartagena, or vice versa.

Bicyclists will not get much respect on Colombian roads, and there are rarely any bike lanes of significance. In Santander and

Medellín's efficient Metro

in Boyacá the scenery is absolutely spectacular, but, especially in Santander, it is often quite mountainous. In the Valle del Cauca, around Buga and toward Roldanillo, the roads are good and flat. Staff at **Colombian Bike Junkies** (San Gil cell tel. 316/327-6101, Medellín cell tel. 318/808-6769, www.colombianbikejunkies.com), based in San Gil, are experts on biking throughout the country, with an emphasis on mountain biking. Another outfitter is **Colombia en Bicicleta** (www.colombiaenbicicleta.com), catering mostly to bike enthusiasts living in Bogotá.

Every Sunday in cities across Colombia thousands of cyclists (joggers, skaters, and dog walkers, too) head to the city streets for some fresh air and exercise. This is the **Ciclovía,** an initiative that began in Bogotá in which city streets are closed to traffic. Except in Bogotá, it may be difficult to find a bike rental place, but you can still head out for a jog. *Ciclorutas* (bike paths) are being built in the major cities as well, and Bogotá has an extensive *cicloruta* network. Again, cyclists don't get much respect from motorists, so be careful!

BOAT

In some remote locations in Colombia the most common way to get around is by *lancha,* or boat. Many of the isolated villages and beaches and the Parque Nacional Natural Utría along the Pacific coast are accessed only by boat from either Bahía Solano or Nuquí. The same goes for Isla Gorgona. To get to this island park, you normally have to take a boat from Guapi or from Buenaventura. All hotels or travel agencies can organize these trips for you.

Although there are some flights from Medellín to the Darién Gap village of Capurganá, it is often more convenient to either fly to the town of Acandí and take a boat onward to Capurganá or take a boat from Turbo or Necoclí. Waters can be rough, especially from November to March. Don't risk this trip if you have a bad back, as the boat ride can be jarring.

In the Amazon region, the only way to get from Leticia to attractions nearby, including Puerto Nariño and the eco-lodges on the Río Javari, is by a boat on the Amazon, which is a memorable experience. All boats leave from the *malecón* (wharf) in Leticia.

The fabulous beaches of Islas del Rosario, off the coast of Cartagena, are accessed only by boat from the Muelle Turístico or from the docks in Manga. The same goes for Barú, although you can technically drive there. If visiting Mompox from Cartagena, you'll need to take a ferry from the town of Magangué along the mighty Río Magdalena.

Visas and Officialdom

PASSPORTS AND VISAS

U.S. and Canadian citizens do not need a visa for visits to Colombia of less than 90 days. You may be asked to show a return ticket.

There is an exit tax (Tasa Aeroportuaría Internacional) of around US$37 (COP$122,000). This is often automatically tacked onto your ticket price, but the airline agents will let you know upon check-in. If you are visiting for under 60 days, you are exempt. Prior to check-in, inquire with the airline if you qualify for an exemption. You may be directed to the Aeronáutica Civil booth across from the airline check-in counter, where you'll show your passport to get an exemption stamp.

To renew a tourist visa, you must go to an office of **Migración Colombia** (www.migracioncolombia.gov.co) to request an extension of another 90 days.

CUSTOMS

Upon arrival in Colombia, bags will be spot-checked by customs authorities.

Duty-free items up to a value of US$1,500 can be brought in to Colombia. Firearms are not allowed into the country, and many animal and vegetable products are not allowed. If you are carrying over US$10,000 in cash you must declare it.

Departing Colombia, expect a pat-down by police (looking for illegal drugs?) at the airport. In addition, luggage may be screened for drugs, art, and exotic animals.

EMBASSIES AND CONSULATES

The **United States Embassy** (Cl. 24 Bis No. 48-50, tel. 1/275-2000, http://bogota.usembassy.gov) is in Bogotá, near the airport. In case of an emergency, during business hours contact the **U.S. Citizen Services Hotline** (business hours tel. 1/275-2000, after-hours and weekends tel. 1/275-4021).

Non-emergency calls are answered at the American Citizen Services Section from Monday through Thursday 2pm-4pm. To be informed of security developments or emergencies during your visit, you can enroll in the Smart Traveler Enrollment Program (STEP) on the U.S. Embassy website. In Barranquilla, there is a **Consular Agency Office** (Cl. 77B No. 57-141, Suite 511, tel. 5/353-2001 or tel. 5/353-2182), but its hours and services are limited.

The **Canadian Embassy** (Cra. 7 No. 114-33, Piso 14, tel. 1/657-9800, www.canadainternational.gc.ca) is in Bogotá. There is a **Canadian Consular Office** (Bocagrande Edificio Centro Ejecutivo Oficina 1103, Cra. 3, No. 8-129, tel. 5/665-5838) in Cartagena. For emergencies, Canadian citizens can call the **emergency hotline** (Can. tel. 613/996-8885) in Canada collect.

Accommodations and Food

Most hotels include free wireless Internet and breakfast (although the food quality will vary). While all the fancy hotels and backpacker places have English-speaking staff—at least at the front desk—smaller hotels may not. Room rates usually depend on the number of occupants, not the size of the room. Except for some international chains and upper-end hotels, most hotels will not have heating or air-conditioning in their rooms.

Note that *moteles* are always, *residencias* are usually, and *hospedajes* are sometimes Colombian love hotels.

VALUE-ADDED TAX EXEMPTION

Non-Colombian visitors are exempt from IVA, a sales tax, which is around 16 percent. To qualify for the exemption, you must make your hotel reservation by email or phone from abroad, there must be at least two services included (such as the room fee and an included breakfast), and you must

show proof of being in Colombia for less than six months.

HOTELS

Midrange hotels are often harder to find and their quality can be unpredictable. Beds can be uncomfortable, rooms may be small, views might be unappealing, and service hit-or-miss. Spanish is the most prevalent language spoken at these types of accommodations.

High-end hotels, including international brands, are in all large cities. In tourist centers such as Cartagena and Santa Marta, boutique hotels are good options for those seeking charm. Expect courteous service and comfort. The only place to expect international television channels and access for travelers with disabilities are at high-end international hotels.

HOSTELS

Hostels catering to backpackers are a relatively new phenomenon, and more are offering private rooms for those not interested in sharing a dorm room with strangers. Young people are drawn to hostels, but an increasing number of older travelers opt for hostels, as these, in addition to offering budget accommodations, are also the best places for information on activities. Most hostel staff speak English. **Hostel Trail** (www.hosteltrail.com) is a good resource for information on Colombian hostels. Hostels generally maintain updated information on their Facebook pages.

FOOD AND DRINK

In Bogotá and Cartagena especially, Colombian foodie culture is alive and well, and visitors will have a wealth of excellent dining options—if they don't mind the occasional Manhattan prices. In the major cities, a 10 percent tip is usually included in the price of a meal, but it is a requirement for the server to ask to include it. You can say no, but that would be considered harsh. If you are truly impressed with the service, you can always leave a little additional on the table.

While seafood, especially *pescado frito* (fried fish), is de rigueur in the Caribbean and along the Pacific, in the interior beef and chicken rule. In the Medellín area, the famed and hearty *bandeja paisa* is a dish made of red beans cooked with pork, white rice, ground

meat, *chicharrón* (fried pork rinds), fried egg, plantains (*patacones*), chorizo, *hogao* sauce, *morcilla* (black pudding), avocado, and lemon. In Bogotá, the dish for cool evenings is *ajiaco*, a chicken and potato soup. In rural areas, the typical lunchtime meal will include soup and a main dish (*seco*) such as *arroz con pollo* (chicken with rice). Eat what you can, but foreigners are forgiven if they can't finish a plate.

Vegetarians have decent options available to them, especially in tourist centers. A can of lentils can be a helpful travel companion in rural areas. In coastal areas it will be hard to avoid eating fish.

Be sure to try the many unusual fruits and juices in Colombia. Juice is either served in water or in milk, and sometimes has a lot of sugar. The same goes for freshly squeezed lemonade.

Tinto (percolated coffee), can be downright dismal in rural areas, where it is served very sweet. For a good cup of coffee, head to a national brand like Juan Valdez or Oma. Non-coffee drinkers will enjoy *aromatica*, herbal tea that is typically served after dinner.

Colombia is a major chocolate producer and has some award-winning local brands, such as Cacao Hunter's Chocolate, which

fresh fruit juices

works with small farmers in different regions including the Sierra Nevada and near Tumaco.

Breakfast almost universally consists of eggs, bread or arepas, juice, and coffee. Fresh fruit is not that common at breakfast. Arepas are important in Colombia: Every region has its own take on these starchy corn cakes. Arepas in Medellín are large, thin, and bland, while arepas in other parts of the country can be cheese-filled.

Travel Tips

ACCESS FOR TRAVELERS WITH DISABILITIES

Only international and some national hotel chains offer rooms (usually just one or two) that are wheelchair-accessible. Hostels and small hotels in secondary cities or towns will not. Airport and airline staff will usually bend over backwards to help those with disabilities, if you ask.

Getting around cities and towns is complicated, as good sidewalks and ramps are the exception, not the rule. Motorists may not stop—or even slow down—for pedestrians.

WOMEN TRAVELING ALONE

Along the Caribbean and Pacific coasts especially, women traveling alone should expect to be on the receiving end of flirting and various friendly offers by men and curiosity by everyone. Women should be extra cautious in taxis and buses. Always order taxis by phone and avoid taking them alone at night. While incidents are unlikely, it is not a fantastic idea to go out for a jog, a walk on a remote beach, or a hike through the jungle on your own. Walking about small towns at night alone may elicit looks or comments. Don't reveal personal information, where you are staying, or where you are going to inquisitive strangers. There have been incidents in the past with single women travelers in remote areas of La Guajira.

GAY AND LESBIAN TRAVELERS

Colombia has some of the western hemisphere's most progressive laws regarding the rights of LGBT people. The Constitutional Court legalized same-sex marriage and adoption in 2016 after a torturous, decades-long struggle marked by court victories, legislative defeats, and much debate.

Colombia is a fairly tolerant country, especially in its large cities. Bogotá is one of the most gay-friendly cities on the continent, with a large gay nightlife scene and city-supported LGBT community centers. In many neighborhoods, passersby don't blink an eye when they see a gay couple holding hands on the sidewalk.

The Caribbean region is generally less open to homosexuality, and this is especially true in rural areas. Nevertheless, the main cities of the region—Cartagena, Barranquilla, and Santa Marta—have gay clubs and are home to active LGBT communities. All bars and clubs, while catering to men, are welcoming to gay women and to straight people. In the San Andrés Archipelago, homophobia is the norm among the native islanders, although violence against gay travelers is unheard of. The online guide **Guia GAY Colombia** (www.guiagaycolombia.com) has a listing of meeting places for LGBT people throughout the country.

Discrimination, especially against transgender people and even more so against trans sex workers, continues to be a problem in many cities and towns, in particular in Cali and the Caribbean. The award-winning nonprofit group **Colombia Diversa** (www.colombiadiversa.org) is the main advocate for LGBT rights in the country, with **Caribe Afirmativo** (www.caribeafirmativo.lgbt) focusing its efforts on the Caribbean region.

Gay men in particular should be cautious

using dating apps, keep an eye on drinks at nightclubs, and avoid cabs off the street when departing clubs.

Same-sex couples should not hesitate to insist on *matrimonial* (double) beds at hotels. Most hotels in cities and even in smaller towns and rural areas are becoming more clued in on this. At guesthouses, hostels, and at some midsized hotels, front desk staff may charge if you invite a guest to the room. At large international hotels and at apartments for rent, this is never the case.

CONDUCT AND CUSTOMS

Colombians are generally friendly to visitors and are often inquisitive about where you are from and how you like Colombia so far. This is most often the case in rural areas. Colombians are also quite proud of their country, after emerging from decades of armed conflict.

With acquaintances and strangers alike, it is customary to ask how someone is doing before moving on to other business. You're even expected to issue a blanket *buenos días* ("Good morning") in the elevator. When greeting an acquaintance, it's customary to shake hands (between men) or give an air kiss on the cheek (for women), although this is mostly the case in urban areas, especially with the upper crust.

Colombians are comfortable with noise—expect the TV to always be on and music blasting almost everywhere. Many Colombians you meet will ask about your family. Family ties are very important to Colombians. Sundays often mean lunch in the countryside with nuclear and extended family members.

While tourists get a pass on appearance, it's preferred that men avoid wearing shorts, especially at restaurants, except on the Caribbean coast. Dress up, like the locals do, when going out on the town.

Indigenous cultures are much more conservative, and women are expected to refrain from showing much skin.

Health and Safety

VACCINATIONS

There are no vaccination requirements for travel to Colombia. At present, proof of vaccination is no longer required in the national parks (namely Parque Nacional Natural Tayrona). However, having proof of vaccination may make life easier, especially if you plan on traveling onward to Brazil or other countries.

The Centers for Disease Control (CDC) recommends that travelers to Colombia get up-to-date on the following vaccines: measles-mumps-rubella (MMR), diphtheria-tetanus-pertussis, varicella (chicken pox), polio, and the yearly flu shot.

DISEASES AND ILLNESSES
Malaria, Zika, Chikungunya, and Dengue Fever

In low-lying tropical areas of Colombia, mosquito-borne illnesses such as malaria, dengue fever, chikungunya, and Zika are common. It is best to assume that there is a risk, albeit quite small, in all areas of the country.

Malaria is a concern in the entire Amazon region and in the lowland departments of Antioquia, Chocó, Córdoba, Nariño, and Bolívar. There is low to no malarial risk in Cartagena and in areas above 1,600 meters (5,000 feet). The Colombian Ministry of Health estimates that there are around 63,000 annual cases of malaria in the country, 20 of which result in death. Most at risk are children under the age of 15. Malaria symptoms include fever, headache, chills, vomiting, fatigue, and difficulty breathing. Treatment involves the administration of various antimalarial drugs. If you plan on spending a lot of time outdoors in lowland tropical areas, consider taking an antimalarial chemoprophylaxis.

The number of cases of **dengue fever** in Colombia has grown from 5.2 cases per 100,000 residents in the 1990s to around 18.1 cases per 100,000 in the 2000s. It is another mosquito-borne illness. The most common symptoms of dengue fever are fever; headaches; muscle, bone, and joint pain; and pain behind the eyes. It is fatal in less than 1 percent of the cases. Treatment usually involves rest and hydration and the administration of pain relievers for headache and muscle pain. **Chikungunya virus** has similar symptoms to dengue, and an infection, involving painful aches, can last for several months. It is spread, like dengue, by the *Aedes aegypti* mosquito, often during daytime.

Zika virus is the latest scare to grip South America, and is a concern to pregnant women, as there is a link between the virus and birth defects. Pregnant women should avoid traveling to low-lying areas (under 2,000 meters/6,000 feet), where Zika is present. This includes much of Colombia. Symptoms include fever, rash, joint pains, and conjunctivitis.

The Centers for Disease Control (www.cdc.gov) remains the best resource on health concerns for worldwide travel.

PREVENTION

Use mosquito nets over beds when visiting tropical areas of Colombia. Examine them well before using, and if you notice large holes in the nets request replacements. Mosquitoes tend to be at their worst at dawn, dusk, and in the evenings. Wear lightweight, long-sleeved, and light-colored shirts, long pants, and socks, and keep some insect repellent handy.

DEET is considered effective in preventing mosquito bites, but there are other, less-toxic alternatives, most available from online retailers.

If you go to the Amazon region, especially during rainy seasons, take an antimalarial prophylaxis starting 15 days before arrival, and continuing 15 days after departing the region. According to the CDC, the recommended chemoprophylaxis for visitors to malarial regions of Colombia is atovaquone-proguanil, doxycycline, or mefloquine. These drugs are available at most pharmacies in Colombia with no prescription necessary.

Altitude Sickness

The high altitudes of the Andes, including in Bogotá (2,625 meters/8,612 feet), can be a problem for some. If arriving directly in Bogotá, or if you are embarking on treks in the Sierra Nevada del Cocuy or in Los Nevados, where the highest peaks reach 5,300 meters (over 17,000 feet), for the first couple of days take it easy and avoid drinking alcohol. Make mountain ascents gradually if possible. You can also take the drug acetazolamide to help speed up your acclimatization. Drinking coca tea or chewing on coca leaves may help prevent *soroche,* as altitude sickness is called in Colombia.

Traveler's Diarrhea

Stomach flu or traveler's diarrhea is a common malady when traveling through Colombia. These are usually caused by food contamination resulting from the presence of *E. coli* bacteria. Street foods, including undercooked meat, raw vegetables, dairy products, and ice, are some of the main culprits. If you get a case of traveler's diarrhea, be sure to drink lots of clear liquids, avoid caffeine, and take an oral rehydration solution of salt, sugar, and water.

Tap Water

Tap water is fine to drink in Colombia's major cities, but you should drink bottled, purified, or boiled water in the Amazon, the Pacific coast, the Darién Gap, La Guajira, and San Andrés and Providencia. As an alternative to buying plastic bottles, look for *bolsitas* (bags) of water. They come in a variety of sizes and use less plastic.

MEDICAL SERVICES

Colombia has excellent hospitals in its major cities. Over 20 hospitals in Colombia (in

Bogotá, Medellín, Bucaramanga, and Cali) have been listed in the *América Economía* magazine listing of the top 40 hospitals of Latin America. Four hospitals were in the top 10. Those were the **Fundación Santa Fe de Bogotá** (www.fsfb.org.co), the **Fundación Valle del Lili** (www.valledellili. org) in Cali, the **Fundación Cardioinfantil** (www.cardioinfantil.org) in Bogotá, and the **Fundación Cardiovascular de Colombia** (www.fcv.org) in Floridablanca, near Bucaramanga. For sexual and reproductive health issues, **Profamilia** (www.profamilia. org.co) has a large network of clinics that provide walk-in and low-cost services throughout the country.

Aerosanidad SAS (tel. 1/439-7080, 24-hour hotline tel. 1/266-2247 or tel. 1/439-7080, www.aerosanidadsas.com) provides transportation services for ill or injured persons in remote locations of Colombia to medical facilities in the large cities.

Travel insurance is a good idea to purchase before arriving in Colombia, especially if you plan on doing a lot of outdoor adventures. One recommended provider of travel insurance is **Assist Card** (www.assist-card.com). Before taking a paragliding ride or white-water rafting trip inquire to see whether insurance is included in the price of the trip—it should be.

CRIME

Colombia is safe to visit, and the majority of visitors have a wonderful experience in the country. For international travelers, there is little to worry about when it comes to illegal armed groups today. The threat of kidnapping of civilians and visitors has been almost completely eliminated.

Even in the worst of times, places like Cartagena and Bogotá have always been less affected by violence from the armed conflict plaguing the rest of the country. Now, with implementation of a peace deal between FARC guerrillas and the Colombian government, the outlook is brighter than ever. However, uncertainty remains and smaller groups of former paramilitaries (*bacrim*) and guerrillas operate in some cities and towns, while drug lords and dangerous gangs rule marginalized urban areas.

There are still places to avoid, even along the peaceful Caribbean coast. In the northwest, avoid the jungle and rural areas in and around Parque Nacional Natural Los Katios in the Darién region, as well as the Parque

Colombian police

Nacional Natural Paramillo in Córdoba. On the eastern side of the country, the Catatumbo region, along the Venezuelan border, remains volatile. In the rest of the country, hot spots include much of the Amazonian rainforest (with the notable exception of Leticia and Puerto Nariño), areas near La Macarena in Meta (but Caño Cristales is safe), rural areas of Cauca (Popayán and Tierradentro are fine), rural areas near Tumaco and Buenaventura on the Pacific coast, and much of the Chocó jungle (except for tourist areas of Bahía Solano, Nuquí, and the capital city of Quibdó).

For updated travel advisories, check the website of the **U.S. Embassy** (http://bogota. usembassy.gov/) in Bogotá. The embassy always errs on the side of caution.

Street Crime

Cell phone theft continues to plague much of the country. Keep wallets in front pockets, be aware of your surroundings, and keep shopping bags and backpacks near you at all times. Muggings in major cities are not unheard of, but are quite rare. Be alert to your surroundings late at night.

Always order cabs instead of hailing them off the street. Fortunately, taxi crimes have diminished greatly in recent years, in no small part due to the advent of apps like Uber and Easy Taxi.

Police

From just about anywhere in the country, the police can be reached by dialing 123 on any phone. Otherwise, many parks are home to neighborhood police stations, called CAI (Centros de Atención Inmediata). Authorities may not be able to do much about petty theft, however.

Recreational Drugs

In Colombia, the legal status of the use, transport, and possession of recreational drugs can be best described as murky. A 1994 high court decision legalized a "personal dose" of recreational drugs for adults. The sale of drugs is prohibited. An attempt by President Uribe to criminalize recreational drugs failed in 2005. In practice, police may harass those caught with drugs, in addition to confiscating drugs, and may solicit bribes.

Medical use of marijuana was legalized in 2015.

Information and Services

MONEY
Currency

Colombia's official currency is the peso, which is abbreviated as COP. Prices in Colombia are marked with a dollar sign, but remember that you're seeing the price in Colombian pesos. COP$1,000,000 isn't enough to buy a house in Colombia, but it will usually cover a few nights in a nice hotel!

Bills in Colombia are in denominations of $1,000, $2,000, $5,000, $10,000, $20,000, $50,000, and $100,000. Some of the bills got a makeover in 2016, so you may see two different versions of the same amount. Coins in Colombia are in denominations of $50, $100,

$200, $500, and $1,000. The equivalent of cents is *centavos* in Colombian Spanish.

Due to dropping oil prices, the Colombian peso has devalued to record levels, making the country a bargain for international visitors. In 2016, one US dollar was the equivalent of COP$3,000.

Most banks in Colombia do not exchange money. For that, you'll have to go to an exchange bank, located in all major cities. There are money changers on the streets of Cartagena, but the street is not the best place for safe and honest transactions.

Travelers checks are not worth the hassle, as they are hard to cash. Dollars are sometimes accepted in Cartagena and other major tourist destinations. To have cash wired to you from abroad, look for a Western Union office. These are located only in major cities.

Counterfeit bills are a problem in Colombia, and unsuspecting international visitors are often the recipients. Bar staff, taxi drivers, and street vendors are the most common culprits. It's good to always have a stash of small bills to avoid getting large bills back as change. Tattered and torn bills will also be passed off to you, which could pose a problem. Try not to accept those.

Consignaciones

Consignaciones (bank transfers) are a common way to pay for hotel reservations (especially in areas such as Providencia and remote resorts), tour packages or guides, or entry to national parks. It's often a pain to make these deposits in person, as the world of banking can be confusing for non-Colombians. On the plus side, making a deposit directly into the hotel's bank account provides some peace of mind because it will diminish the need to carry large amounts of cash. To make a *consignación* you will need to know the recipient's bank account and whether that is a *corriente* (checking) or *ahorros* (savings) account, and you will need to show some identification and probably have to provide a fingerprint. Be sure to hold onto the receipt to notify the recipient of your deposit.

ATMs

The best way to get cash is to use your bank ATM card. These are almost universally accepted at *cajeros automáticos* (ATMs) in the country. *Cajeros* are almost everywhere except in the smallest of towns or in remote areas. Withdrawal fees are relatively expensive, although they vary. You can usually take out up to around COP$300,000-500,000 (the equivalent of around US$150-250) per transaction. Many banks place limits on how much one can withdraw in a day (COP$1,000,000).

Credit and Debit Cards

Credit and debit card use is becoming more prevalent in Colombia; however, online credit card transactions are still not so common except for the major airlines and some of the event ticket companies, such as www.tuboleta.com or www.colboletos.com. When you use your plastic, you will be asked if it's *credito* (credit) or *debito* (debit). If using a *tarjeta de credito* (credit card) in restaurants and stores, you will be asked something like, *"¿Cuantas cuotas?"* or *"¿Numero de cuotas?"* ("How many installments?"). Most visitors prefer one *cuota* (*"Una, por favor"*). But you can have even your dinner bill paid in up to 24 installments! If using a *tarjeta de debito,* you'll be asked if it is a *corriente* (checking) or *ahorros* (savings) account.

Tipping

In most sit-down restaurants in larger cities, a 10 percent service charge is automatically included in the bill. Waitstaff are required to ask you, *"¿Desea incluir el servicio?"* ("Would you like to include the service in the bill?"). Many times restaurant staff neglect to ask international tourists about the service inclusion. If you find the service to be exceptional, you can leave a little extra in cash. Although tipping is not expected in bars or cafés, tip jars are becoming more common. International visitors are often expected to tip more than Colombians. In small-town restaurants throughout the country, tipping is not the norm.

It is not customary to tip taxi drivers. But if you feel the driver was a good one who drove safely and was honest, or if he or she made an additional stop for you, waited for you, or was just pleasant, you can always round up the bill (instead of COP$6,200 give the driver COP$7,000 and say *"Quédese con las vueltas por favor"* ("Keep the change"). Note that sometimes a "tip" is already included in the fare for non-Colombian visitors!

In hotels, usually a tip of COP$5,000 will suffice for porters who help with luggage, unless you have lots of stuff. Tips are not expected, but are certainly welcome, for housekeeping staff.

Value-Added Tax

Non-Colombian visitors are entitled to a refund of value-added taxes for purchases on clothing, jewelry, and other items if their purchases total more than COP$300,000. Save all credit card receipts and fill out Form 1344 (available online at www.dian.gov.co). Submit this to the **DIAN office** (tel. 1/607-9999) at the airport before departure. You may have several hoops to go through to achieve success. Go to the DIAN office before checking your luggage, as you will have to present the items you purchased.

INTERNET AND TELEPHONES

Being connected makes travel throughout Colombia so much easier. Free Wi-Fi is available at most hotels, restaurants, and cafés in major cities. An important Spanish phrase to learn is *"Como es la contraseña para el wifi?"* ("What's the password for the Wi-Fi?")

Obtaining a SIM card for your cell phone will ensure connectivity in all but the most remote locations. Sometimes low-tech phones work better than smartphones in very rural or remote locations like Providencia. SIM cards (*datos de prepago*) are available at mobile-phone carriers in all major towns and cities. Three main cell phone companies are Claro, Movistar, and Tigo.

Facebook and Whatsapp are often the best bets for contacting hotels, restaurants, and shops.

The telephone country code for Colombia is 57. Cell phone numbers are 10 digits long, beginning with a 3. To call a Colombian cell phone from abroad, you must use the country code followed by that 10-digit number. Landline numbers in Colombia are seven digits long. An area code is necessary when calling from a different region. To call a landline from a cell phone, dial 03 + area code + 7-digit number. To reach a cell phone from a landline, dial 03 + 10-digit number.

Resources

Spanish Phrasebook

Knowing some Spanish is essential to visit Colombia, as relatively few people outside the major cities speak English. Colombian Spanish is said to be one of the clearest in Latin America. However, there are many regional differences.

Spanish commonly uses 30 letters—the familiar English 26, plus four straightforward additions: ch, ll, ñ, and rr, which are explained in "Consonants," below.

PRONUNCIATION

Once you learn them, Spanish pronunciation rules—in contrast to English—don't change. Spanish vowels generally sound softer than in English. (*Note:* The capitalized syllables below receive stronger accents.)

Vowels

a   like ah, as in "hah": *agua* AH-gooah (water), *pan* PAHN (bread), and *casa* CAH-sah (house)

e   like ay, as in "may:" *mesa* MAY-sah (table), *tela* TAY-lah (cloth), and *de* DAY (of, from)

i   like ee, as in "need": *diez* dee-AYZ (ten), *comida* ko-MEE-dah (meal), and *fin* FEEN (end)

o   like oh, as in "go": *peso* PAY-soh (weight), *ocho* OH-choh (eight), and *poco* POH-koh (a bit)

u   like oo, as in "cool": *uno* OO-noh (one), *cuarto* KOOAHR-toh (room), and *usted* oos-TAYD (you); when it follows a "q" the u is silent; when it follows an "h" or has an umlaut, it's pronounced like "w"

Consonants

b, d, f, k, l, m, n, p, q, s, t, v, w, x, y, z, and ch
   pronounced almost as in English; h occurs, but is silent—not pronounced at all

c   like k as in "keep": *cuarto* KOOAR-toh (room), *casa* KAH-sah (house); when it precedes "e" or "i," pronounce c like s, as in "sit": *cerveza* sayr-VAY-sah (beer), *encima* ayn-SEE-mah (atop)

g   like g as in "gift" when it precedes "a," "o," "u," or a consonant: *gato* GAH-toh (cat), *hago* AH-goh (I do, make); otherwise, pronounce g like h as in "hat": *giro* HEE-roh (money order), *gente* HAYN-tay (people)

j   like h, as in "has": *Jueves* HOOAY-vays (Thursday), *mejor* may-HOR (better)

ll   like y, as in "yes": *toalla* toh-AH-yah (towel), *ellos* AY-yohs (they, them)

ñ   like ny, as in "canyon": *año* AH-nyo (year), *señor* SAY-nyor (Mr., sir)

r   is lightly trilled, with tongue at the roof of your mouth like a very light English d, as in "ready": *pero* PAY-roh (but), *tres* TRAYS (three), *cuatro* KOOAH-troh (four)

rr   like a Spanish r, but with much more emphasis and trill. Let your tongue flap. Practice with *burro* (donkey), *carretera* (highway), and Carrillo (proper name), then really let go with *ferrocarril* (railroad)

Note: The single small but common exception to all of the above is the pronunciation of Spanish y when it's being used as the Spanish word for "and," as in "Ron y Kathy." In such case, pronounce it like the English ee, as in "keep": Ron "ee" Kathy (Ron and Kathy).

Accent

The rule for accents, the relative stress given to syllables within a given word, is straightforward. If a word ends in a vowel, an n, or an s, accent the next-to-last syllable; if not, accent the last syllable.

Pronounce *gracias* GRAH-seeahs (thank you), *orden* OHR-dayn (order), and *carretera* kah-ray-TAY-rah (highway) with stress on the next-to-last syllable.

Otherwise, accent the last syllable: *venir* vay-NEER (to come), *ferrocarril* fay-roh-cah-REEL (railroad), and *edad* ay-DAHD (age).

Exceptions to the accent rule are always marked with an accent sign: (á, é, í, ó, or ú), such as *teléfono* tay-LAY-foh-noh (telephone), *jabón* hah-BON (soap), and *rápido* RAH-pee-doh (rapid).

BASIC AND COURTEOUS EXPRESSIONS

Colombians use many courteous formalities. Whenever approaching anyone for information or some other reason, do not forget the appropriate salutation—good morning, good evening, etc. Standing alone, the greeting *hola* (hello) can sound brusque.

Hello. *Hola.*
Good morning. *Buenos días.*
Good afternoon. *Buenas tardes.*
Good evening. *Buenas noches.*
How are you? Colombians have many ways of saying this: *¿Cómo estás/como está? ¿Qué hubo/Qu'hubo? ¿Cómo va/vas? ¿Que tal?*
Very well, thank you. *Muy bien, gracias.*
Okay; good. *Bien.*
Not okay; bad. *Mal.*
So-so. *Más o menos.*
And you? *¿Y Usted?*
Thank you. *Gracias.*
Thank you very much. *Muchas gracias.*
You're very kind. *Muy amable.*
You're welcome. *De nada.*
Goodbye. *Adiós.*
See you later. *Hasta luego. Chao.*
please *por favor;* (slang) *por fa*
yes *sí*

no *no*
I don't know. *No sé.*
Just a moment, please. *Un momento, por favor.*
Excuse me, please (when you're trying to get attention). *Disculpe.*
Excuse me (when you've made a mistake). *Perdón. Que pena.*
I'm sorry. *Lo siento.*
Pleased to meet you. *Mucho gusto.*
How do you say . . . in Spanish? *¿Cómo se dice . . . en español?*
What is your name? *¿Cómo se llama (Usted)? ¿Cómo te llamas?*
Do you speak English? *¿Habla (Usted) inglés? ¿Hablas inglés?*
Does anyone here speak English? *¿Hay alguien que hable inglés?*
I don't speak Spanish well. *No hablo bien el español.*
Please speak more slowly. *Por favor hable más despacio.*
I don't understand. *No entiendo.*
Please write it down. *Por favor escríbalo.*
My name is . . . *Me llamo . . . Mi nombre es...*
I would like . . . *Quisiera . . . Quiero . . .*
Let's go to . . . *Vamos a . . .*
That's fine. *Está bien.*
All right. *Listo.*
cool, awesome *chévere, rico, super*
Oh my god! *¡Dios mío!*
That's crazy! *¡Qué locura!*
You're crazy! *¡Estás loca/o!*

TERMS OF ADDRESS

When in doubt, use the formal *Usted* (you) as a form of address.

I *yo*
you (formal) *Usted*
you (familiar) *tú*
he/him *él*
she/her *ella*
we/us *nosotros*
you (plural) *Ustedes*
they/them *ellas* (all females); *ellos* (all males or mixed gender)

Mr., sir *señor*
Mrs., madam *señora*
miss, young lady *señorita*
wife *esposa*
husband *esposo*
friend *amigo/a*
girlfriend/boyfriend *novia* (female);
 novio (male)
partner *pareja*
daughter; son *hija; hijo*
brother; sister *hermano; hermana*
mother; father *madre; padre*
grandfather; grandmother *abuelo;*
 abuela

TRANSPORTATION

Where is . . . ? *¿Dónde está . . . ?*
How far is it to . . . ? *¿A cuánto*
 queda . . . ?
from . . . to . . . *de . . . a . . .*
How many blocks? *¿Cuántas cuadras?*
Where (Which) is the way to . . . ? *¿Cuál*
 es el camino a . . . ? ¿Por dónde es...?
bus station *la terminal de buses/terminal*
 de transporte
bus stop *la parada*
Where is this bus going? *¿A dónde va*
 este bús?
boat *el barco, la lancha*
dock *el muelle*
airport *el aeropuerto*
I'd like a ticket to . . . *Quisiera un pasaje*
 a . . .
roundtrip *ida y vuelta*
reservation *reserva*
baggage *equipaje*
next flight *el próximo vuelo*
Stop here, please. *Pare aquí, por favor.*
the entrance *la entrada*
the exit *la salida*
(very) near; far *(muy) cerca; lejos*
to; toward *a*
by; through *por*
from *de*
right *la derecha*
left *la izquierda*
straight ahead *derecho*
in front *en frente*

beside *al lado*
behind *atrás*
corner *la esquina*
stoplight *la semáforo*
turn *una vuelta*
here *aquí*
somewhere around here *por aquí*
there *allí*
somewhere around there *por allá*
road *camino*
street *calle, carrera*
avenue *avenida*
block *la cuadra*
highway *carretera*
kilometer *kilómetro*
bridge; toll *puente; peaje*
address *dirección*
north; south *norte; sur*
east; west *oriente (este); occidente*
 (oeste)

ACCOMMODATIONS

hotel *hotel*
Is there a room available? *¿Hay un*
 cuarto disponible?
May I (may we) see it? *¿Puedo*
 (podemos) verlo?
How much is it? *¿Cuánto cuesta?*
Is there something cheaper? *¿Hay algo*
 más económico?
single room *un cuarto sencillo*
double room *un cuarto doble*
double bed *cama matrimonial*
single bed *cama sencilla*
with private bath *con baño propio*
television *televisor*
window *ventana*
view *vista*
hot water *agua caliente*
shower *ducha*
towels *toallas*
soap *jabón*
toilet paper *papel higiénico*
pillow *almohada*
blanket *cobija*
sheets *sábanas*
air-conditioned *aire acondicionado*
fan *ventilador*

swimming pool *piscina*
gym *gimnasio*
bike *bicicleta*
key *llave*
suitcase *maleta*
backpack *mochila*
lock *candado*
safe *caja de seguridad*
manager *gerente*
maid *empleada*
clean *limpio*
dirty *sucio*
broken *roto*
(not) included *(no) incluido*

FOOD

I'm hungry. *Tengo hambre.*
I'm thirsty. *Tengo sed.*
Table for two, please. *Una mesa para dos, por favor.*
menu *carta*
order *orden*
glass *vaso*
glass of water *vaso con agua*
fork *tenedor*
knife *cuchillo*
spoon *cuchara*
napkin *servilleta*
soft drink *gaseosa*
coffee *café, tinto*
tea *té*
drinking water *agua potable*
bottled carbonated water *agua con gas*
bottled uncarbonated water *agua sin gas*
beer *cerveza*
wine *vino*
glass of wine *copa de vino*
red wine *vino tinto*
white wine *vino blanco*
milk *leche*
juice *jugo*
cream *crema*
sugar *azúcar*
cheese *queso*
breakfast *desayuno*
lunch *almuerzo*
daily lunch special *menú del día*

dinner *comida*
the check *la cuenta*
eggs *huevos*
bread *pan*
salad *ensalada*
lettuce *lechuga*
tomato *tomate*
onion *cebolla*
garlic *ajo*
hot sauce *ají*
fruit *fruta*
mango *mango*
watermelon *patilla*
papaya *papaya*
banana *banano*
apple *manzana*
orange *naranja*
lime *limón*
passionfruit *maracuyá*
guava *guayaba*
grape *uva*
fish *pescado*
shellfish *mariscos*
shrimp *camarones*
(without) meat *(sin) carne*
chicken *pollo*
pork *cerdo*
beef *carne de res*
bacon; ham *tocino; jamón*
fried *frito*
roasted *asado*
Do you have vegetarian options? *¿Tienen opciones vegetarianas?*
I'm vegetarian. *Soy vegetarian(o).*
I don't eat ... *No como ...*
to share *para compartir*
Check, please. *La cuenta, por favor.*
Is the service included? *¿Está incluido el servicio?*
tip *propina*
large *grande*
small *pequeño*

SHOPPING

cash *efectivo*
money *dinero*

credit card *tarjeta de crédito*
debit card *tarjeta de débito*
money exchange office *casa de cambio*
What is the exchange rate? *¿Cuál es la tasa de cambio?*
How much is the commission? *¿Cuánto es la comisión?*
Do you accept credit cards? *¿Aceptan tarjetas de crédito?*
credit card installments *cuotas*
money order *giro*
How much does it cost? *¿Cuánto cuesta?*
expensive *caro*
cheap *barato; económico*
more *más*
less *menos*
a little *un poco*
too much *demasiado*
value added tax *IVA*
discount *descuento*

HEALTH

Help me please. *Ayúdeme por favor.*
I am ill. *Estoy enferma/o.*
Call a doctor. *Llame un doctor.*
Take me to ... *Lléveme a . . .*
hospital *hospital, clínica*
drugstore *farmacia*
pain *dolor*
fever *fiebre*
headache *dolor de cabeza*
stomach ache *dolor de estómago*
burn *quemadura*
cramp *calambre*
nausea *náusea*
vomiting *vomitar*
medicine *medicina*
antibiotic *antibiótico*
pill *pastilla, pepa*
aspirin *aspirina*
ointment; cream *ungüento; crema*
bandage (big) *venda*
bandage (small) *cura*
cotton *algodón*
sanitary napkin *toalla sanitaria*
birth control pills *pastillas anticonceptivas*

condoms *condones*
toothbrush *cepillo de dientes*
dental floss *hilo dental*
toothpaste *crema dental*
dentist *dentista*
toothache *dolor de muelas*
vaccination *vacuna*

COMMUNICATIONS

Wi-fi *wifi*
cell phone *celular*
username *usuario*
password *contraseña*
laptop computer *portátil*
prepaid cellphone *celular prepago*
post office *4-72*
phone call *llamada*
letter *carta*
stamp *estampilla*
postcard *postal*
package; box *paquete; caja*

AT THE BORDER

border *frontera*
customs *aduana*
immigration *migración*
inspection *inspección*
ID card *cédula*
passport *pasaporte*
profession *profesión*
vacation *vacaciones*
I'm a tourist. *Soy turista.*
student *estudiante*
marital status *estado civil*
single *soltero*
married; divorced *casado; divorciado*
widowed *viudado*
insurance *seguro*
title *título*
driver's license *pase de conducir*

AT THE GAS STATION

gas station *estación de gasolina*
gasoline *gasolina*
full, please *lleno, por favor*
tire *llanta*
air *aire*
water *agua*

oil (change) *(cambio de) aceite*
My . . . doesn't work. *Mi . . . no funciona.*
battery *batería*
tow truck *grúa*
repair shop *taller*

VERBS

Verbs are the key to getting along in Spanish. They employ mostly predictable forms and come in three classes, which end in *ar, er,* and *ir,* respectively:

to buy *comprar*
I buy, you (he, she, it) buys *compro, compra*
we buy, you (they) buy *compramos, compran*

to eat *comer*
I eat, you (he, she, it) eats *como, come*
we eat, you (they) eat *comemos, comen*

to climb *subir*
I climb, you (he, she, it) climbs *subo, sube*
we climb, you (they) climb *subimos, suben*

Here are more (with irregularities indicated):

to do or make *hacer* (regular except for *hago,* I do or make)
to go *ir* (very irregular: *voy, va, vamos, van*)
to walk *caminar*
to wait *esperar*
to love *amar*
to work *trabajar*
to want *querer* (irregular: *quiero, quiere, queremos, quieren*)
to need *necesitar*
to read *leer*
to write *escribir*
to send *enviar*
to repair *reparar*
to wash *lavar*
to stop *parar*
to get off (the bus) *bajar*

to arrive *llegar*
to stay (remain) *quedar*
to stay (lodge) *hospedar*
to rent *alquilar*
to leave *salir* (regular except for *salgo,* I leave)
to look at *mirar*
to look for *buscar*
to give *dar* (regular except for *doy,* I give)
to give (as a present or to order something) *regalar*
to carry *llevar*
to have *tener* (irregular: *tengo, tiene, tenemos, tienen*)
to come *venir* (irregular: *vengo, viene, venimos, vienen*)

Spanish has two forms of "to be":

to be *estar* (regular except for *estoy,* I am)
to be *ser* (very irregular: *soy, es, somos, son*)

Use *estar* when speaking of location or a temporary state of being: "I am at home." *"Estoy en casa."* "I'm happy." *"Estoy contenta/o."* Use *ser* for a permanent state of being: "I am a lawyer." *"Soy abogada/o."*

NUMBERS

zero *cero*
one *uno*
two *dos*
three *tres*
four *cuatro*
five *cinco*
six *seis*
seven *siete*
eight *ocho*
nine *nueve*
10 *diez*
11 *once*
12 *doce*
13 *trece*
14 *catorce*
15 *quince*
16 *dieciseis*
17 *diecisiete*

18 *dieciocho*
19 *diecinueve*
20 *veinte*
21 *veinte y uno* or *veintiuno*
30 *treinta*
40 *cuarenta*
50 *cincuenta*
60 *sesenta*
70 *setenta*
80 *ochenta*
90 *noventa*
100 *cien*
101 *ciento y uno*
200 *doscientos*
500 *quinientos*
1,000 *mil*
10,000 *diez mil*
100,000 *cien mil*
1,000,000 *millón*
one half *medio*
one third *un tercio*
one fourth *un cuarto*

TIME

What time is it? *¿Qué hora es?*
It's one o'clock. *Es la una.*
It's three in the afternoon. *Son las tres de la tarde.*
It's 4 a.m. *Son las cuatro de la mañana.*
six-thirty *seis y media*
quarter till eleven *un cuarto para las once*
quarter past five *las cinco y cuarto*

hour *una hora*
late *tarde*

DAYS AND MONTHS

Monday *lunes*
Tuesday *martes*
Wednesday *miércoles*
Thursday *jueves*
Friday *viernes*
Saturday *sábado*
Sunday *domingo*
today *hoy*
tomorrow *mañana*
yesterday *ayer*
day before yesterday *antier*
January *enero*
February *febrero*
March *marzo*
April *abril*
May *mayo*
June *junio*
July *julio*
August *agosto*
September *septiembre*
October *octubre*
November *noviembre*
December *diciembre*
week *una semana*
month *un mes*
after *después*
before *antes*
holiday *festivo*
long weekend *puente*

Suggested Reading

HISTORY

Bushnell, David. *The Making of Modern Colombia: A Nation in Spite of Itself*. Berkeley, CA: University of California Press, 1993. Mandatory reading for students of Colombian history. Bushnell, an American, is considered the "Father of the Colombianists".

Hemming, John. *The Search for El Dorado*. London: Joseph, 1978. Written by a former director of the Royal Geographical Society, this book explores the Spanish gold obsession in the New World. It's a great companion to any visit to the Gold Museum in Bogotá.

Lynch, John. *Simón Bolívar: A Life*. New Haven, CT: Yale University Press, 2007. This biography of the Liberator is considered one of the best ever written in English, and is the result of a lifetime of research by renowned English historian John Lynch.

Palacios, Marco. *Between Legitimacy and Violence: A History of Colombia, 1875-2002*. Durham, NC: Duke University Press Books, 2006. Written by a Bogotano academic who was a former head of the Universidad Nacional, this book covers Colombia's economic, political, cultural, and social history from the late 19th century to the complexities of the late 20th century, and drug-related violence.

THE DRUG WAR AND ARMED CONFLICTS

Bowden, Mark. *Killing Pablo: The Hunt for the World's Greatest Outlaw*. New York: Grove Press, 2001. This account of U.S. and Colombian efforts to halt drug trafficking and terrorism committed by drug lord Pablo Escobar was originally reported in a 31-part series in *The Philadelphia Inquirer*.

Dudley, Steven. *Walking Ghosts: Murder and Guerrilla Politics in Colombia*. New York: Routledge Press, 2004. Essential reading for anyone interested in understanding the modern Colombian conflict, this book is written by an expert on investigating organized crime in the Americas.

Gonsalves, Marc, Tom Howes, Keith Stansell, and Gary Brozek. *Out of Captivity: Surviving 1,967 Days in the Colombian Jungle*. New York: Harper Collins, 2009. Accounts of three American military contractors who were held, along with former presidential candidate Ingrid Betancourt, by FARC guerrillas for over five years in the Colombian jungle.

Leech, Garry. *Beyond Bogotá: Diary of a Drug War Journalist in Colombia*. Boston: Beacon Press, 2009. The basis for this book is the author's 11 hours spent as a hostage of the FARC.

Otis, John. *Law of the Jungle: The Hunt for Colombian Guerrillas, American Hostages, and Buried Treasure*. New York: Harper, 2010. This is a thrilling account of the operation to rescue Ingrid Betancourt and American government contractors held by the FARC. It's been called a flip-side to *Out of Captivity*.

NATURAL HISTORY

Hilty, Steven L., William L. Brown, and Guy Tudor. *A Guide to the Birds of Colombia*. Princeton, NJ: Princeton University Press, 1986. This massive 996-page field guide to bird-rich Colombia is a must for any serious bird-watcher.

McMullan, Miles, Thomas M. Donegan, and Alonso Quevedo. *Field Guide to the Birds of Colombia*. Bogotá: Fundación ProAves,

ETHNOGRAPHY

Davis, Wade. *One River: Explorations and Discoveries in the Amazon Rain Forest.* New York: Simon & Schuster, 1997. From the author of *The Serpent and the Rainbow,* this is a rich description of the peoples of the Amazonian rain forest, and the result of Davis' time in the country alongside famed explorer Richard Evan Schultes.

Reichel-Dolmatoff, Gerardo. *Colombia: Ancient Peoples & Places.* London: Thames and Hudson, 1965. A thorough anthropological investigation of the indigenous cultures across Colombia by an Austrian-born anthropologist who emigrated to Colombia during World War II.

——. *The Shaman and the Jaguar: A Study of Narcotic Drugs Among the Indians of Colombia.* Philadelphia: Temple University Press, 1975. An examination of shamanic drug culture in Colombia, particularly among indigenous tribes from the Amazon jungle region.

ARCHITECTURE

Escovar, Alberto, Diego Obregón, and Rodolfo Segovia. *Guías Elarqa de Arquitectura.* Bogotá: Ediciones Gamma, 2005. Useful guides for anyone wishing to learn more about the architecture of Bogotá, Cartagena, and Medellín.

TRAVEL

Lamus, María Cristina. *333 Sitios de Colombia Que Ver Antes de Morir.* Bogotá: Editorial Planeta Colombiana, 2010. Colombian version of *1,000 Places to See Before You Die* (only available in Spanish).

Mann, Mark. *The Gringo Trail.* West Sussex: Summersdale Publishers, 2010. A darkly comic tale of backpacking around South America.

Nicholl, Charles. *The Fruit Palace.* New York: St. Martin's Press, 1994. A wild romp that follows the seedy cocaine trail from Bogotá bars to Medellín to the Sierra Nevada and a fruit stand called the Fruit Palace during the wild 1980s. The English author was jailed in Colombia for drug smuggling as he conducted research for the book.

PHOTOGRAPHY AND ILLUSTRATED BOOKS

Often only available in Colombia, coffee table books by Colombian publishers Villegas Editores and the Banco de Occidente are gorgeous, well-done, and often in English. Save room in your suitcase for one or two.

Cobo Borda, Juan Gustavo, Gustavo Morales Lizcano, and César David Martínez. *Colombia en Flor.* Bogotá: Villegas Editores, 2009. This book features fantastic photographs of flowers you will see in Colombia.

Davis, Wade and Richard Evans Schultes. *The Lost Amazon: The Photographic Journey of Richard Evans Schultes.* Bogotá: Villegas Editores, 2009. A fantastic journey deep into the Amazonian jungle by famed explorer Richard Evans Schultes.

Díaz, Hernán. *Cartagena Forever.* Bogotá: Villegas Editores, 2002. A tiny little book of stunning black-and-white images of the Cartagena of yesteryear, by one of Colombia's most accomplished photographers.

Díaz, Merlano, Juan Manuel and Fernando Gast Harders. *El Chocó Biogeográfico de Colombia.* Banco de Occidente Credencial Cali, 2009. A spectacular trip through the unique and biodiverse Chocó region.

Freeman, Benjamin and Murray Cooper. *Birds in Colombia.* Bogotá: Villegas Editores, 2011. Dazzling photographs of native bird species found in Colombia, a veritable birding paradise.

Hurtado García, Andrés. *Unseen Colombia*. Bogotá: Villegas Editores, 2004. Photos and descriptions of the many off-the-beaten-track destinations in the country.

Montaña, Antonio and Hans Doering. *The Taste of Colombia*. Bogotá: Villegas Editores, 1994. A thorough survey of Colombian cuisine by region, with recipes included.

Ortiz Valdivieso, Pedro and César David Martínez. *Orquídeas Especies de Colombia*. Bogotá: Villegas Editores, 2010. Jaw-dropping photos of orchids, from the unusual to the sublime, found in the forests of Colombia.

Rivera Ospina, David. *La Amazonía de Colombia*. Cali: Banco de Occidente Credencial, 2008. An excellent souvenir of your visit to the Amazon region.

———. *La Orinoquía de Colombia*. Cali: Banco de Occidente Credencial, 2005. One of the least visited areas of Colombia is the Río Orinoco basin in the Llanos and Amazon regions.

Various. *Colombia Natural Parks*. Bogotá: Villegas Editores, 2006. Gorgeous photos from all of Colombia's spectacular national parks.

Villegas, Liliana. *Coffees of Colombia*. Bogotá: Villegas Editores, 2012. Everything you'd like to know about Colombian coffee in one charming and compact book.

Villegas, Marcelo. *Guadua Arquitectura y Diseño*. Bogotá: Villegas Editores, 2003. Profiles of minimalistic and modern constructions throughout Colombia all made from guadua.

Internet and Digital Resources

ACCOMMODATIONS

Hostel Trail
www.hosteltrail.com
Run by a Scottish couple living in Popayán, this is an excellent resource on hostels throughout South America.

Posadas Turísticas de Colombia
www.posadasturisticasdecolombia.gov.co
Find information on interesting accommodations alternatives, like home stays.

BIRDING

ProAves
www.proaves.org
Excellent website for the largest birding organization in the country.

CARTAGENA

This is Cartagena
www.tic.com
Experience Cartagena like a local.

ECO-TOURISM

Parques Nacionales Naturales de Colombia
www.parquesnacionales.gov.co
Colombia's national parks website has information on all of the natural parks and protected areas in the country.

Aviatur Ecoturismo
www.aviaturecoturismo.com
Package tours of the Amazon, PNN Tayrona, PNN Isla Gorgona, and more are available

from one of Colombia's most respected travel agencies.

Fundación Malpelo
www.fundacionmalpelo.org
This nonprofit organization works to protect Colombia's vast maritime territory, including the Santuario de Flora y Fauna Malpelo.

Fundación Natura
www.natura.org.co
The Fundación Natura operates several interesting eco-tourism reserves in the country.

EMBASSIES AND VISAS
U.S. Embassy in Colombia
http://bogota.usembassy.gov
The Citizen Services page often has security information for visitors, and is where you can register your visit in case of an emergency.

Colombian Ministry of Foreign Relations
www.cancilleria.gov.co
Offers information on visas and other travel information.

ENTERTAINMENT, CULTURE, AND EVENTS
Vive In
www.vive.in
Updated information on restaurants, entertainment, and cultural events in Bogotá.

Plan B
www.planb.com.co
Competitor of Vive In, Plan B offers information on what's going on in Bogotá, Medellín, and Cali.

Tu Boleta
www.tuboleta.com
The top event ticket distributor in the country, Tu Boleta is a good way to learn about concerts, theater, parties, and sporting events throughout Colombia.

Banco de la República
www.banrepcultural.org
Information on upcoming cultural activities sponsored by the Banco de la República in 28 cities in the country.

HISTORY AND HUMAN RIGHTS ISSUES
CIA World Factbook Colombia
www.cia.gov
Background information on Colombia from those in the know.

Centro de Memoria Histórica
www.centrodememoriahistorica.gov.co
Excellent website on the human toll of the Colombian conflict.

International Crisis Group
www.crisisgroup.org
In-depth analysis of the human rights situation in Colombia.

Colombia Diversa
www.colombiadiversa.org
Covers LGBT rights in Colombia.

LANGUAGE COURSES
Spanish in Colombia
www.spanishincolombia.gov.co
Official government website on places to study Spanish in Colombia.

MEDELLÍN
Medellín Living
www.medellinliving.com
This website run by expats is an excellent purveyor of insider information on the City of Eternal Spring.

NEWS AND MEDIA

El Tiempo
www.eltiempo.com
El Tiempo is the country's leading newspaper.

El Espectador
www.elespectador.com.co
This is Colombia's second national newspaper.

Revista Semana
www.semana.com
Semana is the top news magazine in Colombia.

La Silla Vacia
www.sillavacia.com
Political insiders dish about current events.

Colombia Reports
http://colombiareports.co
Colombian news in English.

The City Paper Bogotá
www.thecitypaperbogota.com
Website of the capital city's English-language monthly.

Colombia Calling
www.richardmccoll.com/colombia-calling
Weekly online radio program on all things Colombia from an expat perspective.

TRANSPORTATION

Moovit
This app will help you figure out public transportation in Bogotá.

Tappsi
To order a safe taxi in Colombia's large cities, first upload this excellent app.

SITP
www.sitp.gov.co
This is the official website of the ever-improving (yet confusing) public bus transportation system in Bogotá.

TRAVEL INFORMATION

Colombia Travel
www.colombia.travel
This is the official travel information website of Proexport, Colombia's tourism and investment promotion agency.

Pueblos Patrimoniales
www.pueblospatrimoniodecolombia.travel
Find a pueblo that suits your needs at this informative website.

VOLUNTEERING

Conexión Colombia
www.conexioncolombia.com
This website is one-stop shopping for the non-profit sector in Colombia.

Index

List of Maps

Photo Credits

Also Available

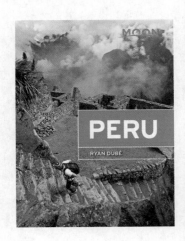

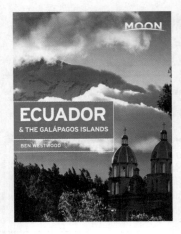

MAP SYMBOLS

≡≡≡ Expressway	○ City/Town	✈ Airport	⚑ Golf Course
≡≡ Primary Road	◉ State Capital	✈ Airfield	🅿 Parking Area
— Secondary Road	⊛ National Capital	▲ Mountain	⛟ Archaeological Site
------ Unpaved Road	★ Point of Interest	✚ Unique Natural Feature	🕆 Church
— Feature Trail	• Accommodation		Gas Station
- - - Other Trail	▼ Restaurant/Bar	🖋 Waterfall	Glacier
·········· Ferry	■ Other Location	♣ Park	Mangrove
≡≡ Pedestrian Walkway	Λ Campground	⬮ Trailhead	Reef
▥▥▥ Stairs		⛷ Skiing Area	Swamp

CONVERSION TABLES

°C = (°F - 32) / 1.8
°F = (°C x 1.8) + 32
1 inch = 2.54 centimeters (cm)
1 foot = 0.304 meters (m)
1 yard = 0.914 meters
1 mile = 1.6093 kilometers (km)
1 km = 0.6214 miles
1 fathom = 1.8288 m
1 chain = 20.1168 m
1 furlong = 201.168 m
1 acre = 0.4047 hectares
1 sq km = 100 hectares
1 sq mile = 2.59 square km
1 ounce = 28.35 grams
1 pound = 0.4536 kilograms
1 short ton = 0.90718 metric ton
1 short ton = 2,000 pounds
1 long ton = 1.016 metric tons
1 long ton = 2,240 pounds
1 metric ton = 1,000 kilograms
1 quart = 0.94635 liters
1 US gallon = 3.7854 liters
1 Imperial gallon = 4.5459 liters
1 nautical mile = 1.852 km

MOON COLOMBIA

Avalon Travel
a member of the Perseus Books Group
1700 Fourth Street
Berkeley, CA 94710, USA
www.moon.com

Editor: Leah Gordon
Series Manager: Kathryn Ettinger
Copy Editor: Brett Keener
Graphics Coordinator: Rue Flaherty
Production Coordinator: Rue Flaherty
Cover Design: Faceout Studios, Charles Brock
Moon Logo: Tim McGrath
Map Editor: Mike Morgenfeld
Cartographers: Brian Shotwell, Austin Ehrhardt
Proofreader: Deana Shields
Indexer: Rachel Kuhn

ISBN-13: 9781631213571
ISSN: 2334-0533

Printing History
1st Edition — 2014
2nd Edition — July 2017
5 4 3 2 1

Front cover photo: village streets and white washed houses, Barichara © Christian Kober/Getty Images
Back cover photo: Caño Cristales © Agap13 | Dreamstime.com

Printed in China by RR Donnelley